LIBRARY

In memory of

Catherine E. Boyd

Professor of History
at Carleton 1946-1966

Derek Watson
MOLOTOV
A Biography

J. N. Westwood
SOVIET RAILWAYS TO RUSSIAN RAILWAYS

Stephen G. Wheatcroft (*editor*)
CHALLENGING TRADITIONAL VIEWS OF RUSSIAN HISTORY

Galina M. Yemelianova
RUSSIA AND ISLAM
A Historical Survey

Studies in Russian and East European History and Society
Series Standing Order ISBN 0–333–71239–0
(*outside North America only*)

You can receive future titles in this series as they are published by placing a standing order. Please contact your bookseller or, in case of difficulty, write to us at the address below with your name and address, the title of the series and the ISBN quoted above.

Customer Services Department, Macmillan Distribution Ltd, Houndmills, Basingstoke, Hampshire RG21 6XS, England

---

Also by Derek Watson
MOLOTOV AND SOVIET GOVERNMENT

Molotov

A Biography

Derek Watson
Honorary Research Fellow,
Centre for Russian and East European Studies,
The University of Birmingham

First published in 2005 by
PALGRAVE MACMILLAN
Houndmills, Basingstoke, Hampshire RG21 6XS and
175 Fifth Avenue, New York, N.Y. 10010
Companies and representatives throughout the world.

PALGRAVE MACMILLAN is the global academic imprint of the Palgrave
Macmillan division of St. Martin's Press, LLC and of Palgrave Macmillan Ltd.
Macmillan® is a registered trademark in the United States, United Kingdom
and other countries. Palgrave is a registered trademark in the European
Union and other countries.

ISBN-13: 978–0–333–58588–7 hardback
ISBN-10: 0–333–58588–7 hardback

This book is printed on paper suitable for recycling and made from fully
managed and sustained forest sources.

A catalogue record for this book is available from the British Library.

Library of Congress Cataloging-in-Publication Data

Watson, Derek.
    Molotov : a biography / Derek Watson
        p. cm. – (Studies in Russian and East European history and society)
    Includes bibliographical references and index.
        ISBN 0–333–58588–7 (cloth)
        1. Molotov, Vyacheslav Mikhaylovich, 1890– 2. Statesmen – Soviet Union –
    Biography. 3. Soviet Union – Politics and government. I. Title. II. Studies in Russian and
    East European history and society (Palgrave Macmillan (Firm))

DK268.M64W38 2005
947.084'092—dc22
[B]   2005043391

10 9 8 7 6 5 4 3 2 1
14 13 12 11 10 09 08 07 06 05

Printed and bound in Great Britain by
Antony Rowe Ltd, Chippenham and Eastbourne

CR0906-7885h6

In memory of R. A. W.

Contents

List of Tables

List of Illustrations

Glossary of Russian Terms and Abbreviations Used in Text

agitparakhod	agitation steamboat
Agitprop	(*Otdel Agitatsii i Propogandy*) Agitation and Propaganda Department
aktiv	activists – politically active members of a community
batrak	rural wage labourer
Byuro Sovet Ministrov	Bureau of the Council of Ministers
Byuro Sovnarkoma SSSR	Bureau of Sovnarkom USSR
CHEKA	(*Chrezvychainaya Komissiya po Bor'be s Kontrrevolyutsiei i Sabotazhem*) Extraordinary Commission for Struggle with Counter-revolution and Sabotage – the secret/ political police (later GPU, OGPU and NKVD)
Cominform	Communist Information Bureau
Comintern	(*Kommunisticheskii Internatsional*) The Communist International
Duma	legislative body of the Russian empire after the 1905 Revolution
Ekonomicheskii Sovet	Economic Council – successor body to STO
etap	halting place – for deported convicts in transit
GKO	(*Gosudarstvennyi Komitet Oborony*) State Defence Committee
glavk (pl. *glavki*)	(*glavnoe upravlenie*) chief administration – directorate
GOELRO	(*Gosudarstvennaya Komissiya po Elektrifikatsii Rossii*) State Commission for the Electrification of Russia
gubkom	provincial party committee
Gosplan	(*Gosudarstvennaya Planovaya Komissiya*) State Planning Commission
guberniya (pl. *gubernii*)	province
Gulag	(*Glavnoe Upravlenie Ispravitel'no-trudovykh Lagerei*) Chief Administration of Corrective Labour Camps – responsible for forced labour
IKKI	(*Ispolnitel'nyi Komitet Kommunisticheskogo Internatsionala*) Executive Committee of Comintern
Instantsiya	The highest authority. Term used to refer to the Politburo and Central Committee
ispolkom (pl. *ispolkomi*)	(*ispolnitel'nyi komitet*) executive committee
Kadets	Constitutional Democrats
KGB	(*Komitet Gosudarstvennoi Bezopastnosti*) Committee of State Security – political police successor to the NKVD

Khlebotsentr	(*Vserossiskii Soyuz Sel'skokhozyaistvennykh Kooperativov po Proizvodtsvu, Pererabotke i Sbytu Zernovykh i Maslichnykh Kul'tur*) All-Russian Union of Agricultural Cooperatives for the Production, Processing and Sale of Grain and Oil Seeds
khozraschet	(*khozyaistvennyi raschet*) economic [profit-and-loss] accounting
kolebanie	oscillation
kolkhoz (pl. kolkhozy)	(*kollektivnoe khozyaistvo*) collective farm
kolkhoznik	collective farm worker
Kolkhoztsentr	(*Vsesoyuzni soyuz sel'skokhozyaistvennykh kollektivov*) All-Union Union of Agricultural Collectives
kollegiya (pl. *kollegii*)	a *collegium* or college/board
komandirovka (pl. *komandirovki*)	official mission
KomIspol	(*Komissiya Ispolneniya*) Commission of Implementation
Komissiya byuro Sovnarkoma SSSR po tekushchim delam	Commission of the Bureau of the Sovnarkom USSR for Current Business
Komissiya Oborony	Defence Commission
Komitet po Evakuatsii	Committee for Evacuation
komendant	commandant, official in charge
Komsomol	(*Kommunisticheskii Soyuz Molodezhi*) Communist League of Youth
kontraktsiya	system of purchase by contract of peasant produce
kulak	rich peasant
MTS	(*Mashinno-Traktornaya Stantsiya*) Machine Tractor Station
NarkomIndel	(*Narodnyi Komissariat Inostrannykh Del*) People's Commissariat for Foreign Affairs
NarkomZem	(*Narodnyi Komissariat Zemledeliya*) People's Commissariat of Agriculture
NEP	(*Novaya Ekonomicheskaya Politika*) New Economic Policy
NKRKI (RKI)	(*Narodnyi Komissariat Raboche-Krest'yanskoi Inspektsii*) People's Commissariat of Workers' and Peasants' Inspection. Also known as Rabkrin
NKVD	(*Narodnyi Komissariat Vnutrennikh Del*) People's Commissariat for Internal Affairs – responsible for the secret/political police from 1934
oblast'	province

OGPU (GPU)	(*Ob"edinennoe Gosudarstvennoe Politicheskoe Upravlenie*) Unified State Political Administration – the secret/political police
Okhrana	secret police in Tsarist Russia
Operativnoe byuro GKO	GKO Operative Bureau
Operativnoe Byuro	Operative Bureau [of Sovnarkom]
opros (instr. *Oprosom*)	procedure by which members of a committee were asked, either by telephone or by circulation of a paper, to indicate their approval or disagreement with a decision
Orgburo	(*Organizatsionnoe byuro*) Organization committee [of party Central Committee]
perelom	turning point
perestroika	restructuring
ploshchad'	square
politkom	(*politicheskii komissar*) political commissar
PolitOtdel (pl. *PolitOtdely*)	(*Politicheskii Otdel*) political department
prikazchik	salesman
prinudite'lnye trud	forced labour
protokol(pl. *protokoly*)	record of proceedings or minutes
pud	measure of weight equal to 0.01638 tons
pyatiletka	five-year plan
Rabkrin	See NKRKI
raikom	(*raionnyi komitet*) district committee
raion (pl. *raiony*)	region/district
real'noe uchilishche	real school
RSDRP	(*Rossiiskaya Sotsial-Demokraticheskaya Rabochaya Partiya*) Russian Social Democratic Workers' Party
RSFSR	(*Rossiiskaya Sovetskaya Federativnaya Sotsialistichekaya Respublika*) Russian Soviet Federative Socialist Republic
SD	(*Sotsial Demokrat*) Social Democrat
serednyak	middle peasant
sheftsvo	patronage, sponsorship
sluzhashchi	office worker
smychka	alliance [between workers and peasants]
Sovet Ministrov	Council of Ministers – the government of the USSR from 1946 – successor body to Sovnarkom
sovkhoz (pl. sovkhozy)	(*sovetskoe khozyaistvo*) [Soviet] state farm
Sovnarkhoz	(*Sovet Narodnogo Khozyaistvo*) Economic Council
Sovnarkom	(*Sovet Narodnykh Komissarov*) Council of People's Commissars
SR	(*Sotsialist-revolyutsioner*) Socialist Revolutionary
Stakhanovite	Emulator of Aleksei Stakhanov who achieved record coal output in a night-shift in August 1935 in the drive for higher labour productivity

Stavka	(*Stavka Glavnogo Komandovaniya*) High Command Headquarters
STO	(*Sovet Truda i Oborony*) Council of Labour and Defence
subbotnik	voluntary unpaid labour day for the state
TASS	(*Telegrafnoe Agentstvo Sovetskogo Soyuza*) Telegraphic Agency of the Soviet Union
tirazh	circulation/edition
tovarishchestvo (pl. *tovarishchestva*)	machine society – forerunner of the MTS
Traktorotsentr	(*Vsesoyuznyi tsentr mashinno-traktornykh stantsii*) All-Union Centre of Machine Tractor Stations
troika (pl. *troiki*)	commission of three persons
TsIK	(*Tsentral'nyi Ispolnitel'nyi Komitet*) Central Executive Committee [of the Congress of Soviets of the USSR]
TsK	(*Tsentral'nyi Komitet*) Central Committee (of the Communist Party)
TsKK	(*Tsentral'nyi Kontrol'naya Komissiya*) Central Control Commission of the Party
TsSU	(*Tsentral'noi Statisticheskoe Upravlenie*) Central Statistical Administration
uezd	district
Upravlenie po Evakuatsii Naseliniya	Administration for Evacuation of the Population
Valyutnaya Komissiya	Commission for Currency
Voennyi Sovet	Military Council
VOKS	(*Vsesoyuznoe Obshchestvo Kul'turnoi Svyazi s Zagranitsei*) All-Union Society for Cultural Links Abroad
vol'nyi trud	free labour
Voprosy Strakhovaniya	Insurance Questions – Bolshevik journal
VSK	(*Vsesoyuznoi Sovet Kolkhozov*) All-Union Kolkhoz Council
VSNKh (Vesenkha)	(*Vysshi Sovet Narodnogo Khozyaistva*) Supreme Council of the National Economy – the government body with the status of a commissariat responsible for industry
VTsIK	(*Vserossiiskii Tsentral'nyi Ispolitel'nyi Komitet*) The Central Executive Committee of the All-Russian Congress of Soviets
VTsSPS	(*Vsesoyuznoi Tsentral'nyi Sovet Profsoyuzov*) All-Union Central Council of Trade Unions
VTUZ	(*Vysshee Tekhnicheskoe Uchebnoe Zavedenie*) Higher Technical Institute

vydvizhenchestvo   policy of promotion of workers from the bench
zemlyachestvo   association, friendly society
zemstvo   local government authority
Zernotrest   (*Vsesoyuznyi Trest Zernovykh Sovkhozov*) All-Union Trust of [New] Grain Sovkhozy
zhenotdel   women's department

Preface and Acknowledgements

I have always been interested in biography, and my earliest attempts at historical writing were about the lives of eighteenth-century English and American merchants and politicians. When I began to study Russian and Soviet history, and became associated with CREES, The University of Birmingham, where historians had a particular focus on the 1930s, I found that there were very few biographies of Soviet politicians except of Lenin, Stalin and Khrushchev, the country's leaders. Among Stalin's supporters, Molotov was prominent and I began to work on his life and consider writing a biography. At that time, however, in the mid-1980s, there was little chance of access to the personal papers of major Soviet politicians, particularly disgraced ones – there were then no cards even for Molotov's collected speeches in the Lenin Library catalogue. This led me to research and write about Sovnarkom, the Soviet government, when Molotov was its chairman between 1930 and 1941. Initially, I based my research on the published decrees and press reports of its meetings, but the opening of the Sovnarkom fond in the Russian State Archive, as I worked, greatly increased the range of material available. This encouraged me to return to Molotov's life when I had completed my book on the Soviet government.

By that time there had been a remarkable change. Not only was access possible to Molotov's papers, but to those of Stalin, other leading politicians, and to major institutions of the Soviet era such as the Politburo. There were also memoirs and substantial collections of printed documents, particularly in Russian, superior to former official publications often printed for the purpose of propaganda. This massive increase in the amount of source material made what had been conceived as a relatively limited and straightforward exercise become a major undertaking, which has taken much longer to write than I had ever envisaged.

I am conscious of the debt of gratitude that I have incurred during the years I have been working on Molotov. I owe a great deal to all the former and present members of CREES, its Directors Professors Julian Cooper, Philip Hanson and Hilary Pilkington, and to scholars from other institutions and countries, particularly Russia, who attend its SIPS seminars. CREES always provides a challenging background against which to work, and I am especially grateful to Professors Bob Davies and Arfon Rees for their help and encouragement at every stage. Professor Davies has been kind enough to read, comment on, and painstakingly correct drafts of the whole book, and make numerous useful suggestions, as has Professor Rees for a major part of it. I would also like to thank Drs. Melanie Ilic and Jeremy Smith for their comments on draft chapters; Dr. Geoffrey Roberts and Professor Jonathan Haslam for advice on and sources for foreign policy; and Mike Berry who discovered much useful information. Omissions, shortcomings, and errors of fact and opinion are of course my sole responsibility.

I would like to express my appreciation to librarians and archivists who have assisted me by providing materials, especially Graham Dix, who was librarian of the former Baykov, now European Research Institute Library, and Nigel Hardware, his assistant; the librarians of The University of Birmingham Main Library; and the Russian State Library, Moscow. Madame V. Somonova of the State Archive of the Russian Federation (*GARF*) made available documents from the Sovnarkom fond, and Dr. Oleg Khlevnyuk assisted with access to invaluable material at the Russian State Archive of Social-Political History (*RGAS-PI*). The Archive of the Foreign Policy of the Russian Federation (*AVPRF*) also provided many useful documents.

I acknowledge the support of the Leverhulme Trust which provided me with a grant which enabled me to work full-time on Molotov from 1995 to 1997; and the British Academy which made available a number of small grants for work related to the biography. Most recently, the Arts and Humanities Research Board has financed a project on Soviet government during the Great Patriotic War, which has provided useful material on Molotov's life. I am also grateful to Tricia Carr and Marea Aries at CREES for secretarial assistance.

Finally, I would like to remember my wife Ruth: her understanding, encouragement, support and assistance whilst she was alive, made me go on after her death. I would also like to thank my sons Alistair and Paul, and Lesley, for their patience and forbearance when I have been preoccupied with Molotov.

DEREK WATSON
January 2005

Introduction

Born when the Tsars ruled the Russia Empire, Molotov died in the Gorbachev era. A revolutionary and active politician in Lenin's time, Molotov became Stalin's first lieutenant but outlived him by more than thirty years, and was prominent during Khrushchev's rise to power. He was Stalin's head of government during the economic transformation of the USSR and Great Terror of the 1930s. As foreign minister, he negotiated with Hitler and Ribbentrop before the Second World War, with Roosevelt, Churchill and Eden during the war, and with Truman, Attlee and Bevin at the end of and after the war. Yet, because he was disgraced and became a 'non-person' in the Khrushchev era, Soviet scholars did not write about him and the material was not available for Western historians to study Molotov. The only memoirs he left were the controversial *One Hundred and Forty Conversations with Molotov*, tape recorded interviews with the Stalinist poet Felix Chuev, made between 1969 and 1986 but not published until 1994. That reliable sources were not available and archives were not accessible are the main reasons why the present volume can claim to be the first major historical biography of Molotov.

I begin my study by examining the origins and activities of a fiery extremist in the revolutionary era and the translation of Molotov – the change was too rapid to be called a transition – to bureaucrat and hard-nosed party functionary during the 1920s. The soubriquet Molotov can mean the 'hammer' to Stalin as 'man of steel'. It was also used more pejoratively and crudely to mean 'stone backside'. Both are appropriate descriptions of Molotov's role in the later 1920s. The first applies to his support for Stalin in his struggle with the oppositions and driving through his policies, particularly in agriculture. The second relates to his patient work as party secretary.

In December 1930, Stalin insisted that Molotov should become chairman of the Council of People's Commissars (Sovnarkom), the nearest Soviet equivalent to 'prime minister'. He continued in this position until Stalin succeeded him immediately before the German invasion in 1941. Both versions of the soubriquet remain appropriate for Molotov as the Soviet government's chief executive. His conduct also gives him a claim to be called a statesman. At one time during the Great Terror of the 1930s, Molotov was in extreme danger of arrest and execution, but unlike many of his colleagues he survived. Indeed, evidence suggests that he

1

participated fully in the terror process, convinced that it was a correct and necessary policy. He played a major role in implementing the purges, and not merely to ensure his own survival.

In addition to his other duties, in May 1939, Molotov was appointed People's Commissar for Foreign Affairs and began a diplomatic career. He learned his craft in the abortive Triple Alliance negotiations with England and France, which, if successful, might have prevented or delayed the Second World War. When these failed he was the Soviet signatory of the Nazi–Soviet Non-Aggression Treaty of August 1939 – the notorious 'Molotov–Ribbentrop Pact' – with its secret protocols in which part of Poland and a large part of the Baltic States were allocated to the Soviet 'sphere of interest'. This led to some of the most shameful behaviour in Molotov's diplomatic career, and I discuss the way in which he managed the take over of these territories for the USSR and negotiated prior to the Soviet invasion of Finland.

Molotov is popularly remembered mostly for the 'Molotov cocktail'. This makeshift weapon was evidence of the crisis in the USSR when Germany invaded in June 1941. The Great Patriotic War saw Molotov not only assisting Stalin in directing the military effort, but also continuing his bureaucratic role in domestic policy. But his main responsibility during the war was foreign policy, where there were two events in his diplomatic career in which he was particularly prominent. The first was his visit to Britain and the United States in 1942 as 'Mr. Brown', to negotiate a treaty of alliance and to try to establish a Second Front for the USSR. His correspondence with Stalin during this visit vividly demonstrates his relationship with the Soviet leader after the Terror. The second event, perhaps the peak of Molotov's diplomatic career, was the Moscow foreign ministers' conference of October 1943. Although his American and British counterparts found him more congenial than at any other time, he dominated the conference and in one famous exchange with Eden rendered the English foreign secretary speechless. Molotov was also present during Churchill's visit to Moscow when the British prime minister and Stalin notoriously agreed 'percentages' of influence on territory in post-war Eastern Europe. Indeed, it was Molotov and Eden who finalised the details of the agreement. Towards the end of the war, Molotov was instrumental in establishing the Council of Foreign Ministers, where, as the Cold War developed, he was to become notorious for implacably pursuing the interests of the Soviet Union, and he became known as 'Mr Nyet' amongst Western politicians. This book contains 'snapshots' of key moments in Molotov's foreign policy activities, selected to throw light on his political biography. I have written elsewhere about certain episodes in his career as foreign minister, which are referred to in the notes and bibliography, and other work is in progress.

After 1945, Molotov had to deal with the aging and increasingly capricious Stalin. He was dismissed as foreign minister in 1949, increasingly fell into disfavour, his wife was arrested, and he seems to have been in personal danger again at the end of Stalin's life. After Stalin's death he was restored to power, and led the struggle against what he saw as Khrushchev's betrayal of Bolshevik principles. His opposition to Khrushchev, and attempt to remove him in 1957, led to his downfall and expulsion from the Communist Party, although he was readmitted shortly before his death.

Obituaries of Molotov in English newspapers were far more detailed than the official notices in the Soviet press. Indeed, Molotov's career is full of paradoxes. Why after a brief resistance did a devoted family man accept the arrest and incarceration of his wife? How was the fiery revolutionary transformed into a bureaucrat? How could someone with statesmanlike qualities be particularly vituperative against former colleagues and support the Terror? Why did Molotov, quite unversed in diplomacy, become the Soviet Union's chief negotiator, first with Nazi Germany in 1939 and 1940, then with the Western allies during the Second World War? How was he then changed into the Cold War diplomat? Finally, if Molotov fell into disfavour during Stalin's last years, why did he remain an unrepentant Stalinist until his death in 1986? This study tries to explain these and other contradictions.

1
The Making of a Revolutionary, 1890–1917

Birth and education

Vyacheslav Mikhailovich Skryabin, to become better known to the world as Molotov, was born on 9 March (24 February) 1890 in Kukarka, (later Sovetsk), Vyatka *guberniya* (province), central Russia.[1] Kukarka, a town of medieval foundations, was an important trading and manufacturing centre, making sledges, carts, baskets and lace.[2] Vyacheslav's father, Mikhail Prokhorovich Skryabin, is described as a *prikazchik*, a salesman, and his origins are generally acknowledged to be petty bourgeois.[3] Molotov qualified *prikazchik* in his memoirs, describing his father as a clerk, who earned sixty rubles a month in 1909.[4] This was considerably above the average yearly wage of 264 rubles for factory workers, equal to that of a teacher in a factory or municipal school, but well below that of 1200 rubles earned by *zemstvo* (local government authority) doctors.[5] Molotov's mother, Anna Yakovlevna,[6] came from a wealthy merchant family, the Nebogatikovs, who ran a flourishing trading house in Kukarka. She was the daughter of Mikhail, Skryabin's employer, whose three brothers took over the business on their father's death. They were sufficiently wealthy to keep two river steamers.[7]

Vyacheslav was the ninth child of a family of ten, three of whom died in infancy. One daughter and six sons survived to adulthood. The family was cultured. They were distantly related to the composer and pianist Aleksandr Skryabin (1872–1915), well known in Moscow polite society in the late nineteenth century.[8] The physical resemblance between him and Vyacheslav, his second cousin, is quite striking, and long after he was better known as Molotov, Vyacheslav wrote Skryabin in brackets on official documents, perhaps partly to remind the reader of his famous musical connections.[9] From an early age, he seems to have displayed the family's musical ability, developing an interest in playing the violin that was to remain with him for the rest of his life.[10] Nikolai, one of his older brothers, became a composer, and although he achieved no prominence, he changed his name to Nolinsk to avoid confusion with the famous Aleksandr Skryabin. Another brother tried to become a painter, and yet another became an army doctor.[11]

It was a conventional late nineteenth century petty bourgeois family: education and religion were important. The father sang in the church choir and remained religious up to his death in 1923, but he also drank and beat his children.[12] Vyacheslav, who as the result of a serious illness, used spectacles to read from the age of eight, and always suffered from a stammer, was educated initially at the local village school, transferring schools at the age of seven when the family moved to Nolinsk. This town some 40 miles away from Kukarka, again of medieval origins, was the administrative headquarters of the district, and a centre for political exiles.[13] The next year he was sent to the local gymnasium, the type of school where pupils were given a traditional education based on the classics and prepared for university entry.[14] This choice, for a younger son, was indicative of the social ambitions of the Skryabin family. Vyacheslav took the preparatory and junior classes, but in 1902, when he was twelve, he failed his examinations, although his mother gave him an ikon to carry in his pocket to help him. In his memoirs, he confessed to having relied on it, but said it did not give him the answers.[15]

Accompanied by his mother, and a younger brother who was put in the preparatory class, Vyacheslav now became a pupil at the *real'noe uchilishche* (real school) in Kazan, which three of his elder brothers also attended. At the end of the first year their mother returned to Nolinsk[16] and the brothers shared and rented a room, living with the family of their cousin, Lidiya Petrovna Chirkova, a midwife. She was married to a Ukrainian, A.S. Kulesh, a prominent member of the Russian Social Democratic Labour Party, the main Marxist revolutionary party, which divided into two fractions, Bolsheviks and Mensheviks in 1903. Kulesh became a Bolshevik and was active in Kazan.[17] The environment in which he now lived and worked was an important factor in turning Vyacheslav into a revolutionary. In contrast, his brothers always seem to have been on the fringes of revolutionary activity, but never prominent. Nikolai, who was four years older, was the most active of the three.[18]

Real schools, introduced under Count Dimitri Tolstoi's reforms in the 1870s, were, in 1902, in a phase of rapid expansion. From 1888, after a preliminary year, they offered a general education for the first four years. Modern languages replaced the classical languages of the gymnasium, and pupils who failed languages or mathematics at the gymnasium, were encouraged to transfer to real schools. They were designed to train local officials and managers, as well as agricultural and industrial technicians. In the fifth and sixth year specialisation began; two courses were offered: general education and business. A specialised seventh grade was introduced in 1901, allowing pupils, like those in the gymnasiya, especially those with higher technical education in view, to qualify for university entry.[19]

Vyacheslav, who claimed in his memoirs that he had most ability in mathematics,[20] achieved the top mark 'five' or 'excellent' in 12 subjects from 14, and the next mark 'four' or 'good' in the other two, at the end of the sixth grade which he completed in June 1908.[21] He was clearly a very intelligent pupil, for Lenin achieved 'five' only in ten subjects, although this was at a gymnasium.[22] When, in exile in 1910, at the age of twenty, Vyacheslav took the examinations at the end of the special seventh grade, he was awarded the top mark in religious studies, German, French, algebra, special course in analytical geometry, physics, history, mathematical geography (cosmography), design and law. He gained the second mark in trigonometry, arithmetic, and Russian language; and the third mark 'satisfactory' in only one subject, natural history.[23] With marks of this standard he was in a position to proceed to higher education. If this was not uncommon among Bolshevik leaders of his generation, it was rather unusual for a Bolshevik leader to have been educated in a 'real school'.[24]

A revolutionary emerges

Kazan, where Lenin had been expelled from university for revolutionary activity,[25] was an important strategic and trading centre. It was full of magnificent churches and had the highest Muslim population in the Russian empire. It was used as a place of political exile and its educational institutions were rife with political ferment. The young Skryabin was there in 1905, when after the disastrous Russo–Japanese war, the Russian Empire was convulsed by a revolution which drew a whole generation into revolutionary politics. It is therefore not surprising that he was attracted to left-wing intelligentsia circles and began to study radical literature.[26] He met Aleksandr Arosev, who was to be a friend and associate until his death during the Terror in the 1930s, and who wrote the official entry for Molotov in the section of the *Granat* encyclopaedia on revolutionaries, the years when he was especially close to Molotov.[27] Arosev was a member of the recently founded Socialist Revolutionary (SR) Party which believed that a new socialist Russia could be built on the co-operative practices of the peasantry and was prepared to use terror amongst its tactics.[28]

Returning home in the summer of 1905, Skryabin began his political career when he came into contact with the Nolinsk district Social Democratic organisation. There was considerable agitation in Vyatka *guberniya* associated with the 1905 revolution. Vyacheslav's grandfather's business had expanded and the family owned a tobacco factory in Nolinsk, at which Vyacheslav tried to organise a strike. His uncles, dependent on the business for their living, naturally disapproved of his activity.[29] He also renewed his acquaintance with Kulesh, now exiled to Nolinsk, who in exile again, a few years later, was killed in a duel. Kulesh's career and death clearly had a deep effect on the young Skryabin.[30] A. M. Vasnetsov, another political exile and brother of the well-known artist V. M. Vasnetsov was also an associate.[31] The organiser of a gang of bomb-makers, Vasnetsov asked the young Skryabin which faction of the Social Democratic Party he thought most appropriate for the present circumstances, and drew his attention to the differences between Bolsheviks and Mensheviks.[32] In the following year, a Social Democratic circle of about ten began meeting in woods outside the town. Here Vyacheslav met a Georgian Menshevik exile who used the sobriquet 'Markov'. The question of a boycott of the elections for the second Duma, the Parliament established at the end of the 1905 revolution, was discussed. His cousin Lidiya (the wife of Bolshevik Kulesh) advocated the original Bolshevik line and supported a boycott in opposition to the Mensheviks, but the young Skryabin was apparently undecided. Nevertheless, he was charged with the production and distribution of a broadsheet on the Duma. This he always considered his first party activity. Molotov claimed in old age that he was reading only Plekhanov at the time: he did not know of Lenin's writings, and was not yet a Bolshevik. This confirms the *Okhrana* (the Tsarist secret police) records, which state only that he was a member of the Social Democratic Party by 1907,[33] and reflects the variety of influences to which he was subject.

Back in Kazan, Vyacheslav became involved in an attempt to found a 'Kazan revolutionary organisation of students'. It began in middle-technical schools and first sought to link all middle school students. According to the *Okhrana*, its influence was mainly restricted to the 'real school', although it did develop in the 'industrial academy'. A further retrospective report of 1913 refers to Skryabin's formation of a revolutionary group in the theological seminary.[34] The organisation aimed to be non-party. Skryabin claimed that it had SR, Social Democrat and anarchist members. It was strongly influenced by members of an SR group, liquidated by the *Okhrana* at the end of 1908, in which university students had been prominent. The central committee consisted of the young Vyacheslav and three others. His collaborators were his great friend Arosev; N. V. Mal'tsev, originally a member of the SR group, with whom he was to be linked for the next few years;[35] and most importantly Victor Tikhomirnov, a fellow student, a year older than Skryabin, who had qualified in 1908. Tikhomirnov was the third of four sons of a rich Kazan landowner. On the father's death the eldest son continued the business, the second son became an actor, but Victor, born in 1889, became a revolutionary activist, one of the founders of the group liquidated in 1908.[36] He and Skryabin used Tikhomirnov family money to finance the new organisation,[37] and Vyacheslav, as tutor to the youngest brother, German Tikhomirnov, strengthened his links with the family.[38]

Skryabin was ranked by the *Okhrana* as second in importance in the organisation, next to Victor Tikhomirnov.[39] He worked under the name *Dyadya* – 'uncle', possibly a reference to his tutoring role, and was made chairman of the committee elected by the student group. A newspaper, *Nasha Zhizn'* – 'Our Life' was published; proclamations were issued; and attempts made to propagandise workers in the factories, as well as students, both in Kazan and in nearby towns. The possibility of establishing an 'All-Russian Revolutionary Union of Secondary Schools and Institutes' was also discussed.[40] From May 1908, Vyacheslav came under *Okhrana* surveillance, after the distribution in the 'real school' of a May Day proclamation by the members of the central committee of the Kazan student organisation. This has been claimed to be Skryabin's first political statement.[41] A further proclamation, published in January 1909, acknowledged that they were now working in a period when repression and reaction were triumphant and reflected the fact that revolutionary movements were very much on the defensive. It concluded:

> The time is not far distant when a new wave of revolution will strike a powerful blow for a new life. ... Form revolutionary organisations! Make ready for a new social upsurge so that you may not be caught unprepared when it comes.[42]

In post-revolutionary party documents, Molotov's date of entry to the Bolshevik Party is invariably stated as 1906, but it seems that it was not until late 1908 or early 1909, under Tikhomirnov's influence, that Vyacheslav first pledged his loyalty to the Bolsheviks. *Okhrana* records indicate that even after this he may have dallied with the SRs. His overzealous protestations, at the height of his career, that he had never been anything else but a strict and loyal Bolshevik, may confirm his SR links,[43] but there were, in any case, close connections between the SRs and the Bolsheviks during the years 1908–1911.[44] Official and sympathetic biographies, written in the Soviet era, that see this period as providing a valuable training in revolutionary activity for the young Skryabin, claim that he engaged in discussions of Marxism, distributed party literature, arranged meetings and was involved in fund-raising amongst the workers. In addition, they assert that he organised collections and relief for political prisoners and exiles in the locality, and attempted to found an all-Russian Bolshevik student society.[45] The *Okhrana* records relating to this period in the Molotov archive, however, demonstrate that these statements relate to his activities in the Kazan student organisation.

By 1909 the Kazan student movement had been penetrated by an *Okhrana* informer, and on 19 March Tikhomirnov and the majority of the group were arrested. Skryabin was seized two days later, and other members of the group, except Arosev, shortly afterwards.[46] When he was arrested and his belongings searched, materials which demonstrated Skryabin's role in the student society, particularly his part in organising its finances and his association with the Social Democratic party, were found.[47] The *Okhrana* list of 122 items included copies of brochures, notebooks, notes, posters, drafts prepared for duplication, and SR and anarchist as well as Social Democratic party pamphlets. There were books of two hundred tickets, each one priced at 25 kopeks, for a lottery organised by the student organisation to replenish their funds and aid political prisoners and exiles. The tickets were stamped 'Society for the Mutual Aid of Political Exiles and Prisoners'.[48] Two letters were found from student groups in Elabuga and Penza. These described their activities, and asked the Kazan group to help to establish an Elabuga student newspaper. Skryabin's draft reply on behalf of the Kazan group, reflected the need for unity, and the dangers of a revolutionary movement split into factions, one of his chief concerns at this time. To the police authorities his attempt to make links with revolutionary student groups in other towns was the most serious aspect of his activities.[49]

The initial reaction of the school authorities was to expel Mal'tsev, Skryabin, and Arosev who was arrested in April, but the first two were pardoned, in response to pleas from their families. In the case of Arosev the decision was upheld, because in addition to his political offences, he had not paid his fees for the first part of the year.[50] Held in prison for two months, a period which he attempted to shorten by a plea of poor health, citing poor circulation, giddiness and serious anaemia, Skryabin was prevented from taking the end of year silver medal examination at the real school.[51] He was sentenced in June to two years exile in Vologda province in northern Russia. A request from his father to release him under the oversight of his family in Nolinsk, and then send him into exile abroad, was refused.[52] According to one account, Stolypin, the Tsar's dreaded minister of the interior, in reply to a plea for clemency from the parents of the group is said to have declared:

> Had they been workers I would have let them go abroad because it is hopeless to try to reform workers. ... But since they are students, members of the intelligentsia, exile, the quiet North, pure air etc., may cure them, and they may still be of use to the State.[53]

Arosev and Mal'tsev, with whom Skryabin had been imprisoned also went into exile, as did Victor Tikhomirnov, but possibly because he came from a wealthy family, Tikhomirnov obtained permission to go abroad, and took his brother Aleksandr with him. Here he established contact with Lenin. Vyacheslav kept in touch with the emigrés, although he knew the Tsarist authorities were opening the correspondence between them. The maintenance of this link with Tikhomirnov was to prove significant.[54]

Skryabin's exile began in the towns of Tot'ma and Sol'vychegodsk. In his first letter to Mal'tsev, he wrote that the journey to Tot'ma by river was uneventful. On arrival, he left Arosev on the quay and went to search for lodgings. This he found difficult, and was initially offered very poor accommodation at a very high price, which made him fear that they might have to stay all night on the landing stage. Then, at the last minute, he was fortunate enough to meet another student exile who had been involved in the Bloody Sunday demonstrations with Father Gapon, the beginning of the 1905 revolution. Through his good offices, a satisfactory room was eventually procured for 2 rubles 50 kopeks a night, although the proprietor raised the rent by another 50 kopeks when it was revealed that there was a second person, and a considerable amount of baggage. In the same letter to Mal'tsev, Vyacheslav enquired about his sister, and how she had taken the news of his sentence.[55]

With an SR exile in the room next to his, with whom he could discuss politics,[56] Skryabin quickly settled down and began work at the local library, which was free for reference purposes, although it charged for borrowing. He focused on nineteenth century radical and revolutionary writing. In December 1909, he wrote that although he was only occasionally able to see newspapers and radical journals, he had been studying Chernyshevsky's *Notes on Gogol's Period in Russian Literature*, and Kagan's *History of Russian Literature*. He described both as good, serious books, and the philosophical basis of the first as 'purely materialistic'. He had also read everything he could about the literary critic V. Belinskii, who he particularly recommended to Mal'tsev.[57] He supplemented an allowance of 11 rubles a month by playing in a quartet in a restaurant, but he complained that he greatly missed serious music, particularly the symphonies of Beethoven.[58]

Skryabin tried to continue his formal studies. In September 1909 he had petitioned the Kazan gendarmerie for the return of his notes and books,[59] but there was no institution with an advanced course in Tot'ma or Sol'vychegodsk, where he could take his final examinations. In April 1910, however, the provincial governor, Khvostov, apparently after considerable pressure from the young man, allowed him to transfer to the town of Vologda itself, so that he could take his examination as an external candidate, at the real school there.[60]

Skryabin's stay was restricted to a month to take the examinations, but he secured an extension, initially to take an additional examination in Latin.[61] He wrote that he was reading P. Milyukov whom he described as clever, good and 'generally sensible'; he found his survey of the Russian economy in the early eighteenth century 'especially interesting'.[62] He was also studying Marx, on whom he did not comment; Dostoevsky's *The Idiot*; A. Tolstoy and Gorky, whom he described as a 'great surprise'. He had not liked him earlier, but was now more sympathetic, possibly because of Gorky's radical political views.[63] He described his reading in some detail in letters to Arosev with whom he disagreed, because the latter was willing only to study subjects that would qualify him for university, and not additional ones recommended by Skryabin, necessary for entry to the Petersburg Polytechnic Institute or Moscow Commercial Institute.[64] Arosev and Mal'tsev, who were to enrol at the Vologda real school prior to higher education, soon joined Skryabin there.[65] They kept in touch with their old friends in Kazan, and despite scrutiny by the police authorities, the group recommenced illegal political work, which for the first time was directed at industrial workers. The railway workers who formed the largest working-class element in town, and whom the authorities considered the most receptive group, were the focus of their activities.[66] Contact was made with them through the Mytishchi workers who had been exiled from Moscow[67] and settled in Vologda, where they were employed mainly on the railways. The three tried to establish a Social Democratic (SD) group in the town. Some *Okhrana* reports indicate that Arosev and Mal'tsev were more active in this work than Skryabin, another slightly later, claims that Skryabin was the leader of the group.[68] Skryabin and Mal'tsev were described as having 'close links' with a Vologda SR group liquidated in August 1910.[69]

Mal'tsev was the driving force behind another May Day proclamation in 1911. This was posted up all over the town and attributed to the 'Vologda group of the Russian Social Democratic Workers' Party'. It used such well-worn slogans as 'Welcome to the First of May, the holiday of the struggling proletariat of all countries' and alluded to Social Democratic policies such as the eight-hour working day and participation in the Third Duma. In addition, the proclamation referred to local working conditions, specifically at the electrical workshop in the town, and called on the Vologda workers to unite in the Social Democratic Party, although contemporary *Okhrana* reports stated that the membership of the local organisation comprised only a few individuals.[70]

By June, Skryabin had moved to the forefront of the group, and tried to organise a meeting in the woods outside the town. This went ahead, despite an attendance of only seven. Skryabin reported on the position in the Social Democratic Party and the need to form a group in Vologda. Arosev had apparently gone to Moscow to try to establish relations with the Moscow organisation, and Skryabin and Malt'sev were entrusted with the formation of a party group. Because of the poor attendance it was decided to meet again.[71] The limited and local nature of this activity is demonstrated by the *Okhrana* report on P. A. Chichikov, another Social

Democratic party member linked with Stalin. He visited Vologda in 1911, and denied that he had any other links with Mal'tsev and Skryabin other than a meeting in prison when they were arrested for a short time.[72] But Skryabin was clearly growing in significance, for a Vologda *Okhrana* report on his activities in 1911 stated that he was:

> a serious party worker and organiser struggling to establish and unite around himself all the criminal element. He is distinguished by his knowledge of the SD [Social Democratic] programme and literature and possesses good organising abilities. Skryabin struggled to influence the town of Vologda and unite the work of the SDs in the whole *guberniya*. He made a collection of money for political purposes. ... In short Skryabin is a strong and dangerous organiser.[73]

He worked under the sobriquet 'Vegun' at this time; the *Okhrana* described him as of middle height and medium build, with a clean oblong face, hazel eyes and a straight nose, no beard but a small light-brown moustache and black hair cut short; and dressed in a black summer suit and black hat.[74]

Accounts of Skryabin's career up to 1912, published before his disgrace under Khrushchev, portray him as the archetypal Bolshevik: he had joined the Party as a youth of sixteen; become a 'professional revolutionary' at eighteen; devoted time to the necessary theoretical study; worked among students and proletarians; and had been subject to arrest and exile by the Tsarist authorities. The truth seems to be somewhat different. He had finally given his allegiance to the Party after dallying with the Socialist Revolutionaries; most of his experience was in student politics; and his work among proletarians was limited. On the other hand, he had undertaken some theoretical study, and a fiery revolutionary, who was impressed by the need for party unity and the dangers of fractional activity, was in the making.

St. Petersburg

At the end of his period of exile, in June 1911, the authorities decided to keep Skryabin under observation, rather than punish him more severely as they did Arosev. He was arrested in September and sentenced to exile in Archangel for three years, from where he escaped to become an emigré in France and Belgium until 1917.[75] From Vologda, Skryabin went initially to Nolinsk to see his father, on whom he still seems to have been financially dependent,[76] the Vologda authorities informing those in Vyatka of his attempt to form an SD group and collect funds in Vologda.[77] After a visit to his family, and to Saratov to meet Tikhomirnov, who had also returned from exile,[78] Skryabin went to St. Petersburg and enrolled at the Polytechnic Institute. He also made a first brief trip to Moscow in December, probably on party business.[79]

The Polytechnic Institute had a reputation for radicalism. Lev Krasin and Nikolai Skrypnik, among the revolutionary leaders of 1917, were former students. Competition for places was intense,[80] and Skryabin's opportunity was apparently provided by the wealth of his maternal uncles,[81] although one popular biography claims that the Tsarist authorities allowed him to take the entrance examination in Vologda, and admitted him to the Polytechnic Institute, in an effort to win him away from the revolutionary movement.[82] In view of the reputation of the institution this seems unlikely. After a short time in the Shipbuilding Faculty, which in old age he described as the most aristocratic and most difficult, Skryabin transferred to the Economics Faculty where he remained registered and continued to study until 1916.[83]

He existed on a small grant from the Vyatka *zemstvo*,[84] and took rooms in *Rakovi Pereulok* (Eel Alley) in the Vyborg district. This was becoming a focus of worker unrest and by 1917 had a reputation for militancy, and as a Bolshevik stronghold.[85] In the Vyborg, prosperous families lived in the same streets as workers; it was also a student district where the Polytechnic Institute was situated.[86] The location of Skryabin's lodgings may have been no more than convenience, but it might also signify that his first loyalty was as a Bolshevik agitator, even if his primary commitment was to students rather than workers. The other reason behind this choice may have been his growing links with the Bolshevik press: his accommodation was next door to the offices where *Pravda* was to be published.[87]

In St. Petersburg, Skryabin immediately continued his revolutionary efforts. He worked to strengthen the solidarity of Bolshevik student groups, to form new ones in the St. Petersburg's higher educational institutions, and to unite them through a committee of the St. Petersburg student organisation.[88] To show their opposition to the Tsarist regime, these student groups attempted to spread Bolshevik literature and disrupt higher educational institutions. Attempts to unite radical student groups in St. Petersburg's higher education institutions predated Skryabin's arrival in the city, and went back to 1909–1910 in the Polytechnic Institute, when there was agitation in support of radical Duma members. In November 1912, when the St. Petersburg Bolshevik Committee of the SD Party, on which Skryabin served, was liquidated, the *Okhrana* asserted that he was the prime organiser of factory demonstrations to mark the opening of the Fourth Duma,[89] but he escaped arrest at this time, although he was forced to go into hiding.[90] Efforts to organise the students were renewed in early 1913, when a new organisation, *Zarnitsa* (Summer Lightning), which aimed to unite all the students of the Polytechnic Institute, was founded. An *Okhrana* report estimated that the number of student activists in St. Petersburg was highest at the Polytechnic Institute, although, because he did not become prominent in the organisation until that year, it is difficult to estimate Skryabin's contribution to this.[91] On 13 March 1913, a proclamation was distributed over the signature of the 'Group of Communists', calling a meeting the next day. There, another proclamation was distributed over the signature of the SD group. This proposed a demonstration on 15 March, in support of students at the military–medical academy, who, it was claimed, were being victimised by the reforms introduced at their institution. Skryabin was the first to address the meeting of 1200 prior to the demonstration.[92] From November 1912, to avoid capture, he had used the name of Nikolai Ivanov Smirnov. On 1 April 1913, when the authorities broke up the 'United Social Democratic Student Committee', he was arrested under this name, and forbidden to live in St. Petersburg and certain other large towns and provinces for three months.[93]

After his return to St. Petersburg from banishment, the SD fraction of the Polytechnic Institute students issued a further proclamation on 30 September. This protested against reactionary government policies, pogroms and anti-Semitism, and mentioned particularly the Beilis affair (the trial of a Jewish workman for the ritual murder of a Christian child). On the same day there was a meeting at the Institute organised by SR and SD groups. Here, Skryabin was prominent in protests against the Beilis trial.[94] Harassed by the *Okhrana* for his activities, he escaped arrest until November 1913, when he was arraigned for participation in the St. Petersburg Bolshevik Committee, but there was insufficient evidence and he was released under police supervision.[95] Then, in April 1914, his lodgings were once again searched and he was arrested in connection with the *Okhrana's* attempt to destroy the St. Petersburg Polytechnic Institute Social Democratic group. Another period of imprisonment followed, after which he was exiled from St. Petersburg[96] for some months, and his residence in large towns and industrial *gubernii* forbidden. Although he lodged outside the boundaries, he was not too far away to continue his party work in the city's Bolshevik organisations, and his writing for *Pravda* (Truth) and the Bolshevik monthly *Prosveshchenie* (Enlightenment), which had begun publication in December 1911. Student groups were an important aid to the Bolsheviks in propagandising the workers. Skryabin also worked in St. Petersburg trade unions, spoke at meetings, reported trade union activities in *Pravda,* and tried to promote the Bolshevik line in the trade union journal.[97] It is clear that his work now extended beyond student groups, and an *Okhrana* report of 1915 stated that

Skryabin can be classified as a Bolshevik Social Democrat who is undertaking party work in the Vyborg *raion* [district] on the instructions of Lenin, with whom he is in correspondence, taking part in the formation of a Social Democratic circle amongst the employees of the Nikolaevskii railway. He is a member of the Social Democratic fraction of the polytechnic students and on 14 March 1913 spoke at a meeting in the Polytechnic Institute proposing the holding of demonstrations against the reforms introduced at the medical–military academy. In 1912 and 1913 he was secretary of *Pravda*, the workers' newspaper.[98]

Pravda

During the years of moderate reform in Russia, at the end of the first decade of the twentieth century, the Social Democrats began, from December 1910, to publish in St. Petersburg, the weekly, *Zvezda* (The Star).[99] From the beginning of 1912 Skryabin worked for this paper,[100] and was therefore in a position to play a part in *Pravda* when it replaced *Zvezda* which was temporarily closed down in April 1912. It was through his old associate Victor Tikhomirnov, that he established his position on the paper. N. G. Poletaev, the publisher of *Zvezda*, was under pressure from Lenin to found a daily. Tikhomirnov promised him 3000 rubles[101] and became the behind-the-scenes business manager.[102] Skryabin worked for *Pravda* from its first issue.[103] Then, when F. F. Raskolnikov, who had been appointed as secretary to the newspaper, was arrested in May 1912, Tikhomirnov pushed Skryabin forward as the SD secretary to the editorial board, responsible for correspondence with the Central Committee abroad.[104] He served in this capacity until forced to go into hiding in late 1912, and then again in the autumn of 1913.[105] When arrested in November 1913 he described his work as 'correcting and copying manuscripts' (*po ispravleniyu i perepiski rukopisei*).[106]

Skryabin's duties brought him into contact with Lenin. On 16 June 1912, he wrote and asked Lenin to contribute because of the very great need for material.[107] In another letter, on 30 July, he informed Lenin when and how his contributions would be published, and warned against too many articles attacking the Kadets (Constitutional Democrats), as these made for 'monotonous reading'.[108] The *Pravda* editors were anxious to avoid factional controversy, and as Skryabin continued to correspond with Lenin in exile, the latter grew furious with the editors because they disallowed some of his articles and censored others in which he attacked the 'Liquidators'.[109] These were SDs who recommended 'liquidation' of underground tactics and participation in legal activities, such as the Duma and trade unions. Lenin wrote to Skryabin on 1 August 1912:

> You write as secretary ... why does *Pravda* persistently and systematically strike out of my articles and out of the articles of other colleagues any mention of the Liquidators? ...
>
>   You know *from experience* that I am showing enormous patience in suffering your censorship of the proofs. For fundamental questions demand *direct answers*. It is impossible to remain a co-worker without information about the intention of the editors to direct the section of the newspaper concerned with the [Duma] elections *against* the Liquidators, clearly and directly, or *not against*. There can be no middle way.[110]

Stalin, newly co-opted to the Bolshevik Central Committee, and responsible for *Pravda*, was also under attack from Lenin, although he was arrested on the day before the first issue of *Pravda* appeared.[111] Stalin and Skryabin became acquainted at this time,[112] and both were supporters of the more conciliatory attitude towards the Liquidators. Towards the end of the year, when Stalin was abroad working on his pamphlet *Marksizm i Natsional'nyi Vopros* (Marxism and the National Question) (1913), Lenin tried to reorganise the Editorial Board and correct *Pravda's* line. He replaced Stalin with Yakov Sverdlov.[113] On 1 November 1912, Skryabin informed Lenin:

> Inside the editorial Board, as you probably know, some changes have been made in the direction you desired. In general there have been no radical alterations – there has been a replenishment of the Board and a rearrangement and possibly more correct distribution of editorial functions. ...

At the same time Skryabin had the effrontery to tell Lenin that the *Pravda* editors in St. Petersburg knew better than the Bolshevik Central Committee in Galicia what the Russian workers wanted to read.[114] This provoked a further outburst from

Lenin who wrote on 12 January 1913:

> We received a stupid and impudent letter from the Editorial Board. We will not reply. They must be got rid of. ... We are exceedingly disturbed by the absence of news about the plan of re-organising the editorial board. ... Re-organisation, but better still, the complete expulsion of all old timers, is extremely necessary. It's managed absurdly. ... Their attitude towards the articles [ie. Lenin's] is monstrous. I've simply lost patience.[115]

The editors, who believed that the Bolsheviks needed to retain credibility with a broad spectrum of the working class in order to increase the circulation of the newspaper and guarantee its survival, published 284 of Lenin's articles, but rejected 47 between 1912 and 1914.[116] They felt that Lenin, who had declared 'irreconcilable war on the Liquidators',[117] and attacked both them and the Mensheviks in his articles, was not supporting them.[118]

The *Okhrana* records make clear that Skryabin was a junior member of the *Pravda* staff. He escaped arrest on 15 November 1912 when he jumped through the window of the *Pravda* editorial offices, but was forced to go into hiding.[119] The Bolsheviks made a special effort in the election campaign for the Fourth Duma and the newly founded *Pravda* was especially important in rallying Bolshevik representation.[120] Skryabin was involved in demonstrations at the opening of the Duma,[121] but claims that he had played a prominent part in the election campaign[122] are difficult to substantiate. A. E. Badayev, a Bolshevik member of the Duma, makes no special mention of Skryabin in his memoirs. He writes:

> Comrades Stalin, Sverdlov, Kamenev, Ol'minsky, Molotov, Krestinsky, Krylenko, Quiring, Concordia, Samilova and other leading Party workers took part in the work of the [Bolshevik] faction. But they appeared in St. Petersburg illegally and for short periods only, between an escape from exile and a new arrest,[123]

and Geoffrey Swain's study of the Social Democrats and the legal labour movement assigns no prominence to Molotov in the election campaign.[124]

Lenin was now becoming increasingly dissatisfied with the work of the *Pravda* Editorial Board. The Central Committee meeting in Cracow, from 28 December 1912 to 1 January 1913, over which he presided, was dominated by the affairs of the newspaper, particularly its conciliatory line during the election campaign and plans to found the joint Bolshevik–Menshevik newspaper *Rabochii Golos* (Workers' Voice).[125] Among the editorial staff, Skryabin, who in his letter of 12 January, Lenin had condemned for 'unpardonable stupidity',[126] was prominent in resistance to Central Committee control over the newspaper, and the Cracow meeting replaced him with K. N. Samilova.[127] Later, Molotov was clearly embarrassed by these events. As an editor of the 1937 edition of the volume of Lenin's works dealing with the period, he had Lenin's letters on the matter omitted. Among these were some which called for the replacement of *Pravda* officials ready to collaborate with the Mensheviks.

Lenin's attack, and his dismissal, made Skryabin rapidly change his position. Within a month, by February 1913, he had accepted the Leninist line, and wrote to Tikhomirnov to ensure that his resistance to the 'Liquidators' was stiffened.[128] This change was probably why he again became secretary to the editors in the autumn of 1913, when the paper was under attack from the Tsarist authorities and the editorial staff were arrested. It is difficult to judge if this was the moment when Skryabin had finally become converted to the Leninist standpoint, or if he was prepared to adopt it to regain his employment. His later association with Stalin provides other examples of the modification of his views to protect his position.

Early contributions to the press and the name Molotov

Skryabin's first contribution to the press was an article under the pen-name 'A. Luchinin' to the first number of a short-lived St. Petersburg student magazine *Utro Zhizni'* (The Morning of Life) in 1911, printed by the presses which were to produce *Pravda*.[129] He then wrote six articles for *Zvezda*, one for its short-lived successor *Nevskaya Zvezda* in 1912, and a further article for the party's theoretical journal *Prosveshchenie* in 1913.[130] For these he used the penname 'A. Ryabin'. He used the same soubriquet and 'V. Mikhailov' (on one occasion 'Vyacheslav Mikhailov'), when he wrote for *Pravda*. It is puzzling why in his early writings he used pseudonyms so closely based on his Christian name, patronymic and surname, that his identity was obvious. By the end of 1912 he had dropped 'Ryabin', and begun to use 'A. Zvanov' and occasionally 'A. Turbin'.[131] He continued to use 'V. Mikhailov' until *Pravda* was closed down in 1914. One early Soviet authority claims that Skryabin also used the pen name 'Akim Prostota' (Akim the Simple) for some of his early *Pravda* articles, but it was a mistake, for it allowed his enemies to claim later that this aptly described his dullness.[132] The use of a variety of pseudonyms was not only a device to protect the author from discovery by the *Okhrana*, it also gave the impression that large numbers of people were involved.

In old age, Molotov maintained that he first used the pseudonym under which he was to become famous in an article in *Voprosy Strakhovaniya* (Insurance Questions) in 1915, but apparently he wrote nothing for the press in that year. This may have been an error of memory, for in 1916 he contributed two articles to that journal under the name Molotov.[133] He claimed that he called himself after the intellectual hero of N. G. Pomyalovskii, portrayed in *Sovremennik* in 1861. In this novel, Molotov is the typical frustrated young idealist of the 1860s, a member of the middle class intelligentsia, who rejected the occupation of his father. He is sturdily independent from the institutions of his society, practical and unromantic, and seeks to make a place for himself in the world. The story is concerned with the conflict caused by the love freely bestowed on him by the heroine, whose family expected her to move in much more conventional channels. It ends with their achievement of bourgeois happiness;[134] but there is no evidence that this element of the novel lay behind Skryabin's choice of name. Again, late in life, he claimed that he gave himself the pseudonym for 'Bolshevik reasons' and denied that there was any connection between the *molot* (hammer) of Molotov and the *stal'* (steel) of Stalin. The connection with Stalin was so slim in 1915 and 1916 that there is little reason to doubt this claim, although by the later 1920s this interpretation of the name was useful to him. He also claimed that Molotov had the practical advantage in that he could avoid stammering over the name Skryabin.[135] When Shlyapnikov wrote his memoirs of 1917 in the 1920s it is clear that he was well known as Molotov.[136]

Molotov's contributions to *Pravda* are mainly concerned with practical politics and it is difficult to gain an impression of his theoretical views from them. During 1912 he contributed 21 short articles, 17 of these between May and August, then 1 in October and 3 in December. The first article he published was about medical insurance. He challenged recent statements and figures by Minister Durnovo in the Duma, about the extent and value of industrial medical insurance, and wrote of the abysmal lack of help to the peasants and in the countryside.[137] In his next article, he pointed out that capitalists in a number of western European countries had come together in organisations to defend themselves against strikes, and that west European workers were uniting to protect themselves.[138] Three weeks later, he wrote a strong protest about the failure of the government to open the Georgian National University in Tiflis.[139] Three further articles commented on Duma politics; attacked the Octobrist Party particularly their links with right wing nationalist groups; and urged workers and peasants to support left wing groups who had recently shown that they were the defenders of democracy.[140]

Against a background of mounting industrial unrest in Russia,[141] Molotov was commissioned to write a series of articles on the strike movement. There were six of these between May and July.[142] Other articles at the end of the year with the same headline were unsigned, so it is difficult to decide if Molotov was the author. The signed articles described the size, duration and location of strikes. They gave most detail for St. Petersburg, with which Molotov was familiar. There was very little comment, although he emphasised the working class basis for the strikes, and denied that the professional classes were involved. He claimed that the industrial base of the strike movement was steadily widening. It seems that at first he was not entrusted with articles of major significance. For instance, on 18 July, when he published one of his reports on the strikes, he was not responsible for the major article 'Workers and the Bourgeois Economy'. In June, following a statement by the Tsarist Minister Menshikov that Russia was only tenth in a list of world powers and below Greece and Denmark, Molotov wrote an article in which he claimed that it stood in the first place with regard to bad harvests, peasant hunger and government repression.[143] Other articles dealt with the attack on workers' organisations, anti-Semitism and the Duma elections.[144]

In August he wrote about wages and productivity of labour, the claimed industrial upsurge in Russia, and commented on its effect on the workers. He maintained that prices had risen but not wages, and that the contemporary boom did not greatly benefit consumer industries such as textiles.[145] In a further series of articles, from October, he attacked the liberal Milyukov, and warned of the increasing danger of war, which only true democrats were opposing, not the Right or liberals.[146] His last article of the year described the early sessions of the Fourth Duma. Entitled 'Running on the Spot' (*Beg na meste*) he condemned the new

Duma, and the socialist fraction within it in particular, for continued support of reactionary policies.[147] On 4 January 1913, he referred to a proposed new law on holidays, and compared the state with serf-owning landlords. Another article, on 23 February, demonstrated that Molotov had come into line to attack the 'liquidators'. His final contribution, before there was a break in his involvement, was a straightforward historical narrative of the writing of the communist manifesto for the thirtieth anniversary of Marx's death.[148]

When he returned to work for *Pravda* again in the autumn of 1913, the quality of the newspaper shows that it was operating under much more difficult conditions, for the era of relaxation by the Tsarist authorities was over. *Pravda*, which had been published under its original name from 1912 to July 1913, was now forced to change its name nine times, each time after a prohibition, until it was finally closed down in July 1914. It retained, however, the word *Pravda* in each title, and the masthead which was familiar to readers.[149] From the time of his reappointment to the paper, until the end of 1913, Molotov was responsible for 35 more articles.[150] Twenty-seven were on trade union affairs, and he emphasised the growth of unions and their importance for the workers. From the nature of his contributions it is clear that he attended workers' meetings as part of his work. Two articles dealt with the Moscow tramway strike.[151] He urged St. Petersburg workers to show solidarity with the strikers and to prevent goods from reaching Moscow. Five further articles dealt with party affairs[152] and included the now conventional attacks on the 'liquidators'. In one, he emphasised the importance of links between SD deputies in the Duma and the workers: the deputies should recognise the authority of organised Marxist interests, or cease to claim to recognise the workers.[153] A further article highlighted the immense cost of the Russian prison system.[154]

There was a short gap in Molotov's contributions to *Pravda* after his arrest in November 1913. When he next published in the paper, in early 1914, his writing assumed far greater authority. He wrote a further nine articles before he was arrested again in April, and one more in June.[155] His first piece, on 21 January, published under the heading 'Workers Newspapers', called on the editors of these journals to portray working class life in all its variety and richness, as the newspapers published for other classes did.[156] This was followed, towards the end of the month, by a strong attack on groups in the Duma that supported a government associated with the 'Black Hundreds' and Jewish pogroms.[157] In an article, on the last day of January, he gave examples of how individual workers had stood up for their rights and better conditions, but went on to argue that the heroes in the struggle should not be individuals but the working class as a whole.[158] On 5 March, he wrote in commemoration of the Paris Commune. He emphasised the role of the Commune's Central Committee, but concluded

> The Commune consisted of workers, a rising of subject people, but those who gave their lives are commemorated by the proletariat of the whole world.[159]

He still wrote about the strike movement, but was now far more prepared to comment, offer advice and draw conclusions. In April he described four small strikes, showed how these could quickly be spread to a number of plants, and how it was necessary for workers to join unions to strengthen their organisation. He emphasised the difficulties for workers in small enterprises and how solidarity was essential for their success.[160] With a new wave of attacks on the St. Petersburg Polytechnic Institute Social Democratic group, Molotov's connection with *Pravda* was one of the reasons for his arrest in April 1914.[161] His last contribution, in June 1914, presumably smuggled out of prison, argued that the strengthening of reaction put great responsibility on Social Democracy to be active in the education of the workers. The first step in this direction had to be the dissemination of a workers newspaper, and the links of the workers with the rural population and with office workers (*sluzhashchi*) had to be reinforced.[162]

Although it is difficult to assess Molotov's importance in the history of the early *Pravda*, it must not be overestimated. A collection of reminiscences mentions his name only once,[163] and if this, and other works written after his disgrace are not likely to emphasize his importance, neither did he, or Soviet sources written when he was at the height of his power. He did, however, say that he considered that his work in *Pravda* was one of the best moments of his party work, and that he was aware that he was playing a part in an important revolutionary movement.[164] If his contribution to the newspaper was not a major one, his experience, in working and writing for it, was an important formative element in his career.

Moscow, exile, and on the eve of 1917

The outbreak of war in August 1914 produced a great upsurge of patriotic feeling in Russia. This, and a new wave of repression initiated by the autocracy, directed against both revolutionary activity and labour unrest, led to the collapse of the strike movement. Revolutionary socialists, who were divided on the question of policy towards the war, were isolated and weakened. The five Bolshevik deputies in the Duma were arrested and exiled after they urged the Russian proletariat to fight the autocracy rather than Germany.[165] The changed circumstances caused Molotov to move the focus of his activities from St. Petersburg to Moscow in April 1915.[166] The claim of one Soviet source that the change was to avoid continual harassment in St. Petersburg, and because of the difficulty in avoiding arrest,[167] appears to be inaccurate. The Party directed him to Moscow. *Okhrana* reports confirm works written in the Soviet period, that the St. Petersburg committee of the RSDRP (Russian Social Democratic Workers' Party) sent him to Moscow on a *komandirovka* (official mission), to restore and strengthen the work of the Party there.[168] Later, he admitted how poorly organised the party was at this time, and told Milovan Djilas, the Yugoslav vice-president:

> I remember ... how at the beginning of the war I came illegally from Petrograd to Moscow on party business. I had nowhere to spend the night but had to risk staying with Lenin's sister.[169]

He was one of at least four representatives[170] sent from St. Petersburg to Moscow, and linked up with his old friend Mal'tsev who had gone direct from exile in Vologda to university in Moscow, in August 1911.[171]

In Moscow, the situation was perhaps even more difficult than in Petrograd. The Bolsheviks were weakened by repression, and many informers existed in the ranks of the revolutionary parties. Molotov, who is described as wearing a grey coat and grey hat with brim, and the pince-nez which were to become characteristic, but at the time without a moustache, initially continued his activities among students, and collaborated particularly with those from the Commercial Institute,[172] where Tikhomirnov was a student.[173] Its students were particularly active and supported the Leninist line.[174] One police report mentions the distribution in Moscow of *Proletarskii Golos'* (Voice of the Proletariat), the organ of the St. Petersburg Committee of the SD Party.[175]

As a cloak for his activities, Molotov worked in a reserved occupation to avoid conscription, and was employed by the Union of Municipalities.[176] Based at Lenin's sister's apartment, he utilised Maria Ulyanov's contacts with Bolshevik activists and was able to lead the revival of the Bolshevik organisation in Lefortovo *raion*, where there was no *raion* committee. He formed a Bolshevik group called 'The Organised Group of Social Democrats'. A 1916 *Okhrana* report noted:

> With the arrival of Skryabin and other agents there was a marked upsurge in the revolutionary spirit of the local Social Democratic underground organisation

The group which Vyacheslav organised in Lefortovo *raion* became the strongest of five groups established by the SD agents sent from St. Petersburg and local Bolsheviks.[177] In commemoration of the Lena massacre (the shooting of strikers in the Lena goldfields in 1912), it published a leaflet which opposed 'civil peace' and advocated a 'democratic republic'. In preparation for May Day 1915, the group issued a proclamation, demanding protests on that day against rising prices and the war.[178] On May Day, another proclamation stated that the class struggle in each state was part of the general class struggle: there was one aim, one freedom, one red flag and one international anthem. The proclamation called for the establishment of a 'European United States – a revolutionary and democratic force'. Another declaration called for a boycott of the government's War-Industry Committee.[179]

With Molotov as one of the principal activists, the different SD groups were brought into contact with each other. Attempts were then made to unite all Moscow groups under the leadership of a single city-wide committee,[180] and revive the former all-city body which had become moribund.[181] To achieve this, a meeting in the Sokol'nicheskii woods on 1 June planned a conference to be held in Izmailovskii Park on 7 June. This was to elect a 'Moscow Committee' and discuss reports and resolutions on three general issues: the war and its consequences, the economic life of Russia, and the position of Social Democracy on ending the war. The meeting was also to consider the text of a leaflet about the looting, on 28 and 29 May 1915, of shops and property in Moscow thought to be owned by those of German extraction. About ten representatives were to participate in this conference, but on the previous night, eight including Molotov were denounced by an *agent provocateur* and arrested. Mal'tsev was amongst others who were seized,[182] and when he was searched, a collection of literature issued by the St. Petersburg Social Democratic Committee, and papers which linked him to Molotov's 'Organised Group of Social Democrats', were discovered.[183] Despite the arrests there was some success. Molotov's work led to the foundation of party organisations in Moscow factories that spread Bolshevik anti-war propaganda,[184] and the *Okhrana* acknowledged his importance in promoting revolutionary activity in Moscow. In Lefortovo *raion* the organisation he had founded continued to develop.[185]

In September, Molotov was banished for three years to the village of Manzurka in Irkutsk *guberniya*, which bordered on Mongolia and was 5000 kilometres from Moscow. This was no easy exile: conditions in the province were naturally harsh and the Tsarist authorities seem to have been more severe on the exiles than usual. Initially, Molotov was imprisoned in Irkutsk for three weeks, and held with six or seven other political offenders in a single cell. He described the conditions as most abominable: the window was either stuffed with rags or open to the elements. The prisoners were deprived of their money and personal food stock, and they often received no breakfast. If their gaolers could do anything to make life difficult, they apparently did so. Vyacheslav was forced to demand a fork to eat his food on one occasion and was held in the punishment cell overnight. He believed that the result of the hardships was to strengthen the loyalty of the political prisoners to each other.

They then left for Manzurka, to travel the last part of the journey by *etap* (by stages, shackled and on foot).[186] More than a month later some of the prisoners had not recovered from the effects of the journey. In his first letter from Manzurka, to his friend Arosev, Molotov wrote:

The Irkutsk administration is repulsive. It is without morals or sense. Evidently they do not take any notice of letters or telegrams. They are obviously Asians [i.e. rude and ignorant]. ... Today I have been in Manzurka a month. I have received so far 4 rubles 20 kopeks for food. According to the rules it should be 12 rubles 50 kopeks as I am privileged. Up to this time I live in a confused way. ...

Regarding books. If you can send anything solid, especially Marxist, I shall be extremely grateful. ... I am desperate for books because the local 'general' library was shut down this summer. There are enough newspapers. ... We receive newspapers, although at third hand.

Later, in the same letter, he requested books by Kautsky, Mazlov and Chernyshevsky, as he intended to use the next few months for the improvement of his mind. He was now dedicating himself to theoretical study. He wrote that he had enough money, but needed warm clothes for the extreme climate. He enquired about his old friends especially Mal'tsev, asked for information on the present attitude of the workers, and about a large protest which he had heard had taken place in Petrograd. He concluded

I look hopefully towards the future. My spirits are good, particularly now that I have heard from many dear friends, and I have no intention at all of getting ill.[187]

There was now a group of twelve exiles in Manzurka, and here Molotov met his future Bolshevik colleagues Martin Latsis, Aleksandr Shcherbakov and G. N. Pylyaev.[188] To see in the New Year, old revolutionaries sang the *Marseillaise*, but Molotov's group sang the *Internationale*. They drank vodka, local beer and *samogon*, which with hunger may have contributed to a serious illness Molotov suffered, in spite of his intentions to the contrary.[189] Then, in May 1916, now classified as a 'party professional', he escaped from exile with a false passport,[190] and returned to Petrograd by way of Kazan. Here he stayed with Tikhomirnov, who had recently been in direct contact with Lenin.[191] Tikhomirnov procured a better passport for him, and joined him for the remainder of the journey to the capital.[192]

In Petrograd, the pair resumed their old activities. They found that the '1915 Bolshevik group', established following the arrest and exile of prominent Bolsheviks, had begun to prepare for the publication of an illegal newspaper, but in the face of intensified government repression it had disintegrated.[193] Molotov, with Latsis, Pylyaev and Comrade Emma,[194] was involved in attempts to rebuild the group and revive the newspaper, which was to be named *Osvedomitel'nyi List'* (Information Bulletin).[195] The situation in the capital was, however, very difficult. There was great danger of arrest, and Molotov for a time went to stay in Orel with a friend from the Polytechnic Institute to avoid capture. On his return to Petrograd he continued to work in the Bolshevik underground. Paid by the Party, he acted as secretary to the journal *Sovremennyi Mir* (Contemporary World) and contributed to the only legal Bolshevik journal, *Voprosy Strakhovaniya* (Insurance Questions).[196] This journal supported a city-wide sickness insurance scheme, and was issued by the 'Workers' Insurance Group'.[197] During 1912–1914 the workers' insurance campaign had been organised under Bolshevik influence and *Voprosy Strakhovaniya* had become the Bolsheviks legal journal. This was closed down after the outbreak of the First World War, and leading activists in the insurance movement were arrested. Early in 1915, the 'Workers' Insurance Group' began to function again and *Voprosy Strakhovaniya* reappeared. The campaign was organised by the Bolsheviks, who, as before, controlled the insurance journal and used it to spread their influence among the Petrograd workers.[198] Molotov's experience with *Pravda* was clearly important. He was associated with both legal and illegal ventures at this time, and worked with Tikhomirnov in the distribution of the material.[199]

Aleksandr Shlyapnikov, who had been active in the St. Petersburg Bolshevik organisation earlier, but more recently had been with the emigré leaders abroad, now returned to the capital and took over the work of rebuilding the city's party organisation. Shlyapnikov was to be associated with the Workers' Opposition, which Molotov was active in crushing, and that his memoirs, published in 1922, pay scant attention to Molotov prior to 1917 is scarcely surprising, although they had met in Irkutsk in 1915.[200] He does acknowledge Tikhomirnov, who as usual remained behind the scenes, but who appears to have played an important senior rôle.[201] Suggestions that Molotov led the St. Petersburg Bolsheviks until Shlyapnikov arrived seem to be inventions of the Stalin period. It was Shlyapnikov who re-established the Russian Bureau of the Bolshevik Central Committee, and had

Molotov, who was a member of the St. Petersburg Committee, co-opted to the Russian Bureau.[202] The biographies of Molotov written in the Stalin period attribute Molotov's co-option directly to Lenin,[203] but this is explicable in terms of Molotov's desire to prove himself a worthy pupil of Lenin, and because the authors needed to write out Shlyapnikov. These works fail to say that in late 1916 and early 1917 there were, in fact, only three members of the Bureau: Shlyapnikov, Molotov and Petr Zalutskii.[204] These were the only Bolsheviks, not in prison or exile, of sufficient rank to merit the honour. Trotsky acknowledges that these were the only members of the Bureau present in February 1917, and sarcastically describes Molotov as a 'college boy'.[205] Molotov, apparently using the name Skryabin again, was in charge of publications and secretarial duties, but on her return from exile, in March, Elena Stasova, who had many years of experience as party secretary, took over Molotov's secretarial responsibilities.[206]

Whilst he was very active in Petrograd during the second half of 1916, Molotov also visited Moscow again, probably with Shlyapnikov.[207] They went to try to strengthen the Moscow Bolshevik organisation, and to improve the links of the party organisation with military units and with the provinces. By 1917, Molotov's experience, training, and presence in St. Petersburg, meant that he was in a position to play a significant if not a leading role, in the year of revolutions.

2
Forging the Bolshevik Regime

1917

In February 1917 there was a wave of mass strikes in Petrograd, partly politically inspired but mostly a response to food shortages and inflation caused by the war. These led to riots and civil disorder, which the Petrograd garrison refused to repress, and the Tsarist regime collapsed. In this chaotic situation, the task of the Russian Bureau, the senior Bolshevik body in Russia, was rendered more complex by the existence of the Sormovo-Nikolaev *Zemlyachestvo* (association/friendly society), which was particularly influential in the Vyborg. The *Zemlyachestvo*, a tightly knit group of about fifty of the most devoted and experienced Russian revolutionaries, had considerable influence through the workers' circles they ran in factories. Shlyapnikov and his associates could not issue orders to this body, and the relationship of the Russian Bureau to the *Zemlyachestvo* was further complicated because meetings of the Bureau and the Bolshevik Party took place in the apartments of *Zemlyachestvo* members.

In February 1917 the *Zemlyachestvo* was at the height of its power[1] and the Bolsheviks were divided.[2] Shlyapnikov, Molotov and Zalutskii were unenthusiastic about the strike movement because they believed that it 'might eventually be detrimental to the cause of the revolution', as the Bolsheviks did not guide it. In contrast, the St. Petersburg Committee and the Vyborg District Committee, the bodies co-ordinating the Bolshevik organisation in Petrograd, attempted to lead and expand the strike movement. As it grew, the breach between the Russian Bureau and the Petrograd organisations widened. Shlyapnikov was apparently among the most pessimistic about the revolutionary potential of the situation,[3] although with Molotov's assistance he eventually issued a leaflet in the name of the St. Petersburg Committee, based on the corrected version of a draft sent by M. S. Ol'minsky from Moscow. This called for the establishment of SD 'committees of struggle, committees of freedom' in each factory, barrack, area of the city, and all over Russia. The leaflet emphasised that it was important to sustain the con-flict,[4] but in line with the more radical policy adopted by the St. Petersburg Committee, which was dissatisfied with Shlyapnikov's leadership, ignored Soviets (Workers' Councils), which were spontaneously emerging, as in the 1905 revolution.

Only the Vyborg District Committee responded positively to demands for the immediate establishment of Soviets.[5]

Molotov added demands for a constituent assembly based on universal suffrage and secret ballot, the eight-hour day, and confiscation of estates: the 'three whales' of the SD party programme, to a manifesto drafted by V. Kayurov. A member of the Vyborg District Committee and of the Sormovo-Nikoloaev *Zemlyachestvo*, he persuaded the reluctant Shlyapnikov that it was essential that such a document be issued in the name of the Bolshevik Central Committee to gain the support of the masses.[6] He was entrusted with the final wording and printing, and persuaded the editors to let it appear as a supplement to the first issue of the *Izvestiya* (News) of the St. Petersburg Soviet.[7] The manifesto stated that the Provisional Government, composed of representatives of the richer bourgeoisie and landowners, which had begun to emerge from the opposition in the Duma, could not be supported. It called on the working class and the army to create a 'provisional revolutionary government', composed of members of parties represented in the Executive Committee of the Petrograd Soviet. This body, besides fulfilling SD demands, was to confiscate and redistribute stocks of food; negotiate 'with the proletariat of the belligerent countries for a revolutionary struggle of all countries against their oppressors'; and end the war. Factory workers and insurgent armies were urged to elect representatives to this government. The Manifesto ended with salutes to the 'red banner of revolution', 'the democratic republic' and 'the revolutionary and insurgent army'. The policies advocated conformed to the Leninist line,[8] which was much easier as the Provisional Government had not yet established itself.

Molotov told Chuev, that he and Zalutskii went to the Soviet early in the morning of 27 February, and were granted membership when they told Kerensky, its chairman, that they were from the Central Committee of the Bolsheviks.[9] Molotov was active in the agitation for the formation of the soldiers' section of the Soviet and encountered opposition because of his support for left wing views.[10] He spoke on 28 February, the day he became a member and opposed the order of M. Rodzianko, the leader of the Duma, which directed officers and soldiers to return to their barracks. He declared that

> Rodzianko's order ... was hostile to the revolution which had been accomplished, which was a worker's revolution, at the 'root' of which was 'property relations'. ... The task of the Soviets was not to settle a conflict with Rodzianko, but to draw the soldiers into a union with the revolutionary masses, which would allow the question of power to be settled outside the Duma Committee.

Molotov proposed to condemn the order as a 'counter-revolutionary attack, a provocative act' which should be publicly retracted and withdrawn.[11]

From 28 February, Molotov, who was involved in the formation of the Executive Committee of the St. Petersburg Soviet, served as a representative of the Bolshevik Party and Russian Bureau.[12] His membership of the Russian Bureau enabled him to be involved in policy discussions prior to meetings.[13] Shlyapnikov was responsible for Molotov's membership of the Executive. At the first meeting of the Soviet, he was dissatisfied with the extreme minority position of the Bolsheviks when the Executive Committee was elected, and moved to include on it two representatives from each socialist party. Molotov and K. I. Shukto were nominated as Bolshevik representatives, although overall the Executive Committee's right wing was strengthened.[14] At the Executive Committee meeting, on 1 March, Molotov did not oppose the transfer of power to the Provisional Government, rather than the Soviet, i.e. he accepted the formation of a propertied regime.[15] Following this, however, he was present at a meeting between the Russian Bureau and the St. Petersburg Committee to discuss tactics, where it was agreed to oppose this policy and to champion a 'provisional revolutionary government'.[16] The next day, the Menshevik leader, Nikolai Sukhanov, confiscated from Molotov a package of tracts, apparently composed by the SRs and a section of the Bolsheviks, which called on the soldiers to massacre their officers.[17] He accused Molotov of making an irresponsible speech in the Executive:

> talking about the necessity of all political power passing into the hands of the democracy. He didn't suggest anything concrete, but he advanced precisely this principle – instead of 'control' over the bourgeois government and 'pressure' on it. Molotov ... could find fault because he was doing nothing and not suggesting anything concrete. ... the opinion he expressed was not that of his party, or at least that of its leaders who were available.[18]

Molotov had apparently said:

> Why [are we conferring. The decision is] already made. Ministers have already been appointed. The task is to conduct a struggle against the Tsar and his lack-eys. The Provisional Government is not revolutionary. Guchkov, factory owners, Rodzianko and Konavolov would make a mockery [of the people]. Instead of land they would give rocks [to the peasant].[19]

Sukhanov commented that Molotov never lost an opportunity to sabotage the 'Right Socialists' and make 'demagogic appeals to the masses'.[20] From this time Molotov showed himself to be a strict Leninist. He adopted Lenin's position on the Provisional Government, that the present situation was very temporary and that there was likely to be a major political polarisation. He also accepted the idea of civil war to secure the triumph of the next stage of the revolution.

On 3 March, the St. Petersburg Committee of Bolsheviks declared that although it would oppose any attempt to restore the monarchy, it would not resist the Provisional Government in as far as its activities corresponded with the interests of the proletariat and 'broad democratic mass of people'. Two days later, Molotov attended a meeting of the Committee to bring it into line, but he was unsuccessful. The Committee claimed that the policy of the Russian Bureau was too 'academic', as it failed to take into account the existing situation. Molotov had proposed a resolution which attacked the Provisional Government as counterrevolutionary: it was 'made up of representatives of the monarchist grand bourgeoisie and landowners'. He demanded its replacement with a government capable of carrying out a programme of democratic revolution. The resolution stated that the St. Petersburg Committee would 'struggle for the creation of a Provisional Revolutionary Government'. The Committee, however, adopted a text promising not to oppose the Provisional Government so long as 'its actions correspond to the interests of the proletariat and of the true democratic masses of the people'.[21] Molotov was also involved in the Russian Bureau's attempts to assert its authority over the Vyborg District Committee. On 3 March, it ordered the withdrawal of a leaflet that did not correspond to Central Committee policy.[22]

On 5 March *Pravda* began to be issued again. Mikhail Kalinin, now as later, valued for his peasant connections, assisted Molotov, who as a member of the Russian Bureau of the Central Committee was senior editor. The other editors were M. S. Ol'minskii and K. S. Eremeev.[23] The first issue was distributed free; the second sold 100,000 copies.[24] In general, the paper adopted the Leninist line. It reflected Molotov's opposition to co-operation with the Provisional Government,[25] denounced it as 'a government of capitalists and landowners' and called on the Soviet to convene a constituent assembly to establish a 'democratic republic'. On 10 March, *Pravda*, on the basis of a resolution drafted by Molotov and Zalutskii, called for the transformation of the imperialist war into a civil war, and for the liberation of the people from the 'yoke of the ruling classes'.[26]

The situation in Petrograd became far more difficult for Molotov after 12 March, with the return from exile of Lev Kamenev, Stalin and Matvei Muranov, all Bolsheviks senior to him and Shlyapnikov. The latter alleged that the new arrivals introduced disagreement and 'deep organisational frictions' into the leading party bodies, and in particular that they launched an attack on *Pravda* and its editors. Molotov, who believed that Stalin and the other senior Bolsheviks were mistaken in their policy,[27] was temporarily replaced on the Executive Committee of the St. Petersburg Soviet, but attempts to adopt a more moderate line towards the Provisional Government were resisted by the Russian Bureau. On 12 March, when Molotov led the opposition to Stalin's candidacy, the Bureau imposed strict conditions on Kamenev, and granted Stalin only non-voting membership, because of 'certain personal characteristics'.[28] At the same meeting, G. I. Bokii, Molotov's nominee, was accepted (five votes for, one against, with two abstentions), and Molotov was in the van of those who resisted pressure from the moderates to co-operate with the Provisional Government. At the next meeting, the membership of Stalin and Zalutskii was accepted, but only because Molotov and Shlyapnikov had been promoted to a newly created Presidium.[29] These manoeuvres can have done nothing to improve relations between Stalin and Molotov.

The records of the afternoon session of the Russian Bureau, on 13 March, begin with an announcement from Molotov that he resigned from the Presidium, Executive Committee of the Soviet and editorship of *Pravda*, as he 'did not consider himself sufficiently experienced'. The real reason, however, seems to have been that Molotov was an orthodox Leninist and that Stalin was using his senior position as a Central Committee member to change the *Pravda* staff.[30] Molotov's resignation was accepted and Stalin took over his positions.[31] The issue of the newspaper, published the next morning,[32] contained an article by Kamenev which called for conditional support for the Provisional Government, and on 15 March, Kamenev's leader appealed for support for the war.[33] Thus, on 14 and 15 March, the moderates seem to have triumphed over the Russian Bureau and the Party was in complete disarray. On 15 March, however, Molotov was restored to a new editorial board of himself, Kamenev and Eremeev, with Stalin as substitute for Eremeev who was temporarily away from Petrograd.[34] *Pravda* now returned, in general, to its former position, but it published only a cut version of the first of the five of Lenin's 'Letters from Afar', and disagreements among the Petrograd Bolshevik leaders continued. Molotov was also reinstated on the Executive Committee of the Soviet where he pressed for peace.[35] He sent a protest to the Russian Bureau on 24 March against daily meetings of its Presidium (possibly an attempt to arrogate power from the Bureau itself), which may be related to friction with Stalin and the moderates.[36]

These events present a very different picture of Molotov's relations with Stalin from the traditional portrayal, and in view of their later association the conflict that occurred between the two at this time is ironic. As well as differences between the strict Leninist and the more moderate, Molotov's previous experience of working with Stalin on *Pravda* may have influenced him. They were sharing lodgings. Stalin admitted that Molotov was 'nearest of all to Lenin … in April', but he stole Molotov's girlfriend, Marusya.[37]

Differences continued at the All-Russian Party Conference, 1–3 April 1917. Shlyapnikov and Molotov headed a left wing supported by Alexandra Kollontai and the Moscow provincial organisation, and unsuccessfully demanded all-out opposition to the Provisional Government and to the war, in conflict with the more moderate line of Stalin, Viktor Nogin, Aleksei Rykov and the Moscow city organisation.[38] When, near its close, the Conference debated the proposal of I. G. Tseretelli to merge the Bolsheviks and the Mensheviks, and Stalin was sympathetic, Molotov opposed it saying

> Tseretelli wants to unite heterogeneous elements. Tseretelli calls himself a Zimmerwaldist and a Kientahlist, and for this reason unification along these lines is incorrect, both politically and organisationally. It would be more correct to advance a definite international socialist platform, we will unite a compact minority.

But Molotov's proposal for the preparation of a separate Bolshevik platform was defeated, and Stalin's motion, for unification with those Mensheviks who accepted the views of the Zimmerwald and Kienthal conferences on the war, was approved unanimously.[39] Following this, after Lenin's promulgation of the April Theses, on 4 April, it was natural for Molotov to support the extreme policies they advocated amongst the Petrograd Bolsheviks.[40]

Molotov was nominated to the Presidium at the Petrograd City Conference, 12–22 April, where, with Lenin, Stalin, Grigorii Zinoviev and Kamenev, he was elected to a seven-man committee to draft a resolution on the Provisional

Government and the war, which he proposed. He was also present at the VII Party Conference, 24–29 April 1917, but he did not make a major speech[41] and now retired into the background. Even though Molotov had, in Lenin's eyes, pursued a more correct line in the early days of the revolution, it was Stalin, who with Lenin's endorsement, was elected to the Central Committee, not Molotov. Slusser argues that Lenin backed Stalin's qualities of leadership, rather than Molotov's ideological correctness. Molotov had local support. He was elected to the newly created Petrograd City Committee as a representative of the Vyborg on 7 May, and its Executive on 10 May, following his report on the 1–3 April All-Russian Conference to the *raion* committee, in which he emphasised the unity which had been achieved.[42] But he had met Lenin for the first time, only when he alighted from the train at the Finland station, late on 3 April, and at the meeting of party workers he addressed immediately afterwards. Moreover, in these May elections to the Central Committee, no member of the group who had led the Bolsheviks until the arrival of the more moderate Stalin and Kamenev was elected. Since conflict with Stalin was to continue, this was not, as Slusser claims, a decisive moment for Molotov, who recognised Stalin's leadership potential and accepted him as his personal leader.[43] Molotov's election to the Executive marked the first step in the revival of his fortunes, after Stalin had ousted him from his positions. He was therefore unlikely to act as a watchdog for Stalin on the Committee, as Slusser suggests.[44] At the same time that Molotov was elected to the Executive he also became secretary of the Vyborg District Duma.[45] It was therefore logical that at the Petrograd Committee on 30 May, where he was elected chairman, whilst he supported the need for strong central action, he emphasised the rights of the *raion*.[46] His experience on *Pravda* now counted in his favour, for at the end of May, Molotov was appointed as the head of a new Central Committee Press Bureau. This was established to strengthen the position of the Bolshevik press in Russia, and Molotov was allocated special funds for this purpose.[47] It was at this time that he first met Lazar Kaganovich, with whom he was to be closely associated in the 1930s. Kaganovich, who had just come to St. Petersburg, recalled that Molotov was working with Arosev and Mal'tsev.[48]

During the July Days demonstrations Molotov was active as a party agent.[49] Then, when many front-rank Bolsheviks were arrested or went into hiding, he became important again. He supported Lenin's arguments on the need to prepare for an immediate armed uprising at the Central Committee Conference on 13 and 14 July,[50] and at the Second Petrograd City Conference on 16 July.[51] Here, in a further clash with Stalin, he asserted that, before the July Days

> the Soviets could have taken power without violence had they desired to do so. ... They didn't. [Instead] the developments of 3 and 4 July impelled the Soviets on a counterrevolutionary course. ... We can't fight for Soviets that have betrayed the proletariat. Our only solution lies in the struggle of the proletariat accompanied by those strata of the peasantry capable of following it.

Stalin, the Central Committee representative, argued that the July political crisis had not ended, and that there was a need for restraint and consolidation. When he proposed the Central Committee's resolution, Molotov and two other delegates introduced eighteen amendments, only one of which was accepted, and Molotov abstained when the resolution was put to the vote, because 'at such a crucial time it is impossible to adopt a vague resolution'.[52]

Whilst Lenin was in hiding in Finland after July, Molotov was in contact with him,[53] and at the VI Party Congress, 26 July to 3 August 1917, he again supported the Leninist line and advocated an immediate armed uprising. On 31 July, he once more asserted that after the critical July days it was no longer possible to transfer power peacefully into the hands of the Soviets.

> The slogan 'All power to the Soviets' signified the peaceful painless develop-ment of the revolution and was a great step forward for all democracy. ... But the revolution was not completed because the peasants did not receive land and peace. ...
> We must show the way they can take power in their hands. ... For us ... there is only one possible result from the established position – the dictatorship of the proletariat and the poor peasantry.[54]

That Molotov accepted the Leninist line for a socialist revolution was clear. He tried to hold the Petrograd Party organisation to that policy,[55] and was now able to co-operate with Stalin who was taking a harder line.[56] On 12 August, he was re-elected to the St. Petersburg Committee by the Vyborg *raion* committee,[57] where on 5 October, he spoke in favour of an armed uprising, asserting that

> Our task at the moment is not to restrain the masses, but to choose every oppor-tune moment for consolidating power. Lenin's theses stated that we must not allow ourselves to be fascinated by dates. ... We must be prepared for action at any moment.[58]

In contrast with the early days of the February 1917 revolution, however, one does not gain the impression from any source that Molotov played a leading rôle in the months prior to the October revolution.[59]

When the revolution came, Molotov was a member of the St. Petersburg Soviet and head of the agitation department of the Military Revolutionary Committee, the body set up by the Soviet to counter the Provisional Government's transfer of soldiers sympathetic to the revolution from Petrograd, which became the tool for the Bolshevik rising.[60] The 1938 *Short Course* names Molotov as one of nine 'specif-ically assigned by the Party to direct the uprising in the provinces';[61] and he may have been the 'comrade' who, as a result of Stalin's motion to the Central Committee on 21 October, was sent to Moscow to demand that their delegation to the Second Congress of Soviets come immediately.[62] He had, however, returned to St. Petersburg before the decisive event. In 1924, he claimed that he was in the Smolny Institute and involved in the events on the night of 25 October 1917, when Kamenev asked him to accompany a delegation of the City Duma to the Winter Palace. The delegation, however, was unsuccessful in reaching the headquarters of the Provisional Government.[63] In his memoirs, in old age, he confirmed that he was in St. Petersburg during October, but did not make any particular claim for his actions during the Bolshevik Revolution.[64]

1917 demonstrated that Molotov was a fiery revolutionary, a staunch Leninist in the front rank of the Bolsheviks. But on no occasion did he challenge for a leadership position. His commitment to Lenin's extreme views was ideological, rather than opportunistic. He had been prepared to differ with Lenin when he worked on *Pravda*, and until late 1917 support for Lenin seemed unlikely to bring political rewards. Molotov's stance, however, might also demonstrate that he needed a strong leader, something that was to characterise his career.

The Northern Sovnarkhoz

Following the victorious October Revolution Molotov supported the Lenin–Trotsky line. He opposed any coalition with other groups in the new government,[65] although the Bolsheviks, who claimed that the Left SRs accepted Bolshevik policies, were in coalition with them until mid-1918. Molotov became one of the Bolshevik leaders in the Soviet.[66] He replaced P. G. Smidovich on 4 November 1917,[67] but he was not senior enough to serve in the new government, the Council of People's Commissars (hereinafter Sovnarkom). He still worked for *Pravda*,[68] continued his party functions, and played an active rôle in the Agitation Department with responsibility for collecting funds and making payments.[69] Molotov was one of eight elected to the Executive Commission of the Petrograd Committee in November, only one candidate secured more votes.[70] At a meeting of the Commission, at the end of the month, his proposal to re-establish the Soviet's departments was accepted unanimously.[71] In the following month, he was the driving force behind the formation of a seven-man commission (two representatives from the Soviet, two from the Red Guard, one from the city administration, one from the *raion* committee and a military staff officer (Kliment Voroshilov was elected)) to defend the city from attack.[72]

Molotov remained a member of the Military Revolutionary Committee which dealt with the threat of counter-revolution, and began to involve itself in civil administration. This included the provision of food supplies for Petrograd.[73] On 30 October, the Petrograd Soviet appointed him to oversee a redefinition of the rôle of the Military Revolutionary Committee,[74] but by mid-November Sovnarkom had re-allocated some of the functions of that body to the new commissariats, and decided to abolish it on 5 December.[75]

In December, the Petrograd Soviet began to establish an Economic Council (*Sovnarkhoz*) for the area, in line with the policy adopted by Sovnarkom's VSNKh (the Supreme Council of the National Economy). At its first meeting, the *Sovnarkhoz* elected a five-man presidium with Molotov as chairman.[76] Its records show that from the start Molotov's duties were onerous.[77] When the national government moved to Moscow in March 1918, and it was decided to invest executive authority for Petrograd in the Soviet, but leave everyday management of the city to be exercised by a new thirteen member Council of Commissars chaired by

Zinoviev, the *Sovnarkhoz*, with Molotov as chairman, became one of the commissariats. A month later, in April, Molotov's area of responsibility expanded. Petrograd, since March called the Petrograd Labour Commune, was reorganised as the Commune of the Northern Region, a much larger area. It included Novgorod, Pskov, Olonets to which Karelia was later added, Arkhangelsk, Vologda, Cherepovets and Severno-Dvinsk.[78] Molotov chaired a body with representatives from seven *gubernii*, responsible for factories, production and nationalisation, in a large area with important industries. In February 1919, however, when the Third Congress of Soviets abolished the Northern Commune, his sphere of operation contracted again to Petrograd.[79] This was an extremely important appointment for Molotov who had no previous experience of economic administration, and can be said to mark the beginning of his transition to a bureaucrat.

When he spoke to the Soviets of the Northern Region, at the time the enlarged Commune was established, he was optimistic about the opportunities provided by the new socialist economy, although he also impressed on his audience the magnitude of the task to be faced. He specified agriculture, transport and fuel, as areas where there were particular problems, and called on the Soviets 'to take all measures to work out a plan of general economic organisation'.[80] The early months of 1918 were months of economic chaos and crisis in Petrograd. The ending of production for the war effort exacerbated an already grave situation. Factories were closed and workers laid off. In May, Molotov, as *Sovnarkhoz* chairman, commented: 'this colossal industrial centre, if it is not dying, is without question asleep'.[81] Nevertheless his *Sovnarkhoz* drew up a constitution for itself, which it hoped would serve as a general model.[82] When this was presented at the First All-Russian Congress of *Sovnarkhozy* in June, Molotov was forced to admit that in April 1918, in Petrograd, 265 factories from 799 were closed, and only 121,000 from a workforce of 208,000 were working. He spoke of severe organisational problems and difficulties, and lack of progress in practically every sector of industry, although he saw this as only temporary. He was critical of those who believed that Petrograd industry could not be revived. Hopeful of progress, he outlined the measures the *Sovnarkhoz* was implementing to remedy matters, and mentioned the potential for electrification in Novgorod *guberniya*,[83] possibly an echo of Lenin's early remarks on electrification a few weeks before.[84] In July, in line with Lenin's current thinking, the *Sovnarkhoz* proposed the introduction of piecework to improve work discipline and productivity, a step that was to prove controversial and earn Molotov, the *Sovnarkhoz* chairman, unpopularity.[85]

He had to deal with nationalisation, and in some autobiographical notes written in the early 1930s, he claimed that under his leadership the *Sovnarkhoz* nationalised industries, instituted workers' control, and acquired the complicated administrative techniques required.[86] He outlined the course of events at a national level in a speech in May,[87] and explained it in a brochure[88] which was summarised in *Novyi Put'* (The New Path), the newspaper of the *Sovnarkhoz*. Quoting Marx on the 'expropriation of the expropriators', Molotov stated that the revolution in Russia, particularly its economic aspects, was taking a very different form to that which most socialists had expected. Much capitalist property was not yet 'expropriated', and it was difficult to predict the timescale for the complete transfer of all the means of production to socialist society. The process of nationalisation had followed 'neither a definite system nor an approximate plan'. Initially large enterprises had been nationalised, often because of opposition to the new Soviet government. Where this had been achieved, not by central government action, but by local initiative or spontaneous acts by workers' organisations, it was '*de facto*' not '*de jure*' nationalisation. The central government discovered it later, and it was difficult to give an estimate of the extent to which industry was nationalised. The decree of 28 June 1918, which nationalised the great majority of larger enterprises, was however, a most important step in 'expropriating the expropriators', and he claimed that Russian industry could be considered as having passed into the hands of the state.[89] Molotov wished to control all food distribution under a strong central authority. He was one of the chief spokesmen of those Petrograd Bolsheviks who disliked the 'co-operatives' that were very active in food distribution. His group were also against any 'district autonomy'. With food in very short supply, they believed that the most efficient means of distribution was centralisation, as it reduced the number of institutions involved and allowed standardisation to be implemented.[90]

By the autumn of 1918 Molotov found himself in conflict with Kalinin, the Commissar for Municipal Services, partly because of an overlap in the area of jurisdiction of the two commissariats, but also because the *Sovnarkhoz* claimed authority to regulate all economic activity.[91] Molotov found the task of leading the *Sovnarkhoz* very difficult. Not only were relationships with other commissariats ill defined, the responsibility of the *Sovnarkhoz* to the national VSNKh on the one hand, and to local factories on the other, was not clear. Molotov reported regularly to the St. Petersburg Soviet, but the *Sovnarkhoz* received very little guidance on policy, and became unpopular because it appeared to consider itself superior to other commissariats. At a *Sovnarkhoz* meeting in September, Molotov claimed that the production plan of the metal section of the *Sovnarkhoz* for the city's metal-working plants, was the first example of socialist planning, and Soviet historians usually accepted this claim. Kalinin commented that, if Molotov had been able to guarantee funds and raw materials, it would have been a significant socialist measure, but his failure to do so prevented this, and it was similar to many other plans.[92] Perhaps this was a clash between someone with bureaucratic inclinations and someone who tried to keep the masses involved.

In August 1918, the technical committee of the *Sovnarkhoz*, chaired by Molotov, was concerned about the supply of fuel to factories. By December, there was an acute shortage, especially of firewood in Petrograd.[93] In October, Molotov and other senior members of the *Sovnarkhoz* were under attack because *Sovnarkhoz* workers had sold the property of nationalised enterprises. Other serious errors in the work of the *Sovnarkhoz* caused alarm in the Petrograd party organisation, and at the request of Petrograd workers the question of improving the work of the *Sovnarkhoz* was repeatedly discussed at local party meetings, the party bureau, and the plenum of the Petrograd Committee.[94] There was, however, little change and when Molotov reported to the VIII Petrograd All-City Conference in the same month, he received a hostile reception. His statement was regarded as 'empty words'. The cumbersome administrative apparatus and bureaucratic nature of the *Sovnarkhoz* was criticised. Whilst there was a shortage of engineers in factories the *Sovnarkhoz* employed them as clerks. It failed to lead industry and transport and prepare enterprises for nationalisation.[95] McAuley contends that of the commissariats, the *Sovnarkhoz* which had 'the strongest combination of proletarian administrators and old specialists among its members, was perhaps the most bureaucratic institution of all' the Petrograd administrative institutions. It had, Molotov admitted in February 1919, a staff of 3000 and found it difficult to maintain good relations with ordinary workers in the factories. He was criticised by union representatives because he ignored the role labour should play in running enterprises in a socialist system, and for being concerned only with capital which was to be nationalised and concentrated under a central management system.[96] In February 1919, at the Second Congress of the *Sovnarkhoz*, Molotov blamed VSNKh, at that time headed by Rykov, for lack of direction. It had failed to take the enterprises for which the *Sovnarkhoz* was responsible under its control, and left the *Sovnarkhoz* to work in isolation.[97] An additional reason for the unpopularity of the *Sovnarkhoz* may have been a concentration of its industrial efforts on agricultural machinery, rather than on industrial or consumer goods.[98]

Despite a crisis in water transport in March, when Molotov pressed for the implementation of the November 1918 decree nationalising all steam ships,[99] he was more confident by the spring. In an optimistic speech, he outlined the successes and failures of the *Sovnarkhoz*, and claimed that a new initiative, the grouping of enterprises of a single industry under a 'branch administration', could serve as a national pattern. But this was not the case. It cut across the *glavki* (directorates) and trusts established by VSNKh. Molotov had opposed the development of the *glavki* the previous October. He accused them of being 'upper class', a home of the old propertied classes, rather than 'proletarian', and of taking over Petrograd plants.[100]

Whilst *Sovnarkhoz* chairman, Molotov made sure that the party leaders in Moscow did not forget him. He attended the VIII Party Congress in March 1919 as a delegate of the IX Petrograd All-city Conference. Here he dissented from a proposal to form a special Bureau of the Central Committee for organisational purposes. He pointed out that previously there had been a special newspaper which played this rôle. He wanted it re-established and issued once or twice a week. Discussion on his proposal was deferred on a point of order, but seems eventually to have led to the foundation of *Izvestiya TsK*, the newspaper of the Central Committee.[101] His activities at the Congress reminded the party leadership of his previous experience with *Pravda* and in party organisation, and kept him in their minds for future assignments.

The Krasnaya Zvezda

With all the difficulties he faced in the *Sovnarkhoz* Molotov was probably pleased to receive a new assignment in the summer of 1919. He may have longed for active military service in the Civil War where some of the friends he had made in exile were killed heroically at the front,[102] but his rôle was to be more limited. As the Red Army re-conquered land from the Whites, special groups of agitators and instructors were sent to stimulate enthusiasm for the Communist regime, and strengthen the Soviet and party machines. Molotov's chief task in the Civil War was to head one of these expeditions. On 26 June 1919, VTsIK (The All-Russian Central Executive Committee) placed him in command of the *agitparokhod* (agitation steamboat) *Krasnaya Zvezda* (Red Star). He was to work in the Volga provinces freed from White forces.[103] On the same day, Lenin's wife, Krupskaya, was authorised to accompany him, as representative of the Commissariat for Education. It proved quite the reverse of the period of rest and recuperation planned for her.[104]

As 'Political Director' *(PolitKom)*, Molotov received practically identical mandates from the government (VTsIK) and party Central Committee. He was to 'instruct and inspect' local state and party organisations, which were commanded to give him full information and assistance. He also carried a note from Lenin, as Sovnarkom chairman, requiring local organisations to give him assistance,[105] and his appointment may have been made on Lenin's initiative.[106]

This was a large and sophisticated expedition. The *Krasnaya Zvezda* towed a barge equipped as an outdoor cinema to show films, such as 'Electricity in the Countryside', to audiences of 1000 strong at a single performance. A number of other Sovnarkom commissariats besides Education, those of Agriculture, Food Supplies, Finance, and VSNKh, sent instructors, as did VTsIK and other government bodies. Molotov represented the Petrograd Committee, the Moscow Committee and other party bodies appointed agitators to represent them.[107] There was a shop that sold books; and the ship had its own press to produce free literature, although initially there were problems in the distribution of this material.[108]

As leader of the expedition, Molotov was in charge of the route, reports to the central government, negotiations with local authorities and obedience to orders. He was financially responsible and accountable for the property of the expedition. Besides Molotov, who headed a list of ten agitators, there was a chief instructor, and a *komendant* and his deputy, who oversaw nine instruction sections. Krupskaya, who continued to try to fulfil her commissariat responsibilities from the ship, was the senior of 14 instructors.[109] At the beginning of the voyage there were 173 persons on the ship, including 48 crew. Molotov was first on the list of passengers, and occupied a two-berth cabin on his own. Only one other person, a member of the *kollegiya* of the Commissariat for Food Supplies, occupied a two-berth cabin alone. Krupskaya was allocated a single berth cabin. Everyone on the steamer used the same dining room where they were allocated a time to eat.[110]

From the beginning, this was a difficult expedition. It involved a great deal of hard work and was not without danger. Sometimes the agitators and instructors met an unfriendly reception and on at least one occasion a hostile group attacked the ship.[111] Very early in the expedition, on 2 July, very worryingly for Molotov, Krupskaya reported sick and claimed increased rations.[112] He eventually felt compelled to telegraph Lenin on 3 August, and inform him that although he had allocated special rations to Krupskaya, due to the difficult conditions of the journey and the hard work, her health had continued to deteriorate.[113] Krupskaya left the steamer in mid-August. She had made thirty-four major speeches, among them, it was claimed, one addressed to 6000 Red Army soldiers.[114] The action Molotov felt obliged to take because of Krupskaya's ill-health may have caused a direct confrontation with her at Kazan on the outward journey, when he was unsuccessful in persuading her to reduce her work. Alternatively, the divided command, whereby Molotov headed the agitators and Krupskaya the instructors, may have caused the altercation.[115] This dispute seems to have been the origin of an antagonism that developed between Krupskaya and Molotov.

The voyage of the steamer, which often travelled by night to make the best use of daytime in meetings, began from Nizhnii Novgorod. It left on the night of 6/7 July, and sailed down the Volga to Kazan, which it reached on 8 July.[116] This allowed Molotov to address the opening of the V Congress of the Kazan *guberniya* Soviet on 10 July. His speech reflected the atmosphere of the time. He claimed that the Whites were nearly defeated in the province, but that after the Treaty of Versailles, imperialists of all countries were united against the new communist regime. Strong central organisation, strong central power and a strong party were needed as a response. He called on the Congress to organise Soviet power in the province correctly. This would assist in 'the mobilisation of all forces in aid of the world socialist revolution'.[117]

From south of Kazan, the *Krasnaya Zvezda's* voyage continued up the Volga's tributary the Kama, to Perm, which it reached on 7 August. In an article written for the press at this time, Molotov claimed that this was a particularly difficult part of the expedition because of the civil war conditions in the area.[118] From Perm, brief expeditions were made into Vyatka province, which gave Molotov the opportunity to visit members of his family.[119] On this phase of the journey, he claimed that there were 92 'business' meetings with local Soviet and party workers, and 89 'agitational' meetings attended by up to 100,000 people, sometimes with 3–12,000 at a single meeting.[120] The steamer finally left Perm on 14 August to return to Kazan (where Krupskaya left it). There was a collision with another vessel on 26 August, which Molotov had to report and which posed a further problem for him.[121]

The voyage now continued down the Volga to Samara, Simbirsk and Saratov, and there was an expedition into Stavropol province before the *Krasnaya Zvezda* finally returned to Nizhnii Novgorod on 20 October. At Simbirsk, Molotov had a special assignment, to report on Josef Vareikis who had spoken against the Leninist line. According to Molotov, Vareikis 'became evasive and contradicted what he had said a short while before'.[122]

During the voyage 75 visits were made. At these, the instructors and agitators, who worked by rota, addressed minor local officials such as teachers. Molotov took his turn. Initially, they spoke on such topics as 'Soviet power and the world socialist revolution'. Gradually, however, the presentation at a locality began to focus on a theme: either 'Where is the Communist Party leading the workers and peasants?' or 'Dual Power' or 'What does the victory of the Red Army signify and how do we deal with the defeated?' The cinema showed films for four or five hours to as wide an audience as possible, and literature was distributed. Meetings were arranged with local Soviet and party officials, and representatives from the steamer attended special sessions of local Soviet executive and party committees. Sometimes a visit centred on a local trade union or factory.[123]

Molotov's summary of the work of the ship for the period 5 July to 5 September, from the time it left Nizhnii Novgorod until it reached Simbirsk, claimed that 55 places and 10 factories had been visited. The expedition had worked with 15 rural district executive committees (*ispolkomi*), 17 rural soviets, 14 town executive committees, 4 provincial executive committees, 30 party organisations and 31 workers organisations. There had been 109 business sessions, 9 lectures and 5 discussions, which he claimed, had involved 200,070 persons. Books had been issued to the value of 748,242 rubles, and 74,159 rubles spent on free literature. The Bureau of Complaints of the *Krasnaya Zvezda* had received 444 complaints.[124] This gives an indication that the activities of the expedition were not always popular with the local population.

There was a meeting of the *PolitOtdel* (political department) of the ship on 15 October, to evaluate the work of the mission, and to provide guidance for future expeditions. Here Molotov stressed a minimum of two days for visits when instructors and agitators should concentrate on the place to which they were allocated. It was generally agreed that the expedition had tried to operate over too vast an area. Whilst generally complimentary about agitational work, Molotov emphasised the need for better lectures, for experts on technical problems, better films and more and better books. He also stressed the need for better internal organisation.[125] There was much more emphasis on the limitations of the work than on its success. Molotov's report at the final session of the ship's *PolitOtdel* on 18 October 1919 was therefore pessimistic. There was general agreement about the weakness of the work carried out, especially in Saratov *guberniya*. The need to strengthen links between local and central authorities was recognised: an echo of the current controversy over the need for centralisation in the Party.[126] It was also felt that in many places that had been visited, local organisation needed improvement.[127] This was scarcely surprising in areas so recently returned to Communist control.

Nizhnii Novgorod

Towards the end of 1919, Molotov was appointed chairman of the *ispolkom* of Nizhnii Novgorod *guberniya*. This suggests that he was not blamed personally for the indifferent performance of the *Krasnaya Zvezda* expedition. Nizhnii Novgorod town was an important commercial centre for a large industrial area in a major agricultural province, where immediately after the Revolution Bolshevism had been weak. There were widespread strikes and peasant risings, and after disturbances associated with the onset of the Civil War, Kaganovich had been sent there in May 1918, as secretary to the provincial party committee. After the fall of Kazan to the Whites in July, the town remained the last bastion protecting Moscow.[128] On a directive from Lenin the Red Terror erupted in an extreme form in the province. It reached its climax at the end of August 1918, after the attempt on Lenin's life and prior to the relief of Kazan in early September.[129] Kaganovich worked to strengthen the party machinery in the province, and continued to do so after January 1919, Then, following the decision that the Party should withdraw from a direct role in administrative affairs, he became chairman of the *ispolkom* of the *guberniya*. With food shortages, strikes in factories, and Admiral Kolchak posing a new White threat, he sought permission to go to the front. When the party committee refused this, he went to Moscow, and in September was reassigned to the defence of Voronezh.[130] Thus, when the *Krasnaya Zvezda* returned to Nizhnii Novgorod, Molotov was on hand to replace Kaganovich. Much later, Molotov suggested that although Lenin made the appointment, Zinoviev, who desired to keep him away from Petrograd, was behind it.[131]

Like Kaganovich, Molotov was to encounter problems because of the withdrawal of the Party from a direct role in administration. Initially he managed to co-operate with some local Bolsheviks in efforts to revive the local economy and seemed to establish his position. In January 1920 he spoke to the VIII *guberniya* party conference on the new party statute and emphasised the need for unity and party discipline. In February, his report on the external and internal position of the Soviet republic to the city all-party conference was received with acclaim; and in March he presented theses on the role and tasks of trade unions to a special *guberniya* party conference.[132]

In late 1919, in Moscow, Molotov reported to Lenin on the state of the timber industry in the province, and on the first regional conference of radio engineers that had been held there.[133] He was keeping himself in the eye of the top party leadership and rose in the party hierarchy; for on another visit to Moscow in March 1920, to attend the IX Party Congress, he was elected a candidate member of the Central Committee, apparently on Lenin's proposal.[134] Lenin knew him better now through his correspondence about Krupskaya's health during the *Krasnaya Zvezda* expedition, even if antagonism had developed between him and Krupskaya.[135]

After the Congress, Molotov continued to try to work with the provincial party leaders. In May 1920 he wrote a front-page article in *Pravda* and congratulated the Nizhnii Novgorod party on their efforts in the *subbotnik* (voluntary unpaid labour day), held on 1 and 2 May, which he had played a significant role in organising.[136] But he failed to break the grip of the local clique of leaders who dominated affairs in Nizhnii Novgorod. Many of these had been Bolsheviks before 1917, were of working class origin, and now sympathised with the 'Workers' Opposition' in the Party. Anastas Mikoyan, who was to succeed Molotov in Nizhnii Novgorod, claimed that Molotov was an intellectual whose links with the workers were weak, and that his main support came from the Bolshevik organisation in the city itself. Molotov, however, claimed that local party officials were degenerate, intrigued with members of the former bourgeoisie, and did not want to accept emissaries from other provinces, i.e. from the central government.

Molotov's attempts to impose central authority were so unpopular that the provincial party organisation split into two warring factions. Molotov led one, and tried to implement his instructions from the Central Committee. He attempted to criticise the group opposing him in his report on the work of the *ispolkom* at the plenum of the provincial committee in June 1920, but the report was rejected. His estimate of the relations of the provincial party committee with the *ispolkom* was condemned as incorrect and he was ordered to present a new statement to the Presidium of the provincial party committee. This was to represent collective opinion and to be objective. Molotov believed that the majority of the provincial committee were struggling to rid themselves of the 'troublesome newcomer'.[137]

The clash between the warring factions continued in more extreme form at the X Provincial Party Conference, 15–19 July 1920. At a special closed session, Molotov accused S. M. Kuznetsov, the presidium chairman, of spreading and encouraging provincial tendencies. Kuznetsov's supporters interrupted Molotov's report, and on the proposal of Khanov, his deputy, Molotov, and his chief supporter Taganov, were censured for

> bringing into disrepute the lofty traditions of our party. They had conducted agitation in place of election ... published a list of all their personal supporters and mistakenly hurled at responsible ... workers a number of vague charges ... abused ten district workers and provincial workers in a most offensive manner ... attempted to discredit all the workers who composed the majority of the former provincial committee in order to clear the way for a new grouping.[138]

Forty-five delegates supported the resolution, 19 voted against and 13 abstained, an indication of how weak Molotov's support was. He threatened to resign from the provincial committee, although prior to this he and others had been elected to the conference as its representatives.[139] The resignation from the provincial committee of the chairman of the *ispolkom*, who was a candidate member of the Central Committee, would clearly have been very abnormal, as well as a great blow to Molotov himself.

Molotov's speech opening the VI *guberniya* Congress of Soviets on 20 July, immediately after the party conference, where he represented the central government gave no hint of the problems,[140] but they became clear in his report as chairman of the *ispolkom* when he said:

> I am not inclined to close my eyes. ... The earlier bureaucratic type of work and former officious red-tapeism which crushes almost all organs of Soviet power without exception, still remains. ... I think we must all struggle mercilessly with bureaucratic survivals and liquidate them in the shortest possible time.

He welcomed representatives from the new Koz'modem'yanovskii *uezd* (district), and remarked that they were not kulaks, but middle and poor peasants, as he knew from his experience when he visited the area 'as a commissar lecturer–agitator and instructor' on the *Krasnaya Zvezda*. He endorsed terror, another reminder of his position as a central government appointee. He admitted that the links of the *ispolkom* with the localities were weak and that there was much unevenness in its work. The resolution, at the end of the Congress, recognised the policies of the *ispolkom* as correct, and its work, carried out 'in conditions of an intense struggle in Soviet Russia on the internal and foreign fronts', to be 'satisfactory'.[141]

Molotov's success at the Congress did not prevent his difficulties with the local party coming to a head. At the Presidium on 27 July 1920, Kuznetsov, its chairman, asked Molotov to work with its representatives elected by the party conference, despite his differences with the local party, and his declarations about the impossibility of working with the old presidium. But Molotov asked 'Can I work with a provincial committee composed in this way?' He drew a distinction between Soviet (state) work and the work of the local party, which Kuznetsov had failed to recognise. He was now in an impossible position, isolated and receiving no support from the party organisation. On 9 August, the party presidium dismissed him, and directed him to report to the Central Committee. As a result, he was forced to leave Nizhnii Novgorod, and the Central Committee reassigned Kuznetsov to Nikolaev, where he was appointed chairman of the *ispolkom*.[142]

This affair came back to haunt Molotov at the end of his political career, when his conduct in Nizhnii Novgorod in 1920 was used against him as a member of the 'anti-party' group. Then, it was said that he had led a demagogic group against the party presidium, and breached the principles of party democracy and discipline. His behaviour showed that he had occupied an incorrect position, attempted to take control of the party organs, and denied the leading role of the Party in the Soviets.[143] Molotov, however, like Kaganovich before him was a central government appointee, sent to impose order at a key strategic point. Kaganovich recalled that, after Molotov's return, Lenin went up to him in the Bolshoi theatre, placed his hand on his shoulder and said:

> Speaking amongst ourselves ... you recently went to Nizhnii and worked there. Many talked about you, this was useful.[144]

The appointment at Nizhnii Novgorod marked an important turning point in Molotov's career. His time as head of the northern *Sovnarkhoz* may have been an initiation, but Nizhnii Novgorod was an important stage in the process of transition from revolutionary, to party official and bureaucrat. This was to take place very rapidly between 1920 and 1922. Molotov's patience and endurance, qualities that had been developed as a revolutionary in the years before 1917; his diligent industry, and willingness to give way to senior party members, which he had learnt when he worked for *Pravda* and during 1917; marked him out as an ideal candidate. As Isaac Deutscher noted in his biography of Stalin

> To save the revolution the party ceased to be a free association of independent, critically minded, and courageous revolutionaries. The bulk of it submitted to the ever more powerful party machine. ... Those who handled the levers of the machine and were most intimately associated with it, those to whose upbringing and temperament the new bureaucratic outlook was most congenial, automatically became leaders of the new era. The administrator began to elbow out the ideologue, the bureaucrat and committee-man eliminated the idealist.[145]

3
Party Secretary

The Donbass and the Ukraine

On his return from Nizhnii Novgorod, Molotov asked to be transferred to party work. Initially, Nikolai Krestinskii, the head of the Secretariat, proposed to relocate him to Bashkiriya, a remote republic, but, Molotov claimed, Lenin helped him in to obtain an appointment in an industrial *raion*. He was reassigned to the Donbass in September 1920, an area in which he was well content to serve, and became secretary to the Artemovskii (Donets) *guberniya* committee.[1] This appeared to be a dangerous mission, for the White general Wrangel was still active in the Donbass, but Molotov soon became preoccupied with administrative matters. As a representative of the *guberniya* committee at the Fifth Ukrainian Party Conference in Khar'kov in November 1920, he was nominated to the Central Committee, and at the plenum after the Conference, he was appointed first secretary of a two-man secretariat of the Ukrainian Central Committee.[2] In his memoirs, Molotov again attributed his good fortune to Lenin.[3]

This Conference marked the beginning of the consolidation of Soviet rule in the Ukraine. No oppositionists were elected to the Central Committee; and from this time emissaries from Moscow exercised tight control of the Ukrainian party. Molotov was among the first of these. At the same time that Molotov was appointed party secretary, Mikhail Frunze, already military commander on the southern front, was appointed as deputy chairman of the Ukrainian Sovnarkom.[4] As party secretary, Molotov supervised co-operation with Frunze's Red Army units charged with the restoration of the Ukraine at the end of the Civil War.[5] He had failed to bring the party in Nizhnii Novgorod under central control, but his new appointment showed that there was no lack of confidence in his abilities. His views on the independence of national communist parties had been clear from as early as 1917, when at the VI Party Congress in August, he with Latsis had voted against the right of national minorities to organise their own sections.[6] This attitude was demonstrated again at the Central Committee plenum of the Ukrainian party, held in February 1921, where Molotov proposed a resolution which called on the Party to implement

> the most energetic struggle against nationalism, anti-Semitism, anarchist Makhnoism and conciliatory parties that create a political atmosphere favourable to the development of banditism.[7]

This resolution reflected not only the attitude to groups who had been hostile in the Civil War, but also the view on Ukrainian nationalism. In early February 1921, as party secretary, Molotov was also involved in the response to the initial stages of the famine in the Ukraine, which was made worse by difficulties on the railways that hindered distribution, and he must have been aware of the growing crisis.[8] It is not clear if he knew that his stay in the Ukraine was likely to be brief, when he attended the X Party Congress as a delegate of the Donets *guberniya* party committee.[9]

Promotion and marriage

At the IX Party Congress 1920, Molotov had come into sharp conflict with Nikolai Bukharin, Mikhail Tomsky, and the 'democratic centralists' who opposed the introduction of one-man management in industry.[10] His election as a candidate member of the Central Committee was a reward for strong support of the Leninist line, but this did not earn him popularity: if the published list is in order of the number of votes cast, Molotov was only eleventh out of 12 candidates elected, after the election of 19 full members.[11]

At the X Party Congress, March 1921, Molotov became a full member of the Central Committee.[12] In the last year he had faithfully supported Lenin against Trotsky on the trade union question: the controversy over the role of the trade unions in controlling industry.[13] In addition, as the notorious *Short Course* of party history, written at the end of the 1930s claims, Molotov never departed from the orthodox Leninist point of view in the 'Workers' Opposition' and 'Democratic Centralist' controversies.[14] His promotion, at the Congress that passed the famous Resolution on Party Unity, may well have been a reward for loyal service. He was among 13 appointed to full Central Committee membership, or candidate membership. Duranty's famous comment on Molotov's election reads:

> It was said that Stalin suggested to Lenin that Molotov, as an old and trusted member of the Party and one of the founders of *Pravda* ... should be a member of the Central Committee of the Party. Lenin squinted his Tartar eyes and said 'Why that one?'
> Stalin repeated Molotov's services, and Lenin said 'Well, if you like. But you know what I think of him: he's the best filing clerk in Russia.' In other words, a mediocrity.[15]

Molotov was eighth in the list of 25 members elected to the Central Committee, and secured 453 from the 479 votes. Lenin received unanimous support, and only Karl Radek (475), Tomsky (472), Kalinin (470), Yan Rudzutak (467), Stalin (458), Rykov (458) and N. Komarov (457), received more votes than Molotov. Trotsky (452), Bukharin (447), Feliks Dzerzhinskii (438), Zinoviev (423) and Kamenev (406) were among the sixteen others elected who received less votes. Five more candidates did not receive the absolute majority necessary for election.[16]

The Central Committee plenum after the Congress appointed Molotov head of the Central Committee Secretariat, a member of the Orgburo and a candidate member of the Politburo. As head of the Secretariat he was first substitute member of the Politburo.[17] This promotion was associated with Trotsky's defeat at the X Party Congress, and the removal of his high-placed supporters from both Politburo and Orgburo, after they failed to secure re-election to the Central Committee. Krestinskii's failure to win re-election to the Central Committee cleared the way for Molotov to become chief secretary, and the promotion of Zinoviev to full Politburo membership in place of Krestinskii, allowed Molotov to become a candidate member. Molotov, V. Mikhailov and Emel'yan Yaroslavskii replaced L. P. Serebriakov, Krestinskii and Evgenii Preobrazhenskii on the Secretariat. Molotov's colleagues on the Secretariat were also critics of Trotsky on the trade union question.[18]

This was a very important moment in Molotov's career. He had not distinguished himself in his assignments since 1917, but he had always ruthlessly attempted to carry out central government policy and shown himself to be a steadfast supporter of Lenin, most recently in the trade union controversy and against the 'Workers' Opposition' and 'Democratic Centralists'. Molotov's temperament and abilities were also important in his promotion. In the new Soviet regime Lenin needed reliable and hard-working functionaries, younger men with no firm ideas of their own, not those who were preoccupied with ideology and interested in challenging him.

In his memoirs, Molotov acknowledged the support of both Lenin and Stalin at this time, but particularly that of Lenin with regard to his appointment to the Secretariat. He emphasised the special position of the first candidate member of the Politburo, frequently able to vote because one of the full members was absent. He believed that Lenin had especially selected him for this position before Kalinin and Bukharin, because he was more reliable.[19] A year later when Stalin, already a Politburo member, became General Secretary, Molotov retained his candidate membership.

It has been suggested that Molotov's appointment as first secretary was because of Lenin's reservations about Stalin.[20] In 1921, however, Lenin was a great enthusiast for Stalin and it seems more likely that the move was part of a more general reallocation of positions with the defeat of Trotsky. This enabled top party bodies to dominate the Central Committee and secured a Secretariat which would act firmly against any opposition.[21] Molotov's skills as an office manager were recognised, although Lenin might sarcastically refer to these on occasions. According to Molotov, whilst walking round the Kremlin, Lenin said to him:

> I will give you only this advice as secretary of the Central Committee. You must occupy yourself with political matters and let your deputies and assistants take care of the technical work. Until now Krestinskii has been … more of a manager than a Central Committee secretary! He has busied himself with all sorts of nonsense, and never politics.[22]

Lenin's advice conflicts with his view of Molotov as recorded by Duranty, but it rings true: as 'responsible secretary', Molotov was appointed to a higher position than his predecessor, although in very difficult circumstances. These may have contributed to his lack of success, and to the appointment of Stalin as General Secretary, another upgrade of the position, in April 1922.[23]

At this time Molotov kept in contact with his family in Vyatka by correspondence. He was particularly attached to his sister Zina (Zinaida). Sometimes his brother Sergei, who often wrote letters home for his more famous sibling, was with him. This, however, ended in tragedy, for in December 1919, Sergei was killed in a fire in his room which was next to his brother's. Vyacheslav had the painful duty of reporting Sergei's death to his parents.[24]

Eighteen months later, shortly after his appointment as Central Committee secretary, Molotov met his wife, Polina Seminova Karpovskaya. She came to Moscow to attend an International Women's Conference in June, but was taken ill and admitted to hospital. Molotov, as one of the party organisers of the conference visited her and a close personal relationship developed. The courtship was short, for they were married in the summer of 1921.[25] After their marriage they each continued to pursue their party career, but a deep and lasting attachment developed.

Born in 1897, Polina was Jewish and came from a small village in Ekaterinoslavska *guberniya*. Her father was a tailor and the fact that as a Kremlin wife, there were comments about her poor manners, is indicative of a lowly background.[26] From 1910 to 1917, she worked in a cigarette factory, then at the cashier's desk in a chemist from 1917–1918 in Ekaterinoslavska. During the Revolution and Civil War, a sister emigrated to Palestine and a brother to the United States. He called himself Sam Carp, and became a wealthy industrialist in the shipbuilding industry. Polina worked in the revolutionary underground, prior to 1917, joined the Party in 1918 whilst serving in the Red Army during the Civil War, and became a political worker. She took the party name Zhemchuzhina (little pearl). In 1919, she was sent as an underground worker for the Party to Kiev, then in 1919–1920 she became a political instructor for work amongst women for the Ukrainian communist party. In 1920 she was promoted to the position of deputy head of the Party's women's department in Zaporozh'e in the Ukraine, and she met her future husband when she attended the conference as a party representative.[27] It seems that she was not completely cured when she was in hospital in 1921, for a year later Molotov sent her to Czechoslovakia for medical treatment where he visited her. In his memoirs he claimed that he took the opportunity of this visit to western Europe to go on to Italy to 'look at Fascism on the rise'.[28] This was Molotov's first foreign journey and only visit abroad before his infamous trip to Berlin in November 1940.

Responsible secretary 1921–1922

Molotov was appointed as party secretary at the time when the Politburo, because of its small size and the frequency of its meetings, which were held at least weekly, was able to develop a coherence and emerge as an effective decision-making body. It replaced the Central Committee and Sovnarkom as the dominant political institution. Stalin and Molotov were members of both Politburo and Orgburo, and this overlap increased in 1922 when Tomsky and Rykov gained Politburo membership. At the time of his appointment Molotov was the only member of these bodies occupied full time in the party apparatus.

The emergence of the Politburo as the leading institution was greatly facilitated by the development of the Secretariat which dealt with organisational and administrative tasks, guided initially by Jakob Sverdlov. Following his death, the VIII Party Congress, March 1919, tried to establish a Secretariat divided into a number of departments directed by one responsible and five technical secretaries. No stability had been achieved, however, by the time of Molotov's appointment, and the departments were subject to frequent reorganisation. The Secretariat also grew rapidly in size: there were 30 members in March 1919, this had become 602 by February 1921, and it decreased by only two members whilst Molotov was responsible secretary. Many of these officials were not party members and performed routine tasks: they were typists, clerks, chauffeurs, etc. This increase in size and lack of organisational stability was to create problems for Molotov.

The replacement of Krestinskii, Serebriakov and Preobrazhenskii in the Secretariat was not solely because of their links with Trotsky. They were criticised for failure to exercise effective central control over lower level party organs, particularly on the trade union question. Molotov and his new colleagues in the Secretariat were more closely identified with centralisation, and it was to improve central direction, efficiency and co-ordination, that Molotov was given candidate membership of the Politburo.[29] Furthermore, the Secretariat's authority was increasing. Whilst Molotov was responsible secretary, it was officially decided that if there were no objections from Orgburo members, the Secretariat's decision would be regarded as a decision of the Orgburo.[30] This ruling increased Molotov's power. His particular task was organisational matters and he was asked by Lenin personally to take responsibility for cadres problems in certain localities. In his memoirs, Molotov specified Tula and Tambov, although he does not appear to have visited these areas until 1925.[31]

Politically and economically, the major issue of the year when Molotov was responsible secretary was the NEP (New Economic Policy), which had been introduced by Lenin at the X Party Congress. No member of the newly selected secretariat was appointed to the Central Committee Commission responsible for implementing the NEP because of their close identification with Lenin,[32] and the policy met huge resistance within the Party. At the X Party Conference, May 1921, held to gain fuller acceptance of the NEP and to extend it, there was further furious controversy. Here Molotov's main task was to report on the previous month's IV Trade Union Congress, where the trade union question had again reared its head. After the Trade Union Congress, Lenin had used the X Party Congress Resolution on Party Unity, in an effort to expel Tomsky from the Party, but found that no procedure had been established to carry out the expulsion.[33] Molotov, in his report to the X Conference, accused both Trotsky's supporters and the 'Workers' Opposition' of a deviation from Bolshevism on the trade union question. He went on to reveal the differences in the Central Committee over Tomsky's expulsion and the NEP.[34] This stirred Lenin into speaking. He emphasised the difficulties of the party leadership and managed to secure greater acceptance of the NEP.

Molotov enthusiastically executed the party purge that followed the conference,[35] and worked closely with Lenin through 1921 and in early 1922. He presented Lenin's proposals on a further party purge at the Central Committee prior to the XI Party Congress, March–April 1922.[36] He was naturally involved in implementing the NEP. In July 1921, he was joint signatory with Lenin, chairman of Sovnarkom and STO (*Sovet Truda i Obrony* – the Council of Labour and Defence) of telegrams which tried to prevent peasants exchanging grain products and enforce collection of the food tax.[37] Since Molotov knew about the famine in the Ukraine, it seems likely that the political leadership were deliberately trying to ignore both the famine, and the shortage of manufactured goods. A month later, on the proposal of Georgii Chicherin, Commissar for Foreign Affairs, Molotov was elected to a Politburo commission for famine relief. Lenin ordered that foreigners who arrived in Russia to distribute the relief were to be spied upon, and Molotov, with Chicherin and Josef Unshlikht from the CHEKA, (the secret police) were appointed to a Politburo commission to conduct surveillance of foreigners.[38]

Molotov's position as responsible secretary gave him his first experience of foreign affairs. He received reports from Chicherin, and relayed Lenin's instructions on them and on other foreign policy matters to the Politburo.[39] In June 1921, Lenin noted that on the question of troops going into Mongolia: 'Molotov and I came to an agreement today and he promised to get it through the P[olit]/Buro by telephone.'[40] Chicherin's letters to Molotov show that they had developed a *rapport*. In March 1921 Chicherin wrote about the proposal of Grigorii Sokolnikov, the Commissar of Finance, to defer payment of the agreed sum of financial aid to Turkey. He claimed that this would disgrace the regime 'in front of the peoples of the Orient ... killing me politically'.[41] The following year Molotov dealt with correspondence from Lenin about the Genoa Conference, where Chicherin led the Russian delegation.[42] He received one letter in which Chicherin had suggested minor changes in the Soviet constitution if the United States pressed for 'representative institutions'. Lenin had endorsed this:

> Madness. ... clearly Chicherin is very ill. We would be stupid not to despatch him straight away to a sanatorium.[43]

Later in the year, Chicherin wrote to Molotov and protested about being forced into a vacation and threatened to resign.[44] Chuev claims that Lenin wished to place Molotov at the head of the Commissariat of Foreign Affairs.[45] If true, it may have been at this point that the proposal was made and shows the reputation that Molotov had earned with Lenin for handling foreign affairs, but there is no corroborating evidence to support Chuev's claim.

As responsible secretary, Molotov received questions from Lenin to be answered, instructions to be carried out, both personally and through the secretariat, and proposals for the Politburo and Orgburo.[46] For instance, in April 1921, Lenin wrote to him about a Central Committee circular which contained instructions 'to expose the lie of religion' in celebrations of the 1 May holiday. Lenin condemned the circular, issued near the date of Easter, as insensitive, and asked Molotov to arrange a supplementary document.[47]

The burden on Molotov increased from the summer of 1921 when he had to take into account Lenin's decline in health and inability to undertake a full workload. In June 1921, the Politburo, on Molotov's initiative, required Lenin to take a month's holiday. Lenin ignored this, but in early July, he wrote to Molotov and requested that the pressure on him be eased.[48] From this time, until after the XI Party Congress, March–April 1922, Molotov was frequently in touch with the ailing Lenin. He sent information, passed his requests and vote to the Politburo when absent, and was responsible for the implementation of Lenin's proposals when approved.[49] These included instructions for others to obtain medical treatment and time for convalescence.[50] In December 1921 Molotov dealt with Lenin's request for further sick leave, and to be excused from reporting at the XI Party Conference and at the Congress of Soviets, because of his continued ill health.[51] The frequency of Lenin's requests increased from this time.[52]

Lenin grew impatient with Molotov because he failed to carry out the improvements in the Secretariat for which he had been appointed, now judged even more necessary because of the introduction of the NEP.[53] He was always a hard taskmaster, and increasingly so when ill. Nevertheless, it is not clear if Molotov, who was working in very difficult circumstances, fell short in fulfilling his duties. As early as 15 April 1921, Lenin wrote angry letters to Molotov in which he stated that a day's delay in issuing decisions was intolerable. He threatened to raise the question of the Central Committee apparatus at the Politburo, and urged Molotov 'to check and to hurry'.[54] Molotov's difficulties led to the appointment of Stalin to assist him in the recently established Agitation and Propaganda Department (*Agitprop*) in the autumn of 1921.[55]

If Lenin was impatient with Molotov's slow bureaucratic methods during his period as responsible secretary, his rigid line against the opposition meant that he was entrusted with such work as the party purge and surveillance of foreigners. He was also the recipient of Lenin's notorious letter of March 1922, for circulation to Politburo members, which called for the execution of priests, and the confiscation of church property.[56] This is indicative of the fact that he was a trusted senior lieutenant.

Yurii Lomonosov, the railway engineer, leader of a group responsible for the import of railway locomotives, recorded his impressions of Molotov as responsible secretary, when he chaired a commission in May 1921:

> The session began after great delay. ... Molotov whom I had not met before deputised for them [Stalin and Mikhailov]. For a long while he could not understand at all what the business of the Mission was and why it existed 'on a Soviet scale'.
>
> Generally he produced on me a strong impression of a narrow-minded but conscientious and diligent man. 'The first student' had been assigned and he was at our service.

Lomonosov was not present at three further meetings of the commission which Molotov chaired, but he became irritated with Molotov's bureaucratic manner, his preoccupation with detail, and suspicions whether or not the mission was Bolshevik in nature.[57] Boris Bazhanov, who worked in the Secretariat at this time, recorded a similar impression:

> Molotov ... was not a brilliant man. An untiring bureaucrat, he worked without stopping from morning to night. ... Molotov, who understood very well the heart of each matter, had great difficulty formulating appropriate wording.[58]

He also recorded Molotov's defensive response to Trotsky:

> I well remember the scene when, staring at Molotov across the table from him, Trotsky made a cutting philippic against 'the Party bureaucrats without souls, whose stone bottoms crush all manifestations of free initiative and free creativity of the labouring masses'. Molotov, whose name Trotsky hadn't mentioned, should have kept quiet and acted as if the matter had nothing to do with him, or better, nodded to indicate a sense of approval. Instead, he declared while adjusting his pince-nez and stuttering: 'We can't all be geniuses, Comrade Trotsky.' It was pitiful and I was embarrassed for Molotov.[59]

An efficient office manager and meticulous hard worker, as demonstrated by his regular contributions to the party bulletin on a variety of issues: education, agitational work, organisational matters,[60] Molotov lacked initiative and authority. Moreover, he had not gained the strength of local party support in his assignments before he returned to Moscow.[61] His experience now was calculated to increase his bureaucratic tendencies and make him the ideal lieutenant.

Second secretary to Stalin 1922–1924

At the XI Party Congress, March–April 1922, Molotov's Central Committee organisational report was a dull speech,[62] confined to the technical and factual matters which were the concern of a party secretary, although he did claim that after his year's work the Party was stronger and that 'basic groupings and tendencies' had disappeared.[63] He reported the defeat of the 'Workers' Opposition' in Samara and the replacement of the *guberniya* committee;[64] but the Secretariat under Molotov, who identified himself fully with these policies, was blamed for the protracted struggle with the Workers' Opposition, and for the great difficulties of the Central Committee at the XI Congress.[65] It was also criticised because it had fallen behind in record keeping.[66] Molotov's replacement by Stalin at the end of the Congress was therefore not unexpected; the latter's appointment as General Secretary was announced one day after the close of the Congress.[67] Stalin's promotion was logical. The appointments following the X Congress had made him the leading figure in the Orgburo and he had been directly involved in Secretariat affairs with Molotov, in the *Agitprop* department. The choice of Stalin for the new enhanced position of General Secretary was little more than recognition and formalisation of the position that he had obtained in securing control over a machine developed by Molotov and his predecessors.[68] Molotov remained as second secretary to Stalin, assisted by Kuibyshev, who was promoted from candidate to full Central Committee member.[69]

The link between Stalin and Molotov was now firmly cemented. Stalin valued Molotov's bureaucratic efficiency and capacity for hard work. He could be relied on to sit in his office and carry out the huge number of clerical tasks which fell to the Secretariat. He could also be entrusted with matters that Stalin wished to delegate, such as issuing instructions and information in the party bulletin.[70] Molotov played an increasingly important role in the Orgburo. From May 1922 he was in charge of an Orgburo commission to work out new party statutes,[71] and from 1923 he was an Orgburo chairman.[72] Stalin and Molotov's offices were close together at the party headquarters and they met frequently during the day,[73] but Stalin may have been more essential to Molotov than Molotov to Stalin.[74] According to Trotsky, Molotov's association with Stalin was now sufficiently clear for Lenin to feel able to aim rebukes at Stalin through Molotov,[75] but he now received very little correspondence from Lenin, whose health had further deteriorated.[76]

Molotov's duties were not confined to Moscow. In June 1922, the Central Committee sent him to Briansk, an important industrial area, to strengthen the weak party organisation. This included the women's section, as one *raikom* (district committee) had liquidated its *zhenotdel* (women's department).[77] Molotov's brief from the Central Committee noted the lack of 'political firmness', ideological leadership and weakness in agitational work in Briansk. It claimed that, although the 'top echelons' of the party organisation were proletarian, they had become 'worker officials' who were narrow-minded.[78] First, Molotov attended meetings of the Dyat'ovskii *raikom* party organisation on 10–11 June, estimated to be the strongest local organisation. Here as a Central Committee secretary he was elected honorary chairman, gave a brief report on the results of the Genoa Conference and worked out a plan of campaign with the leaders.[79] A full meeting of the Briansk organisation followed on 12 June, where Molotov introduced resolutions to strengthen party work. These included new party cells in the factories.[80]

Molotov was in Briansk from 6 to 16 June. He was then immediately sent to the Urals, and arrived in Ekaterinburg for 23 June, to resolve differences between the Urals party bureau and the *guberniya* committee at a special conference. Personal differences between leading local officials were a factor in this dispute. It was a difficult position. Molotov felt compelled to introduce proposals in support of the senior party authority, and only a narrow majority carried these. The speech he made on behalf of the Central Committee again dealt with the results of the Genoa Conference, but this time in considerable depth. He also spoke about internal politics, the XI Party Congress, the party purge and party organisation, before he dealt with the local problem which he been sent to solve. His efforts were successful, and to close the conference he led the singing of the *Internationale*.[81]

It is possible that Molotov's absence from the capital so soon after Stalin's appointment was to allow the new General Secretary to consolidate his position, but, by August 1922, Molotov was back in Moscow at the XII Party Conference. Here he introduced the new party rules, formulated by his Orgburo commission.[82] He had visited Georgia in November 1921 to assist in planning the Transcaucasian federation.[83] This allowed him, in the autumn of 1922, to be closely associated with Stalin, the Commissar for Nationalities, when the federal relationship of the different republics was defined, prior to the formation of the USSR in 1924. Stalin's proposals involved extreme centralisation and Molotov served as an alternate to him as chair of a Central Committee commission which supported them. This angered Lenin.[84] The friction culminated in the well-known breach between him and Stalin over the Georgian affair.[85] This matter dragged on: Molotov felt compelled to mention it in his report on 'Work in the Countryside' at the Central Committee plenum, October 1924, when he also commented on Sergo Ordzhonikidze's report on Georgia.[86]

Molotov continued to ally himself with Stalin and support him against Lenin's criticisms.[87] In early February 1923, he supported Stalin when he unsuccessfully opposed the publication of Lenin's *Better Less but Better* in *Pravda*.[88] Later, in the same month, at the Politburo, he and Kuibyshev backed Stalin's opposition to Lenin's proposal to reorganise Rabkrin (People's Commissariat of the Workers' and Peasants' Inspectorate – NKRKI), and amalgamate it with the Central Control Commission (TsKK).[89] At the XII Party Congress, in April, he gave the report on party organisational problems, and commented on the TsKK. He chaired one of the specially elected organisational sections which examined the plan for the reorganisation of the central party apparatus, including TsKK. This appears to have been a part of the procedural tactic designed to neutralise Lenin's proposals for reform.[90] Molotov chaired the commission which formulated the principal resolution on the unification of TsKK and Rabkrin. This located the unified body within a reorganised central party apparatus. The scheme differed markedly from Lenin's plan, and deflected the threat to Stalin's organisational base in the Secretariat. Indeed, it seems to have turned the reform to Stalin's advantage.[91] Molotov's support for Stalin continued when, at the XIII Party Conference in January 1924, with Kamenev and Mikoyan, he defended the official party line on the NEP, and attacked Georgii Pyatakov who demanded more centralised planning and a greater role for state enterprises.[92]

On 7 October 1923, at a course for party secretaries, Molotov made a detailed report on Lenin's health, which reflected the line taken by other political leaders at the time.[93] He said that the leader's condition had been very serious in the summer, but it had now improved, and that the chief concern was his speech. He was sanguine about Lenin's complete recovery.[94] Molotov's optimism, if real, was in vain, and when Lenin died on 21 January 1924 he was immediately appointed to the eight-man commission to organise the funeral.[95] He was sufficiently important to take his stand at Lenin's bier on 27 January 1924, and was named fourth out of eight, after Stalin, Zinoviev, and Kamenev in the list of those who finally lowered Lenin's coffin into the vault. He was, however, not sufficiently prominent to write a memorial article in the issue of *Pravda* of 24 January[96] which reported Lenin's death, or to speak at the commemorative meeting of the Congress of Soviets on

26 January.[97] There were no issues of *Pravda* on 28 and 29 January, but on 30 January, Molotov, along with Yu. Larin and V. Kviring contributed obituary articles. In his piece, Molotov twice stressed the importance of the new Rabkrin, a mark of his allegiance to Stalin. There can be no doubt, however, that Lenin's death, lying in state, funeral and the decision to embalm the body and place it in a mausoleum – the beginnings of the Lenin cult, had a profound influence on Molotov as on other Bolshevik leaders.

As the second member of the Secretariat Molotov played a prominent rôle in the Lenin Enrolment, the decision to increase party membership by the recruitment of 'workers from the bench', and the party purge which accompanied it.[98] He explained and defended the policy at the Central Committee Plenum, 31 March–3 April 1924,[99] when he stated that he saw the Enrolment as the basis for the future development of the Party.[100] His duties as party secretary gave him increased responsibility for organisational problems and he often made arrangements for party plenums, conferences and congresses. He chaired commissions to plan them, and reported on organisational matters.[101] Throughout the 1920s, party administrative matters of this type continued to be one of Molotov's specialisms; the range of these was to extend, and led him into the sphere of agriculture.[102] By late 1925 he saw a strong party organisation as a cure for many problems, including agricultural deficiencies which led to food shortages.[103] He was also increasingly prominent in the press. In October 1924, he wrote a major article for *Bol'shevik* in support of the campaign for increased productivity of labour. He concluded in Leninist style:

> Our path to socialism lies through increased productivity of labour on the basis of electrification.[104]

This was one of an increasing number of reports and articles on party organisation, policy and ideology, that he was to publish in the 1920s.[105]

The bureaucrat

If the years from 1921 to 1924 had seen his transition from revolutionary to bureaucrat, Molotov's experience in the Secretariat from 1924, served to consolidate his personality as a hard-nosed party functionary. The job of party secretary was a heavy burden. From January 1926 to December 1927, Molotov was available for consultation on two days a week: on Monday with Stalin, and on Friday with Stanislav Kosior.[106] Alexander Barmine described an interview with him at this time:

> The room was huge, badly kept, and poorly furnished … Several people were waiting, seated near the door. At the far end … was a smaller table covered with papers and with several telephones. Molotov sat there talking with a workman. He had a very large and placid face, the face of an ordinary, uninspired, but rather soft and kindly bureaucrat, attentive and unassuming. He listened to me

carefully, made one or two notes, asked a few questions, and said, stuttering slightly: 'All right. I'll do what I can for you.'

Four days later my sentence of expulsion [from college] was reversed.[107]

In 1923 the Central Committee offices moved from Vodvizhenka Street to *Staraya Ploshchad'* (Old Square). Here, on the fifth floor, only a large room in which they held frequent meetings, both alone and with others, separated the offices of Molotov and Stalin. According to one source, Stalin saw Molotov every day from 9.40 am and then again from 4.16 pm to 4.48 pm with other leading politicians.[108] Molotov had two personal secretaries: V. N. Vasilevskii who headed his secretariat and his former tutee, German Tikhomirnov, the youngest of the Tikhomirnov brothers.[109] His job involved not only the continual grind of clerical work, but he also served on Central Committee commissions and committees, both important and more humdrum. Molotov presided over the budget commission and allocated money to sections of the Central Committee;[110] he was also a member of a commission to determine the price of newspapers in March 1924.[111] In addition, he had to take his turn in minuting Secretariat meetings. He arranged Central Committee plenums, held every two or three months at this time,[112] as well as the larger party conferences and congresses. At many of these party assemblies, he was called upon to give important and detailed reports on 'party construction', as at the XIII Congress, 1924; XIV Conference, 1925; and the November 1928 plenum.[113] He also had responsibilities for local party organisation. A long speech at the Orgburo on 2 February 1926 was concerned with the need for local party branches to purge their membership, attack bureaucratism, strengthen their leadership and ensure that work was finished.[114]

A Politburo decision of January 1926 made Stalin responsible for preparation of business for the Politburo, and general direction of the work of the Secretariat. The same Politburo decree appointed Molotov to arrange matters for discussion at the Orgburo. He was also to preside over Central Committee meetings on 'work in the countryside', and direct the work of the Central Committee press, information and party history departments.[115] In April 1927, as part of this work, he addressed newspaper editors on their agitation campaign in support of three important aspects of economic policy: the reduction of industrial prices, rationalisation in production, and the 'regime of economy' in the state apparatus. He stressed that 'the role of the press must be [to] strengthen the trust of the broad mass for the proletarian dictatorship ... reinforce the links between the workers and the peasantry'. He pointed out that the press, like the state's economic organs, had a monopoly position that placed special responsibilities upon it 'to strongly criticise deficiencies, mistakes and distortions, without demagogy or panicky exaggeration', and to emphasise achievements.[116] Later in the year, Sergei Gusev, subsequently described by Trotsky as Molotov's right hand man in cultural repression, took over the Central Committee press department.[117]

An additional duty, as party secretary, until September 1927, was to act as one of the regular Orgburo chairmen. The Orgburo met on a Monday from 7 to 11 pm, the

Secretariat on Friday at 7.00 pm.[118] Of 157 Orgburo sessions, between January 1926 and December 1927, Molotov presided over 60. This did not always involve chairing a formal meeting, since about a quarter of the business was dealt with by the *opros* process (consultation and voting by the circulation of a paper or by telephone).[119] As well as the organisation of large party meetings, the Orgburo dealt with minor appointments to state and party bodies, questions of party membership and the expulsion of members, sometimes at the request of lower party organisations.[120]

In September 1927, Molotov relinquished the Orgburo chairmanship, but became one of its secretaries, perhaps a more onerous position. That there were 207 sittings of the Orgburo and Secretariat between December 1927 and July 1930,[121] is some measure of the size of the task.[122] With this burden one may ask how he had time for anything else? However, in both the Orgburo and the Secretariat, his was an administrative role, he did not have to speak and express an opinion, nor did he have to vote at the Orgburo.[123] This left him in a safe position there, but at the Secretariat he did vote, and in early 1926 still demonstrated a measure of independence from Stalin: his votes on minor matters differed from those of the General Secretary.[124]

Yet even technical reports at party congresses could arouse controversy! At the XIII Congress, 1924, which was marked by clashes between Trotsky, and Zinoviev and Kamenev, and where Krupskaya tried to reveal the contents of Lenin's Testament which condemned Stalin, Molotov, in his report on party construction, caused the one incident where the party leadership lost control of the proceedings. He proposed, for technical reasons, that *guberniya* conferences should be held twice yearly, not once as agreed by the XII Congress. This provoked considerable hostility and was defeated by 266 votes to 259. He then proposed a compromise resolution which allowed the Central Committee to permit some party organisations to hold only one conference. This was passed by 322 votes to 246, but as in the case of the first vote, with a large number of abstentions.[125]

Most significant for the future was Molotov's promotion to full membership of the Politburo at the Central Committee plenum in January 1926, after the XIV Party Congress. He was now, without doubt, one of the foremost Soviet politicians. Other full members of the Politburo were Bukharin, Voroshilov, Kalinin, Rykov, Stalin, Tomsky, Trotsky and Zinoviev. This meant that Stalin could rely on Molotov, Voroshilov and Kalinin, and he was in alliance with Bukharin, Rykov and Tomsky until 1928.[126] In 1926, the Politburo met weekly and sometimes more often. Regular Politburo meetings took place on Friday and were phased with meetings of the Secretariat and Orgburo. The number of formal sittings declined slowly as the decade progressed, but as Table 3.1 shows, Molotov always attended a high proportion (82.26% overall) of these meetings; his most significant periods of absence were during his summer vacation.

The duties of a Politburo member were onerous: meetings were long and even in the early years, with weekly sessions, there were sometimes more than 50 items on the agenda, regularly 20 or 30, although naturally only a few major questions would be discussed. By 1930, with fewer formal meetings, the agenda could be up

Table 3.1 Politburo meetings and Molotov's attendance 1926–1930[127]

Year	No. of sittings	No. of sittings Molotov attended
1926	69*	60*
1927	65	54
1928	54	43
1929	55	44
1930	39	31
Total	282	232

* From date of Molotov's appointment as full member in January.

to 70 items, and interim meetings were held between the formal sessions to ratify decisions.

Initially, as a full member of the Politburo, Molotov's role as party secretary determined his participation in business. He contributed most often on the arrangements for Central Committee plenums, party conferences, other party meetings, the work of the Orgburo, Politburo and Secretariat, and on the appointment and dismissal of party and government officials.[128] His responsibility for rural party organisation is also reflected in the agenda items against which his name appears,[129] and up to 1928 he had a responsibility for defence industry matters.[130] In the later years of the decade his contributions on agriculture and collectivisation increased,[131] and by 1930 he took the lead in items on industrialisation and the Five Year Plan,[132] evidence that he was a senior politician. By this time, he was also responsible for items on the appointment of senior government officials and the reorganisation of commissariats.[133] From 1928 to 1930 his role in *Comintern* (The Communist International) was also reflected in his Politburo contributions.[134] His concern with foreign policy matters also increased, particularly in 1930.[135]

As Central Committee secretary, and because of his personal association, Molotov acted as Stalin's deputy in the summer months whilst the General Secretary was absent from Moscow, often on holiday at Sochi. He received correspondence and instructions from Stalin for transmission to his colleagues, the Politburo and other bodies; sent Stalin responses and generally kept him informed. Between 1925 and 1930 there were at least 71 of these letters.[136] They show that Stalin could rely on Molotov's faithful support, and although he might offer alternatives and modifications he unquestioningly accepted Stalin's decisions.[137] A striking example of this is a letter to Dzerzhinskii, dated 7 August 1925, enclosing two letters from Stalin; the first protested about the financial implications of the plan for the immediate electrification of the Dnepr rapids; the second questioned the decision of the Textile Syndicate for only a small increase in production. Molotov reproached Dzerzhinskii for running VSNKh from his sickbed, and stated that he would have a serious conversation with him about a vacation in the near future. Nevertheless, he asked Dzerzhinskii to note particularly the part of the second letter marked in red pencil, to conduct an enquiry about Stalin's questions, and to write two reports. He said that he was completely in agreement with Stalin who had 'peppered' him with questions about the issues. Finally, he asked Dzerzhinskii to return Stalin's letters.[138]

'Face to the Countryside'

Molotov had written about agriculture during his period as responsible secretary,[139] and it became an increasing preoccupation. In rural localities the communist regime had failed to establish a strong role for the Soviets, the key institution of the proletarian dictatorship. The commune, the traditional peasant institution, which still controlled the budgets of the Soviets, overshadowed these. In his last writings, Lenin envisaged that through the 'patronage' or '*sheftsvo*' movement, the proletariat would carry socialism to the peasantry, but the weakness of the Soviets impeded this process.[140] Molotov's duties as Central Committee secretary involved him in the campaign to 'revitalise' the Soviets, an attempt to increase the strength of the Party in rural areas, and confirmed that agriculture was a top priority.[141]

In February 1924 he was appointed to a Central Committee commission on 'Work in the Countryside', to prepare for the XIII Party Congress (May 1924). At the Central Committee plenum on 2 April he was one of those charged to prepare the report.[142] Later in the year, he took over leadership of the commission.[143] At the Central Committee plenum, in October 1924, where Stalin and Bukharin, opposed by Zinoviev and the Leningrad party organisation, called for improved work in the countryside, Molotov gave a progress report. He admitted that the basic questions, which determined the political opinion of the peasantry, were taxation, and the prices of bread and industrial goods. Then, after a detailed survey of the strength and weaknesses of the Party in a number of localities, he turned to the question of the kulaks (richer peasants who hired the labour of poor peasants) on which he conceded that the Party was not united. The chief problem was that:

> instead of ... isolating and dividing ourselves from the relatively small percentages of kulaks in the countryside, we sometimes include in the general rubric of kulaks a large percentage of the rural population which ... is not hostile ... to Soviet power.

He called for the Party to take great care when it determined its relationship with the peasant mass.[144] The chief challenge to Molotov's report came from Sokolnikov, a supporter of Zinoviev, who insisted that the main priority in the countryside was now political, not economic. But Molotov insisted on the primacy of the economic task, which was to be carried out by strengthening rural party organisations.[145]

On 5 January 1925, at a special Central Committee conference on 'Work amongst the Peasantry', Molotov emphasised that the small peasant farm was the essence of Soviet agriculture. The Party, he insisted, needed to pay particular attention to the opinions of the poor and middle peasants, strengthen its organisations amongst them by concentrating on land tenure, scientific help, co-operatives, rural Soviets, courts, schools and reading rooms. The question of party leadership in the countryside was vital, and he insisted that it was essential for workers from the towns to go into the countryside.[146] These, through the rural Soviets, would help to form a 'non-party *aktiv*' (group of active members) which would stand between party cells and the non-party mass of peasants. This would be fundamental in reinforcing the Party in the countryside, and strengthen the unity of the working class and peasantry. 'Revitalising' the Soviets was crucial. The slogan 'Face to the Countryside' was the essential condition for the further development of the dictatorship of the proletariat in current conditions. In conclusion, he spoke about the need to encourage 'co-operation' (agricultural co-operatives – the lowest form of collectivised agriculture) and how difficult a task this was.[147] At the Politburo, later in the month, in reply to Kamenev, Molotov again stressed the importance of 'co-operation' and the importance of involving poorer peasants as elected officials in the management of collectives.[148] His work as party secretary increasingly led him into the sphere of agriculture.

Komandirovka to Tambov, Kursk and Tula provinces, February 1925

In February 1925, Molotov was sent on a month-long *komandirovka* to Tambov, Kursk and Tula provinces, areas for which he had been entrusted with special responsibility since his appointment to the Secretariat.[149] The aim of the mission was to assess peasant opinion and the strength of rural party organisations.[150] He visited rural communities and farms, and attended party meetings and assemblies of farm workers. He began the tour, on 3 February 1925, when he spoke about the recent Central Committee plenum, to 1600 members of the Tambov party organisation. This speech was not adapted to a rural audience and was typical of a member of the 'patronage movement', criticised for its 'parade-style' activities in the countryside.[151] Molotov talked about international relations, the Comintern, the economy and the struggle with Trotsky and the opposition. The only part of his speech of direct concern to his listeners was the section where he talked of the need to strengthen the Party in the countryside, and when he apologised for a recent flood of memoranda (70 in three months) from central and local party bodies.[152]

For the next few days, Molotov toured villages in the *guberniya*, where initially he made similar or identical speeches.[153] He listened to reports on the achievements of the villages, but more often tried to answer criticisms about the level of taxation, land ownership, poor living conditions, and seed and bread shortages.[154] His response was to fall back on pure ideology: socialism, which meant the abolition of private property and capital, was the answer to these complaints. As for the heavy burden of taxation, the root of the problem was that there was nothing in the fields to harvest, to provide the wherewithal to pay the tax.[155] He summarised the questions he received after his report at the first village, and noted that of 17, eight were concerned with rural problems and four with internal problems, three of which related to the price of bread and consumer goods.[156]

By 7 February, when he visited a third village, he had modified his approach and concentrated on agricultural problems. In response, his audience raised the negative effects on struggling co-operatives of the reduction of the price of grain; the high price of goods the peasant had to buy; and the need for credit. He was asked why the handicraft industries so vital to peasant agriculture were heavily taxed, when it was difficult for the peasant to raise the productivity of the land.[157]

Molotov's growing awareness of agricultural problems was reinforced at another village on 9 February, where he may have given his original address. There was a barrage of protest about peasant conditions. He was quoted as saying that the living conditions of workers had improved, but, he was told, the peasants lived in poverty, were poorly paid and burdened with heavy taxes. There were very few opportunities for trade, educational facilities were non-existent, and when they elected 'honourable' officials, as Molotov directed, they were only told to obey the Party.[158]

When he addressed the Kozlovskii *uezd* Party Committee on 10 February, he showed that he was prepared to take an unpopular line. He supported the local officials' decision to reduce staff on the railway to improve productivity; he backed price rises for consumer goods sold to peasants on local collectives; and he attacked the officials for their speeches at the meetings, and told them how to behave and deal with complaints. He called on them to support the peasants, warned against the SRs, spoke of the necessity of 'defending the collective line of the party, and decrees of Soviet power'.[159] When he spoke about stronger rural party organisations, he referred to one district where a note had been received 'Down with Communists who are our exploiters!' This, he said, was a 'direct counter-revolutionary act', but less serious because its authors had not voted against party resolutions, and therefore it could be ignored. He explained how to prepare party workers, and referred to recent discussion at the Secretariat and Orgburo.[160] In conclusion, he insisted that the key question was the formation of strong links with the peasant mass: 'revitalising' the Soviets and the formation of a non-party peasant *aktiv* as the core of the local party organisation.[161]

Molotov continued his visit in Kursk *guberniya* where he stayed for at least ten days.[162] In his speech to the Kursk *gubkom* (provincial party committee) on 12 February, he omitted the more general part of his speech and concentrated on the importance of the slogan 'Face to the Countryside'. In an echo of his statement at the Politburo the previous month, he said that the basic problem in the countryside was the development of co-operatives, which were at the heart of the transition to socialism. He referred to the bad situation in Tambov *guberniya* where, he claimed, one *volost* was dominated by 'former bandits' with the slogan 'Down with the Communists – exploiters of peasants', and another by kulaks. He stressed the importance of the forthcoming elections to the Soviets and the need to prepare for them.[163]

At the end of his report in another *uezd*, he was probed on the question of land tenure reform and the position of the poor peasant.[164] At another time, of 10 written questions, four were concerned with rural problems and three with party organisational matters – all related to Trotsky.[165] This can have left him with no doubt that, if agriculture was the chief anxiety of his audience, they were also interested in political matters, particularly when they related to popular leaders.

Molotov now varied his approach. In one village, he confined his report to the internal and international position of the USSR, and left it to local officials to talk about matters such as agriculture. However, the audience then turned on him and raised detailed questions on farming, the poor peasantry, land tenure and taxation.[166] In Tula province there was one of the oldest kolkhoz (collective farm) associations, but it had always been subject to difficulties and attacks, which were put down to the fact that the chairman was a former SR. Here, Molotov felt obliged to intervene personally to improve the situation.

The whole tour must have been a chastening experience after the period he had spent in Moscow. He could have no doubt now of the importance for the Party of agriculture and rural conditions, although, his absence from the capital meant that he did not attend a conference of kolkhoz members held in February.[167] His report to the Central Committee i.e. the Politburo, focused on the need to strengthen party organisations rather than on economic matters, but he admitted that there had been areas of harvest failure in the previous year, and that the situation had been especially severe in Tambov.

> Living conditions were extremely poor ... on one of the collectives, the members were living in small evil-smelling rooms (and this in what had been the fine house of a nobleman).

He blamed the grain shortage partly on administrative deficiencies in collecting the agricultural tax, which had provoked the peasants. He stressed the importance of 'co-operative' agriculture, and alleged that shortcomings in the work of the local party organisation were responsible for the feeble performance on collective farms. Although he claimed the slogan 'revitalising the Soviets' was not understood in many of the rural localities he had visited, he believed that it was within the power of the party organisation to make collective farms successful in two to three years, and emphasised the need for strong party leadership in the Soviets. The weak development of handicrafts industries was due to the activities of kulaks and speculators.[168]

The Central Committee decree promulgated in response to Molotov's report, focused on strengthening of party organisation in the areas he had visited.[169] He followed up the report with three articles in journals on the same theme.[170] In a fourth, 'The Party Line in the Peasant Question' (*Liniya partii v krest'yanskom voprosom*) published in *Pravda*, on 24 March 1925, he cited what Lenin had written, especially in one of his last works, 'On co-operation'. He emphasised the importance of the campaign for 'revitalising the Soviets' in the development of 'co-operative' (collective) agriculture, and the significance of the slogan 'Face to the Countryside' for the Party. He was to find that agricultural policy was at the heart of the struggle with the oppositions in which he was now to become involved.

Molotov's growing reputation was demonstrated, in March 1925, when the Central Committee of the Ukrainian Communist Party, in which the divisions over the oppositions reflected the struggle in the Russian party, tried to insist that he be sent to Khar'kov as General Secretary for the Ukraine, and claimed that he had sufficient authority to unite the whole party. But the Politburo rejected the demand. Possibly Stalin could not afford to lose Molotov, although Kaganovich, who went in his place, asserted that Molotov himself rejected the position.[171]

4
The Struggle with the Oppositions 1925–1927

In the mid-1920s, as Stalin gathered a group of supporters in his struggle with the oppositions, and formulated and refined his policies, Molotov strengthened his association with the General Secretary. He was prominent in his support for Stalin in the conflicts with Trotsky, Zinoviev and Kamenev, and in the development of agricultural policy. This was an important stage in the construction of Stalin's dictatorship. The oligarchy that was to rule the Soviet Union during the early years of the next decade began to emerge with Molotov as one of its leading members.

Trotsky – the Eastman Affair

Molotov had never avoided controversy, and his senior position meant that he was bound to become involved in high-level struggles within the Party. In 1924, as he was not first secretary, he was able to protect himself from the main attack when he supported Stalin in the struggle against Trotsky and the Left Opposition.[1] As early as October 1923, he had been one of the signatories of the Politburo's reply to Trotsky's letter to the Central Committee. This attacked the increased power of the Secretariat in appointments, and the Politburo's domination of economic policy, which Trotsky claimed was erroneous and an abandonment of NEP.[2]

With Stalin and Bukharin (two articles each), Molotov contributed 'Ob urokakh Trotskizma' (The Errors of Trotskyism) to the collection Za Leninizm[3] (For Leninism), published in 1925 in response to Trotsky's 'O Lenine' (About Lenin). He extended attacks that he had made in a Pravda article the previous December,[4] and made the standard accusations about Trotsky's Menshivism and lateness in joining the Bolsheviks in 1917. He described 'O Lenine' as an act of self-justification and glorification by Trotsky, and alleged that he had disparaged Lenin, as he portrayed him not as the leader and inspirer of the Party and masses in October 1917, but as 'a conspirator and quite unsuccessful conspirator at that'.[5]

The next stage in the struggle with Trotsky was the 'Eastman affair'. In the summer of 1925, Max Eastman, an American Trotskyite, published Since Lenin Died, which contained an inaccurate and highly politicised description of the contents of Lenin's Testament. In this, uncomplimentary references to Trotsky were removed, as were favourable references to the other political leaders. This embarrassed Stalin and the other party leaders, because they had decided to withhold 'Lenin's Testament' from the XIII Congress, although it was read 'off the record' to delegations. Stalin and his allies pressed Trotsky to repudiate Eastman, and for a memorandum by Stalin on the Eastman book, and other material, to be published in the newspapers.[6] Stalin was on holiday at Sochi at the time, and Molotov became his representative and channel of communication with the rest of the Politburo. He did not escape criticism. When he and Bukharin voted against a resolution to allow Politburo material on Eastman's book to be transmitted to foreign communist parties, Stalin told him 'they had done the wrong thing', because they prevented foreign colleagues from receiving information about Eastman.[7] The documents would have included Stalin's memorandum and Trotsky's repudiation.

Agricultural policy and the Leningrad Opposition 1925–1926

Before the Eastman Affair, Stalin's alliance with Zinoviev and Kamenev was under strain. In January 1925, Kamenev proposed that Stalin should take Trotsky's place at the Commissariat of War. Molotov believed that this was a plan by Kamenev and Zinoviev to remove Stalin from the position of General Secretary.[8] Molotov's speeches in 1925 reflected the divergence on agricultural policy, already apparent in the autumn of 1924.[9] On 10 March 1925, when he spoke to a congress of correspondents of the two journals *Bednota* ('Poor Peasant') and *Krest'yanskaya Gazeta* ('Peasants' Gazette'), he again underlined the importance of a 'wide peasant non-party *aktiv*' as the means of strengthening the Party in the countryside.[10] When he met the editors of the *Krest'yanskaya Gazeta*, on 25 March, he stressed 'revitalising the Soviets', and concluded with the slogan 'strengthen the proletarian links of our countryside'.[11]

In his report to the Central Committee plenum, April 1925, Molotov emphasised, possibly because of his earlier clash with Sokolnikov, that political work in the countryside was inextricably bound up with economic problems: they were in essence one question. The political question could only be resolved through correct economic policies. For the development of large-scale industry, the basis of the socialist state, agricultural development was essential. He noted the growth of the kolkhoz (collective farm) movement, but the priority was to strengthen the small, individual peasant economy, prior to the development of 'co-operative' farming. This would lead to the isolation of the kulak, although he had an important role in the development of agriculture and the market. Molotov repeated that it was necessary to 'strengthen the confidence of the peasant in Soviet power' by 'revitalising the Soviets', and claimed that this had already been accomplished by re-elections in some *guberniya*.[12]

He was now in charge of a Politburo committee on agriculture to examine the hiring of labour and the leasing of land.[13] When he reported to the XIV Conference on 27 April, he called for rapid growth in agriculture to support industrial development, for which state help to the peasantry was essential. He declared that a turning point (*perelom*) had been reached: party policy was to develop trade relations in the countryside and strengthen the work of the Soviets.[14] This meant the transfer of 'important political tasks from the worker's *raions* to the peasant mass' in 1925.[15] The growth of 'co-operation', the basic form of organisation in the countryside which united the peasantry, was to be achieved by proletarian influence on the peasantry through revitalised Soviets, and by state assistance to the poor peasant.[16] This was the last occasion when there was superficial unity among the party leadership on the question of concessions to the peasant.[17]

On 30 April 1925, the day after the close of the XIV Party Conference, Molotov submitted to the Central Committee plenum a resolution on agriculture, basically written by Bukharin, which established the principle of carefully guarded encouragement for the kulaks.[18] At this point Molotov was associated with an extreme interpretation of the policy. He claimed

> We struggled against the Nepmen not only by administrative measures, but also by economic. It is the same in the countryside. We will allow ... the growth of kulakism in the economy at least for the immediate period, so that a wealthy and worthy kulak–peasant population will grow. Of course, this will go on very slowly, and now it will not endanger Soviet power. ... But ... in no way do we end the fight. ... This is a new economic policy. ... The struggle with the kulak economy will be conducted not by dispossession of the kulaks, not by arrests, not by fines, but ... [by] tax policy, by a policy of a system of land tenure, by co-operative work which will play a supremely important role.[19]

Because of the controversy among the party leadership about Bukharin's slogan that the kulak should be encouraged to 'enrich' himself',[20] Molotov found it necessary, when he spoke at the TsKK, on 5 May, to say that there was now unity on an agreed line.[21] On 9 May he wrote of 'poor peasant illusions about the collectivisation of the broad peasant masses.'[22]

In the summer of 1925, Zinoviev began to attack the policy of concessions to the peasant and the NEP as 'state capitalism' and a retreat, not as the road to socialism as envisaged by Stalin and Bukharin.[23] There were as yet, however, no open divergences on policy. Disagreements over Stalin's doctrine of 'socialism in one country', which he intended to announce at the XIV Party Conference, had been concealed in a compromise resolution at the April Central Committee meeting. This was followed by a summer when there were grave agricultural difficulties and the export of grain was halted. Food became scarce in the towns and the price of bread increased. In these circumstances, Bukharin urged the Politburo to make new concessions, offer incentives to farmers and call on them to enrich themselves. Discontent with this policy was particularly marked in Leningrad, and Zinoviev the party leader there, placed himself at the head of it.[24] Molotov was to play a major role in the campaign against Zinoviev and the Leningrad Opposition. In August, he sent his proposals for the agenda of the October Central Committee plenum to Stalin, on holiday at Sochi. Stalin modified them to include an item on 'Party Work among the Village Poor', with instructions that Molotov should give the report personally.[25] In his report, Molotov spoke of two potential deviations: for and against the kulak.[26] He claimed that party organisation in the countryside had been strengthened, although political leadership still needed consolidation. He said that kulaks took the initiative, not the poorer peasantry, and that it was essential for the Party to organise the poor peasants, and build on 'close links with the middle peasant mass'. He warned against an attack on either the kulak or the middle peasantry,[27] but went on to announce a series of measures to organise the poor peasants, to help them economically, enlist them in the 'co-operative' movement, and strengthen their role in the rural Soviets and other village institutions. He also gave notice of further exemptions from the agricultural tax for poor peasants.[28]

This report was essentially a compromise.[29] In September 1925, Zinoviev had submitted to *Pravda* his famous article '*Filosofiya Epokhi*' ('The Philosophy of an Epoch'), which advocated 'equality' as against 'differentiation', implied in Bukharin's encouragement of the kulak. Kalinin and Molotov were, however, the only Politburo members in Moscow and they were candidate members. Molotov, as acting head of the Secretariat, sent the document to Stalin. He supervised its revision before a sanitised version was published.[30] As Molotov's report to the plenum demonstrated, neither side was ready for conflict yet.

Kamenev criticised Molotov's report when he spoke to the Moscow party organisation after the plenum.[31] In response, Molotov led the initial attack against him at the Moscow province party conference in December 1925.[32] Then, at the XIV Party Congress, immediately after this, where Stalin and he gave the major Central Committee reports, Molotov for the most part, like Stalin, maintained a posture of reasonableness and moderation. In accordance with Stalin's line, he admitted that 'the task of rallying the poor and middle peasant round our Party ... we still perform weakly'. He talked about raising the percentage of communists in the Soviets,[33] noted the growth of 'co-operatives', and claimed that workers sent into the countryside were influencing its 'socialist reconstruction'.[34] He demanded that the Party should fight against the kulak danger, isolate the kulak and drive him from the rural economic and political position which he still retained.[35] This was a marked contrast, almost a contradiction to what he had said in April, and indicative of the situation into which the opposition had driven him and Stalin. Molotov had to defend a policy that favoured the kulaks whilst he argued the case to limit their power. He was trying to refute the attacks of Zinoviev, Kamenev and their allies.

When, at the Congress, Zinoviev demanded 'a Politburo with full powers and a Secretariat of functionaries subordinate to it', Molotov called Zinoviev 'Gregory the Bountiful'. He asserted that this sort of Politburo meant one that Zinoviev and Kamenev would dominate. Kamenev, he said, raised questions 'by way of discussion', and abandoned them like a weakling when he met opposition, although, at least, he tried to put forward a complete range of opinions. In contrast, Zinoviev dealt in high-sounding phrases that contained 'nothing new, nothing concrete, no class content'.[36]

At the Congress Molotov was censured in Krupskaya's famous speech which warned that the majority were not always right:

> I see in comrade Molotov's report the same kind of optimism about the state apparatus. ... I felt great satisfaction when I listened to comrade Molotov's

report about how quickly we are growing and how everything is proceeding smoothly and well. ... The point is how together we can find the right policy. It seems to me that there was nothing of this in comrade Molotov's report. ... We cannot simply satisfy ourselves by thinking that the majority is always right.

She went on to remind delegates of the Stockholm conference of 1906 where the Mensheviks were in a majority.[37] In old age, Molotov admitted that his report had been a weak one.[38] Nevertheless, at the end of the Congress, the Leningrad Opposition was routed, and it was at this point that Molotov was elevated to full Politburo membership. Zinoviev's ally Kamenev was demoted to candidate member and Molotov wisely played no part in the debate when he was downgraded.[39]

Molotov's promotion preceded his leading a strong team, the so-called 'savage division', to Leningrad in January 1926. It included Voroshilov, Tomsky, Andrei Andreev, Grigorii Petrovskii and Sergei Kirov, soon to replace Zinoviev as head of the Leningrad Party apparatus. This visit was undertaken ostensibly to report to the Leningrad Party apparatus on the results of the XIV Congress, but the real object of the expedition was to propagandise the official line of the Central Committee, and to discredit and remove Zinoviev. The tactics were to ignore the upper ranks of the regional party organisations initially, and to address workers and factory groups directly. Molotov later described the visit

> Zinoviev politely welcomed us into his office: 'Perhaps you will explain what you need. ... When will you begin work?' 'We shall begin tomorrow. ... We shall go to the factories, deliver reports, take votes.'
>
> Well. The group distributed itself throughout the factories. The next day I spoke at the Lenin shipyards, a famous factory. I don't remember the others. ...
>
> We removed Zinoviev. How? We went to all the factories, and everywhere they endorsed the resolution of the XIV Congress that criticised the Leningrad group.
>
> It was essential that we did not lose the chief factories. To avoid this we first of all won over the second level factories, as they had strong organisations in the big factories. ... It was my task that we should not fail. Zinoviev asked, 'Well, when will you go to the Putilov Works?'
>
> I replied, 'In good time. We are in no hurry.'
>
> The Putilov works was their main base. ... A delegation of Putilov workers came to me, 'Dear comrade, why don't you visit us? We, Putilovites also are workers!' I said, 'We will visit you, we will pay you a good visit, the whole team will visit you. Give us a chance to see how things are at other factories.'
>
> It was important to encircle them. So we saved for last the two most doubtful institutions – the Triangle rubber works ... and the Putilov works.

The meeting at the Triangle Rubber works was chaotic and it was not clear if the 'savage division' had won a majority. Molotov tried to remedy this by 'selective' press reports and won a 'thumping majority' at the Putilov works.[40] He claimed that members of the 'savage division' addressed 652 out of 717 workers' groups, and that although a significant number of party activists voted against the party line, 96 per cent of the votes of the Leningrad organisation had been won over for the Central Committee from the opposition.[41] This made it easier to carry the Central Committee (i.e. Stalin's) line at the Leningrad provincial party conference in February.[42]

There were echoes of the XIV Congress and the attack on Zinoviev's Leningrad party apparatus in Molotov's report to the Orgburo in March 1926. He criticised the way in which the power of party conferences to elect leading organs was undermined by prior decisions in higher organs, or by deals between different party organisations, often by local party leaders who attempted to gain the leadership they wanted.[43] The part Molotov played in the struggle with the Leningrad Opposition and his mission to Leningrad, is indicative of the rôle of Stalin's troubleshooter that he had now assumed, and which continued during the later 1920s.

The United Opposition 1926–1927

1926

The first signs of a *rapprochement* between Trotsky, Zinoviev and Kamenev, and the formation of the United Opposition, appeared at the April 1926 Central Committee plenum. Here, in defence of Stalin, Molotov took the lead against Trotsky, who, supported by Kamenev, attacked the resolution of the XIV Congress on industrialisation. Molotov challenged them for doubting (in accordance with Stalin's formula of 'socialism in one country') that 'the internal resources' of the USSR were sufficient to construct socialism. He condemned Kamenev's interpretation of 'co-operation' because it conflicted with the decision of the XIV Congress, and extended the attack to take in recent articles by Zinoviev. Molotov's chief support came from Kaganovich. Stalin remained in the background and made only a short speech.[44]

The opposition predicted that industrialisation and market relations with the peasants presented serious problems. Stalin and his supporters did not accept this view until 1927, and Molotov's response to the challenge, in a speech to the Orgburo on 24 May 1926, was to emphasise the importance of the poor peasants. He asked: 'How can you be a communist in the countryside when you do not put as your first duty work amongst poor peasants?' He argued that it was crucial to organise the poor peasants and form a 'non-party *aktiv*'. If rural Soviets were to be 'revitalised', groups of poor peasants had to be actively involved in the work of the Soviets and in 'co-operatives'. This, he claimed, would strengthen the bonds between the poor and middle peasants.[45]

In the same month, Molotov defended Stalin when he was accused of responsibility for the medical murder of Frunze in October 1925, at the height of the struggle with Kamenev and Zinoviev. Frunze submitted unwillingly, on orders from the Politburo driven through by Stalin, to an operation for a stomach ulcer which proved to be unnecessary. Stalin and Molotov were amongst the leading politicians who visited Frunze on the day of his death, but Stalin then laid himself open to accusation by some odd comments in his rather brief funeral oration. Moreover, the death of Frunze allowed the promotion to Commissar for Military and Naval Affairs of Stalin's ally, Voroshilov, who had been passed over in January 1925, when Frunze replaced Trotsky.[46]

The accusation of medical murder was made in B. Pil'nyak's 'Tale of the Unextinguished Moon'; the story of an army commander forced to submit to an unnecessary operation, during which he was murdered, an almost exact parallel to Frunze's death. The narrative included a portrait of a political leader, described as 'number one' and 'the unbending man', with a personality and physical appearance similar to Stalin.[47] The 'Tale of the Unextinguished Moon', was published in *Novyi Mir* (New World) in May 1926. Molotov headed a Politburo commission that condemned and banned Pil'nyak's story as a 'malicious counter-revolutionary and slanderous attack against the Central Committee and Party'. The commission arranged for the offending issue of *Novyi Mir* to be immediately confiscated by the OGPU (secret police). Only a few copies escaped, and a replacement number was issued without Pil'nyak's story. The June issue of *Novy Mir* contained disavowals and the apology of the editorial board, headed by Anatolii Lunarchaskii. Pil'nyak himself, who had gone abroad on a trip to the Far East, after he submitted the story in January, escaped for the time being: the commission ordered only his dismissal from the posts he held on Leningrad journals and the writing of a recantation which was published in *Novyi Mir* in January 1927.[48]

In May and June 1926, with Stalin away from Moscow in Tiflis, the struggle with the opposition continued over Zinoviev's theses on the lessons of the British General Strike. These claimed that Stalin and Bukharin had been mistaken in their policy on the international trade union movement. On 28 May, Molotov sent Stalin a detailed account of Zinoviev's theses; four days later he and Bukharin wrote to Stalin:

> It is extremely important for you to study these theses immediately and send us your opinion. ... Zinoviev is re-evaluating our analysis of capitalist stabilisation and the tactics of Comintern, slinging mud at the Comintern's existing policy and making references to the party and to individual Central Committee members. ... He is ready to take upon himself the initiative of breaking immediately with the General Council [of the British TUC]. I believe that this is consummate stupidity. ... and the Central Committee should ruthlessly oppose it. ... Opportunism disguised by 'leftist' phrases should be ruthlessly exposed. ... We're expecting your immediate reply.[49]

In a second telegram, the same day, Molotov wrote that Bukharin was preparing counter-theses against Zinoviev and that

> Our theses should expose not only ultra-leftism but that which screens it, that is, leftism in the Comintern as Lenin taught. ... Simultaneously we must (1) emphasise the conditional nature of the stabilisation and the growth of complications that may lead to revolution in the capitalist countries, although

the outcome may go either way. ... Your opinion is needed immediately. It would be better if you came in person to Moscow ...[50]

Stalin replied in two telegrams two days later, with a detailed analysis of the errors in Zinoviev's theses. He gave instructions as to the content of Bukharin's counter-theses and on other measures that the Politburo should take with regard to the British General Strike. At the Politburo, Zinoviev's theses were rejected and Bukharin's counter-theses were accepted.[51]

At the July 1926 Central Committee plenum, Molotov turned on Trotsky and Zinoviev and attacked them for failure to support the campaign to 'revitalise' the Soviets.[52] He argued that the development of the country depended on robust rural Soviets which would strengthen the *smychka* (alliance) between workers and peasants. It was insufficient to rely on the proletariat, as the opposition maintained. He claimed that his was the true Leninist position, for it recognised the workers as the vanguard of the proletariat.[53] Molotov chaired the commission which edited the plenum resolution, based on his draft Politburo resolution. It stated:

> The increased activity of the basic mass of the peasantry, especially the middle peasants, the strengthening of their trust in the party, will form favourable conditions for the formation of a poor–middle peasant (*bednyatsko-serednyatskogo*) bloc against the kulak. The formation of a non-party peasant *aktiv*, as the core of the Party and Soviets, is critical for the success of this.[54]

At the end of the plenum, when Zinoviev was deprived of his Politburo membership,[55] Molotov was the second signatory after Kalinin, with Tomsky, Kuibyshev, Bukharin, Rykov and Rudzutak, of a declaration which supported Stalin and condemned the attack of the opposition group on him.[56]

The affair rumbled on through the summer of 1926. Stalin, who had returned to Moscow, wrote to Molotov, now on holiday at Sochi, that Kamenev, who had resigned from the Commissariat of Trade, continued to vote at the Politburo as a candidate member, where the opposition kept a low profile.[57] Later he wrote about the need to remove Zinoviev from Comintern.[58] By September, Molotov was back in Moscow and Stalin warned him

> It's possible tomorrow that Zinoviev will come out with a statement on Molotov's and Bukharin's 'lack of principle' [saying] that Molotov and Bukharin 'offered' Zinoviev ... a 'bloc' and that he, Zinoviev, 'rejected this intolerable flirtation with disdain', and so forth and so on.[59]

Following the clash with Zinoviev over the British General Strike, Molotov now attempted to organise a campaign in support of the British miners, and wrote to Stalin that this should have 'political slogans (dissolution of Parliament, "Down with the conservative government, for a genuine workers' government")'.[60] He also tried to assist Stalin in mollifying Ordzhonikidze, another important Stalin supporter, whom Molotov had known since 1917 and with whom he was friendly.[61] Ordzhonikidze had taken offence over his recall from Transcaucasia, and resisted Stalin's pressure to serve in the central state apparatus. He preferred to remain a provincial leader, rather than aid Stalin in Moscow.[62] Molotov suggested that Ordzhonikidze should be made head of TsKK-NKRKI and a Sovnarkom-vice chairman.[63] Ordzhonikidze's appointment was announced in November.[64]

In a speech to the Orgburo in September, Molotov underlined the importance of party work with the rural wage labourer (*batrak*) and among the rural unemployed, to increase their numbers in the Party and Komsomol (Communist Youth Movement).[65] But in a further speech to the Orgburo, in October, he emphasised that more than half of the party should be from workers actually involved in production, and that stricter criteria should be used to judge applications from peasants, especially middle peasants, who should play an active role in support of the Soviet regime.[66] At the XV Party Conference, October–November 1926, he echoed Stalin when he hailed Kalinin, Smirnov, Voroshilov, Tomsky, Nikolai Uglanov and Vasily Shmidt as 'all workers, the very flower of our party'.[67]

In early October, Molotov made a fierce onslaught on the opposition, in a speech to students beginning courses at party schools. He noted that an oppositional bloc had formed in the Party, which united 'tendencies from those of [G] Medvedev and Shlyapnikov [The Workers' Opposition] to those of Trotsky and Zinoviev.' In the first third of the speech, he described in detail the differences with Trotsky before 1917. He compared the contemporary bloc to the August bloc of 1912–1914 organised by Trotsky. This had shared the fate of the Menshevik party, and the Bolshevik party had become 'the powerful leader of the proletarian revolution'.[68] The emphasis on the August bloc had been agreed previously with Stalin.[69] He admitted that the contemporary 'opposition bloc' (Trotsky, Zinoviev, Pyatakov, Kamenev, Radek and others) had 'no little talents' especially in the use of words. He demanded strict adherence to the party line in the construction of socialism and accused the opposition of endangering the regime by encouraging bourgeois elements.[70] This attack was in preparation for the Central Committee plenum later that month, where Molotov introduced the Politburo resolution which deprived Trotsky of his full membership and Kamenev of his candidate membership in the light of their fractional activity since the July plenum.[71] Zinoviev was also expelled from his Comintern position.[72]

In December 1926 Molotov was absent from Moscow for a month in the campaign against the opposition. Among his chief duties was attendance at the VIII All-Georgian Party Conference where he made an important statement of his current ideological position. This clearly reflected Stalin's view. Stalin had been a sceptic on industrialisation in 1925, and as late as 1926 opposed to large-scale schemes, such as the construction of the Dnepostroi power station. Political expediency and the need to defeat the opposition now, however, drove him to favour industrialisation and Molotov reflected this view.[73] Molotov emphasised that next year would see the anniversary of ten years of revolutionary government (not three months as in the case of the Paris Commune). He claimed that 96 per cent of industry was now in the hands of the proletariat. The economy had been restored to its pre-revolutionary level, but 'without large-scale industry we cannot think about the victory of socialism'. NEP Russia had to be transformed into socialist Russia. He admitted that industrialisation based on the internal resources of Russia was a very difficult task. Bourgeois elements within the country believed it was impossible, and they 'infected' the Party. He referred to the success of industriali-sation in the previous year, but claimed that the reduction of prices was a central task. The opposition might accept this, but there were differences on the question of trade development: the Party could not support the development of large-scale private trade, especially in rural localities. He claimed that, this year, the procurement campaign, now out of the hands of the opposition, was satisfactory.

He now attacked the opposition, particularly Trotsky, for saying that the con-struction of socialism based on the link between the peasants and workers was not possible because of encirclement by international capitalism, and that socialism could not be built without international revolution. This, he claimed, was the basic difference between Lenin and Trotsky in 1915, when Lenin wrote about the possibility of the victory of socialism in a single country. Lenin's doctrine had led to the 1917 revolution and the construction of the proletarian state during the last ten years. This was where social democracy departed from Communism.

Molotov broadened his attack to include Kamenev, Radek and others who claimed that the Party had departed from Leninist policy. In a full-blooded con-demnation of recent opposition speeches Molotov asserted that the opposition was struggling to form a new party

> But for us there cannot be another party, besides the united Bolshevik party, the leaders of the proletariat. For communists there can only be one task, the unity of our party, the struggle against all who try to break its unity.
>
> We need to carry out the liquidation of the opposition bloc ... so that the leaders ... are excluded from the party mass, that they are generals without armies.[74]

Whilst he was absent from Moscow Stalin wrote to him on 23 December:

> We published ... documents that slaughtered Kamenev politically. We consider that Kamenev is knocked out of commission and won't be in the Central Committee any longer, ...[75]

1927

Molotov welcomed the new year with an article in *Pravda* in which he claimed that elections to the Soviets would show up more clearly the 'class interests and class contradictions of the peasantry', but that the aim should be 'the complete take over of the whole state apparatus by the working class'. He emphasised the importance of the 'non-party peasant *aktiv*' in the Soviets. Shortly afterwards, in a further article, he condemned Soviets packed with nominated candidates which divorced these institutions from the mass of non-party peasants.[76] He made a particularly fierce attack on the opposition leaders at the Leningrad *guberniya* party conference, 26 January 1927. He said that whereas industry was 'already pre-occupied with the radical work of formation of the socialist industrial base', in the countryside there was 'only preparatory work' for co-operation (collectives) 'which was said by Lenin to be the basic path to socialism for the countryside'. There were different paths for town and country, different types and tempos of socialist construction. He accused Zinoviev and Kamenev of panic because of the pro-kulak policy, which they misunderstood as capitulation before difficulties. He pointed to the improvement in procurements, increased revenue from the agricultural tax, the growth in collectives and the spread of party influence through the Soviets, and emphasised again the importance of the 'non-party peasant *aktiv*'.[77] The contradictions in what he said show the position to which he and Stalin had been driven by the attacks of the opposition.

Initially, Molotov made only a brief speech at the February 1927 Central Committee plenum, in support of the official policy on the price of agricultural machinery as established by the April 1925 plenum. When he could not secure agreement he had the matter referred to the Politburo.[78] On 11 February, however, he spoke again, and made a very full statement about the 'non-party *aktiv*', where 'heightened activity of the leading workers and peasants from the non-party mass ... will mean a colossal increase in Soviet power'. He warned that rural communists must be wary of the rise in strength of the kulaks as the Party struggled to make the middle peasant its ally and isolate the kulaks, although they were only a very small minority.

> Our slogan is 'the kulak has no place in the Soviets', but ... amongst the ranks of those disenfranchised by the electoral law, we must not find even the smallest percentage of middle peasants.[79]

He castigated Trotsky and Zinoviev for their lack of faith in the campaign to revitalise the Soviets, and there was a sharp exchange with them about how socialism could be constructed on the basis of this policy. He defended the official policy of reduction of the price of industrial goods against Trotsky's attacks, and shielded Kalinin from Zinoviev's denunciation of a speech he had recently made. In conclusion he condemned the systematic attacks of the opposition on party policy: they behaved like a parliamentary opposition.[80] The next month, at the Orgburo, Molotov warned about poor recruitment to the Party. He called for improved party educational machinery, and for senior party and commissariat members to be sent on *komandirovki* to strengthen the Party.[81]

Molotov's specialism in agriculture enabled him to defend official economic policy with increased assurance.[82] At the July 1927 Central Committee plenum he also attacked the opposition more generally. He dealt with the development of the international socialist revolution, the 'war scare' situation of 1927 and the defence of the USSR from a possible attack, and demonstrated his ideological commitment to Stalin's line. He accused Zinoviev, in a recent article, of lack of faith in the USSR as 'an authentic proletarian republic', and was prepared to challenge

Trotsky on theoretical issues, such as his differences with Lenin on interpretations of the First World War. He continued:

> The Soviet Union exists in extremely difficult international conditions. The danger of imperialist intervention at the present moment has been significantly reinforced ... but comrade Trotsky cannot find anything better, than to say, at the moment when the imperialist onslaught is 80 kilometres from Moscow,[83] than that it is necessary to strike out decisively against the policy of the party, as if deficient in courage, as if deficient in boldness, as if deficient in leftism. To follow this path signifies sinking into defensist ideology.

He went on to accuse Trotsky and his supporters of an attempt to form a new party, but, he said, 'I would like to remain a member of the *old* party'. The policy of the opposition was like the policy of the Left SRs of the NEP period: it was a struggle against Soviet legality. This was especially dangerous in the present international situation – the time of the war scare.[84] He returned to the question of the activities of the opposition at a time of heightened danger of war later in the plenum, and dragged in the opposition's lack of faith in the theory of 'Socialism in One country'.[85] Molotov also announced plans for the forthcoming XV Congress at the end of the plenum, which the opposition, suspecting the pre-congress plenum would be used to secure their expulsion from the Central Committee, again opposed.[86] At this point Stalin joined Molotov in his attacks on the opposition.[87]

In preparation for the XV Congress, Molotov chaired the commission that prepared the theses on 'work in the countryside'.[88] A commission of which he was a member, but which Petrovskii chaired, produced the final version.[89] The theses called for 'further reinforcement of *planned* action on the peasant economy ... a decisive break-through in the direction of the isolation of the kulak'.[90] By this time, Stalin and his supporters realised the significance of the poor 1927 harvest and were beginning to retreat from a policy of market relations with the peasants towards a return to forcible procurements.

When he introduced the theses to the October 1927 Central Committee plenum, Molotov asserted that they placed relations between the town and the countryside on a new basis, and represented stronger links with the middle peasant – 'one of the central tasks of our Party in the countryside'. He maintained that the opposition increased the kulak danger in the countryside, and he called for 'the development of ... agriculture by state planning, and ... co-operation'. The theses were 'one of the most important indices of the correctness of party policy'.[91] Molotov claimed that one-third of the peasantry were members of 'co-operatives', and that the growth of the socialist element in the countryside produced panic among kulaks, the struggle against whom was entering a new decisive stage. Part of the poor peasants had been proletarianised, whilst others had been helped into the middle group, yet the opposition denied that there was any radical difference in the countryside since 1917. Although he admitted that there had been a growth of 'kulakism', he claimed that the 'central figure' in the countryside had been, was, and would continue to be the middle peasant (*serednyak*). He quoted Lenin, and alleged that the opposition ignored and denied the growth of the socialist element in the countryside. They did not understand the 'Leninist co-operative plan'; and failed to recognise the success of co-operation in the countryside. The opposition behaved not as members of a Leninist Central Committee, but as representatives in a provincial parliament, 'sitting in the seats of left-bourgeois chatterers'. He reminded them of the X Congress Resolution on Party Unity.[92] Counter-theses by the opposition, described Molotov's theses as 'a revision of Leninism in the peasant question', but these were defeated, and the victory over the opposition completed with the expulsion of Trotsky and Zinoviev from the Central Committee.[93]

After the plenum, in a speech to the Moscow party *aktiv* Molotov poured scorn on the opposition when they complained about the use of the OGPU and the planting of an *agent provocateur* in their underground printing press.[94] In November 1927, in a *Pravda* article, he defended Stalin from the personal attacks of the opposition, which he indicated might lead to a terroristic attempt against the General Secretary. He wrote of open attacks on 'Soviet legality' and that 'a certain Left SR odour exudes from the opposition cess-pit'.[95] His article on the tenth anniversary of the 1917 revolution was also used to attack 'Trotskyism',[96] and on 7 November he was personally involved in dispersing a meeting that Trotsky addressed. Trotsky's response was to make his famous accusation that Stalin and his supporters were the 'gravediggers of the revolution'.[97] Despite the expulsion of the opposition from the Central Committee, now cast in the role of Stalin's first lieutenant, Molotov still found it necessary to attack Trotsky's economic policy at the XV Congress, December 1927.[98]

5
Stalin's Lieutenant 1927–1929

The XV Congress

Molotov chaired the Central Committee commission that prepared for the XV Party Congress, December 1927.[1] By the time that the Congress met there was growing anxiety about the grain collections. Stalin did not specifically admit this, but said that the rate of growth in agriculture was inadequate, and called for the 'collective cultivation of the soil on the basis of a new and higher technique'.[2] This marked a fundamental change in policy. Driven back to the forcible requisition of grain to solve the immediate crisis, Stalin committed himself to collectivisation and rapid industrialisation. The change in direction was an embarrassing *volte face*, although Stalin and his supporters tried to pretend it had always been their policy. It provoked widespread opposition in the party leadership, and the loyalty of his supporters, especially Molotov, was of key importance to Stalin.

Early on at the Congress, on 11 December, Molotov, with approving comments by Stalin, condemned forcible requisitioning.[3] Five days later he argued that an increase in agricultural production, in the conditions of 1927, symbolised the expansion of the productive forces of a market economy, which inevitably involved the development of rural capitalism. He said that it was 'an almost impossible task to calculate any sort of general percentage of agricultural bourgeoisie (kulaks) for the entire USSR', although he gave a figure of 3.7 per cent of peasant households. He warned that the kulak element had increased, which meant that the struggle with them was likely to grow fiercer,[4] 'Speeding up the attack on the kulak' combined with 'the development of co-operation, the development of the collective element in our agriculture ... [was] an attack on the capitalist element in the countryside'.[5] He continued:

> Up to now, when we have revitalised the Soviets, the *kulaks* have often turned to the communes and have tried to entrench themselves there. ... Now we will finally beat them out of even these last trenches, ...[6]

He claimed that when he spoke of 'speeding up the attack on the kulak', he spoke of nothing new. This ignored the huge policy shift which had taken place between 1924 and late 1927. Molotov was moving towards the policy of 'liquidation of the kulak',[7] and with Stalin he was harsher against them at the Congress than any other speaker.[8]

Prior to this he had reminded his audience that although the rural proletariat was growing, half of it was in the 'individual peasant economy', and the middle peasant remained the central figure in agriculture. The slow development of socialism on this basis meant that it was imperative to change to 'social' (collective) economy and the party recognised 'co-operatives ... as the basic path of the peasant mass to socialism'.[9] He mentioned some letters from peasants who asked to have their tiny holdings taken away and organised in large units, to put them in the position of workers. The Party had to place itself at the head of initiatives of this type. He praised *kontraktsiya* (the system of purchase by contract) as the beginning of planning and of industrialised agriculture. All types of collectives, not only kolkhozy, had to be supported in the transition from individual peasant agriculture, and he commended 'machine societies' (*tovarishchestva*), the forerunners of the MTSs (*mashinno-trakto naya stantsiya* – Machine Tractor Station).[10]

Later, he continued:

> What are our methods? ... *Persuasion plus encouragement* by the proletarian state ... *this is our method of collectivising the countryside. ... Forward the countryside to large scale collective economy!*[11]

He attacked the opposition and alleged that their proposal for a 'union of poor peasants' would isolate the poor peasant, separate him from 'co-operation', from the kolkhoz, and from socialist construction in general.[12] He said that the slogan 'face to the countryside' was deficient in the new stage:[13] the development of a large-scale collective economy would destroy hostility between town and country and everyone would be a member of a single socialist society.[14] Following Stalin's initial comments, Molotov was announcing in more detail, a major shift in policy, away from the NEP. It was also a declaration of war against the Right.

There seems no evidence to support A. Antonov-Ovsyenko's assertion, that Stalin, who did not warn Molotov, criticised the speech to test Molotov's loyalty and confuse the opposition; and that a distraught Molotov complained to Polina that Stalin attacked what they had previously agreed.[15] Indeed, Stalin punctuated the final theses on agriculture, worked out by a commission that Molotov chaired, with encouraging remarks. They announced a more decisive offensive against the kulak and claimed that the growth of heavy industry would transform agriculture through improved technique and collectivisation. They described small peasant holdings as 'the fundamental evil of the countryside, its basic economic contradiction', and Molotov called for 'the unification and transformation of individual peasant holding into large collectives', which he described as 'the fundamental task of the Party in the countryside'.[16]

'Extraordinary Measures'

In the crisis at the end of 1927, despite the condemnation of forcible grain requisitioning at the Congress, leading politicians visited key areas to remedy the shortfall in procurements. Molotov was sent to the Ukraine from 28 December 1927 to 6 January 1928, then from 11 to 19 January 1928 to the Urals and Bashkiriya.[17] During Molotov's second *komandirovka*, before Stalin left on his famous journey to Siberia where the withholding of grain had followed a record harvest, he sent instructions to Molotov and other visiting officials to make the procurement campaign more forceful and step up measures against kulaks and speculators. He specified Siberia and the Urals as key areas.[18] This presaged the introduction of grain confiscation and a change of policy to forced collectivisation.[19] Molotov worked closely with Stalin. Their proposal for 'peasant self-taxation' was introduced to the Politburo prior to their departure for the grain producing areas.[20]

During his visit to the Ukraine, Molotov visited Khar'kov, Melitopol' and towns and villages in their vicinity. He arrived in Melitopol' on New Year's Day, when everyone was celebrating the holiday. He insisted on an immediate meeting of party activists. 'I turned on the pressure: "Give us grain! It is high time to put a squeeze on the kulak!" ' He later admitted:

> We took away the grain. We paid them in cash, but of course at miserably low prices. ... I applied the utmost pressure to extort the grain. All kinds of rather harsh methods ... had to be applied.

Molotov lived on a special train protected by members of the OGPU. He saw officials from Zaporozh'e and some other areas on the train. When he travelled to villages, he always returned to the train at night. Following his visit, the Ukrainian Central Committee intensified the procurement campaign and repression was stepped up. In his memoirs, he claimed that Stalin said to him: 'I would cover you in kisses for your action down there.'[21]

Molotov's report, presented to the Politburo on 26 January, ascribed the shortfall in procurements in the Ukraine to non-compliance of the local agencies, and a clear underestimation of the grain surplus. He claimed that in co-operatives, the elected leadership was deficient because of the influence of a middle peasant and kulak elite. He noted conflict between Union and Ukrainian agencies, particularly the Ukrainian Commissariat of Agriculture, and emphasised that a single union authority was necessary – perhaps foreshadowing the creation of the Union Commissariat in 1929, a process in which he was to be central. He stressed the need to strengthen the role of party organisations in grain procurement and stated that the self-taxation policy that he and Stalin were promoting had made good progress in the Ukraine. He produced figures which showed the improvement in the collections after his visit.[22]

During his expedition to the Urals, Molotov based himself at Sverdlovsk and Chelyabinsk, and in Bashkiriya at Ufa. He disagreed with M. Frumkin, the deputy Commissar for Finance, who had visited the Urals a short while before. Molotov believed that it was possible to collect the Commissariat of Trade's figure of 44,000,000 puds (707,143 tons). Frumkin thought this figure was unrealistic and 39,000,000 puds (626,785 tons) to be a more accurate estimate.[23] Molotov's attitude was clear when he told the Urals province party committee: 'we must deal the kulak such a blow that the middle peasant will snap to attention before us'![24]

Molotov considered that in Bashkiriya the procurement campaign was handicapped by slipshod organisation and the failure to take measures against kulaks, although these were only 2.6 per cent of the population, a figure below the average for the country as a whole. In the conclusion to his report, he emphasised deficiencies in leadership and the importance of the policy of self-taxation, because it would strengthen the middle-poor peasant bloc. He called for a toughening of Soviet discipline.[25] His policy was to extend repression through the lower party apparatus.[26]

Before Molotov's return from Bashkiriya, Stalin, in Novosibirsk, wrote to tell him that he had insisted that the Politburo send him immediately to four central Russian *gubernii*, to stay two or three days in each, and check progress of the procurement campaign.[27] Consequently Molotov, accompanied by Jacob Yakovlev,[28] chairman of the All-Union Kolkhoz Council, went to Tambov, where the provincial committee had reduced the control figure. His tactics were confrontational. He told the committee on 26 January

> No *guberniya* committee has the right to change a directive of the Central Committee of the Party. ... From the point of view of party discipline ... [it] must declare: we support the directive of the Central Committee and we will fulfil it. ... The Central Committee can issue an incorrect directive. But you do not have the right to change this directive without requesting its revision.

He asserted that the peasant had grain, and that failure to collect it 'totally discredits the working class before the peasantry and the party leadership before the peasant mass'.[29] Molotov exhorted the committee to 'heroic measures',[30] told them that they had not read the law on taxation, and sarcastically referred them to the appropriate number of *Izvestiya TsK*. When there were protests about the arrests of kulaks, he said that it was not necessary for the OGPU to arrest them all: the *guberniya* committee should decide. He was firm, however, that the law must be obeyed, and accused the committee of behaving like landlords.[31] The local representatives now protested that they needed agricultural machinery to fulfil the procurements, but Molotov insisted that the directive must be fulfilled irrespective of deliveries of machinery, and that kulaks who did not pay taxes should be arrested.[32]

When the meeting resumed in the evening and it was proposed to send telegrams to local committees Molotov remarked 'We need to show there are communists here.'[33] He accused anyone who opposed him of a 'kulak deviation' and was adamant that each area should fulfil the control figures. He made members of the *guberniya* committee personally responsible and demanded strict measures, which included the use of the OGPU.[34] The evening session ended when members of the committee were despatched, on Molotov's initiative, on *komandirovki* to ensure fulfilment of the collections.[35] The next morning Molotov insisted on a firm figure for each area and the name of the individual responsible: it was that individual's communist duty to see that the control figures were achieved. He told the committee: 'If you vote for the measure you are for the Central Committee, against you are an Oppositionist!'[36]

On his return to Moscow, Molotov was the Central Committee secretary who signed the directive on the spring sowing campaign 1928.[37] In March he was quoted as saying 'Feeding the middle peasant with credit can lead to him outgrowing himself into a kulak.'[38] His attitude towards the kulak was reflected again when he interrupted Petrovskii at the April 1928 Central Committee plenum, where he also interjected comments into Vlas Chubar's speech, to reinforce the importance of the procurement campaign.[39] If the atmosphere of this plenum was to celebrate the success of the 1927–1928 collections,[40] there was another temporary crisis shortly afterwards. The Politburo, on 19 April, had to deal with the shortfall in the first half of the month,[41] and called a meeting of local representatives on 24 April, chaired by Molotov. This was followed by a top secret Politburo directive to local party organisations to reinforce the procurement campaign. At the meeting, supported by Mikoyan, Molotov defended 'extraordinary measures' and the collectives. He stressed the improvements in procurements in the current year and called for further development of the kolkhozy and of sovkhozy (large state farms).[42] Stalin had first proposed sovkhozy at a Politburo meeting the previous day.[43]

Molotov occupied a key position during collectivisation. By December 1926, Stalin's agricultural policy began to favour the kolkhoz, and a discussion of collectivised agriculture at the Politburo in that month had resulted in measures to strengthen the All-Union Kolkhoz Council – VSK (*Vsesoyuznoi Sovet Kolkhozov*). Molotov chaired a commission which was responsible for establishing *Kolkhoztsentr* RSFSR in April 1927, a body set up to promote, organise and direct the kolkhozy.[44] Its administrative organs were its Congress, Council (*Sovet*) and Administration. Political leaders, including Stalin and Molotov, were members of the Council, and from the end of 1928, *Kolkhoztsentr* became very active. In 1929, MTSs began to be formed, and *Traktorotsentr* (All-Union Centre of Machine Tractor Stations) was organised separate from *Kolkhoztsentr*. Molotov became chairman of the Council (*Sovet*) of *Traktorotsentr*. These bodies were amalgamated under the leadership of the All-Union *Kolkhoztsentr* in October 1929. Prior to this, at the First All-Union Congress of Kolkhoz Workers (i.e. of *kolkhoztsentr*), 1–6 June 1928, Molotov was appointed chairman of the All-Union Council (*Sovet*) and he reported on behalf of *Kolkhoztsentr* at the crucial November 1929 Central Committee plenum.[45] Kalinin claimed that a Politburo commission on the kolkhozy, established under Molotov's chairmanship in 1927, achieved a 'mental revolution',[46] and from February 1928 he chaired a further Politburo commission to develop them.[47] His reputation as an authority on agriculture was now sufficient for a collection of 21 of his articles, speeches and reports, written between October 1924 and January 1927, suitably edited and revised to fit current party policy, to be considered worthy of publication. Four editions were issued between 1926 and 1928, the third in 1927 had a *tirazh* (circulation) of 7000 copies.[48]

The growing breach with the Right

The rift in the party leadership was demonstrated on 15 June 1928, when Frumkin, who had clashed with Molotov earlier in the year, wrote his famous letter of protest to the Politburo. He attacked policy since the XV Congress, especially 'extraordinary measures', and claimed that 'the countryside, with the exception of a small section of the poor peasants, is against us', because a restricted attack against the kulak had been turned against the middle peasant. Molotov, in particular, distorted policy by his extreme hostility towards the kulaks.[49] Stalin replied, in a letter to the Politburo on 20 June, and Molotov in another letter on 25 June. Molotov stated that he agreed with Stalin that Frumkin's analysis of the situation in the countryside 'signifies a complete condemnation of the conduct of party policy'. He cited figures to show the increase in the grain procurements. He defended his hostility towards the kulak, and alleged that Frumkin opposed development of kolkhozy and sovkhozy. He quoted from the report on his January *komandirovka* to justify his January statement to the Urals province party committee about middle peasants 'snapping to attention', and his March statement that condemned giving credit to them.[50] Nevertheless, on 30 June 1928, he was very cautious when he spoke to the Moscow party committee. He stressed the backwardness of Russian agriculture and the danger of relying on planning alone.[51]

At the Central Committee plenum, in early July 1928, there were preliminary skirmishes over the grain procurement figures reported by Valerian Osinskii (formerly head ot TsSU [*Tsentral'noe Statisticheskoe Upravlenie* – the Central Statistical Administration] but now Gosplan [State Planning Commission] representative), and with Bukharin, who protested against the continuation of 'extraordinary measures'. Mikoyan then gave the main speech on behalf of the Politburo, and emphasised that there was no intention that 'extraordinary measures' should become a permanent policy.[52] Molotov, in his report on the procurement campaign, which was frequently interrupted, spoke of the end of 'extraordinary measures' for the forthcoming harvest. He attributed difficulties in the grain collections to the 'small-peasant economy', to the activities of kulaks and speculators, and perhaps to mistakes in planning. He called for price rises in agricultural products and bread to remedy this, and alliance with the middle peasants. He went on to attack both 'Left' (Trotskyist) and 'Right' errors.[53] He criticised amongst others, V. Astrov, a follower of Bukharin, for a *Pravda* article which claimed that 'extraordinary measures' had negative effects on the middle peasant, and drove them towards the kulak. He also attacked Sokolnikov because he underestimated the 'leading role' of the proletariat in the struggle with the peasantry.[54] He admitted, however, that 'the middle peasant has become stronger and come into collision with us'.[55] The remedy was to organise the poor peasants, which would strengthen middle peasant–poor peasant links against the kulaks.[56] This was the essential preliminary to ending 'extraordinary measures' and a rise in the price of agricultural goods. He attempted to give a theoretical underpinning to 'extraordinary measures', and said that those who forgot their real class basis committed a crime against Marxism. In conclusion he quoted Lenin on the union of the proletariat and the peasantry as the 'guarantee of the victory of socialism'.[57] The next day Stalin endorsed his comments.[58]

In August, Molotov cautioned against any measures that might benefit the kulaks as 'essentially petit-bourgeois' as they led 'to rejection of the leading rôle of the proletariat in the worker–peasant alliance'. He described the rise in grain prices as a necessary 'concession to the middle peasant', and following Stalin's lead, criticised Bukharin without naming him, when he attacked those who spoke of a 'break in the link'. He argued that the main source of the crisis was that the peasantry, 'especially the top strata', was stronger after the 1927 harvest than after the 1926 harvest, and warned that a whole 'transition period' was necessary to get rid of classes, 'the main stages of which we have not yet passed through'.[59]

In September, Molotov described to a meeting of newspaper editors an organised beating of poor peasants by a group of well-to-do peasants with the connivance of the village Soviet in Votsk province.[60] As Carr and Davies have commented

> The pronouncements of Stalin and Molotov at this time were the utterances, not of men ... who believed that mass collectivisation of the peasantry was a practicable policy for the near future, but of men hesitant and bewildered in the face of an intractable problem, and still hoping somehow to muddle through.[61]

It was now clear that there was a crisis in the 1928 grain harvest. Bukharin called for a decrease in the rate of collectivisation, and conflict with the Right became open.[62] In these circumstances, Molotov's report at the November 1928 Central Committee plenum was gloomy. He cited statistics to prove that the rise of the richer peasant element in local party organisation was out of proportion to their numbers, and that the Party was very weak in kolkhozy and sovkhozy. In rural communities agricultural workers and poor peasants represented only 5 per cent of the party membership. How, in these conditions, he asked, could social reconstruction in the countryside or the attack on the kulak be accomplished?[63]

This plenum focused on local difficulties in the harvest, and there was no open breach with the Right. Molotov admitted that prevailing conditions were 'completely inadequate for the rapid transfer of the basic mass of peasants to a large scale collective economy'. This was a task for a long period.[64] In his closing remarks, before he introduced the resolution on 'the recruitment of workers and regulating the growth of the party', he talked, however, of strengthening the attack on the kulaks, of collectivisation and the construction of sovkhozy on the basis of the decisions of the XV Congress.[65]

Shakhty – the 'New Specialists'

A forerunner of the terror and repression campaigns of the 1930s, the Shakhty Affair involved the discovery of a supposed counter-revolutionary group, which had been engaged in wrecking and sabotage in the mines of the Donbass since 1922. 'Bourgeois specialists' (engineers and technical specialists) appointed during the NEP were the focus of the attack and the case gave rise to the theory of 'wrecking'.[66] The Shakhty Affair became associated with the struggle with the new opposition – the Right, since one of its leaders, Rykov, chairman of the Sovnarkom until 1930, was especially active in defence of the 'specialists'.

Stalin had expressed to Molotov his unease about the 'specialists' as early as 1925,[67] and Molotov's involvement marked the earliest participation of a national political leader in the Shakhty Affair and the question of the specialists. It was also his first significant intervention in the industrialisation debate and put him at the forefront of developing the Party's new cadres policy.[68] Accompanied by Yaroslavskii and Tomsky, he was leader of the three-man investigatory team sent by the Central Committee to probe the Shakhty Affair in March 1928. Stalin closely watched the commission, and Molotov, on his return, reported immediately to the April 1928 Central Committee plenum.[69] After a 40-minute break in the proceedings, perhaps to allow him time to confer with Stalin, Molotov announced that the Shakhty Affair had grave implications for the industrialisation programme, and plunged into an attack on the 'bourgeois specialists' as the core of the counter-revolutionary group. He quoted a Lenin speech of 1918 about the rôle and control of the specialists in the early Soviet period, but maintained that that time had now passed. He again referred to Lenin, and called for a 'new "proletarian" method' for employment of the specialists 'by accountability to the entire nation and control from below'. This would 'accomplish the inevitable transition of the mass of the specialists to the side of the proletarian state', although it placed particular demands on the trade unions, and implied the development of the planning process.[70] In conclusion he spoke of the need to train 'red' specialists, and to promote workers from the bench – the policy of *vydvizhenchestvo*. He demanded that his audience become

> fully occupied with the direction of economic work ... work to strengthen the training of new cadres and involve the wide mass in the administration of the economy.[71]

Unsurprisingly Stalin endorsed Molotov's comments.[72] A challenge from Rykov followed, but controversy was defused because Rykov was appointed to chair the commission that produced resolutions on the Shakhty Affair, and Molotov chaired the session when this reported at the end of the plenum.[73]

At the next Central Committee plenum, in July 1928, Molotov introduced the Politburo resolutions on 'the training of new specialists'.[74] In a wide-ranging speech, he spoke of the need for engineers, and used statistics to compare the proportion of engineers in the USSR workforce with that in some advanced European industrial powers. He described the situation in the higher technical institutes (*VTUZ*) and the curriculum necessary for training specialists. He insisted that both a high level of skill and a broad range of specialisms were necessary. In conclusion he called for

> 1000 communists, who possess good economic, professional or party practice ... [to be] placed in favourable material conditions and ... rapidly increase the cadres of specialist-communists for us[75]

Policy, however, varied with the demands of the industrialisation drive. Later in the year the need for skilled labour was so great that Molotov not only called for labour discipline, but also warned against specialist baiting.[76]

In 1929 he again attacked the old specialists. At the Moscow regional party conference in September he berated 'White Guard groups of wreckers, linked to the foreign bourgeoisie' and condemned officials who 'firmly impose their bourgeois line on particular agencies'. They had to choose: 'Either – or! – There is not and cannot be any third road.'[77]

The attack on the Right and the Moscow party apparatus

The summer of 1928 was marked by a swing in party policy towards the Left, towards rapid industrialisation, and by a growth in Stalin's power.[78] It was a crucial period for Molotov who was caught up in the beginnings of the struggle against the new opposition – the Right; and next to Stalin, he now replaced Bukharin as the Party's chief ideologist. This may have led to particular animosity between him and Bukharin,[79] especially as Molotov replaced Bukharin in Comintern.[80] Molotov seems to have disliked Bukharin from the mid-1920s, and described him as 'Shuisky' to his closer colleagues.[81]

In his first direct attack on the Right, at the Moscow Party Committee on 30 June, Molotov deprecated a leading article on self-criticism in *Bol'shevik* by A. Slepkov, a follower of Bukharin. Slepkov asserted that all the members of the editorial board had approved the article except Molotov, who had not commented on the proofs sent to him. In response, Molotov, who had been appointed to the Board of Editors by the XV Congress, stated that he had not received the proofs, as he had been in the Crimea on leave. He accused Slepkov of a deliberate untruth, and called on the party Central Control Commission to consider the matter. This body reprimanded Slepkov for failure to check his allegations.[82] Molotov followed this up with criticism of *Pravda* editorials which attacked the procurement campaign – an implied criticism of Bukharin. He seems to have been especially annoyed by Bukharinist attacks on 'extraordinary measures'.[83] In August, as Stalin consolidated his position, he wrote to Molotov that Ordzhonikidze was loyal, and that the allegiance of Kuibyshev and Mikoyan had to be maintained.[84]

In September, with Stalin on leave, Molotov restrained extremists in the Institute of Red Professors who wanted to attack the leaders of the Right by name, as Stalin was not yet ready for this.[85] On 22 September, at the end of a speech to newspaper editors, in which he noted that Trotskyism was only 'one of the varieties of opportunism in our conditions', Molotov quoted a recent Comintern resolution about intensification of the struggle against Right deviations. He also cited the resolution of the July Central Committee plenum about pressing on with the campaign against the kulak.[86] He was now fully engaged in the struggle with the opposition, and published an attack on them in *Pravda* on 14 October.

The November 1928 Central Committee plenum was dominated by controversy with the Right. In his report, on 23 November, Molotov spoke of the 'openly hostile relations of some specialists to Soviet power and socialist construction'.[87] He referred to the struggle with the Trotskyite opposition to introduce his attack on the 'present petty-bourgeois deviation', the 'open-opportunist right deviation from the Leninist line'. When the Party was engaged in the 'radical work of constructing the fundamentals of socialism', it was essential to struggle 'on two fronts' – against both the Trotskyites and the Right – a theme to which he was to return many times in the next two years. He cited Lenin's formula: 'the idea of the **union** (*soyuz*) of the workers and the peasants and the idea of the **leadership** of the working class in this union': the Trotskyites denied the union of peasant and working class, the Right deviation denied the leadership of the working class. Taking his lead from Stalin, however, the only person Molotov attacked was N. I. Frumkin.[88]

The next morning, Molotov made a number of interruptions to endorse those who supported him and condemn those who dared to sympathise with the Right.[89] In his closing remarks, he talked of the 'sharpening of the struggle between the socialist and capitalist elements'; and of attacks from all sides by the bourgeois intelligentsia (the specialists). He mentioned the Moscow party organisation to which he was soon to be appointed, and called for a 'decisive blow at the Right deviation'.[90] Nevertheless, to preserve the appearance of accord, the plenum adopted a resolution that affirmed the unity of the Politburo and the absence of disagreements within it.[91]

From the time of the July 1928 plenum, Bukharin's strongest support had developed in the Moscow party organisation, but even prior to this Molotov had criticised the Moscow authorities for neglect of heavy industry in favour of the local textile industries.[92] During the summer, Stalin and Molotov clashed increasingly with the Right leaders of the Moscow organisation, particularly Nikolai Uglanov,[93] and Molotov endeavoured to ensure that members of the apparatus were loyal to him and Stalin.[94] In September, he had his speech to the plenum of the Moscow Party Committee amended, before publication in the press. He made it more vicious, accused the Right of 'a direct departure from Leninism', and demanded 'a merciless struggle with elements of putrefaction and bourgeois–philistine degeneration'.[95]

At the next Moscow Party Committee plenum, on 18 and 19 October, Uglanov's speech was interrupted by a standing ovation when Stalin and Molotov entered the hall.[96] Molotov, then Stalin, attacked the Right, particularly its supporters in the leadership of the local party organisation, and praised their own followers.[97] At the Moscow party Committee, on 27 November, Molotov emphasised the need to struggle against the 'right danger', and cautioned against a conciliationist attitude towards it.[98] Uglanov was now forced to resign. One version of the story of his resignation claims that he stalked out of a meeting followed by Stalin. When Stalin returned alone, Molotov asked him 'Where is Uglanov'?[99] Molotov replaced him as secretary of the city organisation. This was only for a short period until April 1929, when he combined this work with his other rôle as Central Committee secretary. Karl Bauman was appointed as second secretary, and was to take over when Molotov had trained him. But Bauman had to be dismissed for excesses during collectivisation and was replaced by Kaganovich in April 1930.[100]

Once in post, Molotov organised a purge of rightists from the Moscow organisation. He removed four of six deputy heads of department of the city committee, four of six *raion* secretaries, and 99 of 157 members of the city committee.[101] His work in connection with this purge led to a revival of his nickname 'stone backside'.[102] He was now regarded as Stalin's chief agent in the struggle with the Right, and his additional appointment was taken as a signal that Stalin was going all-out for industrialisation and rapid collectivisation.[103]

When he reported the Central Committee plenum to the Moscow party organisation on 30 November, Molotov again took his lead from Stalin and cited only the name of M. Frumkin as a member of the Right deviation, although he gave notice that a party purge, to rid the Party of alien elements, would be discussed at the forthcoming party conference.[104] In December 1928, at the congress of VTsSPS, (*Vsesoyuznyi Tsentral'nyi Sovet Profesessionalnykh Soyuzov* – All-Union Central Council of Trade Unions) Molotov disavowed the action of Kaganovich, whose motion condemning the policy of the Council's presidium had been defeated. The motion was an attempt to remove Tomsky from the chairmanship of the body, and Molotov thus redeemed the position of the Central Committee.[105] Bukharin was not yet attacked by name, but in a report to the Moscow provincial party conference at the end of February 1929, Molotov poked fun at 'the peaceful growing of the kulak into socialism', and the conference condemned the Right. He also called for the 'most rapid possible growth of industry'.[106] Then, in March, to assist Stalin to guarantee the loyalty of Kalinin, Molotov, although he did not speak, was prominent with Stalin and Mikoyan, in the press pictures of the meeting to celebrate the tenth anniversary of Kalinin's appointment as President of TsIK (*Tsentral'nyi Ispolnitel'nyi Komitet* – Central Executive Committee [of the Congress of Soviets of the USSR]) – the Soviet parliament.[107]

The climax in the struggle with the Right occurred at the April 1929 Central Committee plenum, prior to the XVI Party Conference. Here, on 18 April, Bukharin quoted what Molotov had said at the XV Congress, on relations with the middle peasants, against the Trotskyite position. Molotov had denied that Lenin's 1918 dictum about 'the neutralisation of the peasantry' was correct for contemporary conditions, and supported Stalin's line that those who held the opposition view could not remain members of the Party. Bukharin therefore argued that either the Molotov of 1927, or the present Molotov, could not remain a member of the Party. He also quoted Molotov's words at the July 1928 plenum, and his August 1928 article, when he had contended that 'extraordinary measures', as a long-term policy, replaced Leninist policy with the Trotskyite policy of an attack on the middle peasant, and damaged the alliance with the peasantry. Bukharin related this to current agricultural policy.[108] He was exposing the inconsistency of Stalin and Molotov on agricultural policy and their lurch to the left in 1928.

Stalin made the main response on the last day of the plenum,[109] but Molotov answered Bukharin on 19 April when he dealt first with accusations by Tomsky. He denied differences within the Politburo over the industrial plan for 1927–1928, and supported the Politburo decision on industrialisation targets. He then answered Bukharin's accusations. Molotov admitted that he had made an ideological mistake in his interpretation of Lenin's formula at the XV Congress, which he had already admitted in a letter published in *Bol'shevik*.[110] In this letter, Molotov confessed that he had applied Lenin's 1918 formula on agreement with the middle peasant and not flinching in the struggle with the kulak, to the period of the 'neutralisation of the middle peasant', rather than to the period immediately after that.[111] Next, he dismissed charges about Comintern and the Moscow party apparatus as part of the campaign of the Right. He cited the attitude of the Right to a number of events in the last nine months, to refute their claim that they were not an opposition. He accused the Right of failure to support party policy in Comintern and their leaders of formulating their own line against party policy. He maintained that in the version of the Five Year Plan supported by Rykov and Bukharin, the central idea was the 'growth of the productivity of labour'. This was a non-party aim.[112] He asked how the theses of Bukharin and Rykov on the *pyatiletka* (Five Year Plan) could entirely omit the struggle with the kulak and the class struggle, especially at a time of its sharpening. When they emphasised the need to accomplish the Five Year Plan within the framework of NEP, Bukharin and Rykov did not occupy the correct Leninist position, especially when they talked about trade turnover as the chief means of 'the normalisation of market relations'. For the kulak this would mean only a change from state regulation of prices, and the removal of the state from the struggle with speculation. The correct interpretation of the formula meant the organisation of the market for the worker, to provide him with bread, other necessities and manufactured goods. Both workers and peasants would support additional measures against kulaks and speculators rather than be without bread and other products. The formula had a clear class character: the worker, relied on by the poor peasant, must implement it in alliance with the middle peasant mass against the kulak.

Molotov attacked as 'opportunist', the 'two-year working plan' that Bukharin and Rykov had proposed as a modification of the *pyatiletka*. He claimed that Bukharin had forgotten the sharpening of the class struggle, and attacked Bukharin's theory of 'the kulak growing into socialism'. In conclusion, he said that because of current agricultural and industrial policies, the struggle with the Right deviation had become of central importance for the Party, and it was necessary to fight against both Right ideology and the Right line 'in practice'. Bukharin, Rykov and Tomsky did not speak openly against the Party, but they did not renounce Right views. He pointed out that in the revolutionary and immediate post-revolutionary era they had serious differences with the Party. They now attacked Stalin and made false charges about the lack of collective leadership of the Party. They were going along the Trotskyite road. This could only lead to one thing – a struggle with the Party.

> Comrades Bukharin and Tomsky ... must take especial responsibility for a policy of sabotage of the work of the Central Committee ... The party will ... denounce the breach of party discipline that has taken place ... Against the vacillations and against the mistakes of these comrades and those who slide with them into the Right deviation we must mobilise the whole party, and not tolerate any wavering in our ranks. ...[113]

Molotov's attack was only of limited success. On the next day, 20 April, he was forced to make a statement which gave 'factual information' of proceedings in the Central Committee and Politburo in answer to charges that Rykov made in support of Bukharin and those of Bukharin against him.[114]

At the XVI Party Conference, April 1929, many speakers denounced the Right, but there was no public mention of the dissension among the leadership at the pre-conference plenum. Molotov's sole contribution to the Conference was a two-hour 'information' report on the proceedings of the plenum, 'at the request of delegates'. He then proposed a short resolution which noted the 'departure of Bukharin's group from the general party line in the direction of the Right deviation', and confirmed the decisions of the pre-conference plenum. This was not included in the 1929 Conference Report but was noted briefly in the 1962 edition.[115]

When he spoke at the Ivanovskii *oblast'* (province) party conference, in July 1929, Molotov noted that the struggle against the Right was still not complete. He contrasted the Right policy of 'capitulation to the kulak' to the offensive against the kulak and mobilisation of the poor–middle peasant against them. He maintained that this had led to a decrease in grain imports in the current year. The policy of the Party was to develop the socialist element in agriculture: the kolkhoz, the MTS and the sovkhoz. He hinted at the creation of the Union Commissariat of Agriculture.[116] He claimed that the difference in policies showed a different understanding of the role of the class war in present conditions. Right ideology was 'no less than a political capitulation before the attack of the capitalist element'. He also felt it necessary in this speech to defend party policy, the *pyatiletka* and 'socialism in one country' against Trotskyite attack. In conclusion, he claimed that the USSR was 'poised at a new upsurge of the international proletarian revolution inextricably linked with the development of the socialist offensive in the USSR'.[117]

During August, Molotov wrote to Stalin that Bukharin was 'going downhill'. In the grain procurement campaign in the autumn of 1929, also the subject of correspondence with Stalin,[118] he later reported with pride that no member of the Right was sent as a Central Committee plenipotentiary to the countryside.[119] At the end of September Stalin wrote to Molotov and condemned a speech Rykov had made to the Moscow region Congress of Soviets that had been greeted with 'stormy prolonged applause'. Rykov had failed to condemn the Right, and Stalin told Molotov that Rykov should be given an alternative:

Either disassociate openly and honestly from the rightists and conciliators, or lose the right to speak in the name of the Central Committee and Council of Commissars.

Molotov endorsed the letter:

Totally agree with everything said. Didn't read Rykov's speech, but only skimmed the headings. Will read.
I do see now, however, that Stalin is right. Just don't agree that we're 'covering' for Rykov. We have to fix things in the way Stalin proposes, however.[120]

Finally, at the Central Committee plenum, November 1929, after a barrage of threats that they should recant, Bukharin, Rykov and Tomsky made a circumspect but unrepentant statement. Although they acknowledged a certain amount of success in party policy, they criticised Stalin's methods in the countryside and their impact on urban living standards.[121] The next day Molotov made a swingeing attack on the Right and condemned

> their declaration about not enjoying equal rights in the party ... written by Comrade Rykov, [as] totally unprincipled, totally deficient in ideology, a document thoroughly false, thoroughly hypocritical, thoroughly two-faced. ... thoroughly lacking in conviction. ... The three leaders of the Right. ... declare that their 'method' ... is a 'less unhealthy path'. ... False, sustained, double-meaning phrases about two specific methods do not fit the facts: the position of the **Right Deviation** is a position of opposition to the **party**. ... Disorganisers in an army are not necessary, especially not in the army staff. ...
>
> Therefore the authors of the document must ... recognise their mistakes in this matter and break with right-deviation ideology or they will be driven into the camp of the enemies of the party. The Right deviation leads to the camp of bourgeois liberalism. That is its root. Understand that the party conducts and will conduct an irreconcilable struggle with this deviation.[122]

For good measure, he also attacked former opposition groups including Trotsky, Kamenev and Zinoviev, and some non-party specialists in Gosplan, and made comparisons with the Right.[123] At the close of the plenum, Molotov was a member of the commission chaired by Rudzutak, which compiled the resolution that expelled Bukharin from the Politburo and censured Rykov and Tomsky most strongly.[124]

Comintern

Comintern was another area where Molotov was to act as Stalin's trouble-shooter and lead the campaign against the Right deviation. He had been a member of IKKI (*Ispolnitel'nyi Komitet Kommunisticheskogo Internationala* – the Executive committee of Comintern) since 1926, originally as an alternate to deputise for Stalin whilst he was on leave.[125] He was co-opted to IKKI's political secretariat for the VI Comintern Congress, July-September 1928, where he was used by Stalin, again on leave, to watch Bukharin, who despite his leadership of the Right, and Stalin's attacks on him, remained formally in charge of proceedings.[126] Molotov served with Bukharin on a five-man drafting committee to work out the final version of the Comintern programme,[127] but used the opportunity of the Congress to develop the assault against the Right. Delegates of the German party recognised that Molotov had been invested with authority, and consulted him, rather than Bukharin, about an internal dispute.[128] In an interview with American communists, although Molotov failed to react to the mention of Bukharin's name, he left a clear impression that there was 'complete support' for those who fought the Right in the American party.[129]

Molotov's new importance was signalled at the end of the Congress when he was entrusted with presenting the customary report to the Leningrad Party organ-isation.[130] For the first time, he warned of the danger of the growth of fascism. In line with Stalin's formula, originally that of Zinoviev, he bracketed fascism with ' "socialist" reformism' – social democracy. This was the main enemy, although the 'Right danger' was also a serious threat, and Trotskyism a menace. He empha-sised the importance of Soviet industrialisation and maintained that the policy of the Soviet state was 'indissolubly linked to the policy of Comintern'. The key ques-tion was that of the preparation of capitalist states for 'a new bloody war'. The summary of the speech in *Pravda* emphasised the potential victory of world communism, but the full speech dwelt more on the struggle for it.[131]

When the presidium of IKKI met in December 1928 to deal with affairs of the German communist party and Stalin attacked the Right element there, Molotov supported him. Stalin became so exasperated with by J. Humbert-Droz, who described his speech as 'an attack on the conception of stabilisation of capitalism set forth in the theses of the sixth world congress', and said that the real target was Bukharin, that he muttered 'Go to the devil'. Molotov backed him by shouting 'hypocrite'.[132] This was to prove an embarrassment to Molotov in the next year.

In the spring of 1929, Stalin attacked the leaders of the American communist party sympathetic to the Right, and again relied on Molotov, who reported the matter to the Politburo, for support.[133] Bukharin's disgrace meant that he had now withdrawn from the scene, and the tenth IKKI, convened in July 1929, at first seemed to be leaderless. Humbert-Droz now challenged Molotov's ability in the international sphere, and claimed that, although he was designated to replace Bukharin, he was ignorant of Comintern's problems and incapable of taking decisions on documents submitted to him.[134] Molotov was silent during the first week of the proceedings, and then asserted his position in an authoritative speech. In this he described the struggle against the Right 'as the fundamental point in the development of the Communist International since the Sixth Congress'. He went on to attack leaders of foreign communist parties who were Right supporters. After this, other delegates felt able to follow suit and assault the Right.[135] When Molotov commented on the international position of com-munism, he claimed that the USSR had gained a temporary respite from capitalist attack, because of tension and crisis in the capitalist world. In 'a new revolutionary wave', however, the majority of the proletariat of capitalist countries would be won over to communist parties, and in the period of intensified class struggle on a world scale that would follow, the danger of war against the USSR would increase.[136] Strikes in Germany, Poland, France, Czechoslovakia and India were evidence of the 'new rev-olutionary wave'. Molotov declared that '*the political mass strike*' was the weapon of the future and called for '*the conquest of the majority* of the working class'. He used the term 'social fascists' to describe the German social-democrats, following the deaths of 25 workers in the May Day demonstrations in Berlin banned by the social democrat mayor, and declared that the events of 1 May 'reveal the true nature of social-fascism to its full extent'. In addition, he used another term of abuse – 'police socialists', an expression that had a long history for Russian communists, and dated back at least to the police trade unions of the pre-revolutionary era.[137]

At this time Molotov seemed more confident when he dealt with Soviet affairs rather than with foreign affairs and international communism. When policy in response to Chinese aggression was criticised as weak at the Moscow regional party conference in September 1929, his response was by no means clear. He played down the significance of the aggression and warned against a hasty response to provocation, but he also admitted that the attack aimed to discredit the Soviet Union as powerless, beset with economic problems and political troubles.[138] His speech to IKKI in February 1930 was confined to the achievements of the USSR.[139] He may, however, have been active behind the scenes, and was much more confident when he reported on Comintern to the XVI Party Congress, June 1930.[140]

6
Change and Consolidation 1929–1930

The struggle against the kulaks – collectivisation

The defeat of the Right removed any restraint on implementing the radical policies of forced collectivisation and 'elimination of the kulaks as a class'. Molotov's prominence in the attack on the Right meant that he was in the forefront of the collectivisation campaign, but he had already demonstrated his own inclination to extreme policies in his attitude towards the kulaks. In February 1929, he wrote of a 'deep chasm' between 'the policy of an offensive against the kulak and the theory of the peaceful growth of the kulak into socialism'. The latter led to 'an emancipation of the capitalist elements, and finally to the re-establishment of the power of the bourgeoisie'.[1] At this time Molotov was preoccupied with the struggle against the Right, and at the Central Committee plenum, 16–23 April 1929, prior to the XVI Party Conference, Kalinin introduced the main proposals on agriculture for the Conference.[2] In mid-July, however, in his speech to the Ivanovskii *oblast'* party conference, one of the first in which he dealt in any detail with industrialisation and the *pyatiletka*, Molotov asserted that 'our chief difficulties lie in agriculture'. He claimed that 'the influence of the petty-bourgeois factor ... puts its stamp on a certain number of party proletarians, especially those who have close connections with the countryside'. Later in the speech he made a clear distinction between the 'offensive' against the kulak and Trotskyite 'panic in face of the kulak'.[3]

During August, with Stalin on vacation, Molotov was central in planning the forthcoming procurement campaign, and with Mikoyan was charged with preparation of the directives to be issued to local party organisations. Stalin wrote to him and criticised a draft Central Committee (Politburo) decree on the grain collections. He condemned speculation, and expressed fears that the campaign would not be successful. Molotov saw that the final decree took into account all Stalin's criticisms.[4]

In his speech to the first Moscow Regional Party Conference, on 14 September, Molotov claimed that the kulak was no longer content simply to obstruct rural socialist construction, but had gone over to the offensive. He had penetrated collective farms and their leadership to overthrow the system from within – 'kulak–SR elements will often hide behind the kolkhoz smokescreen'. He called for a 'merciless struggle' against the kulak, for better organisation of poor peasants, and the alliance of poor and middle peasants within every kolkhoz. The examples of opposition to state policy he cited: grain speculation on the private market, and refusal to surrender surpluses to the state; reflected his recent correspondence with Stalin. He also condemned 'Menshevik–SR influences' in grain statistics, and attributed them to 'bourgeois-kulak ideologists in the centre and in the localities'.[5] In October, Stalin still on vacation, wrote to Molotov that he had to maintain the pressure, but 'Generally, I'd have to admit that things are going pretty well for you (that is for us), at least for the time being. That's good.'[6]

In early October, Molotov told the Moscow regional party organisation that the 'broad middle-peasant mass ... [was convinced that] kolkhozy with tractors and large-scale agricultural machines have tremendous advantages over small farms'.[7] This was a reflection of the decision of the party leaders to launch an all-out collectivisation drive.[8] In a *Pravda* article, on 7 November, immediately before the Central Committee plenum, Stalin proclaimed a 'great change' in agriculture and the 'revolution from above'. He asserted that the peasant masses, which included middle peasants, were voluntarily quitting their private plots and 'joining collective farms ... by whole villages, groups of villages, districts, and even regions'. It was a call for immediate wholesale collectivisation.

It is not clear if, at this point, Molotov was personally in favour of rapid forced collectivisation, or if he was driven by Stalin's policies, but his extreme position against the kulaks suggests he would have no difficulty in supporting them. He was prominent at the crucial November 1929 Central Committee plenum. He broke protocol when he made two major speeches, as well as a brief statement to introduce the Politburo proposals to establish the Union Commissariat of Agriculture.[9] His first major speech, on 13 November, included a bitter attack on the Right for lack of confidence in the collectivisation campaign, and stressed the need for ultra-rapid collectivisation.[10] The second, on 15 November, his main speech on agriculture, was in support of Grigorii Kaminskii's report 'On kolkhoz construction', which praised the great increase in the rate of collectivisation. Molotov quoted Lenin's *Left Wing Communism* to support the view that the transformation of petty commodity producers required rigid centralisation, and discipline within the party to prevent reversion to 'petty-bourgeois spinelessness, disintegration, individualism and alternate moods of ecstasy and misery'. He maintained that in collectivisation, as elsewhere, the authorities lagged behind the poor and middle peasant because they were too bureaucratic, and that the struggle with bureaucratism was the task of the working class.[11] He described the pace of collectivisation as 'really frantic', gave regional examples, and declared that the five-year plan targets would be exceeded in all the main agricultural areas. When he introduced the resolution to form the Union Commissariat of Agriculture, he asserted that 'as soon as next year we will be able to talk not only of collectivised regions, but of collectivised republics'. He claimed that a region was collectivised 'in the main' if more than fifty per cent of households belonged to the kolkhozy.[12] The agencies that had been responsible for the grain procurements would now concentrate on the spring sowing campaign:

> This will be **our Bolshevik sowing campaign**, which will give a decisive victory to kolkhozy in the USSR. ... the question of comprehensive collectivisation of a number of very large agricultural areas will be decided, and the question of collectivisation of the USSR as a whole will develop in a completely new fashion.[13]

Molotov's insistence on the urgency of collectivisation was more outspoken than anyone else's. He interrupted other speakers, including such senior figures as Andreev, to press for a higher rate of collectivisation.[14] This surprised some delegates. His enthusiasm was now becoming personal; it reflected his earlier preference for extreme policies and he was more than Stalin's mouthpiece. His comments on the pace of collectivisation were also part of the general euphoria in the party, in late 1929 and early 1930, about the success of collectivisation, with competition between regions to outdo each other when they set targets. The optimism was a tactic designed to ensure that the campaign pressed on at the fastest rate possible. The speeches of Stalin and Molotov encouraged regional party organisations to press for a high rate of collectivisation in January and February 1930.[15]

Molotov referred to the construction of two huge new tractor factories, and the importance of the development of electric power in rural localities. He described the recent stage as one in which 'the middle peasant has moved into the kolkhozy'. This marked 'a new period in our revolution'. It was now necessary

> to attack the capitalist elements on the whole front, ... and not fail in necessary cases to use extraordinary measures. ... [or] to fold up one's line opportunistically under the furious attack of the class enemy.[16]

In the rest of the speech he was much vaguer on kolkhoz organisation and gave a strong warning against the danger of kulak penetration of the kolkhoz. He was harsher on the kulaks than anyone before him, and in a much referred-to phrase he urged 'Treat the kulak as a most cunning and still undefeated enemy.' He noted the mobilisation of 25,000 industrial workers and the use of the Red Army for work in the kolkhozy.[17] Molotov claimed that the Union Commissariat of Agriculture was made essential by the 'socialist reconstruction of agriculture', which demanded 'united leadership on an all-union scale'. This would liquidate semi-feudal elements and 'kulakism', particularly in the more backward eastern republics. The 'proletarian centre' of the USSR would assist in this.[18]

After the plenum, with Stalin in Moscow, Molotov took a vacation in December, something which had become common in recent years. Stalin wrote in familiar style to report on the grain collections:

Hello Molotshtein,
    Why the devil have you burrowed into your lair like a bear, and why are you not talking? How are things there, good or bad? Write something.[19]

This is one of the few occasions when Stalin's correspondence with Molotov shows a personal relationship; and may reflect a particular appreciation of Molotov's support in recent months.

Molotov's absence on vacation may be the reason why he was the only one of Stalin's leading supporters who did not contribute to the panegyrics for their leader's fiftieth birthday on 21 December 1929, an event important in establishing the Stalin 'cult'.[20] *Pravda* and *Izvestiya* contained pieces written by Kaganovich, Kalinin, Kuibyshev, Ordzhonikidze, Voroshilov, Mikoyan and others, but nothing by Molotov. But both papers contained a picture of him with Stalin, with whom he continued to correspond on collectivisation. He sent Stalin telegrams which criticised the moderate rate proposed by a Politburo Commission, and the new decree being prepared:

> I do not understand the need for a new lengthy resolution ... in parts obviously diffuse and departing from reality and the decision of the plenum ... For me ... it signifies bureaucratic planning, especially inappropriate in relation to the turbulent widespread popular movement.[21]

Stalin announced the 'elimination of the kulaks as a class' as a policy on 27 December 1929,[22] and at a conference of delegates from collectivised areas, held in mid-January 1930, Molotov again said that collectivisation of individual districts was now enhanced by 'comprehensive collectivisation of whole regions and republics'. He urged his audience 'to break the enemy at the very beginning and deprive him of any wish to make any attempt to resist'. He warned that 'in certain districts the class struggle may acquire in the next few months a sharpness against which the facts of the preceding period look pale'. He called for immediate new elections to those village Soviets which could not cope with their task.[23]

Two days after this speech, on 15 January 1930, Molotov was appointed as chairman of a 21-person Politburo commission, 'to elaborate measures in relation to the kulaks'.[24] This had representatives from all the main grain regions, and from regions where kulaks were to be exiled, and organised the mass exile. The decree 'On Measures for the Elimination of Kulak Farms in *Raiony* of Wholesale Collectivisation', submitted to the Politburo on 30 January, divided the kulaks into three categories: supposed counter revolutionaries, to be shot and their families exiled; those to be exiled; and a third less dangerous category who could be left on inferior land outside the collectives.[25] As chairman of the commission Molotov raised the number of kulaks to be exiled.[26] He was now the central figure in the collectivisation campaign, and gained a reputation for harshness. Possibly this and his personal enthusiasm for the campaign, was responsible for his appointment as head of the commission. In late February, he received a report that kulaks disembarking from trains were 'pleasantly surprised' that they were not to be shot, but settled in special villages.[27]

'Dizzy with Success' and after

By the end of January 1930, Stalin and Molotov advised caution on the accelerated rates of collectivisation unless 'the masses were really involved', although they still seemed to hope that the kolkhozy might be consolidated by the elimination of the kulaks, and that the grain procurement system would bring about better organisation.[28] At a conference of party officials from national areas in mid-February, Molotov warned against 'kolkhozy on paper', and again urged prudence in less advanced areas.[29] He notified delegates that the conference would take secret decisions to be carried out by all party organisations. He then arranged and chaired a further commission from among those who attended the conference, to implement the Politburo decree on dekulakisation.[30]

Later in the month, supported by Stalin and Genrikh Yagoda, the deputy head of the OGPU, Molotov dominated another conference of the major grain consuming areas. He dictated policy and nominated himself as the chairman of the commission established to work out the decree on collectivisation and dekulakisation of those areas.[31] At a further meeting on 23 February, he proposed the amalgamation of the Politburo commission he chaired with another presided over by Serge Syrtsov. The combined commission prepared a decree on the spring sowing campaign, further measures on collectivisation and on the liquidation of the kulak.[32] The next day, he was appointed to a Politburo commission to draft the new collective farm statute, and on 10 March became a member of another commission to deal with the mobilisation of workers to help with collectivisation in national areas.[33]

Ultra-rapid collectivisation had now, however, created a crisis; and the political leadership was faced with a mass exodus from the kolkhozy and the failure of the spring sowing campaign. On 2 March, Stalin urged restraint and caution in his famous article 'Dizzy with Success'.[34] To deal with the situation, in the second half of March 1930, in what had become a routine response to crisis, Molotov and other senior party leaders were despatched to the provinces. Molotov went to the North Caucasus, and visited the chief towns and some collective farms, first on the Don, then in the Kuban, where his itinerary included Krasnodar. As on previous *komandirovki*, he met local party officials and collective farm managers. Perhaps his personal enthusiasm for collectivisation showed through, on 18 March, when he approved the regional party decision, although it conflicted with the Central Committee decision that collectivisation should now be voluntary. He asserted:

> our approach is to manoeuvre, and by securing a certain level of organisation not entirely voluntarily, consolidate the kolkhozy and strengthen the nucleus of collective farmers during the spring sowing.[35]

When he spoke to the party *aktiv* at Rostov-on-Don, a few days later, he said that the situation in the Don area was satisfactory. In the Kuban, however, there was a very strong 'oscillation' *(kolebanie)* among the peasant mass; it was not an 'anti-Soviet wavering but they are anti-kolkhoz'. They were badly prepared for the kolkhozy, party work was weak and the influence of white guard elements and kulaks, who were cunning and organised, was so strong, that the kolkhozy were 'paper kolkhozy'. He questioned the use of the principle of voting as the method of forming the kolkhozy in such areas, because the influence of the minority swayed the majority.[36] Molotov warned that in areas like the Kuban, the problem of the kulak would be dealt with by the OGPU. He claimed that the 'oscillation' was chiefly of the middle peasant – 'today he oscillates to our side, tomorrow to the side of the kulak'. This occurred when collectivisation was carried out badly, 'without explanation, without the voluntary participation of the middle peasant'. He failed to point out that, by official calculations, the middle peasants involved in the 'oscillation' formed up to 65 per cent of the peasantry.[37] His remedy was to organise the poor peasants, strengthen repression against the kulaks

> and enhance the judicial organs ... because terrorist attacks by *kulaks* against poor and middle peasants remain unpunished. ... In such cases it is necessary to pass the matter to the courts and shoot without any hesitation the perpetrators ... and those who descend to the last resort of kulakism.[38]

If, in a given locality there was the firm support of 80–90 per cent of the poor and middle peasants, it could be said that collectivisation had been carried out on the 'voluntary' principle.[39] In this way Molotov attempted to reconcile the threat of direct physical intimidation with the voluntary principle. He elaborated on this in another speech, in the same area, on 26 March.

> For us retreat is impossible, there can be no going back. ... Of course the voluntary principle is the ultimate basis. ... but if [the peasant] does not wish to enter ... the kolkhoz, I do not think he should be excluded because he opposes us. To the majority, to the proletariat, I understand the principle of voluntaryism to mean that the majority will dictate its will to a certain part of the minority on the question of collectivisation as well. [This is not] in conflict with our Bolshevik understanding of the voluntary principle.[40]

The attempt to reconcile the 'voluntary principle' and the use of force makes clear the grave errors in the policy that had been adopted.

In a speech to the Leningrad *oblast'* party conference prior to the XVI Congress, on 5 May 1930, Molotov spoke more generally on agricultural policy. He referred to the 1928 Central Committee decision, acknowledged Stalin's initiative on the formation of sovkhozy and their success, and in the foundation of *Zernotrest* (All-Union Trust of Grain Sovkhozy).[41] He referred to 'dizzy with success' – mistakes in the implementation of party policy by local party organisations were 'a huge crime in the *smychka* with the middle peasant, in the construction of socialism in our country'. He emphasised the importance of tractors in the further development of collectivisation and described the need to develop livestock farming as 'a colossal new task'. He maintained that at the core of all these questions was the problem of class relations in the countryside: the great mass of the poor peasants and a significant part of the middle peasants had entered the kolkhozy. For the further development of collectivisation, 'the liquidation of the kulak as a class' had to be implemented through the kolkhozy.[42]

When he spoke to the same party organisation, a month later (6 June 1930), Molotov contrasted success in industry with shortfalls in agriculture. To achieve a decisive turning point in the development of the USSR depended not only on industrial production, but also on large-scale socialist construction in agriculture. Later in the speech, having emphasised the importance of the struggle with Trotskyism, he specified the Right deviation as the main enemy when agriculture was the priority. The Right refused to recognise that the key task in the construction of socialism was an attack on the capitalist element – the kulak. This policy of socialist construction, to be adopted by the forthcoming XVI Congress, was the hardest path.[43]

At the time of the Congress, June 1930, Molotov was still preoccupied with agriculture. He spoke at the Politburo about the next procurement campaign on 15 June, and was responsible for a Politburo directive on the collections in August.[44] His tasks increased in September, when Stalin was on leave. He was in telegraphic contact with Stalin who advised him not to support a more flexible form of co-operative farming,[45] and then congratulated him when he reported the Politburo decision of 13 September which raised the projected procurement figures.[46] He took his cue from Stalin when he was prominent at the session of the Central Committee conference on the collections, the next day. Here, protests that the very ambitious procurement figures allocated to the kolkhozy could not be met, resulted in their modification and an increase of those assigned to the individual sector that was finalised four days later.[47] Molotov was involved in stormy exchanges with delegates. He quoted Stalin's telegram, defended the current official line and challenged those who questioned it, particularly M. N. Belenkii, deputy chairman of *kolhoztsentr* and chairman of *khlebotsentr* (All Russian Union of Cooperatives for Grain and Oil Seeds). He charged Belenkii with opposing first a Central Committee resolution, then a Politburo decision. When Belenkii denied the existence of the decision, Molotov read it out to him, and accused him of being a defender of the individual sector (i.e. a supporter of the Right).[48] When he spoke at the end of the conference, he attacked Belenkii:

> Only you comrade Belenkii, you alone fail to understand that there are two lines – one line for the kolkhoz, another line for the individual sector. One leads to socialism the other to capitalism; this for the tenth time is the explanation. ... We do not force the peasant to go into the kolkhoz, but we must show the peasant all the economic advantages on the side of the kolkhoz, then he will understand ... and enter the kolkhoz. ... This is not a policy of persuading the peasant to enter the kolkhoz. This is a hard policy carried out by the party, the policy of collectivisation.

When Belenkii said he entirely agreed with this, Molotov replied:

> You do not agree at all. ... because you do not see the difference between two fundamentally opposed lines. It seems that you wish to give an advantage to the individual farmer before the *kolkhoznik*. ... We are at this time defending and implementing a policy of privilege for the *kolkhoznik*. ... Note that these are two completely irreconcilable policies.

He went on to say that it was essential to fulfil the ambitious procurement plan because it was connected with the liquidation of the kulak, and he insisted on a hard line for the kolkhozy, 'a single demanding plan. In addition, not one *pud* in the private market for speculation'.[49]

Molotov now became preoccupied with the industrialisation campaign and the reorganisation of the government apparatus which culminated in his appointment as Sovnarkom chairman. It was not until 22 December 1930, the day after his appointment as head of government, that he made a further major intervention in agricultural policy. At the Central Committee conference on the outcome of the autumn sowing and the forthcoming 1931 spring sowing campaign, Yakovlev, Commissar for Agriculture, gave the major report. This reflected the new role Molotov had just assumed, but perhaps also signified it was now a matter of implementation rather than formulation of agricultural policy. If, however, agriculture had moved from the top of Molotov's agenda, his continued preoccupation with this vital area was shown when, towards the end of the conference, he strongly supported Yakovlev and Josif Kosior, and referred particularly to what he described as 'organisational problems'. He told G. F. Goleshchkin, who tried to blame the poor development of sovkhozy in Kazakhstan on harvest failures, that 'Soviet power must take into account that your harvest failures often happen', and that the *Zernotrest* system was in his opinion 'absolutely correct', because it embodied the fundamental principle of centralisation. He supported Kosior that the central problem, as far as improved technique was concerned, was the problem of spare parts, which both the Commissariat of Agriculture and VSNKh were trying to resolve. He continued with a fierce attack on the way that collectivisation had been discussed at the conference, particularly with regard to *Traktorotsentr* and *Kolkhoztsentr*, and asserted that the role of these institutions had been misunderstood. The key problem in the kolkhoz organisation was the 'labour day'. This was the system introduced in the spring of 1930, whereby the number of units (labour days) worked by a collective farmer were recorded, and the available income after the harvest, distributed according to the labour days worked, with skilled work allocated more units than unskilled. Molotov claimed that on the 'labour day', depended not only how successful the spring sowing campaign would be, but also the whole question of construction and organisation of kolkhozy. Agriculture was similar to industry. Success was decided by the organisation of production. It was necessary to think not only of the sowing campaign but also of the harvest.[50] In this speech there was an indication that he was conscious of the new broader responsibilities he had now assumed.

Molotov is often regarded purely as a stalking horse for Stalin in agricultural policy, particularly in the collectivisation campaign, but his own beliefs influenced policy and its implementation, as did his work as party secretary, and his experience when he visited rural areas. His authorship of works on 'socialist reconstruction in the countryside' had been acknowledged by the end of 1930.[51] In 1940, an article by Andrei Vyshinskii, to celebrate the tenth anniversary of Molotov's appointment as chairman of Sovnarkom, noted specifically his contribution to agricultural policy 1927–1930, and the assistance that he had given to Stalin.[52] Sources from the late Soviet period coupled his name with that of Stalin on agricultural policy, and some suggest that he was especially responsible for the excesses in early 1930.[53] The chief instrument in applying Stalin's policy of ultra-rapid forced collectivisation, evidence points to the fact that he became a personal enthusiast.

Comintern and the XVI Congress

Molotov's responsibilities for Comintern continued in early 1930, alongside his preoccupation with agriculture and work as party secretary. When he spoke at IKKI, on 25 February 1930, he developed the attack on the 'Rubin school' of economists first made by Stalin in December 1929. This was extended in early February 1930 to an attack on all advocates of 'mechanism' on the economic front.[54] Molotov supported Stalin's first major intervention into intellectual theory, and stressed that 'a certain Menshevik Rubin' had exercised great influence in the Institute of Red Professors and diverted attention away from urgent problems of the Soviet and world economies into abstract and scholastic paths. This he associated with the Right deviation, and claimed that a change had been achieved in recent times only with the help of the Central Committee.[55]

Molotov's Comintern duties influenced his speeches to the Leningrad *oblast'* party conferences, on 5 May and 6 June 1930, prior to the XVI Congress. He claimed that 'the construction of socialism along the whole line, on all fronts', in which collectivisation was an essential element, would form the basis of the international proletarian revolution, and he contrasted the situation in the USSR with the capitalist world. A long description of recent events in Comintern was an indication that he was preparing his report for the XVI Congress. He warned that the danger of capitalist military intervention against the USSR had increased and called for the Soviet Union to strengthen its defences.[56]

Like other leaders, Molotov praised the ultra-ambitious plans for industrialisation. He asserted that dependence of industry on imported equipment had fallen from 50 per cent to 23 per cent, but he noted shortfalls in the current year, especially in capital construction, 32 per cent in Leningrad *oblast'*. He also alleged that there was 'not one branch of large-scale industry where there was not revealed some or the other counter-revolutionary wrecking organisation' – a comment on events at the time. He emphasised the need for new skilled cadres, the importance of socialist emulation, shock work, and the individual responsibilities of each worker to raise production.[57] The remedy to shortfalls in agricultural production, which had harmed the standard of living of the working class, was the attack on kulakism for which the Party had mobilised the middle and poor peasant mass. This led Molotov into an attack on the Right who opposed this policy.[58] He spoke of the penetration of the Moscow party organisation by the Right, and criticised a recent speech by Krupskaya who had condemned collectivisation as 'panic before difficulties'. The greatest achievement of the Party, Molotov asserted, was that there would not be any open opposition at the XVI Congress, a mark of the success of the correct line of the Party.[59]

Molotov's contribution to the Congress, June–July 1930, was limited to a report from IKKI. This demonstrated growing confidence when he dealt with theoretical questions and international issues. The speech included attacks on Bukharin and other leaders of the Right, and on Trotsky. He began with a 'few notes' on themes from Stalin's Central Committee report. The western world had been plunged into the Great Depression and he spoke of the sharpening of the crisis of capitalism – as predicted by Marx. It was a crisis of over-production, not only in industrial states but also in agricultural countries. He referred to the growth of monopoly capitalism, of protectionism and of the falling standard of living in capitalist countries. The crisis increased the likelihood of an attack of capital on the working class. The very existence of the USSR, with its planned economy, undermined the foundations of world capitalism, and the chances of an attack on the USSR grew, as did the chances of a new imperialist war – a struggle for world hegemony between the United States and Great Britain. As at the tenth IKKI, 1929, he referred to a 'revolutionary upsurge' that had become apparent among the workers of many countries. He cited the number of strikes in England and France and noted China and India as examples. He again attacked social democracy, which would be on the side of the bourgeoisie if there was an attack on the workers, as 'social-fascism'. Communists made two mistakes in their attitude towards it. The Right error denied the degeneration of social-democracy into social-fascism; the Left error, and Molotov put much more stress on this,[60] was to attack the whole body of social-democratic workers as 'rotten elements' irredeemably corrupted by social-fascism, and not draw a line between the mass of the workers and 'social-fascist bureaucracy'. He referred once more to a struggle 'on two fronts'.

Molotov referred to the increasing strength of the fascist party in Saxony in recent elections to demonstrate the bourgeoisie's attack on the working class. In response, he offered 'the tactics of the united front from below' and the slogan 'class against class'. He noted the growing strength of national communist mass parties, with the important exceptions of the United States and Great Britain. Communist mass parties were particularly significant in the struggle against social democracy. He concluded

> The strongly developing crisis of world capitalism forms the preconditions for the victory of the proletariat. The practical talents of the working class for a decisive self-sacrificing struggle ... will decide the question.[61]

After the debate on his report, he once more emphasised the importance of the slogan 'class against class', 'to win back the working mass from the social-fascist path, by the realisation of a united proletarian front from below' and called on communist parties to assist the workers in their preparations for the growing class war.[62]

Molotov's comments were in line with the *Theses* adopted by the VI Comintern Congress. He did not draw any particular conclusions about the danger to the USSR from the growth of Nazism.[63] Indeed, Soviet policy recognised the growth of a German fascist party as a desirable phenomena. In addition to preventing a Franco-German rapprochement directed against the USSR, as desired by the German Social Democratic Party, the Nazis could even attract workers because of their radical programme. Then the masses would soon realise that Hitler was a tool of the capitalists and turn to the communists. Thus, if Hitler became a member of, or even formed a government, he would be fully unmasked and the communists could only gain.[64] Molotov served as Stalin's faithful lieutenant when he faithfully adopted this line. The conclusions were completely false, but may have made him more suspicious of capitalist states, and eventually of the policy of collective security, something which was to be influential when he became responsible for foreign policy.

New responsibilities

Molotov's emphasis on the world economic crisis, in his report to the XVI Congress, was an indication that the main preoccupation of the Soviet political leadership was now focused on the industrialisation campaign. Stalin, on leave during the summer, as usual, directed policy by correspondence with Molotov. He sent detailed instructions on a wide range of topics: the nature of confessions to be obtained from the recently arrested group of 'wreckers'; the shortage of coinage; party affairs in Siberia and Azerbaijan; and especially industrial policy. With Stalin and his supporters intent on pursuit of the highest possible rate of growth, the leader was especially concerned over a shortfall in planned production.[65]

In September, the Central Committee's counterplan to raise production by 'storming' methods was published,[66] and in October, Molotov attended the Ukrainian Central Committee as a plenipotentiary of the USSR Central Committee to deal with the crisis in the coal industry. As a result of his visit, the Ukrainian Central Committee recommended to the Politburo a restructuring of wages with rewards for higher productivity, greater mechanisation and better skills.[67] He addressed party *aktiv* meetings in Donbass mining towns, condemned 'Right deviationist and Trotskyite elements prophesying disaster that the tempo is beyond our strength'. He called for 'a Bolshevik repulse to the class enemy choristers by fulfilling the industrial plan ... by the liquidation of the bottle neck'.[68] 'A new Bolshevik mechanised Donbass', and the formation of a skilled permanent labour force would achieve this. He also stressed the significance of the use of shock workers to overcome the coal crisis.[69]

Molotov reported to the Politburo by telegram, and stressed the importance and urgency of speeding up of the mechanisation of the Donbass coal industry and the reorganisation of labour. He remained in the Donbass to implement the Politburo decree arising from his report, and the resolutions of the Ukrainian Central Committee and local party organisations.[70] He gave instructions to the local party authorities,[71] and Stalin wrote to him:

> Your work on the Donbass turned out well. You've achieved a sample of Leninist checking up on fulfilment. If it is required, let me congratulate you on your success.[72]

Pressure for moderation in the industrialisation campaign created conflict in the state administration, in particular in the economic commissariats responsible for the industrialisation programme. This naturally raised the issue of Rykov, a Right leader who remained as Sovnarkom chairman. In mid-September, Stalin on vacation wrote to Molotov:

> Rykov and his lot must go. ... It is impossible to go on tolerating this rottenness in government economic management. **But for the time being this is just between you and me.**

A week later he wrote:

> It seems to me that the issue of the top government hierarchy should be finally resolved before the autumn. This will also provide the solution to the matter of leadership in general, because the party and Soviet authorities are closely interwoven and inseparable from each other, My opinion on that score is as follows. ...
>
> You'll have to take over Rykov's place as chairman of the Council of Commissars [Sovnarkom] and Labour Defence Council [STO]. This is necessary. Otherwise, there will be a split between the Soviet and the party leadership. With such a set-up, we'll have complete unity between Soviet and party leaders, and this will unquestionably double our strength. ...
>
> The existing *Conference of Deputies* [meetings of the Sovnarkom chairman with his deputy chairmen to arrange business] should be dismantled, and the chairman of the Council of Commissars should be allowed to consult with his deputies (bringing in various officials) at his own discretion.
>
> All of this is just between you and me for the time being. We'll speak in more detail in the autumn. Meanwhile, consult with our closest friends and report on any objections.[73]

Stalin also proposed the establishment of a Commission of Implementation, (*Komissiya Ispolneniya – KomIspol*). A week later, he wrote to Molotov that if Ordzhonikidze refused to chair this new body, Molotov would have to.[74] He apparently consulted members of the Politburo about the person to be appointed as the new Sovnarkom chairman. Among those who recommended Molotov was Kaganovich, although this was partly because he did not think that Stalin could be both General Secretary and Sovnarkom chairman.[75] Stalin's proposals, implemented almost to the letter, were to determine Molotov's position for the next decade.

Until 1930, Molotov's experience had been in the party machine and not in the state/government machine. In 1927, he had become a member of the Presidium of TsIK RSFSR (Russian Soviet Federative Socialist Republic), and in 1929 of TsIK USSR, but these were purely formal positions.[76] They were, however, a necessary prelude to his appointment to a senior position in the state apparatus. The Union Council of People's Commissars (Sovnarkom) was a very different body to the Sovnarkom created immediately after November 1917, which had been 'Lenin's government' during the early years of Bolshevik rule. Established in 1924 with the creation of the USSR, besides its standing commissions, the most important of which were STO and Gosplan, it consisted of eleven commissariats. There were five 'unified' commissariats: food supplies, labour, workers' and peasants' inspection, finance and VSNKh. These theoretically functioned through parallel apparatuses in identically named republican commissariats. The Commissars of five 'all-union' commissariats: foreign affairs, war and naval affairs, foreign trade, transport, and posts and telegraphs; had plenipotentiaries directly subordinate to them attached to republican Sovnarkoms.[77] As already noted, Molotov was central in the creation of a further all-union commissariat, for agriculture, in October 1929.[78] By 1927, in addition to its central staff, the Union Sovnarkom had a large supporting bureaucracy of 9267 employees in the commissariats.[79] To call this sophisticated bureaucracy a government, or cabinet, and to term its chairman 'prime minister', is to give a misleading impression of its powers, although these terms indicate the best parallels with western democracies and give an indication of the importance of the post to which Molotov was to be promoted. The party decided policy; there was no sense of cabinet responsibility; and Sovnarkom functioned as a high level committee which implemented policy, especially in economic and social affairs.[80]

Rykov had been chairman of the Union Sovnarkom from the time of its creation. As a consistent supporter of moderate policies he became a natural ally of Bukharin and Tomsky. His place as head of the chief government institution and a member of the Politburo forced him into the centre of the political arena, but after 1928 his ability to reconcile departmental claims, the key to success as Sovnarkom chairman, became increasingly difficult, because the views he represented were so out of step with Stalin and his leading supporters.[81] Fiercely attacked at the XVI Congress, that he was allowed to remain a Politburo member and Sovnarkom chairman until the end of the year, shows only that Stalin was not yet ready to replace him. The economic difficulties of the summer and autumn delayed the sweeping changes in the government apparatus which culminated in Molotov's appointment as Sovnarkom chairman.[82]

The restructuring of Sovnarkom to consolidate the Stalinist position, began with Rudzutak's replacement as head of the Commissariat for Transport by Moisei Rukhimovich in June, although Rudzutak retained his Sovnarkom vice-chairmanship and was important as an assistant to Molotov when the latter became the new chairman. If Molotov had foreign policy links with Chicherin, the latter's replacement as head of the Commissariat of Foreign Affairs by Maksim Litvinov, at the end of July, was a clear indication of the direction in which policy was moving. Chicherin's anti-Western polices were out of step with the idea of peace and security during Soviet industrialisation. Uglanov, a prominent Rightist, was replaced by Anton Tsikhon as Commissar for Labour in early August; and Grigorii Grin'ko appointed as head of the Commissariat for Finance in place of Nikolai Bruyukhanov in October. In November, the Commissariat of Trade was divided, Mikoyan, the former Commissar for Trade, took over the new Commissariat of Supply: food supplies was an area in which he had specialised since 1926.[83] Arkadii Rozengol'ts was appointed to lead the new Commissariat of Foreign Trade. Before the decision was taken to divide the commissariat, Stalin, whilst on vacation, had sent instructions to Molotov that Rozengol'ts should be appointed as deputy to Mikoyan responsible for foreign trade.[84] In November, Kuibyshev, who was replaced by Ordzhonikidze at VSNKh, took over Gosplan from Gleb Krzhizhanovski and became a Sovnarkom vice-chairman. He had worked with Molotov in the Secretariat in 1922; Molotov was on good terms with him and he was a loyal Stalinist. Ordzhonikidze's position as head of the Commissariat for Workers' and Peasants' Inspection was left vacant until after the appointment of Molotov to the Sovnarkom chairmanship. It was then filled by the less senior loyal Stalinist Andreev,[85] perhaps a sign that the days when that commissariat was the driving force behind the government machine were over.[86]

The replacement of Rykov, and Molotov's appointment to the chairmanship of Sovnarkom, took place at the Central Committee plenum held 17–21 December 1930. The first and most substantive item on the agenda was a report by Kuibyshev, the new head of Gosplan, 'The National Economic Plan for 1931 (Control Figures)'.[87] In his concluding words, Kuibyshev condemned Rykov as an enemy of rapid industrialisation, and stated that he had not become an active supporter of the 'general line' after the XVI Congress, despite the undertaking made there by the leaders of the Right. Consequently, a disruptive breach had appeared between the party and government leadership, which could not be allowed to continue because of the complete unity required to achieve the 1931 plan.[88] The adoption of the resolution on the Plan, on 19 December, was followed by a series of motions proposed by Stanislav Kosior on the chairmanship and vice-chairmanship of Sovnarkom, and Politburo membership relating to these positions. The most important of these proposals relieved Rykov of his Sovnarkom chairmanship and Politburo membership, and proposed Molotov in his place as Sovnarkom chairman. When he introduced his resolutions Kosior stated:

> We need a chairman of Sovnarkom who will direct the whole of our Soviet and economic apparatus, who will stand as the chief leader in the struggle for the line of the Party, who will … fight with frantic energy to implement the party line as the first priority in Soviet and economic work.

The proposal of Molotov as Sovnarkom chairman was greeted with 'prolonged applause by the entire hall'. A supplementary resolution relieved Molotov of his Central Committee secretaryship and Orgburo membership, in the light of his new responsibilities.[89] This was clearly a necessary step if he was to lead the state apparatus.

Molotov's major contribution to the plenum was a report, in support of Kalinin, on re-elections to the Soviets. He said that he was speaking for the first time as chairman of Sovnarkom, as well as a Central Committee member, and that he would apply his experience of party work to the Sovnarkom chairmanship. He then spoke about restructuring (*perestroika*) the work of the Soviets to make them conductors of the 'general line' of the Party. He admitted that recently the Central Committee had been forced not only to direct the work of central Soviet organs, but also to stand in their place, and this was not normal. The restructuring was to strengthen the struggle against bureaucratism and remedy deficiencies in the state apparatus. He attacked the Right and the recently defeated 'Right–Left bloc' of Syrtsov and Lominadze.[90] The attack on this group is evidence of the serious divisions between Stalin and some of his supporters revealed by their criticisms of the pace of industrialisation, the pressure on the peasantry and excessive centralisation, which were partly responsible for the reorganisation of Sovnarkom and Molotov's appointment as chairman. Molotov associated recent 'wrecking', particularly in the food industry, and the Industrial Party trial, with the Right. He attacked its leaders, particularly Bukharin. Here he raised theoretical issues, and cited criticism of Bukharin's 'Organisation of Capitalism'.[91] Finally, he repeated phrases from Stalin's September letters to him about the reorganisation of the government apparatus. STO, Sovnarkom's chief standing commission, was to become a 'militant organ of economic leadership' with Stalin amongst its members; a new Commission of Implementation, as suggested by Stalin, was to be created, and he specified its membership including his own chairmanship. He claimed that, with a reinvigorated Gosplan, staffed with new, young communist cadres, this would mean that Sovnarkom would have three important standing commissions.[92] A year later he was to say that checking implementation and ensuring effective leadership were essentially two sides of the same question.[93] He concluded:

Now in view of my new appointment I would like to say a few words about myself and about my work.

I grew up in the Bolshevik party and have been connected with it by many years of uninterrupted work. As a communist I cannot desire anything more than to be a student of Lenin. For a short while I was able to work under the immediate leadership of Lenin, but as a communist, my chief task will always be and will remain to master the study of Marxism–Leninism and actively participate in realising Marxist-Leninist doctrine. During the last ten years as a Central Committee secretary I attended the school of Bolshevik work under the immediate tutelage of a personal student of Lenin's, under the immediate leadership of Comrade Stalin. I treasure this.

Up to the present time I have had to work chiefly as a party worker. I declare to you comrades that at the work in Sovnarkom I will continue as a party worker, as an instrument of the will of the Party and its Central Committee.[94]

Even if it is incorrect to describe Sovnarkom as the 'government', and to equate the post of Sovnarkom chairman in the USSR with that of prime minister in western democracies, Molotov had become the head of the state machinery of the USSR at the age of forty. If, at times in the campaign for collectivisation, there had been opportunities to use the abilities of Molotov the revolutionary, and these were apparent to all, the transformation from fiery revolutionary to bureaucrat, now appeared to be complete. Molotov was, however, to display new qualities as Stalin's head of government.

7
Head of Government

Official duties

Molotov's appointment as Sovnarkom chairman not only involved him relinquishing his Secretariat and Orgburo positions, he was also replaced by Kaganovich as Stalin's deputy in the party whilst the general secretary was on leave, when Kaganovich also assumed chief responsibility for correspondence with Stalin.[1] Any relief that this may have given to Molotov, however, was more than outweighed by the burden of new duties. As head of government, Molotov's attendance at Politburo meetings was vital. The Politburo, now dominated by a group of Stalin's leading supporters, met at least weekly in 1931;[2] and by tradition it was chaired by the Sovnarkom chairman.[3] Table 7.1 shows that Molotov, as in the period 1926–1930, attended a high proportion of meetings (86.26% overall for 1930–1941), and again his most frequent absences were during his summer vacation.

Molotov also had to attend and preside over government committees. There were 34 Sovnarkom meetings in 1931, about one every ten days, and of these Molotov chaired 25. The main break was whilst he was on his annual leave in August and early September, after which he chaired all nine meetings held between October and December 1931. The incomplete data available for the remainder of the decade suggests that he continued to chair a high proportion of meetings.[5] As Sovnarkom chairman, Molotov was also chairman of STO. He presided over most of the STO sessions, held regularly at ten-day intervals in 1931. The small amount of data available after this time, we know only that there were 15 STO meetings in 1935, again indicates that he continued to chair a high percentage of the sittings.[6] In addition, he presided over the new *KomIspol* up to 1934, when the body was abolished.[7] The meetings of all these bodies were scheduled to allow senior politicians who were members to attend all meetings.[8]

When the state apparatus was reorganised at the time of Molotov's appointment as head of government, two further joint Politburo–Sovnarkom commissions, the Defence Commission (*Komissiya Oborony*) and the Commission for Currency matters (*Valyutnaya Komissiya*) were established. Molotov served on both and chaired the defence commission.[9] He managed important new committees of Sovnarkom

Table 7.1   Politburo and Sovnarkom meetings and Molotov's attendance 1931–1941[4]

Year	Politburo No. sittings	Politburo No. sittings Molotov attended	Sovnarkom No. sittings	Sovnarkom No. sittings Molotov chaired
1931	61	51	34	25
1932	47	39	26	X
1933	24	23	25	X
1934	18	15	22	X
1935	16	14	21	X
1936	9	9	12	9
1937	7	7	9	9
1938	4	2	19	X
1939	2	2	12	11
1940	2	2	12	11
1941	0	0	0	0
Total	172	149	192	

X – data not available.

and STO as they were formed, such as the STO Price Committee, and Committee for Reserves, which he was instrumental in forming.[10] He was also a member of numerous *ad hoc* committees of Sovnarkom. These included those responsible for such minor matters as the preparation of individual decrees.[11]

As chairman of Sovnarkom, Molotov gained the power to make authoritative statements on foreign policy, and a supervisory responsibility for the commissariat of foreign affairs, as for other commissariats. At first sight this does not seem important, as an analysis of Sovnarkom's business during the 1930s shows that foreign policy was not discussed there and the commissar attended only infrequently – seven out of 34 meetings in 1931.[12] As head of government, however, Molotov outranked Litvinov when it came to meeting ministers from foreign states who visited the USSR.[13] In addition, foreign policy was one of six main areas on which the Politburo concentrated its attention,[14] and it was a matter to which Stalin devoted considerable personal interest,[15] clearly of importance to Molotov.

His official duties were broadened by his new position. By late May 1931, he had succeeded Voroshilov as chairman of the commission to build the new Palace of Soviets, established in February 1931,[16] and introduced its business to the Politburo. He arranged for the Cathedral of Christ the Redeemer, which stood on the proposed site, to be blown up in December 1931.[17] The commission did not announce the final winning design until July 1933.[18] Molotov believed that this design was absurd, in that the structure was so huge, that Lenin's head, on the statue that surmounted it, would not be visible from the entrance. Consequently, he would not authorise work to begin on construction until forced to do so by Stalin and Voroshilov when they attended the commission, a rare example of Molotov taking an independent line based on his personal judgement.[19]

There were also ceremonial duties, for example, visits to new factories and higher education institutes. In May 1935, Molotov was among the delegation that opened the new Moscow metro. They inspected the entrance to the station at *Ploshchad' Sverdlova*, rode on the escalators, travelled on a train that stopped at each station to inspect equipment, and congratulated the chief engineer, P. Rottert.[20]

Public life and politics

1931

Molotov's position as chairman of Sovnarkom made him responsible for explaining and justifying government policy. He reported to the equivalent of the Soviet Parliament (TsIK, and the Congress of Soviets), on the work of the government. He was also called upon to address important conferences and other meetings. If less specialised than his former reports to party bodies, these speeches were wide-ranging and more in the public eye and international arena. Initially they reflected both his radical views on agriculture and the official line on industrialisation, but his ideological orthodoxy and a new concern for balance in the economy as Sovnarkom chairman soon became apparent.

His first major commitment was a report to open the meeting of TsIK, 4–8 January 1931, on the 1931 Annual Plan, the third year of the *pyatiletka*. The speech reflected the ultra-ambitious rates of growth aimed at in early 1931: he spoke of completion of the *pyatiletka* in four years.[21] Against a background of the impending renewal of the collectivisation campaign,[22] he extolled the 'halting of the growth of the capitalist element in agriculture', and the transition to 'complete collectivisation in new and large regions of the country'. These factors, he claimed, would 'allow the completion of the construction of the fundamentals of the socialist economy in the Soviet Union'.[23] He was already hinting at his completely orthodox position on the 'foundations of socialism', which was to cause considerable controversy.

Later in the speech he talked about the development of Soviet foreign trade, and the campaign against Soviet 'dumping' by Western powers. In answer to British accusations of the use of forced labour, he cited the end of unemployment in the USSR and the introduction of the seven-hour working day. He contrasted accusations of 'forced labour' (*prinudite 'lnyi trud*) in the USSR with unemployment and the long working hours of 'free labour' (*vol'nyi trud*) in Britain. Forced labour was a topic with which he was to deal more specifically in another speech two months later.[24]

During the debate that followed, I. M. Gordienko challenged Molotov and claimed 'everything depends on the poor peasant'. Molotov responded that everything depended on the kolkhoz, which united the poor and middle peasant and built a Bolshevik peasantry. He quoted Stalin's speech to the XVI Congress on a 'Bolshevik Offensive'. Finally, he returned to what Lenin had said about the need to check implementation and the establishment of *KomIspol*, which showed the important role envisaged for this new committee.[25]

Hard on the heels of the speech to TsIK, was a major speech at the 'First All-Union Conference of Employees of Socialist Industry', held 30 January to

4 February 1931, where Molotov spoke to 700 senior industrial officials and factory managers. Organised to focus attention on the need for financial discipline and cost reduction in the industrial plan for 1931, the conference would be remembered for Stalin's speech which included the words

> We are fifty to one hundred years behind the advanced countries. We must close the gap in ten years. Either we do this or they will crush us.[26]

Ordzhonikidze, the new chairman of VSNKh, opened the conference and stressed the importance of *khozraschet* (cost accounting). Molotov vigorously supported him on 2 February, the fourth day of the conference. He argued that the growth of planning did not lessen the need for *khozraschet*, and opportunistically used his speech to condemn the former Trotskyite, Ivan Smirnov, who, as an alternative to Ordzhonikidze's proposals, had advocated a central industrial supply system, similar to that which had existed in the period of War Communism. Molotov emphasised that in early 1931, *khozraschet* had to be strengthened. He assumed, however, that this was a temporary phenomenon: an outcome of NEP that would end when NEP was completed.[27] His view was that *khozraschet*, in the state sector, reflected the market relations outside that sector, and would not be a feature of a proper socialist economy. Again this demonstrated his strictly orthodox position on the nature of socialism. He did not contradict the line Stalin had taken a year earlier, but his view of *khozraschet* was strikingly different to that of Ordzhonikidze, who treated *khozraschet* more as a thing in itself.[28] This interpretation of a significant point of Marxist economic theory was to cause considerable perplexity among Molotov's colleagues.[29] By 1934, the line that *khozraschet* was a feature of socialism and not of NEP, was the new orthodoxy, but it was something that Molotov was never to acknowledge.

A month later, on 9 March 1931, he reported on the work of the Soviet government to the Congress of Soviets. The fragmentary correspondence with Stalin available for this period shows that Stalin had read and corrected the draft of the speech. He wrote that the section on 'dumping' was good, but made major alterations to the section on forced labour.[30] Molotov informed his audience that in the USSR 'the victory of Socialism is completely and fully assured', but he warned of the danger from international imperialism if there was a slackening of tempo in industrialisation. He dismissed accusations of 'dumping' of Soviet goods,[31] and made an authoritative but very careful statement on the use of forced labour in the USSR to answer the widespread campaign against it in the Western press, particularly its use in the timber industry.[32] He began by citing Marx and Engels on labour exploitation in capitalist countries, and claimed that in contrast to capitalist slavery, labour in the Soviet Union was free. He compared unemployment in the capitalist countries with the abolition of unemployment in the USSR, where, he asserted, the working day was shorter and wages were rising.[33] He categorically rejected British and American accusations about the use of forced labour in the timber industry. This was a barefaced lie, but it was the official line propagandised by senior Soviet politicians.[34] He did admit that:

> we have never refuted the fact that healthy prisoners capable of normal labour are used for road and other public works. We have used such labour in the past, are using it now, and will continue to use it in the future. This is very good for society. It is also good for the prisoners themselves who are thereby accustomed to regular work and assisted to become useful members of society.[35]

He denied that forced labour was used in the production of any commodities exported, but explained that the labour of prisoners was used in road-building in Karelia and other northern districts, and in the construction of the White Sea–Baltic canal. He asserted that the working day of these prisoners, who he said numbered 60,000, never exceeded eight hours, that they were provided with board and a monthly salary of 20–30 rubles, and that they could move about freely in the penal colonies where there was intensive cultural and educational work and training.[36]

He again stressed the importance of the newly established *KomIspol* and emphasised the need to master technique, on which he quoted Stalin's speech to the recent industrial conference. He claimed that in the last ten years the NEP had been implemented on Bolshevik lines, and emphasised that 1931 was the decisive year in achieving the *pyatiletka* in four years. In conclusion he spoke of the struggle to build socialism in a world where 'our class enemy has set himself the task of sweeping the Soviet system of Socialism, from the face of the earth'.[37]

This was a very busy period for Molotov. As he made clear in his speech to the industrial conference, there was a transport crisis in the USSR, and on 13 March a high level 'Committee for Freight' attached to STO, was formed, with Molotov as chairman, a further addition to his already onerous duties.[38] In the same month, he chaired an important Sovnarkom commission 'on the industrial plan for 1931', which included Stalin as well as Kuibyshev, Ordzhonikidze and other senior commissars, among its members. The commission was responsible for a substantial increase in investment to VSNKh, a reflection of the ambitious targets at this time.[39] Shortly afterwards, Molotov chaired another Sovnarkom commission on 'the reconstruction of rail transport'.[40]

Molotov's speech at the 'First All-Union Conference for Planning of Scientific-Research Work', on 11 April, was notable for the reassurance he gave to the 'old-specialists', a mark of his new responsibility for the priority of industrialisation. The conference was organised by Bukharin, as head of the scientific research sector of VSNKh, and early on he warned the delegates in very strong terms on severe punishments for those suspected of wrecking. It is not clear whether Bukharin had not kept up with the shift in policy, or whether he was advising the specialists that he could no longer protect them,[41] but the role reversal of him and Molotov, who had been deeply involved in attacks on specialists from the time of Shakhty, is remarkable. Molotov made the conventional attack on wrecking, but went on to say that with the decisive victory of socialism in the countryside, 'vacillations among scientific-technical workers are now ending'. He drew a distinction between the evil intent of the wrecker and the bold initiative and justifiable risk of scientific research work, and he advocated a comradely style of criticism of specialists who did not accept the superior Marxist–Leninist dialectical method, so that they might be won over in slow stages.[42]

When the Central Committee plenum met, 11–15 June 1931, Molotov, on Stalin's proposal was elected as chairman.[43] He was not responsible for a major report, indicative of his new role as head of government. His work on transport continued, however, with his membership of a commission formed to edit the theses of Rukhimovich, the Commissar for Transport, in which Molotov played a prominent role.[44] Rukhimovich was a personal friend, and Molotov tried to support him later in the year and in 1934.[45] Immediately after the plenum Molotov presided over a major conference of business managers, 20–22 June 1931, called to emphasise the need to fulfil the 1931 plan in the second half of the economic year.[46] Kuibyshev gave the major report, and there was so much comment that Molotov found that he had to take stern measures to limit discussion.[47] In his speech, he dwelt on the need for new skilled workers, and warned against overzealous attacks on the 'old specialists'. He deplored that there was little success yet with *khozraschet*, the need for which had to be instilled into the working masses – 'the ruble must control our economic work'.[48] After his colleagues had spoken, Stalin, who had frequently interrupted them, made his famous 'six conditions' speech, and when Molotov closed the conference he insisted: 'Fulfilment of the plan is obligatory'.[49]

In July 1931 Molotov was appointed by the Politburo to convene a commission to consider 'the foreign currency debt in the first half of 1932',[50] but the summer of 1931 was a period of less tension in economic, internal and foreign policy.[51] This allowed him to take a lengthy summer leave in Sochi, in close proximity to Stalin also on vacation.[52] During this period, when Kaganovich corresponded with Stalin on policy, he also asked for comments from Molotov, and Stalin consulted Molotov on various matters.[53] Among the most important of these was the question of the resignation of Kuibyshev from the Gosplan chairmanship. In August, Kuibyshev wrote to Kaganovich to say that he could not cope with the job. One factor, he explained, was the domination of Ordzhonikidze, who pressed the case of VSNKh, his commissariat. Kuibyshev stated that Ordzhonikidze had 'triumphed' over Molotov as well, and that there were bad relations between them. Kaganovich forwarded Kuibyshev's memorandum to Stalin, who was alarmed by the conflict between his lieutenants, because it might undermine the 'leadership group'.[54] He was clearly instrumental, when Molotov wrote to Kuibyshev to say that his proposal to resign would receive no support, that the time was not right, that it was necessary to strengthen Gosplan, and that he would help him.[55]

Stalin became very critical of Ordzhonikidze. He wrote to Kaganovich that the Politburo was used to bypass Sovnarkom to assure the supremacy of VSNKh and other People's Commissariats,[56] and that the friction between Molotov and Ordzhonikidze that Kuibyshev had mentioned, was continuing. When, on 30 August, the Politburo accepted a proposal made by Ordzhonikidze and the VSNKh leadership to increase imports from Germany, which overturned an earlier decision of 30 July made before Stalin went on leave, Molotov supported Stalin's protest to the Politburo. On 6 September, Stalin and Molotov sent an ultimatum, and demanded a special meeting, to which they would be summoned if Ordzhonikidze's proposal of 30 August was not revoked. The Politburo now reversed its decision.[57]

The hostility between Molotov and Ordzhonikidze became even more marked in late 1931, when the Politburo, on Stalin and Molotov's initiative, considered reorganisation of the economic commissariats, particularly VSNKh, to create separate commissariats for heavy industry, light industry and the timber industry; appointing three additional vice-commissars to VSNKh, responsible for specific branches of heavy industry. This reduced the range of Ordzhonikidze's authority, and allowed Molotov, as Sovnarkom chairman, more power to control the industrial commissariats and reconcile conflicting interests. Ordzhonikidze threatened to resign over the matter, but was overruled in the Politburo by Stalin's proposal to carry out the reorganisation and reject the resignation. The Politburo then agreed 'to schedule a special meeting of the Politburo to review Comrade Ordzhonikidze's statement about his relationship with Comrade Molotov'.[58] Mikoyan recorded in his memoirs 'Sergo did not love Molotov very much',[59] and there is correspondence between Ordzhonikidze and Stalin, where Ordzhonikidze calls Molotov an obscenity *(negodniai)* and complains that he opposed him from the beginning. The two apparently began to ignore one another.[60]

In late September 1931, Molotov who had by now returned to Moscow, proposed Rukhimovich, strongly criticised by Stalin and about to be removed as Commissar for Transport, as chairman of Gosplan. Molotov's support for Rukhimovich seems to have been based on personal friendship. There is no evidence to suggest that Molotov sympathised with Rukhimovich's view that the problems on the railways were due to lack of investment.[61] This support for Rukhimovich, which would also have allowed Kuibyshev to resign, angered Stalin. He wrote that he was astonished at Molotov's proposal. It would mean that Rukhimovich, who had failed as People's Commissar for Transport and conducted the 'most malicious agitation <u>against</u> the practical line of the Central Committee', would be promoted and become deputy chairman of Sovnarkom *ex officio*. He also dismissed Ordzhonikidze's proposal to make Rukhimovich a VSNKh vice-chairman. In a telegram to Stalin, Kaganovich described Molotov's proposal as 'simply laughable', and in line with Stalin's instruction to send him away from Moscow, Rukhimovich was demoted to head the Kuzbass coal corporation.[62] In June 1934, however, when Rukhimovich was appointed a deputy commissar for heavy industry with responsibility for fuel, Molotov supported him again. He proposed that Rukhimovich should be appointed to head a new commissariat of the fuel industry, which would be removed from Ordzhonikidze's commissariat of heavy industry.[63]

Molotov's correspondence with Stalin in the autumn of 1931, on the economic plan for the fourth quarter of the year[64] and the need to reduce imports,[65] demonstrated that from being an extremist, in his role as Sovnarkom chairman, he attempted to keep a balance in the economy and resist the demands of powerful high-spending commissariats, such as VSNKh. At the end of the year, and in early 1932, Molotov mediated on the level of defence expenditure between Gosplan on one side, and VSNKh, the Commissariat of Defence and the Gosplan vice-chairman responsible for military questions on the other. He received complaints from Yan Gamarnik, the deputy commissar for defence, and VSNKh representatives, about Gosplan cuts in capital construction. The dispute was resolved when in January 1932, the Sovnarkom commission on the armaments industry, headed by Kuibyshev, recommended an increase in armaments investment.[66]

In the last months of the year, Molotov was preoccupied with the fulfilment of the 1931 plan and preparation of the control figures for 1932, on which he reported to the Politburo on 20 November.[67] After this he was concerned with the detailed development of the 1932 Plan in Sovnarkom.[68] He still found time for agricultural policy. In August, he was appointed chairman of a high level Politburo commission on the autumn sowing.[69] When he addressed a conference on drought, called by the Central Committee and Sovnarkom on 30 October, he pointed out the significance of drought as it affected the harvest in grain producing areas. His broader responsibilities as Sovnarkom chairman were apparent when he claimed that the new large-scale agricultural institutions: the kolkhozy, sovkhozy and the MTS, demanded that everyone should be an economic administrator.[70] The following day, at the Central Committee plenum, 28–31 October, which he once more chaired but where he did not make a major speech, he was involved in sharp exchanges about the size of the harvest. When delegates from the Volga region emphasised that it had been very poor, he supported Stalin's criticism of the lack of precision in their figures.[71] In December, he was appointed chairman of another high level Politburo commission on the spring sowing plan. Stalin was among the members of the commission.[72]

When he spoke on the anniversary of the October Revolution, Molotov warned that the biggest battles with capitalism were ahead and claimed that the most vital task now was to raise the productivity of labour.[73] His concern to maximise production was again evident in May 1932, when in an interview, a Czech mining engineer told Molotov that bad working and living conditions were partly responsible for poor production in Soviet mines. In response he asked the engineer

> to write to the papers about it and then he (Molotov) would take the matter up with the appropriate commissariat. But so far the government officials had only talked and talked about the subject.[74]

Molotov's behaviour as Sovnarkom chairman suggests that one of his basic economic policies was to try to maximise production whilst restricting investment. His attempts to keep a tight rein on investment were reflected in his conflicts with Ordzhonikidze and other powerful commissars, and his attitude towards planning.

Foreign policy came to the top of Molotov's agenda in the last months of 1931. In response to the Japanese invasion of Manchuria in September, which meant that there was a very real danger of war, the Politburo on 23 November 1931, established a foreign affairs commission to make proposals for measures on the international situation. Molotov served on this commission.[75] The alarm of the political leaders was reflected in Molotov's speech to TsIK in December 1931 in which the emphasis on foreign policy matters was very different to that in previous speeches. He focused on the Far East, and specified the Japanese threat and the crisis in Manchuria as the most crucial problems for the Soviet Union. He repeated almost word for word, Stalin's statement to the XVI Party Congress, June 1930, 'we emphasise anew our basic principle: we need no one else's land, but not one inch of our land will we cede to anyone else'. He asserted that all provocations would be answered with a policy of peace.[76] This speech marked the beginning of a new policy of appeasement towards Japan, followed on 31 December 1931, by the offer of a non-aggression pact. Whilst, however, TsIK was in session, the Politburo had, on 23 December, established a 'commission to develop measures to reduce the military danger in the Far East'. This commission, with Stalin, Molotov, Voroshilov and Litvinov amongst its members, was responsible for a rapid rise in defence expenditure.[77] In April 1932, Molotov warned again about the danger of the situation in the Far East.[78]

1932 – The XVII Party Conference and after

The XVII Party Conference, 30 January–4 February 1932, was preceded by controversy at the Politburo over the Second Five Year Plan, between Kuibyshev, the chairman of Gosplan, and the industrial commissariats. The proposals to be presented to the Conference were apparently prepared very hurriedly,[79] and Molotov, as Sovnarkom chairman, would without doubt have tried to reconcile differences. He opened the Conference, and declared that the First Five Year Plan had been fulfilled in four year,[80] but the proceedings reflected the changing atmosphere from the reckless planning of 1930, to the more sober atmosphere of the XVII Congress of 1934. Stalin did not speak, and left it to Kuibyshev and Molotov to report on the preparation of the Second Five Year Plan. In a return to caution after the great enthusiasm for collectivisation, Molotov tried to define the place of the Plan in the construction of socialism in the USSR. He claimed that, 'in the main', collectivisation would be completed in 1932–1933, which would lead to 'the liquidation of the principal part of the capitalist element in the countryside'.[81] Molotov's strictly orthodox position was apparent when he was less optimistic on the development of socialism than Kuibyshev, and continued:

> we have entered the first, lower phase of communist society (socialism), but this will be far from completion during the Second Five Year Plan. ... The final victory of socialism will occur only when all distinctions between peasants and workers have disappeared.[82]

He stressed that the aim of the Second Five Year Plan was not that the USSR should 'catch up and overtake' the leading capitalist countries 'in a technical and economic respect overall', but that it would catch up in a number of branches of the economy and occupy the first place in Europe in technology.[83] He dismissed demands for restoration of cuts in the iron and steel plan and pointed out that the revised projections were 'beyond the capacity of capitalist countries'. He challenged certain areas, especially the Urals, to fulfil the projected targets. He was again more cautious than Kuibyshev when he estimated the growth in supply of consumer goods over the period of the Second Five Year Plan.[84]

At the conference, Molotov was involved in a controversy over the relative importance of engineering and electrification. The resolution on the Five Year Plan specified that 'Soviet engineering' would play the 'principal role in completing technical reconstruction', and Molotov criticised those who advocated that only electrification should be considered a leading principle. He stressed that 'the creation of an up-to-date energy base' depended primarily on the development of the engineering industry.[85] His comments were aimed at Krzhizhanovskii, the author of the GOELRO (State Commission for the Electrification of Russia) plan, and the great advocate of electrification. In support of Krzhizhanovskii, a Gosplan official quoted Lenin's remark that Communism equalled 'Soviet power plus the electrification of the whole country'.[86] Molotov, however, noted that under the Second Five Year Plan electric power production was planned to increase 600 per cent, whilst engineering figures projected only an increase of 300–350 per cent,[87] and Krzhizhanovskii did not reply. The exchange demonstrated the extent to which Stalin's lieutenants, men like Molotov, the new generation of administrators, had ousted the older generation of more idealistic planners.[88]

In April 1932, at the IX Trade Union Congress, Molotov claimed that the First Five Year Plan had 'brought about considerable improvement of the standard of life of the working class and the toiling peasantry'.[89] It is not clear if he believed this, or knew that it was untrue,[90] but on 8 May, the Politburo put Molotov at the head of a commission established to check implementation of decisions on consumer goods production.[91] At this time Smirnov, who he had condemned in 1931, described Molotov as

> in general ... the leader of the left wing of the Stalinist bureaucracy. It was said that he personally was against any retreat or modification in the questions of collectivisation and industrialisation.[92]

In 1932, partly for reasons of health, Stalin took a long and early vacation.[93] As usual, from the beginning he was in contact by letter and telegram with Kaganovich and Molotov, especially about the forthcoming harvest and procurement campaign.[94] In early June he corresponded with Molotov about the new government decree on 'Revolutionary Legality', approved by the Politburo on 25 June, aimed at preventing illegal coercion in connection with procurement campaigns.[95] On 20 July, however, Stalin wrote about the notorious law of 7 August, on the 'defence of socialist property'. Stalin personally drafted this decree, which was to be used mercilessly in the ongoing procurement campaign.[96] He sent Molotov and Kaganovich instructions on how to deal with opposition to his proposals; they discussed the decree in correspondence; and returned drafts of the decree as it was developed. After it was issued, Stalin sent instructions on its implementation.[97]

Molotov was also concerned with the decree on the management of industry. From May 1932, he chaired the commission that prepared a draft, only to find, in early August, that Stalin, who described it as 'schematic and unspecific', was extremely critical. He criticised particularly as 'slipshod', arrangements for the sale of output, and for supply allocated to the Commissariat for Heavy Industry. Molotov had submitted the draft to the Politburo before he received Stalin's comments, but was able to defer the issue until the autumn as Stalin suggested.[98] In July, Molotov's preoccupation as Sovnarkom chairman with maintaining a balance in the economy was again evident. Because of the financial situation, Grin'ko, the Commissar for Finance, proposed a reduction of the allocations to capital construction by 1.5 billion rubles. Molotov first recommended a billion rubles, and when Grin'ko accepted this appears to have suggested 500 million rubles. Stalin, however, supported Grin'ko.[99] At the same time, Molotov tried to mediate in disputes on the control figures for the third quarter of the annual plan. Kaganovich wrote to Stalin that 'our chairman' was trying to satisfy everybody, and to avoid disputes.[100]

On his return from six weeks leave, the first few days spent with Stalin in Sochi,[101] Molotov chaired the Central Committee plenum, 28 September–2 October 1932, where Sovnarkom commissars and vice-commissars delivered the main reports on economic policy.[102] Molotov, however, neither made a major speech at the plenum, nor was he prominent in the repression of the opposition, which included the Ryutin Platform, and was a response to harsh policies.[103] Indeed, as the senior political figure present at the Fifth Congress of Engineers and Technicians, on 26 November, he went out of his way to reassure the 'old specialists' and to emphasise the important role of the new technical intelligentsia.[104]

In December 1932, Molotov was once more involved in efforts to keep expenditure in check and control powerful high-spending commissariats. Yakovlev, the Commissar for Agriculture, appealed to Molotov against a Sovnarkom resolution that reduced the financial allocation to his scientific research institutes. Molotov replied to his letter:

> I am surprised at your manner of dealing with the Union Sovnarkom. In spite of the fact that you are aware of Sovnarkom's final decision, reached only yesterday, 25 December, (of course you were not present, i.e. your 'being busy' prevented you staying until the end of the sitting) – you have the nerve to write a letter like this to Sovnarkom.
>
> Since I cannot take such an attitude to the matter seriously, I am returning the paper to you for <u>you</u> to decide what to do with it.[105]

Molotov's response, if harsh, also indicates that he behaved in a statesmanlike way when he mediated between colleagues and conducted Sovnarkom proceedings. A similar case occurred in January 1934 when Voroshilov complained to Stalin that he had not been allocated an adequate number of tractors for use in the Far East, and wrote 'Comrade Molotov evidently did not consider it necessary to satisfy me nor even to inform me'.[106] Despite increases in defence expenditure the controversy continued, and Voroshilov complained about the lack of deliveries of new aircraft in 1935.[107]

In the autumn of 1932, Molotov, who had accompanied Stalin on two earlier visits, in 1931 and 1932,[108] was with Stalin when he called on Gorky during the night of 26–27 October 1932 and Stalin made his famous comment about writers as 'engineers of human souls'.[109] Twelve days later, on the night of 8–9 November, Molotov and his wife were the closest witnesses to the suicide of Stalin's wife, Nadezhda Alliluyeva. In his memoirs, Molotov recalled that he was present at the dinner at Voroshilov's that took place that night. Nadezhda, apparently angered either by Stalin's flirting or by his boorish behaviour, left with Polina Molotov, with whom she walked in the Kremlin grounds prior to shooting herself. Polina later told Stalin's daughter that Nadezhda was calm when she left her. It is often claimed that Nadezhda's suicide was a protest against the harsh policies of Stalin and his supporters, rather than a mark of disapproval of his personal behaviour. Polina, with Abel Enukidze, were the first persons to be called when the body was discovered. Molotov arrived shortly afterwards and no one dared to wake Stalin. In his memoirs, Molotov contradicted the traditional story that Stalin turned away from the coffin, and he twice recalled Stalin's grief.[110]

Agriculture 1931–1933 and famine in the Ukraine

The conference on drought, and the clash at the Central Committee plenum in October 1931, indicated the anxiety of the political leadership over the 1931 harvest.[111] With alarm over the collections, Molotov, as chairman of the Politburo Commission on Procurements,[112] went on a *komandirovka* to the crucial area of the Ukraine between 28 December 1931 and 3 January 1932. At the Ukrainian Politburo and Central Committee, on 28 and 29 December 1931, he was adamant about the need to meet the procurement targets and forced acceptance of the central authorities' decision. He denied that the Ukrainian harvest had been poor: 'There is no district in Ukraine with a bad harvest this year, but the RSFSR had a huge drought'.[113] He blamed the shortfall on bad organisation, which was to be remedied by dividing the Ukraine into six territorial sectors.[114] The decree of the Ukrainian Politburo stated that Molotov had insisted that the complete fulfilment of the procurement targets was essential, 'dictated to the USSR by the total political and particularly the international situation'.[115] The last phrase was indicative of Molotov's concern with foreign affairs at that time.

He sent three telegrams to Moscow to order the distribution of goods and maize to assist in the collections, although before the end of his visit he was to complain that these resources were badly allocated.[116] He visited rural districts and collective farms and the industrial construction in Dnepropetrovsk.[117] Wherever he stopped he spoke about the need to meet the procurement targets. He attacked the management of poorly performing kolkhozy as 'agents of kulaks' and 'kulak swine', and ordered the dismissal of some managers. He threatened to dissolve the kolkhozy and tax their members as individual peasants.[118] He condemned the grain plenipotentiaries sent from Khar'kov, and described one as 'not only not useful but harmful ... utterly undesirable as a collection official in 1932'. Shortly after Molotov's visit, one kolkhoz party secretary suffered a heart attack.[119] The *komandirovka* culminated in a final meeting with the party *aktiv* and procurement workers in

Khar'kov, on 2 January 1932, where Molotov did not hesitate to specify the reasons why individual kolkhozy had not fulfilled the targets, or to criticise individuals.[120]

Later in January, after his return, Stalin and Molotov, in a telegram to the Ukrainian Politburo, demanded complete fulfilment, without conditions, of the procurement plan for the Ukraine.[121] They insisted that Politburo member Stanislav Kosior, the Ukrainin leader, on vacation in Sochi, should return to Khar'kov immediately and take personal responsibility for the matter.[122] This, however, was only the beginning of Molotov's concern with the agricultural situation in the Ukraine in 1932.

By March, it was clear that there were famine conditions in the far east of the USSR, exacerbated by an inflow of troops in response to the Japanese invasion of Manchuria, and Stalin and Molotov authorised purchase of grain from abroad to alleviate the situation. By May, there were widespread reports of famine, which the political leadership hoped to remedy partly by foreign purchases, and partly by diverting grain from the Ukraine, although, in the same month, orders were issued to cancel some of this, which was to be retained for Ukrainian needs.[123]

In mid-May 1932, Molotov was sent on a mission to the Urals because of the problems with the spring sowing.[124] Scarcely had he returned when, on 25 May 1932, the Politburo decided that, because of the critical position, he should head a special five-man commission to the Ukraine, the commission to leave Moscow that day.[125] This resulted in the provision of additional resources to assist the sowing campaign, but not in a modification of the procurement figures.[126] Following Molotov's appointment, on 7 June, as chairman of the Politburo commission on the 1932 harvest,[127] he and Kaganovich received a telegram from the Ukrainian party leaders, on 17 June, which requested food assistance because of the emergency. This was refused by the Politburo on 23 June, and before this, on 21 June, Molotov and Stalin had signed a telegram to the Ukrainian Politburo and Sovnarkom to confirm that the Ukrainian procurement figures would not be modified.[128] On 28 June, Molotov spoke to a meeting of party secretaries, chairmen of provincial government executive committees and representatives from the commissariats, called especially to discuss the forthcoming harvest and procurement campaign. He read out a letter from Stalin, approved by the Politburo, to emphasise that the Politburo figures had to be fulfilled by all areas.[129]

Stalin now instructed that Molotov as Sovnarkom chairman, and Kaganovich as party secretary, should attend the Third All-Ukrainian Party Conference. Molotov apparently doubted if he should go, possibly questioning his role as Sovnarkom chairman at a party conference, but the Politburo confirmed Stalin's instructions on 3 July:[130] Molotov and Kaganovich were to make clear that the Politburo decision on the collections had to be implemented.[131] Prior to the conference, on 6 July, Molotov and Kaganovich attended a meeting of the Ukrainian Politburo, which confirmed the USSR Politburo figures, as proposed by Stalin, as the basis of the resolutions produced for the conference.[132]

At the party conference, the Ukrainian leaders stated that some areas were already seriously short of food, and that the procurement figures were unrealistic.[133] In response, Molotov, who noted that without improvements in agricultural performance industrialisation could not be successful,[134] and reminded his listeners of the important position of the Ukraine in Soviet agriculture, blamed poor party organisation and kulak agents for the shortfall in the last procurement campaign. He declared that it was 'necessary to give a decisive blow to this anti-Bolshevik attempt' to assign responsibility to an unrealistic plan,[135] and that this time there would be 'no concessions or vacillations on the question of fulfilling the task set by the party and Soviet power'. He ordered the conference to organise 'a Bolshevik mobilisation,'[136] and he and Kaganovich reported to Stalin that the Politburo figures had been enforced.[137]

Although later Molotov warned the Politburo that they faced the spectre of famine in the Ukraine,[138] he implemented the harsh coercive policy pursued in the autumn and winter of 1932–1933,[139] which was a major factor in the disastrous Ukrainian famine. He visited the Ukraine again, on two occasions, in late October and November 1932. During the first ten-day visit, made on Politburo orders to strengthen the procurement campaign,[140] he attended the Ukrainian Central Committee plenum. He wrote to Stalin that he recommended acceptance of the Ukrainian Politburo's proposal for a further reduction of the procurement figures, already decreased in August.[141] But he also asked that 50–70 experienced party workers be sent from Moscow to work on the campaign,[142] and proposed a series of measures to assist in its implementation.[143] Repression was the chief instrument he used. With Mendel' Khataevich, the Ukrainian Party Second Secretary, he directed the enforcement of the notorious law of 7 August to achieve a decisive turning point (*perelom*).[144]

Appointed chairman of a new Politburo commission on grain yields on 12 November,[145] on 17 November, Molotov returned to Khar'kov,[146] where he forced through the Ukrainian Politburo a further decree, 'Measures for Strengthening the Procurement Campaign', described by one authority as 'a draconian measure to pressurise the peasantry of the Ukraine and the Kuban'.[147] In a report to Stalin on a meeting of the Khar'kov party *aktiv*, he described a large part of its members as 'opportunist waverers'.[148] He attacked local officials who had used their initiative to try to vary the procurement targets, and tried to recruit the help of local communists who could be considered 'reliable'.[149] Molotov's hostility to the individual peasant farmer was especially significant. In mid-November he proposed to the Politburo a special levy on the individual peasant to be worked out and implemented immediately. His suggestion was acted upon and created great hardship.[150]

He now turned on Khataevich who had published a speech in which the Second Secretary suggested that procurements should be limited to 'commodity grain'.[151] Khataevich sent Molotov a copy of the brochure with a letter that argued

> if ... in the future production can increase in accordance with the needs of the proletarian state we must take into consideration the minimum need of collective farmers, or there will be no one left to sow next year's harvest.[152]

In response, Molotov drafted a vague statement to show that Khataevich was theoretically wrong, which he did not forward.[153] Instead he sent a curt memo that said that he did not have time to answer the letter, and continued

> your position is radically incorrect and non-Bolshevik. We Bolsheviks cannot afford to put the needs of the state – needs that have been carefully defined by party resolutions – in second place, let alone discount them as priorities at all. ... The satisfaction of the needs of the proletarian state is the immediate priority.

He did, however, add, that to 'take <u>any</u> grain, wherever we can', was 'an opportunist extreme' and 'non-Bolshevik'. When Molotov reported the matter to Stalin he wrote 'we are in danger of sinking into a left-wing deviation'.[154] Khataevich was forced to recant before the Ukrainian Politburo,[155] but Molotov continued to pursue him. In December, he wrote on a letter from Khataevich that he 'sinks deeper into his false position'.[156] Molotov's position in this dispute, as in his line on *khozraschet*, and his greater caution on the future of socialism than Kuibyshev at the XVII Party conference in 1932, again reflected his ideological orthodoxy. He was far less willing to adapt the classic definition of socialism than other leaders and this was to culminate in the famous dispute of 1955.[157]

At this point, Kaganovich was sent to the Ukraine and took control, although Stalin and Molotov continued to direct measures from Moscow.[158] In January 1933, Stalin and Molotov signed a joint Sovnarkom and Central Committee decree, which blamed the mass exodus of peasants from famine areas on the activities of 'enemies of Soviet power, SRs and Polish agents'. The OGPU was ordered to prevent the exodus, immediately arrest the counter-revolutionary element, and return the remainder to the places they had left.[159]

Molotov's activities in 1932 lend support to the view that with Stalin and other Soviet leaders, he must be found personally guilty for the famine.[160] The verdict of a 1990 commission formed by the 'World Congress of Free Ukrainians', that the thesis of genocide against the Ukrainian people in 1932–1933 could not be excluded, may be tenuous. There is, however, more evidence to support its conclusion that the chief blame for the 1932–1933 Ukrainian famine lies with Stalin, and that 'this responsibility is shared with other members of the Politburo, especially V. Molotov and L. Kaganovich'.[161]

Challenged years later by Chuev 'that the famine of 1933 was deliberately organised by Stalin and the whole of your leadership', Molotov replied:

> Enemies of communism say that! They are enemies of communism! People who are politically blind.

He argued that the figures for the number of deaths had not been substantiated and were exaggerated, that he had travelled to the Ukraine twice and saw 'nothing of the kind'. He did, however, admit that in the Volga region, which he did not visit because it was not possible to procure grain there, people might have been worse off.[162]

1933 – The Second Five Year Plan, industry and opposition

Molotov chaired the Central Committee plenum, 7–12 January 1933,[163] which he addressed on 'The Tasks of the First Year of the Second Five Year Plan'. After Stalin had ominously announced a new attack on wrecking and on the 'old specialists', Molotov emphasised 'the mastery of technique' and the need to increase labour productivity, particularly in the industrial commissariats. He demanded that heavy industry, Ordzhonikidze's commissariat, should give a lead. He condemned an article by Trotsky, of October 1932, which called for a delay of the Second Five Year Plan by one year and proposed that 1933 should be 'a year of capital repair'. Molotov declared 'We stand on the road of the attack'. In response to Zinoviev, who had mentioned the possibility of a retreat in October 1932, he sarcastically remarked 'Zinoviev is very sensitive to the attitudes of petty bourgeois elements'.[164] On the last day, the plenum turned its attention to the 'anti-party grouping of Eismont, Tolmachev, A. P. Smirnov and others'. The first two were already under arrest, and the fire was concentrated on Smirnov, who although sick was made to attend the plenum, Molotov wrung from him an admission that the arrest of Eismont and Tolmachev was 'correct'.[165]

Later in the month, on 23 January, Molotov spoke to TsIK on 'The Results of the Five Year Plan and the Plan for 1933'. Stalin wrote to him shortly afterwards:

> I read the section on international affairs. It came out well. The confident, contemptuous tone with respect to the 'great' powers, the belief in our own strength, the delicate but plain spitting in the pot of the swaggering 'great powers' – very good. Let them eat it.[166]

In March and April, Molotov was deeply involved in the problems of the Donbass coal industry.[167] In May, he signed jointly with Stalin the famous decree that called for a reduction in the prison population and the end of the 'orgy' of mass arrests which were blamed on local officials. The decree also strictly defined the authorities empowered to make arrests. It is evidence of relaxation at the end of the mass collectivisation campaign,[168] and that Molotov was closely associated with the large-scale repression carried out in connection with the anti-kulak campaign.

Friction with Ordzhonikidze was renewed in late July 1933. Molotov, as Sovnarkom chairman, received several telegrams from different regions which complained that the Zaporozh'e factory, Communard, was supplying combine-harvesters that lacked certain vital parts,[169] and on 28 July he signed a Sovnarkom decree 'On the Criminal Dispatch of Incomplete Combine-Harvesters to MTS and State Farms'.[170] This decree ordered Orzhonikidze's Commissariat for Heavy Industry to cease delivery of incomplete harvesters and to make good the deficiencies. It also initiated the arrest and trial of the factory managers responsible. Molotov received a protest from Khataevich who defended the factory, and claimed that it was inexpedient to try the factory managers. He replied:

> We are well aware of the achievements of Communard and so is the Prosecutor. ... The trial is certainly not merely significant only for the factory itself, and to cancel it is entirely inexpedient.[171]

The wider ramifications that Molotov implied became clear, when at the trial, in his final address, Vyshinskii, the deputy public prosecutor, questioned the work of the Commissariats for Heavy Industry and for Agriculture.[172] This angered Orzhonikidze and Yakovlev, especially as Vyshinskii gave a 'broad hint' that pointed at the commissars themselves, and Molotov apparently personally approved that this should be included in the press report.[173] Ordzhonikidze raised the matter at the Politburo on 24 August and attempted to have Vyshinskii censured. Besides Ordzhonikidze, all members of the Politburo present, Kaganovich, Kalinin and Molotov himself, who edited the final Politburo decision, voted to condemn Vyshinskii.[174] Kaganovich reported to Stalin who was on vacation, that on this occasion both Molotov and Ordzhonikidze tried to show restraint.[175]

The attempt to censure Vyshinskii angered Stalin. On 29 August, he sent a telegram to Kaganovich, Molotov and Orzhonikidze which maintained that the Politburo decision was 'incorrect and harmful', that People's Commissars should be held accountable for 'incomplete output' in their area of responsibility, and concluded:

It's sad that Kaganovich and Molotov could not stand up to the bureaucratic onslaught of the Commissariat for Heavy Industry.[176]

Three days later the Politburo reversed its decision, but only Kaganovich, of those who had agreed to censure Vyshinskii, signed the resolution. Ordzhonikidze had gone on vacation on that day, and Molotov was to leave the next.[177] On the same day, Stalin wrote again to Molotov and accused Ordzhonikidze of hooliganism, and of 'wishing to disrupt the campaign of Sovnarkom and the Central Committee to provide proper equipment'. He asked 'Did Kaganovich pull a fast one? So it seems. And he's not the only one'.[178] Kaganovich's response was to blame Molotov for Stalin's criticism. He wrote to Stalin:

Comrade Molotov managed this trial by himself and did not tell anyone anything. This largely accounts for the fact that instead of a direct and simple statement that the People's Commissariats bear responsibility ... hints were given that were so 'subtle' that they ended up as explicit raps on the knuckles.[179]

Stalin was now so angry that he wrote again to Molotov (and to Kaganovich) to condemn Ordzhonikidze and those who supported him (including Kaganovich) as being 'in the camp of the reactionary elements in the party'.[180] He seemed to ignore Kaganovich's accusation of Molotov's sole and poor organisation of the trial. Molotov, however, replied to Stalin that the episode 'should be a lesson to us and particularly to me', although he thought the trial 'hadn't gone too badly'.[181] If this is another example of Molotov's independence in taking an initiative, even on the basis of an agreed policy, it had not turned out well. He was, however, compelled to work with colleagues even whilst he was at odds with them. On 18 August 1933, he had been appointed as chairman of a new high level Politburo commission on transport, with Kaganovich, responsible for party oversight over the railways, as his deputy.[182]

Confusion about the vacation arrangements for Politburo members at this time makes clear Stalin's opinion of Molotov's key role. Molotov insisted on his usual six-week period and in the same letter of 1 September, in which he accused Ordzhonikidze of 'hooliganism', Stalin wrote:

> To be honest, neither I (nor Voroshilov) like the fact that you are leaving for vacation for six weeks instead of two weeks as was agreed upon when we made the vacation schedule. ... Why did you change the schedule – I don't understand it. Are you running away from Sergo [Ordzhonikidze]? Is it so hard to understand that you can't simply leave the Politburo and Council of Commissars to Kuibyshev (he may start drinking) or to Kaganovich for long?

Molotov had to return from vacation early, and on 12 September, Stalin was a little apologetic.

> I am a little uncomfortable with being the reason for your early return from your vacation. But this awkwardness aside, it's obvious that it would be rash to leave the centre's work to Kaganovich alone (Kuibyshev may start drinking) for any length of time, because Kaganovich must divide his time between his central and local responsibilities. I will be in Moscow in one month, and you will be able to go on vacation then.[183]

1934–1936

The XVII Party Congress provides a rare example of Molotov, whilst he was Sovnarkom chairman, adopting an extreme position. On 3 February 1934, he and Kuibyshev introduced theses on the Second Five Year Plan that proposed an expansion of industrial production by 19 per cent a year between 1933 and 1937. The figures, which had apparently been revised upwards whilst they were prepared, included increases proposed by Stalin personally. In his famous intervention, on the next day, Ordzhonikidze objected to increases made while the plan was in preparation and proposed cuts. In his reply, Molotov accepted cuts to 16.5 per cent and referred to them as a symptom of 'Bolshevik caution'. He insisted, however, that there must not be the slightest reduction in the 16.5 per cent and that for 1934 the rate of growth should not be reduced below 19 per cent.[184] If Molotov had been forced to accept higher figures in the preparatory discussions, he was now reverting to a more familiar role. He also made clear in his speech to the Congress that he insisted that any increase in investment should be accompanied by increased production.[185]

Whilst on vacation in the Crimea in this year (1934), he was still preoccupied with restricting investment. He wrote to Kuibyshev, his deputy, on the annual plan:

> I've been thinking about the third quarter. I consider that it would be wrong to adopt a plan for the third quarter larger than the plan for the second quarter.

It would be more correct if we adopt an <u>even lower construction</u> plan, particularly in view of the threat of drought.[186]

In 1933, Molotov had been central in a redistribution of Gosplan's functions by which authority for preparation of both quarterly and annual material balances was transferred from Gosplan to the economic commissariats concerned. His 'great initiative' in the reform was acknowledged by Kuibyshev.[187] This reform demonstrated both Molotov's faith in reorganisation as a remedy for problems, in line with Stalin's views, but it was also, perhaps, an attempt to make the burden of his friend Kuibyshev more manageable.

In 1933 and 1934, Molotov supported by Kuibyshev, took the initiative in persuading Stalin to accept moderate investment plans,[188] but in 1935 Kuibyshev died, and Molotov was on vacation at the time of the critical discussion of the 1936 plan. During the first six months of that year the Politburo accepted a rapid increase in the 1935 investment plan, and in the summer, when the 1936 investment plan was prepared, a further very large increase was agreed. Stalin wrote to Molotov that Valerii Mezhlauk, successor to Kuibyshev as head of Gosplan, had presented a memorandum proposing 19 milliard rubles and that he had recommended an increase to 22 milliard rubles.[189] Molotov replied that it was 'possible and necessary' to keep the figure to 22 milliard and that

> I consider it extremely undesirable to increase the construction programme above 22 milliard rubles. I am guided in this by the desire to strengthen the ruble and also to reduce the cost of construction.[190]

Stalin now wrote a conciliatory letter to Molotov[191] and Molotov replied:

> I would have preferred a smaller amount of capital construction, but I think we shall cope if we put our shoulders to the wheel (*ponatuzhivshis*). ... The possibility of increasing industrial production by 23–22% favours this outcome.[192]

This incident demonstrates not only Molotov's desire to restrict investment and keep a balance in the economy, but it is also a striking example of the difference made when he was able to control the situation. When, by April 1936, increased investment and the early stages of the Stakhanovite movement failed to increase production, Molotov, quite consistently, supported Stalin's move to save money and chaired a commission to implement measures to reduce prices to make more foodstuffs available.[193]

The same attitude was apparent in the major report Molotov gave on the abolition of bread rationing at the November 1934 Central Committee plenum, presented in the press as a major victory for the Soviet system: 'the beginning of the abolition of rationing for all food products and commodities'. Molotov emphasised the need to move from the supply of flour to the supply of baked bread, and that prices were to be arranged to stimulate the purchase of bread rather than flour. He argued that expenditure on higher wages and the higher prices of industrial crops must be balanced by the revenue from increased bread prices: the reform should be 'planned so that the state should not suffer a loss'. When Stalin interrupted to say that 'It evidently comes out fifty-fifty (*tak na tak*) it is equal', Molotov replied that 'so far it is still with a surplus (*s gakom*)' and that revenue was planned to exceed expenditure by two milliard to two and a half milliard rubles, but that precise financial estimates could not yet be made.[194]

On 1 February 1935, at the Central Committee plenum, Stalin introduced a resolution for Molotov, as chairman of Sovnarkom, to present a proposal to the VII Congress of Soviets on amendments to the constitution. Five days later the Congress directed TsIK to elect a commission to prepare revisions. Chaired by Stalin, this commission included Molotov, Voroshilov, Kaganovich, Litvinov, Mikoyan and Vlas Chubar' amongst its members. The commission met for the first time on 7 July 1935, when Stalin made clear that its task was to draw up a new constitution. Molotov and Kalinin were appointed as vice-chairmen, and twelve sub-commissions were established, with Molotov chairing the sub-commission on economics.[195] In September 1935, Stalin, while on leave, wrote to Molotov with his outline for the constitution. Molotov included this outline with his report in February 1936, and asked for Stalin's comments; Stalin replied 'Reviewed. Not bad. See comments in text'.[196] During these discussions Molotov advised Stalin that it was impossible to include in the constitution Lenin's words 'from each according to his ability to each according to his labour', because the principle could not be realised. Stalin disagreed with him. He argued that people must see the future and strive for it, and the words were eventually included. Molotov commented in old age that experience over the years showed that people received more, but not according to their labour, support or opposition to the principle not counting.[197] He retained his ideological orthodoxy, apparent in 1935 and 1936, even in old age.

Molotov – politician and statesman

As Sovnarkom chairman Molotov played a crucial political–economic role. His standing was strengthened by his Politburo membership and as a member of its leading group. This was especially true in the period up to 1933 whilst a vestige of collective leadership remained.[198] After this, his close association with Stalin was especially significant in maintaining his position. In 1930, the former senior Soviet diplomat G. Bessedovsky, described a ruling circle in the USSR led by a triumvirate of Stalin, Molotov and Kaganovich, in which Stalin dominated his two chief lieutenants by sheer willpower, but was also very dependent on them as assistants and advisers.[199] In its April 1932 edition of 'Who's Who in Soviet Russia', the British Embassy reported that Molotov was

> said to be a creature of Stalin, and is probably closest to him in the Kremlin circle. Has a considerable reputation as an organiser. In person he is undistinguished and suffers from a painful stammer.[200]

In the years between 1931 and 1936, when Stalin took long vacations, Molotov supplemented Kaganovich as his agent, sought his advice and implemented his decisions, as Stalin's correspondence demonstrates. The positions of Molotov and Kaganovich also gave them tremendous influence,[201] and the leading group was held together by joint participation in ruling the USSR.

The number of Politburo and Sovnarkom commissions Molotov chaired, some examples of which are given in the earlier part of this chapter, provide evidence of the vital role he played. A further remarkable example is provided by the Politburo *protokol* (minutes) of the meeting on 8 January 1932, where at one session he was appointed to chair five commissions: one on sowing, one on preparing theses on the Second Five Year Plan for the XVII Party Conference, one on the MTS, one on the railways and one on consumer co-operatives.[202] The diverse nature of these commissions also shows the widespread nature of Molotov's responsibilities.

Further evidence of Molotov's key position is that he was a member of the small inner group selected to receive three types of key information. First, there was data on armaments production and the output of the Gulags (Corrective Labour Camps) which was not included in the monthly statistical bulletins. Second, there were OGPU/NKVD reports on the state of the economy and social unrest,[203] and third, information on certain aspects of agriculture. The vital documents on the grain harvest, grain procurements and grain loans were sent only to Stalin, Molotov, Kaganovich (as Stalin's party deputy) and Kuibyshev (head of the committee of procurements). They were not sent to the other Sovnarkom deputy chairmen, or to Yakovlev, the Commissar for Agriculture.[204] With Stalin, Molotov was one of the very few people with the information to be able to take an overview of the economic, social and political landscape.

If, in his role as Stalin's chief lieutenant for agricultural policy and general 'trouble shooter', he had appeared to be an extremist, in his new position as head of government, Molotov was transformed to a moderate. Mikoyan, referring to the years 1932 and 1933, recalled in his memoirs:

> Molotov as chairman of Sovnarkom felt responsible to maintain a balance in the economy, and in particular was very concerned to preserve the stability of our currency, to reduce the losses of economic establishments and to seek sources of profit. This was natural and arose out of his position. ... I remember that Ordzhonikidze and I often quarrelled with him when he restricted capital investment in the construction of new industrial organisations after the successful completion of the First Five Year plan early. He was strongly influenced by Grin'ko, the Commissar for Finance. ... He particularly influenced Molotov on the reduction of expenditure.

Mikoyan asserted that Molotov often made mistakes in pursuit of his objectives, and cited an occasion when Molotov argued that the land of unprofitable sovkhozy should be transferred to kolkhozy because the expenses of loss-making kolkhozy was not borne by the state. In this case Stalin overruled Molotov because of the social importance of the sovkhozy, but also said that measures should be taken to eliminate deficits.[205]

As Sovnarkom chairman Molotov was compelled to keep the overall interest of the state as his priority; make the commissariats obtain the maximum from the resources allocated to them; reconcile the interests of powerful economic controllers, each striving for the maximum resources for their commissariat; and settle disputes between them. Molotov could be harsh and authoritarian in his efforts to keep expenditure in check as demonstrated by his treatment of Yakovlev and Voroshilov.[206]

As this chapter has shown, Ordzhonikidze, as head of VSNKh and its successor the Commissariat of Heavy Industry, and the commissars of other high spending commissariats, often pressed for more investment. Molotov to resist this pressure, allied himself with Kuibyshev, head of Gosplan until 1934, with whom he was on good terms,[207] and whom he supported as early as 1931.[208] Molotov, as chairman of Sovnarkom, and Kuibyshev, as head of Gosplan, were responsible for overall policy and maintaining balance in the economy, whereas commissars such as Ordzhonikidze were responsible only for the performance of their commissariats.[209] Kaganovich had a similar experience to Ordzhonikidze later in the decade. He recalled that he worked well with Molotov when they were both party secretaries. Although they were never close friends, Molotov supported him when he introduced proposals to the Orgburo. After his appointment as head of the Commissariat of Transport, in 1935, however, there were often arguments. When Kaganovich demanded more capital investment and was opposed by Mezhlauk, head of Gosplan after Kuibyshev, Molotov supported Mezhlauk.[210] Molotov was offended when Kaganovich and Ordzhonikidze complained to Stalin when they were overruled, and asked why they did not take their complaints to Sovnarkom. Kaganovich and Ordzhonikidze excused themselves by saying that the Politburo was the highest authority, and Stalin acted as the supreme arbiter.[211] Later, when Kaganovich became deputy chairman of Sovnarkom in 1938, Molotov was more supportive.[212]

Molotov's behaviour as Sovnarkom chairman suggests that he behaved in a statesmanlike way in mediating departmental interests. It does not support the thesis that during the 1930s he was a prominent member of a group of radicals in the Politburo opposed to a group of moderates.[213] Further evidence of statesman-like behaviour is the high proportion of Sovnarkom and STO meetings he chaired, his attempts to make Sovnarkom run smoothly by regular meetings, efforts to fix the dates of meetings and agendas, deal with procedure at meetings, make the institution's workload manageable, attempt to streamline its operation, and allocate responsibility to the vice-chairmen.[214] His concern for Sovnarkom's reputation is shown by a December 1932 decree which required the commissariats to establish a 'wage fund' for each of the institutions for which they were responsible. This bears an endorsement in Molotov's hand: 'Do not publish as an order of Sovnarkom. Decrees of the commissariats can be published on the basis of this decision.'[215] The commissariats were to be blamed for the restriction in wages not the central body for which Molotov was responsible. His aim was statesmanlike if the method he adopted to achieve it was not.

The meticulous attention that Molotov paid to detail in documents he received is also evidence that he was more than a mere bureaucrat and possessed states-manlike qualities. His papers show that he usually annotated documents as he read them, underlined key points and made marginal comments. In July 1933 he received a 14-page document on the 1932 harvest, from Osinskii, Chairman of the State Commission for Determining the Yield and Scale of the Gross Grain Harvest. On this he has marked the key points. There are 34 separate underlinings, rings round and marginal lines. In one place he correctly altered 1932 to 1933, in another he queried what appeared to be an arithmetical error.[216] On a later, November 1936 document from Osinskii, as usual carefully marked by Molotov, he has written 'Is there *recent* information about the harvest? M.' In response, Molotov received a memorandum from Bruyukhanov, deputy to Osinskii, endorsed that he was sending to Molotov a copy of a memo of Osinskii to Stalin, of 7 December 1936, with all the appendices 'according to the request of Comrade Molotov passed to me by telephone by Comrade Moiseev'. This document is again carefully marked.[217] A further example is provided by Molotov's deletion of the words 'free trade', and replacement of them with 'open trade' in a draft decree 'On the Plan for the Open Sale of Meat and Meat Products in 1935', submitted to him by the Commissar for Internal Trade, I. Ya. Veitser, in March 1935. Veitser was an enthusiastic protagonist of 'free trade', but this was a sensitive term and Molotov changed every reference.[218]

A further aspect of Molotov's behaviour that might be regarded as statesmanlike is the treatment of colleagues who he regarded as friends. His support for and attempts to relieve Kuibyshev have been discussed above. There is also the case of Rukhimovich. As Molotov believed in restricting investment whilst maximising production, it seems unlikely that he supported Rukhimovich because he pressed for increased investment in rail transport, although he may have been more sympathetic when he recognised that Rukhimovich was a realist when he suggested what could be achieved on the railways.[219] Whatever the case, Molotov's surprising suggestion that Rukhimovich should be promoted, when Stalin suggested that he should be sacked as head of the Commissariat of Transport and demoted, demonstrates Molotov's independence of judgement and friendship. Support for friends and colleagues was changed by the Terror, Molotov denounced Rukhimovich, now Commissar for the Defence Industries, in 1937. He was also involved in the repression of Chubar' and Nikolai Antipov, two Sovnarkom vice-chairmen, and a number of other former colleagues.[220]

1. The Skryabin family about 1900. Vyacheslav (Molotov) sits at the left front

В. М. МОЛОТОВ, 1909 г.

2. 1909. As a student in Kazan

B. M. МОЛОТОВ, 1910 г.

3. 1910. Molotov in exile in Vologda

B. M. МОЛОТОВ—СТУДЕНТ ПЕТЕРБУРГСКОГО ПОЛИТЕХНИЧЕСКОГО ИНСТИТУТА

4. As a student at the Petersburg Polytechnic Institute 1912

5. Chairman of the Northern *Sovnarkhoz* 1918

6. Military training on the *Krasnaya Zvezda* 1919. Molotov is on the extreme left of the picture, back row

7. On shore during the expedition of the *Krasnaya Zvezda* 1919. Molotov on the extreme left of the picture

8. Addressing a meeting, early 1920s

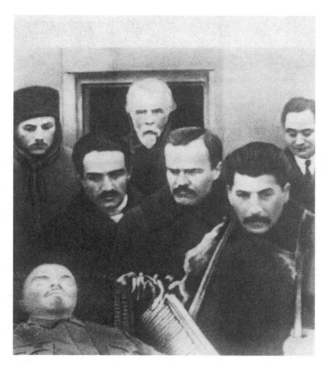

9. Around Lenin's coffin 1924. Molotov stands slightly behind Stalin to his right. Mikoyan stands to Molotov's right. Behind him to his right is Voroshilov

10. On a walk in the Alexander Gardens whilst party secretary in the 1920s

11. 1920s – The Party Secretary emerges from a meeting

12. Meeting Young Communists during the 1930s

13. Family portrait. Molotov with wife Polina and daughter Svetlana, mid-1930s

14. Walking with Stalin and Litvinov in the Kremlin grounds, late 1930s

15. Molotov, Sovnarkom chairman with Valerii Mezhlauk, Gosplan chairman, about 1935

16. Ordzhonikidze's funeral 1937. Kaganovich is behind Stalin to Molotov's left with Voroshilov behind Molotov

17.   Voting at the elections for the new 1938 Supreme Soviet. Stalin follows Molotov

18.   1938 bust of Molotov by G. V. Neroda

19. Signing the Molotov–Ribbentrop pact, August 1939. Ribbentrop stands to Stalin's right behind Molotov

20. Molotov arrives in Berlin, November 1940

21. Meeting Hitler in Berlin, November 1940

22. Molotov meets Anthony Eden on his arrival in Moscow, December 1941

23. Molotov meets Roosevelt on his visit to the USA, 1942

24. Wearing the new Foreign Ministry uniform, 1943

25.   Molotov stands behind Stalin at the Yalta Conference, 1945

26.   Talking with Stalin at the Potsdam Conference, 1945

27. Molotov and Polina with Vyshinskii and wife, Moscow 1945 or 1946

28. Politburo poster between 1945 and 1947. Molotov is second to Stalin in prominence

29. Molotov carries Stalin's coffin, 1953

30. Molotov's grave, next to Polina's with that of his daughter and son-in-law in front of it at the Novodevichii Cemetery, 1999

8
Molotov and the Terror 1934–1938

Amongst Stalin's lieutenants Molotov is conspicuous for his commitment to and consistent support of the Terror. He not only supported it during the 1930s, but convinced of its necessity, he sought to justify it even in old age. In 1982 he told Chuev:

> I consider that we had to go through a period of terror, because we had conducted a struggle for more than ten years. This cost us dearly, but without it things would have been worse. . . . I believe the terror carried out towards the end of the 1930s was essential. Of course, there would have been fewer victims if we had operated more cautiously. But Stalin insisted on playing safe: spare no one but guarantee absolute stability in the country for a long period of time – through the war and post-war years which was certainly achieved. I don't deny I supported that line.[1]

Molotov saw the origins of the Terror of the 1930s in Lenin's call for a merciless struggle against the opposition at the XI Congress and argued that, with Lenin removed from the scene, Stalin had to take the lead.[2] At another time, he said that the policy of repression was the only policy in accordance with the basic principles of Leninism.[3]

Mikoyan and Nikita Khrushchev also strongly supported the Terror, but, it seems, more to protect themselves, than because of their belief in the policy. Their opportunism was demonstrated when they both denounced the process at the XX Congress, 1956, and cited examples from the period when they strongly supported it. Ordzhonikidze, although he went some way to support the Terror, eventually tried to restrain it, and his suicide was a reaction to terror. Kaganovich clearly had reservations, and gave the process his full support only after a disagreement with Stalin in the summer of 1936, when he saw how committed the leader was to the process. At this time, Molotov himself was in considerable personal danger, but his differences with Stalin were not connected with his support for the Terror. He had been fully identified with the repression of the kulaks and mass peasant resistance in the collectivisation campaign, and with the condemnation of the political oppositions in the early 1930s, particularly that of A. P. Smirnov in 1932.[4] Even if one can quibble with the description of his features, Molotov's reputation on the eve of the Terror is clear from Osip Mandelstam's poem on Stalin, written in November 1933, and later to cost him his life:

> Around him a rabble of thin-necked leaders –
> Fawning half-men for him to play with.
> They whinny, purr or whine
> As he prates or points a finger,
> One by one forging his laws to be flung
> Like horseshoes at the head, the eye or the groin.[5]

Mandelstam's wife commented:

> The adjective 'thin-necked' was inspired by the sight of Molotov. M[andelstam] noted his thin neck sticking out of his collar and the smallness of the head that crowned it. 'Just like a tomcat' said M, pointing at his portrait.[6]

From the XVII Congress to the Kirov murder

There is still no agreement amongst historians as to Stalin's accountability for the Kirov murder, which is often accepted as a focal point in the development of the Terror.[7] If Stalin was responsible, it would strengthen the argument that he already had a grand plan to launch a campaign of terror against the political elite, and use the assassination as evidence of a widespread conspiracy against the Soviet state and its leaders to justify his actions.[8] If this was the case, Molotov's attitude to the Terror means that he was either naïve and deceived by Stalin, or party to the plot. His activities at this time are clearly crucial.

At the XVII Party Congress, 26 January to 10 February 1934, the famous Congress of Victors, there was a superficial atmosphere of unity and note of optimism, inspired by the good 1933 harvest and the apparent justification for economic policies pursued during the First Five Year Plan. Many former oppositionists addressed the Congress and accepted the party line.[9] Molotov spoke twice in the early sessions. He made the formal opening address on 26 January, and the major report on the 'The Tasks of the Second Five Year Plan' on 3 February.[10] Towards the end of this he made an attack on both Left and Right oppositions. Like the criticism by most other delegates, however, the attack was notably low key and represented a much smaller proportion of the speech than normal. Perhaps this was because it was vital to secure the acceptance of the Plan over which there was considerable controversy.[11]

In old age, Molotov denied rumours that at the XVII Congress Stalin received fewer votes than Kirov in the elections, although he admitted that both he and Stalin had received 'black balls', and maintained that this was perfectly normal.[12] He confirmed that there was a move to nominate Kirov as General Secretary, but Kirov refused the approach and reported the matter to Stalin.[13] When Stalin saw Kirov at the end of the Congress and suggested that he should be transferred to work in Moscow, Molotov supported Stalin and noted Kirov's angry reaction.[14] There is a story that, at this time, Stalin offered his resignation at a meeting of the Politburo. Molotov is rumoured to have taken the lead in urging him to stay on and said: 'No one can replace you'; although in another version, Molotov is supposed to have said: 'for the time being the party still had confidence in Stalin; they would see how things were in a year's time'.[15] If true, either version confirms that he was standing staunchly with Stalin.

The XVII Congress was followed by a period of dispute between Kirov and the Leningrad party apparatus on the one hand, and Stalin and his Politburo allies on the other. They pressed for an improvement in Leningrad's economic performance and an acceleration of collectivisation in the Leningrad areas.[16] As chairman of Sovnarkom, Molotov was deeply involved in this controversy, and challenged the decision of the Leningrad Soviet to set up a special account for funds acquired from goods sold at commercial prices. He peremptorily summoned Kirov to appear at Sovnarkom.[17]

In early August, following the abolition of the OGPU and the creation of the NKVD (People's Commissariat for Internal Affairs), supposedly part of a new drive to respect 'legality', Molotov spoke at a meeting of procuracy officials. He contended that the main defect in the work of the OGPU had been to rely on the confession of defendants – it decided questions in a political way, and did not attach importance to the investigation. He went on to emphasise the more limited powers of the new secret police apparatus, and said that many of the special powers of the OGPU had been transferred to the normal judicial apparatus.[18] If these statements reflected what was supposed to be the official view of the time, they were rather ironic in view of what was to follow.

In September, when senior politicians visited different regions to oversee the procurements, Molotov went to western Siberia.[19] On his journey to Prokop'evsk in the Kemerovo mining area, the car in which he was travelling came off the road. He was not injured, and apparently had the reprimand given to the chauffeur cancelled,[20] but the incident was to figure as an attempt on his life in the Pyatakov trial of January 1937, and the true nature of the event was not revealed until the XXII Party Congress.[21] In November 1934, Molotov was back in Moscow for the Central Committee plenum, which with Stalin and Kaganovich he dominated, and which focused on the question of the abolition of bread rationing.[22]

The Kirov murder and after

In old age, when asked about Stalin's implication in the Kirov murder, Molotov ascribed the speculation to hints in the Secret Speech, and cited the conclusions of the commission he chaired in the Khrushchev era, which naturally enough decided that Stalin was not implicated.[23] Irrespective of the issues of Stalin's culpability and Molotov's truthfulness, next to Stalin he was probably more closely involved than anyone else in the immediate response to Kirov's death.

When Mikhael Chudov, Kirov's deputy in Leningrad, telephoned Stalin between 4.30 and 5.30 pm, on 1 December 1934, to report Kirov's murder, Molotov with Kaganovich, Voroshilov and Andrei Zhdanov had been with Stalin in his office since 3.05 pm. Genrikh Yagoda, the head of secret police, presumably summoned, arrived shortly afterwards, followed by other NKVD officials.[24] At 6.20 pm, other Politburo members, including Kalinin, joined them. Stalin presumably consulted this group as he drew up the notorious law of 1 December, which speeded up trials of those accused of terrorist acts, forbade appeals for pardon and ordered immediate execution of those convicted. Enukidze, the secretary of TsIK, whose signature with that of Kalinin was necessary for the decree, joined at 6.45 pm.[25] Stalin, Molotov, Voroshilov, Zhdanov and Yagoda left for Leningrad by train that evening, for Stalin to conduct a personal investigation into the murder. A. Vyshinskii, deputy USSR prosecutor, and senior investigators from the central NKVD apparatus in Moscow, accompanied them.[26]

When they arrived, early the next morning, the group called at the hospital where the post-mortem on Kirov took place, and visited Kirov's wife. The party then divided. Molotov remained with Stalin and other senior colleagues when Stalin interrogated the assassin, Leonid Nikolaev, Leningrad NKVD officials and others.[27] The investigations continued on 3 December, when Nikolaev apparently continued to insist that he had acted alone.[28] Then, after they had performed the last half-hour vigil over Kirov's catafalque at 9.30 on the evening of 3 December, where Molotov 'appeared very calm, his face expressionless', the group departed for Moscow on the train carrying Kirov's coffin.[29] Molotov also took his turn in the vigil over Kirov's body whilst it was lying in state in Moscow on 4 and 5 December, and was one of the pallbearers at the funeral on 7 December. He spoke first at the funeral and his speech was given prominence in the press.[30] His close involvement with Stalin in these events throws no light on the question of whether there was a conspiracy in which he was involved.

On 8 December, Stalin held a three-hour meeting in his office with NKVD officials and the colleagues with whom he visited Leningrad. Knight implies that after this meeting former Zinovievite oppositionists began to be blamed for the murder, although Molotov glosses over this in his memoirs.[31] When the formal indictment against the group was published on 27 December, they were accused of a plot to kill Stalin, Molotov and Kaganovich, as well as Kirov.[32] There was now a wave of arrests in Leningrad, but it is not clear if these were centrally directed or a reaction of the Leningrad NKVD.[33] Thirty thousand 'social aliens' were expelled: members of the intelligentsia, former nobles, tsarist officials and their families. Molotov, as chairman of Sovnarkom, received protests from the internationally renowned physiologist, academician I. Pavlov, who stated that the arrests and expulsions were against the interests of international cultural co-operation, and requested the release of certain intellectuals and their families. Molotov's reply, apparently approved by Stalin, was to explain the wave of terror as a response to the capitalist threat to the construction of socialism in the USSR, and the need to take action against 'malicious anti-Soviet elements' in Leningrad, a city very near to the border. In a final letter, in December 1935, Molotov, who had referred the cases that Pavlov had mentioned to Yagoda, whilst he insisted on the need for the arrests, was conciliatory, and admitted that mistakes had been made in some cases, which would be remedied by the thorough investigations. He was, however, totally negative with regard to former clergy and their dependants: they were needed in their time, but Marxist philosophers were necessary now to build a new communist culture.[34] Molotov's position on the Terror was thus established very early.

The sudden death of Kuibyshev, his closest ally in Sovnarkom, on 23 January 1935,[35] put Molotov under increased pressure, but the early months of 1935 were quiet, as the case against Zinoviev, Kamenev and others accused of Kirov's murder was developed. There seems no evidence to support Trotsky's statements in his diary that Molotov was under a cloud at this time and was about to be replaced by Chubar'.[36] He was involved in the intensification of repression. As Sovnarkom chairman he was signatory to the 7 April decree which extended the death penalty to children as young as twelve; of the 9 June decree which imposed the death penalty for flight abroad;[37] and of the 17 June decree 'On Procedures for the Conduct of Arrests', which hinted that senior party leaders might be arrested.[38] In addition, he must have been fully identified with the Central Committee (Politburo) decrees of 25 May and 25 June that abolished the Society of Old Bolsheviks and the Society of Former Political Prisoners. These societies had apparently organised a petition against the use of the death penalty on former leaders of the opposition.[39]

Tension increased in early summer of 1935 with the revelation of the 'Kremlin affair'. One hundred and ten Kremlin employees were accused of planning terrorist attacks against the country's leaders, among whom Molotov was named. Enukidze, as head of the Kremlin staff, was accused of lack of vigilance, and Nikolai Ezhov, a Central Committee secretary at this time, attacked him at the June 1935 plenum. Molotov chaired the session that expelled Enukidze from the Party, and Ezhov accused Zinoviev, Kamenev and Trotsky of direct involvement in the Kirov murder for the first time.[40]

Late in the year, with the rest of the political leadership, as his correspondence shows, Molotov was fully committed to repression against those who attempted to sabotage or resist the Stakhanovite campaign.[41] On 15 October, in the Kremlin, with Andreev, he congratulated a group of Stakhanovites; and at the first Stakhanovite conference, 14–17 November, he lashed out at 'bureaucrats, enemies of the Stakhanov movement' as a new 'kind of saboteur of the workers' cause'. He claimed that production plans did not fix maximums, only minimums.[42] Molotov then presented the resolution on 'industry and transport and the Stakhanovite movement' at the Central Committee plenum in December 1935.[43]

1936–1938

In early 1936, the party leadership attempted to ease repression. In February, Procurator Vyshinskii wrote to Molotov, as Sovnarkom chairman, and called for a reduction in the NKVD's administrative powers. He pointed out that abuses were likely to increase, and asked for cases to be transferred to the regular courts.[44] He also complained to Stalin that the NKVD refused to release prisoners whom procurators had ordered to be freed because of lack of evidence, and Stalin wrote to Molotov to say that he believed that Vyshinskii was right.[45] This mood seemed to continue. In June 1936, when the Central Committee plenum met, Stalin seemed to be against mass expulsion of ordinary members, but attempting to turn the repression on to former leading oppositionists, perhaps partly because of the impending trial of Zinoviev and Kamenev.[46] In the debate on Ezhov's report on 'party members expelled and their appeals', Molotov, as chairman, raised the question of a request by Enukidze to be reinstated in the Party. He supported a motion that the ban on his re-admission be lifted, and that a local party organisation should decide the matter. When it was suggested that the plenum might re-admit Enukidze as no local organisation would dare to, Molotov claimed that the plenum was 'too solemn an occasion' for this. Stalin supported him, and pointed out that it would mean that Enukidze had been expelled from the Party at one plenum and reinstated at the next. The motion that the matter should be left to a local party organisation, was then carried.[47]

Final preparations were now in hand for the trial of the 'Trotskyite–Zinovievite Centre'. This was to be a most difficult time for Molotov. There was a deep rift with Stalin, and for a period he was in considerable personal danger. Molotov's behaviour at this time does not suggest that he had any reservations about the attack on former oppositionists. A not very reliable source records that Sergei Mrachovsky, on his way to see Stalin, whilst under interrogation for the Zinoviev–Kamenev Trial, met Molotov in Stalin's reception room. Molotov advised him:

> You are going to see *him*. Be frank with him my dear Sergei, hide nothing. Otherwise you will end before the firing squad.[48]

In 1937, Trotsky claimed that there were differences between Stalin and Molotov over Stalin's change in line from the theory of 'social-fascism' to the policy of the 'Popular Front'.[49] This may be linked to an attempt to commit Stalin to a pro-German policy at an interview with Shastenet, the correspondent of *Le Temps*, on 19 March 1936, and the most likely cause of the breach with Stalin.[50] During the interview, when asked if a rapprochement between Germany and the Soviet Union was possible in the present circumstances, Molotov replied:

> There is a tendency among certain sections of the Soviet public towards an attitude of thoroughgoing irreconcilability to the present rulers of Germany, particularly because of the ever repeated hostile speeches of the German leaders against the Soviet Union. But the chief tendency, and the one that determines the Soviet government's policy, thinks an improvement in Soviet–German relations possible. Of course, this might happen in several ways. One of the best would be the re-entry of Germany into the League of Nations, provided of course, that Germany gave real proof of its respect for international treaties, that it showed on its part, that it would observe its international responsibilities in accordance with the real interests of peace in Europe and the interests of universal peace. With the fulfilment of these conditions the participation of Germany in the League of Nations would be in the interests of peace and would meet with a positive response on our part.
>
> *Shastenet.* Even Hitler's Germany?
>
> *Molotov.* Yes, even Hitler's Germany.[51]

This statement was quite remarkable. Molotov admitted differences of opinion among the political leadership, and by references to the 'chief tendency', made Stalin's position clear, and committed him to a specific pro-German policy. Moreover, the statement was made shortly after an interview in which Stalin had condemned Hitler's threats against the Soviet Union, and shortly after Hitler had occupied the Rhineland.[52]

In the same interview, Molotov said that the internal situation of the USSR no longer demanded 'administrative measures' carried out previously, and that the strength of the opposition: 'terrorists and the wreckers of social property and their allies' grew weaker.[53] These statements must throw considerable doubt on Molotov as party to a Stalinist terror conspiracy. If, however, they were a legacy of the slackening of repression in early 1936, they were at odds with the campaign to shake up the economic bureaucracy which arose from the Stakhanovite movement, and the upsurge in Terror at the time of the Zinoviev–Kamenev trial. They may have been an additional cause for Stalin's displeasure. Resistance to repression at this time, by Ordzhonikidze and Kaganovich, was to cause friction between them and Stalin. Kaganovich came into line in the summer, after which he consistently supported the Terror, but Ordzhonikidze continued to try to support his cadres.[54]

The crisis in Molotov's relations with Stalin took some while to mature. With Stalin and Voroshilov, he visited the dying Gorky on 8 June, and was a pallbearer and leading speaker at Gorky's funeral on 20 June.[55] His name was, however, omitted from the list of potential victims whom the 'Trotskyite–Zinovieivite' conspirators aimed to kill in the letter from the Central Committee to national, regional and local committees, dated 29 July 1936,[56] and from the indictment of 'The Trotskyite–Zinovievite Centre' trial of August 1936. Press reports and the official record of the trial confirm that this was no accident. On more than fourteen occasions, when the defendants specified the names of the leaders they allegedly conspired to assassinate, and four times in Vyshinskii's closing speech, Molotov's name was never mentioned, although he was head of the Soviet government and the phrase 'leaders of the Soviet state' was used more than once.[57]

According to Alexander Orlov, a not very reliable authority, Stalin personally crossed out Molotov's name from the interrogation record of I. Reingold, one of the accused, and from that point onward the NKVD omitted Molotov's name.[58] If the veracity of this is open to question, it cannot be doubted that the name of the head of the Soviet government would not have been omitted from the list of potential victims without Stalin's personal approval. Nadezhda Mandelstam's comment 'I have heard of a woman who heroically went through torture rather than give "evidence" against Molotov', which referred to her husband's portrayal of Molotov as 'thin necked', may relate to this time,[59] as may Molotov's comment to Chuev,

> My first secretary got arrested, then my second secretary got arrested too. I sensed danger gathering around me.[60]

His daughter's nursemaid, a Volga German, was apparently also arrested.[61]

Stalin's office diary provides no further evidence of the breach. In July 1936, as Sovnarkom chairman, Molotov was involved in organising the Commissariats of

Justice and Health created in the new constitution.[62] He continued to meet Stalin in his office up to 20 July, but there was then no interview until 25 October.[63] Molotov was away from approximately 27 July until 1 September,[64] and Stalin was on leave from 14 August to 25 October. Unusually, however, Molotov was not mentioned in Kaganovich's correspondence with Stalin whilst on leave, and there was no mention of consulting him. Indeed, Kaganovich and Chubar' referred a telegram from the Second International, addressed to the chairman of Sovnarkom, to Stalin. He ordered the telegram, a plea for impartial procedures in the Zinoviev–Kamenev trial, to be published in the press, with a statement that this was the business of the Supreme Court, not of Sovnarkom. When Molotov returned from vacation he joined Kaganovich in correspondence with Stalin, which suggests that the breach was now healed.[65]

Orlov suggests that whilst Molotov was on leave, a convenient preface to his arrest, Stalin had him watched to prevent his suicide. He claims that Stalin did not go to the station to see Molotov depart, then sent a message to say that he had missed the train: again an attempt to reassure Molotov to prevent suicide.[66] During this period, as Trotsky noted, Molotov was not quoted or praised, nor did his photograph appear in the press.[67]

A Russian historian, K. A. Zalesskii, states that Molotov resisted an *open* trial of Kamenev and Zinoviev.[68] Conquest also suggests that Molotov 'in some way dragged his feet about the plan to destroy the Old Bolsheviks'.[69] This seems to be extremely unlikely. The most that can be said is, that if it was the reason for the rift, the vacation of one and a half months, authorised by the Politburo on 19 June 1936,[70] was very opportune. It meant that Molotov was away whilst Stalin and the Politburo finalised the indictment, list of defendants and sentences for the trial.[71] Molotov, however, did not oppose the practice of show trials. As Central Committee secretary, as early as February 1922, he had been responsible for distribution to the Politburo of copies of Lenin's letters to Commissar of Justice, Dimitrii Kurskii, which pointed out their educational value.[72] He had also been at the forefront in the Shakhty Affair, and believed that its chief value was for propaganda.[73] In 1930, Stalin and he had corresponded about the advisability of the Industrial Party trial,[74] and by 1931 Molotov accepted that show trials were useful to discredit former oppositionists. In 1933 he had taken the initiative in the Communard trial.[75] At the end of his life Molotov still offered weak Stalinist justifications for the trials during the Terror. He maintained that no other evidence besides confessions were required because the party leaders were certain the defendants were guilty. He denied that cases were fabricated, and within six months, in 1973, gave two slightly different explanations for the improbable confessions. First, he explained them as an opposition stratagem to carry on the struggle against the Party at the public trials: they maligned themselves to show how preposterous the trial was. Alternatively, he argued that the testimony was reduced to the point of absurdity because the accused were so embittered. He claimed that the idea that defendants at the trials were promised life in return for a confession was a 'White Guard' version.[76]

Molotov apparently did nothing to restore himself to favour. One can only hypothesise that Stalin, whatever Molotov had done to incur his wrath, eventually felt that he could not do without his right-hand man. That he was not a member of the Politburo commission present at the confrontation between Bukharin, Rykov and the arrested Sokolnikov, on 8 September,[77] was perhaps a sign that he had not yet fully recovered his position. On 21 September, however, the attempt on his life was mentioned in an interrogation to be cited in the trial of Pyatakov.[78] On 25 September, he and Kaganovich were the named recipients of the famous telegram from Stalin and Zhdanov which demanded that Yagoda should be replaced by Ezhov as Commissar for Internal Affairs.[79] Molotov signed the decree that appointed Ezhov head of the NKVD the next day, together with those that dismissed Rykov from the post of Commissar for Communications, and replaced him with Yagoda.[80] Molotov's view on Yagoda was that he was always too sympathetic to former oppositionists.[81] This is in line with David Shearer's view that the reason for the replacement of Yagoda with Ezhov in August 1936 was because the former concentrated on 'social disorder'. Yagoda failed to distinguish this from political crime, when Stalin believed that the threat of counter-revolution had become more dangerous.[82] Molotov also offered the lame excuse that 'oppositionists' like Yagoda succeeded in retaining top positions for a long while, and corrupted the Terror process, when they encouraged excesses and made mistakes unavoidable.[83]

In the Kemerovo trial in Novosibirsk, in November 1936, the attempt on Molotov's life was again mentioned,[84] a further sign that his relations with Stalin were restored, as was the fact that when he was denounced for 'improper behaviour', Ezhov forwarded the denunciation to him on 3 November.[85] Then, at the Central Committee plenum, 4–7 December 1936, when Ezhov attacked Bukharin, Rykov and Tomsky, he not only mentioned the plot to kill Molotov, but also spoke of a further attempt on the lives of Stalin, Kaganovich and Molotov in 1936, and Molotov intervened at one point to secure clarification. With Kaganovich, Lavrentii Beriya and other leading supporters of Stalin, Molotov joined in the attack on Bukharin and Rykov, and reminded Bukharin that Kamenev and Zinoviev had been party members for thirty years.[86] In his own speech, when he summed up for the Stalin group – a sign that he had fully recovered his position, Molotov early on attacked Tomsky who had already committed suicide. He reflected Stalin's view that recent suicides were an attack on the Party:

> Tomsky's suicide is a premeditated conspiracy, in which Tomsky arranged with not one, but several people to commit suicide and once again strike a blow against the Central Committee.[87]

This extraordinary charge was clearly dictated by the circumstances of the time. He attacked Bukharin for

> always acting as a lawyer. . . . You know how to make use of tears and sighs. But I personally do not believe these tears. . . . so much and so thoroughly has Bukharin lied through his teeth these past few years.

When Bukharin claimed that he had the right to defend himself, Molotov continued:

> I agree . . . a thousand times over. But I consider it my right not to believe your words. Because you are a political hypocrite. And we shall verify this through the courts. . . . We are not political cowards. It is rather you who are the coward.[88]

Molotov reminded the plenum of Bukharin's struggle with the Party over collectivisation, and of the Right deviation.[89] In response, Bukharin accused Molotov of shouting 'directed slogans'.[90] If this reflected the particular animosity between Molotov and Bukharin, in December 1936 Molotov may have been seeking to consolidate his own position with Stalin when he was especially vituperative against Bukharin.[91] He must also have been well aware that Bukharin did not conceal that he had a low opinion of his intellect.[92]

Despite this attack, and Stalin and Molotov taking the lead at a confrontation between Bukharin on one side, and Pyatakov, Radek and several other prisoners on the other;[93] the plenum, on Stalin's proposal, postponed a decision on the question of Bukharin and Rykov.[94] Molotov was present at the confrontation between Radek and Bukharin on 13 January 1937, but made only brief interventions especially on the matter of Bukharin and Radek's contacts with foreigners. He branded William Bullitt, the American ambassador, as a fascist. Radek was plainly puzzled that Zinoviev and Kamanev had not named Molotov as a potential victim.[95]

In the Pyatakov Trial, 23–30 January 1937, the attempt on Molotov's life in 1934 was referred to on seven occasions; this time a plot to derail the train on which he was travelling at Sverdlovsk, was added to the story.[96] Medvedev claimed that 'Molotov made up the whole story for the sake of provocation'.[97] If it is unlikely that he personally invented the assassination attempts, the fact that attempts on Molotov's life were mentioned more than those on any other Soviet leader was a sign that he had recovered his position with Stalin.

Following this trial, a Central Committee plenum scheduled for 19 February was postponed because of the death of Ordzhonikidze on 18 February. Molotov had seen him on Sovnarkom business the previous day, when they both attended a Politburo meeting about the plenum. He arrived with Stalin and other Politburo members soon after Ordzhonikidze's death, in the evening of 18 February.[98] Molotov's brother Nikolai apparently photographed Stalin, Molotov and other party leaders round the body.[99] Molotov took his turn at Ordzhonikidze's lying in state and spoke first at his funeral. He accepted the official line that his death was from a heart attack,[100] but knew otherwise, and commented in his memoirs:

> By his last act he proved that ultimately he was unstable. He had opposed Stalin, of course, and the party line. Yes, the party line. This was such a very bad step. It couldn't be interpreted any other way.[101]

When the plenum opened on 23 February 1937, Ezhov reported on the charges against Bukharin and Rykov. Bukharin replied first, and Molotov, although he was chairman, was amongst those who interrupted to abuse him. He shouted that

Bukharin confirmed his fascist connections when he cast doubt on previous confessions. Stalin cut him off. Molotov's attacks on Rykov, who followed Bukharin, were even more vituperative.[102] On the third day, no longer in the chair, it was Molotov's turn to lead the attack on Bukharin and Rykov. With interruptions in support from Stalin's other lieutenants, he traced Bukharin's differences with Lenin from 1916, reminded his listeners of the struggle with the Right in the later 1920s, and Bukharin's career in the 1930s. He concluded

> If rightists and Trotskyists now say to us – not all, but many: 'Yes, we have committed sabotage, yes, we are engaged in terrorism, yes, we have contaminated the workers' water, we have poisoned the workers with gas in their workshops'. ... this means they are people who have now broken with the working class, with our party, with Marxism and Leninism. It means that they are in another camp ... If you begin to struggle against the party and change to open counterrevolutionary action, we will deal with you as is appropriate to deal with such gentlemen.[103]

On 26 February, when Bukharin and Rykov were given another chance to speak, Molotov again interrupted and attacked Bukharin. He asked 'Is there at least one Rightist who gives plausible testimony or are there no such Rightists'?[104] When it was Rykov's turn to speak, Molotov was again in the chair, but this did not prevent him asking questions to make Rykov look like a deliberate liar which greatly damaged him. After this, Molotov figured prominently in the commission and sub-commission which compiled the resolution that expelled Bukharin and Rykov from the Party and ordered that their case be handed over to the NKVD.[105]

Molotov was allocated the report on 'wrecking' in heavy industry that Ordzhonikidze had been preparing at the time of his death; the dispute on the repressions, which arose from Stalin's criticism of Ordzhonikidze's draft, having led to Ordzhonikidze's suicide.[106] On 28 February, in his statement: 'Lessons of the wrecking, diversionist and espionage activities of the Japanese–German–Trotskyite agents', Molotov cited and criticised the reports which had been prepared for Ordzhonikidze.[107] Stalin had approved the draft of the harsh speech, and made comments that indicate his fear of the increased danger of disloyalty during a war.[108] Molotov warned that despite apparent success in plan fulfilment in industry, the wrecking, sabotage and espionage of Japanese–German–Trotskyite agents had caused serious damage. He described the supposed activities of Pyatakov and his supporters, and claimed that the distinguishing feature of the present wrecking campaign was that the culprits held party cards: they masqueraded as communists – 'ardent supporters of the Soviet regime'. He was also emphatic that the Rightists: Bukharin, Rykov and their supporters, were 'in one company with the Trotskyites as wreckers, diversionists and spies'. He called for an expansion of self-criticism as demanded by Stalin in connection with the Shakhty affair, in 1928. New cadres had not only to 'master technique', but they also had to develop their capacity for self-criticism, and be especially vigilant. He attacked bureaucratic methods of leadership and singled out Moisei Kalmanovich, the head of the Commissariat for

Sovkhozy, soon to be arrested. He said that his 'unconcern' was 'incomprehensible', that he and his assistants should 'set about purging their apparatus': this responsibility could not be passed to the NKVD or the Commission for Soviet Control. He then attacked the commissariats in general where

> the situation with regard to the political understanding of the exposed cases of wrecking is far from satisfactory. ... *We are still not vigilant enough with regard to the enemy and we must improve the education of cadres in Bolshevism.*

In conclusion he asserted that it was necessary to defeat the wreckers, saboteurs and spies, if the USSR was to 'catch up and overtake' the capitalist countries.[109] If Molotov made clear that he did not support a campaign against everyone who had ever opposed the party line, but was following Stalin's line that former oppositionists were to be evaluated on their merits,[110] his attack on the government, the body he headed, was devastating. In his concluding remarks on this agenda item, on 2 March, he listed the number of wreckers discovered in the government apparatus. These totalled 2132. They included 585 in the Commissariat for Heavy Industry, as well as 5 in the Administration of the White Sea Canal, 77 in the Academy of Science and higher technical education, 68 among the editorial bodies of the press and 17 among court and procuracy workers. He singled out the Commissariat for Light Industry and the Commissariat for Water Transport for attack, and went back to the reports prepared for Ordzhonikidze. He claimed that in two, there was not one word about 'wrecking' in 54 pages. One of these reports was on Kemerovo, and Molotov was perhaps reminding his audience about the supposed attempt on his life, but it was also an indirect charge of 'lack of vigilance' against Ordzhonikidze himself. Molotov also spoke of the need to check for wrecking in the armed forces, and laxness there against enemies of the people. With some officers already under arrest, this was taken as a directive for the arrest of Tukhachevsky and other military leaders.[111]

For the remainder of the plenum, Molotov contented himself with occasional interruptions hostile to those under attack when Ezhov delivered his report on 'Lessons of wrecking sabotage and spying of Japanese–German–Trotskyite agents in the NKVD' – the beginning of the attack on Yagoda; and during Stalin's report on 'Deficiencies in Party work'. In this, his statement that the class struggle sharpened the closer the USSR came to socialism, provided the theoretical underpinning for the repressions.[112]

Molotov was now fully identified with promoting the Terror. In early April, after Yagoda was arrested, at a meeting of Sovnarkom presided over by Molotov,[113] the Molotovs took over his dacha.[114] The arrest of the generals and important civilian figures in May, such as Molotov's deputy and close associate Rudzutak, not linked to previous oppositions, marked a turning point. The Terror was now turned against anyone suspected of disloyalty to Stalin and his lieutenants.[115] Questioned by Chuev, about his visit with other Politburo members to Rudzutak whilst under investigation, Molotov excused himself by saying that there were incriminating materials against Rudzutak, and that although he was not 100 per cent convinced, he could not do anything to protect Rudzutak because of personal impressions. Molotov was also present at NKVD headquarters when Antipov and Chubar', both deputy chairmen of Sovnarkom, were investigated. He said of Chubar' in his memoirs, 'I felt he might be lying'. Rudzutak complained of torture and although Molotov admitted that this was probable,[116] he was generally very reticent about torture, and ignored comments by Chuev that people were beaten up.[117] He denied that he had issued a directive on the use of torture with Stalin, but in fact, counter-signed a decree which approved its use in 1937.[118]

To the end of his life, Molotov insisted that the case of Tukhachevsky and the other generals was not a mistake. He maintained that Tukhachevsky feared arrest and was preparing a coup from mid-1936, and that the date of this was known.[119] His belief in Tukhachevsky's guilt is not surprising. As early as September 1930, Stalin wrote to Molotov about a possible plot by Tukhachevsky, and urged Ordzhonikidze to discuss the matter with him, although on this occasion Tukhachevsky was exonerated.[120] Molotov signed the Politburo decree which replaced the military leaders[121] and was fully identified with the Politburo resolution proposed by Stalin, on 24 May 1937, that expelled Rudzutak and Tukhachevsky from the Central Committee, two days after Tukhachevsky's arrest.[122] He was present with Stalin and other senior Politburo members at the meeting of the Military Council (*Voennyi Sovet*), 1–4 June, when Voroshilov presented a report on the military conspiracy.[123] He also added 'a perfect description' to Stalin's endorsement: 'Scoundrel and prostitute' on Iona Yakir's letter protesting his innocence[124] and worked with Stalin to arrange and direct the trial of the officers and the application of the death penalty, as Stalin's office diary shows.[125] One Russian historian, who claims to have used an archival source, states that between 27 February 1937 and 12 November 1938, Stalin, Molotov and Kaganovich sanctioned the execution of 38,679 Red Army officers and 3000 naval officers.[126] These figures seem, however, to be an exaggeration. Roger Reese cites a total of 34,301 officers removed from the Red Army and Air Force during the Ezhovshchina. Of these, 11,596 were reinstated by May 1940, which leaves 22,705 either dead, in the Gulag or in civilian society in disgrace.[127] In his memoirs Molotov claimed that '1937 was necessary' to ensure that in war time there was not a fifth column.

> It is doubtful if these people were spies, but they were connected with spies, and the main point is that at the critical moment they could not be relied on. ... If Tukhachevsky and Yakir and Rykov and Zinoviev, when there was a war, went into opposition ... it would mean disaster.[128]

Self-justification was the basis for Molotov's explanation, but the need for stability in war time and the elimination of a potential fifth column, was a motivation for the Terror.[129]

At the June 1937 Central Committee plenum, Molotov's chief concern was with the forthcoming elections to the new Supreme Soviet and the turnover tax, although he did make reference to 'enemies of the people'.[130] When, however, Josif Pyatnitskii, head of the political-administrative department of the Central

Committee, said he opposed the use of the death penalty in the case of Bukharin, Rykov and other Right leaders, Molotov, on Stalin's instructions, with Kaganovich and Voroshilov, tried to persuade Pyatanitskii to withdraw his remarks. Molotov told Pyatnitskii to think of the fate of his young wife and two sons if he persisted in the line he was taking. Pyatnitskii was arrested in early July.[131]

In August, Molotov led a Politburo delegation with Ezhov amongst its members, to 'verify' the party leadership to the Ukraine.[132] When he arrived in Kiev, Molotov called a meeting of the Central Committee of the Ukrainian Party, where he made accusations of wrecking in agriculture, and demanded that S. Kosior, USSR Politburo member, General Secretary of the Ukrainian Party and leader of the Ukrainian Politburo, and two of his colleagues be expelled from the Party. When he encountered opposition, he dissolved the plenum and called a meeting of the Ukrainian Politburo, but this again resisted his pressure. Molotov therefore returned to Moscow, and the leaders of the Ukrainian Politburo were summoned there shortly afterwards. In 1938, Khrushchev replaced Kosior, who for a short while served in Sovnarkom USSR before he was arrested; but from the time of Molotov's visit there was a notable increase of repression in the Ukraine.[133] In December 1937, Molotov was present but not prominent at the celebrations for the twentieth anniversary of the founding of the NKVD, which were chaired by Mikoyan and from which Stalin was noticeably absent.[134]

The Terror was now entering a new phase. With the issue of Politburo Order no. 00447 in July 1937, against 'anti-Soviet elements', which set quotas for each region for arrest, imprisonment and execution of 'ex-kulaks', and established three-man commissions (the *troiki*) to carry this out, a mass operation by the NKVD commenced. Similar campaigns against other groups, which included members of national minorities, followed.[135] In this mass terror which consumed the country, sometimes known as the 'kulak operation', Molotov supported Stalin and agreed to requests from local authorities to increase the numbers that could be arrested, shot and imprisoned.[136] This whipped up hysteria and increased the Terror. It has been suggested that there was a feeling amongst the population in the summer of 1938 that only five men: Stalin, Molotov, Kaganovich, Voroshilov and Ezhov were 'insured against repression'.[137] The 1987 Politburo commission formed to study the repressions of the 1930s, concluded that 383 lists of persons to be arrested were sent to the Politburo in 1937 and 1938. These lists divided the victims into three categories: those to be shot, those to be imprisoned for a period from eight to twenty-five years, and those subject to imprisonment for less than eight years and exile. The lists included 44,000 names. Of these, 39,000 persons were to be shot, 5000 were in the second category and 102 in the third. Of the 383 lists, Stalin signed 362, Molotov 373, Voroshilov 195, Kaganovich 191 and Zhdanov 177; Ezhov, Mikoyan and S. Kosior signed less frequently. This seems to leave no doubt that Molotov was one of the principal perpetrators of the Terror, and Conquest claims that he suggested sentencing by list.[138] Volkogonov notes one list, dated 26 July 1938, of 138 persons arrested, to be executed if found guilty by the military tribunal, sent by Ezhov to Stalin, which has been endorsed 'Shoot all 138' by Stalin and Molotov. Another memo, which enclosed four lists with

736 names, is endorsed 'Yes' to shooting, by Stalin and Molotov; and they agreed the death penalty for a list as late as 12 December 1938, with the huge figure of 3167 names.[139] In his memoirs, Molotov admitted that he signed 'most, in fact, almost all, the arrest lists' as chairman of Sovnarkom, and that Stalin signed on behalf of the Party. He maintained that there was discussion. At another time, however, he admitted that because of haste, decisions had to be based on NKVD reports.[140] On the lists he received, Molotov underlined the numbers, not the names.[141]

After his devastating attack at the February–March 1937 plenum, it is not surprising that repression in the commissariats was stepped up. From 19 commissars and heads of two standing commissions who had the status of commissars, there were 13 changes in the last six months of 1937.[142] At the meeting of the Supreme Soviet, in January 1938, Zhdanov criticised the work of the Commissariat for Foreign Affairs and attacked the Commissariat for Water Transport. He also attacked Platon Kerzhentsev, the chairman of the Sovnarkom Committee for the Arts, because he did not encourage talent in youth and the nationalities. Other speakers, who attacked Nikolai Krylenko, the People's Commissar for Justice, and the Sovnarkom Committee for Procurements, supported Zhdanov.[143] When Molotov, who 'spent most of his time writing diligently, presumably preparing his speech, and seemed quite oblivious of his surroundings',[144] replied, he promised changes in the Commissariat for Foreign Affairs; made clear that this was the last chance for the present leadership of the Commissariat for Water Transport; and broadly accepted the criticisms of Krylenko. He was replaced, as was the leadership of the Committee for Procurements, which was reorganised into a commissariat. Kerzhentsev was also dismissed.[145] The 1987 commission noted that Molotov, as chairman, was particularly associated with the Terror in Sovnarkom, and that 20 out of 28 commissars and nearly 2000 workers from the commissariats were repressed in 1938. This did not include the Commissariat for Defence, the NKVD and the Commissariat for Foreign Affairs.[146] T. J. Uldricks has calculated that 34 per cent of the 'responsible' staff of that commissariat was purged; certain departments experienced three or four changes of command in 20 months. Among the top leadership of over 100 people: deputy commissars, members of the Soviet and ambassadors, 62 per cent were purged; only 16 per cent remained in their posts unscathed.[147] The commissariat was to suffer a further purge on Molotov's appointment as its head in 1939.

The situation at the fortnightly meetings of Sovnarkom in 1938[148] must have been very strange when its chairman knew that some of the commissars were about to be arrested. The effect of the purge was, however, not entirely negative for Molotov personally. In November 1937, Polina Molotov was selected as a deputy to Mikoyan at the Commissariat of the Food Industry,[149] and in January 1939 she was appointed as head of the newly created Commissariat of the Fish Industry. She was the first woman to achieve full membership of Sovnarkom since Molotov had been appointed chairman in December 1930.[150]

As early as October 1935, Molotov had approved Yagoda's proposals to deport groups of Poles from the Ukraine.[151] The 1987 commission put particular blame on him for supporting the repression of various national groups, especially the attack on those of Polish nationality, August to December 1937. Stalin, Molotov,

Kaganovich and Kosior authorised Ezhov's proposal that resulted in the repression of 18,193 persons. Molotov personally amended some verdicts from imprisonment to death.[152] He was also a key figure in the deportation of Koreans from the Far East to Kazakhstan and Uzbekistan at this time, described by one authority as 'the first ethnic cleansing of an entire nationality'.[153]

Molotov denounced Rukhimovich as a wrecker at the October 1937 Central Committee plenum.[154] He joined in the attack on Pavel Postyshev at the January 1938 Central Committee plenum, although he did say that those who made mistakes should be distinguished from 'wreckers'.[155] According to Khrushchev, Molotov was personally responsible for signing the death sentences for Postyshev and other leading Ukrainians, and for Kosior's wife.[156] In old age he admitted that he had amended verdicts, but was less clear when accused of altering one case to the death sentence.[157] Asked in 1986 why family members had been repressed, Molotov gave the excuse that it was necessary to isolate them to avoid the spread of complaints and negative political feeling.[158]

Molotov told Chuev that the NKVD might have distorted the evidence on the guilt of Bukharin and Rykov at their trial, and that there was a lack of concrete evidence, but 'we knew they were guilty, that they were enemies'![159] Two months after the trial, in his May 1938 speech on higher education, Molotov fully endorsed the terror process publicly, and emphasised the importance of ideological-political education in training new cadres, essential to build socialism and achieve victory in the struggle with spies and wreckers.[160] In the summer of 1938 he was present when Ezhov arranged for Boris Mel'nikov to testify against Pyatnitskii before Krupskaya and a group of Politburo members, to convince Krupskaya of Pyatnitskii's guilt. When Krupskaya called on Molotov to defend Pyatnitskii, he failed to say anything.[161]

When the Bukharin trial took place, in March 1938, there were already hints of attempts to bring the Terror under control, and Molotov received correspondence from Vyshinkii to this effect.[162] In the summer he is reputed to have clashed with Ezhov at a Sovnarkom meeting. In response to a question from Molotov, Ezhov replied:

> If I were in your place, Vyacheslav Mikhailovich, I would not ask competent organs those kinds of questions. Do not forget that one previous chairman of Sovnarkom, A. I. Rykov, has already been in my office. The road to me is not off limits even for you.

The fact that Molotov, on Stalin's suggestion, was able to secure a personal apology from Ezhov is evidence that the latter's power was now past its peak.[163] About this time, on Stalin's orders, with Mikoyan, and Beriya who had been appointed as Ezhov's deputy, he served on a commission to investigate the charges against the recently arrested deputy commissar, Ivan Tesovyan. In his memoirs, Molotov left the impression that he was partly responsible for Tesovyan's acquittal, but Mikoyan claimed that when the commission reported to Stalin, 'Molotov's face was like a mask'.[164] He was playing safe.

Molotov served with Malenkov, Beriya and Vyshinskii on the commission set up to investigate the NKVD, prior to Ezhov's fall,[165] and Stalin and Molotov began to question Ezhov's contacts with F. M. Konar, executed as a Polish spy in 1933.[166] Molotov was also involved in the meetings in November 1937 when Ezhov offered his 'resignation' as head of the NKVD.[167] In January 1939, as Sovnarkom chairman, Molotov reprimanded Ezhov for neglect of his duties as Commissar for Water Transport.[168]

In his memoirs, Molotov argued that Ezhov overreached himself and committed all sorts of mistakes because Stalin demanded greater repression. He specified particularly the plan to allocate a number of arrests and executions to districts in the 'kulak operation', and said that Ezhov had not been subject to supervision.[169] There may be some truth in this, but when he claimed that Ezhov had turned 'limits' into 'quotas', and assigned figures to *oblasti* and divided these to allocate totals to individual *raiony*,[170] he seems to offer no more than a very lame excuse for the mass terror.

By November 1938, before Ezhov's replacement by Beriya, Stalin and Molotov had signed decrees that halted the work of the notorious *troiki* and called for closer supervision of NKVD arrests and investigations.[171] Molotov's speech on the anniversary of the Revolution focused on the USSR's economic achievement and the dangerous foreign situation. Although he referred on several occasions to 'wrecking' he said nothing about the NKVD.[172]

Conclusion

Molotov's actions during the Terror demonstrate his commitment to the process, he stood alongside Stalin and never showed any remorse for the deaths for which he was responsible. He believed that the Terror was defensible for the survival of Stalin's government and justified Stalin's actions by saying 'there is no smoke without fire' and Stalin 'let an extra head fall' so that there was no vacillation during and after the war.[173] Perhaps, influenced by his own experience as a revolutionary constantly involved in conspiracy, he continued to assert the guilt of many of those accused, although he admitted that many others were persecuted unjustly.

His views were summarised in a book, *Facing New Tasks, on Completing the Construction of Socialism*, which he prepared in retirement, but which was never published. In this, he wrote that all the opposition groups, Trotskyites, Zinovievites and the Right, eventually developed links with foreign (capitalist) states, including Hitler's Germany, which aimed at the overthrow of the communist regime with their assistance. He excused grave errors in rooting out these counter-revolutionary groups, which were to be regretted, by saying that they were largely caused because the investigations fell into the hands of people later exposed as traitors, and because the emergency situation meant that no delay could be permitted in punitive measures.[174] At another time, he accounted for excesses because tests for loyalty and reliability were a very complicated process, which required harsh unquestioning discipline, and because of the shortage 'of ready-made pure people' who would carry it through. This meant that many who were honest and spoke frankly were expelled, while those who concealed everything and were eager to curry favour with the party chiefs, retained their positions.[175]

Molotov's dealings with his lifetime friend, Arosev, sum up his attitude to the Terror. Arosev left St. Petersburg for Moscow in 1917, then completed his higher education in western Europe and served as a Soviet diplomat. His appointments included ambassadorships to Latvia, Lithuania, Sweden and Czechoslovakia in the 1920s and early 1930s, but he was removed from the diplomatic service in 1932 as the result of a denunciation.[176] A writer and literary scholar, Arosev had then served as head of the All-Union Society for Cultural Links Abroad (VOKS) from March 1934.[177] After his return to Moscow, Arosev and his family resumed friendship with Molotov and Polina. They relaxed together and discussed literature. Molotov relayed to Arosev, on one occasion, Stalin's displeasure at his translation at the latter's meeting with Roman Rolland.[178] They also seem to have been close at the time of the death of Stalin's wife.[179] By late 1936, however, relations had become more distant, although Arosev still sent letters to Stalin via Molotov.[180] About to be arrested in June 1937, Arosev tried to telephone Molotov who on the first two occasions put the phone down, but Arosev then told Molotov he could hear him breathing. After several calls, Molotov said only two words, which implied that he would make arrangements for the children.[181]

In contrast to her husband, Polina Molotov continued to help the family of an 'enemy of the people' after the arrest. Molotov apparently chose not to help or remember his friend.[182] In 1955 Arosev was rehabilitated, and his daughter Olga Arosev, an actress, wrote to Molotov to tell him that his old school friend had been found not guilty, but received no reply. Polina, however, invited Arosev's daughter to visit them in the Kremlin. Molotov would say very little, except that it was a long while ago, but Polina, who had returned from the camps, maintained her friendship. There was a further interview after Molotov had been expelled from the Party when Olga Arosev challenged Molotov about his behaviour. Polina, however, excused him, saying that Molotov could do nothing and that Olga Arosev did not understand the situation in 1937.[183]

9
1939 – Molotov Becomes Foreign Minister

After the Great Terror, Molotov, like Stalin's other lieutenants, became more preoccupied with trying to retain the leader's confidence and repel possible rivals to ensure their own survival.[1] Moreover, after 1936, Stalin no longer took long vacations: he was a constant presence as he consolidated his tyrannical authority. The increase in his despotism was reflected in a decline in the number of meetings of top-level institutions: the Politburo met only six times in 1937, on four occasions in 1938, and only twice in 1939 and 1940.[2] Sovnarkom convened on 19 occasions in 1938, but met only 9 times in 1937, and there were only 12 meetings in 1936, 1939 and 1940. In addition, compared to the early years of the decade, when there could be twenty or thirty items on a Sovnarkom agenda, the number of agenda items was normally less than ten,[3] and discussion was often replaced by use of the *opros* procedure.[4] The new tyranny was reflected in the way that Molotov conducted Sovnarkom business. Nikolai Kuznetsov, who became Commissar for the Navy in 1939, wrote:

> When I was appointed ... in my ignorance I at first attempted to bring all questions to V. M. Molotov, Chairman of the Council of People's Commissars. But it was very difficult. Minor, daily affairs, still moved, but important ones got stuck. Whenever I was persistent it was suggested that I turn to Stalin.[5]

Another change was that authority was often delegated to permanent *ad hoc* committees. For instance, on 14 April 1937, the Politburo established a group for 'speedy resolution' of urgent foreign policy questions which consisted of Stalin, Molotov, Voroshilov, Kaganovich and Ezhov, and a parallel group for economic matters with Molotov, Stalin, Chubar', Mikoyan and Kaganovich as members, and Molotov as chairman.[6] This removed the necessity to obtain formal assent from the full Politburo for these matters and increased the power of the leading group of Stalin and his supporters, particularly as Stalin, Molotov and Kaganovich served on both committees.

Formal meetings of the Politburo, Sovnarkom, and other top-level party and government bodies, were partly replaced by meetings in Stalin's office. Unfortunately we know little about how business was transacted at these meetings and less about the part played by individuals. It can, however, be assumed that in the case of the Politburo, where even the *opros* practice soon fell into disuse, and Politburo *protokoly* merely listed decisions of the Politburo (*reshenie Politbyuro*), the 'decisions' were made in Stalin's office[7] and Molotov was party to them.

The meetings in Stalin's office increased in number throughout the 1930s. In 1931, Stalin's office diary records a total of 832 visitors, 1155 in 1938. In 1931 he saw Molotov 100 times, by 1938 the number had risen to 170.[8] Molotov was by far the most frequent visitor to Stalin's office. Between 1930 and 1953 he met Stalin there on 2927 occasions, for 8169 hours and was present for 76.5 per cent of Stalin's official meetings. Next to Molotov came Georgii Malenkov who from 1937 met Stalin for 3153 hours, then Voroshilov and Kaganovich, who between 1930 and 1953 met Stalin for 3484 and 3329 hours, respectively. The fact that Molotov was Sovnarkom chairman up to 1941, and responsible for foreign policy from May 1939 to March 1949, goes some way to explain why he was with Stalin for so many more hours than the dictator's other close associates.[9] It is also indicative of the close association between Stalin and Molotov, something on which Molotov was now far more dependent than the fact that he was a senior member of the Politburo.

The XVIII Congress

At the beginning of March 1939, Molotov was involved in the funeral arrangements for Krupskaya, and took his turn at the lying-in-state and was one of the pall bearers of the coffin.[10] At this time he was preparing for the forthcoming party congress. If there were no controversy now, and congresses were celebrations of the achievements of Stalinism, the long reports were still onerous. When he opened the Congress on 10 March 1939, Molotov immediately claimed that 'socialism had been built in the main', but reminded his audience of the Terror, when he referred to foreign intervention and spying. He hinted at plans for improvements in the standard of living and in education that he was to describe in more detail in his main report on the Third Five Year Plan. He claimed that 'No enemy can break down our Soviet Union. Any aggressor who attempts to, will only break his stupid head against our Soviet boundary posts'.[11] He did not know how prophetic his reference to foreign policy was to be for his career over the next few years. Molotov's short speech was followed by Stalin's report on the work of the Central Committee in which he mispronounced NarkomZem (*НаркомЗем*) – the Commissariat of Agriculture – as NarkomZyom (*НаркомЗём*). All subsequent speakers, including Molotov, repeated the mispronunciation, indicative of Stalin's new tyrannical power. Molotov explained in old age that if he had corrected Stalin he would have taken offence.[12]

On 14 March, Molotov delivered the major report on the Third Five Year Plan. He gave details of the Plan, and immediately noted that it marked a new period: the USSR had entered upon the stage of the gradual transition from socialism to communism. He repeated his claim that socialism had been achieved in the main, and said that Soviet society now consisted of two friendly classes, workers and peasants united in a common cause – the construction of communism. He told his audience: 'We think that it is high time the young but robust Soviet forces entered the arena of international competition for economic primacy'. He admitted, however, that the USSR had yet, in Lenin's words 'to catch up and overtake the advanced countries', particularly in industrial output per head of population. His orthodox views on the development of socialism were again apparent and he was still concerned with extracting the maximum from resources allocated.

The increased concern of the political leadership with the international situation was reflected when Molotov claimed that the USSR was confident of victory in a capitalist world where there was a growing danger of war, particularly from fascism. He also noted that German fascists were copying the concept of planning, although capitalism, even its fascist version, was incompatible with economic planning.[13]

Molotov becomes Foreign Minister

Molotov and foreign affairs 1931–1939

Following Molotov's first involvement in foreign affairs as party secretary in the early 1920s,[14] Chicherin, when he was in difficulties with his pro-German policy between 1925 and 1927 and threatened to resign, suggested that Molotov should replace him on more than one occasion.[15] If this was an early indication of Molotov's reputation for competence in foreign affairs and pro-German views, Chicherin's efforts came to nothing. In 1930, Litvinov, who was to pursue a policy of improved relations with the Western powers during Soviet industrialisation, replaced him. Throughout the 1930s, Molotov seems to have had a particular concern with Soviet–German relations. His report to the Congress of Soviets, in March 1931, for the first time demonstrated a noticeable pro-German stance. He pointed out that German foreign policy had of late been one of 'amicable co-operation,' and he recalled traditional Soviet–German friendship.[16] In his speech to TsIK in January 1933, before Hitler became Chancellor of Germany, his next major statement on foreign affairs, Molotov spoke of the 'special place' Germany occupied in the USSR's relations with foreign states and the strong economic ties with that country.[17]

After Hitler came to power in 1933, with increasing fear of a resurgent Germany, there were two foreign policy options for the USSR. The strategy of 'collective security' – a defensive alliance against an aggressor, particularly Germany, with France and Britain as the chief partners, was one. The alternative was a policy of conciliation and an attempt to reach an understanding with Germany, which had been the only real ally of the new communist regime during the early years of its existence.[18] It seems likely that, rather than an internal political struggle over which policy to adopt, between 1933 and 1939 Stalin allowed the pro-Western Litvinov and NarkomIndel (the Commissariat for Foreign Affairs) to take the lead in pursuit of the first alternative, and as a reinsurance, Molotov, as Sovnarkom chairman, became particularly associated with the second, on behalf of the Politburo.[19]

In early 1933 Soviet–German relations were poor, with Alfred Hugenberg's anti-Soviet speech at the World Economic Conference, and the public appearance of Stalin and Molotov at the Moscow funeral of the veteran German Communist,

Clara Zetkin, on 22 June 1933.[20] Molotov attempted to improve the situation, on 4 August 1933, at a meeting with Herbert von Dirksen, the German ambassador.[21] According to his record of the conversation, Molotov emphasised that the USSR did not consider the 1922 Treaty of Rapallo 'inexpedient' or 'disadvantageous', nor were there any grounds for Germany to raise this question. He assured the ambassador that the Soviet attitude to Germany remained unchanged, despite recent hostile German acts and statements, and that 'our future relations with Germany will depend exclusively on the position Germany assumes towards the USSR'. Molotov stressed that Dirksen grew emotional, but that he remained calm and correct.[22] In his report on the interview, Dirksen stated that the anxiety of Molotov, 'one of the really authoritative men and closest co-workers of Stalin', about 'German policy towards Russia seemed to be genuine'.[23]

In October 1933, Molotov was involved in attempts to maintain connections with Germany, after that country's sudden departure from the League of Nations: he cancelled a visit to Turkey and saw Dirksen.[24] His speech to the Moscow Soviet, on the anniversary of the revolution in November 1933, however, reflected alarm about Germany's actions. He noted that 'reactionary forces of a fascist type have become stronger ... inflaming the dark passions of nationalism and particularly anti-semitism'.[25] On 15 December, the American ambassador W. Bullitt, who was impressed by Molotov's dignity and intelligence, found him preoccupied with Japan. Molotov told Bullitt that 'the primary desire of the entire Soviet government was to avoid war and to obtain time to work out the domestic reconstruction which had scarcely begun', but he feared greatly that Japan would attack this spring; he considered an attack inevitable at some point, 'and 1935 as the probable limit of peace'.[26]

It would be consistent with Molotov's position that a month later, as Jonathan Haslam argues, he and Kaganovich were the least enthusiastic members of the Politburo about the Resolution of 12 December in favour of a collective security agreement and membership of the League of Nations on certain conditions.[27] In his speech to TsIK on 28 December 1933 Molotov emphasised the theme of a coming war, but said little about the League of Nations and collective action, in marked contrast to Litvinov the next day.[28] Molotov was prepared to talk of a 'reactionary fascist camp', but he was not willing like Litvinov to speak of 'pacific' powers in the capitalist world.[29] He, more strongly than Litvinov, still held out the possibility of reconciliation with Germany, and blamed deteriorating relations on the 'reactionary desires and aggressive imperialist plans' of 'the ideologues of National Socialism', which were 'incompatible with the great future before Germany'.[30] When he spoke to the Congress of Soviets, on 28 January 1935, he left the door slightly open for a reconciliation with Germany, when he said 'we make no secret of our profound respect for the German people as one of the great peoples of modern times', but he quoted *Mein Kampf* and warned that the statement 'when we [the National Socialists] speak of new lands in Europe today, we can only think of Russia and her border states', remained in force.[31]

A few weeks later, at the end of March 1935, when Anthony Eden, then Lord Privy Seal, visited Moscow, Molotov was present as head of government when

Eden saw Stalin in Molotov's office in the Kremlin. The record of the meeting shows that Molotov made the first official response for the USSR in the dialogue. He stated that the policy of the USSR was peace; it did not want new lands and did not seek to interfere in the internal affairs of the British empire. Apart from one jocular remark about Ivan Maiskii, the Soviet ambassador to Great Britain, after this, however, Molotov was silent, and it was left to Stalin to deal with foreign policy in detail, something that was to become typical of Molotov's behaviour in interviews with foreign politicians when Stalin was present.[32]

The signing of the Treaty of Mutual Assistance with France, in May 1935, the high point for Litvinov's policy of collective security, did not achieve the improvement in relations hoped for, and because of the failure of the French to implement the military clauses, fears about security remained in the USSR.[33] Molotov announced an increase in the defence budget in his speech to TsIK on 10 January 1936, but he also tried to initiate a rapprochement with Germany, since relations with that country had remained poor since the autumn of 1935. His comments have been taken as evidence that he was always in favour of a *rapprochement* with Germany.[34] He recalled and repeated his references to *Mein Kampf*, made in 1935, and claimed that by its silence on the matter, the German fascists had not disowned the policy of territorial conquest. They had

> openly transformed the country which has fallen into their hands into a military camp ... and [were] armed with everything which converts modern warfare into a mass slaughter not only of soldiers at the front, but also of simple, peaceful citizens, women and children.

He continued straightaway, however, to note the credit agreement of 1935 and German proposals for a further agreement:

> The development of commercial and economic relations with other States, irrespective of the political forces which are temporarily ruling those countries, is in conformity with the policy of the Soviet Government. ... It is the business of the government of Germany, to draw practical conclusions from this.

Molotov claimed that the USSR alone stood for the principle of the equality and independence of Abyssinia, and that by membership of the League of Nations the USSR had stiffened that body's resistance to Italy's aggression. He made only a perfunctory reference to collective security, and warned that although every diplomatic effort would be made to avoid war, ultimately:

> we toilers of the Soviet Union must rely on our own efforts to defend our affairs, and above all on our Red Army in the defence of our native land.[35]

L. W. Henderson, the American *chargé d'affaires*, believed that Molotov's speech signalled a change in Soviet foreign policy. The USSR was not prepared to rely any longer on the League of Nations or collective security and would put its faith in its armed forces.[36] Litvinov, who drew attention to the emphasis on increasing armaments, told the French ambassador 'he had to struggle against certain of his colleagues who desired that the Soviet government should demonstrate more clearly its desire for autarchy', and renounce the Franco-Soviet pact.[37]

Molotov was now to overplay his hand in his attempts to seek improved relations with Germany, the most likely cause of the breach with Stalin in the summer of 1936. In his interview with the American newspaper proprietor, Roy Howard, on 1 March, Stalin told him that 'Hitler ... tried to say peaceful things, but ... sprinkled his "peacefulness" so plentifully with threats against both France and the Soviet Union that nothing remained of his "peacefulness" '.[38] A week later Hitler occupied the Rhineland. In the interview with Shastenet, on 19 March, Molotov claimed that although the remilitarisation of the Rhineland was a danger to the countries to the east of Germany, it was 'in the first place' a threat to Germany's western neighbours, France and Belgium. It was more a threat to Locarno to which the Soviet Union was not party, than to Versailles, as suggested by Litvinov.[39] He continued by committing Stalin to a pro-German policy and a rapprochement with Hitler's Germany on certain conditions.[40] Molotov's words were in marked contrast to Stalin's comments to Howard made before the occupation of the Rhineland. They were also at odds with Litvinov's speech to the Council of the League of Nations, and Ambassador Maiskii's speech in London, which warned the Western powers not to agree to new proposals by Hitler and called for united action by the League of Nations.[41]

By the autumn, Molotov had come into line. With the deterioration of relations with Germany and the signature of the anti-Comintern pact, he included attacks both on the Japanese and German regimes in his speech to the Congress of Soviets in November, and mentioned such issues as anti-Semitism and concentration camps.[42] On 23 December 1936, however, he saw F. W. von der Schulenburg, the German ambassador, about the arrest of German citizens during the Terror. This was unusual in that the chairman of Sovnarkom did not normally see ambassadors on routine matters; evidence perhaps of Molotov's pro-German feelings. Schulenburg applied to see Molotov through NarkomIndel and received an invitation 'exceptionally quickly'. Litvinov, who accompanied Schulenburg, seemed to be relieved that the ' "Minister President" – one of the really important and really influential people in the Soviet Union' was dealing with the 'outrages'. Schulenburg believed that Molotov 'was naturally in an awkward position and did not really know what to say about these matters' and summed him up as 'soothing but non-committal'.[43]

In early 1937 Molotov confirmed the undertaking he made to Schulenburg, that 'proceedings against the [arrested] German will not be inflated and will be carried out on a "minimal scale" ', but there were strong anti-German overtones in the Pyatakov trial, where it was claimed that the accused relied on the support of the German government, and German espionage was alleged.[44] In addition, in his speech on wrecking, to the February–March 1937 plenum, Molotov failed to distinguish between the capitalist powers, in marked contrast to his own preference for Germany, but he was following Stalin's line.[45]

From 1937, Stalin, whose views on foreign policy were decisive, was increasingly active as the issues became more critical,[46] but Molotov's influence on foreign policy also grew. He was a member of the new Foreign Policy Commission of the Politburo established in April 1937,[47] and in 1939 acted as chairman of this commission. Andrei Gromyko, who was appointed to the Commissariat of Foreign Affairs in 1939 by a Politburo commission of which Molotov was a member, stated that Stalin delegated certain areas of foreign policy to Molotov.[48] As chairman of the Foreign Policy Commission Molotov settled many matters referred by NarkomIndel. If he felt unable to settle the question personally, he would consult Stalin and/or put it on the Politburo agenda. By 1939 he regularly received copies of intelligence which Litvinov sent to Stalin. In these reports, often sent daily, Litvinov asked for decisions or approval of his proposals.[49] Molotov's position had been strengthened, on 7 April 1937, when the Politburo confirmed its decision to appoint Vladamir Potemkin, the Soviet ambassador to France, as first deputy commissar for foreign affairs. Potemkin directed the Western section of NarkomIndel, which had been Litvinov's preserve.[50] There was no love lost between Litvinov and Molotov. In old age Molotov commented that Litvinov, although an 'opportunist', was not a bad diplomat. He was, however, not trusted, because it was believed that he sympathised with Trotsky, Zinoiviev and Kamenev, and did not always agree with the policy that Stalin pursued.[51] Litvinov had a very low opinion of Molotov's abilities. His daughter remembers him calling Molotov a fool (*durak*) during telephone conversations, and said he was prepared to express this opinion quite openly.[52]

Both the thesis that the Western powers were trying to turn Hitler eastwards against communism, and the idea that the USSR had the strength to defend itself, were clear in Molotov's speech on the anniversary of the Bolshevik Revolution, in November 1938. He referred to Czechoslovakia and the Munich agreement, and condemned both fascist and 'democratic' countries. He argued that Britain and France had sacrificed Czechoslovakia in the mistaken belief that the aggressors would be satisfied.[53] Molotov had again faithfully adopted Stalin's line and there was nothing in this speech to distinguish him from other Soviet politicians including Litvinov.

Volkogonov has argued that Stalin, who was forced to pay more attention to foreign policy issues in 1939 because of the international situation, came to increasingly rely on Molotov in foreign policy matters, and was heavily influenced by his ideas. Only Molotov had the right combination of flexibility and firmness, and with his help Stalin drafted his speech on foreign policy for the XVIII Congress, March 1939.[54] Here, Stalin made the famous statement that the USSR would not 'be drawn into conflict by warmongers who are accustomed to have others pull their chestnuts out of the fire for them'[55] and stated that the USSR wanted to maintain relations with all states, indicative of the reluctance of the USSR to be driven into war with Germany. In this speech, which is often taken as the basis of Soviet foreign policy until the last years of his life, Stalin's analysis of the international situation did not differ essentially from that presented by Molotov in November 1938. There was, however, a contrast between the speeches of Molotov and Stalin at the Congress; Molotov emphasised that the Western powers would not interfere with Germany because of workers' movements, and Stalin that they were endeavouring to drive Germany to seek aggrandisement in the east.[56]

Molotov's appointment as Commissar for Foreign Affairs

Stalin's office diary reveals Molotov's increased participation in foreign policy, prior to his official appointment as Commissar for Foreign Affairs. It shows that he was present on every occasion when Litvinov saw Stalin in 1937, 1938 and 1939.[57] As early as June 1938, Molotov suggested to the American ambassador that Litvinov might be ignored in negotiations on the questions of the USSR's debts to the United States, incurred by the Kerensky government.[58] On 27 March 1939, acting both as deputy for Stalin, and as chairman of Sovnarkom, he met Robert Hudson, the British Overseas Trade Secretary, with Mikoyan and Litvinov. There was 'an amicable exchange of opinions on international politics', as well as discussion of commercial matters.[59]

By February 1939, there was a rumour that Litvinov was likely to be dismissed because his hostility to Nazi Germany militated against the improvement of relations with that country.[60] Hostility between Litvinov and Molotov, whom he regarded as 'an accomplice' in the Terror, increased,[61] and Litvinov found that he was not consulted about staff appointments to the commissariat. The appointment of Potemkin was the beginning of a process whereby an increasing number of staff owed loyalty to Molotov.[62] Diplomats reported directly to him, and articles on foreign policy from members of the commissariat, including Potemkin, appeared in the press without Litvinov's knowledge. Recently released Soviet documents do, however, make clear that it was Litvinov, not Molotov, who initiated the notorious Merekalov–Weizsäcker meeting of 17 April 1939, that the talks were primarily about economic issues, and that it was the German side which was more concerned with political matters.[63] There are thus no grounds to believe that this was the beginning of Molotov's efforts to secure a political understanding with Germany, to culminate in the Nazi–Soviet pact.

After Britain and France had issued guarantees to Poland and Romania, they approached the USSR about joint action to assist those countries, if they were attacked. Molotov, Stalin, and other members of the Politburo Foreign Policy Commission, were involved in preparation of the response to the British and French proposals,[64] which led to the Triple Alliance negotiations.[65] Molotov was responsible for the modification of Litvinov's draft counter-proposals for a mutual assistance pact, to include the need for joint negotiations with Turkey and to emphasise Balkan security.[66] In mid-April, as chairman of Sovnarkom, he approached Turkey to explore joint action against aggression in the Balkans and Black Sea area.[67]

The internal discussions culminated in meetings in Stalin's office on 19 and 21 April, in which both Stalin and members of the Politburo Foreign Policy Commission, as well as Litvinov and Potemkin, were involved. Maiskii, the ambassador to Britain, Jacov Surits, the ambassador to France and A. Merekalov, the ambassador to Germany, were recalled for the meetings.[68] On the second occasion there was radical criticism of Litvinov's policy of 'collective security', and Molotov emphasised alternatives which included the possibility of better relations with Germany.[69] Stalin was hostile to Litvinov and 'Molotov became violent, colliding with Litvinov incessantly, accusing him of every kind of mortal sin'.[70]

Litvinov appeared near Stalin on the podium above the Lenin mausoleum at the May Day parade,[71] but late in the evening of 2 May, Molotov, Beriya, Malenkov (a Central Committee secretary) and Vladimir Dekanozov, a close associate of Beriya, assembled in the commissariat to interrogate its high-ranking members. Eugeny Gnedin, who worked in the press department of the commissariat, recalled:

> Molotov had already replaced his earlier suppressed excitement and odd embar-rassment with a haughty unfriendly attitude. When I made a 'seditious' statement about censorship he assumed a still more dissatisfied expression, simultaneously making a mark on his paper.[72]

Litvinov appears to have carried out his duties as normal, until about 4.00 pm, on 3 May.[73] He was then summoned to the Kremlin where the policy of collective security was discussed and criticised. Litvinov's passive reaction to this so infuri-ated Molotov that he screamed as Litvinov left the room, 'You think we are all fools.'[74] Politburo resolutions dated the same day, ordered Litvinov to hand over to Molotov within three days, and appointed Dekanozov as a deputy commissar for foreign affairs.[75] Late on 3 May, the embassies in China and Prague received telegrams bearing the mysterious initial 'M'.[76] At 11.00 pm a message signed by Stalin was circulated to all ambassadors which informed them that

> In view of the serious conflict between Comrade Molotov, Chairman of the Council of People's Commissars, and Comrade Litvinov, People's Commissar for Foreign Affairs, over Comrade Litvinov's disloyal attitude to the Council of Peoples' Commissars USSR, Comrade Litvinov has asked to be relieved of the duties of People's Commissar. The CPSU(b) Central Committee has complied with Comrade Litvinov's request and relieved him of the duties of People's Commissar. Comrade Molotov, chairman of the Council of People's Commissars, has been appointed to serve jointly as People's Commissar for Foreign Affairs.[77]

On the night of 3 May, the commissariat building was surrounded by NKVD troops. The next morning, Molotov, Beriya and Malenkov arrived, informed Litvinov that he had been removed from his post, and Molotov called a meeting of the commissariat to announce his appointment and that of Dekanozov.[78] Molotov was involved in the investigation of senior staff in the next few days.[79] Gnedin, who was to be arrested within ten days, was questioned by foreign correspondents about Molotov's knowledge of foreign languages and international affairs. In response, he had a statement issued which said that Molotov was a significant state figure and had a knowledge of all important questions including international affairs. When he saw his new chief immediately after this, he recalled:

> Molotov stood at a table, obviously agitated. If the foreign correspondents could have seen me at this minute they would have all reported 'Moscow has gone mad'. Shaking my statement, Molotov furiously attacked me. He spoke in a haughty tone ... the sense of his words was that he was playing the role of Hercules in the Augean stables (he put it in this way). 'We do not need your recommendation' screamed Molotov. ... 'You are not a genius nor a wise man and that must be understood'.[80]

When Molotov summoned V. G. Korzhenko, head of personnel, and Fedor Gusev, the commissariat's party secretary, on 4 May, he gave them a lecture

> delivered in a steady shout, about the need to reverse an era of political short-sightedness cleansing the staff of class enemies. Referring to his Jewish predecessor Molotov roared 'Enough of Litvinov liberalism. I am going to tear out that kike's wasp's nest by the roots.'[81]

Litvinov later accused Molotov of removing 'every important individual who had any experience of the outside world', in his first few years at NarkomIndel,[82] and the huge turnover of staff is generally acknowledged.[83] Molotov, clearly had orders to purge the commissariat and bring it more closely under central control. His actions also reflected an upsurge of anti-Semitism in the USSR. In old age he admitted that in 1939

> Stalin said to me 'Purge the ministry of Jews.' Thank god for these words! Jews formed an absolute majority in the leadership and among the ambassadors. It wasn't good. Latvians and Jews ... and each one drew a crowd of his people along with him. Moreover, they regarded my arrival in office with condescension and jeered at the measures I began to implement.[84]

At a meeting at the commissariat in July 1939 Molotov stated that under Litvinov the commissariat was 'not quite Bolshevik because comrade Litvinov clung to a number of people alien and hostile to the Party and to the Soviet state'. Not surprisingly the meeting resolved that only with Molotov's appointment 'did a Bolshevik order begin to be established at the People's Commissariat. ... Unsuitable, dubious and hostile elements' were expelled.[85]

Ten years later, at a meeting of the commissariat, Molotov made a statement about his appointment, which paralleled his comments when he took over the chairmanship of the Sovnarkom in December 1930. He stated:

> The decision of the CPSU(b) Central Committee in May 1939 was prompted by the need to bring the Ministry of Foreign Affairs closer ... and make it a more direct agency of the Central Committee, in order to end the period when the Ministry was a refuge for the opposition and various kinds of dubious semi-party

elements. Accordingly corrupt workers or those with any such entanglements were removed.[86]

The NKVD purge of the commissariat reached a climax in the first years of Molotov's tenure of power.[87] In July 1939, the American *chargé d 'affaires* reported that

> with very few exceptions almost the entire staff ... has been changed. ... Their places without exception have been taken by unknown individuals who have had no experience of matters pertaining to foreign affairs, no knowledge of foreign languages, nor any contacts in general with foreigners or foreign countries. ... Among the minor officials ... at least ninety per cent have been replaced.[88]

Foreign affairs were considered to be in a state of crisis when Molotov took over. Purge was Stalin's reaction to crisis and he and his chief lieutenant applied this formula to the Commissariat of Foreign Affairs.[89] With Molotov's appointment, for the first time since 1918, a Politburo member was responsible for foreign policy.

The dismissal of Litvinov, a Jew with an English wife, strongly committed to collective security, and his replacement by Molotov, in May 1939, is often explained as the appointment of a pro-German, possibly the leader of a body of opinion in the Soviet leadership critical of Litvinov's policies, as a preliminary to the negotiation of an alliance with Hitler.[90] Allied to this is the idea that Litvinov's dismissal came on the day after Stalin was convinced that France and Britain would fight if Germany attacked Poland or Romania. Now that he had gained security in the west he could turn his attention to Japan, and make an agreement with Hitler to protect his western frontier.[91]

An opposite explanation has also been advanced: the appointment of the pro-German Molotov was to enable the proposal for an alliance with England and France to be pursued more resolutely than it was by Litvinov who had become very pessimistic and negative. It was to put pressure on Britain and France to make a positive response to Soviet collective security proposals. That there was no immediate change in policy in favour of an alliance with Germany; Molotov's diplomatic activity before he was appointed Commissar; his involvement in the formulation of the Triple Alliance proposals to Britain and France; and his attitude to those countries immediately after he was appointed, is cited in support of this hypothesis.[92]

Another theory sometimes used to explain Molotov's appointment is that, in the face of the growing threat from Germany, the policy of 'appeasement' pursued by the Western powers, and his fear of another Munich, Stalin decided to take direct personal control of foreign policy, and give it a more strongly nationalist flavour. There were certainly tighter constraints from early 1939.[93] In addition, the power of the NKVD in the Commissariat of Foreign Affairs at the time of Molotov's appointment, and his diplomatic activity from the time of his appointment until the German attack in June 1941, particularly his attitude towards the Baltic States, suggest greater personal control by Stalin.[94]

The urgency of foreign affairs and Molotov's closeness to Stalin were key factors in his appointment to an office that he was to dominate for the rest of his career. In a crisis situation Stalin appointed his close colleague as Commissar for Foreign Affairs so that he could personally take direct action and seize any opportunity that presented itself. This explains both the attempt to negotiate an alliance with France and Britain, and when that failed the negotiations of the Nazi–Soviet pact. The replacement of Litvinov by Molotov sent a signal to Germany, the same signal was a warning to Britain and France on their dilatory response to the Soviet Triple Alliance counter-proposals. Molotov's complete lack of diplomatic skills was a price well worth paying for someone in whom Stalin had confidence as a tough negotiator.

Molotov's apprenticeship in foreign policy – the Triple Alliance negotiations

The Triple Alliance negotiations provided Molotov's official introduction to international diplomacy and established his negotiating style. This was based less on the traditional civilities of the diplomatic world than on his experience as a Politburo member, Sovnarkom chairman and party leader, where he was prepared to hand out rude and rough treatment to others. The importance of these negotiations cannot be overrated. Hitler commented that if they were successful he would be unable to attack Poland, 'but should the western powers return home with empty hands, I can smash Poland without the danger of a conflict with the West'. Furthermore, after the signature of the Nazi–Soviet pact, Stalin told Georgii Dimitrov, the Comintern Secretary, that the USSR would have preferred an alliance with 'the so-called democratic countries'.[95]

Molotov immediately indicated to his ambassadors in Britain and France that he intended to pursue the negotiations seriously.[96] On 8 and 11 May, he reassured the British and French ambassadors, that his appointment did not indicate a change in Soviet foreign policy.[97] To Sir William Seeds, the British ambassador, he also made the cryptic comment that policy 'was liable to be altered if other states changed theirs'. He compared Moscow's response time of three days to the British proposals to London's three weeks to Soviet counter-proposals. He attacked Seeds for ten minutes because the French and British had made independent and different responses and pressed him on the British government's willingness to start military conversations.[98] Seeds reported to Halifax, the British Foreign Secretary that 'we are faced with a more truly Bolshevik as opposed to diplomatic or cosmopolitan *modus operandi*'.[99]

An article entitled 'The International Situation', in *Izvestiya*, on 11 May, directed, if not written, by Molotov, formed the basis for ongoing discussions. It deliberately ignored the existence of the Franco-Soviet Treaty of 1935, demonstrated when an official at the Commissariat of Foreign Affairs who drew Molotov's attention to the error was promptly dismissed.[100] At his interview with the French ambassador, Molotov used the omission to question the validity of the treaty,[101] which put more pressure on the French to sign a new treaty and military convention. The article condemned revised English proposals because they did not mention British and French help to the USSR if it became involved in hostilities in fulfilling obligations it had made to eastern European countries. It concluded: 'Where there is no reciprocity there is no possibility of establishing real co-operation'. This was restated in Molotov's formal response to Seeds on the British proposals on 14 May. He rejected suggestions that he might meet Halifax in Geneva, at the meeting of the Council of the League of Nations, for an informal discussion, presumably because the British still resisted a full alliance.[102] He insisted that there must be a military convention. He refused, however, to say if the absence of the principle of reciprocity was more important than the question of a guarantee to Estonia, Latvia and Finland.[103] At his 11 May interview with the French ambassador, he had stressed that this was important to the Soviet government because they had a border with the Soviet Union, and should be given the same protection as Poland and Romania.[104]

Molotov took the opportunity to set the stage and tone for the negotiations on 27 May, when Seeds and Jean Payart, the French *chargé d'affaires*, formally presented a revised Anglo-French draft. Seeds reported:

> The interview took place, exceptionally, in the Kremlin, with M. Molotov sitting at a large desk on a raised dais, and M. Potemkin (who acted as interpreter), M. Payart and I at his feet below. ... M. Potemkin then proceeded ... to translate aloud the draft into Russian. I noticed that M. Molotov had before him a paper on which he seemed to be checking M. Potemkin's translation.[105]

To the astonishment of Seeds and Payart, Molotov stated that his personal opinion was that the proposals were unacceptable because Great Britain and France merely wanted to continue conversations *ad infinitum* and not achieve concrete results. The introduction of references to the League of Nations in the Anglo-French draft, which made effective co-operation dependent on the interminable delays of the League procedure, was clear evidence of this. Seeds believed that Molotov was 'either blindly acting on instructions or incapable of understanding'. He continued to amaze Seeds and Payart when he argued that in Point 5 of the proposals, the British and French proposed to safeguard the rights and position of an *aggressor* state. When Seeds explained that the phrase referred only to states to which it was proposed to lend assistance, Molotov retorted that this was typical of the 'reserve' that he read into the Anglo-French proposals. He repeated that the Soviet government wanted immediate and concrete action, and that a military convention was absolutely essential. Molotov asserted that Russia would be bombed whilst Bolivia blocked action, if disputes were referred to the League of Nations. He had clearly seen through why references to the League of Nations had been introduced. Finally, Molotov gave what was to become a standard response: he agreed to refer the proposals to his government,[106] i.e. he would consult Stalin.

The next meeting took place on 29 May, at 10.30 pm: Molotov had already adopted Stalin's late-night methods of work for foreign policy. He stated that it was essential to conclude simultaneous military and political alliances. This became increasingly important for Molotov, who believed that otherwise the USSR was making an open-ended commitment to French security.[107] He raised the question of guarantees to Estonia, Latvia and Lithuania, to protect them from absorption by Germany after an agreement with that country. In response, Seeds warned that neither the British government, nor public opinion, would accept the imposition on independent nations of guarantees against their will. Molotov retorted that Britain might argue in that way with regard to the Baltic States, but would not remain 'loftily aloof', if it were Belgium. Seeds concluded:

> It is my fate to deal with a man totally ignorant of foreign affairs and to whom the idea of negotiation – as distinct from imposing the will of his party leader – is utterly alien. He has also a rather foolish cunning of the type of the peasant as shown by his arguments about safeguarding the rights of *aggressor* states on 27 May.[108]

Perhaps if Molotov did not have the skills of the professional diplomat, he had a surer grasp of the realities of the situation and the determination to fight his corner.

Despite reservations about the Soviet response to the Anglo-French proposals,[109] the British government decided to send William Strang, head of the Central Department at the Foreign Office, to Moscow to expedite matters. Molotov's telegram to Maiskii showed that the negotiations were a top priority for him at this stage, for he told Maiskii to hint to Halifax that a visit from the British Foreign Secretary would be welcome.[110] This was a proposal of major significance, for negotiations at the ministerial level could well have clinched a treaty at this time. It came when Molotov was under considerable pressure, for on 7 June, Germany had signed a non-aggression treaty with Latvia and Estonia.[111] He must have suspected that the British were not serious about the negotiations when he learned that, on 21 and 26 June, Chamberlain had been asked in the House of Commons to send a minister, but had refused to do so, even though he was reminded that he had travelled three times to see Hitler.[112] Molotov resented the failure to send a senior member of the British government. This is confirmed by two reports of the French government to the British Foreign Office to that effect; his comments to Schulenburg in August, when he described Strang as 'an official of the second class';[113] and his speech to the Supreme Soviet on the ratification of the Nazi–Soviet pact, on 31 August. Here he described the British and French negotiators as 'minor individuals who were not invested with adequate powers'.[114]

Molotov saw the French ambassador, Seeds and Strang, on 15 June, at a meeting which lasted two and three-quarter hours. The two ambassadors now found Molotov less stiff and hostile and more genial, although he still arranged the setting to his advantage, and sat at a large desk, raised on a dais.[115] His visitors were in a semi-circle below him. All, except Molotov, had to nurse their papers and make notes on their knees. Nobody suggested that they should use a table which was in the room. Behind Molotov, to the left, was a door always left slightly open as if someone were listening. No one took any record of the conversations, although Molotov, who occasionally left the meeting, sometimes fiddled with a switch under the left-hand side of his desk. Strang assumed that he was relaying those parts of the talks that he wanted recorded.[116] Determined to have no respect for diplomatic niceties and prepared to take the greatest advantage possible from his seniority, Molotov's behaviour also minimised the disadvantage of his own insecurity and inexperience as a diplomat. He was, as usual, in daily contact with Stalin throughout the negotiations. Earlier in the negotiations, Molotov and Potemkin had seen Stalin on 11 and 27 May. On 15 June, Stalin's diary records no interviews until 23.00 hours, so it is quite possible that he was a hidden observer of the talks. On 21 June, the date of another important session in the afternoon, Stalin's office diary records no meeting with Molotov, and no interview until 18.15, which suggests a similar situation.[117]

Like Seeds, Strang was struck by Molotov's unfamiliarity with diplomatic technique. There was little give and take, nor was there the informal contact between assistants and experts, normal in such negotiations. He also noted Molotov's apparent ignorance of foreign languages, although with his top grades in French and German at school, Strang may have been mistaken about this.[118] He wrote that: 'Molotov's technique is stubbornly and woodenly to repeat his own point of view and to ask innumerable questions of his interlocutors'.[119] Later, he recalled:

> With Molotov ... one had to say exactly what one meant, neither more nor less, and to say it over and over again in the same words. There was no other way of convincing ...[him] that one really meant what one said.[120]

The Soviet government's written reply to the revised Western proposals, handed by Molotov to the British and French representatives on 16 June, emphasised that the lack of reciprocity in the Anglo-French proposals humiliated the USSR.[121] Molotov stressed that every time his government had made suggestions, one of its proposals had been rejected. He said that if the British and French governments treated the Soviet government as 'naïve or foolish people' he, personally, could smile, but he 'could not guarantee that everyone would take so calm a view'. He used the words *naivnyi* and *duraki*, rendered later by Strang as 'nitwits and nincompoops' and by Seeds as 'simpletons and fools'. To emphasise the phrase Molotov confirmed with an embarrassed Potemkin, that the latter had translated the last word appropriately, as 'imbeciles'.[122] He had become exasperated and lost patience; he was prepared to apply to the negotiations tactics he had learned outside the field of diplomacy, and implied that it was the French and British who were the 'simpletons' and 'fools'.

On 1 July, Molotov conceded that there were possibilities in an Anglo-French draft which gave the Soviet Union the right to decide if any aggression against any one of Estonia, Latvia and Finland, constituted a threat to the independence or neutrality of that state, and forced the Soviet Union to go to war against the aggressor.[123] He stressed, however, that the USSR was required to guarantee far more countries on the borders of the Western powers than *vice versa*, and raised the need for a definition of and reference to 'indirect aggression', as in the case of President Hácha's capitulation to Hitler in March 1939. He was returning to the question of internal subversion by Germany in Estonia and Latvia where there was increased German penetration. When challenged that this was a new point, Molotov said that the Soviet government had the same rights as France and Britain, to raise new issues.[124] Although he would have been encouraged that he had gradually gained ground from Western concessions, this objection must have reinforced fears that the Western powers were not serious in their desire for a treaty and were willing to wrangle eternally on issues that affected the vital interests of the USSR.

The French government, angered by Molotov's attitude, described his arguments about equality of obligations as 'unjustifiable in theory and indefensible in fact'. It feared that the concept of 'indirect aggression' gave one state the right to interfere in the internal affairs of another,[125] and believed that since the Baltic States feared Soviet interference in their internal affairs, it would drive them 'gratuitously' into the arms of Germany. Molotov appeared 'impervious' to this argument.[126]

On 8 July, Molotov suggested that 'indirect aggression' should be defined as 'the use by a European power of the territory of one of the undermentioned states for purposes of aggression either against that state or against one of the three contracting countries'.[127] Seeds believed that Molotov put forward this formula spontaneously, in an effort to be helpful.[128] This was the high point in the negotiations. Strang described Molotov as 'affable and co-operative',[129] and there was now some chance of agreement.[130] This change in Molotov's attitude may have been caused by alarm over the warm reception of a German military mission in Finland, Latvia and Estonia in late June,[131] or he could have been lulling the Western negotiators into a false sense of confidence to secure more concessions. On the next day, he had refined the definition to make it less acceptable,[132] and possibly because of the deteriorating European situation, he again insisted on the simultaneous signature of political and military agreements, on which he said the Soviet government was unanimous.[133] Whilst he maintained the priority of Soviet interests in the Baltic countries which bordered on the USSR, and drove the British and French to discuss the vital military compact, Molotov may also have aimed to put pressure on Hitler to offer a treaty, by forcing the pace on military staff talks with the two Western powers.

Seeds described the atmosphere of the next meeting, on 17 July, as 'unfavourable'.[134] German approaches about the possibility of a German–Soviet trade agreement may explain the change in Molotov's manner. Perhaps he wanted to force an outcome so that the USSR could choose if another option became available.[135] In addition, Molotov had heard from Maiskii that Chamberlain was still reluctant to accept a pact with the USSR.[136] The British and French representatives agreed to the inclusion of a definition of 'indirect aggression', but pressed Molotov to accept their interpretation of the term. He asked if the French and British were willing to open military negotiations immediately,[137] and wrote to his ambassadors in France and England on the same day:

We ... categorically reject the Anglo-French proposal that we should first agree on the 'political' part of the treaty. ... This dishonest Anglo-French proposal ... contradicts our basic proposal about concluding the whole treaty simultaneously, including its military part, which is the most important and most political part of the treaty. ... Only crooks and cheats such as the negotiators on the Anglo-French side have shown themselves to be ... could pretend that our demands ... are something new in the negotiations. ... It seems that nothing will come of these endless negotiations. Then they will have no one but themselves to blame.[138]

Strang, who was astonished that British and French governments were expected 'to talk military secrets with the Soviet government' before there was a political understanding, commented:

> Molotov does not become any easier to deal with as the weeks pass. He has ... now made himself familiar with the details of our problem; and ... the drafts he produces ... are ingeniously constructed, though they are, I am told, couched in inelegant Russian. But it is difficult to get to grips with him. He seems to be bored with detailed discussion. ... It took us ... an inordinate time trying to make clear to him the difference between initialling an agreement, signing an agreement, and bringing an agreement into force, and even now we are not sure that he has grasped it. ... And yet we have usually come to the conclusion ... that Molotov has seen clearly the extent of the differences between the respective positions on both sides.

The fact that Molotov saw these as very fundamental may well explain his lack of patience on detail. Strang went on to say that the negotiations had been humiliating because the British and French had continually made concessions and changed their position and Molotov seemed to sense this.[139] Paul-Émile Naggiar, the French ambassador, described Molotov's implacable method of negotiation as the reverse of that employed by an oriental government, echoing Chamberlain's comment in Cabinet when he spoke of 'bazaar haggling'.[140]

On 23 July, Seeds told Molotov that the British and French governments accepted the simultaneous implementation of political and military agreements. Molotov expressed his 'keen satisfaction', and after some prevarication, the British and French representatives agreed that military negotiations should begin immediately.[141] Molotov was concerned about the delay of eight to ten days before the Western military missions could be dispatched.[142] He would not agree to press statements about the military talks. Perhaps he feared that it would give the impression to the Germans that an agreement with the Western powers was ready for signature, and that the USSR was about to throw in her lot with them.[143]

Molotov's concern about the delay in sending the military missions would have been increased by the low priority given to their journey to Moscow,[144] which meant that they did not arrive in Moscow until 11 August.[145] Nor would the composition of the military delegation have impressed Soviet leaders. The members may have been experts in their fields, but they were not front-rank military personages of the seniority of Voroshilov.[146] Stalin observed to Molotov about this time:

> They are not serious. These people cannot have proper authority. London and Paris still wish to play poker, but we would like to know if they have the ability to carry out European manoeuvres.

Molotov replied that it was essential that the talks should continue. 'Let them show their cards', he added. 'Agreed, if we must' replied Stalin.[147]

What proved to be the final meeting in the political negotiations took place on 2 August, in an atmosphere that Strang later described as 'extremely cool'. Seeds reported that Molotov was 'a different man' since the previous interview, and that he felt that the negotiations had received a 'severe setback'.[148] Molotov's attitude may have been a tactic to pressurise the British and French and disappointment at the low priority given by them to the military conversations. It was also an indication that Stalin and he had decided to try to reach an agreement with Germany; Molotov's first interview with Schulenburg in the negotiations that were to lead to the Nazi–Soviet pact, took place on 3 August.[149] The British government's withdrawal of Strang, on the excuse that the military talks meant his presence in Moscow was no longer necessary,[150] must have further undermined Molotov's confidence in the seriousness of the British negotiators.

The ambassadors presented the military delegations to Molotov on 11 August. Whereas Voroshilov had been most welcoming, it was a short and formal interview. Seeds put the difference down to

> the personal inability of M. Molotov to unbend and be affable on official occasions than to any coldness on his part. He said indeed that he regarded the arrival of the Missions as being 'the greatest help'.

But Molotov did not attend the dinner given that evening for the mission,[151] further evidence that Stalin and he had now begun to put their faith in an agreement with Hitler.[152] Hopes for a treaty with the Western powers had, however not been abandoned, for when Molotov saw Lawrence Steinhardt, the American ambassador, on 16 August, he emphasised how important the discussions with Britain and France were for the USSR and tried, through him, to use his interview with Schulenburg the previous day to pressurise the British and French negotiators.[153] In addition, as late as 20 August, he spoke enthusiastically to the new Turkish ambassador about a positive and speedy result; and his stalling on the date of a visit by Ribbentrop to Moscow indicates that there were still hopes for a successful outcome of the Triple Alliance negotiations.[154]

On 22 August, Molotov saw the British and French ambassadors individually. He told Naggiar that the Soviet government had signed a number of non-aggression agreements and in negotiating another with Germany, he did not consider that his government had deviated from its fundamental policy of the maintenance of peace and resistance to aggression. When asked what the USSR would do in the event of German action against Danzig, Molotov neatly turned the tables, and replied that the Soviet government could hardly assist Poland, as it was reluctant to accept Soviet help.[155] In his interview with the British ambassador, Seeds accused

> the Soviet Prime Minister to his face of 'bad faith'. ... That the accusation had to be made through a subservient and very frightened M. Potemkin, as interpreter and witness, was particularly galling to the recipient, who savagely asked whether these words figured textually in my instructions.[156]

Molotov was learning diplomatic niceties. He angrily

> rejected the accusation of bad faith: he would not admit the right of His Majesty's Government to employ that expression, or to stand in judgement on the Soviet Government. ... His Majesty's Government did not inform Soviet Government of modifications in their policy.

But he soon recovered his composure and the interview ended normally. Molotov claimed that during the negotiations he had constantly reproached the British with insincerity. The arrival of the military missions in Moscow, quite unprepared to deal with the question of Soviet troops passing through Poland and Romania, a question that the USSR had raised in the past on several occasions at the time of the Czech crisis, confirmed that the English and French were only 'playing' with the Soviet Union, and '(either yesterday or the day before) the Soviet Government ... had accepted the proposal made to them by the German Government'. If Molotov's statement on the final decision to negotiate with Germany is accurate, he was sincere throughout the negotiations with Britain and France. He was clearly embarrassed when Seeds asked him if the USSR would now allow Germany to overrun Poland.[157] Considerable personal animosity had developed between Seeds and Molotov. When he was asked, in September 1939, if Great Britain should declare war on the USSR as well as Germany, Seeds replied that he saw no advantage for Great Britain in this 'though it would please me personally to declare it on M. Molotov'.[158]

After the conclusion of the Soviet pact with Germany, Seeds and Naggiar saw Molotov on 25 August. He told them that the political situation had changed and that the Soviet government did not consider that the negotiations should be continued. He confirmed Voroshilov's comments to the military delegation, that the question of the passage of Soviet troops through Poland and Romania was the reason for failure.[159] Molotov told Naggiar that 'a great country like the USSR could not go and beg Poland to accept help which she did not desire at any price'. When asked if the agreement with Germany did not have secret clauses, he inquired ominously if France did not conclude treaties which contained them.[160]

Molotov displayed in the Triple alliance negotiations many of the characteristics for which he was to become notorious and which were to become the trademarks of Soviet diplomatic method. He was not guided by the conventions of diplomacy;

he began with almost automatic opposition to the proposals of the other side and uncompromisingly advocated the Soviet point of view. He used the trivial as the first line of defence when his opponents attacked crucial Soviet interests; he appeared to be in agreement then reverted to his own point of view.[161] He employed bad manners, invective, rudeness (his description of the Western nego-tiators as 'simpletons' and 'fools') and calculated delays, although he did not at this time walk out of meetings. These were tactics skilfully employed to wear down the opposition. He was an 'iron civil servant' rather than a revolutionary hero.[162] The Triple Alliance negotiations showed that he was logical and precise, that he worked almost to a mathematical precision and dispensed with rhetoric.[163] He showed very little personal initiative, but implemented Stalin's instructions, and when there were problems, said that he would have to consult his 'government'.[164]

10
The Nazi–Soviet Pact and After 1939–1941

Molotov became preoccupied with foreign affairs from the time of his appointment as head of NarkomIndel, although he remained Sovnarkom chairman until 1941. The significance of his new duties was evident at the Central Committee plenum, March 1940 where his contribution was limited to foreign policy.[1] The rise of Nikolai Voznesenskii as Gosplan chairman, his promotion to Sovnarkom first vice-chairman in March 1941, when he replaced Molotov as chairman of the *Ekonomicheskii Sovet* (Economic Council), the successor body to STO as Sovnarkom's main standing committee, confirms Molotov's preoccupation with foreign affairs. It was also apparent in his lack of prominence at the XVIII Party Conference, February 1941, where he said nothing following Malenkov's report that criticised the work of the commissariats, or in support of Voznesenkii's report on planning.[2]

This was a period when Molotov achieved great personal prominence. If it was normal to commemorate the fiftieth birthday of senior figures with public celebrations, those which marked Molotov's, on 9 March 1940, were exceptional. Articles in *Izvestiya* commenced on 8 March and continued until 11 March. He was awarded the Order of Lenin; Perm became Molotov, and Perm *oblast'* Molotov *oblast'*. The town and *oblast'* of his birth were renamed after him; and the house in which he was born, and the one in Manzurka in which he had lived in exile were recorded to be of historical note.[3]

The Nazi–Soviet Pact

When Molotov was appointed as head of NarkomIndel, Tippelskirch, the German *Chargé* in Moscow, reported that he was not a Jew, and as one of Stalin's closest collaborators was likely to implement a policy strictly based on Stalin's wishes. In May, however, the efforts of Georgii Astakhov, the Soviet *Chargé* in Berlin, to discover if German–Soviet relations could be improved, were fruitless.[4] A sign of change in Soviet policy was that Molotov immediately began to keep the Soviet embassy in Berlin informed of the negotiations with Great Britain and France,[5] a significant departure from Litvinov's procedure.[6] In addition, Molotov reprimanded the Soviet ambassador to Turkey when he brushed aside a possible approach by his German counterpart for an improvement of relations.[7] These actions indicate that Molotov believed that other options were open besides an alliance with the Western powers.

His first interview with Schulenburg, the German ambassador, on 20 May 1939, was difficult. Molotov used a new young interpreter who translated carefully but slowly from the French, perhaps to give him time to formulate his replies, for he was not as ignorant of foreign languages as Schulenburg, like the British negotiators, assumed. He impressed Schulenburg with his suspiciousness, and said that the economic negotiations, which had made slow progress, could only be renewed if the necessary 'political basis' had been established. When pressed by Schulenburg to explain this, Molotov would only say that this was something that both governments would have to consider.[8] This seems more like a delaying tactic than an attempt to use commercial relations as a 'hostage' for the improvement in political relations.[9] It was hardly surprising when Ribbentrop was still trying to persuade Japan to join the German–Italian pact.[10]

Hitler echoed Molotov's comments about the need for a 'political basis' a few days later,[11] and the situation changed on 30 May. The German Foreign Office was ordered to undertake 'definite negotiations' with the USSR, and in the light of Molotov's comments about a 'political basis', not to confine these to economic matters.[12] In his speech to the Supreme Soviet on 31 May, Molotov hinted that the trade discussions of 1938 and 1939 might be resumed;[13] the only public reference a Soviet politician was to make to the Nazi–Soviet pact negotiations.[14] Suspicions remained on both sides; Molotov and the Commissariat for Foreign Affairs were not aware of high-level German decisions; the negotiations with Britain and France continued; and for the whole of June discussions with Germany focused on economic questions.[15] Initial moves were, however, made to sound out the Germans on the possibility of a non-aggression treaty if an agreement with Britain was not concluded, indicative perhaps that by late May, Stalin and Molotov were considering the idea.[16]

On 28 June, Schulenburg, newly returned from Berlin, reassured Molotov that Germany wanted a normalisation of relations. Asked what he had meant by a 'political basis', Molotov stated that the USSR aimed to cultivate good relations with all countries, and that he was pleased that Schulenburg confirmed that Germany considered that the 'Berlin Treaty'[17] was still in force. According to one second-hand report, Schulenburg asked if the USSR wanted a non-aggression treaty, but Molotov did not reply,[18] and Schulenburg, who was left with an overwhelming impression of 'distrust' for Germany,[19] did not report this in his dispatch to Berlin. The Anglo-French Alliance was still the priority for Molotov.

There were no further developments until 26 July, when K. Schnurre, the German economic negotiator, informed Astakhov that Germany was serious about normalisation of relations, had renounced aspirations for expansion in the Ukraine, and was prepared to respect the integrity of the Baltic States. Astakhov felt that he was out of his depth, and sought Molotov's advice.[20] He immediately endorsed Astakhov's action in referring to Moscow, and when he had consulted Stalin, sent detailed instructions the next day, the first the *Chargé* had received since Molotov's appointment. These insisted that an improvement in Soviet–German relations depended on a concrete proposal from the Germans.[21] On 2 August, Ribbentrop told Astakhov that 'in all problems relating to territory, from the Black Sea to the Baltic, we can come to terms without difficulty',[22] and negotiations now passed directly to Molotov. In a one-and-a-half hour interview on 3 August, however, Schulenburg found Molotov less than enthusiastic. He asked questions about aspects of German foreign policy and suggested that exclusion from the Munich agreement had been an attempt to outlaw the USSR. Schulenburg concluded that, although Molotov wanted an improvement in relations, the 'old mistrust' of Germany persisted. By 7 August, however, he claimed that Molotov was much more amiable towards him than to the British and French negotiators.[23]

Astakhov now reported to Molotov that the Germans proposed to update Rapallo and other German–Soviet political treaties, even if the USSR signed the Triple Alliance agreement.[24] Molotov's response on 11 August was guarded: the list of points was interesting, but a period of preparation and transition from the 'trade–credit' discussions was necessary.[25] This was the first indication that any wider agreement with Germany was a possibility,[26] and Molotov began to press Astakhov on a deal.[27] On 14 August, Schulenburg, who was reluctant to return to Germany for the Nuremberg rally, wrote to Ernst von Weizsäcker, State Secretary, German Foreign Ministry, that although it was likely that political conversations would be carried on in Berlin, he should remain in Moscow to expedite matters with Molotov, a

> remarkable man and difficult character [who] has now grown accustomed to me and has, in conversations with me, in great measure abandoned his otherwise always evident reserve.[28]

The next day Schulenburg proposed that Ribbentrop should visit Moscow for direct negotiations with Molotov and Stalin. Molotov, clearly ready for the approach, embarrassed the German ambassador when he called the proposal the 'Schulenburg plan'. He indicated that the successful conclusion of the 'trade–credit' talks was a preliminary, and resorted to his now standard response that he had to report to his government. Molotov pressed Schulenburg about the possibility of German pressure on Japan to improve Japanese–Soviet relations. He also tried to explore the possibility of a non-aggression pact between Germany and the USSR, a joint guarantee of the Baltic States, and the prospects for a broadly based economic treaty between the USSR and Germany. The conversation and issues were used as a test of the real desire of Germany to improve relations with the USSR, and indicated vital Soviet interests. Schulenburg suggested these matters as an agenda for Ribbentrop's visit to Moscow, but Molotov said that he would have to make a further reply on this and emphasised that detailed preparation would be necessary. Molotov's behaviour was a sign that negotiations with Britain and France were about to fail, and that the USSR was feeling its way towards an alternative policy.[29] After the meeting, Schulenburg noted that Molotov who had been 'unusually compliant and candid', had been particularly flattered by the proposal that Ribbentrop should visit, after the failure of Britain to send a minister for the Triple Alliance negotiations, and that his priority was a non-aggression pact.[30]

On 17 August, Schulenburg reported that Ribbentrop could come to Moscow any time after 18 August,[31] but Molotov had only the official Soviet response to the German proposals of 15 August. This stated that the first step was the conclusion of a trade and credit agreement. The next was a non-aggression pact, or the renewal of the Rapallo Treaty, which should include a protocol which dealt with the interests of the two powers in certain areas of foreign policy – an indication that the initiative for a 'secret protocol' was Soviet, perhaps Molotov's personal idea. Ribbentrop's proposed visit was approved as evidence of Germany's seriousness, but was to be made only after thorough preparation. Stalin's appointments diary confirms Molotov's statement that Stalin was following the conversations with great interest. There is also another earlier version of the official reply amongst Stalin's papers on which Stalin has written marginal notes. This draft states that the non-aggression pact is the 'second and chief step'; a draft is attached endorsed by Stalin that its use was rejected.[32]

Despite Schulenburg's pressure, Molotov refused to bring forward the date for Ribbentrop's visit. He suggested that both sides worked on drafts for the treaty and supplementary protocol, a similar tactic to that which he had employed for the definition of 'indirect aggression' in the Triple Alliance negotiations.[33] This makes it clear that Molotov was seeking an offer from the Germans, but it was also the first formal mention of the format of the document that was to become infamous, and often referred to as the 'Molotov–Ribbentrop Pact'.

In view of the imminent German attack on Poland, Schulenburg was now pressed by Ribbentrop to arrange an early visit, but, at 2.00 pm on 19 August, Molotov insisted that more preparation was necessary. He also asked for a specific statement on what points were to be covered in the protocol. At a second meeting, at Molotov's request, at 4.30 pm on the same day, he said that he had reported to his government, and agreed to Ribbentrop's arrival on 26 or 27 August, on condition that the economic agreement, which to put pressure on the Germans the Soviet negotiators seem to have delayed signing,[34] was concluded on 20 August. He also provided Schulenburg with the draft for a pact, which contained the essence of the final agreement, identical to that which two days earlier Stalin had not wished to use. It included a stipulation that the pact was only valid if a special protocol was signed to 'cover the points in which the High Contracting Parties are interested in the field of foreign policy'.[35] Molotov concluded the interview by saying 'This is after all a concrete step'.[36] Schulenburg's assumption that Stalin had intervened is correct. He had seen Molotov (and Mikoyan) before the first meeting with Schulenburg, he had no appointments until 5.15; he was personally involved in preparation and amendment of the draft, and could well have been involved in telephone discussions with Molotov. In any case, Stalin saw him again after the second interview.[37]

On 21 August, Schulenburg met Molotov at 3.00 pm, and delivered a personal message to Stalin from Hitler. This accepted the Soviet draft of the non-aggression pact, but requested clarification of the content of the supplementary protocol. This was to be settled by Ribbentrop in a personal visit on 22 or 23 August, his stay restricted to one or two days because of the international situation.[38] At 5.00 pm Molotov delivered Stalin's reply, which welcomed a non-aggression pact and agreed to Ribbentrop's visit on 23 August.[39]

On Ribbentrop's arrival, he was shown into Molotov's office in the Kremlin where he found not only Molotov, but Stalin as well.[40] Within hours the infamous pact and its secret protocol were signed.[41] It came into force immediately after signature, not on ratification by both parties as was customary with similar agreements previously negotiated by the USSR: an indication that Hitler was about to attack Poland. Stalin took the initiative on the 'secret protocol',[42] on which Ribbentrop had to refer to Hitler on one issue: Stalin's desire that the Latvian ports of Libau (Liepaya) and Windau (Ventspils) should be in the Soviet sphere of influence, with the whole of Lithuania originally in the German zone. The secret protocol was still negotiated in such haste that two days later Molotov had to ask for clarification and a correction to be made, because due to inaccurate maps the name of the river Pissa had been omitted from the frontier line that divided the German and Soviet zones of influence.[43]

At the conversations afterwards, both Stalin and Molotov condemned the British mission to Moscow 'which never told the Soviet Government what it wanted'. In the toasts at the end of the discussion, besides Stalin's famous toast to Hitler, Molotov toasted Stalin, and said that by his speech at the XVIII Congress in March 1939, which had been well understood in Germany, Stalin had brought about the reversal in political relations.[44] One of the German diplomats present noted that 'Molotov was the only subordinate who could talk to his chief as one comrade to another', and this may have been a time when Molotov's influence on foreign policy was at its peak.[45]

Geoffrey Roberts has pointed out that no documents have been discovered which relate to the drafting and detail of the 'Secret Additional Protocol'. The originals were found with the originals of the pact and the drafts with Stalin's amendments in the Presidential Archive, but these documents do not include any draft copies of the secret protocol.[46] Roberts suggests that this may have been because Stalin and Molotov were embarrassed by the agreement and possibly only they, and not other members of the Politburo, knew of the existence and content of the 'Secret Additional Protocol'. This undermined the socialist foundations of Soviet foreign policy by an imperialist division of spheres of interest, and resolved a territorial question with a small third power by imperialist means.[47] The practical advantages of the pact had ideological costs. Roberts's thesis is supported by a number of assertions in the media in the *glasnost* era;[48] the transfer of the original documents from one of Molotov's secretariats to another in April 1946, which signified that he wished to keep the original documents under his personal control;[49] and their eventual deposit in a secret sealed packet in the Central Committee archive in October 1952.[50] Possibly the fact that after the conversations on 23–24 August Molotov met Stalin alone in his office for an hour and a half in the early hours of 24 August also indicates that they alone knew of the secret protocol.[51]

Molotov's denial that it existed until the end of his life, although challenged on the matter more than once when Chuev recorded his memoirs, also supports this thesis.[52] No institution approved the secret protocol and he had no authority to sign it.

Molotov delayed three days before he requested ratification of the treaty by the Supreme Soviet, and claimed that there was more essential business. This allowed time to assess the impact of the pact both on the behaviour of Germany and on the Western powers.[53] In his speech, on 31 August, Molotov set out the new neutral, not yet expansionist, Soviet foreign policy. He stated that as negotiations with France and Great Britain had reached an impasse, the USSR had to ensure peace and eliminate the danger of war with Germany. He asserted that the Germans had understood the implications of Stalin's remarks at the XVIII Party Congress about the USSR being drawn into conflicts by warmongers, who are accustomed to have others pull chestnuts out of the fire for them. As in earlier speeches he denied that the different 'outlook and political systems' of the two countries was an obstacle to good relations. Molotov, however, did point out that the agreement was a non-aggression pact, and not a treaty of mutual assistance which the USSR had sought with Britain and France.[54] Ominously, he omitted all reference to assistance to countries that were the victims of aggression, which he had maintained was an essential component of Soviet foreign policy in all his references to foreign affairs since November 1938. He compared the treaty to other non-aggression treaties signed by Germany, and claimed that this was why it did not contain a clause which made it invalid if one of the signatories committed an act of aggression against a third party. He also said that it was not necessary to 'dwell on individual clauses of the treaty', and gave no details of its terms, and thus skilfully diverted attention from the secret protocol, which was not submitted for ratification.[55]

After the Pact: Poland and the second treaty with Germany

In the few days between the signature of the pact and the outbreak of war, Molotov tried to allay German fears, caused by press reports that Soviet troops had withdrawn from the Polish border, that unless Poland appeared to be threatened from the Soviet side as well as the west, the Western powers would intervene when Hitler attacked. He also came under pressure from Schulenburg for the USSR to appoint a new ambassador and military representatives, but resisted attempts to make the new delegation appear like a military mission.[56]

Reluctance to give in to German pressure, to make the collaboration of the two powers official, continued after Germany attacked Poland and Britain and France declared war. As late as 5 September, Molotov offered aid to W. Grzybowski, the Polish ambassador. With the rapid collapse of Polish resistance, however, he refused to see Grzybowski for two days, then on 8 September withdrew the offer, and said that the British and French declaration of war meant that the Soviet Union needed to consider its own security. Grzybowski noted some reluctance on Molotov's part to slam the door; he said that circumstances might change.[57] Meanwhile Schulenburg had pressed Molotov for Soviet forces to occupy the part of Poland allocated to the USSR by the secret protocol. Molotov's official response stated that the USSR considered this premature, but he also warned off Germany from permanent encroachment on the Soviet sphere.[58] This exchange allowed the Soviet Union to clarify the vague phrases in the secret protocol that referred to 'spheres of influence' and 'the question of ... the maintenance of an independent Polish state'. The protocol did not refer specifically to a partition of Poland and military occupation.[59] On 9 September, Molotov announced to Schulenburg that the Soviet army would begin action in the next few days, but it was not ready to cross the Polish border until 17 September.[60]

The USSR needed an excuse to invade Poland, and initially Molotov suggested protection of the White Russians and Ukrainians from the Germans. On 16 September, he said that the Soviet government would explain the invasion by the Soviet Union's obligation to protect 'its Ukrainian and White Russian brothers' from the chaos caused by the collapse of the Polish state. He admitted that this argument might offend German sensibilities, but said no other explanation of the Soviet action was possible as it had never before concerned itself with the plight of minorities in Poland. Stalin modified the draft and emphasised that the collapse of Poland threatened the security of the Soviet state, which satisfied Schulenburg.[61] This established the basis of Molotov's radio broadcast on 17 September.[62] Red Army units invading Poland were recommended to study the speech,[63] in which he also spoke of Poland's internal bankruptcy, claimed that the whereabouts of the Polish government was unknown, and that the Soviet government proposed 'to deliver the Polish people from the disastrous war into which they have been plunged by their unwise leaders'.[64] The reference to 'the Polish people' may be a sign that the USSR intended to occupy a considerable part of ethnic Poland, as well as White Russian and Ukrainian lands, which Soviet armies proceeded to do, and take even more territory than allocated by the secret protocol.[65] On 17 September, Molotov also gave a note to all the other powers with which the Soviet Union had diplomatic relations. This indicated that the Soviet Union aspired to stay neutral whilst it occupied Poland, and attempted to reassure the Baltic States.[66] There were, however, a series of minor frictions with Germany. Stalin and Molotov were apparently suspicious that Hitler did not intend to keep to the boundaries agreed in the secret protocol, and an agitated Molotov complained to Schulenburg on 19 September:

> This way of drawing the boundary is at variance with the agreements which have been reached in Moscow. ... The Soviet government as well as Stalin personally are surprised at this obvious violation of the Moscow agreement.[67]

The final act in this part of Molotov's dealings with Poland came in March 1940. With Voroshilov and Mikoyan, he followed Stalin in endorsing Beriya's request to execute Polish officers and prisoners at Katyn. Kalinin and Kaganovich, consulted by the *opros* process, also supported the application.[68] This is the worst and best-documented case of Molotov's direct complicity in mass murder, and exceeded his activities during the Terror. To the end of his life, however, he ascribed the Katyn massacre to the Nazis,[69] an obvious lie.

The collapse of Poland prefaced Ribbentrop's second visit to Moscow, which marked the high point of Nazi–Soviet friendship. On 20 September, after an alarm over where the Germans would draw the demarcation line between the zones of influence of the two powers,[70] Molotov told Schulenburg that the USSR believed that 'the time was ripe' for the two powers to establish a permanent new structure for the Polish area. The USSR had reconsidered its ideas on the continuing existence of a residual Polish state; it now wished to partition the country, and divide it with Germany along the Pissa–Narew–Vistula–San line. This was a decision that Stalin seems to have taken in early September. Molotov pressed Schulenburg that the negotiations, which needed to begin at once, should take place in Moscow, because Soviet negotiators were senior persons who could not leave the USSR.[71] This was an indication that Stalin wished to control the discussions.

Prior to Ribbentrop's arrival on 27 September, Stalin suggested that Germany should have the province of Lublin and a large part of the province of Warsaw, in exchange for the inclusion of Lithuania in the Soviet zone of influence. This formed the basis of the additional and secret protocols of the second Soviet treaty with Germany, signed by Molotov on 28 September. The main treaty established the frontier between the German and Soviet zones of influence in Poland along the 'four rivers line'. During the conversations with Ribbentrop, Molotov ceded to Stalin the right to negotiate 'because he would unquestionably do it better', but supported him when he refused to cede more of Lithuania to Germany. Stalin admitted his intention to 'penetrate' Estonia and Latvia and 'incorporate' Lithuania.[72]

A declaration, signed by Molotov and Ribbentrop at the end of the talks, expressed their intention, in view of the settlement of the Polish problem – 'a foundation for a lasting peace', to seek an end to the conflict between Germany and Britain and France. If they failed, Britain and France would be responsible for the continuation of the war.[73] Molotov repeated this in his speech to the Supreme Soviet on 31 October, when he said that by aiming at the 'destruction of Hitlerism', Britain and France were declaring an 'ideological war'.[74]

In mid-October Molotov declined an invitation to make a return visit to Berlin for economic negotiations because of pressure of business. In response to Schulenburg's suggestion that it would take only three or four days if he flew, Molotov said that since he was a poor sailor he shrank from air travel.[75] This was the first of a number of invitations that Molotov declined, before Stalin authorised his visit in November 1940.

The Baltic States and the Balkans

Molotov was now involved in the expansion of Soviet influence in the Baltic States, and signed agreements with Estonia, Latvia and Lithuania, cynically described as 'mutual assistance treaties'. In all cases, the USSR insisted that the pacts were necessary for Soviet security and to protect the independence of the Baltic States. Germany was identified as a potential threat in the negotiations with Latvia and Lithuania. In each case the foreign minister of the Baltic state concerned resisted Soviet demands, insisted that the proposed treaty would compromise the neutrality and independence of his country, and would cause friction with the USSR. Counter-proposals more acceptable to the individual states were rejected, and as a last resort the Baltic States were forced to accept Soviet demands or face invasion.[76]

In these negotiations the traditional pattern of Stalin–Molotov diplomacy was established. Molotov played the 'hard' role; he bullied and threatened the use of military force, which allowed Stalin to act as the conciliator to clinch the negotiations.[77] After their first meeting, on 6 June, A. Rei, the Estonian minister in Moscow, wrote of Molotov:

> I began to understand why Sir William Seeds ... noted with anger and concern that ... it was quite difficult to carry on a conversation as his manner was completely different to that which we diplomats were accustomed. ... On the question of political neutrality ... with Molotov it was necessary ... to start again from the very beginning.[78]

Molotov insisted that the non-aggression treaties signed by Latvia and Estonia with Germany, on 7 June, favoured Germany rather than the USSR and were not purely guarantees of peace. He took the same position with Schulenburg, and very soon after the signature of the 23 August pact with Germany, which placed Estonia in the Soviet 'sphere of influence', the USSR began to amass forces along the Estonian frontier.[79]

On 18 September, a Polish submarine, which the Estonians had attempted to intern, instead of permitting it to leave after twenty-four hours as required by international law, had escaped from Talinin. Molotov told Rei that the Soviet navy would track it down, and this became the excuse for the violation of Estonian territorial waters and air space.[80] On 22 September, K. Selter, the Estonian Foreign Minister, who was invited to Moscow to sign a trade agreement, found himself confronted with an ultimatum to sign a treaty of mutual assistance. Molotov used the escape of the submarine as an excuse. He told Selter that although the USSR had no desire to impinge on Estonian sovereignty, and would not force communism on Estonia, the Soviet army would be used to safeguard Soviet security unless he signed the treaty.[81]

When he returned to Moscow after consultations, Selter was told that there would be no negotiations: he must be prepared to say 'yes' or 'no' to the agreement. Molotov confirmed this, and added that Soviet planes were about to fly over Estonia: if they were fired upon, Estonian fortresses would be shelled.[82] Selter was now confronted with new demands, which included the garrisoning of Soviet troops all over the country as well as in defined bases. These requirements were based on Soviet press reports that Polish submarines operating in the Baltic, supplied from Estonian ports, had sunk a Soviet ship.[83] At one stage in the negotiations, Selter and his colleagues emerged from Molotov's office to find Ribbentrop and the German delegation waiting. When it came to detailed negotiations on the military clauses of the treaty Molotov once more increased the USSR's demands, and when it was finally agreed, in the hearing of the Estonian delegates, he telephoned Voroshilov to cancel an order to invade Estonia which was apparently about to be implemented.[84]

Molotov pursued similar tactics with V. Munters from Latvia. He presented him with an ultimatum at their first meeting and gave him forty-eight hours to reach a decision.[85] He insisted that neutral Baltic States were too insecure to protect the Soviet Union's access to the Baltic Sea.[86] Stalin was on hand to soften the threats. In so doing, he admitted that a division into spheres of influence of Poland and the Baltic areas had taken place, and thus acknowledged the existence of the secret protocol.[87] Troops were massed on the Latvian border, and Voroshilov and Boris Shaposhnikov, the Soviet Chief of Staff, were present during the negotiations.[88] The most significant clauses of the agreements with Estonia and Latvia leased naval and air bases to the USSR, the strength of Soviet forces at the bases to be defined. This gave the USSR the potential to threaten the countries. In addition, the treaties specified mutual assistance against aggression; a pledge not to become involved in diplomatic arrangements directed against the signatories; and a dis-avowal to interfere in each other's affairs.[89] Stalin and Molotov had cynically imposed treaties, the basic clauses of which they had no intention of keeping, and Estonia and Latvia were in no position to assist the USSR.

In the case of Lithuania, the mutual assistance agreement was slightly different: no actual bases for troops were specified, and the treaty included a provision for the cession by the USSR to Lithuania of the city and province of Vilna, occupied by the USSR on the invasion of Poland. This was to be in return for Lithuania ceding to Germany, territory allocated to her by the German–Soviet pact of 28 September.[90] Initially Molotov hoped that there would be simultaneous agreements to exchange territory, one between Germany and Lithuania, the other between Lithuania and the USSR. Schulenburg objected to this, as he believed that it would make Germany appear to be 'robbers' of Lithuanian territory.[91] Before the German objection had been considered, however, Molotov revealed the arrangement to the Lithuanians, who were taken aback. He extricated himself from the situation by telling Schulenburg that, to prevent a crisis, Stalin personally asked that the Germans should not insist on the cession of the 'Lithuanian strip' for the moment.[92] He then gave an undertaking not to occupy it with Soviet troops, and to leave Germany to decide when to take it over.[93] The atmosphere during the negotiations was similar to those with Estonia and Latvia.[94] Molotov and Stalin left the Lithuanian delegates in no doubt that the Lithuania was far more impor-tant to the security of the USSR than Estonia or Latvia.[95]

Molotov maintained the charade that the treaties were to protect the approaches to the USSR and the security of the Baltic States in his speech to the Supreme Soviet on 31 October. He ingenuously claimed that the USSR did not intend to interfere with their internal affairs.[96] The pretence continued when, at first, on Molotov's orders, Soviet representatives in the Baltic States tried to honour the promise of non-interference.[97] In the case of Lithuania, Molotov went as far as to advise the shooting of local communists, and called on the Soviet garrisons for assistance. He also tried to reduce pressure for additional bases in Estonia.[98]

The final phase in Molotov's dealings with the Baltic States occurred in May and June 1940, when the German offensive in the west commenced. He presented ultimatums to the leaders of the three states which accused them of provocation.

He demanded free passage of Soviet troops, and governments acceptable to the Soviet Union to guarantee fulfilment of the mutual assistance treaties. Molotov named individuals who were acceptable and unacceptable. Military occupation followed, and plebiscites held by the new puppet governments requested the annexation of the countries by the USSR. He now supervised negotiations with Germany on the resettlement of and compensation to German citizens.[99]

Molotov was less successful in extending Soviet influence in the Balkans. He proposed a mutual assistance pact with Bulgaria, but his efforts were rebuffed, although the Bulgarian government did agree to consider a non-aggression pact if the USSR provided a draft of an agreement.[100] Similar unsuccessful efforts were made with regard to Turkey. Attempts to negotiate a pact, when prospects for the Triple Alliance with Britain and France were good, were rejected by the Turks. On the failure of those negotiations, Molotov, who told the Turkish ambassador, on 4 September, that the international situation had changed and required careful study, became preoccupied with securing the neutrality of Turkey for his German ally.[101] But the Turkish Foreign Minister, who was in Moscow for three weeks from 25 September, refused to concede to the demand that Turkey should not sign a pact with Britain and France and close the Dardanelles. Here Molotov was not in a position to threaten, and the Turkish Minister returned home without signing an agreement.[102]

War with Finland

If there was some justification on the grounds of national security, for the acquisition of Polish territory and for Molotov's treatment of Estonia, Latvia and Lithuania, the attack on Finland marked the end of the Soviet commitment to non-aggression in foreign policy, and Molotov's behaviour in the negotiations over the Finnish war was particularly repugnant. Prior to his appointment, the USSR had failed to obtain leases on Finnish islands in the east of the Gulf of Finland to improve the security of Leningrad, and Molotov began by instructing Maiskii, the Soviet delegate to the League of Nations Assembly, to block joint Finno-Swedish proposals for the refortification of the Åland Islands.[103] In his speech to the Supreme Soviet on 31 May, he reminded his listeners that 'for more than a hundred years these islands belonged to Russia', and claimed that their refortification would be a threat to the USSR. He was clearly alarmed at the prospect of Swedish–Finnish co-operation. The next day the Swedish government withdrew its support from the scheme to refortify the islands.[104]

In early October 1939, emboldened by his success with Estonia, Latvia and Lithuania, Molotov attempted similar tactics with Finland. He invited the Finnish foreign minister to Moscow to discuss a number of 'concrete questions', and requested a reply within twenty-four hours.[105] Shortly afterwards he expressed irritation over the delay in a Finnish delegation arriving. In the negotiations, Molotov played only a secondary role; he left centre-stage to Stalin who acted 'graciously', which allowed him to assume a tough stance.[106] According to one Finnish representative he acted like an 'automaton ... as though he were merely executing someone else's orders'.[107]

The Finnish delegation declined the initial Soviet proposals for a mutual security pact. Stalin and Molotov then rejected, as insufficient, a Finnish offer to cede certain islands in the Gulf of Finland and adjust the frontier to improve the security of Leningrad. Fears for Finland's independence produced notes from the three Scandinavian countries, and a personal letter from President Roosevelt to Kalinin, the Soviet Head of State, expressing hopes that peaceful relations between the United States and Moscow would be continued.[108] Molotov replied to this in his speech of 31 October:

> One might imagine that the relations between the USA and, let us say, the Philippines or Cuba, which have long demanded independence without getting it, are better than those between the Soviet Union and Finland which long ago received its liberty and independence from the Soviet Union.

In this speech he revealed details of the ongoing negotiations,[109] a tactic the Finns regarded as a manoeuvre to frighten them, and which stiffened their opposition. In addition, it meant that the discussions ceased to be negotiations in the true sense of the word. Molotov also asserted that the influence of outside powers affected the talks, an indication that the Soviet leaders believed that France and Britain were supporting Finland. Molotov confirmed this with Schulenburg on 13 November; and it became enshrined in official Soviet histories of these events.[110]

On 3 November, Stalin was absent when Molotov saw the Finns, and he concluded the discussion with the comment, 'We civilians can see no further in the matter; now it is the turn of the military to have their say.'[111] The talks, however, continued until mid-November, but then broke down because the Finns would not make concessions which threatened their independence.[112]

At this time, the Old Bolshevik Madame Aleksandra Kollontai, prominent in the 1917 revolution, who in 1939 was Soviet Minister in Stockholm, returned to Moscow to inform Molotov of Swedish opinion on the crisis. He kept her waiting for several hours, and then dismissed her warnings that although the Swedes were determined to stay neutral, Britain, France and the United States were likely to support Finland. Molotov 'pointedly repeated several times that it was completely impossible to come to terms with the Finns' who 'keep on obstinately and recklessly rejecting' Soviet proposals. He instructed Kollontai to return to Sweden at six am the next morning and work to keep that country neutral.[113]

Early on 26 November, the famous frontier incident of the 'seven shots' occurred. In his note of protest, Molotov claimed that four Red Army soldiers had been killed and seven wounded by the 'provocative firing'; and that the concentration of Finnish troops near Leningrad was a 'menace' to the city, and 'an act hostile to the USSR'. He demanded that Finnish troops be withdrawn 20 to 25 kilometres from the border; and ignored the Finnish minister's reminder that, by the Soviet–Finnish Treaty of 1928, all incidents were to be investigated by a joint border commission. The reply of the Finnish government delivered the next day, which sought to prove that the shots could not have been fired from the Finnish side of the border, and proposed a mutual withdrawal of forces, enraged Molotov. On 28 November, he claimed that a withdrawal would mean that Soviet forces were posted in the suburbs of Leningrad, which would be under a perpetual threat, and that the Finnish refusal to withdraw troops meant that Helsinki did not intend to comply with the Soviet–Finnish non-aggression agreement of 1932. The Soviet government therefore now considered itself released from its obligations under that treaty. On 29 November, the Finnish Minister was asked to call on Deputy Foreign Commissar Potemkin, who read a statement which broke off diplomatic relations. The Finnish Minister, who had received additional instructions to make concessions, asked to see Molotov, but before he received a reply,[114] in a radio broadcast at midnight, Molotov stated that

> The present Finnish government, embarrassed by its anti-Soviet connections with the imperialists, is unwilling to maintain normal relations with the USSR. ... From such a government and from its insensate military clique nothing is now to be expected but fresh insolent provocations. ... The [Soviet] government [which] can no longer tolerate the situation created for which the Finnish government is entirely responsible. ... gave the order to the supreme command of the Red Army and Navy to be prepared for all eventualities and to take immediate steps to cope with any new attacks.

He claimed that allegations that the USSR wished to seize Finnish territory were malicious slander,[115] an obvious lie, for Stalin and Molotov were clearly intent on this. Most authorities suggest that the 'seven shots' were a deliberate Soviet provocation. Molotov's proposal for a withdrawal of Finnish forces in his first note, which left the Finns with a diplomatic solution to the crisis, was purely tactical, for when the Finns proposed one, he ignored it.[116] Steinhardt, the American ambassador, who saw Molotov at this time, believed that he was refusing third party mediation as the USSR wished to 'liquidate the Finnish question' immediately, so that it was free to deal with issues that might arise in the Balkans or Black Sea area, or from Germany.[117]

Molotov's broadcast did not contain a declaration of war, because on 1 December the USSR recognised the 'People's Government of Finland', composed of Finnish communist emigrants resident in the USSR, headed by O. Kuusinen. This stratagem seems to have been arranged by Stalin, Molotov and Kuusinen.[118] The next day, Molotov signed a treaty of friendship and mutual assistance with that government. This allowed him to reject the approaches of a new Helsinki government formed in an effort to bring the USSR to the conference table. Molotov described W. Tanner, the head of this new government, as the 'evil genius' of the Moscow talks.[119] Tanner's government now asked the League of Nations to take action on Soviet aggression, but Molotov stated that the USSR would not take part in the proposed session, because the USSR was not at war with Finland and maintained 'peaceful relations with the Democratic Republic of Finland'.[120] On 14 December, at the end of what was to be its last official session, the League expelled the USSR for breach of its covenant,[121] a decision that produced a sharp negative reaction from Molotov.[122]

The initial stages of the war were disastrous for the USSR, and by 7 January 1940, Molotov was not entirely dismissive of peace feelers made by the Finns through Schulenburg. He described them as 'late, very late' and said 'it would have been better for the Finns to have accepted Soviet demands in the first place'.[123] Schulenburg was active throughout the peace negotiations, since Germany did not want supplies from the USSR interrupted.[124] Initially, Molotov explained the slow Soviet advance because of the presence of numerous mines, but by the end of 1939 he referred to the unbelievable strength of the Mannerheim line.[125] From late January 1940, nothing more was heard of the Kuusinen government, and Molotov used Kollontai in Stockholm in preliminary exchanges to bring the war to an end. He pressed Soviet military leaders to conclude peace with Finland as quickly as possible,[126] and he tried to use Steinhardt as an intermediary.[127] With an improvement in the Soviet military prospects (rather than victories), however, Molotov increased Soviet demands and the negotiations made no progress. One note from Molotov stated that

> because ... blood has been shed on both sides ... contrary to our hopes and through no fault of ours, [it] calls for augmented guarantees for the security of the frontiers of the USSR.[128]

The end of the Kuusinen government meant that Finland was no longer fighting for its existence, but only for its frontiers. It was a sign that Stalin, possibly influenced by fear of French and British intervention, had decided to cut his losses in the Finnish campaign.[129] In late February, Molotov asked Halifax to act as a mediator in the war, in an effort to prevent British military assistance to the Finns.[130] By early March, however, the Finnish military situation was so grave that their representatives were forced to accept peace and armistice terms dictated by Molotov, Zhdanov and General Aleksandr Vasilevskii. Stalin's absence strengthened their position, as they had no power to modify the terms. When fresh demands were introduced, Molotov ingenuously replied that 'Madame Kollontai must have forgotten to mention them before',[131] and would agree only to very minor modifications to the text of the treaty.[132] When a Finnish delegate pointed out that Peter the Great had paid substantial monetary compensation when he established the frontier, Molotov replied: 'Write a letter to Peter the Great, if he orders it we will pay compensation.'[133]

Molotov's 'logic of war' policy: the need for the USSR to guarantee its security with a large-scale international war raging, provided the theoretical basis for Soviet actions. In his speech to the Supreme Soviet, on 29 March 1940, he admitted Soviet losses of 48,745 Soviet dead and 158,863 wounded during the war,[134] but a more accurate figure would seem to be in the order of 131,476 killed and 325,000–330,000 wounded.[135] In the same speech, he declared that the Kuusinen government had dissolved itself of its own volition, and accused the Finns of atrocities.[136] The Treaty of Moscow, 12 March 1940, if notorious for the USSR's acquisition of Karelia, did provide a permanent basis for Soviet–Finnish relations. It was the foundation for the settlement concluded in 1944, although on that occasion Finland lost the Petsamo area; and attempts to make new demands at the time of the annexation of the three Baltic states, drove Finland to fight with Germany when that country attacked the USSR in 1941.[137]

When the peace treaty had been signed, the Finns tried to negotiate a defensive alliance with Sweden and Norway to avoid further loss of territory. Molotov objected, and told the Finnish delegates that 'all questions between ourselves and Finland have been settled once and for all'; that the term 'defensive alliance' made no difference: 'the question is not solely one of defence but also of attack, of military revenge'.[138] He warned that if the alliance were concluded, the USSR would assume that the Finns had broken the peace treaty,[139] and his threats were sufficient to prevent it. He did, however, agree to the renewal of the Soviet–Finnish Non-Aggression Pact, instead of a mutual assistance treaty, as with the three Baltic States. When he reported to the Central Committee plenum in the same month that the pact was renewed, Molotov played down the importance of this concession, which one authority claims was a significant failure in Soviet foreign policy.[140] He spoke of improved relations with Germany and the hostility of France and Britain to that country.[141] In response, in a ten-minute speech, Litvinov attacked foreign policy since his removal from office, and insisted that Germany would try to attack the USSR. Molotov tried unsuccessfully to interrupt him although Stalin remained silent.[142]

Relations with Finland continued to be poor throughout 1940, partly because of the increased influence of Germany in Finland. Molotov found it necessary to threaten the Finns in his speech to the Supreme Soviet, on 1 August 1940, the last major foreign policy statement he made before the German invasion. He justified the agreement with Germany whilst he denied rumours about a breach in relations.[143] In December 1940, he attempted to influence the Swedish presidential elections in favour of a candidate acceptable to the USSR;[144] and when the Finns revived the plan for an alliance with Sweden, Molotov again threatened them that it would be a breach of the peace treaty.[145]

Relations with Germany 1940, Romania and Molotov's visit to Berlin

In 1940, difficulties with Germany over border incidents and the fulfilment of economic obligations increased[146] after Hitler's famous meeting with Mussolini at the Brenner Pass on 18 March 1940, where he undertook to work out a Balkan compromise between the USSR and Italy. There were rumours in Berlin that Molotov was about to visit for conversations with Hitler. These were denied both in Moscow and Berlin.[147] At the end of the month, when Ribbentrop, perhaps on Hitler's initiative, suggested that Schulenburg should remind Molotov of his undertaking to make a return visit made during one of Ribbentrop's missions, Schulenburg advised against it. He argued that Molotov would not come because the Soviet Union was determined to demonstrate to the world in general its commitment to strict neutrality, and feared the reaction of the Western powers to such a public demonstration of Soviet–German friendship. He wrote

> that Molotov, who has never been abroad, has strong inhibitions against appearing in strange surroundings. ... Furthermore, Molotov, who never flies, will need at least a week for the trip, and there is really no substitute for him here.[148]

In April, Molotov told Schulenburg of the Soviet government's wishes for Germany's 'complete success in her defensive measures' in Norway and Denmark, and promised a resumption of Soviet deliveries which had lapsed, but the fulfilment of the economic agreement continued to be a source of friction.[149]

Molotov now took the lead in the acquisition of Romanian territory for the USSR. Germany had declared herself 'disinterested' in Bessarabia in the Nazi–Soviet Pact, and in September 1939, Molotov complained of Polish military units crossing into Romania. Further action was delayed until the conclusion of the war with Finland, but from April 1940, with Germany preoccupied with the invasion of Norway, and unlikely to intervene to protect her oil supplies, pressure was stepped up. It was, however, not until 26 June 1940, when he had checked German agreement to the acquisition of Bessarabia and northern, but not all Bukovina, that Molotov presented an ultimatum to the Romanian Minister. By this time Germany had overrun Belgium and Holland and was advancing rapidly into France, an event which caused considerable alarm in the Kremlin.[150]

The ultimatum claimed that the Soviet Union had never been reconciled to the 'robbery' of Bessarabia in 1918, and raised the question of northern Bukovina as compensation, a new demand. The map attached to the note mistakenly included a corner of Moldavia as well, but Molotov refused to rectify this. In response to a Romanian attempt to play for time by asking for a 'friendly examination' of the Soviet proposals, one report alleges that Molotov replied: 'My colleagues, especially the military, are very dissatisfied with the answer.' The official Soviet report states that he asked the Romanian Minister if Soviet demands were accepted and received an 'affirmative' reply. Romania capitulated early on 28 June 1940, and like Finland was driven to fight with Germany in June 1941.[151]

When the Germans entered Paris in June 1940, Molotov offered Schulenburg his 'warmest congratulations'; at the same time he notified him of the Soviet occupation of the Baltic States.[152] Disputes with Germany continued, however, over the 'Lithuanian strip'.[153] Ribbentrop raised the matter in July 1940 and Molotov, in response, quoted Stalin's view that it was impossible for the USSR to cede it and offered financial compensation. As a result of Soviet military occupation of the strip, the Germans raised the price of compensation, and the situation became more complicated in August with the 'Vienna award': Romania's cession of a great part of Transylvania to Hungary under German pressure, whilst Germany guaranteed the rest of Romanian territory. On 21 September 1940 Molotov handed Schulenburg a long memorandum that protested about the guarantee of Romanian territory, and asserted that Germany had promised to support Soviet claims to southern Bukovina, a statement that he modified when Schulenburg disputed its correctness. The memorandum claimed that as the USSR had not been consulted about the guarantee, Germany had violated Article III of the Non-Aggression Pact. Counter-claims by Germany, that the USSR had already violated the pact, by occupation of the 'Lithuanian strip', followed.[154]

Differences over Romania formed an element of the background to Molotov's visit to Berlin in November 1940. If Hitler had been alarmed by the Soviet seizure of northern Bukovina, Molotov and Stalin were taken aback by the German guarantee of Romanian territory that thwarted any Soviet ambitions for southern Bukovina. The arrival of German troops in Romania, a few days later, further worsened relations, as did German attempts to revise the arrangements for commissions which controlled the navigation of the Danube, and the entry of German troops into Finland.[155] The Tripartite Pact signed between Germany, Italy and Japan on 27 September 1940, an attempt to prevent the United States from entering the war, created more difficulties. Molotov demanded to see the text before the pact was signed, and considered that the Soviet Union was entitled to consultation by the terms of the non-aggression treaty. He was also suspicious that there were secret codicils that related specifically to the USSR.[156]

At this point, on 13 October 1940, Ribbentrop wrote to Stalin and invited Molotov to come to Berlin, to 'give the Führer the opportunity to explain to Herr Molotov personally his views regarding the future moulding of relations between our two countries'. He stated that Hitler's opinion was that it was the historical mission of the Tripartite Pact powers and the USSR 'to adopt a long range policy', and agree 'their interests on a worldwide scale'.[157] Schulenburg handed the letter to Molotov on 18 October, which provoked a protest from Ribbentrop as to why the letter had not been given to Stalin personally. Schulenburg explained that if he had given the letter to Stalin directly it 'would have caused serious annoyance to Herr Molotov' and that it was 'imperative to avoid this', as 'we will have to deal with him on all the great political issues in the future'.[158] Molotov admitted that he owed a visit to Berlin, but reserved his reply until he had studied the letter (i. e. he had discussed the matter with Stalin). On 19 October, he informed Schulenburg that Stalin's response would be favourable, and that he would come to Berlin after the celebrations for the anniversary of the Revolution on 7 and 8 November.[159]

Hitler had favoured an invasion of the USSR since July 1940, and Ribbentrop's initiative seems to have been a last attempt to see if war was inevitable, or if the USSR could be drawn into an ant-British power bloc through the extension of the Tripartite Pact.[160] Stalin's directive to Molotov makes clear his aims for the mission, and shows no sign that he and Molotov were aware that Hitler was planning an invasion. Molotov was not to seek a new agreement, which could be deferred until a future visit of Ribbentrop to Moscow. He was to ascertain the 'real intentions of Germany', and other members of the Tripartite Pact, in 'the realisation of the plan of forming a "New Europe" ' and discover the USSR's role in this. Molotov was also to investigate Germany's idea of 'spheres of influence' in Europe and in the Near and Middle East. Stalin regarded Soviet interests in the Balkans as crucial for the talks. Molotov was to establish Soviet control over the mouth of the Danube;

resolve dissatisfaction with German guarantees to Romania; make a demand for Soviet involvement in a decision on the 'fate of Turkey' and consultation on the future of Romania, Hungary and Yugoslavia. Bulgaria, 'the main topic of the con- versations', was to be allocated to the Soviet sphere of influence. There were also directions on what Molotov should say on such matters as the USSR's relations with Britain, the United States and Japan.[161] Molotov's visit was therefore of extreme importance and it created much diplomatic comment in Europe.[162] Indeed one authority writes that these conversations

> rank among the most significant negotiations of the entire war. Had they followed the course Ribbentrop intended, Great Britain and, indirectly the USA would have been faced with an overwhelming aggregate of power in the form of an alliance between Germany, Italy, Japan and the USSR to which would be added as associated powers Spain, Vichy France and Germany's satellites and client states in central and south-eastern Europe. Moreover, the position of certain neutrals, notably Turkey would have been seriously compromised.[163]

Molotov and his entourage of over sixty, which included Vice-Commissar Dekanazov, Commissar for Ferrous Metallurgy Ivan Tevosyan, personal security guards and a personal physician, arrived by train in Berlin on 12 November, to be greeted by Ribbentrop. A guard of honour was inspected, the *Internationale* was played and the Red Flag prominently displayed, although the streets were not decorated and the pomp in no way approximated to that which Mussolini had received.[164] Molotov summarised Stalin's nine-page 'directive' of detailed instructions, and had met Stalin at his dacha to discuss them prior to the visit.[165] During the conversations he reported to Stalin by telegram and received further instructions, in which Stalin corrected what he considered to be Molotov's mistakes.[166] This is the first example what one authority has described as a system of Stalin's 'remote control' of Molotov's foreign policy negotiations.[167]

An hour after his arrival, Molotov had a preliminary discussion with Ribbentrop who was very affable, although Molotov responded only with an occasional frosty smile.[168] Ribbentrop claimed that the war was won and that England was defeated. He tried to reassure Molotov about the Tripartite Pact, and asked him if the USSR might not now 'turn south' for its natural outlet to the sea. In response to Molotov's question, he specified the Persian Gulf and Arabian Sea as the area. Ribbentrop then suggested that Italy, Germany and USSR should try to draw Turkey away from the British, and suggested that 'in the Black Sea, Soviet Russia and the adjacent countries should enjoy certain privileges over other countries of the world'. Molotov referred to the Tripartite Pact and asked for definition of Japan's 'Greater East Asian Sphere' of influence. He warned that 'particular vigilance was necessary in the delimitation of spheres of influence between Germany and Russia', a clear reflection of the directive he had received.[169]

When he reported this discussion to Stalin, Molotov claimed that he had told Ribbentrop that the 1939 treaty was 'exhausted', with the exception of the Finnish question. Stalin's reply, four hours later, was very critical. He found

Molotov's phrasing inaccurate: it was the secret protocol that was exhausted, not the main treaty. The Germans might conclude that the Non-Aggression Pact, which Stalin regarded as the basis of German–Soviet relations, had become meaningless. Amendments could be attached to it.[170]

At Molotov's first meeting with Hitler, the Führer, who was surprisingly affable, initially made an hour-long statement about his general plans, and about German–Soviet co-operation. Molotov sometimes expressed agreement. When the time came to reply he stated that Stalin had given him exact instructions.[171] Then, as P. Schmidt, Hitler's personal interpreter, who recorded the conversations for Germany, recalled: 'The questions hailed down upon Hitler. ... Until now, no foreign visitor had spoken to him in this manner in my presence.'[172] Molotov asked if the German–Soviet agreement with regard to Finland was still in force; what was the meaning of the new order in Europe and Asia; and what would the role of the USSR be in it? There were issues to be clarified regarding the Soviet Union's Balkan and Black Sea interests with reference to Bulgaria, Romania and Turkey. What were the boundaries of the so-called Greater East Asian sphere? Hitler's reply to this onslaught, surprisingly, was polite. He tried to reassure Molotov about the Tripartite Pact, and said that any settlement in Europe or Asia needed Soviet co-operation. He talked again about his 'new order' throughout the world, and suggested that the Soviet sphere of influence might lay to the south of its frontier, in the direction of the Indian Ocean. In response, Molotov said that he could see no point in discussing schemes of this kind: the USSR was interested only in the preservation of peace and security in the countries on its borders. Hitler ignored this comment and explained his plan for the division of the British Empire.[173] Valentin Berezhkov, who interpreted for Molotov, commented: 'The conversation began to assume a strange character with the Germans seeming not to hear what was said to them.'[174] In view of a possible air raid, the talks were then adjourned until the next day; although Molotov dined with Ribbentrop that evening. He apparently commented to one of his German hosts that Hitler was 'not nearly so stern as I had imagined him'.[175]

In his report to Stalin, Molotov insisted that he had followed instructions on the Non-Aggression Pact and had been cautious with regard to the Tripartite Pact. He said that German 'replies during the talks were not always clear and required further elucidation'. He asked for further detailed directives, and was told not to stray from his original brief, or become involved in the German proposals on 'spheres of influence'. He was to continue to demand explanations of issues that affected Soviet security.[176]

In a second three-hour discussion with Hitler and Ribbentrop, on 13 November, Hitler first raised the issue of Lithuania, which he claimed had much greater importance than the Polish area he had received. Molotov replied that the USSR would not have insisted on this revision if Germany had objected, but he was adamant on the importance of southern Bukovina to the USSR, and protested against the German guarantee of Romanian territory. Hitler replied that, for the time being, the repeal of this was impossible. A long argument over Finland followed. Molotov protested about the presence of German troops and German sympathy for the Finns. Hitler claimed that Finnish nickel and timber were vital for Germany, and feared that a new conflict in the Baltic area would give Britain an opportunity to establish air bases in Finland, and might involve the United States. He called for broader collaboration between the two powers than the insignificant revisions now under discussion. Molotov agreed that broad collaboration was desirable, but insisted that there was a need to clarify secondary issues which spoiled relations. Hitler maintained his position on Finland, and Molotov eventually conceded that he saw no danger of a new war. This seemed to reassure Hitler. He went on to talk again about the division of the British Empire, and the need to decide in outline the shares allocated to the victorious powers (Germany, Italy, France, Spain, Japan and the USSR). Molotov listened with interest, but was non-committal. He raised the question of the Straits – 'England's historic gateway for attack on the Soviet Union'. He stated that the USSR was particularly interested in Bulgaria, and asked what the German reaction would be to a guarantee similar to the Axis guarantee to Romania. Ribbentrop was conciliatory about the Straits, but Hitler refused to reply on Bulgaria and said that he needed to consult Mussolini before he expressed an opinion. He wondered if the USSR could gain sufficient security for her Black Sea interests by a revision of the Montreux Convention (the 1936 agreement that regulated navigation of the Straits). Molotov described this as a 'paper guarantee' and said that the USSR needed a 'tangible' one. He continued to press on the question of a guarantee to Bulgaria. The discussion was then adjourned again at Hitler's request, because it was late and there was danger of an air raid. In conclusion, Molotov stated that a number of new and important questions had been raised for the USSR, which as a powerful country could not keep aloof from the great issues in Europe and Asia. He thanked the Reich Government for its help in the recent improvement in Russo-Japanese relations, and anticipated that the upturn would continue at an even faster rate.[177] At this meeting, Molotov's comments about the Straits, as England's gateway to attack Russia, echoed Stalin's words. His emphasis on the importance of the agreement with Bulgaria were a clear reflection of both his original instructions and the additional ones he had just received from Stalin, who now approved the way in which Molotov conducted the negotiations.[178]

That night, after a dinner at the Soviet embassy, Molotov had a supplementary conversation with Ribbentrop between 9.45 and midnight. This was the meeting that took place in an air raid shelter because of a British air raid, where, in the story Stalin liked to recount, Molotov, in response to Ribbentrop's claim that England was defeated, asked why they were in a shelter and whose bombs were dropping?[179] Ribbentrop introduced the draft of a revised version of the Tripartite Pact to include the USSR, and a further secret agreement for Molotov to take back to Stalin, which defined the spheres of influence of the four powers. He offered his assistance with Soviet–Japanese relations. In response, Molotov repeated that relations with Japan were improving and again emphasised the importance of the Straits issue and the Black Sea powers for the USSR. He raised a number of other issues noted in his instructions: the Axis attitude to Greece and Yugoslavia, Germany's intentions with regard to Poland, and Swedish neutrality. Ribbentrop was clearly in no position to reply to these questions, but went on to claim that the key issue was the USSR's willingness to co-operate in the liquidation of the

British Empire. Molotov echoed Hitler's comments and replied:

> If ... Germany was waging a life and death struggle against England, he could only construe this as meaning that Germany was fighting 'for life' and England 'for death'.

He stated that he would have to consult Stalin and his colleagues about the delimitation of spheres of influence; and that if the issues of tomorrow could not be separated from the issues of today, it was necessary to complete the latter before undertaking new tasks. With regard to the draft documents, he said that 'paper agreements were insufficient ... [the USSR] would have to insist on effective guarantees of her security'. Finally, Molotov stressed 'that he did not regret the air raid alarm, because he owed to it such an exhaustive conversation with the Reich Foreign Minister'.[180]

On 13 November, Molotov had also met Hess and Göring. Molotov questioned Hess about the structure of the Nazi state and seemed particularly interested in the precise functions of the deputy Führer (Hess's position and parallel to his own). He enquired about party–state relations, but reported to Stalin that 'the talk with Hess had no political significance'.[181] In old age, in his memoirs, Molotov was scathing about the interview and said that he constantly tripped up Hess.[182] The meeting with Göring was concerned with Soviet–German trade relations.[183]

When Molotov and his delegation departed, there was no pomp or ceremony and merely an official exchange of words.[184] His conversations with Hitler and Ribbentrop had settled none of the problems between the two countries, although the TASS statement noted that 'the exchange of views ... established mutual understanding on all important questions of interest to the USSR and Germany'.[185] Molotov's reports to Stalin emphasised 'Hitler's great interest in reaching an agreement and strengthening friendly relations with the USSR with respect to spheres of influence'. He returned convinced that Germany would not attack, a stance he maintained until the last days before the war. If, as one authority claims, Stalin and Molotov knew of Hitler's plans to attack the USSR before the talks,[186] their behaviour at the time conflicts strangely with this. Molotov, however, admitted that his talks had not produced the 'desired results', and that during the second meeting Hitler had become 'obviously agitated' over the guarantee to Romania, the Soviet guarantee to Bulgaria, and the question of the Straits.[187] In addition, he had failed to resolve the detailed problems of Turkey and the Balkans. The German attitude to the talks reflected Hitler's desire to divide the British Empire after British defeat, while the Soviet attitude reflected the fierce rivalry between the USSR and Germany over the Balkans. In all the conversations, Hitler and Ribbentrop were preoccupied with generalities and their statements were vague, but Molotov consistently raised concrete issues in accordance with Stalin's instructions.

When he reported to members of the Politburo on 15 November, Molotov found that Stalin interrupted with anti-German comments. He accused the Nazi leaders of not being bound by any moral standards and is supposed to have said 'the chief principle of their policy is perfidy'.[188] On 25 November Molotov informed Schulenburg that the USSR was willing, on four conditions, to participate in the 'four power pact' outlined by Ribbentrop, but Hitler never responded to Molotov's offer.[189]

11
The Great Patriotic War

The last months of peace

Molotov continued to be preoccupied with foreign affairs in early 1941. From late January he was protesting to Schulenburg over the entry of German troops into Bulgaria and was involved in negotiations with Italy and Germany over the question of the Dardanelles and Bosphorus.[1] He was particularly concerned with the 'Treaty of Friendship and Non-Aggression' with Yugoslavia in April. Gorodetsky claims that Molotov pressed Stalin to sign the agreement as a deterrent to Hitler, as it was not a military alliance which the Germans were bound to see as a provocation.[2] At this time Molotov established a pattern of dismissing the German threat as 'only a bluff' with Sir Stafford Cripps, the new British ambassador, and as late as June, despite warnings of an imminent German attack including those from Dekanazov, now ambassador in Berlin,[3] he made the comment: 'Only a fool would attack us!'[4] It is therefore not surprising that in the early weeks of the war he appeared embarrassed when Steinhardt reminded him that he had rejected warnings of a German attack as false rumours,[5] but there can be little doubt that he was copying Stalin's line.

Molotov was deeply involved in negotiations with Japan. He had made a cautious response to Japanese approaches for an improvement in relations in early 1940, but became more enthusiastic with the fall of France. Pressure was stepped up with the creation of the Axis and increased tension in the Balkans in the autumn, and in November Molotov considered proposals for a non-aggression pact, similar to the one that he had signed with Germany. These efforts failed because of Soviet insistence on recognition of sovereignty over northern Sakhalin, to reverse the humiliation of 1905, but Matsuoka, the Japanese Foreign Minister, revived the non-aggression proposal with Molotov when he visited Moscow in March 1941, *en route* to Berlin. The fall of Yugoslavia produced a dramatic change in the Soviet outlook by the time of his return on 6 April. Matsuoka found Molotov 'considerably softer', although his insistence on the return of southern Sakhalin led to deadlock in the negotiations. With Matsuoka about to leave on the Trans-Siberian express, Stalin intervened and a neutrality pact was hastily signed on 13 April, followed by celebrations at the Kremlin. The train was delayed for Matsuoka, and

Stalin and Molotov appeared to say farewell to him. Molotov, apparently the least inebriated of both Japanese and Soviet representatives, 'kept saluting all the time, shouting: "I am a pioneer, I am ready!" '[6]

The crisis in relations with Germany was clear in late April when G. Berzheri, the new ambassador from Vichy France, presented his credentials to Molotov. He confined himself to a formal greeting and farewell, and made only one comment as he listened to Berzheri's statement about the purpose of his mission, the policies of Vichy France and the 'new Europe'.[7] On 5 May, Molotov was present when Stalin addressed the graduates from the Red Army military academy and at the banquet in the Kremlin that followed.[8] According to one report, in one of his speeches, Stalin said:

> If V.M. Molotov and the apparatus of the People's Commissariat of Foreign Affairs are able to delay the start of war for two to three months, this'll be our good fortune.[9]

A Politburo decree of the same date, 'strengthening the work of central Soviet and local organs' appointed Stalin as chairman of Sovnarkom. By the same decree, Molotov became a deputy chairman although not first deputy, and 'leader of the foreign policy of the USSR remaining at the post of Commissar for Foreign Affairs'.[10] The decree that relieved Molotov of chairmanship referred to 'repeated declarations that it was difficult for him to exercise the responsibility together with the executive responsibility of a commissar'.[11]

Schulenburg noted that the official reason given for Molotov's replacement was pressure of work and commented that it meant an abridgement of his former authority. He speculated that the move was a response to the cooling of German–Soviet relations and Molotov's obstinate negotiating tactics.[12] But Molotov's continued responsibility for foreign policy, and Stalin's comments about his ability to delay the German attack, call into question this observation. Stalin's prominence in the negotiations with Japan influenced the change. It allowed him to assume direct control over dealings with Germany in a crisis situation, after his experience of personal negotiation with Matsuoka. Press reports had stated that Stalin had a conversation with Matsuoka and only that 'Molotov was present'.[13] For Molotov, the end of his official period as Sovnarkom chairman, in effect, produced little change. If there was some diminution in his workload, this was only temporary, for with Stalin's preoccupation with the military aspects of the war, Molotov undertook many duties that he would have performed had he remained Sovnarkom chairman.

The outbreak of war – Molotov's broadcast

Direct contact between Molotov and Schulenburg had been frequent until March 1941, and as late as 13 June 1941, after frequent British government warnings to Maiskii, Molotov passed to Schulenburg press statements which denied rumours of German demands and 'an impending war between the USSR and Germany'.[14]

Attempts were made to preserve an atmosphere of normality. With a great show of publicity, Stalin, Molotov and other important members of the Politburo attended a performance of *On the Steppes of the Ukraine* one or two days before the outbreak of the war – perhaps an indication to Germany of their interest in the Ukraine, and about this time Molotov dined with Schulenburg.[15]

On Saturday 21 June 1941, Molotov summoned the German ambassador at 9.30 pm to protest about increased violations of Soviet airspace. He used this as an introduction to more general remarks about Soviet–German relations, said that there were a number of indications that the German government was dissatisfied with its Soviet counterpart; that there were rumours of war; and that German businessmen and the wives and children of embassy staff had left the country. This left Schulenburg, who knew that Hitler planned to attack the USSR, in an impossible position. He could say only that he had no information from Berlin and mention the Soviet pact with Yugoslavia as a cause of Hitler's displeasure. Molotov then seems to have given up his efforts 'with a resigned shrug of the shoulders'.[16] A desperate last effort to try to negotiate with Germany had failed.

At 3.25 am on 22 June Marshal Georgii Zhukov, Chief of the General Staff, woke Stalin to report German air attacks on Soviet forces. Stalin summoned Marshal Semën Timoshenko Commissar for Defence, Beriya, Molotov, Malenkov and other members of the Politburo. After reports from the military leaders Stalin told Molotov to telephone the German embassy. He found that the ambassador had requested an interview.[17] Molotov left the meeting at 5.30 am to see Schulenburg who stated that he was charged to deliver a note to Molotov. This stated that the German government could no longer tolerate the growing Soviet troop concentrations along its border and felt forced to take military countermeasures. Molotov, apparently looking tired and worn out, asked what was the meaning of the note and Schulenburg replied that in his opinion it was the beginning of war. Molotov denied the Soviet troop concentrations and protested against the German attack on a country with which it had a treaty of non-aggression. According to unofficial reports he called the German attack 'a breach of confidence unprecedented in history', and concluded the interview by saying 'surely we have not deserved this?', although in his memoirs he denied that he had made this statement.[18] Molotov now reported to Stalin and his colleagues that 'The German government has declared war on us', and at about 6 am instructed Alexei Shakhurin, the Commissar of the Aviation Industry, to go to his commissariat.[19] It was, however, only at 7.15 am, after devastating Soviet losses, that Stalin authorised the issue of 'Directive no. 2', which ordered 'active offensive operations', although Soviet troops were still forbidden to cross the frontier.[20]

Molotov was given the task of announcing the outbreak of war to the country at noon. Mikoyan claimed that Stalin refused to speak because he believed that people would remember that he had denied that there would be an invasion.[21] In his memoirs, Molotov excused Stalin because, as the political leader, he wished to obtain a clearer picture before he spoke. Molotov drafted the speech with Stalin's assistance, and other members of the Politburo were involved in the final editing.[22] He was so distressed when he spoke that his stammer re-appeared.[23] He announced the German attack without a declaration of war and losses of 200, clearly a deliberate gross understatement. He called the German invasion 'an unparalleled act of perfidy in the history of civilised nations', made despite the non-aggression treaty which had been scrupulously observed by the USSR, and without any complaints by Germany. Molotov described his interview with Schulenburg; denied an announcement over Romanian radio that morning that Soviet planes had bombed Romanian airfields; and stated that Soviet forces had been ordered to repel the invader. He absolved the German people of responsibility for the war 'inflicted upon us ... by the clique of the bloodthirsty fascists who ruled Germany', and listed the countries in Europe they had 'enslaved'. He went on to say that he did not doubt that the Soviet armed forces would smash the aggressor and recalled Napoleon's invasion of Russia when the whole Russian people (*narod*) had responded with 'patriotic war' and defeated Napoleon. The same would happen to Hitler. He stressed duty, hard work, discipline, organising ability, selflessness and the need for unity, and called the Red Army and the whole nation to a 'victorious patriotic war for the motherland, for honour, for freedom'. He urged Soviet citizens to rally round the Bolshevik Party, the Soviet government, and Stalin, and concluded with the famous words, 'our cause is just. The enemy will be smashed. Victory will be ours.'[24] The use of the term 'motherland' (*rodina*) introduced a nationalistic element to the appeal from the first hours of the war and was a significant change. Listeners immediately commented on it.[25] The phrases 'patriotic war' and 'our cause is just' were to become much used slogans, but one contemporary observer believed that, because of the general tone of the broadcast, and because Molotov said that Germany had made no demands on the USSR, it left a feeling of unease, almost of humiliation.[26] Stalin himself, apparently thought Molotov's performance 'lacking in lustre'.[27]

Leading the war from the Kremlin

The early crisis months

On the day war broke out Molotov was appointed a member of the *Stavka* (*Stavka Glavnogo Komandovaniya* – high command headquarters). Due to the reorganisations of the defence commissariats in the 1930s,[28] no effective high command organisation existed in 1941 and the creation of the *Stavka* was a response to the German invasion. There were two reorganisations before this body was stabilised when Stalin became Commander-in-Chief and then Commissar for Defence on 19 July,[29] but Molotov's membership of the *Stavka* from the time it was set up, placed him at the centre of military strategic planning from the first day of the war.

For the first few days of the war he was with Stalin in his office for much of the time.[30] On 27 June, he confirmed with Sir Stafford Cripps that although the possibility of war had been anticipated, it was 'never expected [that] it would come without any discussion or ultimatum'.[31] There is no evidence to support the traditional story that Stalin was incapacitated for a period of two to three weeks. Mikoyan, in his memoirs, says that, on 30 June, Molotov told him that Stalin had been prostrate for two days, but Molotov himself in his conversations with Chuev claimed that

Stalin was agitated, 'not quite himself', but not incapacitated. Stalin's office diary shows that he continued to work and was extremely busy, although he had no appointments on 29 and 30 June and had retired to his dacha.[32] The last event before Stalin's brief withdrawal was a visit made to the Defence Commissariat by Stalin, Molotov and Beriya on 28 June, following the fall of Minsk, when Stalin supported by Beriya attacked Zhukov. Zhukov became emotional and was apparently comforted by Molotov.[33] Up to this time, Molotov had 'sat and listened' and 'never asked questions'; but in his memoirs, Ya. E. Chadaev, the Sovnarkom secretary, claimed that in Stalin's brief absence, Molotov showed a willingness to assume control.[34] If this was an indication that Molotov was regarded as second man in the state, that it was only for this short period demonstrated his reliance on the strong leadership of Stalin and the effect of the Terror in destroying initiative. It was in this brief interval, according to Sergei Beriya's memoirs of his father, that Aleksandr Shcherbakov turned to Molotov and said 'Vyacheslav, be our leader!', although in Mikoyan's unpublished memoirs this outburst is attributed to Voznesenskii.[35]

On 30 June, Molotov summoned Mikoyan and Voznesenskii by telephone. They found Malenkov, Voroshilov and Beriya with Molotov. Beriya proposed the formation of a State Defence Committee (*Gosudarstvennyi Komitet Oborony* – GKO), and it was agreed to ask Stalin to head the body because of his position and 'reputation with the people'. On Voznesenskii's initiative, Molotov was delegated to lead the deputation to Stalin, the others promised their support and said that if Stalin was unfit to lead the body they would support Molotov,[36] further evidence that Molotov was second man in the state.

When the group arrived at Stalin's dacha, he appeared to be worried, perhaps thinking they had come to arrest him because of his refusal to recognise the imminent German attack in early 1941. Molotov, as spokesman, talked of the need to create GKO to concentrate power and put the country on a war footing. Stalin asked who was to lead the body, and Molotov said that Stalin should. Stalin looked astonished, but then agreed.[37] After discussion, Beriya's suggestion of Stalin, Molotov, Voroshilov, Malenkov and himself as members was adopted, and Molotov was appointed vice-chairman,[38] a further indication of his position. If Beriya, not Molotov, was the driving force behind the creation of GKO, Molotov had led the delegation to Stalin. As vice-chairman of GKO, a body which concentrated in its hands 'the complete plenitude of power in the state',[39] a member of the *Stavka*, Sovnarkom vice-chairman, and Commissar for Foreign Affairs, he was in a position of immense power and responsibility.

Molotov's activities during the early months of the war reflected the crisis situation. Very soon after GKO was established he signed the decree which ordered the manufacture of 'Molotov cocktails'. These 'bottles filled with inflammable liquid', used against German tanks, were first made by army units near the front, but the decree ordered factories, such as lemonade factories, and workshops of all kinds to produce them and consignments began to arrive at the front.[40] On 16 August, with Stalin and other members of the *Stavka*, Molotov signed the infamous Order 270 which directed that any soldier taken prisoner was to be considered a traitor and enemy of the people and their families were also to be subject to repression.[41]

On 26 August, Molotov, as deputy chairman of GKO, led a group of six plenipotentiaries to Leningrad to strengthen the defence of the city and to arrange evacuation of the civilian population and vital factories.[42] This was reminiscent of his earlier missions. On 27 August, Stalin wrote to Molotov and Malenkov that he feared that 'Leningrad will be lost by foolish madness' and questioned the actions of the military leadership, particularly Voroshilov.[43] The delegation responded to Stalin's letter. Senior military officers were dismissed, the High Command structure was reorganised, and Voroshilov's position was abolished, although he remained in command until mid-September and Molotov did not dismiss him as he claimed in his memoirs.[44] On 29 August, Molotov, Malenkov, Aleksei Kosygin and Zhdanov submitted to Stalin their plan for the evacuation of some important Leningrad works within ten days and the evacuation of 91,000 of the population.[45] In addition, they proposed that the city and region should be cleansed of 96,000 people of German and Finnish origin. Beriya sent a telegram which ordered deportations the next day, but these were interrupted by the encirclement of the city.[46] After the return of the mission to Moscow, Stalin, Molotov, Malenkov and Beriya telegraphed Voroshilov and Zhdanov, on 9 September, still angry at the unsatisfactory defence operations and demanded information on the state of the front and the measures taken.[47] This telegram prefaced Voroshilov's recall.

On 10 October, when the Germans broke through at Vyaz'ma, and threatened Gzhatsk and the Mozhaisk fortified line – Moscow's main defence, the capital was in great danger. Molotov, Malenkov, Voroshilov and Marshal Aleksander Vasilevskii undertook another GKO mission to assess the situation and recommend how to localise the German breakthrough. Molotov had orders to dismiss Marshal Ivan Konev, and the commission recommended his replacement with Zhukov. But when Zhukov protested to Stalin, Konev was retained as his deputy. Medvedev criticises Molotov for failure to make concrete suggestions, but this is hardly surprising, for Molotov was not a military man. The military leaders led by Vasilevskii put these forward.[48]

Between these two missions Molotov took the chair at the 'three-power conference': the visit of Lord Beaverbrook and Averell Harriman to Moscow, 29 September–1 October 1941, where the 'lend–lease' scheme was extended and large quantities of aid promised to the USSR. Harriman found Molotov overbearing, lacking in humour and inflexible.[49] He had stayed in the background at the preliminary visit of Harry Hopkins, Roosevelt's special envoy, at the end of July when the conference was arranged; his one long meeting with Hopkins was dominated by discussion of the Japanese danger. Molotov suggested that the United States warn Japan about attacking the USSR;[50] an indication of how seriously Soviet political leaders still regarded the threat from Japan.

By 15 October, the Germans had broken through the Mozhaisk line. GKO issued an urgent directive that ordered the immediate evacuation of the government to Kuibyshev. Molotov was charged to notify foreign missions, and as deputy chairman of Sovnarkom to go to Kuibyshev as head of government.[51] He summoned the British and American ambassadors at 12.30 pm. Sir Stafford Cripps, the British ambassador, wrote that he had never before looked 'so tired and ill ... he was deadly pale and his collar all awry where he is generally very neat and tidy'. Molotov told the ambassadors that the military situation was so grave that the whole diplomatic corps had to depart for Kuibyshev immediately. Pressed by Cripps and Steinhardt, on whether the Soviet government intended to go or remain in Moscow, he eventually admitted that the government would not leave that evening. He assured them, however, that he would fly to Kuibyshev very shortly and would almost certainly be there before them. In fact, Molotov did not arrive in Kuibyshev until 22 October.[52] Later, on 15 October, Molotov called the people's commissars to the Kremlin and ordered them to leave Moscow at once.[53]

On 19 October, when GKO took the crucial decision to defend the capital, Molotov was strongest in support of the decision which Beriya opposed.[54] Asked later, by the novelist I. Stadnyuk, what would have happened if Stalin had left Moscow at this time, Molotov replied that 'Moscow would have burned': the Germans would have taken the city, the Soviet Union would have collapsed and this would have led to the break-up of the anti-Hitlerite coalition.[55] It may have been at this point, if the incident occurred at all, that Stalin considered making peace with Germany on very humiliating terms which Molotov is said to have described as a 'second Brest'.[56]

Soon after his arrival in Kuibyshev on 22 October, Molotov saw Stanislaw Kot, the ambassador for the Polish government-in-exile. Kot described him as 'incredibly overworked, obsessed with the seriousness of the situation, but endeavouring nevertheless to master his exhaustion'.[57] When Walter Citrine, who was visiting with a British trade union delegation, saw Molotov with Cripps on 23 October,[58] he noted that Molotov was pale, and gesticulated with his hands as he spoke in short sharp sentences.[59]

With Deputy Commissar for Foreign Affairs Vyshinskii to deputise for him in Kuibyshev, Molotov flew back to Moscow on 23 October[60] and seems to have remained there, especially in the crucial period that followed, although he made occasional visits to Kuibyshev. The evacuation left Stalin, Molotov, Malenkov, Beriya, a small group of general staff officers led by Vasilevskii, and certain people's commissars, who were recalled from Kuibyshev, in control of the government in Moscow during the crucial period of the German assault. For part of this time Molotov headed a GKO commission to the western front. He warned Zhukov that if he did not halt the German advance he would be shot.[61]

On 14 November, the Katyn question reared its head. At an interview with Stalin and Molotov, Kot pressed for the release of imprisoned Polish officers. Stalin telephoned the NKVD and claimed that he was assured that they had all been released. Molotov then angered Stalin when he deliberately misread a document to restrict the size of the Polish army to be formed from these officers, and Kot seized the document to correct him. The next day Molotov told Kot that the 'military situation of Moscow had changed for the better.'[62]

Wartime politics

The position of Stalin, now not only General Secretary, but Chairman of Sovnarkom, Chairman of GKO, Commissar for Defence, Supreme Commander and Chairman of *Stavka*, and the overlapping membership, with Molotov and other senior lieutenants, members of the Politburo, GKO, the Stavka and Sovnarkom, gave him and this group great power. It facilitated centralised direction, and the continuation of the system that had developed in the years before the war. This was acknowledged by Mikoyan in his manuscript memoirs where he writes of a nucleus of five, later six, of Stalin's leading supporters meeting, often in Stalin's office, on a daily basis, with an *ad hoc* agenda.[63] As Table 11.1 shows, Molotov was present in Stalin's office more than anyone else in the war years. This reflected not only his closeness to Stalin, but particularly among the positions he held, that of Commissar for Foreign Affairs. This was linked to Molotov's significance in Stalin's dealings with Dimitrov, both before and after the dissolution of Comintern in 1943, and Molotov often acted as Stalin's agent with Dimitrov from this time.[64] Molotov visited Stalin's office 86 times from June to December 1941, on 198 occasions in 1942, 191 in 1943, 134 in 1944 and 102 between January and August 1945. In 1942 Malenkov and Beriya were present more often (201 times each), but this is explained by Molotov's absence whilst in Britain and the United States in May and June.[65]

The meetings in Stalin's office replaced formal sessions of the Politburo and other party bodies. Only one Central Committee plenum was held during the war years, in January 1944. Stalin did not attend but Molotov was present, presumably as one item of business was the proposal to form commissariats of foreign affairs in each of the republics.[66] At the informal meetings in Stalin's office, decisions and decrees were formulated as necessary, presented to Stalin for signature and issued in the name of the institution, GKO, the *Stavka*, the Politburo or Sovnarkom, thought to be most appropriate. Sometimes Stalin would personally dictate the decree, and use Molotov as an amanuensis.[67] In his published memoirs, Mikoyan recorded that when he went to see Stalin he usually found Molotov there and that he was party to all conversations and reports. He claimed, however, that foreign affairs were Molotov's special preserve, and that Stalin kept certain matters from him and did not really trust him. He speculated that Stalin kept Molotov in his office because he feared what the latter would do if left to himself. Mikoyan thought that this was because Stalin believed that Molotov was regarded as the second man in the state and therefore a possible replacement for him at this time.[68]

Table 11.1   Attendance of GKO members in Stalin's office during the war[69]

Year	Molotov	Beriya	Malenkov	Voroshilov	Mikoyan	Voznesenkii	Kaganovich	Bulganin
1941 June–December	86	74	69	27	41	1	18	6
1942	198	201	201	24	75	24	9	20
1943	191	165	163	63	70	1	12	5
1944	134	109	119	11	67	0	0	26
1945 January–August	102	82	88	2	49	2	2	46

Zhukov records that Molotov was present when the strategy for the attack on Berlin was formulated. In another place, he acknowledged that he was of great influence on Stalin and 'almost always present when operative-strategic and other important questions were discussed', although 'differences and serious arguments quite often arose between them'.[70] Mikhail Pervukhin records an instance in August 1941, when Molotov attacked him for delegating authority as deputy chair of the Committee for Evacuation, but when the *Stavka* met, Stalin supported him.[71] If, however, Molotov was prepared to differ with Stalin at times, his support or fear of Stalin seems to have outweighed any strategic sense he had. He is recorded as backing Stalin's pressure on Marshal Konstantin Rokossovskii to abandon his plan for a two-pronged attack on Bobriusk in May 1944. Stalin told Rokossovskii to go out and think over his proposal for a single attack, Malenkov reminded Rokossovskii where he was and to whom he was talking. Molotov then said 'You'll have to agree Rokossovskii. Agree – that's all there is to it.' Stalin, however, eventually gave way to the intransigent Rokossovskii.[72] Molotov again supported Stalin against Zhukov and Rokossovski at the end of October 1944, when they called for a delay in the advance into eastern Europe to the Vistula to allow Soviet forces to regroup. Molotov interrupted Zhukov's report and said 'Comrade Zhukov, you are proposing to end an attack ... when a defeated enemy is not in a condition to resist the pressure of our forces. Does your proposal make sense?' In a replay of the earlier incident Zhukov and Rokossovski were sent away to think over the proposal, but Stalin gave way.[73]

Molotov remained a member and vice-chairman of GKO throughout the life of the institution. According to one authority, like other GKO members, he worked for the entire war period without leave.[74] Among Molotov's early responsibilities was oversight of the GKO Committee for Evacuation (*Komitet po Evakuatsii*), responsible for relocation of industrial enterprises to the east where they were out of reach of the German invasion. GKO also formed an Administration for Evacuation of the Population (*Upravlenie po evakuatsii naseliniya*) headed by Konstantin Panfilov who reported to Molotov.[75] As deputy chairman Molotov signed more than half of the 9971 decrees issued by GKO, especially those not concerned with military matters and the defence industries.[76]

In February 1942, members of GKO were assigned particular areas of responsibility.[77] Molotov was allocated tank production and related questions, including metallurgy and chemistry related to the war. This made him responsible for the development of atomic weapons.[78] The importance of tank production may be why this was assigned to Stalin's leading lieutenant, although Stalin intervened personally when there were shortfalls and difficulties.[79] Each member of GKO was assigned deputies for the sectors of industry for which he was made responsible; P. M. Zernov was assigned to Molotov. In addition, Molotov's working group of specialists, up to 75 in number, included experts in motors, armaments and tank chassis. He regularly received reports on the output of tanks and self-propelled guns, the fulfilment of production plans and numbers of tanks manufactured by individual factories from three specially appointed officials.[80]

In July 1943, Molotov was relieved of the responsibility for oversight of tank production 'in the light of overloading with work',[81] and was replaced by Beriya. In his published memoirs, Mikoyan claimed that very soon after Molotov's appointment Stalin had questioned his performance and Beriya had said that Molotov did not have links with the factories, did not direct strategy, did not investigate production problems. When V. A. Malyshev, the Commissar for Tank Production, or others, raised problems he just called a large meeting, discussed the matter for hours and formulated a resolution that was of little use.[82] If, however, inefficiency caused Molotov's replacement, he was not disgraced, for he was awarded the decoration of 'Hero of Socialist Labour' for his contribution to the increase of tank production in October 1943.[83]

Molotov's responsibility for atomic weapons continued after July 1943. Very soon after the outbreak of war he took the initiative in the appointment of Sergei Kaftanov, chairman of the Sovnarkom Committee for Higher Education, as the GKO plenipotentiary for science, and in founding a Scientific–Technical Council under Kaftanov's chairmanship, responsible for the organisation of war work in research establishments and the evaluation of research proposals. In September or October 1942, Molotov showed Pervukhin, People's Commissar of the Chemical Industry, the intelligence material on foreign atomic research. He forbade Pervukhin to show the reports to scientists but told him to find out what they knew about it and what research was being carried out in the USSR. A few days later, in response to Pervukhin's report, Molotov gave instructions to work out measures for renewed research efforts into the feasibility of an atomic bomb, the time it would take to make one, and he appointed Igor Kurchatov as scientific director of the nuclear project.[84] He recalled in his memoirs:

> I was charged with the responsibility of finding a man who would be able to create an atomic bomb. The Chekists gave me a list of reliable physicists ... I made the choice. I summoned [Peter] Kapitsa. ... He said that we were not ready. ... We asked [Abram] Ioffe – his attitude was also not clear. In short I was left with the youngest and least known, Kurchatov, they had been holding him back. I summoned him, we talked, he made a good impression on me.

Molotov gave Kurchatov the intelligence data and he said that this provided the information Soviet scientists lacked.[85] Molotov remained in charge of the project until August 1945, but there was a lack of urgency about the development of the bomb, and apparently a lack of understanding of the significance of the new weapon. When Truman told Stalin about the bomb at the Potsdam Conference, Zhukov recalled that Stalin turned to Molotov and said 'We must talk to Kurchatov today about speeding up our work.'[86] In August 1945, Stalin intervened personally, and discussed the project with Kurchatov and B. L. Vannikov, the People's commissar for Munitions. A GKO decree then established a special committee on the atomic project chaired by Beriya. Kurchatov remained as director of the project,[87] but Molotov lost responsibility for it.

That Molotov was relieved of his responsibility for oversight of tank production in October 1943 is not surprising. In December 1942 the GKO Operative Bureau (*Operativnoe byuro GOKO*) had been established. This body was given direction and oversight of the defence industry commissariats, the commissariats of communications, power stations, coal, oil and petrol industries, and ferrous and non-ferrous metallurgy. Sovnarkom lost responsibility for these commissariats. Molotov was the first chairman of the Bureau, with Beriya, Malenkov and Mikoyan as members.[88] In 1943, Molotov chaired all 21 meetings, and 13 out of 14 of the meetings in 1944 up to mid-May when Beriya took over the chairmanship from him and he ceased to attend. Whilst chairman, Molotov acted as executive officer of the Bureau.[89] The reasons for Molotov's replacement by Beriya as chairman of the GKO Operative Bureau are not clear. Perhaps it is an indication that Stalin was dissatisfied with his bureaucratic methods, hinted at by Mikoyan, and/or of Beriya's growing power, and one authority suggests that Molotov's position as Stalin's first lieutenant was challenged during the later stages of the war.[90]

In his last months as Sovnarkom chairman Molotov had been responsible for the weekly meetings of the seven-man Bureau of Sovnarkom, formed on 21 March 1941, and entrusted with the powers of the full Sovnarkom.[91] On the outbreak of war, the Commission of the Bureau of Sovnarkom USSR for Current Business (*Komissiya byuro Sovnarkoma SSSR po tekushchim delam*) superseded this body.[92] Molotov, although a Sovnarkom vice-chairman, attended and chaired only one of the 42 meetings of the Commission from June until December 1941. This meeting took place on 22 October, the day of his arrival in Kuibyshev, and was presumably held there. Six of the seven items on the agenda were concerned with the evacuation of the government to Kuibyshev, a matter for which Stalin had made Molotov responsible.[93]

In 1942, however, Molotov attended 41 of the 55 meetings. He took over the chairmanship of the Commission in August, when he was appointed 'first deputy chairman of Sovnarkom for all questions of the work of Sovnarkom USSR'.[94] He chaired 22 meetings in 1942 and continued as chairman when the Commission was reformed as the Bureau of Sovnarkom (*Byuro Sovnarkoma SSSR*) in December 1942. In 1943 the Bureau met only five times and Molotov chaired all five meetings: the GKO Operative Bureau, with Molotov as chair, had been given responsibility for many vital commissariats.[95] The brief given to the Operative Bureau meant, in effect, that Sovnarkom's work was divided between the two committees; Molotov oversaw both until Beriya assumed responsibility for the Operative Bureau.

The work of the Sovnarkom Bureau and Molotov's role in its proceedings increased in 1944. It held 31 meetings; Molotov attended and chaired 28, including two joint meetings of the Sovnarkom Bureau and the GKO Operative Bureau held in October.[96] The focus of Molotov's administrative work in the Sovnarkom Bureau may indicate that in domestic politics he was being relegated to more routine business and that Beriya's power was increasing. In 1945, up to the time of its abolition, in August, the Bureau met 36 times, but Molotov attended only nine of these meetings, all of which he chaired. This fall in attendance was presumably because of his preoccupation with international affairs.

If Stalin was dissatisfied with Molotov this may have been because he failed to adapt to wartime conditions, and used the bureaucratic methods of the 1930s. He formed commissions, and on at least one occasion he circulated a draft resolution he had written to ten people and asked for their opinion. This included Malyshev, although the resolution did not concern the tank industry. Mikoyan recorded one meeting chaired by Molotov in the very early days of the war, called to discuss questions raised by Malyshev. Twenty persons were present: commissars, deputy commissars and members of the Gosplan *kollegiya*. Molotov did not allow free discussion, but invited people to present different points. He contributed nothing to the discussion of the questions personally and had a strange manner. Mikoyan concluded that the meeting was not useful and the whole thing could have been settled by telephone.[97]

The Jewish Anti-Fascist Committee

Besides the main areas for which he was responsible Molotov took a personal interest in the Jewish Anti-Fascist Committee. There can be little doubt that this was because of the leading role in Jewish affairs played by Polina Molotov, who possibly acted as an intermediary between the Committee and Molotov.[98] The Committee was created in 1942 to encourage Western Jewish support for the alliance with the Soviet Union. It operated under the supervision of Solomon Lozovskii, appointed as a Deputy Commissar for Foreign Affairs in May 1939, shortly after Molotov's appointment as Commissar. From the experience he had gained from his own visit, Molotov briefed the famous actor Solomon Mikhoels and the poet Israel Fefer before they travelled to Britain and America in 1943 to raise support for the Committee.[99] Soon after their return, they saw Molotov, possibly on Polina's initiative, and raised with him the question of the creation a Jewish Republic in the Crimea, or in the area of the former Volga German Republic.[100] Molotov dismissed the second suggestion because the Jews were an urban people who would not adapt to agricultural work, but with regard to the Crimea he said 'you write the letter and we will have a look at it'. Lozovskii supervised the composition of the letter that was sent to Stalin and Molotov.[101] According to Khrushchev, Stalin reacted in a very hostile manner to the proposal,[102] and if there was ever any sympathy for this idea it soon faded with Soviet military success, although Molotov continued to interest himself in the work of the Committee. A further letter of 15 February 1944, addressed to Stalin, was referred to Lozovskii, but when Molotov saw it he arranged to have it edited and readdressed to himself. On receipt of it he had copies distributed to Malenkov, Mikoyan, Voznesenskii and A. S. Scherbakov, the Moscow party chief.[103]

In August 1944, Molotov received complaints from the Committee that Jews in reconquered territories were being neglected and failed to receive Western aid sent to them. He immediately ordered an investigation, but noted on the memorandum he sent to the Commissariat of State Control that the Jewish Anti-Fascist Committee 'was not created to handle such matters and the Committee apparently does not have a completely accurate understanding of its functions'.[104] It was becoming too dangerous to support the Committee.

12
The Diplomat at War

Molotov's visit to Britain and the United States 1942

Molotov's lukewarm attitude towards Britain, a reflection of his pro-German sentiments, and the treaties with Germany, meant that despite the efforts of Sir Stafford Cripps, British ambassador to the USSR from May 1940, there was little change in Anglo-Soviet relations from 1939 until Hitler launched Barbarossa.[1] On 12 July 1941 Molotov and Cripps signed a joint agreement between Britain and the USSR. This pledged mutual aid and affirmed that neither country would conclude a separate peace. A trade and credit agreement was signed in August, but even after the 'three-power conference'[2] relations between the two countries remained poor. Stalin and Molotov were clearly dissatisfied with the limited aid they were receiving from Britain, which had not responded to enquiries about a Second Front, raised by Molotov with Cripps, and by Stalin with Churchill, as early as 18 July.[3] Eden's visit to Moscow, in December 1941, was a half-hearted and unsuccessful British attempt to foster improved relations and closer co-operation.

Molotov was responsible for the formalities of the Eden visit, meeting Eden in the Kremlin 'dressed in a little buff uniform coat and Russian boots'.[4] Stalin led the talks, however, and Molotov played his typical secondary role. He supported Stalin in pressing Eden for Britain to accept the USSR's 1941 frontiers.[5] Eden recorded on one occasion 'Molotov was most unhelpful', adding in his memoirs 'and the close of our discussion frigid'.[6] He did not accept the Soviet demands, but left Stalin and Molotov with the impression that he recognised *de facto* Soviet claims to the Baltic States, and from this time, in negotiations with the British, they behaved as if the future of these states was settled, a useful bargaining position.[7] At the banquet, at the end of the visit, Stalin blamed Molotov for the Nazi–Soviet pact. He also narrated the story of Molotov's comments to Ribbentrop about the British bombs during Molotov's visit to Berlin in November 1940, which Churchill claimed Stalin told him when he visited Moscow in August 1942. According to Eden, in response to Stalin's story, Molotov smiled and nodded.[8]

Shortly after Eden's departure Molotov tried to persuade Cripps that, as the original belligerent powers, Britain and the USSR should act independently of the United States against Germany, but Cripps did not respond favourably.[9] This, a clear reflection of Molotov's commitment to an ideological framework, appears to be his first attempt to create divisions between the 'imperialist powers'. It is less certain that he was proposing an Anglo-Soviet alliance which could eventually be directed against the United States, although his hostility was evident. When Litvinov, now ambassador to America, with whom Molotov's relations continued to be strained, suggested he should approach Roosevelt about the Second Front, Molotov forbade him to raise the matter, because they had already had three refusals and did not want a fourth.[10]

With British military reverses in the Far East, Churchill, by March 1942, was prepared to negotiate with the USSR, and make concessions on the frontier question. He suggested that Molotov come to London to negotiate a treaty.[11] Not to be out-done by the British initiative, Roosevelt invited Molotov to Washington, hinting at the possibility of a Second Front.[12] On 13 April, Maiskii told Eden that Molotov was unable to accept 'because he had been charged by Stalin with more important duties in connection with [tank] production'.[13] On 20 April, however, Stalin wrote to Roosevelt that it was essential to arrange a meeting between him and Molotov about opening a Second Front as quickly as possible, and that he agreed that Molotov should visit London, as well as Washington.[14] Molotov was to go to London first as Britain might make concessions on Soviet territorial claims. If he went to Washington first, he might have to trade possible concessions for the promise of a Second Front.[15] Stalin and Molotov were trying to divide the 'imperialist camp'.

Knowledge of the mission was limited to Molotov, Stalin and General A. E. Golovanov, responsible for planning it. Molotov travelled as 'Mr. Brown', Stalin and Molotov insisting on keeping the date of Molotov's arrival secret.[16] Clearly this was essential for Molotov's personal safety, but Molotov would have become suspicious and alarmed when the USSR air attaché to Britain and three other Soviet officials, including a member of the advanced party for the Molotov visit, were killed in late April, when an RAF plane in which they were flying burst into flames.[17] He arrived on 20 May[18] after an overnight flight of ten hours and 15 minutes. He travelled over the front and occupied Europe at an altitude of 30,000 feet, to avoid German fighters.[19] Sir Alexander Cadogan, the Permanent Under-secretary of State at the Foreign Office, who met Molotov, found him 'at the top of his form and most chatty'.[20] He brought with him, not only his male NKVD bodyguards, but also a female attendant to look after his clothes and guard his room at Chequers, where the party stayed for the visit. On Molotov's arrival his police guard made a meticulous search of the room. The bedding was so arranged that Molotov could spring out of it at a moment's notice, and a revolver was placed next to Molotov's briefcase by the bed each night. Churchill's comment on these arrangements was that Molotov should have asked if anyone on the English side had any interest in his assassination.[21] Molotov scathingly recorded in his memoirs that Chequers was old-fashioned: he had a bathroom, but there was no shower. At the White House, however, it was up-to-date: he had a bathroom with a shower.[22]

Molotov worked under 'remote control', as on his visit to Berlin. He began the negotiations by stating that he was authorised to negotiate on an alliance and the

Second Front, which the Soviet government considered to be especially/more important, and to be primarily a political rather than military matter.[23] This brought the question of the Second Front to the top of the agenda, and the negotiations demonstrated that the post-war security of the USSR could be traded off for it if the Soviet military situation deteriorated. On both issues, Molotov could exploit differences between Britain and the United States.

The early meetings were mainly occupied by a long wrangle over Soviet post-war frontier claims in a draft treaty.[24] When the Second Front was discussed, Molotov, who Cadogan thought 'had all the grace and conciliation of a totem pole',[25] insisted on a political focus. He argued that, since Britain would be primarily responsible, it should be discussed before he went to the United States. He pointed out that the main burden of resisting Hitler was falling on the USSR, and in the light of the desperate situation his country faced, asked if 40 German divisions could not be diverted to fight in Western Europe in the summer of 1942. This, he argued, might determine the eventual outcome of the war that year. Rather than begging for help, he was suggesting a strategy to achieve a quick victory at minimum cost to the USSR. In response, Churchill spoke of the lack of British and American resources to mount a European offensive in 1942. During the discussion, Molotov (perhaps looking for divisions in the 'imperialist camp') repeatedly tried to clarify whether Churchill was stating an agreed Anglo-American position, or if he was speaking only on behalf of Britain.[26] Embarrassingly, he insisted on reminding the British prime minister of the small proportion of British forces actively engaged in military operations in May 1942, and of the relatively minor losses the British had suffered.

After his return from Downing Street, on 22 May, Molotov was taken aback when Churchill and Eden arrived at Chequers for a final meeting that day. This was an attempt by Churchill and Eden to browbeat Molotov into concessions. After a long analysis of the military situation by Churchill, Eden introduced the draft of a 'reserve' treaty, which did not mention frontiers. This was clearly meant as a threat if Molotov continued to insist on the Soviet proposals for the Polish eastern border. Interestingly, there is no record of this meeting in the British archives, only hints in diaries. Molotov's report to Stalin and the Russian foreign ministry archive, however, make clear that this additional meeting took place and also its significance.[27]

In three reports to Stalin on 23 May, Molotov, who stressed the personal pressure Churchill and Eden were placing on him, stated that that they were now withdrawing concessions on Soviet post-war frontiers. They were falling back on Eden's 'reserve' document, unless Molotov agreed to discuss the original proposal in the United States and then return to Britain. He had resisted this, because a second visit to Britain was not in his instructions. He knew that discussions with Roosevelt were not going to strengthen his position on the frontier question.[28] When Eden formally presented his alternative document Molotov's response was guarded: the Soviet government would have to be consulted. He asked to conclude discussion on the original drafts.[29] He sent to Stalin the new draft treaty proposed by Eden and reported: 'Eden ... was prepared to derail the two treaties under discussion, and gave the draft of a new, emasculated, treaty as cover'.[30]

With the Germans having broken through in the Crimea, 22–24 May, Stalin replied promptly, on 24 May, with an abrupt change of policy. He instructed Molotov to accept Eden's 'reserve' treaty because it left the USSR a free hand, and the question of frontiers 'will be decided by force'. Molotov was to sign the document as quickly as possible and fly on to the United States.[31] There, Stalin believed, Roosevelt offered the prospect of a Second Front.[32] When, late on 24 May, Molotov received Stalin's instructions on the second treaty, he sensed Stalin's impatience and immediately fell into line on the new policy, writing to Stalin: 'I believe that the new draft treaty can also have a positive value. I failed to appreciate it at once. … I shall present our consent … as a big concession to Churchill, and especially to Roosevelt'.[33] The telegram makes clear that Molotov accepted the new treaty and abandoned Soviet territorial claims because of instructions from Stalin, not, as some older authorities suggested, as a result of his interview with J.G. Winant, the American ambassador to Britain.[34]

When Molotov met Eden, on 25 May, he was enthusiastic for the new document. He introduced two minor technical amendments to wording, proposed by Stalin, and one of his own referring to the 'security interests' of the signatories.[35] The Treaty was signed on 26 May, and Molotov departed for the United States the next day.[36] Churchill wrote to Roosevelt: 'We have completely transformed the treaty proposals. … Molotov is a statesman, and has a freedom of action very different from what you and I saw in Litvinov.' … [37] Clearly, Churchill had reached the wrong conclusion on the reasons why Molotov accepted the new treaty.

Immediately after landing in the United States, Molotov, 'somewhat dishevelled and unwashed', as he admitted, went to meet Roosevelt.[38] Later the same day, he emphasised that despite signing the 'reserve treaty', the USSR's position on the frontier question had not changed.[39] In a seven-and-a-half hour discussion on the Second Front with Hopkins and Roosevelt, the American President said that he was trying to persuade his military leaders to risk landing from six to ten divisions in France in 1942. Molotov, in response, stressed the perilous military position of the USSR, and the strategy of diverting forty German divisions to the west in 1942. Clearly the figure was in Molotov's brief for the mission.[40] Hopkins sensed the nature of the correspondence between Stalin and Molotov, commenting: 'the word has gone out from Mr. Stalin to be somewhat more agreeable than is Mr. Molotov's custom'.[41]

The next day, in discussions with Roosevelt and American military leaders, Molotov emphasised that Hitler was at that time able to use most of the resources of Europe against the USSR. Captured Soviet assets, particularly oil, would strengthen Hitler's position, if the military situation deteriorated. General George Marshall stated that the only assistance possible in 1942 was the use of American planes against the Luftwaffe.[42] A crestfallen Molotov, who had been led by the British to believe that Marshall was a supporter of the Second Front, wrote to Stalin 'They told me nothing concrete' and later 'The insincerity of this reply was obvious to me.'[43] At lunch, after the meeting, Roosevelt tactlessly asked Molotov to give his impressions of Hitler. He replied that it was possible to arrive at a common understanding with anyone, but he had never dealt with two more disagreeable people than Hitler and Ribbentrop.[44]

At a further meeting on 1 June, Roosevelt suggested that the USSR should reduce its demands for supplies from 8,000,000 to 2,000,000 tons, to free ships to transport men and arms to Britain.[45] This clearly faced Molotov with a dilemma, and according to one American report, he 'bristled'. He agreed to convey the proposal to 'the Soviet government', but stressed the need for equipment. When Roosevelt referred to the matter again, Molotov, according to an American record of the conversation

> retorted with some emphasis that the Second Front would be stronger if the First Front still stood fast, and inquired with deliberate sarcasm what would happen if the Soviets cut down their requirements and then no Second Front eventuated. Then, becoming still more insistent ... he asked ... What is the President's answer with respect to the Second Front?[46]

Molotov reported to Stalin Roosevelt's proposal for the reduction of supplies, noting a discrepancy between Roosevelt's figures and the Soviet calculations.[47] He drafted a bland communiqué on the talks, for Stalin's approval. There was no mention of the Second Front or Soviet frontiers.[48] But Stalin was now alarmed and furious, writing to Molotov on 3 June:

1. The *Instantsiya*[49] is dissatisfied with the terseness and reticence of your communications, You convey to us ... only what you yourself consider important and omit all the rest.
2. This refers to the draft of the communiqué as well. You have not informed us ... why ... there could not be two communiqués. ... we are having to guess because of your reticence.
3. ... We further consider it absolutely necessary that both communiqués should mention ... the subject of creating the Second Front ... [and] the supply of war materials to the Soviet Union from Britain and the USA.[50]

Instructions from Stalin were to dominate the rest of Molotov's negotiations. His response to Stalin reflected the relationship of the two men since the end of the Terror. When Molotov met Cordell Hull, the American Secretary of State, the same day, Hull found him 'very insistent on the question of the Second Front', totally preoccupied with the war situation, and not interested in post-war questions.[51] He suggested amendments to the communiqué, the most important of which were statements that 'full understanding' had been reached on the Second Front – these were Stalin's words, and that supplies from the United States to the USSR were to be increased.[52] This, no doubt, was meant as a reassurance that he had not accepted Roosevelt's proposal to reduce them. A long telegram to Stalin began:

> I have taken into account the *Instantsiya's* direction to provide complete information about my meetings and talks. ... Of course, all my talks are thoroughly recorded and the records will be submitted by me to the *Instanstiya* in addition to the code messages. ... I agree that it would be better to have two communiqués on the talks in Britain and the USA.

He concluded by mentioning a visit he had made to New York.[53] This was when, in the back of a car, the famous argument with Litvinov, witnessed by Gromyko, took place. Molotov criticised British and French pre-war policy, which he claimed was aimed at pushing Hitler into war against the USSR, and Litvinov defended Britain and France.[54]

Molotov's revised communiqué on his talks in the United States – no longer a joint communiqué on the two sets of talks – was now described by Stalin, in a terse telegram, as satisfactory.[55] In response to Stalin's angry complaint of 3 June, Molotov sent a further five telegrams between 4 and 7 June, in which he described in detail the talks in which he had participated.[56] 'Mr. Brown' finally left the United States on 5 June.[57] Roosevelt wrote to Churchill that Molotov had 'warmed up more than I expected and ... he has a far better understanding of the situation here than when he arrived'.[58] He returned to Britain to receive two more telegrams from Stalin; the first gave more directions on the joint communiqués; the second instructed him to press Churchill on the Second Front.[59] He did this on 9 June, saying that he had received a message from the 'Soviet government' that if Britain could attack the continent in 1942, the USSR would reduce its requirements for military supplies. He emphasised again the need to draw off 40 German divisions, and mentioned an idea of Roosevelt's for a limited expedition – a 'second Dunkirk'. This angered Churchill. Molotov asked him why, if he was so hostile to a 'second Dunkirk', he had suggested an attack on France with only six divisions. In response, Churchill referred to 'successful operations', and the difficulty of landing troops from boats.[60] When he met Eden on the same day, ominously, the British Foreign Secretary said that statements about the Second Front in the communiqué 'might be a means of worrying and deceiving the Germans'. To this Molotov replied that 'there must be no deception between friends'.[61] His realisation that there was little chance of a Second Front in 1942 was confirmed at a final private dinner party, which like the after-dinner meeting on 22 May, does not appear to be recorded in English archives. For three hours, Churchill tried to persuade Molotov of the impossibility of opening the Second Front in 1942.[62] As the visit drew to a close Molotov was punctilious in correcting the Soviet reports on the negotiations, on one occasion deleting a passage reading 'there seem to be a few deficiencies on our side'.[63] He now asked Stalin, whose anger he had aroused once, to approve everything.[64] Clearly, he did not wish to antagonise him further, particularly as the mission had not really achieved its major objectives. Molotov left Britain in his plane in the evening of 9 June, again flying over German occupied Europe where German fighters attacked the plane. In addition, before finally landing in Moscow it was mistakenly attacked by Soviet aircraft.[65]

Churchill made the comment that the only time he obtained 'a natural, human reaction' from Molotov was at their farewell meeting on this visit:

> I gripped his arm and we looked each other in the face. Suddenly he appeared deeply moved. Inside the image there appeared the man. He responded with an equal pressure. Silently we wrung each other's hands.[66]

The treaty Molotov had signed provided the basis for an alliance which achieved the destruction of Nazi power and a new balance in Europe, but the Grand Alliance was never an end in itself. From the beginning it is clear that Molotov approached the negotiations with multiple objectives. Initially, as a top priority these included the post-war balance of power in Europe, reflected in demands for Soviet frontiers to guarantee the security of the USSR. With the deteriorating military situation, however, these broader objectives had to be abandoned for a Second Front, to relieve pressure on the USSR and ensure its survival.

The Moscow Foreign Ministers Conference, October 1943[67]

Molotov played his typical secondary role during Churchill's visit to Moscow in August 1942.[68] He headed the official welcome at the airport and had one private interview with Churchill to which he 'contributed nothing'.[69] At the Moscow Conference of October 1943, the first meeting of the foreign ministers of the major allied powers, however, he was centre stage, and took the lead in establishing Soviet post-war policy. The Soviet Union basked in the sunshine of the foreign ministers of the United States and Great Britain having come to Moscow to negotiate with the USSR on its own ground, on terms of equality.[70] It was the longest wartime conference, and the Western allies found Molotov more affable than at any other time. Crucial in laying the foundations for the post-war world, the Moscow Conference is often taken as the peak of Molotov's diplomatic career.

A major factor that influenced the conference was continuing Soviet military success after the victories at Stalingrad in January 1943 and at Kursk in July.[71] There was no doubt now about the outcome of the war, and the precise timing of the American and English cross-channel invasion of Europe was of less importance. The Russians were not, as Mastny contends, 'playing a weak hand'.[72] The question at issue was the post-war settlement when Germany was defeated. Soviet military victories meant that Stalin and Molotov were moving into a strong position to dictate this.

The origins of the conference lay in Roosevelt's proposals, dating back to December 1941, for a personal meeting between himself, Churchill and Stalin to discuss post-war problems. This had long been delayed because of difficulties in finding a venue, and the deteriorating relations between Stalin and his Western allies, particularly over the 'Second Front', although, in May 1943, Molotov hosted celebrations to mark the first anniversary of the agreements with Britain and the United States.[73] The recall of Maiskii and Litvinov, Soviet ambassadors to Britain and the United States, was not, however, a protest against the failure to open a 'Second Front', as argued by some older authorities, nor was it a result of Stalin's desire to handle relations with his allies personally.[74] Litvinov and Maiskii were appointed as deputies to Molotov in Moscow, to assist the Commissariat of Foreign Affairs in the end-of-war planning it was undertaking on the Politburo orders. In May 1943, Molotov made clear to Sir Archibald Clark Kerr, the British ambassador, the need for Maiskii in Moscow.[75] Another factor that caused friction between the allies was mutual suspicion that one of them might make a separate peace. When Clark Kerr raised this question in April 1943, Molotov told him that no one had approached the Soviet government with peace suggestions on behalf of Germany, and that if anyone did they would 'send him to all the devils'.[76] In August 1943, when Clerk Kerr told Molotov of 'an approach ... by a certain Veres', Molotov was suspicious and asked many questions.[77]

Soviet military successes made the Western allies redouble their efforts to obtain a meeting. In early August 1943, Churchill offered to send his foreign secretary to Moscow 'to stroke the bristles of the bear', as Eden put it.[78] Stalin refused this offer: he had no wish to hear again British excuses about the Second Front and Arctic convoys. He proposed a meeting of 'responsible representatives' to prepare the ground for a meeting of the three heads of government.[79] On 18 August, Roosevelt, with Churchill's consent, accepted an exploratory meeting at foreign minister level.[80] In response, Molotov passed the American ambassador a note from Stalin insisting that the meeting 'should not be of a narrow exploratory character but of a practical preparatory character', and that the agenda and draft documents should be agreed beforehand.[81]

Two months of discussion to agree time, place and personnel followed.[82] Stalin insisted that the conference should be held in Moscow despite a number of alternative suggestions.[83] He was adamant that unless the conference was convened there, Molotov, whose presence he considered indispensable, would be unable to attend.[84] Both the proceedings, and his Commissar for Foreign Affairs, would be easier to control in Moscow. Rather than 'a system of remote control', Stalin's control could be direct, and his appointments diary shows that Molotov met him daily during the conference, after each meeting, except on one day, 22 October, when Stalin had no appointments.[85] After his experience in trying to follow Stalin's wishes in 1942, to negotiate in Moscow must have been a relief for Molotov!

He was deeply involved in advanced planning for the conference. When, in January 1942, the Politburo established 'a commission for plans for the post-war state structure of the countries of Europe, Asia and other parts of the world', Molotov chaired a sub-commission to prepare diplomatic materials.[86] Two further commissions established under the auspices of the Commissariat for Foreign Affairs (*pri* NKID), in September 1943,[87] provided briefing papers for Molotov at the conference, particularly one chaired by Litvinov on the 'peace treaties and post-war structure'. On almost every agenda item Molotov followed the line of these papers.[88] Among the most important is one on mechanisms for permanent consultations among the allies. In another, Litvinov argued that any post-war international organisation would not be able to function effectively without a division of the world into Soviet, American and British zones of responsibility, although he also advised that the USSR should avoid revealing that it advocated a division into spheres of influence.[89] On the key question of the future security of the USSR from German aggression, evolving Soviet policy aimed at the long-term occupation of a dismembered Germany, which was to be disarmed and denazified, and from which punitive reparations were to be extracted.[90] The briefing materials related not only to policy but also to tactics, for example they included plans to defer discussion so that Molotov and his colleagues could discuss matters with the Litvinov commission.[91]

Because the British and American agenda items were submitted first, Stalin was able to select the topic he knew he could use to put pressure on the Western powers. In addition, with Soviet military victories, it is clear that the USSR was less enthusiastic about discussion of its post-war boundaries, particularly the frontiers of Poland and Romania in dispute with their Western allies, which could now be settled without Western aid. The Soviet proposals, therefore, submitted over Molotov's signature on 29 September, consisted of one item: 'Measures for Shortening the War'. The Second Front, and a cross-channel invasion by Great Britain and the United States in 1943, were specifically mentioned.[92] This caused consternation in London and Washington, and there was speculation that the USSR wished the conference to be abandoned.[93] Molotov's reference to 'questions concerning European countries' in documents sent to the Americans, may have been intended to be provocative, referring to the West's delay in invading the European mainland. He had used similar ploys in earlier negotiations.[94] It is also evidence of his interest in the peace settlement with Italy. The Soviet view appeared intransigent and self-centred to the Western powers, but it was conditioned by prolonged hardship and suffering following the Nazi invasion, and suspicions about the Western powers' failure to launch a cross-channel invasion.

The conference and the 'Hero of Socialist Labour' award to Molotov were announced on the same day, 1 October.[95] The British Ambassador commented it was the 'rarest award in the USSR', although it was for 'increasing tank production' and not for achievements in foreign policy.[96] It obviously increased Molotov's status for the forthcoming negotiations. On their arrival in Moscow, he met both Hull and Eden. The latter found Molotov 'very affable,' and talked to him about 'harmony' and the need to 'keep in step' (suggested by the guard of honour).[97]

Held in the huge, ornate Spiridonovka Palace,[98] the conference opened on 19 October.[99] Diplomatic uniforms had been reintroduced in the USSR especially for the event.[100] Molotov, although proud of his uniform, 'looked somewhat ridiculous. … The uniform was black trimmed in gold, with a small dagger at the belt … much like that of Hitler's elite S.S. troops'.[101] After a show of reluctance, he accepted the chairmanship on a permanent basis,[102] which placed the full responsibility for the success of the conference on his shoulders. A preliminary discussion of the agenda and the powers of delegates demonstrated that Molotov remembered the Triple Alliance negotiations.[103] He then introduced the Soviet item 'Measures for Shortening the War' pressing for an invasion of northern France in 1943, and for Turkish entry into the war to relieve pressure on Soviet forces.[104]

The second session was preceded by a hearty luncheon hosted by Molotov, at which there was a profusion of toasts,[105] and protests from the Western delegates about the heat of the room. Molotov had arranged for its temperature to be increased because Hull had felt cold and sent for his coat during the first session.[106] His vain attempt at this session to obtain information about the precise timing of the invasion of north-west Europe in 1944 is not recorded in the British report of the discussion of 'Measures for Shortening the War'[107] which, seeking room to manoeuvre, he tried unsuccessfully to avoid chairing.[108]

When the Western proposal for a 'Four Power Declaration', which included Roosevelt's scheme for a new international organisation and a statement on 'unconditional surrender', was discussed, Molotov made clear that he was seeking a free hand for Soviet forces in the post-war world in territories that it had re-conquered. He tested the West to see if it would acquiesce to an enormous expansion of the Soviet sphere of influence.[109] This same tactic was apparent in discussion of the main British proposal, for a 'politico-military commission' (to become known as the European Advisory Commission) for three-power discussion of current problems.[110]

Prior to formal proceedings on 23 October, Molotov had a private meeting with Hull who raised the questions of the USSR trying to spread communism in the United States and of religious freedom for Soviet citizens.[111] Molotov clearly did not view these as serious issues, and must have been astounded to discuss what he regarded as trivia when the fate of Europe was at stake. In the negotiations that day, he obtained Soviet representation on the Italian Advisory Council proposed previously by Eden, and went on to secure limitation of the powers of the European Advisory Commission to dealing with the end of hostilities and the immediate post hostilities period. He resisted the commission having wider powers to consider current European questions and played off Eden against Hull to achieve a notable success.

At the close of this session, Molotov obtained deferment of discussion on Germany to give time for the Soviet delegation to study proposals that Hull had given him at their informal meeting.[112] These recommended unconditional surrender, total disarmament and occupation by the three powers, and thus went at least part of the way to meet Soviet requirements as formulated by the Litvinov commission. Molotov must have been delighted to take these proposals to Stalin whom he saw that night, with Litvinov, Voroshilov and his fellow delegates.[113] According to Hull, Molotov was 'radiant', and stated that Stalin's first response to the American proposals on Germany had been enthusiastic.[114] Valentin Berezhkov, Molotov's interpreter at the conference, was more guarded. He reported that Molotov told Hull that Stalin's 'reaction was on the whole favourable'; that the proposal corresponded to Soviet ideas about the treatment of Germany; and was the basis for 'work on an appropriate document'.[115] Molotov was going to press the Western powers for more concessions.

On 24 October, Eden's plan for a 'self-denying ordinance' was discussed.[116] This scheme, for neither the USSR nor Britain to make agreements with smaller states about the post-war world without the approval of the other party, was quite clearly aimed at checking Soviet expansionist aims.[117] Molotov's immediate concern was the Soviet–Czech treaty[118] awaiting signature, on which, he claimed, Eduard Beneš, the head of the Czech government in exile, had taken the initiative. Eden was unwilling to agree to this as an exception because the exiled Polish government had not been consulted, but Molotov used Hull's indifference to ask if the United States would accept whatever Britain and the USSR agreed. He also had ready a Soviet government statement, amending the draft 'self-denying ordinance', to allow its signatories to conclude agreements with bordering states on the security of their frontiers, without consultation of the other party. In these circumstances, Eden agreed to the Soviet–Czech treaty.[119] Molotov later confided to Beneš that he was surprised at the lack of debate.[120] This may have been because, during discussion, the famous exchange between Molotov and Eden, not recorded in any of the official reports of the conference, took place. Eden said 'I may be mistaken, but. ...'; Molotov leant across the table and cut him short saying, 'You are mistaken.' It is not clear if Eden was unnerved by this 'undiplomatic' behaviour, but he did not reply and had suffered a major defeat. It is, however, too much to claim that this marked a turning point in the conference giving Molotov the upper hand over Eden.[121]

The next day, Molotov tried to gain agreement to further punitive measures against Germany. He emphasised the importance of reparations for the USSR, and stated that the Soviet Union would not oppose the dismemberment of Germany by force, saying that Eden was less resolute towards Germany than the United States. When Hull tried to moderate the attack, indicating that the United States was looking less favourably on dismemberment,[122] Molotov was clearly annoyed. He said that the USSR was backward in the study of the question because of the military preoccupations of its leaders. This may have meant that no final decision had yet been taken on the matter.[123] Molotov's view, that Germany must be restored to her pre-*Anschluss* frontiers, was supported. This allowed the question of Austria to be referred directly to the conference's drafting committee[124] where the Soviet delegates insisted on inserting reparations claims. Controversy over these, in which Molotov participated, contributed to the delay in the Austrian peace treaty until 1955.[125] Molotov's suspicions of the Western powers were clear at this session of the conference in his insistence on unconditional surrender in a discussion of peace feelers from enemy states. He was particularly concerned with Hungary, Romania and Finland, countries that had voluntarily supported Hitler, and was adamant that there should be no negotiations with opposition groups, a strategy aimed at preventing the West from restoring 'bourgeois' governments.[126]

On 26 October, Molotov managed to dispose of Eden's awkward proposal for a joint declaration on 'spheres of influence' and confederations in eastern Europe, because Hull's support was only lukewarm. This would have committed the signatories to the restoration of freedom and self-determination in countries conquered by the Nazis; to encourage larger groupings of states provided they were not hostile to other states; and to renounce any intention of creating 'spheres of influence'. Molotov argued that commitment to respect self-determination and renunciation of 'spheres of influence' were general principles which should be included in the Four Power Declaration. This was embarrassing to Great Britain in view of the British Empire, and to the United States in the light of the Monroe Doctrine. Clearly the real Soviet objection was to the formation of a bloc of states in eastern Europe hostile to the USSR. Molotov referred to a *cordon sanitaire* (*sanitarnyi kordon*).[127] Eden hastened to reassure Molotov: Britain was interested in a *cordon sanitaire* against Germany, not against the USSR. When Eden did not persist with his proposals,[128] Molotov had scored another notable victory.

When the Four Power Declaration was discussed on the same day, Molotov was particularly suspicious about Article 6. This defined when military forces might be used 'within the territory of other States' and had already been modified at his request. He had defeated British plans for federation in eastern Europe and was not likely to accept American proposals that might limit Soviet action. On this occasion, however, he seemed to be reassured when Hull proposed that a further article to which he had raised objections be withdrawn. Molotov then submitted an additional resolution that the three powers should appoint representatives for preliminary discussions of the proposed international organisation. He suggested meetings in any of the three capitals, with invitations to other allied powers if necessary. Hull called Molotov's proposal – if it had been successful he might have been regarded as the father of UNO – a 'practical step', but it was eventually agreed that the best results would come from informal meetings of the three heads of state.[129] This had been a triumphant day for Molotov. Not only had he put an end to British aspirations for eastern Europe and obtained a free hand for the USSR, but he had also secured the modification of the Four Power Declaration where it appeared to limit Soviet freedom of action.

On 27 October, Molotov supported Eden in referring the British foreign secretary's proposal for a declaration of allied policy in liberated territories to the European Advisory Commission. The declaration sought to extend to the smaller countries in Europe the principles of democracy and self-determination on which the conference already had proposals for liberated France, Germany and Italy.[130] Eden tactfully referred to Norway, Belgium and the Netherlands, but Molotov could have had little doubt that his real concern was Poland and other eastern European countries that the USSR was likely to re-conquer.[131] Molotov had again managed to protect Soviet interests.

On 28 October, after a meeting between Stalin, Molotov and Eden the previous evening, where Eden indicated that the cross-channel invasion might have to be postponed a little,[132] Molotov could obtain no reassurance that the decision taken at the Quebec Conference on the invasion of France in the 'early spring' of 1944 was still valid. Eden would say only that he felt sure that 'a generally accepted agreement' could be worked out.[133] This was the most unsatisfactory day of the conference for Molotov.

The following day, on post-war economic co-operation, he was enthusiastic about US aid to the USSR for reconstruction, but on long-term assistance to other countries would only agree that negotiations would be desirable, in due course. The British and Soviet accounts of the discussion show that Molotov was particularly concerned with reparations, and insisted that they should be punitive. He did not want these restricted to Germany alone, but applied to her allies as well. He stated specifically that the living standards and the general interests of Germany's victims should be regarded as equally important to those of the Germans.[134] This discussion was a portent for the future: American economic strength was to be confronted by Soviet military power.

Eden and Molotov had already clashed on Poland during a visit to the opera arranged for the visiting foreign ministers.[135] When Eden introduced the Polish issue, regretting that there were no diplomatic relations between the USSR and the Polish government-in-exile, and requested aid for the Polish resistance, Molotov was hostile. He said that arms should be only in safe hands, and there were none in Poland. He emphasised that since Poland was the USSR's neighbour, the question of good relations was primarily a Soviet–Polish concern. The Soviet Union wanted an independent Poland, but one with a government friendly to the USSR. He quoted a Russian proverb about a chariot remaining in the same place, saying that General K. Sosnkowski, who had replaced General W. Sikorski as leader of the Polish government in exile, was hostile to the USSR. Molotov stood his ground and there was no progress.[136] At an informal meeting with Hull on that day, when Hull suggested that he might deputise for Stalin at a forthcoming meeting of the three heads of state, Molotov 'instantly dissented from this suggestion by saying that he was in no sense a military man and would not fit into that sort of situation'.[137]

At the final session of the conference, on 30 October, Eden noted Molotov's 'business-like' approach. He believed that it was a response to orders from Stalin after his interview.[138] Molotov used Litvinov to repel a further attempt by Eden to secure a declaration in favour of democracy and independence in Europe and against spheres of influence, and was skilful in glossing over the differences between the three ministers to secure the signing of the documents. At the conclusion of the session Eden and Hull complimented Molotov on his chairmanship.[139] Clark Kerr reported to the Foreign Office:

Molotov conducted the proceedings with sustained tact and skill and growing good humour, deferring any matter that seemed to threaten prickliness and only reverting to it when its thorns had been drawn by talks over food and wine. The way he handled the debates compelled our respect and in the end our affection also. He has travelled a long way during the last year and a half.[140]

He seems to have failed to realise the extent of Molotov's success and the crushing blow to British aims for eastern Europe. In the House of Commons Eden was complimentary about Molotov's chairmanship,[141] as was Hull in his report to Congress.[142] There was no indication of a diplomatic defeat, although comments in the American press recognised the potential dominance of eastern Europe by the USSR.[143] Later, however, in his memoirs, Eden noted that during the conference, for the first time, he became uneasy about Soviet ambitions.[144]

The conference was dominated by exchanges between Eden and Molotov. The Second Front on which Molotov had gained little, despite reports in the Soviet press afterwards,[145] was now a much lower priority. Indeed, it was becoming a good stick with which to beat the Western powers, and as the USSR re-conquered more territory it was in the Soviet interest to delay it as long as possible. In other spheres, blocking a Balkan confederation; achieving maximum freedom of action for the USSR by blocking Eden's 'self-denying ordinance'; establishing the European Advisory Commission with strictly circumscribed powers; seeing that the question of Poland was left to the USSR to settle; and laying the basis for a new international order in the Four Power Declaration; Molotov's achievements were considerable. One authority claims

> The Moscow meeting stands out as the only one where issues were clearly defined, systematically discussed, and disposed of through genuine bargaining. ... Molotov was at his very best at Moscow. ... It was because of the superior Soviet diplomacy ... that Stalin could look forward with confidence to his impending talks with Roosevelt and Churchill at Teheran.[146]

Harriman noted that 'Molotov expanded as the days passed ... he showed increasing enjoyment in being admitted for the first time into the councils as a full member with the British and ourselves'.[147] He did not really understand the real reasons for Molotov's growing confidence. Charles Bohlen was a little more suspicious:

> Like almost all Soviet leaders a man of mystery, Molotov maintained that air at the conference. Although he was trying to be affable, he had a hard time smiling, and his face remained impassive through most of the talks. The first close-up impression of Molotov as a careful, sober negotiator, the epitome of an intelligent Soviet bureaucrat, deepened the more I came in contact with him.[148]

Comments by Hull and Eden in their memoirs, that at the dinner on the last night of the conference, Stalin indicated to each of them, that although he could not leave the 'military-emergency' situation, he was willing to send Molotov as his deputy to meet Roosevelt and Churchill, may indicate Stalin's approval of Molotov's success at the conference.[149] At this dinner, Molotov agreed to drink a toast proposed by Harriman to their fighting together against Japan, saying 'Why not – gladly – the time will come.'[150] According to Harriman, Stalin repeated the story he had told Eden and Churchill about Molotov's question to Ribbentrop about British bombs during his visit to Berlin in 1940.[151] Eden then

> assured Stalin that his confidence in Molotov was not diminished by the Soviet Foreign Minister's past associations. Stalin ... responded that his Foreign Minister was really responsible for Neville Chamberlain's behaviour in the Munich crisis, although 'not 100 per cent'.[152]

It is not clear if there was more in Stalin's comment than ridicule of his lieutenant, or if he was reminding him that he had fallen into disgrace in 1936 by pressing for friendly relations with Germany.[153] Molotov, however, must have found this comment more damaging than the compliment in Stalin's offer to send him as his deputy to negotiate with Churchill and Roosevelt. Equally embarrassing for Molotov was the fact that Litvinov, whom he had displaced as Commissar for Foreign Affairs, who thought he was a fool and was prepared to say so quite openly, provided the briefing material for him and served as a Soviet delegate at the conference.[154]

The last years of the war

After the Moscow Conference Stalin stood firm on Teheran for the meeting of the three heads of state, although he did offer to send Molotov as his deputy if the conference was located elsewhere.[155] Roosevelt and Churchill arranged to meet in Cairo on the way to Teheran. Roosevelt invited Molotov and requested a Soviet military representative to join the British and American military leaders.[156] On 10 November Stalin accepted the invitation,[157] but two days later withdrew his acceptance, citing 'reasons of a serious nature'.[158] He later pleaded an illness that made it impossible for Molotov, his first deputy, to be spared, but the real reason, as he made clear to Churchill at Teheran, was that he had discovered that discussions with Chiang-Kai-Shek and Chinese nationalist representatives were to take place in Cairo.[159]

Prior to the conference, Molotov was involved in discussions with Harriman, Eden and Clark Kerr about Roosevelt's residence whilst in Teheran. The British and Soviet embassies were located close to each other, but the American some distance away. Both the British and the Soviets tried to persuade Roosevelt to move into their compounds, but Molotov won. He persuaded Harriman that there were German agents in Teheran who might assassinate Roosevelt.[160] No doubt this allowed conversations between the American representatives to be monitored. During these preliminary discussions Molotov asked Harriman if he had an agenda for the conference – the Soviets had insisted on one for the Moscow Conference. Harriman explained that Roosevelt envisaged an informal 'get together'. Molotov then approached Clark Kerr and as a professional diplomat found him more receptive. The British tried to compile a document, which led to acrimonious discussions with the US representatives, and there was no agenda.[161] Molotov had managed to drive a wedge between the British and American representatives before the conference commenced.

The formal sessions and banquets at the Teheran conference, 27 November to 1 December 1943, were dominated by the discussions between the three heads of state, the supporting representatives from all three powers playing a very minor role.[162] Molotov was involved in the incident at a dinner hosted by Stalin, on 29 November, where he insisted that 50,000 or 100,000 German officers should be shot. Roosevelt tried to defuse Churchill's anger by jokingly suggesting it was necessary to shoot only 49,000. Churchill was so angry that he left the room. Stalin and Molotov followed him laughing, and said that they were 'only playing'.[163]

On 30 November, there was a separate meeting of foreign ministers where Hopkins represented the United States. This established a procedure for future wartime conferences, and the post-war conferences of foreign ministers where Molotov was able to ruthlessly press Stalin's views. At Teheran, the foreign ministers met at Churchill's request to confer on the political situation in the eastern Mediterranean. Hopkins and Molotov, however, plunged into a discussion of 'strong points' (bases) the allies should control after the war. This was a proposal Stalin had made, with the aim of holding Germany in check.[164] Bizerte and Dakar were mentioned, and various points in the Far East. Molotov linked Bizerte to

Stalin's view of punishing France for collaboration with the Nazis. Eden propounded the British view that France should be treated as a liberated and friendly country, and Molotov was forced to concede that some form of voluntary French collaboration might be appropriate.[165] On Turkey, the real purpose of the meeting, Molotov agreed that Soviet views had changed since the Moscow Conference. He stated that if Turkish entry into the war meant that military resources had to be committed to the Aegean, and the invasion of Europe delayed, the USSR would object. Hopkins tried to reassure him that Stalin's demands: a continental invasion in May 1944, the immediate appointment of a commander for this operation and a supporting operation in southern France, could be met. Molotov replied that if this was the case Turkey could be fitted into the priorities.[166]

A provisional arrangement made on Eden's initiative, for the three foreign ministers to discuss Poland's frontiers over lunch the next day, was replaced by a full meeting of the three leaders and their foreign ministers. Here, on 1 December, Molotov raised the question of Turkish rights in the Straits. Blocked by Churchill, who said he would have to consult his 'war cabinet', Molotov did not press the point. Stalin and Molotov were satisfied with Churchill's proposal that he and Roosevelt would discuss the matter with the Turks and if they did not co-operate they would not be given Western help against future Soviet demands.[167] When the question of the Soviet peace treaty with Finland was discussed, in support of Stalin's demands for reparations, Molotov declared that the Finns, allied with the Germans, had bombed and bombarded Leningrad for two years.[168] During discussion of the future Polish frontiers at this meeting, when Eden referred to the 'Molotov–Ribbentrop line', Molotov was quick to correct him – the 1939 frontier corresponded to the Curzon line.[169]

After the conference it was clear that Stalin and Molotov had not agreed the Soviet line on the Second Front. In mid-December, Molotov told Beneš that the question of the Second Front had been settled at Teheran 'to our complete satisfaction'. A few days later Stalin questioned Beneš about the intentions of the Western powers to invade the continent of Europe.[170] The purpose of Beneš's visit to Moscow was to define the post-war relations between Czechoslovakia and the USSR, but Stalin clearly ranked the visit of secondary importance. He delegated most of the negotiation to Molotov, who was irritated by Beneš's volubility. During the discussions, Molotov revealed Soviet concern that knowledge of the policy of dismemberment of Germany might encourage sterner resistance whilst there was still fighting on Soviet territory.[171] A few weeks later, on 1 February 1944, in a major speech to the Supreme Soviet Molotov claimed that the Soviet Union's relationship with Czechoslovakia was a model for other countries, and attempts were made to apply the model to both Italy and France.[172]

When the USSR's major allies invaded France and the Red Army was entering east central Europe, Molotov received briefing materials from the Commissariat of Foreign Affairs commissions established in 1943. There were, however, major differences between Soviet diplomats on the post-war structure of Europe[173] and in the early autumn of 1944 Molotov raised the question of the definition of a Soviet security zone at a meeting at the commissariat.[174] This served as a preparation for his participation in the notorious 'percentages' agreement discussions, when Churchill visited Moscow in October 1944. Churchill suggested the amount of influence to be exercised in post-war Europe, by the Soviet Union on the one hand and the British and Americans on the other, should be 90:10 in the Soviet Union's favour in Romania, 90:10 in the West's favour in Greece, 50:50 in Yugoslavia and Hungary, and 75:25 in the Soviet Union's favour in Bulgaria.[175] The proposals for Greece and Romania were accepted without further discussion, recognition of Britain's disinterestedness in Romania and Stalin's unwillingness to be drawn into the problem of Greece. Stalin, however, objected to the 25 per cent influence proposed for the west in Bulgaria, 'because it did not harmonise with the other figures in the table'. He suggested a ratio of 90:10 in favour of the Soviet Union and insisted on this figure. After further haggling it was agreed that Eden, who had accompanied Churchill, and Molotov who had met them at the airport and who with Eden was present at the conversation, should consider the matter further.[176] Molotov's sole contribution to this first discussion had been to raise the question of Turkey, which allowed Stalin to introduce the issue of Soviet rights to the navigation of the Straits.[177] In later discussions during Churchill's visit, he asked Eden to define what he meant by 'international control', when the question of the occupation of Germany at the end of the war was discussed, but he did not contribute on the difficult issue of Poland.[178]

When the two foreign ministers met, it was clear that Stalin and Molotov had worked out their position. Molotov proposed a change in the ratios, especially in the case of Hungary, where he suggested 75:25 in the USSR's favour. He argued that with the high Soviet casualties in Hungary, a country which bordered the USSR, Soviet military leaders would be disappointed if the Soviet share of influence was not increased. He also demanded a change in the ratio for Bulgaria. There was considerable argument and Eden tried to get the final agreement referred to the European Advisory Commission. Molotov, however, presumably on Stalin's orders, made clear the Soviet priority. He suggested that if they could agree to figures of 90:10 for Bulgaria, a country that had fought as an ally of Germany, the remainder of the problems could be easily settled. Eden indicated that he was prepared to make a concession in the case of Hungary, but not for Bulgaria. Molotov then suggested, if Eden insisted on 75:25 for Bulgaria, a ratio of 60:40 in favour of the Soviet Union for Yugoslavia. Both sides put forward other possibilities for Hungary, Bulgaria and Yugoslavia. They could, however, come to no agreement, and at the end of the meeting Molotov said he wished to resolve the question of Bulgaria within twenty-four hours if possible.[179] Eden commented on this meeting: 'It didn't go well. I found [Molotov's] difficulty over Bulgaria and general attitude more unyielding than last night'.[180]

The next day it was agreed that the ratios in the case of Hungary and Bulgaria would be 80:20 in favour of the Soviet Union.[181] Eden noted in his journal: 'all was smooth as it had been rough yesterday. ...'[182] At this second meeting, Molotov explained how he and Stalin understood some of the percentages: 60:40 for Yugoslavia meant no Soviet interference along the Adriatic coast, but a right to exert influence in the interior; 80:20 for Bulgaria meant the establishment of a Soviet rather than joint allied control commission.[183] In this way, Molotov was responsible for finalising what has often been regarded as a despicable and immoral carve up of the Balkans, which has caused much discussion amongst historians.[184] The United States, however, would never accept an agreement between the USSR and Great Britain which divided Europe into spheres of influence, and Harriman, now the American ambassador, believed that Stalin realised this.[185] Bulgaria was already under Soviet control, and in the case of Hungary an armistice delegation had arrived in Moscow a few days before Stalin's meeting with Churchill. The high ratio in favour of the USSR gave the Soviet Union maximum power in negotiations with it. In the case of Yugoslavia, Mastny suggests that Stalin was willing to recognise a high proportion of British influence because he felt it would help him control Tito.[186]

In January 1945, Molotov, in a surprising breach of diplomatic protocol, approached Harriman for a $6 billion loan to be repaid over thirty years at an annual interest rate of 2 per cent. He portrayed this as a favour to the United States, because it would help solve the vast unemployment and economic dislocation in that country at the end of the war.[187] Molotov raised the matter again at the Yalta Conference, but nothing came of it,[188] and the reasons behind the approach are not clear. At this time there was concern in the West, not only over the advance of Soviet armies into Europe, but also over Soviet demands for territory. In November 1944, following the liberation of a small part of northern Norway by Soviet forces, Molotov claimed Spitzbergen and Bear Island for the USSR, a claim on which he was still insisting in November 1945. Stalin's demands for extensive territory in the Far East followed this.[189] In addition, it was believed that Soviet actions in countries such as Bulgaria and Romania, limited the possibility of establishing 'democratic' governments in those countries.[190] This was an important factor at the Yalta Conference, February 1945.

Molotov met Roosevelt and Churchill at Saki airport, eight miles from Yalta, on 3 February 1945. The first sessions of the conference took place the next day. Molotov remained in the background when Stalin negotiated, but provided more detailed support than before on such questions as Polish frontiers, the post-war Polish government, the dismemberment of Germany and reparations.[191] At the plenary meeting, on 7 February, he read the Soviet counterproposals on the Curzon and Oder-Neisse lines as the basis for Polish frontiers, and on the new Polish government. Roosevelt and Churchill had proposed that a number of Poles, representing a range of political opinions, be brought to Yalta to agree on its formation. Molotov now ingenuously announced that it had been impossible to contact these by telephone. He acknowledged the need for elections, but used the word 'general' rather than 'free'. This proved a turning point at the conference and in the establishment of post-war Poland. From this time, British and American political leaders, whilst they pressed on Poland's western frontier, made less effort to establish a Western style democracy in the negotiations at the Polish Commission chaired by Molotov.[192] Molotov made the Soviet position plain at a plenary session at Yalta, on 9 February. His amendment to the American drafted

'Declaration of Liberated Europe', which promised all liberated countries the right to shape their political future, read: 'support will be given to the political leaders of those countries who have taken an active part in the struggle against the German invaders'.[193] It was apparent that he regarded the whole document as 'interference in the liberated territories'.[194]

At Yalta, there were eight separate meetings of the foreign ministers to discuss the many issues referred to them by the three heads of state. At the first sitting, on 5 February, Molotov hinted that the post-war treatment of Germany was at the top of the Soviet agenda, but he was co-operative once Edward Stettinius, the new American Secretary of State, had agreed to insert a reference to 'dismemberment' in the draft of the surrender document. He maintained, however, that the Soviet government was interested only in studying the problem.[195] On 8 February, he interrupted Eden, as at the Moscow conference, in a way that was becoming typical. When Eden said that he would be ready to say at an appropriate moment, that he was sympathetic to membership of the Soviet republics in the proposed United Nations Organisation, Molotov commented 'the sooner the better'. He then compared the status of the Soviet republics with that of the British Dominions.[196]

In April 1945, Molotov was present at the foundation conference of the United Nations Organisation in San Francisco. Initially, Stalin refused to allow Molotov to go, because it was imperative for him to attend a session of the Supreme Soviet.[197] The real reason was, however, the rapidly deteriorating relations with the United States and Great Britain over Poland. Molotov first agreed to allow Western representatives into Poland, then reversed his decision. In addition, Harriman had clumsily refused Molotov's request to allow Soviet participation in surrender negotiations with the commanders of the German forces in Italy. Molotov, in response, charged the Americans with bad faith and arrogantly insisted that the German approach be abandoned.[198] He seemed genuinely moved on the death of Roosevelt on 12 April. He immediately called on Harriman, and stayed for some time, but was already making preliminary enquiries if Roosevelt's policies were to continue.[199] Stalin, on Harriman's prompting, now changed his decision, and agreed that Molotov should attend the early part of the San Francisco Conference, and meet Truman in Washington before it began.[200] This was an opportunity to assess the new president and the possibility of a change in policy. Molotov confided to ex-ambassador Joseph Davies, before the first meeting with the President, his government's unease about the uncertainty created by Roosevelt's death.[201]

Molotov had two conversations with Truman on 22 and 23 April 1945,[202] the main issue was the dispute about the new Polish government. This was also discussed twice with Eden and Stettinius between the two conversations and once afterwards.[203] According to Truman, the second conversation culminated in the famous exchange where Molotov said, 'I have never been talked to like that in my life' and Truman replied, 'Carry out your agreements and you won't get talked to like that'.[204] Some authorities take this to mark the end of wartime co-operation which led to the divergence between the great powers and to the Cold War.[205]

Although Truman may have spoken bluntly even roughly, there is considerable doubt if the exchange, as reported, ever occurred. It is not included in either the official American or Soviet reports of the conversation, nor did Bohlen, Truman's interpreter, record it in his memoirs. The official record of the conversation shows that it is more likely that Molotov was reassured, and able to report to Stalin that Truman was committed to continue Roosevelt's policies. Co-operation with the United States was likely to continue; and agreements reached at Dumbarton Oaks and Yalta, on the UNO and Soviet entry into the war against Japan, remained in place.[206]

In San Francisco, during the final preparations for the conference, there was a further acrimonious exchange over Poland when Molotov unsuccessfully tried to insist that the Polish 'provisional government' be represented. He strenuously opposed Argentine participation, arguing that in contrast to Poland, Argentina had assisted the enemy throughout the war.[207] Molotov and the Soviet delegation stayed at the St. Francis Hotel in the centre of San Francisco and were apparently popular with the American public. They clustered round Molotov's car, besieged him in the hotel lobby, and asked for his autograph, much to the alarm of his NKVD guards. His response, to what must have been a unique experience, was to appear genial and smile.[208] The opening of the conference was marked by a dispute because the Americans, as hosts, expected Stettinius to be chairman throughout. This conflicted with a system of rotating chairmanship the Soviets anticipated, although Molotov had of course chaired the entire Moscow Conference, and he now became one of four chairmen. In this capacity, he found the vehement demands of the smaller nations for an equal voice in affairs difficult.[209] With Stalin's approval, however, he co-operated with the American drafters of the United Nations Charter,[210] and later supported New York rather than a European city as the future headquarters for the new international organisation, 'as it would enjoy greater popularity in the New World'.[211]

Meetings with Stettinius and Eden over Poland continued,[212] and at a private lunch, on 3 May, when Stettinius enquired about the Polish political leadership, who Molotov had said at Yalta it had not been possible to contact, he replied quite casually, 'Oh yes, I forgot to tell you, the Red Army arrested them.'[213] This resulted in a further stormy meeting with Eden and Stettinius. Molotov repeatedly referred to Genereral L. Okulicki, who he claimed was 'an enemy of the Soviet Union', and Eden said that he had no knowledge of him, but pressed Molotov on the other arrested leaders.[214] Challenged on 8 May, that his leaving would interfere with the work of the conference, he is said to have replied: 'On the contrary I expect it to proceed more smoothly after my departure.'[215]

With the surrender of Germany, on 7 May 1945, Molotov presided over a victory reception for military and government leaders, scientists, representatives from the arts and worker representatives, held in the Kremlin on 24 May, the first reception held since 2 May 1941.[216] At the victory banquet presided over by Stalin a few days later Molotov was the only one of his lieutenants to be toasted by Stalin.[217] In late May 1945, when Hopkins visited Moscow, he enquired if Molotov had recovered from the 'battle of San Francisco'. Molotov replied that he did not recall any battle, but merely arguments.[218] Hopkins's visit was to prepare for the next 'big three' conference, which Stalin proposed for Potsdam, although it became clear that he had not consulted Molotov about this.[219] Molotov contributed to discussion of the question of the Polish political leadership and showed a detailed knowledge of the arrangements for the forthcoming British general election,[220] but conformed to his usual pattern of saying little when Stalin negotiated. Harriman reported to Truman that Molotov did not report accurately to Stalin in all cases, and that he was more suspicious of the United States than Stalin.[221]

Prior to the Potsdam Conference, the British and American governments consulted on the agenda,[222] and Harriman submitted the American items to Molotov on 8 July. He said he would inform the Ambassador if Stalin wished to comment or add other issues.[223] Molotov, however, waited until the day before the conference opened before he presented the Soviet agenda items to Eden,[224] and then to Truman in Stalin's presence the next day. The content of additional items which included Tangier, Syria and the Lebanon, Spain (a proposal for joint action to remove the Franco regime) and what proved to be a Soviet claim to a share of Italy's former African colonies, made clear why Stalin and Molotov had delayed.[225]

At the first session of the Potsdam Conference, 17 July to 2 August 1945, Truman formally proposed that a Council of Foreign Ministers should be established. In preparation for a peace conference, this would have a brief to draw up peace treaties with Italy, Romania, Bulgaria and Hungary, and settle territorial questions outstanding at the end of the war. Representatives of China and France were to join the foreign ministers of the 'big three'.[226] It was soon obvious that this was likely to become a semi-permanent body. The three foreign ministers met 11 times at Potsdam with a rotating chairmanship.[227] They were responsible for the transaction of much of the business of the conference.[228] Molotov, at their first meeting, suggested that Finland be added to the list of countries for which the Council was to draw up peace treaties.[229] He doggedly fought for Soviet policies. The most important issues from the Soviet point of view were Germany, Poland's western frontier and reparations.[230] This was the major area of disagreement, on which Molotov pressed hard, although Stalin avoided antagonising his wartime allies.[231]

On 24 July, when Truman revealed to Stalin that the United States had successfully exploded an atomic bomb, Stalin's comment about speeding up the Soviet atomic energy project, was apparently in response to Molotov's remark: 'They are raising the price.'[232] This indicated that he regarded Truman's announcement as an attempt to blackmail the USSR into concessions at the conference. The view that he and Stalin already knew about the 'secret' is confirmed by Molotov's reference to Harriman about the 'revelation', 'with something like a smirk on his face', shortly after his return to Moscow, although it may have only been after Hiroshima and Nagasaki that the Soviet leadership realised the full significance of the new weapon.[233]

Molotov was genuinely surprised when Churchill was defeated at the British general election. He believed that Churchill had failed to arrange the election properly, a view he retained to the end of his life.[234] He was extremely hostile to

E. Bevin, the new British Foreign Secretary who he regarded as the worst kind of trade union leader, 'a "man of the people" who read Marx and quoted him back at Molotov'.[235] At a luncheon party Molotov held for Bevin, on 31 July, Molotov probed him on likely changes in foreign policy by the new British government. He then jokingly asked Bevin when the Labour government was going to establish its Gestapo.[236] Bevin replied that the British government proposed to consult Russia since most of the Gestapo documents were in Soviet hands, which Molotov denied. He then enquired of the new Foreign Secretary how soon the conference would end, and Bevin jovially replied that it would finish as soon as Molotov agreed to all his proposals. His response was to tell Bevin that an equally speedy end could be secured if Bevin accepted all of his. Both sides agreed, however, that it was essential to secure real agreement, working slowly if necessary.[237] If there was now little doubt that the wartime alliance was over and the Potsdam Conference was not a success for the USSR,[238] Molotov did not realise this. He told Bevin that the USSR should enjoy a lasting peace for two generations, although the new United Nations Organisation was not strong enough. If peace lasted to the end of the century, he claimed that 'people would get out of the habit of settling their disputes by war and eternal peace would follow'. There was an exchange about Marx. Bevin said that he was a brilliant economist, but the world had progressed since his day. Molotov agreed that Marx's theories needed to be further developed before they could be applied to contemporary problems.[239]

At the final plenary session of the conference Molotov reminded the meeting that it was Stalin's turn for his name to be the first signature on the communiqué.[240] On arriving home, he told Dimitrov that the conference had been a success, 'in particular about decisions affecting Bulgaria and the Balkans. ... In effect, this sphere of influence has been recognised as ours'.[241]

13
Stalin's Last Years 1945–1953

Diplomacy and foreign policy 1945–1949

Among Molotov's most important activities in the immediate post-war years was the part he played at the Council of Foreign Ministers and at the Paris Peace Conference, 1946. Representation of the USSR at the United Nations was delegated to Vyshinskii, but Molotov attended one session in November–December 1946, because on his initiative, a meeting of the Council of Foreign Ministers in New York was made to coincide with the UN session.[1] His behaviour at these meetings reflected his background as party secretary and Sovnarkom chairman, the diplomatic experience he had gained during the war and his relations with the aging Stalin.

The early sessions of the Council of Foreign Ministers and the Paris Peace Conference

The London meeting of the Council of Foreign Ministers, September–October 1945, was the first diplomatic meeting of the Allies since the Potsdam Conference, which had referred to the Council the preparation of peace treaties with Germany's allies,[2] and the trusteeship of the Italian colonies. The participants added other items to the agenda; the Soviet additions included reparations and the repatriation of Soviet citizens.[3] Molotov's task was to consolidate the Soviet security position in eastern Europe and Germany achieved at the wartime conferences; to try to expand Soviet influence in the Mediterranean, if possible without confrontation with the Soviet Union's wartime allies; and to obtain maximum reparations for the USSR. The system of 'remote control' by Stalin, evident when Molotov negotiated in Berlin in 1940, in London and in the United States in 1942, and in San Francisco in 1945, again operated. Molotov was given a detailed directive from Stalin. It ordered him to insist on a sole trusteeship for the USSR in Tripolitania.[4] He received instructions from and reported to Stalin during the conference, and they discussed issues by telephone and telegram.

At the first session, on 11 September, Molotov resisted attempts by James Byrnes, the US Secretary of State, to have the additional Soviet items removed from the agenda,[5] and in response to a procedural question from Bevin, agreed that all five members of the Council, including France and China, might participate in discussion of all issues. This included the peace treaties, although only countries that had signed the armistice with the country concerned were to vote on the treaty.[6] By the third meeting, on 14 September, Molotov was changing his position.[7] On 20 September, he tried to have discussion of the Finnish peace treaty restricted to Great Britain and the USSR, on the grounds that they were the only powers 'directly concerned', and that the decision taken at the beginning of the conference was erroneous, as it conflicted with the agreement made at Potsdam.[8]

On 14 September, Molotov argued for individual rather than collective trusteeship of the former Italian colonies. He used Italian involvement in the invasion of the USSR as an excuse for the Soviet bid for trusteeship of Tripolitania, and asserted that the USSR's 'experience in establishing friendly relations between different nationalities' could be used to advantage.[9] The aim to expand Soviet influence in the Mediterranean was obvious to the Western powers.[10] Molotov found that Bevin and Byrnes opposed both individual trusteeship and Soviet trusteeship of Tripolitania, although at the next meeting he continued to press his case.[11] Outside the formal meetings, he reminded Byrnes of an acceptance in principle to Soviet participation in trusteeship, Stettinius, Byrnes's predecessor, had given to Gromyko in New York in April 1945.[12]

During the first week of the conference Molotov received repeated instructions from Stalin to stand firm and stick to the agreed line, particularly on Romania.[13] The peace treaties with Romania and Bulgaria, a priority for Molotov, were the key areas of conflict, for the United States and Great Britain refused to discuss these until the Romanian and Bulgarian governments were re-organised on a 'broadly representative' basis. After Byrnes made this clear on 20 September,[14] Molotov asked if the Italian government was more democratic, a hint that the USSR might not sign the Italian peace treaty, a priority for the West. This was a tactic suggested by Stalin.[15] Molotov was quite specific about it when he met Byrnes informally on the previous day.[16] He also pointed out that the United States maintained diplomatic relations with fascist Spain and Argentina.[17] On 21 September, he refused to accept Bevin's proposal to appoint a new commission to look into the problem of the Romanian government and there was deadlock.[18] Two days before, he had written to Stalin that the Americans and British had agreed in advance, and that 'ahead lies bargaining and an intense search for compromise'.[19]

Stalin had now become alarmed about the participation of France and China in discussion of the peace treaties. Molotov lamely excused his initial agreement to this 'because we did not consider this issue a significant one', when Byrnes and Bevin insisted on it. In response, on 21 September, he received an angry telegram from Stalin, on the pattern of those he had received in 1942, in which Stalin dropped the familiar *ty* (you) and used the formal *vy*, signing the telegram *Instantsiya*. He ordered Molotov to 'adhere to the decisions of Potsdam about the participation of involved states', and pointed out that Molotov's agreement to the new arrangement had allowed Byrnes to question the procedure of taking decisions on the basis of unanimous agreement. Stalin also criticised Molotov for expressing interest in Byrnes's proposal for a treaty on the demilitarisation of Germany for 20–25 years. He believed that it was an attempt to divert Soviet attention from the Far East, and an American attempt to play a role in Europe equal to that of the USSR.[20] On French and Chinese participation in discussion of the peace treaties, Molotov admitted that he had made a 'grave oversight'. He stated that he would at once take measures to 'insist on immediate cessation of common sessions of the five ministers. ... although it would be a sharp turn in the proceedings of the Council of Ministers'.[21]

Molotov's assessment was correct. On 22 September, he said that he was unable to attend the scheduled Council meeting, and asked Byrnes and Bevin to meet him. He told them that the conference was not following the procedure established at Potsdam, and that he could not continue to participate 'unless an interpretation of the Berlin protocol were adopted which met his point of view'. He refused to give way despite compromise suggestions. In response to a plea for harmony from Molotov, Bevin observed that when there were two interpretations, Bevin's and Molotov's, 'harmony was only obtainable by Mr. Bevin accepting M. Molotov's interpretation. He (Mr. Bevin) was quite ready to try and harmonise the two interpretations.' The meeting ended with Molotov saying that 'it would be difficult for him to take part in discussions on that basis'.[22] At a second meeting with Bevin and Byrnes on the same day, Molotov specifically referred to Stalin's telegram and his view that the decision of 11 September was 'a violation of the Potsdam agreement'.[23] He refused to deviate from Stalin's instructions and proved obdurate to further attempts to resolve the procedural difficulty, both at formal sessions of the Council and at more informal meetings with Bevin and Byrnes.[24] At the close of a meeting with Bevin on 26 September, in response to Bevin's question 'So you stand firm?' He replied, 'unquestionably'.[25] Bevin, however, was not as sure of his ground as he pretended to be, for in a note to Byrnes, he wrote that 'we are all agreed that Molotov is strictly legally right, although morally unsound'.[26] At a further meeting with Bevin, on 1 October, however, Molotov described the procedural issue as a 'misunderstanding' and 'of trivial importance', and made clear that it was recognition of the governments in Romania and Bulgaria that were 'the main cause of the difficulty'.[27]

The Council met on a further sixteen occasions, but did not discuss the peace treaties. No progress was made, and much time was spent on procedural matters until the conference broke up on 2 October. On 25 September, Molotov, because of Stalin's suspicions of American procrastination, tried to have the formation of a fully-fledged Allied Control Council for Japan placed on the conference agenda.[28] In his telegram to Molotov, Stalin had suggested that American and British seizure of Japanese gold reserves was the reason for the delay. Molotov hinted at this to Bevin and Byrnes, who said they had never heard of the gold. Despite Molotov's efforts, however, the Americans, with British support, still refused to discuss the Allied Control Council for Japan at the conference.[29]

On 26 September, in an attempt to break the deadlock, Byrnes suggested an agreement on convening a peace conference in exchange for accepting the Soviet position on procedure for discussion of the peace treaties.[30] Stalin, however, refused to accept Molotov's plea for compromise. He wrote:

> The Allies are pressing on you to break your will and force you into making concessions. It is obvious that you should display complete adamancy. ... It is

possible that the Americans ... would make some concessions to provoke you into some serious concessions, using the 'tit-for-tat' principle. I think that even in this case you should display complete adamancy.

Molotov agreed with Stalin that a fiasco of a conference that could be blamed on Britain and the United States, was preferable to fruitless negotiations and Soviet concessions, but he still hoped to gain something from the Western powers giving way. He wrote to Stalin, on 28 September:

> I agree that the decisive moment has come. ... I believe that we can now rip off the veil of optimism whose appearance the Americans would like to maintain, or obtain from them ... substantive concessions in favour of the USSR. Perhaps we will not obtain American concessions both on the Balkans and on Japan. ... But if the Americans (and the British) give in on at least one of these questions, we should make a deal with them.

On repatriation, he suggested the publication in the Soviet press of 'scandalous facts', regarding the treatment of Soviet citizens in American hands, about which the Soviet government had demanded urgent measures, and concluded, 'This may help us get under their thick skin'.[31]

In the closing stages of the conference, during the attempt to prepare the protocol, Molotov said, 'If anyone denounces the decision adopted by us in common, that decision ceases to be a decision.' In the famous interchange which followed, Bevin responded: 'Someone takes part in a decision, then he denounces it and is free. That is the nearest thing to the Hitler theory I have ever heard.' Molotov shouted in reply: 'Unless Mr. Bevin withdraws his words, I shall leave the room', rose to his feet, and began to make for the door. Bevin apologised when he understood what Molotov was doing and Molotov returned to his seat when one of his aides told him that Bevin had apologised.[32]

The failure of the conference was now obvious. Molotov reported to Stalin that the Americans and British had decided to break it off:

> It means that that we should be ready for an open anti-Soviet demarche from our 'respected allies'. Our response will have to depend on the character of their assault.

Stalin now approved of Molotov's position: 'I confirm your position. ... We will lose nothing, only they will.'[33] The conference ended not only without the usual glowing reports of unity and optimism, but also without a protocol. In his report, Molotov tried to claim a moral victory in repelling 'a diplomatic attack on the foreign policy gains that the Soviet Union made during the war'.[34] Described by a British observer as 'outstanding for his mastery of the negotiation procedure ... stubborn and unyielding to an almost incredible degree',[35] he had dominated and decided the outcome of the London conference. Byrnes wrote: 'I had no experience that prepared me for negotiation with Mr. Molotov.' He capitalised on Byrnes' habit of speaking 'off the cuff' by asking him to clarify and explain, hoping for mistakes, and on Bevin's quickness of temper by trying to provoke him.[36]

In an effort to restart negotiations, Byrnes, who believed that Stalin would put pressure on Molotov, proposed a meeting of the three foreign ministers, in Moscow, in December. Molotov was positive in response, asking 'Do you wish me to find out if Stalin will be in Moscow at that time?'[37] Stalin's instructions to Molotov on the meeting, in a telegram in which he reminded him that he had achieved success in London by returning to a sterner policy on his (Stalin's) instructions, were 'The same policy of tenacity and steadfastness should be our guide ...'.[38]

At the Moscow Conference, 15–27 December 1945, there were 14 meetings of the three foreign ministers, seven formal and seven informal. In addition, Stalin met Byrnes twice and Bevin twice, and Molotov saw each of his opposite numbers twice.[39] By agreeing to small alterations in the governments of Bulgaria and Romania, the USSR was able to move towards Western recognition of those governments. Agreement was also reached on establishing a Far Eastern Commission, the Control Council for Japan, procedure for a peace conference and the creation of a United Nations Commission on Atomic Energy.[40] At the final meeting, when the three ministers met to sign the protocol, the Russian version was not ready for Molotov's signature. When it was produced, it included the Soviet draft on Bulgaria, which had been rejected by the British and American delegations. Molotov proposed that this version be signed because 'he hoped such good work would not be wasted'. Byrnes and Bevin refused to agree to Molotov's attempt to trick them and he meekly gave way.[41] His summary of the results of the conference stated that decisions had been reached on a number of important matters, and co-operation with the Western powers had been 'sustained'.[42]

At a banquet hosted by Stalin on Christmas Eve, after agreement on the Atomic Energy Commission, Molotov said that he would toast J. B. Conant, the US atomic energy adviser, 'who, perhaps had a bit of atomic bomb in his waist-coat pocket'. Stalin angrily interrupted Molotov. He asserted that the bomb was too serious a matter to joke about, and proposed a toast to the American scientists and what they had accomplished. Molotov's remarks may have been a reflection of the light-hearted public attitude that the Soviet leaders had agreed to adopt towards the atomic bomb from the time of Potsdam, a policy now abruptly changed by Stalin. Alternatively, Stalin may have intended another deliberate personal humiliation of Molotov, perhaps a sign of the relations between the two men at this time. Molotov did not alter his expression after Stalin's comments.[43]

The pattern for the meetings of the Council of Foreign Ministers and for the Paris Peace Conference was established at the first London meeting and consolidated in Moscow. Molotov continued to rigidly follow Stalin's line, but never dominated the proceedings to the extent that he had done in London. The Moscow Conference was followed by Stalin's election speech, of 9 February 1946, in which he asserted that a peaceful international order was impossible because of the inevitable clash between communism and capitalism. Kennan's 'Long Telegram', of 22 February, also claimed that that the USSR believed that there could be no permanent peaceful coexistence with capitalism; and Churchill's Iron Curtain speech was made in March.[44] Molotov made the fullest statement on Soviet foreign policy in his election speech of 6 February, in which he warned of the dangers of a new war against the USSR provoked by the 'warmongers' of the United States and Britain.[45] The Iran crisis had also occurred: the Soviet Union failed to honour its pledge to withdraw its troops and Molotov did not respond to two notes from Byrnes on this question.[46] The Paris session of the Council of Foreign Ministers, beginning in April 1946, met against this background of deteriorating international relations, and was marked by deadlocks, although some progress was made.[47] Molotov continued to respond negatively to Byrnes's proposal for German demilitarisation, and press for Soviet trusteeship of Tripolitania jointly with Italy. He was strongly reprimanded by Stalin for failing to respond when Byrnes asked him if the goals of Soviet foreign policy were a 'search for security, or expansion'. Stalin instructed him to 'avoid excuses and a defensive posture, but instead to hold a position of denunciation and attack against the imperialist trends of the United States and Great Britain'. He was also to tell Byrnes that he shared the 'slanderous attitude that Churchill expressed in his anti-Soviet speech'. At a dinner at the Soviet embassy, on 5 May, when Byrnes refused Molotov's offer of Yugoslavia abandoning its reparation claims against Italy, in return for US acceptance of Yugoslav territorial claims for Trieste, Molotov, supported by Vyshinskii, attacked US imperialist expansion. The attack provoked the departure of Molotov's American guests, but the next day he also attacked Bevin for imperialism, bracketing him with Churchill.[48]

When the Paris session resumed in June after an adjournment, Molotov, who was personally reluctant to make concessions, proposed two compromise solutions, suggested by Stalin, on the question of Yugoslav claims to Trieste, and it was eventually agreed to make Trieste a 'free territory'. Molotov believed that this was of great importance to the British and Americans, as they considered it 'a beach-head for their control and influence in the Balkans'.[49] During the protracted discussions on Trieste there was a typical exchange between Molotov and Bevin. The British Foreign Minister observed that 'the procedure of the conference was not to decide anything'. Molotov replied that 'Bevin should not underestimate his services in helping to produce that result.'[50] Byrnes's plan for the demilitarisation of Germany was again rejected, following extensive and unusual high-level consultations by Stalin in Moscow. Molotov's declaration stated that the plan sidestepped the issues of reparations and the promotion of German democracy.

This session agreed drafts of the peace treaties with Bulgaria, Romania, Hungary and Finland on the basis originally desired by the USSR. Molotov reported that 'we reached solutions acceptable to us',[51] but much of the success in reaching agreement was due to Byrnes, who was now using Molotov's tactics against him.[52] The Council also settled a date for the peace conference, but Molotov refused to allow invitations to be issued until procedure had been agreed. On this he was most obstinate, probably, on Stalin's instructions, trying to protect the USSR's minority position at the forthcoming conference. It led to bitter wrangling. At one point in the proceedings Bevin became so frustrated that he raised his fists to attack Molotov, who apparently ignored the furore he was creating.[53]

The last item on the Council's agenda was the peace treaty with Austria. Molotov offered to expedite this, providing the Council first agreed upon the denazification of Austria and the immediate evacuation of '437,000 foreign nationals so-called displaced persons'. These included the followers of General A. Vlasov, the Soviet general captured by the Germans, who had chaired the German sponsored Committee for the Liberation of the Peoples of Russia. Byrnes opposed this because of the role of the United States as a sanctuary for refugees, but Bevin found himself in difficulties and abruptly ended the conference.[54]

The first sessions of the Paris Peace Conference, July–October 1946, were again dominated by procedure, when Molotov endeavoured to obtain the most favourable voting conditions for the Soviet minority bloc.[55] During statements from the former enemy states, Molotov attacked A. de Gasperi, the Italian Foreign Minister, ferociously. Asked by de Gasperi why he was so hostile, he replied, 'Oh, you must not take that seriously. That was just polemics,'[56] but his antagonism reflected the hostility between the USSR and the Western powers over Italy. The conference made very slow progress and the Council of Foreign Ministers met to expedite its work, but had little success. On 3 October, Byrnes approached Molotov and suggested limitations on debate in the closing plenary sessions. Molotov agreed, but said he wanted minority rights protected because 'he expected to be speaking for the minority view, which was harder than speaking for the majority as Mr. Byrnes would be doing'. Shortly after this he went to Moscow to consult Stalin. On his return he appeared to be more co-operative, although he considered the conference 'unsatisfactory'.[57] In his opinion, the main achievement of his delegation was the frustration of 'the Byrnes–Bevin plan to isolate the USSR and impose their superiority', and he claimed 'we managed to prove the moral superiority of the Soviet Union over our adversaries'. Stalin congratulated his diplomats on their 'tenacity and steadfastness'. He wrote to Molotov: 'Your assessment of the Soviet delegation's work … is absolutely correct. The delegation fulfilled its mission well.' Molotov had already received one endorsement for his behaviour. He left a military parade staged by the French during the conference, because he was assigned a seat in the second row with representatives of the small countries, and wrote to Stalin, 'I am not sure I did the right thing'. Stalin informed him that he behaved 'absolutely correctly', for 'the dignity of the Soviet Union must be defended not only in big matters, but also in minutiae'.[58]

The Novikov Long Telegram

In mid-September, Molotov approached Nikolai Novikov, the Soviet ambassador to the USA, who was a member of the Soviet delegation to the Peace Conference, and asked him to write a report on the tendencies of US foreign policy. As he insisted that the report be written by the end of the month, he perhaps hoped to use it with the delegation at the conference. He asked to see drafts, suggested changes, and essentially dictated to Novikov the conclusions he should reach.[59] This document is often seen as a parallel to the Kennan and Roberts 'Long Telegrams'.[60] The report, particularly the phrases Molotov marked with blue pencil, denoted here by underlining, reflects his views on the international situation at this time: the movement away from co-operation towards a 'bi-polar' world with the emphasis on confrontation with the United States. It demonstrates his commitment to an ideological framework and hostility towards the United States, reinforced by the experience of the Paris Peace Conference.

The document began by stating that the United States had abandoned its pre-war tradition of 'isolationism', and was bent on 'world supremacy'. The economic devastation caused by the war gave America 'prospects for enormous shipments of goods and the importation of capital' into countries starved of consumer goods and to infiltrate their economies. This was a stage on the road to world domination for the United States. The USSR had, however, retained its economic independence and its international position was 'currently stronger than in the pre-war period', particularly because of the new 'democratic' regimes established in eastern Europe.

The report continued by saying that American foreign policy was no longer based on the desire to strengthen co-operation between the three great powers. The increasing size of American armed forces and military budget, and the building of new bases near the USSR's borders, demonstrated the major role to be played in America's plans for world dominance by its military. In this section Molotov underlined words and figures which showed the increased military strength of the United States and the number of new bases.

In a part of the report about a United States 'understanding with England concerning the partial division of the world on the basis of mutual concessions', that is, 'spheres of influence', he underlined the names of the key places specified. By this 'understanding', Britain recognised American 'control' of China and Japan, and the United States acknowledged the English sphere of influence in India and the Far East, although the 'nature of relations' about the Near East was 'irregular'. The United States, however, regarded Great Britain as its 'greatest potential competitor' as well as a 'possible ally'. Despite co-operation between the two powers at recent international conferences, at the United Nations, and on military questions, there was not, as yet, however, any formal 'military alliance'. American loans to aid Britain were allowing American capital to penetrate the British economy and increase American influence in the British Empire. There were 'great internal contradictions' in the relations between Britain and the United States, in which the Near East might become a 'centre' that would destroy the Anglo-American alliance.

The final sections of the report, devoted to the United State's ' "hard-line" policy with regard to the USSR', stated that this was designed to undermine co-operation between the 'big three'; allow the United States to form new alliances directed against the USSR; and rid Eastern Europe of Soviet influence. Plans for a revived Germany as an American ally were a key element in this strategy. All this was intended by the United States 'to prepare the conditions for winning world supremacy in a new war ... against the Soviet Union'.[61]

The United Nations and the New York meeting of foreign ministers

At the United Nations General Assembly meeting in New York, November–December 1946, Molotov was on the defensive because the Soviet Union was in a minority and likely to remain so. There were two major issues for the USSR: the formation of a Trusteeship Council for former mandated territories of the League of Nations, and reduction of armed forces and armaments. When Molotov suggested that he should not insist that the USSR be included in the list of 'immediately interested states' for the Trusteeship Council, Stalin immediately corrected him. He was to take a position of 'active interest' because of the USSR's great power status, and because mandated territories gave the USSR a bargaining weapon.

On the reduction of armed forces, Bevin constantly tried to modify Molotov's proposal for the provision of data on armed forces of the great powers on foreign territories, and negate it. Stalin told Molotov, because of the number of times he was speaking, not to get nervous and upset, but to behave more calmly. He was, however, to 'stand firm', because if the Soviet proposal was defeated, it would reveal that the Western powers did not want to provide the data. When Molotov replied that he could not stop speaking altogether, Stalin told him 'to speak at the decisive moment to crown the whole affair', and when the Soviet proposal was rejected, that the Soviet delegation had scored a 'moral-political victory'.[62]

The task of the New York meeting of the Council of Foreign Ministers, November–December 1946, which met concurrently with the UN General Assembly, was to draw up final versions of the peace treaties, and to consider German issues. This proved the most difficult meeting of the Council. Molotov was determined that the treaties should favour the USSR: he ignored the peace conference recommendations and constantly introduced modifications.[63] Asked by Byrnes how many amendments he had on the Statute on the Free Territory of Trieste, Molotov replied 'A whole box of them.' Byrnes' retorted 'Let's see what you have in the box.' This gave Molotov the initiative in the ten sessions on Trieste that followed. He tirelessly introduced amendment after amendment and forced Byrnes and Bevin on to the defensive.[64] Progress was made, however, when the foreign ministers again resorted to informal meetings and when Molotov began to offer concessions on one point for agreement on another. This provoked Bevin to accuse Molotov of horse-trading. Molotov responded that he did not know how to horse-trade. Byrnes replied that he would give a gold medal if a horse-trader as hard as Molotov could be found. Molotov responded that he was learning, and Bevin finished the exchange by saying 'God help us when you have learned!'[65] The claim of Byrnes and Bohlen that Molotov made concessions on Trieste after Byrnes threatened him with an adjournment is an exaggeration: he had received instructions from Stalin.[66]

Besides Trieste, Molotov's priority was Italian reparations for the smaller powers. He consulted Stalin on precise figures, and there was considerable haggling. Agreement was reached on the major issues on the basis of bargaining, and the foreign ministers agreed to hold a further meeting in Moscow in March 1947 on the German and Austrian peace treaties.[67] Molotov reported to Stalin that 'the peace treaties are acceptable to us in all points of substance and meet the criteria set for the delegation.' With Stalin's approval he informed Soviet ambassadors that an improvement in the reparations settlement in the treaty with Italy had been obtained and that the 'Anglo-American bloc … had to retreat under our pressure'.[68]

If Molotov was not as dominant after the first session of the Council in London, he remained the central figure. As one authority has written on the sessions up to the end of 1946:

> Unhindered by the press, public opinion, or Congress, aided by definite goals, ... Molotov introduced the Council and then the world to a new brand of diplomacy. Chain-smoking Russian cigarettes and stroking his moustache, Molotov manipulated the others like a puppet master, time after time reducing Bevin to fury, Byrnes to impatience, and Bidault [the French Foreign Minister] to new compromise suggestions.[69]

The Marshall Plan

The key foreign policy issue in which Molotov was involved in 1947 was the Soviet response to the Marshall Plan; its rejection by the USSR is often seen as a turning point in the development of the Cold War.[70] The speech of Marshall, now American Secretary of State, on 5 June 1947, which offered American aid to Europe to prevent economic catastrophe, was made in response to a rapidly deteriorating situation: the failure of the Council of Foreign Ministers to reach agreement on German economic unity and immoderate Soviet demands for reparations.[71] Molotov's initial response to the pessimistic report by ambassador Novikov on Marshall's speech was cautiously favourable. In the translation of the speech he received, although he underlined phrases which show that he believed that the reasons for Marshall's proposals were American economic self-interest, and that they were directed against the USSR, he also noted the plan's mechanism. European countries had to take the initiative and come to an agreement about the economic aid required; and the American role was limited to support of this programme. This indicates that Molotov believed that the USSR might obtain loans for reconstruction from the USA.[72] He may also have believed that the Plan might be used to exploit capitalist contradictions – promote discord between the United States and Western European nations.[73] He requested a report from the economist, Eugene Varga, about the motives for the plan, and before the end of June, he instructed the Soviet ambassadors in Poland, Czechoslovakia and Yugoslavia, to tell the governments of those countries that they should show their interest in taking part in drawing up an economic agreement.[74]

Despite growing suspicions in the USSR that Marshall's proposals were aimed at forming a European alliance headed by the United States directed against Soviet interests, particularly in eastern Europe, Molotov led a delegation of more than 100 to discuss Marshall's proposals with British and French representatives at the Paris Conference, held in late June 1947. The size of the delegation indicates that the USSR wished to engage in serious discussion of the proposals. Molotov's draft instructions to the delegation – sent to Stalin for approval – indicated the terms on which the USSR would take part in the American aid programme. They also show that the priority for the delegation was to discover how much and what sort of aid the United States was prepared to offer. The delegation was to call for the formulation of economic plans by individual countries, rather than on a European-wide basis, thus preventing an anti-Soviet alliance. They were to object to any conditions that either meant 'economic enslavement'; or prevented the industrial development of eastern Europe; or utilised German resources, unless agreement was reached on the payment of reparations to the USSR. Because of the centrality of Germany in any European economic recovery programme, the last condition meant that concessions would have to be made on Soviet reparations, if there was to be any agreement to which the USSR was party. If the terms of the instructions were cautious and rather negative, they do show that the acceptance of American aid on certain conditions was not ruled out.[75]

Molotov's speech on the first day of the conference was moderate. Its purpose was to obtain further details of the proposed aid programme from the Americans, who were not present. After this, however, the conference failed because the Soviet delegation would not agree to a multinational committee to co-ordinate aid requests; and Britain and France refused to give assurances that German participation in the programme would not endanger reparations, or lead to increased German industrialisation. The Western powers were not meeting the Soviet conditions. When this became clear, Molotov denounced the Western states and walked out of the conference. In his closing speech, on 3 July, he accused Britain and France of aiming to split Europe into two hostile camps. Detailed work on the Marshall Plan seemed to the Kremlin to confirm Novikov's 1946 report: it was an attempt to use American economic might to penetrate the east European economies and imperil the security the USSR had so recently gained.[76] Molotov, at the conference, had also received a detailed intelligence report from his deputy Vyshinskii, that Britain and the United States had agreed that the Marshall Plan should be regarded as a plan for the reconstruction of Europe under the leadership of one main committee. This would operate outside the framework of the United Nations, with Germany as one of the key bases, and they would oppose the payment of German reparations to the USSR.[77]

Initially, the Polish and Czech governments were allowed to continue to show interest in the Plan. Molotov, through the Soviet ambassador, on 5 July, instructed the Czech government to participate in the next Paris Conference,

> demonstrate ... the unacceptability of the Anglo-French plan, prevent adoption of a unanimous decision, and then leave the conference, taking as many delegates of other countries as possible.[78]

By 9 July, however, Soviet policy had changed, and Molotov urged Klement Gottwald, the Czech premier, to withdraw his acceptance of the invitation to attend the conference. He gave as reasons that the French and British were persisting with a European-wide aid programme. This ignored the economic independence of small states; and they intended to establish a Western bloc that included western Germany.[79] The view that the Marshall Plan aimed at forming an anti-Soviet alliance and would imperil Soviet security in eastern Europe had prevailed. Stalin reinforced the change in policy when he met a Czech delegation the same day, and neither Czechoslovakia nor Poland was represented at the second conference.[80] A major shift in Soviet policy had occurred. It was no longer believed that limited co-operation with the west was possible. The Marshall Plan seemed to demonstrate that the United States was hostile, bent on building up anti-Soviet alliances and attacking Soviet power in eastern Europe. The foundation of Cominform in September 1947, for which Andrei Zhdanov acted as Stalin's chief agent and propounded the 'two camp' thesis, followed.[81]

The Moscow and London sessions of the Council of Foreign Ministers 1947

The last two sessions of the Council Molotov attended were not a success, despite initial high hopes. At the March–April 1947 session, the French vetoed proposals for central administrative agencies in Germany strongly advocated by the USSR, although these were supported by the United States and Britain. Molotov's efforts to salvage elements of the scheme by making concessions on reparation demands were unsuccessful.[82] The United States now began to make clear that it would not tolerate a demilitarised unified Germany that might fall under Soviet influence, and the Western powers began to move towards a separate West German state. At its meeting in London, November–December 1947, called chiefly to discuss the German question and the Marshall plan, which Molotov attended after a long vacation with Stalin, and during which they no doubt prepared for the meeting, Molotov found himself isolated. He tried to find differences of opinion among the Western powers on Germany, and asked particularly for intelligence on disagreements between the United States and Britain on West Berlin. He did not seem to realise that attempts to find divisions between the Western powers only drove them closer together on the decision to found a separate West Germany.[83] Molotov faced an impossible task. He had been instructed to reach an agreement on a united Germany that would allow Soviet influence to expand, and protect Walter Ulbricht's emerging communist power in the Soviet zone. Bevin was confrontational.[84] On some days Molotov was optimistic about the future for a united Germany, on others he just re-iterated Soviet demands. His constant rejection of Western proposals led Western ministers and reporters in London to call him 'Mr. *Nyet*'.[85] Finally, one of his harangues provoked Marshall to propose adjournment, and the Council of Foreign Ministers broke up without agreement on a German peace treaty, or the date for another meeting. Molotov, clearly taken aback, was left sitting alone in his seat. General Lucius Clay, an American delegate who had attended many meetings, recorded that it was the only time he had seen Molotov visibly wince.[86] His recommendation to Stalin, in March 1948, for a meeting of east European states to press for a further meeting of the Council of Foreign Ministers became part of the policy of the Berlin blockade. Alongside Stalin, Molotov played a key role in the unsuccessful negotiations over the blockade in July and August 1948, during which he constantly pressed the Western powers to abandon their decision to establish a separate West German government.[87]

Before this, Molotov had become deeply involved in Stalin's dispute with Yugoslavia, the Cominform expulsion of the Yugoslav Communist Party in

June 1948 marking the climax of Stalin's quarrel with Tito. Molotov was central in the development of Soviet policy in response to Tito's initiatives on such matters as a Yugoslav–Bulgarian Treaty of Alliance and a Balkan Federation, and in Stalin's negotiations with the Yugoslav leaders from 1946, as the dispute developed.[88] Following his dismissal as Minister of Foreign Affairs in 1949, Molotov continued to take an orthodox line, and in July 1951 condemned the Yugoslav regime.[89]

Senior politician at home

Some older authorities have portrayed the last years of Stalin's life as a period when his political lieutenants tried to usurp his power or even conspired to kill him. Alternatively, it has been suggested that these were years when a moderate 'faction' was defeated.[90] More recent research based on archives now available indicates, however, that during this period, Stalin's despotic rule, firmly established by the end of the 1930s, continued. He sought to preserve his position and keep his leading supporters loyal by a system of collective responsibility for decision-making, concentrated in the 'leading group', the 'quintet' of Stalin, Molotov, Beriya, Mikoyan and Malenkov. The last four of these, having acted as Stalin's deputies during the war, had come to exercise a degree of freedom in the fields for which they were responsible. They sought to maintain a balance of power among themselves, whilst the ageing dictator tried to ensure that there was no challenge to his position by launching attacks against individuals in this group. Molotov's very senior position meant that he was particularly likely to be attacked by Stalin, for believing that he was his most likely successor, the dictator was very wary of him.[91]

The post-war bureaucrat

The 'leading group' took the decision to dissolve GKO[92] on 4 September 1945, its business being transferred to Sovnarkom.[93] On the abolition of GKO, Molotov was made responsible for one of two Operative Bureaus (*Operativnoe Byuro*) of Sovnarkom. These replaced the former Sovnarkom Bureau in which he had played a leading role during the war, although with his absence at Potsdam, he attended and chaired only three from 18 meetings of that body between 11 May and 30 August 1945. The Operative Bureau headed by Molotov had a brief for defence, agriculture, foodstuffs, trade, finance, and Sovnarkom committees and administrations. It met 27 times up to 7 March 1946, and Molotov attended and chaired ten of the sessions. His responsibilities were more limited than before: the second Operative Bureau, which Beriya chaired, was answerable for industry and transport.[94]

Indicative of Molotov's continuing senior position was the fact that in March 1946, when Sovnarkom was reorganised as the Council of Ministers (*Sovet Ministrov*), he was named first among eight deputy chairmen. He was not at this point officially designated as first deputy chairman and retained his post of foreign minister.[95] Responsibility for oversight of the work of ministries and state committees was distributed between the chairman and deputy chairmen of the Council. As Minister of Foreign Affairs and senior vice-chairman, Molotov's role was the most limited among the deputy chairmen. He was assigned oversight over the Ministry of Justice, the Committee for Higher Education, the Committee for Radio and Broadcasting and TASS, the last clearly linked to his foreign policy role.[96] A Politburo resolution of February 1947 confirmed that foreign policy questions, defence, internal security and government appointments were the responsibility of the Politburo.[97]

When the Council of Ministers was created, a single Bureau (*Byuro Soveta Ministrov*) with a membership of the deputy chairmen of the Council of Ministers, replaced the two Sovnarkom Operative Bureaus. Initially, Beriya, with Voznesenskii and Kosygin as vice-chairmen,[98] chaired this important decision-making body[99] and Molotov's role in it was limited. He attended only three sessions from 44 in 1946.[100] When the Council of Ministers was reorganised in February 1947, at which point Molotov was formally appointed as First Deputy Chairman and made responsible for Union-Republican questions, his commitment to the Bureau increased. Alongside eight sectoral bureaus, each chaired by a council vice-chairman, the main Bureau's chief responsibilities were direct oversight of finance, state control, justice, reserves – both human and material, and supply; and Molotov chaired half of the 46 meetings held during the remainder of 1947.[101] At the end of March 1948, a Politburo decree relieved him from participation in sittings of the Bureau so that he could be 'occupied chiefly with matters of foreign policy'.[102] Up to this time, he had chaired half of the 16 meetings held in 1948, but he did not attend again for the remaining 41 sessions in that year, Beriya taking over as the main chairman.[103] In 1949, up to the end of July, Molotov attended 12 from 29 sessions of the Bureau, although he did not now serve as chairman.[104] The Bureau was now reformed as the Presidium of the Council of Ministers. It met 38 times from August 1949 to April 1950. Molotov, who had now lost his ministerial responsibility, did not attend the first seven sessions up to the end of August 1949, but was then present at every session of the Presidium.[105] In April 1950, the Bureau of the Presidium was formed in addition to the Presidium of the Council of Ministers.[106] From April 1950, these bodies met a total of 180 times, up to Stalin's death in March 1953, and Molotov was present at all but 25 of the meetings.[107] His government administrative duties thus continued very much in the same way as during the war.

Molotov's Politburo responsibilities also continued. Of the nine recorded meetings of the full Politburo held between December 1945 and October 1952, Molotov attended six: the one taking place in December 1945, four from six in 1946, he was absent from the single meeting held in December 1947, but attended the meeting held in June 1949.[108] Stalin's meetings with members of the 'leading group' were, however, more significant during these years than formal meetings of the full Politburo (see Table 13.1).[109] Molotov's frequent attendance in Stalin's office, where he continued to be one of the most frequent visitors until 1952 and 1953,[110] demonstrates his continuing very senior position.

Conflict with Stalin

From the end of the war Stalin spent increasing periods away from Moscow in his dachas in the south of the USSR. In his memoir interviews with Chuev, Molotov

Table 13.1   Attendance of the 'leading group' in Stalin's office 1945–1953[111]

	1945	1946	1947	1948	1949	1950	1951	1952	1953*
Molotov	123	76	97	99	84	59	37	27	0
Malenkov	118	76	103	100	107	43	44	37	9
Beriya	114	95	109	110	102	45	47	38	7
Mikoyan	63	79	86	98	82	30	31	24	1

* to 1 March.

said that after the war Stalin intended to retire, and said over an informal dinner 'Let Vyacheslav take over now. He is younger'; but abandoned his intention after Churchill's Iron Curtain speech.[112] In the autumn of 1945 Stalin went on leave for a lengthy period, the first time since 1936, leaving government in the hands of the 'quartet' of Molotov, Malenkov, Mikoyan and Beriya, with Molotov unofficially in charge. *Pravda* noted prominently that Molotov was carrying out the functions of head of government.[113] On vacation, Stalin's suspicions were aroused by a number of reports in the foreign press, which stated that he was about to step down in favour of Molotov, who was described as the second man in the USSR.[114] These rumours were fuelled partly by the fact that when Molotov gave the main address on the anniversary of the October revolution, he figured prominently in the press.[115] Immediately prior to this, continuing wartime practice, he had authorised the publication in *Pravda*, on 9 November, of extracts from a speech by Churchill in the House of Commons in which he praised the Soviet people and Stalin in particular. Stalin condemned Molotov's action as 'servility before foreigners'. Already under attack from Stalin for his independent mood and conciliatory line at the London Foreign Ministers Conference, and in negotiations with Harriman over the Control Commission for Japan, Stalin wrote to the 'quartet' early in November: 'Molotov's manner of separating himself from the government, to picture himself as more liberal and compliant than the government, is good for nothing.' Molotov's colleagues recognised his behaviour as 'incorrect' and joined in the attack on him. He attached a postscript to their response to Stalin, saying 'I will do my best not to repeat these mistakes,' and was forced to make another apology over the publication of the Churchill speech. He admitted a further mistake because it was printed without Stalin's authorisation, and 'praise of Russia and Stalin served Churchill to camouflage his hostile anti-Soviet aims'.[116]

At precisely this time, Molotov, as Commissar for Foreign Affairs, gave way to lobbying from foreign journalists and embassies and pressed Stalin to relax the censorship on foreign correspondents. At a reception for the diplomatic corps in the Kremlin, on 7 November, he was supposed to have gone up to an American press correspondent with a glass of wine in his hand and said: 'I know that you journalists want to remove Russian censorship. What would you say if I agree to this on conditions of reciprocity?' Reports of this produced an angry reaction from Stalin. He telephoned Molotov and asked who had authorised the lifting of censorship. Molotov denied he had done it, and Stalin then accused him of being drunk.[117] Following this, there was speculation in the *New York Times* as to why

Stalin had not yet returned to Moscow, and on 3 December, Reuters again announced a relaxation of press censorship in the USSR, attributing the change of policy to Molotov. On 5 December, Stalin ordered the 'quartet' to discover if Molotov or the Commissariat of Foreign Affairs press department was responsible, call the guilty party to account and prevent further 'libels against the Soviet government'. They offered excuses, denied that Molotov had said the words ascribed to him at the November reception, but admitted that there had been some slackening of censorship as a result of Molotov's instructions to the press department of the Commissariat of Foreign Affairs.[118] Stalin became furious. He telegraphed the other three members of the 'quartet' that their response was 'absolutely unsatisfactory', accused them of 'naivety', and Molotov of 'sleight of hand' and of taking 'individual decisions to change our foreign policy line'. He concluded:

> I thought we could limit ourselves to a reprimand of Molotov. But now it is no longer sufficient. I am convinced that Molotov does not really care about the interests of our state and the prestige of our government, all he wants is to win popularity in certain foreign circles. I cannot think of such a comrade as my first deputy any more.[119]

On Stalin's instructions, Molotov's three colleagues summoned him to a meeting, where, as commanded, they read him Stalin's telegram. Molotov must have been very afraid; the only consolation was that Stalin still considered him a comrade. At the very least his dismissal was likely. His three colleagues informed Stalin that Molotov had admitted his mistakes and wept, although he claimed that the lack of trust in him was unjust. They reported that they had already corrected him by making him cancel a proposed press appointment for Randolph Churchill. They further separated themselves from Molotov when they reminded Stalin of the London Foreign Ministers Conference and the negotiations with Harriman, and resurrected the charge that Molotov was pursuing his own policy rather than that of the government.[120] Molotov sent a grovelling letter, on 7 December, the same day as the report from his colleagues. He conceded that he had shown 'false liberalism', had made a 'gross opportunistic mistake which has brought harm to our state', and that he had attempted to blame officials for his own errors. He concluded:

> Your ciphered telegram is imbued with a profound mistrust of me as a Bolshevik and human being, and I accept this as a most serious warning from the Party for all my subsequent work, whatever job I may have. I will seek to excel in deeds to restore your trust in which every honest Bolshevik sees not merely personal trust, but the Party's trust – something that I value more than life itself.[121]

Stalin's initial response, on 8 December, was to inform the other members of the 'quartet' that he disagreed with their interpretation of the affair, and that he would take up the matter when he returned to Moscow.[122] Now, however, fortunately for Molotov, there were indications that Soviet foreign policy was bringing rewards.

On the following day Stalin addressed the 'quartet'. This implied that Molotov was not to be dismissed, and he pointed out the success which Molotov had achieved by implementing his (Stalin's) instructions at the London Conference, where Stalin had ended the concessions Molotov was making and returned him to a sterner policy.[123] On 17 December, Molotov tried to ensure the affair did not continue. He wrote to Stalin that A. Bogomolov, the Soviet ambassador to France, had on his own initiative, spoken to de Gaulle about the attacks on Stalin in the French press and allowed de Gaulle to attack the USSR. Molotov stated that the Commissariat of Foreign Affairs was taking measures to prevent further errors.[124]

Stalin's proposal at the Politburo, on 29 December, to form a group of 60 leading workers to prepare for important work in the area of foreign relations may have been an attempt to weaken Molotov's power in foreign policy, as may the appointment of Zhdanov as chairman of the foreign policy department of the Central Committee Secretariat in April 1946.[125] He seems, however, to have decided not to press the attack on Molotov any further for the time being. In August 1946, the USSR sent a threatening note to Turkey demanding concessions on the Black Sea Straits, but had to back down when the Western powers sent warships into the Aegean. One Soviet source ascribes the mistake to Molotov personally, the only occasion in which he is mentioned in this study of post-war Soviet foreign policy, but he seems to have escaped censure from Stalin.[126] In November, however, when Molotov was at the Council of Foreign Ministers meeting in New York, the Academy of Sciences, at its first post-war meeting, nominated him as an honorary member. Molotov hesitated before he replied, until Stalin suggested that he should accept, which he did, and on 1 December, the Soviet press, in which reports on Molotov's negotiations in New York had been prominent, published the greetings of the Academy to its new member. But Molotov's telegraphed response to the 'high honour' never appeared. He received a telegram from Stalin asking him why he was 'so ecstatic' about his election, which was a 'second-rank matter'. Stalin told him that, as 'a statesman of the highest type', he should care more about his dignity. In response, Molotov wrote another abject apology in which he said that the election did not make him 'ecstatic', that he had made a fool of himself, and thanked Stalin for his telegram.[127]

During the war years, in an abrupt change in Soviet policy, Soviet scientists had been allowed to exchange information with their Western colleagues, and in 1946, at a reception held for visiting foreign scientists held at the Kremlin, Molotov proposed a toast 'for the development of close collaboration between Soviet and world science'. Shortly afterwards, in November 1946, he authorised, without Stalin's permission (a request for permission having not reached Stalin and therefore no reply being sent) the release of information to American scientists on a supposed new cancer cure discovered by Soviet scientists. This led to the 'Klyueva–Roskin' or 'KR affair' during the first half of 1947. Zhdanov initiated an attack on N. Klyueva and G. Roskin, the two scientists concerned. A three-day public show trial was held, Klyueva and Roskin escaped with a public reprimand, but Stalin seems to have taken no action against Molotov even though he had acted without his authorisation, perhaps because policy on international scientific co-operation changed after Molotov's action.[128] Indeed, at this time, Molotov's position seemed to be growing stronger, when he acquired responsibility for foreign intelligence. In the autumn of 1947, the Committee for Information was created, possibly on Molotov's initiative. This brought together the First Directorate of State Security, formerly the responsibility of Beriya, and the Main Intelligence Directorate (Military Intelligence) from the Ministry of Defence. Molotov chaired the Committee as Minister for Foreign Affairs,[129] and was responsible for presenting a daily report to Stalin.[130] He organised intelligence so that the Soviet ambassador in each country served as the 'resident' of the Committee there.[131] The new institution, however, to Beriya's delight, was a disaster.[132] Perhaps this was because with his other duties, the time that Molotov could allocate to the Committee was limited.

Molotov in decline

From 1948, again under attack from Stalin, Molotov's status began to noticeably decline. His release from participation in the Bureau of the Council Ministers to concentrate on foreign policy, at Stalin's request, was the result of a Politburo censure for an unauthorised speech of the ambassador to the United States.[133] The next sign of Stalin's displeasure was when, whilst on leave, in October 1948, he criticised Molotov's amendments to the draft German constitution as 'politically incorrect'. He ordered the telegram containing the reprimand to be circulated to Molotov and other members of the 'leading group', although Beriya and Mikoyan were away.[134] In December, according to Mikoyan's unpublished diary, at one of his informal dinner parties, Stalin arranged for Molotov and Mikoyan to be accused of organising a conspiracy against him whilst he was on leave. Molotov turned pale and 'sat like a statue'. Mikoyan concluded it was to test their reaction.[135]

The position of Polina Molotov was a key factor in the deteriorating relations between the two men. Her connection with Jewish Anti-Fascist Committee[136] made her one of the targets of the growing anti-Semitic campaign in which the attack on the Committee was central. Polina's career had begun to falter after 1939; she lost her Central Committee candidate membership at the XVIII Party Conference, March 1941,[137] although from 1939 to 1948 she was manager of the main administration of the textile industry in the Commissariat of Local Industry of the RSFSR. In that year, however, her department was transferred to the USSR Commissariat of Light Industry, and she was placed on the reserve list of the Commissariat,[138] perhaps a sign of her declining position. From 1945, Molotov followed Stalin's line, hostile to the Jewish Anti-Fascist Committee, and with Stalin he received the report on the case against the Committee from Viktor Abakumov, the Minister of State Security, in March 1948.[139] This did not name Polina, but shortly afterwards Stalin came up to Molotov and said 'You will have to divorce your wife!' Polina's response was apparently to say 'If the party needs this then we shall get a divorce!' They were divorced shortly afterwards and lived apart.[140] Polina, however, remained prominent amongst the Jewish community, and met the Israeli Ambassador, Golda Meir, very publicly in November.[141] On 29 December 1948 she was expelled from the Party[142] and accused of 'links with Jewish nationalists'. Molotov recalled, that when Stalin read out the charges at a meeting of Politburo members, his knees began to tremble,[143] but on the vote to expel her from the Party, taken by the *opros* process, he abstained. This clearly infuriated Stalin. On 19 January 1949, he ordered that the correspondence on Molotov's 1945 mistakes be circulated to Bulganin, Kosygin and Voznesenskii, who had now become members of the 'leading group'. This made it appear as if Molotov was deliberately taking up a 'position'.[144] The next day Molotov wrote to Stalin, saying that when he abstained it was a 'political mistake'. He had thought the matter over, and was now voting in favour of the decision to expel Polina

> which meets the interests of the party and of the state and conveys a correct understanding of communist party-mindedness. In addition, I acknowledge my heavy sense of remorse for not having prevented Zhemchuzhina, a person very dear to me, from making her mistakes and from forming ties with anti-Soviet Jewish nationalists ...

To humiliate him further, on Stalin's instructions, Molotov's statement was distributed to all Politburo members and candidate members. Stalin's displeasure therefore became more widely known than in previous incidents. Asked, in 1955, about his lack of opposition to Polina's arrest on 21 January 1949,[145] he said, 'I must obey Party discipline. ... I submitted to the Politburo, which had decided that my wife must be put away'.[146]

On 4 March 1949, Molotov was dismissed as Minister of Foreign Affairs, but remained as a deputy chairman of the Council of Ministers. Mikoyan was sacked as Minister for Foreign Trade on the same day. The Politburo resolutions dismissing them were taken at a meeting of Stalin, Malenkov, Beriya and Bulganin. The *opros* process was used to canvass Molotov, Mikoyan, Voznesenskii, Kosygin, Shvernik and Voroshilov by telephone. All voted for the resolutions including Molotov and Mikoyan. Only Voroshilov expressed any reservation. He said 'If everyone is in favour, so am I.'[147] It has been suggested that Stalin's nervousness at the measure he was taking was the reason for using the *opros* process rather than a vote at a full meeting.[148] Although he apparently told Molotov that he could relieve himself of day-to-day operational matters but direct overall strategy through the Foreign Policy Committee of the Politburo,[149] it seems likely that Stalin had decided to end Molotov's power in foreign policy. It may have been at this time that Stalin first mentioned his suspicions, aroused by Molotov's visits to the Unites States, that Molotov was an American spy.[150]

Molotov, although not a member, was given oversight of a new foreign policy commission of the Central Committee, responsible for links with foreign communist parties and Cominform, and the international activities of Soviet public organisations. This restricted him to the secondary propaganda aspects of foreign policy.[151] In addition, a Politburo resolution of 9 April 1949 stated that

Vyshinskii, Molotov's successor, should present foreign policy questions directly to the Politburo. Stalin personally deleted from the draft resolution a clause that read

> Questions ... that have a bearing on foreign relations will be presented directly to the Politburo by comrade Molotov.[152]

In April 1949, Molotov was also made chairman of a new sectoral bureau of the Council of Ministers responsible for metallurgy and geology.[153] This seems to have been a further attempt to detach him from foreign policy. His personal humiliation was continued when his nominee for deputy chairman was twice rejected, on the second occasion, because of an appeal to Stalin from Tevosyan, the Minister for the Metallurgical Industry, after a Politburo decision had approved the appointment.[154] Stalin's decision to dismiss Molotov as foreign minister may have been related to the failure of Soviet policy in Germany – the Berlin blockade. The appointment of a new foreign minister was a signal to the West that the USSR was ready to negotiate.[155] Later in the year, with the creation of the German Democratic and Federal Republics, Molotov was blamed for the final decision that Germany should be divided.[156] If, however, he was being made a scapegoat for foreign policy failures, Molotov's behaviour over Zhemchuzhina's arrest must have aroused Stalin's suspicions, and Mikoyan's dismissal, which occurred without the complications of Molotov's, suggests that Stalin was, in addition, trying to introduce younger men into senior positions.[157]

Molotov's divorce from foreign policy proved very temporary. On 12 June 1949, the Politburo relieved him of the responsibility of chairing the Bureau for Metallurgy and Geology 'to concentrate on leadership of the Ministry of Foreign Affairs and the Foreign Policy Commission of the Politburo'.[158] In December 1949, with Bulganin, he met Mao Tse-tung on his arrival in Moscow and participated in the negotiations with him, although he created bad feeling by refusing a meal on Mao's train to which the Chinese leader invited him.[159] Molotov was again given a role outside foreign policy from February 1950, when he was appointed chairman of the sectoral Bureau for Transport and Communications, until it was abolished in March 1951,[160] and in March 1950 he became chairman of a commission for planning rail and water transport of the Council of Ministers.[161] His main work, however, was foreign policy where he remained a central figure until the autumn of 1952. The practice established when he was minister continued. Foreign policy questions from the Politburo Foreign Policy Commission and the Ministry of Foreign Affairs were referred to him, especially matters concerning the East European satellites. He was present with other members of the 'leading group' at Stalin's interviews with the East German leaders in May 1950 and April 1952.[162] Stalin and he settled some issues between themselves.[163] Indeed, O. Troyanovskii, a former ambassador who worked in the ministry, claimed that after 1949, the Ministry of Foreign Affairs, rather than Molotov, lost status, for it was no longer headed by a Politburo member and played a smaller part in foreign policy decision making.[164]

In April 1950, when the Bureau of the Presidium was formed additional to the Presidium of the Council of Ministers, Bulganin replaced Molotov as First Deputy Chairman of the Council of Ministers.[165] Until 1952, however, he remained a member of the 'leading group', the 'quartet' having become a 'septet' with the addition of Khrushchev, Bulganin and Kaganovich. This acted in a genuine collective fashion when Stalin was absent from Moscow. The regular sessions of the Bureau of the Presidium of the Council of Ministers of which, Molotov, as already noted, attended a high proportion, provided opportunities for meeting, even when Stalin was present in Moscow.[166] Molotov still played an important role in the political decision-making process.[167] There were disagreements amongst the 'leading group'. Molotov was involved in a conflict with Kaganovich in May 1952 when he resisted his proposal to increase the plan for rail transport.[168] This echoed the disputes of the 1930s when Molotov was Sovnarkom chairman. Stalin still attacked individuals; Molotov joined in the censure of Khrushchev for his proposal of 'agrocities' in 1951.[169] His article, which appeared second from thirteen after Malenkov's, alongside those of other leading party members, on Stalin's seventieth birthday in December 1949, was relatively restrained,[170] perhaps a reflection of his relations with Stalin at the time; and the celebrations in the press for Molotov's sixtieth birthday, in March 1950, were noticeably more muted than for his fiftieth in 1940.[171] His decline in importance from 1949 is also clear in the reduction of the number of documents he was now receiving from the Ministry of Internal Affairs, 225 in 1946, 180 in 1948 and 153 in 1951.[172]

In the summer of 1952, Molotov headed a commission to examine Maksim Saburov's draft report on the five-year plan to be presented at the forthcoming XIX Party Congress, October 1952.[173] At the Congress, Molotov, as often in the past, chaired the opening session,[174] but was dissuaded from making a major speech by the 'entire Politburo', for fear of displeasing Stalin.[175] Malenkov, Khrushchev and Saburov gave the main reports. After the first few days, Stalin was absent from the Congress. He returned on the last day, 14 October, and made a very brief speech, devoted to encouraging communist parties in 'fraternal' countries.[176]

At the post-Congress plenum of the Central Committee, on 16 October, Stalin announced a Presidium of 25 members and 11 candidates to replace the Politburo, which in 1952 consisted of 11 members and one candidate.[177] He also announced the creation of a nine-man Presidium Bureau.[178] Molotov was a member of the Presidium, but not of the Presidium Bureau, a mark of the decline in his position. A number of explanations have been suggested for Stalin's proposals: he was planning a new purge after which the Presidium would be reduced to the size of a workable Politburo;[179] it was an extension of the 'job-slot' system whereby those occupying senior positions in the state were given representation on the Party's top committees;[180] Stalin was putting the old guard under pressure by bringing in a younger cohort; he was protecting himself from his successors in the same way that Lenin had tried to.[181] Whatever the rationale, Molotov was under threat. This was made quite clear when Stalin attacked him and Mikoyan at the plenum. He reminded the meeting of Molotov's 1945 attempt to relax press censorship, alleging that he drunkenly gave an 'assurance to a British diplomat that the capitalists can start to publish bourgeois newspapers in our country'. He accused Molotov of attempting to give the Crimea to the Jews, Molotov's dealings with the Jewish Anti-Fascist Committee during the war having resurfaced in the trial of the Committee earlier in the year.[182] He also alleged that Molotov revealed Central Committee and Politburo decisions to his wife immediately after they were made. The charges implied cowardice and surrender to capitalism, but most significantly meant that Molotov was disloyal to the Party; Stalin stated specifically that Molotov did not trust the USSR constitution and nationality policy. Molotov attempted his time-honoured response of abject apology and claimed that he was a faithful disciple of Stalin. Stalin replied that he had no disciples; they were all students of Lenin.[183] This is as far as the only published report of the speech goes, but some recollections are more extreme. Stalin is said to have accused Molotov and Mikoyan of right wing deviation and talked of a split in the leadership with Molotov pursuing an anti-Leninist position.[184] The writer, Konstantin Simonov, who was present, stated that the whole audience was taken aback by the attack and by Stalin's fury, particularly the members of the Politburo who were seated behind Stalin. Molotov and Mikoyan turned 'deathly pale'.[185] Mikoyan, in his memoirs, claimed that Stalin had to limit his attacks because they raised questions about the whole Stalinist system.[186] This casts doubt on more extreme reports of the speech. Stalin may have been trying to finally destroy any pretensions that Molotov might have to succeed him. His attacks since 1945 had already done a great deal to undermine Molotov's standing at senior party levels.[187] At this point, Stalin may have compelled him to return to the Central Committee Secretariat the originals of the Nazi–Soviet pact and the secret protocols.[188]

Despite the condemnation, and the new structure, whereby the Presidium Bureau from which he was excluded became the body where the 'leading group' met collectively,[189] Molotov continued to play a part in politics. He attended the two sittings of the Central Committee Presidium held in October and December 1952, the only sessions before Stalin's death.[190] At the first, he was appointed as a member of the Presidium Commission for Foreign Affairs, but relieved of responsibility for supervision of the Ministry of Foreign Affairs. This duty was allocated to the Commission.[191] In addition, on 27 October, the Presidium Bureau again gave him oversight of transport, the Ministry of Communications and the newly formed commission for links with foreign communist parties.[192] This was an echo of the situation when he had been deprived of his foreign policy responsibilities in 1949.

Molotov, with Mikoyan who was also out of favour, continued to arrive at the 'leading group's' informal meetings at Stalin's Kremlin flat or dacha, without receiving an invitation. They persisted after Stalin said 'I don't want those two coming round any more.' Beriya, Malenkov and Khrushchev had agreed to advise them of the meetings. The attempts of Molotov and Mikoyan to 'save themselves' was brought to an end when Stalin singled out Malenkov and attacked him for relaying the information;[193] and Stalin seems to have attacked Molotov again at the December meeting of the Presidium.[194] Molotov claimed in his memoirs that he did not see Stalin for four or five weeks before his death.[195] With his knowledge of Stalin's murder of his close associates from the 1930s onwards, the arrest of Polina, and Stalin's continuing ferocious attacks, Molotov clearly thought he was trying to preserve his life as well as his position. He told Chuev that if Stalin had lived another year he would not have survived.[196] Khrushchev indicated in his memoirs and Secret Speech to the XX Congress that he believed that Molotov was in danger at this time.[197] Molotov's fears would have been reinforced by his knowledge of the 'Doctors' Plot', which was soon to be made public.

Since July 1951, Stalin, through the secret police, had been pressing the investigation of a group of Jewish Kremlin doctors.[198] On 13 January 1953, *Pravda* alleged that they were responsible for a vast conspiracy to murder members of the Soviet military leadership; claimed that they had already murdered Zhdanov and Shcherbakov; and had connections with British and American intelligence. The anti-Semitic overtones were quite clear and Polina Molotov was brought back to Moscow to be reinvestigated.[199] This may indicate, as a recent work argues, that Molotov himself was to play a central role in the plot. The same work states that Stalin denounced Molotov and Mikoyan as spies at the December 1952 Central Committee Presidium meeting where the Doctors' Plot was discussed.[200] The arrest of Maiskii in February 1953 also indicates this.[201] There were, however, no further developments affecting Molotov before Stalin's stroke on 1 March 1953 and death on 5 March, and, as a recent discussion of the Doctor's Plot concludes, Stalin's intentions are unclear.[202]

Molotov did not serve on the commission to organise Stalin's funeral, but he did speak at the funeral after Malenkov and Beriya.[203] Both in his speech and general behaviour, he was seen to be the only member of the political leadership to feel genuine grief.[204] The funeral took place on Molotov's birthday, and Khrushchev and Malenkov asked him what he would like as a present. He replied 'Give me back my Polina.' The next day, Beriya, who had occasionally whispered to Molotov 'Polina is still alive', released her.[205] He is reputed to have met her with a bunch of roses and gone on to one knee. Beriya's son claimed that in 1954, out of gratitude, Molotov intervened to secure his release from prison following the arrest of his father.[206]

14
Unrepentant Stalinist 1953–1957

Foreign Minister and Deputy Head of Government again

Molotov was restored to a very strong position on Stalin's death. He was called to two meetings of the Central Committee Presidium Bureau, held to discuss Stalin's illness, on 2 March 1953. At the end of three further sessions in the next two days, in the early hours of 5 March, it was decided to convene a joint meeting of the Central Committee, Council of Ministers and Presidium of the Supreme Soviet that day. Such a joint meeting was unprecedented.[1] At its forty-minute session, chaired by Khrushchev, the joint party and government body appointed Malenkov head of government, with Beriya, Molotov, Bulganin and Kaganovich (listed in this order) as first deputy chairmen of the Council of Ministers. Molotov was also re-appointed as Minister of Foreign Affairs. The Bureaux of the Presidium of the Council and Central Committee were abolished. Molotov became a member of the 15-person Central Committee Presidium, where he was listed third in seniority (fourth if the dying Stalin who was listed first, is counted) behind Malenkov and Beriya, but before Khrushchev, who was listed fifth.[2] Whilst most of the 'leading group' seemed to show relief, Molotov sat stony-faced and immobile through these and other proceedings.[3] The abolition of the Central Committee Presidium's Commission for Foreign Affairs enhanced Molotov's status as Minister for Foreign Affairs,[4] although a move, in April or May, to have foreign policy questions discussed only in the Presidium of the Council of Ministers, which Molotov ascribed to Beriya, but possibly by Malenkov, may have weakened his position temporarily.[5] Vyshinskii, who had replaced Molotov in 1949, was appointed permanent representative of the USSR to the United Nations, apparently departing on the steamer for New York with tears in his eyes.[6]

Malenkov, Beriya and Khrushchev worked closely together in the days immediately after Stalin's death. Beriya initiated a series of liberalising and de-Stalinising reforms, particularly a de-Russianising nationality policy. These were partly designed to gain popular support for the new leadership, but Beriya's contemptuous attitude to his colleagues alarmed them.[7] The political manoeuvres that led to the fall of Beriya and Malenkov and the rise of Khrushchev to supremacy, demonstrated that Molotov wished to play a leading role. When, however, his opposition to Khrushchev drove him to challenge the First Secretary, it led to his downfall. Resistance to policies that he considered wrongheaded, and unwillingness to move from the Stalinist line, were a main cause of the conflict with Khrushchev. Molotov's behaviour was also influenced by the belief that he was the senior member of Stalin's successors. It is not clear how far he had ambitions to succeed him.

The 'peace offensive' and the fall of Beriya

Malenkov, Beriya and Molotov launched a 'peace offensive' in their speeches at Stalin's funeral on 9 March to counter the growing hostility of the West. Molotov's speech developed the 'peace' theme in most detail. He spoke of 'the Stalinist peace-loving foreign policy. ... the unwavering defence and strengthening of peace ... a policy of international co-operation ...'.[8] In his speech to the Supreme Soviet, on 15 March, Malenkov emphasised that disputed questions, particularly those with the United States, could be settled peacefully;[9] and Molotov was involved in formulating a new policy to speed up the Korean armistice negotiations.[10] These and other gestures of *rapprochement* were rejected by the Eisenhower administration. A precise translation of Eisenhower's 'Chance for Peace' speech of 16 April, in which he set out preliminary conditions for high-level talks, was published in *Pravda* on 26 April with a front-page article which was not entirely hostile. The headline in the *New York Times* on 29 April, however, read 'US, in Effect, Bars Molotov Peace Bid'.[11] The change in Soviet foreign policy seems to have originated with Beriya not Molotov. Beriya made other moves to reduce international tension, encouraged reform in eastern Europe, and tried to arrange a secret meeting with Tito to discuss better relations with Yugoslavia. Beriya's son claims Molotov approved of this;[12] although in the light of his past attitude and future behaviour it seems unlikely. Molotov had reservations about the 'peace offensive', particularly in the light of Eisenhower's response to it, which he regarded as propaganda and provocation. He also refused to respond to Malenkov's suggestions to begin separate talks on the Austrian peace treaty, separating it from the German question.[13] With Molotov's reluctance to depart from the Stalinist position, Beriya's son also asserts that his father suggested that Molotov should resign if he could not support the new line.[14]

The economic crisis in East Germany was a key factor in Beriya's downfall. When the Presidium of the Council of Ministers met, on 27 May, the recommendations to the East German leaders compiled by Molotov and the Foreign Ministry, to which he had restored many of his former aides and assistants,[15] contained a clause that they should 'abandon the policy of the forced construction of socialism'. According to one version of the story, Beriya is reported to have proposed the deletion of the word 'forced', thus recommending the abandonment of the building of socialism. He maintained that all that the USSR needed was a peaceful Germany, and that socialism in East Germany was maintained only by Soviet troops. A set of agreed resolutions, however, that adopted Molotov's formula, was eventually produced on 2 June. The East German political leadership was forced to accept the proposals, but the reluctance of Ulbricht and his supporters to implement reform resulted in the East German rising, for which, in Moscow, Beriya took most of the blame.[16]

Later in the month, when he knew that Malenkov and Bulganin supported Khrushchev, Molotov strongly backed Khrushchev's plan to remove Beriya from office. He argued that Beriya was very dangerous and that they had to 'resort to more extreme measures'. Khrushchev responded, 'You think we should detain him for investigation?'[17] On 26 June, with Khrushchev, Malenkov and Bulganin, Molotov briefed the military detachment that was to arrest Beriya that day,[18] and prior to the arrest, spoke in support of Khrushchev and Bulganin at the Presidium of the Council of Ministers meeting called by Khrushchev. Molotov expressed 'the proper party position' on Khrushchev's accusations that Beriya was a 'careerist' and 'no Communist'.[19]

A Central Committee plenum met, from 2–7 July, to legitimise the arrest of Beriya and his supporters. Malenkov and Khrushchev spoke first. Malenkov ascribed Stalin's attack on Molotov at the plenum after the XIX Congress in 1952, to information given to him by Beriya's agents. He described Molotov as a 'true and faithful warrior for Communism ... a most well-known activist of the Party and of the Soviet State'.[20] Khrushchev was particularly derisive about Beriya, branding him as 'careerist' and 'great intriguer'.[21] Molotov spoke next. He was not as scathing about Beriya as Khrushchev, although he did describe him as a 'traitor' and 'enemy of our party and the Soviet state'. He claimed that in the period after Stalin's death, 'Beriya was uncontrolled and unduly presumptuous. As a result he was exposed, arrested and imprisoned'. He thus revealed that certain members of the Presidium had decided in advance to arrest Beriya. Molotov described the discussion of East Germany in the Presidium in May. He asserted that Beriya insisted on 'untying the hands of German imperialism', an echo of the accusations he had hurled at Britain and the United States at the Council of Foreign Ministers in 1947. He denigrated Beriya's attempt to use agents of the Ministry of Internal Affairs to arrange a secret meeting with Tito, and maintained that the Presidium of the Central Committee had already decided to establish the same relations with Yugoslavia as with other bourgeois states. He then attacked Tito for calling himself a Communist – a sign that he still held fast to the orthodox Stalin line in foreign policy. He claimed that in his attempt to seize power, Beriya had relied on support from the 'imperialist camp', that Beriya had penetrated the party leadership because of lack of vigilance, including insufficient vigilance by Stalin himself! Finally, he spoke of the growing alarm in the capitalist world at the increased power of the USSR and its allies, and referred to the 'peace initiative', 'which has caused great doubts in the ranks of our aggressive enemies'.[22] He thus capitalised on something he had not fully supported. In prison, before his trial and execution in December 1953, Beriya wrote pathetic letters to the political leadership, begging forgiveness. In a letter to Malenkov, he emphasised the good relations he had enjoyed with Molotov and how he had supported him, although he did not mention his part in Polina Molotov's release.[23]

Very quickly, after the arrest of Beriya, the political leadership took sides. Most members of the Central Committee Presidium, including Molotov, supported Khrushchev, and not Malenkov. Throughout 1954, Khrushchev steadily built up his support and power, at first taking care to listen to the opinions of his colleagues.[24] Initially, he and Molotov co-operated and Khrushchev did not interfere in foreign policy, Molotov's special preserve.[25] Khrushchev claimed that fear of Beriya and co-operation in his removal strengthened his association with Molotov. They had a 'good, trusting relationship', and were particularly friendly after Beriya's arrest.[26]

According to Khrushchev, Molotov had tried to have him appointed as Deputy Commissar for Foreign Affairs in 1939, a move which was rejected with Stalin's help. He acknowledged that he had considerable respect for Molotov, who more than most, questioned Stalin's decisions, and was prepared to defend him and others before Stalin.[27] In his memoirs, Khrushchev maintained that Molotov's unwavering adherence to Stalinist policies caused the breach between them. He was, however, able to use this to defeat Molotov and somewhat contradictorily, in the light of his comments about respect for Molotov, he ascribed Molotov's support of Stalinism to stupidity.[28]

Foreign policy 1953–1954

In response to the 'peace offensive', Churchill made an independent British approach to improve relations with the Soviet Union.[29] Before his famous initiative in the House of Commons on 11 May 1953, Molotov and the Soviet Foreign Ministry had, however, already adopted the position that although ready to improve relations with Great Britain, they were reluctant to become involved in any proposal of Churchill for high-level talks.[30] Churchill sent a personal message to Molotov on 2 June. He expressed the hope that the forthcoming Bermuda Conference might result 'in bridges being built, not barriers between east and west'. Molotov received the approach coldly. He was apparently receptive when the British ambassador delivered the message, but his reply to Churchill was cynical about the outcome of the Bermuda Conference, although he did express a willingness to resume his wartime personal correspondence.[31] As well as suspicion of Churchill and his ability to win Eisenhower's support for his scheme, Molotov's behaviour is consistent with scepticism about the 'peace offensive', and wariness of the ambitions of Beriya and Malenkov. When the Bermuda Conference was delayed because of Churchill's illness, and he approached Molotov again on 11 November 1953, Molotov remained sceptical of Churchill's intentions. Malenkov took the same line with Sir William Hayter, the new British ambassador, in the same month, which one authority claims, demonstrates that he was in no position to challenge Molotov in foreign policy, although Malenkov may have made an independent approach for a meeting with Churchill in March 1954.[32] On 13 November 1953, the day after he had received Churchill's note, Molotov held a press conference for foreign correspondents where he demanded the immediate 'unification of Germany', and at which it was reported he used the phrase 'lessening of international tension' (*umen'sheniyu/smyagcheniya napryazhennosti v mezhdunarodnykh otnosheniyakh*) 24 times.[33] In the last six months of 1953, eleven notes were exchanged between Molotov and Western governments about the possibility of international conferences, and Molotov's tone became increasingly bitter.[34] He was clearly unwilling to depart from a Stalinist foreign policy.

The meeting of the foreign ministers of USSR, the United States, Great Britain and France in Berlin, 25 January–18 February 1954, which it was eventually agreed to hold, was the first since 1949. Molotov, without the restraining influence of Stalin, was at his most extreme. At the head of a delegation of 72, he rode about in a limousine with tinted bullet-proof windows and brown curtains, possibly to draw attention to himself as the person who would have the predominant voice in the settlement of Europe.[35] At first, he refused to accept the Western agenda of two items: Germany and Austria, and insisted on the discussion of 'measures for lessening international tension'. This led to four days of fruitless dispute on issues such as Communist China and disarmament. Much time was then spent on Molotov's proposal to invite delegates from both East and West German States to the conference, countered by Eden, again serving as British Foreign Secretary, who put forward free elections as a way to reunite Germany. Molotov then recommended the formation of a new German government to arrange elections, a scheme he and his advisers had been preparing in the Foreign Ministry since the previous summer. It was based on the assumption that the Western powers, seriously divided over the European Defence Community, would find the proposal difficult to resist, and a German settlement favourable to the Soviet Union could be secured.[36] In a further attempt to divide the Western powers, as a rejoinder to the European Defence Community, Molotov's proposals included a new treaty for 'collective security in Europe', to be signed by all European states, whereby the European community would assist any of its members attacked by another power. This caused amusement amongst Western delegates and Molotov became angry. He demanded the abandonment of the European Defence Community, NATO, and the scrapping of US bases in Europe. In a note to the Western powers after the conference, he agreed to include the United States in his European security treaty, and expressed the willingness of the USSR to join NATO![37]

The German problem was eventually discussed on 13 February, but Molotov still insisted that the future of Austria should be linked to it, although there was no agreement with his Kremlin colleagues about this. When the Western powers indicated that they were willing to accept Austrian neutrality, Molotov was taken aback and began to stammer, but continued to insist on non-withdrawal of foreign troops until a peace treaty with Germany was signed.[38] It was clear that the discussion was going to produce no results and the only positive outcome of the conference was that the foreign ministers agreed to meet again in April 1954, to discuss Korea and Indo-China.[39]

On one occasion Molotov appeared to let his guard down in Berlin. At a reception he held, when the wife of Sir Frank Roberts, who had served in Moscow between 1945 and 1947, said he might not remember her, Molotov replied:

> Oh no, I remember you well, because you remind me of the good old days. You do not know what my wife and I have been through since then.[40]

At the Geneva Conference, April–June 1954, Molotov served as one of three chairmen for each of the two sets of negotiations, one on Korea, and the other on

Indo-China. If Communist China profited most, by being invited to an international conference for the first time, Molotov's position, as the senior member of the USSR delegation, meant that he was recognised as the leader of the communist delegations and the line he took was crucial for the communist states. The proposals for the reunification of Korea, submitted by the North Korean foreign minister, were an almost exact replica of Molotov's proposals at Berlin for the reunification of Germany: a commission with equal representatives from both North and South Korea (which had more than twice the population of North Korea), to arrange a general election. Initially, it seemed that some concessions might be made to meet the Western objections, but after Molotov returned to Moscow for two days (31 May and 1 June) he was quite uncompromising. His speech of 8 June was particularly hostile, and it became clear that the conference would make no progress.[41]

The negotiations on Indo-China were marked by a change in Soviet strategy, which prevented them from breaking down. The Chinese were anxious to arrange an armistice and it was clear that the Western powers were divided. As soon as Pierre Mendès-France, who was known to be hostile to the European Defence Community, became head of the French government and undertook to resign unless he could arrange a truce in Indo-China in five weeks, a Chinese delegation headed by Chou-En-Lai negotiated a truce.[42] If the change in Soviet policy represented continuing attempts by Molotov to split the 'imperialist bloc', he treated the Chinese prime minister with 'ostentatious deference', a new experience for him in dealing with a politician from another socialist state.[43] On the other hand, Molotov's greater confidence and authority, now that Stalin was not alive, struck the American Under-Secretary of State Walter Bedell Smith, who headed the American delegation for part of the conference. When the American Secretary of State and the French Foreign Minister departed, before the Indo-China stage of the negotiations, Molotov was concerned about negotiating with people 'inferior in status to himself'.[44]

Molotov sent a sympathetic but vague reply, apparently approved by the Central Committee Presidium, to a further approach by Churchill for a meeting with Malenkov in July 1954, and was very non-committal when Eden approached him personally at the end of the Geneva Conference about the possibility of such a meeting.[45] Three days later, however, he proposed a four-power conference at foreign minister level, to discuss European security and the settlement of the German problem. Churchill rejected this on 27 July because it cut across his plan for two-power high-level talks. Although one Soviet diplomat tried to explain Molotov's proposal as a reply to an earlier Western note, Molotov, personally, used this opportunity to end Churchill's initiative. He secured approval from the Central Committee Presidium for a response which refuted Churchill's contention that an informal high-level meeting without an agenda could not follow a four-power foreign minister conference on Germany, although he deleted the final clause from the document. This stated that the Soviet government doubted whether personal contacts between Churchill and Malenkov could be preliminary to a broader high-level conference.[46] Molotov clearly refused to allow Malenkov to interfere in foreign policy. He rejected a further letter from Churchill expressing determination to pursue Anglo-Soviet high-level talks, and explained why the USSR had proposed a foreign ministers conference.[47] Molotov's control of Soviet foreign policy and implementation of the Stalinist line were now, however, to be challenged.

The defeat of Malenkov and the struggle with Khrushchev

In March 1954, Malenkov, with whom Khrushchev's relations steadily deteriorated, declared that the development of the hydrogen bomb meant that a new world war would mean the destruction of civilisation. This denial of the Marxist–Leninist position that any war would lead to crisis in the capitalist world and the expansion of socialism, was strongly criticised by Khrushchev and Molotov at the Central Committee plenum in April 1954, and Malenkov was forced to repudiate his statement.[48] An open split occurred at the Central Committee plenum, January 1955, and in February 1955, the Supreme Soviet demoted Malenkov from Chairman of the Council of Ministers to Vice-chairman and Minister for Electric Power Stations.[49] At the Central Committee Presidium meeting preceding the plenum, Molotov proposed Khrushchev as Malenkov's replacement as Chairman of the Council of Ministers, but Khrushchev secured the election of his candidate Bulganin. He argued that it was necessary for him to strengthen the work of the Central Committee and party organisations.[50] Molotov's move was either in support of Khrushchev, or an attempt to replace him in the party position, but Khrushchev was later to use it to accuse him of denigrating the role of the Party.[51]

At the plenum, Khrushchev accused Malenkov of being Beriya's 'right hand'; Molotov supported him. When Khrushchev attacked Malenkov's support of light rather than heavy industry, as an attempt to win cheap popularity, Molotov, according to Khrushchev, asked 'Why did he join the Party, if he doesn't know whether he's following a Communist or capitalist course?' Molotov declared that Malenkov's warning that a nuclear war would destroy civilisation was nonsense. Marx had predicted the end of capitalism; Malenkov should speak about the necessity of preparing for the destruction of the bourgeoisie. His prediction showed that he 'didn't have his head on his shoulders, but at the other end of his body'.[52] In his foreign policy statement to the Supreme Soviet, on 8 February 1955, Molotov again condemned Malenkov's statements about the consequences of nuclear war. He maintained that it would not be world civilisation that would perish, but the 'social system with its imperialist basis, soaked in blood, which is moribund'.[53]

Conflict between Molotov and Khrushchev began even before the defeat of Malenkov. Khrushchev told the July 1955 Central Committee plenum that there was not a single important issue on which Molotov did not oppose him.[54] Initially, the most important domestic questions on which there were clashes were agriculture and housing. Molotov opposed Khrushchev's Virgin Lands campaign consistently; from the time he first proposed it at the September 1953 Central Committee plenum; and when it was elaborated and the area to be cultivated extended the following year, at the February–March plenum.[55] Molotov favoured 'intensification': investment to raise the productivity of traditional agricultural areas. Khrushchev recognised that this was important for the future development of agriculture, but argued that bread was needed now.[56] Molotov told Chuev in 1979 and 1982, that at the Central Committee Presidium, he had used statistics to demonstrate that the harvest yield could be improved by ploughing land where the crop prospects were better, and that Khrushchev was unwilling to consult experts. Molotov also maintained that, although in the 1957 resolution against the 'anti-party group', he was branded as the principal opponent to the scheme, he was in favour of much more limited and gradual development of the Virgin Lands. He described Khrushchev as being like a 'runaway horse' and 'small-time cattle dealer'.[57] When the split on this matter became open at the July 1955 Central Committee plenum, Khrushchev alleged that Molotov knew nothing about agriculture and never visited the collective farm next door to his dacha.[58] If the last part of the accusation was true, Khrushchev was ignoring Molotov's role in the later 1920s and early 1930s. As well as opposition to the Virgin Lands scheme, Molotov resisted Khrushchev's proposal to transfer control of the MTSs directly to the kolkhozy. He described the measure as 'anti-Marxist' and as 'destroying our socialist achievements'. Molotov believed that if collective farms had their own machinery they would be too independent of state control; opposition which Khrushchev correctly described as political and not economic.[59] Molotov and those who supported him succeeded in delaying the change until 1958.[60]

Khrushchev claimed that Molotov reported to the Presidium about popular dissatisfaction with housing conditions in Moscow 'with panic in his voice'. His response was to propose the amalgamation of the different administrations responsible for housing construction. This angered Molotov, who according to Khrushchev asked, 'How can you suggest such a thing? ... What makes you think that a single organisation will do a better job than all these separate ones?'[61] Molotov, the bureaucrat and traditionalist, was defeated, but it is not clear if he was opposing Khrushchev's plans to build inexpensive prefabricated five-story apartment blocks.[62]

After visits to Warsaw and Prague in 1954, which he justified by party (rather than state) links,[63] Khrushchev began to challenge Molotov on foreign policy. Molotov was evasive about the Austrian peace treaty when questioned by an American journalist in late January 1955. He said 'You are quite well acquainted with the Soviet Union's point of view,'[64] but in his statement to the Supreme Soviet on 8 February 1955, he hinted at a change of policy.[65] This was forced on him by Khrushchev[66] and announced in a Foreign Ministry statement on 11 March.[67] Following negotiations with Austrian representatives in which Khrushchev played a prominent part, an agreement was reached; and in May, Molotov signed the Austrian State Treaty in Vienna with the three Western foreign ministers,[68] which marked an important break in the Cold War.

Yugoslavia, another issue on which there were clear foreign policy differences, now became central in Khrushchev's conflict with Molotov. After the resumption of formal diplomatic relations in 1953 with Molotov's approval, he and the Foreign Ministry resisted a Central Committee Presidium directive of February

1954 to improve relations with Yugoslavia. Molotov believed that Yugoslavia had repudiated the principles of Marxism–Leninism in 1948 and was no longer a socialist state. A commission established by Khrushchev, however, declared Yugoslavia to be socialist and allowed direct contact with the Yugoslav government.[69] On 10 March 1955, *Pravda* printed extracts from a speech by Tito that included a direct criticism of Molotov. Tito stated that his declarations about Yugoslavia did not correspond with reality. This enabled Khrushchev to defeat Molotov's proposal that the Yugoslav leaders should be asked to come to Moscow, and obtain support to send a delegation.[70] The attitude of the Soviet leadership to Yugoslavia and the directive for the delegation was discussed at three sessions of the Presidium. Molotov, who received scarcely any support, insisted on 19 May 1955 that 'In 1948 Yugoslavia left the position of national democracy for the path of bourgeois nationalism. Yugoslavia is trying to leave our camp.'[71] On 23 May, he challenged the directive which stated that the USSR could work more closely with Yugoslavia than with a capitalist state. He stated that the present position of Yugoslavia was that they thought that they occupied a Marxist–Leninist position, but 'they do not give the impression that they are truly Marxist–Leninist'.[72]

A delegation, led by Khrushchev, but without Molotov, visited Yugoslavia from 26 May to 2 June and produced a significant improvement in relations with Tito.[73] Khrushchev's report on the mission was discussed at the Presidium, on 8 June, in preparation for the forthcoming Central Committee plenum. Molotov, whilst he admitted that the mission had achieved substantial and pleasing results, was very critical of the draft report, especially claims that discussions were based on a Marxist–Leninist position, and that relations with Yugoslavia were worsened by Beriya and not by a nationalist deviation. Molotov claimed that Yugoslav national interests were put before the interests of the USSR and 'our party'. He was heavily criticised, and Khrushchev, who was probably seeking an opportunity to publicly attack Molotov, secured support for his proposal to inform the plenum that there were differences amongst presidium members.[74]

At first, when Molotov defended his position before the July plenum, Khrushchev made only minor interruptions. When, however, Molotov accused him of 'saying anything that happens to come into his head', he attacked Molotov's foreign policy for uniting the world against the USSR.[75] After an exchange on the truth of Molotov's complaint that the Presidium decided Yugoslav issues in his absence,[76] all Presidium members joined in the onslaught on Molotov. Malenkov claimed that Molotov now considered Tito a fascist and Yugoslavia a fascist state. Molotov, who as the next year was to show, had considerable justification in pointing out the danger of 'nationalist deviations' for the 'socialist camp', strenuously defended his position, but in the end was forced to make a recantation, reminiscent of those made in his correspondence with Stalin:

> I consider that the Presidium has correctly pointed out the error of my position on the Yugoslav question. ... I shall work honestly and actively to correct my mistake.[77]

This did not satisfy Khrushchev. He charged that Molotov had sat in the Politburo for 34 years, but had talked nonsense for the last ten, and suggested that Molotov should retire. He alleged that he had provoked the biggest clashes which had occurred in the Presidium, because he 'aspired to the role of grandee'. Finally he condemned Molotov for presenting the East Germans with buses so that he received a 'grand welcome when he visited Berlin'; for permitting Polina Molotov to receive the US ambassador Charles Bohlen and his wife; and for allowing her to accompany him to Berlin and Geneva.[78]

Despite condemnation, both devastating and petty, perhaps because with the XX Party Congress scheduled for early 1956, it was important to show unity, Molotov was allowed to remain in the Presidium and as foreign minister. He accompanied Bulganin and Khrushchev to the Geneva Summit in the same month as the plenum, and apparently suggested that Khrushchev who held no ministerial post should be included in the delegation.[79] Bulganin, in March 1955, had responded positively to Eisenhower's initiative for a heads of state meeting, a change in policy and further example of Molotov's declining power. The summit conference, where Molotov played only a minor role, was fruitless: the only outcome was an agreement to hold another foreign ministers conference.[80] At this meeting, 27 October–16 November 1955, on the main subject of the discussions, 'European Security and Germany', Molotov emphasised 'European security', and re-iterated Soviet proposals for a 'collective security treaty'.[81] During a recess, he returned to Moscow where the conference was discussed at the Presidium on 6 and 7 November. This shows Molotov now had to seek approval for the line he was taking.[82] Western delegates expected him to be more amenable when he returned, but he was as inflexible as before, and the conference was a complete failure.[83]

Khrushchev's next attack was on Molotov's theoretical orthodoxy, scarcely surprising in the light of Molotov's emphasis on Marxist theory in the Yugoslav dispute. In his foreign policy report to the Supreme Soviet, on 8 February 1955, Molotov had stated that:

> Side by side with the Soviet Union where the foundations (*osnovy*) of a socialist society have been built, there are also people's democracies which have taken the first ... steps in the direction of socialism.[84]

Molotov's statement was challenged by P. N. Pospelov, a Khrushchev supporter, former arch-Stalinist and *Pravda* editor, who was to become director of the Institute of Marxism–Leninism, and by A. M. Rumyantsev. They published a letter, sent to Presidium members, that pointed out that Molotov's phrase, which implied that socialism was yet to be attained, was erroneous: a revision of the official view that it had been reached long ago, as enshrined in the 1936 Stalin Constitution. Molotov tried to defend his position before the Presidium. He argued that there was no difference between 'the basis (*osnovy*) of socialism' and 'socialism in the main' (*v osnovnom*). Khrushchev's response was to attack Molotov for belittling the accomplishments of socialism,[85] and in September he was forced to publish his famous retraction in *Kommunist* in which he stated that the 'erroneous formulation' in his speech led to

> the mistaken view that a socialist society has not yet been built in the USSR, that only the foundations of a socialist society have been built ... which does not correspond with the facts.

He concluded:

> I consider that my formulation ... is theoretically erroneous and politically harmful. ... It brings confusion into ideological matters, contradicts the decisions of the party on the questions of building a socialist society in the USSR, and casts doubt on the existence in our country of a socialist society which has already in the main (*v osnovnom*) been built.[86]

The assault on Molotov as an ideologist was emphasised in the editorial to the same issue of *Kommunist*. This criticised attempts to carry over obsolete formula and 'the theoretical bankruptcy of using the formula of a state passed through long ago'.[87]

In the light of the last phrase in Molotov's retraction, in which he reminded Presidium members of his defence, it may be asked how far he was truly repentant of ideological heresy, and regarded himself mainly as a victim of an attack by Khrushchev. His strictly orthodox views on building socialism, which he was less willing to adapt than other Soviet leaders, were apparent in his statement to the Supreme Soviet in 1955, just as they had been in the early 1930s when he was Sovnarkom chairman.[88]

The XX Congress and Khrushchev's Secret Speech

When Khrushchev's draft Central Committee report for the XX Congress was discussed at the Presidium on 30 January 1956, Kaganovich, Molotov and Voroshilov were in a minority in their criticisms. Molotov questioned Khrushchev's statement which denied the fatal inevitability of war. He contended that it was inaccurately formulated, and asked why Khrushchev did not quote fully Stalin's dictum 'peace will be defended and consolidated if the people see that the defence of peace is in their hands and will remain there to the end'. He also asked why Khrushchev did not acknowledge Stalin, and challenged him about the 'parliamentary path' to socialism. He rejected the socialist governments in Britain, Norway and Switzerland as roads to socialism.[89] Quite clearly he was still prepared to challenge Khrushchev on theoretical matters. At the Congress, Khrushchev in his report, although he did not name Molotov, said that the Central Committee had corrected those whose 'speeches ... contained erroneous formulations, such as the one that so far only a basis of socialism, only the foundations of socialism, had been erected in our country'.[90] In response, Molotov, who played only a minor part at the Congress, admitted that he and his ministry had often been 'prisoners of old habits', and that he was guilty of mistakes which had been corrected by the

Central Committee and Presidium. He did not report on foreign policy and did not speak until the seventh day.[91]

The previous October, Khrushchev had suggested that delegates should be informed of Stalin's crimes. On 31 December, when he proposed a commission to look into them, Molotov asked 'Who will benefit?'[92] Whilst the Commission, which according to Khrushchev was to be primarily concerned with Beriya's 'violations of socialist legality', was at work, the Presidium, on 1 February 1956, interviewed Boris Rodos, the former NKVD deputy head of 'specially important investigations' who had been personally responsible for torturing Chubar' and others. He admitted that he had acted on orders, not only from Beriya, but from Stalin personally. In the exchange that followed, Molotov, supported by Kaganovich and Voroshilov, opposed informing the Congress.[93] Molotov said that he took his stand on the distinguished leadership of Stalin, who was a worthy continuer of Lenin's work. Mikoyan interjected that Molotov had supported Stalin.[94]

On 9 February, the Presidium discussed the report of the Commission. This provided evidence of Stalin's personal responsibility for the Great Terror, the number of arrests and executions, the fabrication of plots, and his personal endorsement of torture. Khrushchev argued that it was necessary to tell the truth to the Congress. Molotov, who responded first, insisted that they should add that they had lived under Stalin's leadership for 30 years; that the country had been industrialised; and that on Stalin's death there was a fine party. As well as the 'cult of personality', they should talk about Lenin and Marx. Kaganovich and Voroshilov supported him. They were no doubt suspicious of an attempt by Khrushchev to implicate them in the evils of the Stalin era, but were unsuccessful in carrying their point, although Khrushchev tried to minimise the differences.[95] After the Presidium approved Khrushchev's report to be given at a closed session of the Congress,[96] a draft was circulated on 23 February, two days before the speech, but there is no evidence that Molotov was among the members who made comments.[97] Like other Presidium members, he sat stony-faced when Khrushchev spoke. According to some reports, Khrushchev tried to provoke Molotov, Malenkov, Voroshilov and Kaganovich into explaining their behaviour under Stalin, but they did not respond.[98] Molotov was mentioned twice in the speech, first as one of the recipients of Stalin's telegram to appoint Ezhov in place of Yagoda in 1936 and increase terror, second as a prospective victim of Stalin after the XIX Congress.[99]

Years later, Molotov told Chuev that by the time Khrushchev delivered his secret speech, 'I was already sidelined. And not only at the Ministry [of Foreign Affairs]. People made it a point to keep their distance from me.' He said that the turning point had been his dispute with Khrushchev over Yugoslavia. Pressed by Chuev as to why he and his 'group' did not speak against Khrushchev, he said that they were not united or prepared; he believed that if he had spoken out, he would have been expelled from the Party. By remaining in the Party he hoped gradually to change things. He therefore chose to keep silent, but unfortunately his silence had been taken as acceptance of the report.[100] Molotov chaired two commissions in the months after the Congress. The first, on the Kirov murder, concluded that Nikolaev had acted alone; the second, on the Zinoviev–Kamenev and Bukharin trials, that there was no basis for re-examining the trials, since the defendants had 'led an anti-Soviet fight against the construction of socialism in the USSR'.[101] Khrushchev had not forced Molotov to change his position.

Among the most serious pro-Stalin responses to the Secret Speech were demonstrations and riots in Stalin's native Georgia, on the anniversary of his death. In Tbilisi, the authorities had to use troops to quell the protests. Twenty demonstrators were killed, 60 wounded and many arrested and imprisoned. That some of the demonstrators carried placards bearing the words 'Molotov for Prime Minister' and 'Molotov to Head the CPSU', was clearly an embarrassment. His relief when V. Mićunović, the Yugoslav ambassador, linked the XX Congress with international relations and not with the Secret Speech was clear.[102] This must have been the only occasion in Molotov's life when there were demonstrations in favour of him being leader of the USSR. At a May Day lunch in the Kremlin, which Mićunović attended, Khrushchev indicated that Molotov had defended Stalin in the Presidium and mentioned Stalin's suspicions of Molotov at the end of his life. Mićunović commented that Molotov 'remained passive throughout the lunch ... unable to share in the festive atmosphere'. He believed that Khrushchev 'was touching him on the raw', especially when he spoke of Stalin's suspicions of Molotov as an 'agent of American imperialism'. It was Molotov, however, who proposed the toast to friendship with Yugoslavia, when Khrushchev mentioned that country.[103] With a visit from Tito scheduled for 1 June, perhaps he realised that his position as Foreign Minister was in danger.

The fall of Molotov

Molotov's dismissal from the Foreign Ministry

When the Presidium deliberated on Tito's forthcoming visit on 25 May, Molotov referred to its effect on relationships between the socialist and capitalist camps, and the attitude of international communist parties. He also talked of 'Tito "In the reign of Stalin" '. Khrushchev responded that 'It pains us that Molotov has not changed since the plenum.'[104] The next day, a discussion of appointments to the Ministry of Foreign Affairs soon focused on Molotov. Khrushchev condemned him as 'a weak minister', an 'aristocrat' who was 'used to being a patron but does not work'. He proposed Molotov's replacement either by Mikoyan, Dimitri Shepilov or Mikhail Suslov.[105] On 28 May, Molotov pleaded that he had sincerely and honestly fulfilled Central Committee decisions, but Bulganin and Saburov emphasised that under Molotov the Ministry of Foreign Affairs took a different line to the Presidium. Most Presidium members believed that Molotov should be replaced, principally because of his attitude on Yugoslavia. Mikoyan had reservations. Although he agreed with Khrushchev about Molotov's faults as foreign minister, he did not believe that either Shepilov or Suslov were suitable as a replacement. Kaganovich proposed the appointment of Shepilov as first deputy, with a view to making him minister in the future, thus delaying a decision because a change now would create a bad impression of the leadership. When Khrushchev, as chair, concluded the discussion, he repeated his accusations that Molotov had not changed his position since Stalin died, and that nothing mattered to him apart from being a grandee. He referred to the Virgin Lands campaign, and his claim that Molotov did not understand kolkhoz problems. Finally, he dismissed comments about Molotov's reputation as foreign minister as incorrect.[106] On 1 June 1956, Shepilov replaced Molotov, the decree dismissing Molotov stating that he had been relieved of his responsibilities at his own request.[107] He did, however, participate in the discussions during Tito's visits and attend formal occasions. He criticised his own and Soviet policy at a dinner given by Tito on 8 June.[108] No doubt, it was with some satisfaction that in early July he supported Khrushchev, when the latter complained to Mićunović about Yugoslav press censorship of his speech during Tito's visit.[109]

The Polish and Hungarian uprisings 1956

Molotov continued to be active at the Presidium[110] as the crises with Poland and Hungary developed in June and July. He was absent throughout August and early September,[111] probably on leave, but in late September and October was again involved in domestic policy, and in the response to the Polish and Hungarian revolts.[112] With Mikoyan, Kaganovich, Zhukov and other Soviet military leaders, he travelled to Warsaw with Khrushchev on 19 October. Although Molotov played only a very minor part in the proceedings,[113] his presence, and that of Kaganovich, indicated how serious the crisis was for Khrushchev.[114] That night, when the delegation returned, Molotov strongly supported Khrushchev in advocating military intervention in Poland, although the latter changed his mind the next day, which allowed Vladislav Gomulka to appease the Poles.[115]

On 23 October, when the security police were unable to control large-scale demonstrations in Budapest, all Presidium members, except Mikoyan, were in favour of armed intervention, Molotov saying 'Hungary is coming apart.'[116] But the presence of large numbers of Soviet troops and tanks only escalated the crisis, as reported by Mikoyan and Suslov who were sent to Budapest on Khrushchev's suggestion.[117] When their telephoned despatches were discussed at the Presidium, on 26 October, most of those present, with Molotov, Kaganovich and Voroshilov prominent, criticised Mikoyan. Molotov endorsed Bulganin's view that 'Mikoyan is maintaining an improper and ill-defined position.' On 28 October, as the situation deteriorated, he claimed that it was 'gradually moving towards capitulation', that Suslov and Mikoyan were 'behaving diffidently', and that Mikoyan was reassuring the Hungarians. He continued:

> 'It is agreed up to what limit we will permit concessions. ... The bare minimum is the question of friendship with the USSR and the assistance of our troops.
> If they don't agree we must consider what will happen with the troops.

Later on the same day, however, when Suslov returned to report directly to the Presidium, Molotov and his co-critiques refrained from direct censure.[118] If earlier they hoped to use criticisms of Mikoyan against Khrushchev, the leadership was now beginning to unite in the face of the acute emergency.[119] By 30 October, even Molotov accepted that it might be necessary to scale down military action and withdraw the troops. The Presidium pinned its hopes on negotiations based on the 'Declaration on the Principles of Development and further Strengthening of Friendship and Co-operation between the USSR and other Socialist Countries', which they had agreed that day.[120]

The next day, with very gloomy messages from Mikoyan and Suslov, the decision was reversed. The danger of Hungary leaving the Warsaw Pact (mentioned by Molotov on 30 October), of unrest spilling over into other Warsaw Pact countries, and the apparent immediate success of British, French and Israeli forces in the Suez Crisis against the USSR's ally, were factors which influenced the change. Khrushchev proposed that 'we should take the initiative in restoring order in Hungary'. Only Saburov, who argued that the discussion was pointless after the previous day's decision, dissented. Molotov, who was first to challenge him, pointed out that it had been a compromise.[121] He was absent from the Presidium the following day, when Mikoyan, who had returned from Budapest, expressed his doubts about the policy. With Khrushchev and Malenkov, Molotov went to Brest, to brief the Poles about the forthcoming invasion of Hungary, a difficult task in the light of the political situation in Poland; and Khrushchev was unsuccessful in convincing Gomulka that military intervention was necessary.[122]

Mikoyan's attempt to change policy on 1 November presaged the break down of the brief period of united leadership. In Presidium meetings, on 4–6 November, the first few days of the invasion, Molotov and Kaganovich disagreed with the others about the post-invasion regime to be established in Hungary. Initially, Molotov advocated Andras Hegedues, who had been prime minister before Imre Nagy in October, as head of a 'Provisional Workers' and Peasants' Government', thus reinstating the legitimate authority. He gave way on this, but insisted that it was dangerous for Janos Kadar's new government to condemn the former Stalinist leaders and that the Hungarian Workers' Party should not be renamed. He claimed that Kadar was calling for a condemnation of Stalinism and shifting to the Yugoslav position. Khrushchev commented: 'I do not understand Comrade Molotov. He produces the most pernicious ideas'. Molotov replied 'you should keep quiet and stop being so overbearing'.[123] On 6 November there were acrimonious exchanges when Molotov 'vehemently' objected to Khrushchev's plans for the new regime that Kadar was establishing in Hungary. He asserted:

A new party will be created on an unknown basis. Where will it lead? ... we must not forget that a change of names is a change in character. The formation of a new Yugoslavia is taking place. We are responsible for Hungary (without Stalin).

Saburov accused Molotov, and Kaganovich who gave him limited support, of being 'simplistic and dogmatic'. Averky Aristov charged that 'they clung to the cult of Stalin, and they are still clinging to it'; and Khrushchev reviled them for 'proposing ... the line of screeching and face-slapping'.[124] The differences were to resurface in 1957 when Molotov, as a member of the 'anti-party group', accused Khrushchev, with some justification, of making 'dangerous zig-zags' in eastern Europe and of 'ignoring the impact of [the USSR's] actions on other countries'.[125]

Continuing opposition

On 21 November 1956, Molotov was appointed as Minister of State Control.[126] This was a relatively junior position, and the ministry was abolished when Molotov was dismissed following the implementation of Khrushchev's proposals for economic reform.[127] The reasons for the appointment are by no means clear. It is difficult to accept the contention of one Russian source that it was 'as compensation'[128] for the loss of his post as Minister of Foreign Affairs, for any unity amongst the leadership over Hungary had now disappeared. With Khrushchev's foreign policy difficulties, particularly on Yugoslavia, it may point to a slight revival in Molotov's fortunes,[129] but the new post was possibly an attempt to divert Molotov into an area where he was less able to authoritatively challenge Khrushchev. If this was the case, the move was unsuccessful, for in the next few months Molotov continued to try to intervene in foreign policy and used his new domain, which gave him the potential to interfere more generally, to mount fierce attacks.

Molotov's opportunities were increased by Khrushchev's weakness at this time, signalled by a tactical retreat from attacking Stalinism. There were not only the Polish and Hungarian crises, but also domestic protests, discontent amongst intellectuals, and the revision of the ambitious targets of the Sixth Five-Year Plan at the December Central Committee plenum.[130] Initially, these difficulties drove the leadership together. Molotov contributed positively to discussion, both on the secret draft letter to party organisations to deal with the disorders, on 6 December, and on the draft resolution on the Sixth Five-Year Plan when it was discussed at the Presidium on 18 December.[131] In November, as Presidium representative, he presided, over a conference organised by the Ministry of Culture on the correct attitude to socialist realism in art, where he took a strong line against those objecting to party leadership.[132]

When Khrushchev's proposals for the reform of industrial management, which involved the abolition of most union and union–republican economic ministries and their replacement with regional economic councils (*sovnarkhozy*), were first discussed at the Presidium on 28 January 1957, Molotov expressed caution. He requested more detailed formulation of the scheme.[133] When the proposals were considered again on 22 March, after approval at the Central Committee plenum, Molotov pressed particularly on the question of central control. He maintained that an equivalent to VSNKh and a number of central committees were needed. He received support from N. K. Baibakov, the Gosplan chairman, but Brezhnev said that this path would be going up a blind alley and Khrushchev denied that there was any necessity for a VSNKh.[134] Molotov now circulated a note specifying his objections. He stated that the scheme was not properly worked out and proposed the immediate formation of a small number of committees attached to the Council of Ministers, and an Economic Council equivalent to the former Council of Labour and Defence (STO).[135]

When discussion was resumed on 27 March, following consideration at the Council of Ministers, Molotov said that he had not changed his opinion and that 'experience teaches us that amendments will be needed to this too decentralised draft'. Bulganin, Chairman of the Council of Ministers, accused Molotov of undermining the Presidium by pressing the matter of committees at the Council, although Kaganovich denied that Molotov was attacking the Presidium. In an exchange about Matyas Rakosi, the former Hungarian leader who was in exile in the USSR, Molotov alone argued that he should be allowed to return to Hungary. This was condemned by Khrushchev. The Presidium then turned to Molotov's note.[136] Khrushchev's written response deplored the stubbornness with which Molotov defended his position, especially as the Presidium had unanimously approved his draft theses. He considered that Molotov's proposal for committees was an effort to retain branch ministries, and his suggestion of an Economic Council an attempt to establish an intermediate link between Gosplan and republican governments.[137] Bulganin supported Khrushchev when he denounced Molotov for circulating the note, and repeated the charge that he endangered the unanimity of the Presidium. Molotov justified his action by saying that on one day committees were going to be allowed, the next they were not. He still considered the proposals underdeveloped. Although Molotov received some support from Voroshilov, Malenkov and Kaganovich, most speakers were alarmed by the threat to Presidium unity and censured Molotov. Finally, in a typical Khrushchevian attack, in which he dismissed Molotov's behaviour as unacceptable for the collective leadership, Khrushchev claimed that Molotov was out of touch with reality. In addition to the dispute on industrial policy, he reminded the Presidium of Molotov's opposition on the Virgin Lands, on foreign policy, and of his behaviour during collectivisation and the Terror.[138]

Khrushchev's proposals, partly because they represented political as well as economic change, in that they gave power in the *sovnarkhozy* to local party leaders who were his supporters, were rushed through and implemented in May 1957. Molotov's criticisms that the scheme was being introduced too hastily, and that there was a need to protect central interests had considerable justification; even some of Khrushchev's supporters at the time recognised this, but did not dare to say so.[139] That Molotov made the criticisms, and in the context of his opposition to Khrushchev, discredited the criticisms.

On the anniversary of Lenin's birthday, 22 April 1957, Molotov published a major article in *Pravda*, entitled 'On Lenin'. He emphasised that he was the only member of the Presidium who had personally worked with Lenin, and that he had met Lenin as early as April 1917. He referred to Stalin's mistakes, saying that sometimes mistakes were inevitable when huge and complex historical tasks were being completed, and that no one could give a guarantee not to make mistakes. He was defending himself and emphasising his senior position in the current leadership.

Clashes between Molotov and Khrushchev at the Presidium continued in April and May. The major exchanges concerned the Ministry of State Control, although there were also arguments over foreign policy, particularly on disarmament.[140] On 18 April, Khrushchev said that he was astonished that the Ministry of State

Control intervened in such questions as deficiencies in aero-engine production. Molotov replied that after initial consideration he proposed to discuss the matter in the Defence Council.[141] On 4 May, the Presidium refused permission for Molotov to publish an article on State Control in *Pravda*,[142] and it never appeared, but the major clash took place on 31 May. Khrushchev immediately condemned as unacceptable Molotov's response to the February 1957 plenum's resolution on the *sovnarkhozy* reform, which had called for the work of the Ministry of State Control to be improved and 'radically restructured'.[143] He objected particularly to Molotov's plan to inspect *sovkhozy*. Bulganin supported him and argued that there was too much centralism. Molotov received support from Kaganovich and Malenkov who said a central control organ was needed, but Khrushchev maintained that Molotov and his supporters had incorrectly interpreted the Leninist position on state control. He was instructed to rework his proposals and base them on local rather than central initiative.[144] These were never presented and following the defeat of the 'anti-party group', the Ministry was abolished.[145]

Khrushchev had talked previously about catching up with America, and on 22 May 1957, in Leningrad, he promised that the USSR's output of meat, butter and milk per capita would overtake that of the United States in a few years. The statement was made without any support from his Presidium colleagues and contradicted figures provided by Soviet statisticians, including those from Gosplan.[146] Khrushchev's opponents naturally enough used this to attack him. According to Kosygin, at the time a Khrushchev supporter,

> Molotov spent a long time gathering materials to show that no one – not the Party, not the people, not the agricultural leadership, not the peasantry – that no one was in a position to overtake the United States in the production of meat.[147]

Khrushchev, however, did not retreat, but continued to insist on his statement. This caused Bulganin to lead a walk out of his Presidium colleagues from a meeting in Moscow a few days later.[148] The last straw appeared to come for Molotov when, at a non-party meeting of Moscow writers with party leaders at about the same time, Khrushchev revealed publicly that he had disagreements with him.[149]

The defeat of the 'anti-party group'

Molotov had consistently resisted Khrushchev's attempts to move away from the Stalin line in both domestic and foreign policy, and his opposition increased after the XX Congress. The strongest support had come from Kaganovich. There had been some from Malenkov, and occasionally other members of the Presidium had stood with him. Relations between Molotov and Kaganovich were, however, not good and Molotov had been instrumental in demoting Malenkov.[150] There was thus little chance of a thoroughgoing alliance. Molotov and other former lieutenants of Stalin were alarmed at the growing wave of rehabilitations, increasing in number from the time of the XX Congress, although slackening in late 1956 when Khrushchev was in difficulties. The fear that they might have to share responsibility for Stalin's misdeeds was clearly a common concern. Molotov's article in *Pravda*, in April 1957, may indicate that he was prepared to become leader, but the catalyst that finally drove the 'anti-party group' together and led it to attempt to oust Khrushchev, was his claim that the USSR would exceed the United States in meat, butter and milk production in a few years. There is no evidence that the group were attempting a 'coup', in the sense of an effort to over-throw the government by violent means. As Zhukov's behaviour showed, the army was loyal to Khrushchev, as was the KGB. Exasperated by the way in which Khrushchev conducted affairs and assumed increasing personal authority, and in Molotov's case his departure from Stalinist policies, the group aimed to remove Khrushchev by a majority vote in the Presidium.

Khrushchev called Molotov the 'ideological leader' of the group, Kaganovich the 'knife sharpener' and Malenkov the 'main organiser'.[151] Voroshilov, Bulganin, Shepilov, Saburov and Mikhail Pervukhin joined them, some at the last minute. All except Shepilov were Presidium full members and constituted a majority there. Three of five other Presidium candidate members seem to have wavered.[152] The first sign of the coming attack was on 10 June. At the Presidium, with Khrushchev and Bulganin in Finland, the former's proposals to purchase papermaking machin-ery in Austria were defeated.[153] On 15 June, after Khrushchev's return, when Molotov and other members of the 'anti-party group' met him at the airport,[154] another scheme to import machinery from abroad was rejected. Molotov was prominent on both occasions.[155] On 16 June, he, Malenkov, Kaganovich and Bulganin left the celebrations for Khrushchev's son's wedding prematurely and very publicly, which should have been a warning to Khrushchev.[156]

The plan was identical to that successfully employed against Beriya. On 18 June, Khrushchev was summoned to a meeting of the Presidium of the Council of Ministers of which he was not a member, seemingly to discuss a visit to Leningrad planned for later in the month.[157] This was used as an excuse to move to a discus-sion of Khrushchev's conduct. The meeting was changed to a joint meeting with the Central Committee Presidium, chaired by Bulganin because of the nature of the business. Malenkov, followed by Voroshilov and Kaganovich, attacked Khrushchev. Molotov supported them, saying:

> No matter how Khrushchev tried to provoke me I did not succumb to the strained relations. It seemed to suffer further was impossible. Khrushchev increased tension not only in personal relations, but also in the Presidium as a whole in settling important state and party questions.

He then attacked Khrushchev's reform of industrial administration and conduct of foreign policy, particularly in relation to Yugoslavia. In conclusion, he declared that it was impossible to work with Khrushchev as First Secretary, and that he was in favour of relieving him of his responsibilities. Bulganin and other members of the group supported him.[158] The First Secretary was shaken, but managed to have the meeting adjourned, so that all full and candidate members of the Central Committee Presidium and Central Committee secretaries could be present at the joint meeting the next day.[159] On 19 June, when Molotov was again prominent in the attack,[160] Shvernik, for the first time, used the expression 'anti-party group', to describe those attempting to remove Khrushchev from the First Secretary position.[161] As Kaganovich pointed out, this was untrue as they were a majority, but the term, which implied factionalism, was reminiscent of that applied to oppositions in the 1930s and helped to seal their doom. A quick victory was essential: Khrushchev would have found it difficult to overturn a Presidium resolution. The delay gave him time to pressurise waverers and mobilise the full Central Committee to which the Presidium was theoretically responsible, and to which many of his supporters had been elected after the XX Congress.[162] By 20 June, Khrushchev's opponents had scaled down their demands from his resignation to the abolition of the position of First Secretary, 'to prevent the appearance of a Khrushchev personality cult', and they were forced to agree to hold a Central Committee plenum.[163]

The plenum of 22–29 June 1957 was one of the most extraordinary in Soviet history. There were no reports. Khrushchev declared that there was one item on the agenda: 'the internal party question'.[164] He used the issue of Stalin's crimes to defeat his foes. Much more detail was given than in the Secret Speech, and statistics on the numbers murdered and the names of those responsible were cited. By the end, only Molotov refused to vote for his own defeat.

As soon as the plenum opened, Molotov challenged Khrushchev's proposal to delay the second sitting: an attempt to give time for his allies to arrive.[165] Suslov spoke first. He described the proceedings at the Presidium and made a general attack on the 'anti-party group'.[166] Zhukov then named Malenkov, Kaganovich and Molotov as the 'chief culprits' in the 'arrest and execution of party and state cadres' and cited the number of death sentences that Stalin, Molotov and Kaganovich had signed in 1938. He noted Molotov's addition to Stalin's vicious endorsement on Yakir's protest of innocence.[167] Malenkov and Kaganovich tried to defend themselves, Kaganovich attempting to make Molotov speak first, saying that he was not prepared.[168]

At the next sitting, Molotov found that his request to speak next had been overruled.[169] Bulganin immediately denied that he had allied himself with Molotov at the Presidium. He claimed that he had opposed Molotov on agricultural questions and on foreign and internal policy, and that his relations with Molotov were not particularly friendly.[170] Saburov and Pervukhin also tried to distance themselves from the core group of Molotov, Malenkov and Kaganovich.[171]

When Molotov spoke, he was frequently interrupted by abuse and insults, but remained defiant. Accused of forming a fractional group he tried to remind the plenum of his long service to the Party, and maintained that it could not have been a group because it did not have a political platform. He insisted that it was necessary to check on the work of the First Secretary, but his attempts to concentrate on Khrushchev's faults were in vain.[172] His contention, that in the light of the collective leadership, Khrushchev's claim that the USSR would overtake America in milk, meat and butter production should have been approved by the Presidium, before being made public in a speech, was countered by assertions that local officials had discussed the matter, although he returned to this question a number of times. He argued that he had been willing to oppose Khrushchev at the Presidium when others remained silent, but found his views on all the major issues on which he disagreed with Khrushchev under attack. He insisted that there was no plot, but an accumulation of complaints against Khrushchev, because he undermined collective leadership by assuming responsibility for all issues himself, and dismissed his colleagues as 'senile old men', 'good-for-nothings', or 'careerists'. Khrushchev called for modesty, but his arrogance had united the group. He had not remained the same person as when he was selected as First Secretary and the situation continued to deteriorate.[173]

When Molotov tried to discuss foreign policy, Zhukov insisted on reminding him of his involvement in Stalin's crimes. He replied

> I was a member of the Politburo and chairman of Sovnarkom, so I cannot deny responsibility. I am accountable with other members of the Politburo.

Molotov referred to a Presidium decision at the time of the XX Congress in an attempt to prevent discussion of the repressions, but Khrushchev asked who authorised torture to produce confessions. Molotov, supported by Kaganovich, replied that it was the whole Politburo. Khrushchev then said that Molotov was second in command to Stalin and must accept blame. Challenged now by Zhukov with a document he had signed in 1945, which sentenced 126,000 freed German officers to concentration camps for six years, he argued that his signature represented a Politburo decision and that he had raised more objections to Stalin than anyone, 'more than you Comrade Khrushchev'.[174]

When the plenum resumed in the evening of 24 June, Molotov again tried to attack Khrushchev's foreign policy. He alleged that Khrushchev had disregarded the XX Congress decision and Leninist principle of exploiting contradictions in the imperialist camp. In an attempt to come to an agreement only with the United States, he had ignored other non-socialist states and forgotten the rest of the socialist camp. He charged Khrushchev with bringing the Ministry of Foreign Affairs into disrepute before bourgeois states by joking about Gromyko and Dulles's disagreements; and behaving in an undignified way by visiting a sauna with the President of the Finnish Republic. Khrushchev replied that it would have been discourteous to refuse the invitation to the sauna – Molotov argued with everyone and wished to lead the country into war. Molotov replied that Khrushchev had invented the details he cited, but Khrushchev supporters introduced the issues of Molotov's visit to Hitler and his attitude to Yugoslavia.[175] When, as before the XX Congress, Molotov asked why Khrushchev ignored Stalin's achievements, Khrushchev responded that Molotov wanted to turn everything back so that he could take up the hatchet. In conclusion, Molotov tried to insist that it was necessary to criticise Khrushchev's mistakes and strengthen collective leadership. Khrushchev accused him of discussing these matters in 'his group' and not at the Presidium. An interrupter asked why he was afraid of a plenum, and Molotov was forced to concede that the matter had to be decided there.[176]

During the remainder of 24 June, and for the next three days, Khrushchev's supporters censured all aspects of Molotov's political conduct. His behaviour in the later 1920s and 1930s including his part in the repressions, his conduct of foreign policy and attempts to criticise Khrushchev's policies were attacked; as were his theoretical errors,[177] failure to restructure the Ministry of State control,[178] and lack of control of Polina Molotov.[179] Criticism by his former protégé Gromyko of his conduct of foreign policy must have been particularly galling.[180] It was made quite clear that he was considered the leader of the 'anti-party group'.[181] Sometimes he tried to intervene and challenge the accuracy of the statements and there were further exchanges with Khrushchev.[182]

On 28 June, first Kaganovich, then Malenkov, prostrated themselves before the plenum.[183] Molotov, however, who admitted that he had gone further than other members of the group, drew a distinction between seeking the dismissal of Khrushchev, which raised an organisational problem and was a serious political mistake; and criticism of the errors of a member of the Presidium, which he considered 'legal'. He was accused of a 'right deviation' and challenged twice to specify the 'political platform' of the group. Charged with plotting against the party line and party leadership, Molotov claimed that, as an honourable communist, he had always recognised the correctness of the party line, defended the interests of the state and tried to implement party policy. He said that the 'conspirators' did not wish to be a group; they had met, but only in the last two or three weeks, and there was no plot against the Central Committee leadership. He recognised his particular personal responsibility as an old party member for his errors, and the plenum would decide. Finally, Khrushchev challenged him again on his resistance to a plenum, and he replied that the group sought to discuss and resolve the matter in the Presidium.[184]

Molotov's statement was followed by the confessions of Shepilov, Pervukhin and Saburov and further attacks on the central group by Khrushchev supporters.[185] Semyon Ignat'ev alleged that they planned to appoint Kaganovich, Molotov or Malenkov as First Secretary, an ally as chairman of the KGB, and Khrushchev as Minister of Agriculture. In his memoirs, Molotov acknowledged that this was what the group had planned for Khrushchev.[186] The attacks continued at the next penultimate session of the plenum. Vasily Kuznetsov, a deputy Minister of Foreign Affairs, asserted that, as Foreign Minister, Molotov had not exploited contradictions in the capitalist camp, but united it. He also reminded the meeting of the repressions.[187] When Khrushchev summed up, he began by labelling Molotov, Kaganovich and Malenkov as the core of the group, but shortly afterwards dismissed all eight as 'pathetic intriguers' and not politicians, although a great danger to the Party.[188] That a large part of his speech was concerned with details of his conflict with Molotov, indicated that he regarded Molotov's opposition as the greatest threat, and that it was Molotov he most feared. Early on he claimed that Molotov had not reciprocated the friendly relations that he had tried to establish with him at the time of Beriya's arrest.[189] He alleged that Molotov, Malenkov and Kaganovich had tried to control the KGB to conceal their criminal activities in the 1930s. He again attacked Molotov's opposition to the reform of industrial administration, and poked fun at Molotov's knowledge of planning, because the phrase 'it is essential to make provision for a rhythm of work for enterprises', which Molotov had insisted on being inserted into the Sixth Five-Year Plan, was elementary for planners.[190] He accused Molotov of 'wrecking' in agriculture by a proposal on procurements in 1956. Molotov interrupted to claim that the proposal was made earlier.[191] He also challenged the accuracy of Khrushchev's statements about his foreign policy,[192] but Khrushchev continued:

> Essentially the international policies of Stalin were Molotov's policies. It must, however, be said that Stalin was much wiser and more flexible in implementing basic foreign policy than Molotov. ... Molotov's policy ... would have helped the imperialists unite their forces against the USSR. It is an adventurist policy. Yet he still has the nerve to quote Vladimir Il'ich Lenin, teaching us Leninist foreign policy. He is an empty dogmatist divorced from life.[193]

When Khrushchev quoted the panegyric to Stalin in Molotov's 1939 toast on Stalin's sixtieth birthday, Molotov again intervened and asked 'Why do you not recite your own speeches?' Khrushchev continued by attacking Molotov's role in the Terror. He maintained that Molotov, after Stalin, had more power than anyone else, and that he had scribbled curses on death sentences, not because Stalin dictated them, but because he wanted to please Stalin, and to demonstrate his vigilance.

> With derision and a smirk you sent innocent people to their deaths. The mothers, wives and children of the innocent who were shot, remained alive. They shed a sea of tears. ... Why do you not talk about when you shot Postyshev ... Eikhe, Kosior, Rudzutak? How can you look in the eye of the innocents who survived? It is necessary to interview and reply to such people in your name.[194]

Molotov did not respond, but unlike the rest of the group, he remained unrepentant, as his interventions demonstrated.

At the plenum's final session, on 29 June, Kaganovich and Malenkov confirmed their contrition.[195] Molotov, however, maintained his position. His declaration claimed that Khrushchev's summing up was 'extremely unobjective' and directed at his statement. He affirmed that he recognised the correctness of party policy, which was successful because of the Presidium's collective leadership to which he recognised Khrushchev's major contribution, although concern about his infringements of this was the chief reason for the meeting of 18 June. He acknowledged that raising the question of abolishing the post of First Secretary was a political mistake, although it was based on the desire to strengthen collective leadership. He admitted that he had met individual members of the Presidium on a number of occasions to discuss this, but there was no basis for calling this a 'conspiracy', although it had the appearance of an 'inadmissible grouping'. He finished by declaring that he was not pursuing any personal interest, but believed that everything he did was in the interests of the Party and the struggle for communism.[196]

All three declarations, particularly that of Molotov, were considered unsatisfactory. The statements demonstrated that the authors had still not renounced their 'anti-party position'. Molotov alone abstained from the vote in favour of the draft resolution the plenum now passed.[197] Kaganovich and Malenkov stated that they supported the resolution in the interests of party unity, because they recognised their mistakes and because they were loyal party members. Molotov, however, said that he had always, as now, had only one basic aim, to be a dutiful and true party member. These were his last words to the Central Committee, for the plenum now expelled him, Kaganovich and Malenkov from both the Presidium and the Central Committee, requiring them to withdraw.[198]

The published resolution on the 'anti-party group', which, *Pravda* noted was supported unanimously except by Molotov who abstained, rehearsed the issues on which Khrushchev's policies had been opposed. Molotov, although described only as a 'participant' (*uchastnik*) in the group, was singled out for 'demonstrating conservatism and a stagnant attitude' to the development of the Virgin Lands. It was stated that Kaganovich and Malenkov had supported his opposition on foreign policy, and this made clear that he was the leader in that sector. All three were denounced for being 'shackled by old notions and methods'; for being sectarian, dogmatic and scholastic; and for seeking 'to return to the erroneous methods of leadership condemned by the XX Congress'. The resolution on Party Unity of the X Congress was cited in support of the condemnation of their fractional activities and their expulsion. Shepilov alone was mentioned from the other members of the group. He was dismissed from his post of Central Committee secretary and lost his candidate membership.[199] That Saburov was removed from the Presidium and Pervukhin demoted to candidate member,[200] was not noted in the published version of the resolution. Bulganin and Voroshilov retained their positions temporarily. This allowed Khrushchev to maintain that he commanded a majority in the Presidium and emphasise the fractional nature of the 'anti-party group's' activities.[201]

The paragraph in the resolution which stated that Molotov, Malenkov and Kaganovich were personally responsible for the mass repressions, and counted on seizing the key positions in the Party and state to hide their criminal activities, was omitted from the published version.[202] It was, however, repeated and elaborated on in the confidential letter circulated to all party organisations, party members and candidate members. This paraphrased the resolution, and expanded on the 'errors' of the core group. It charged Molotov, as deputy chairman of the Council of Ministers, with neglecting his responsibility for strengthening cultural work. It repeated the accusation that he was a candidate to replace Khrushchev as First Secretary. Before specifying the measures taken against the 'anti-party group', the letter was careful to state that in their speeches on 28 June, Molotov, Malenkov and Kaganovich had recognised their erroneous position. It quoted extracts from their speeches where they acknowledged this. Molotov's speech was especially carefully edited.[203]

Molotov's defeat at the plenum was immediately followed by the loss of his government posts. On 29 June, he, Malenkov and Kaganovich were dismissed as deputy chairmen of the Council of Ministers. Molotov and Malenkov were also deprived of their ministerial positions.[204] This was the reverse procedure to the 1930s: then Stalin's victims lost their state positions before their party membership. Nearly two months later, following a Presidium decision on 3 August, Molotov was appointed as ambassador to the Mongolian Republic on 30 August.[205] V. Pissarev, the former ambassador, accompanied Molotov in an advisory capacity. Malenkov had already been sent to manage a power station in Kazakhstan, and Kaganovich appointed as director of a potash works in the Urals.[206] If there was an attempt to use the skills of those Khrushchev had defeated in these appointments, there was also irony. If Khrushchev's appointment of Pissarev as adviser to Molotov was meant to demonstrate his incompetence, it also showed that Khrushchev believed he still had to be watched.

15
The Outcast

Molotov's departure from Moscow was unexpected. Driven out of his apartment, he was forced to abandon a large library that was later ruined in a flood.[1] Initially, he was greeted with considerable respect in Mongolia,[2] but soon found himself shunned by the diplomatic staff of other socialist countries, except by Mićunović, the Yugoslav ambassador to the USSR, who took care to maintain contact with Molotov as Khrushchev's relations with Tito deteriorated.[3] At the Mongolian Party Congress in 1958, Molotov was treated with contempt by the Soviet delegation. He was not allowed to meet the representatives when they arrived or attend their meetings with the Mongolian government.[4] Perhaps, because when he did speak to them, he unwisely criticised the disbandment of the MTSs,[5] the leader of the delegation, N. G. Ignatov, attacked him as a factionalist and a member of the 'anti-party group'. Molotov was kept away from the session of the Congress when this occurred.[6]

In the harsh climate of Mongolia Molotov became increasingly concerned over Polina's health; she was hospitalised for surgery[7] and he suffered from bouts of pneumonia. Molotov, however, had time on his hands and travelled round the country, staying in yurts.[8] As Khrushchev's relations with the Chinese deteriorated Molotov managed to move closer to Chinese diplomats, and the Chinese used every opportunity to demonstrate that they respected Molotov because of his close association with Stalin.[9] He clearly relished the opportunity to continue to support the Stalinist line in foreign policy, and as early as September 1958 the Soviet Foreign Ministry was complaining to the Central Committee Presidium of Molotov's incorrect behaviour towards the Chinese.[10]

Shortly before the XXI Party Congress in February 1959, where the 'anti-party group' was again attacked, there was talk that Molotov was to be transferred from Mongolia to the Netherlands, and at the time of the Congress there were rumours of his close contact with the Chinese.[11] The close proximity of Mongolia to China and Molotov's contacts with Chinese diplomats seem to have been the main reasons why, in September 1960, he was moved to Vienna to become Soviet co-chairman of the United Nations International Atomic Energy Agency.[12] In Vienna, although Molotov continued to be treated as a figure from the past, he worked hard and earned the respect of his staff.[13] When Khrushchev arrived to meet the newly elected President Kennedy, in June 1961, Molotov was among those greeting him at the station and received a casual recognition. He was, however, invited to be present at Khrushchev's meeting with Kennedy.[14]

At Ulan Bator, and in Vienna, Molotov resumed his theoretical studies. He also kept up an active interest in politics in Moscow. He wrote frequently to the Central Committee Secretariat expressing his views. In May 1959 he put forward a scheme for a new 'Confederation of Socialist States', aimed at improving relations with China. Individual members would retain control over most matters of domestic and foreign policy, but questions of war and peace and defence would be centrally controlled. The USSR and China were to be the founder members.[15] In the same year, Molotov wrote to the Central Control Commission to protest about Khrushchev's remarks to Vice-President Nixon that he had opposed signing the Austrian State Treaty. He complained that Khrushchev's comments were 'slander similar to the sorts of poisonous attacks which the Mensheviks directed against the Bolsheviks'.[16] In early 1960, he submitted to *Kommunist* an article to mark the ninetieth anniversary of Lenin's birth. In this, as in his *Pravda* article of 1957,[17] he emphasised his personal conversations with Lenin, reminding his readers of his seniority. The article was not published, but the editor wrote to Molotov and criticised him for not recognising his errors; for describing the February revolution as a blow against imperialism as if there had been no October Revolution; and for saying that in conversation with him Lenin had described the country as weak and had criticised communists.[18]

Preparations were being made for the XXII Party Congress from the summer of 1961, when a draft of the new party programme was published for discussion. Shortly before the Congress, Molotov sent the Central Committee a detailed criticism of the draft programme, which naturally enough was not published, but was referred to in detail in Pavel Satyukov's speech to the Congress. Molotov described the new programme as 'antirevolutionary', 'pacifist' and 'revisionist'. He refuted the idea that the avoidance of war was possible. He insisted that Lenin had never believed in 'peaceful co-existence', and called upon the Party to step up its support for the 'revolutionary struggle of the working class'.[19] In conversation with Chuev in 1981 Molotov said Khrushchev was like 'a bridleless horse who dictated the programme with his left foot',[20] but it is not clear whether his attack on the programme at the time was so strong.

Khrushchev's new programme made little reference to the anti-Stalin campaign, which had not been prominent since 1957. His comments on Stalin and the 'anti-party group,' in his two formal reports at the Congress, October 1961, were restrained,[21] but he did say

> certain stars, which are very far removed from earth, seem to shine on although they have been extinct for a long time. ... some people ... imagine they continue to radiate light, even though they have long since become nothing but smouldering embers.[22]

His comments were followed by an onslaught on Stalin and his 'accomplices in terror' by other speakers, and new vituperation against Molotov, Malenkov and

Kaganovich, as leaders of the 'anti-party group'. This dominated proceedings, and during the Congress Stalin's body was removed from the Lenin mausoleum. It is difficult to decide to what extent the attack was provoked by Molotov's letter; how far it was a spontaneous outburst; or engineered by Khrushchev, insecure because of the limited success of his foreign and domestic policies.[23] Amongst the most notable of the attacks was one by Shvernik. He alleged that in 1937, when a professor working in the Commissariat for Foreign Affairs had pleaded for his arrested father, Molotov, as Sovnarkom chairman, had sent the letter to Ezhov endorsed 'Why is this professor still in NarkomIndel and not in NKVD?' Shvernik also claimed that the 1934 plot against Molotov's life in a motor accident was a fake.[24] Shelepin accused Molotov of writing on a letter sent to him by Stalin, which accused G. K. Lomov of maintaining friendly relations with Rykov and Bukharin, 'I am for the immediate arrest of the swine, Lomov.'[25] Khrushchev joined in the onslaught in his closing speech.[26] He now openly accused those responsible for the mass repressions of trying to prevent 'all measures for the exposure of the personality cult' to conceal their own guilt.[27] He claimed that at the Presidium, when Molotov, Kaganovich and Voroshilov had said they were in favour of rehabilitating Tukhachevsky, Yakir and Uborovich, he had told them that they had executed the generals and asked 'when were you acting according to your conscience, then or now?'[28]

Many delegates at the Congress demanded that Molotov and the other leaders of the former 'anti-party group' should lose their party membership, but no immediate action was taken. On 8 January 1962, the Soviet Foreign Ministry announced that Molotov was returning to his post in Vienna, but the statement was withdrawn shortly afterwards.[29] Then, on 17 January, an article in *Pravda* criticised Molotov's views on foreign policy, particularly his attitude to 'peaceful co-existence'. Shortly afterwards, Molotov was dismissed from his post in Vienna and expelled from the Party by the Council of Ministers primary party organization; his part in the repressions being one of the charges against him. He appealed unsuccessfully against the expulsion three times in the following weeks.[30] All the towns, other places and institutions named after Molotov were now renamed,[31] although he continued to be employed by the Foreign Ministry until placed on pension in September 1963.[32]

As a former member of the Council of Ministers Molotov was awarded a pension of 120 rubles a month. Partly because Polina retained her party membership, he and his wife were allowed to keep a Moscow apartment in Granovskii Street.[33] She remained active, attended party meetings, and because of her pressure their pension was increased to 250 rubles a month in 1967. They were also awarded a ministerial dacha at Zhukovka, although a deduction was made from the pension for this.[34] On one occasion Polina met Khrushchev in Granovskii Street and pressed him to restore Molotov to the Party. In response Khrushchev took Polina and showed her lists that Molotov had endorsed 'To be shot'. The names included Postyshev and other Ukranians, and Kosior's wife.[35]

There were few visitors during these years. Svetlana Stalin recorded the embarrassment of Molotov's daughter and son-in-law, caused by the Molotovs outmoded views, on the one occasion she visited, when Polina praised Svetlana's father for destroying a 'fifth column' in the 1930s.[36] There were similar embarrassing incidents with the Arosevs.[37] Polina died in 1970. Local party representatives attended her funeral, where Molotov made the last public speech of his career, praising her work for Communism and the USSR.[38] His pension now reverted to 120 rubles a month, but was raised again to 250 in 1977 on the sixtieth anniversary of the 1917 revolution.[39] Following Polina's death Molotov lived with Tanya, a housekeeper, and Sarah Mikhailovna, a niece of his wife who was a party member.[40]

There were rumours that Molotov was writing his memoirs during the final years of his life and he was seen working in 'Reading Room No. 1' of the Lenin Library. As he had been expelled from the Party, however, he was refused access to the Kremlin archive and said that without this he could write nothing.[41] He was recognised on occasions by passers-by on the streets of Moscow and at the theatre and cinema. Most of his contacts were Stalinists,[42] like the poet Felix Chuev, who recorded his *Sto sorok besed s Molotovym* (One Hundred and Forty Conversations with Molotov) between 1969 and 1986, the only memoirs Molotov left.[43] He continued his theoretical studies, but his attempts to publish comments on the writings of authors on Leninism were not published.[44]

Molotov submitted regular applications for the restoration of his party membership, although he sometimes denied it.[45] Eventually, in July 1984, in the anachronistic period of Konstantin Chernenko, he was summoned to Communist Party headquarters in *Staraya ploshchad'*, where in a two-minute interview, Chernenko personally informed him of the Politburo decision to restore his membership. The resolution ignored his period of expulsion, and indicated membership since 1906. This gave him the longest continuous record of service of any member. As stubborn as ever, he had refused to write any recantation, and now told Chernenko that he knew neither the reason for his expulsion, nor for his reinstatement.[46] According to Chernenko, Molotov 'heard the decision with great happiness and almost started crying'. He said 'You are doing things right, and for this you have the people's support.'[47]

The last press interview with Molotov, in July 1986, quoted him as saying 'I am happy in my old age. … I wish to live to be a hundred'. It reported that he rose at 6.30 am, did exercises for 20 minutes and then walked in the forest for an hour. He still studied Marxist theory, read and kept abreast with current political developments and enjoyed spending time with his children, grandchildren and great grandchildren.[48] He died on 8 November 1986. Notices in the Soviet press were brief; there were longer obituaries in English newspapers.[49] There were only 500 rubles in his bank account, enough money to cover the cost of his funeral.[50] Two hundred official mourners attended. Police were present to keep unofficial mourners away.[51] Long after the Khrushchev era it seemed there was still fear of the memories that Stalin's chief lieutenant might awaken.

Conclusion

Molotov's career was similar to that of many other front-ranking Soviet leaders who did not achieve the dominating General Secretary position, but in other ways was markedly different. His longevity/survival and role as foreign minister from 1939 were fundamental in distinguishing it.

His life as a revolutionary, one of agitation, protest and attempted insurrection, alternating with periods of exile and imprisonment, was parallel to that of many of Stalin's lieutenants. In Molotov's case, his presence in St. Petersburg and the part he played in the early *Pravda* were important factors in defining the role he played in the revolutions of 1917 and in putting him in the front rank of Bolshevik leaders. From the beginning his tendency towards extremism was apparent. The earliest example was perhaps his attempt to organise a strike at the family tobacco factory in 1905, and then his sympathy for, and perhaps association with, the SR Party. It is not clear, however, if Molotov's acceptance of the Leninist line on the Liquidators in 1913 reflects a rejection of a more moderate for an extremist position, or if he was trying to preserve his employment and place on *Pravda*, and hence perhaps, his future career in the Party. His behaviour under Stalin, perhaps most noticeably his apologies for errors, show that he was prepared to go to great lengths to protect his position, although in the last years of Stalin's rule he was probably trying to protect his life as well as his career. His support for the Terror was, however, from a conviction that it was a correct and necessary policy and this must have made it easier for him to protect himself.

Molotov's acceptance of the Leninist position, and the events of 1917, demonstrate another important characteristic: his need for a strong leader. He was willing to assume the front rank, but was always more comfortable supporting a dominant personality. Initially he was prepared to quarrel with Stalin, but as Stalin became established, Molotov attached himself to Stalin as a leader. The opinions and policies of the leader had, however, to command Molotov's respect. This factor seems to have been at the heart of his differences with Khrushchev.

Molotov's initial ventures into administering the new Russia after 1917: his chairmanship of the northern *Sovnarkhoz*, his command of the *Krasnaya Zvezda* and his stay in Nizhnii Novgorod, were not marked by success. If he did as well as anyone could have done in very difficult circumstances, his performance demonstrated that Bolshevik leaders, as well as shaping the new regime by their beliefs, personalities, outlook and experience, were confronted with problems which so constrained them, that their policy options were moulded by circumstances. Their performance in this situation also helped to mould their own careers.

If Molotov managed to keep himself in the eye of the party leadership during his early missions after 1917, in which he appears not to have harmed his reputation, and they were crucial in turning him into an administrator, they must have made him more than welcome the relative security of the Central Committee Secretariat from 1921. Here his diligence, patience, tenacity and endurance – qualities inculcated as a revolutionary – led to his achieving a senior position amongst the top party leadership as he cemented an alliance with Stalin. There can be no doubt that Stalin valued Molotov's abilities as 'the best filing clerk in Russia', and his other abilities which refer to one translation of his soubriquet. With Molotov's preference for a strong leader, however, perhaps Stalin was more essential to Molotov than Molotov to Stalin.

This period was important in consolidating Molotov's position as the hard-nosed party functionary; his qualities of ruthlessness and extremism also came to the fore. His ruthlessness was particularly valuable as he served as Stalin's trouble-shooter in the campaign against the Leningrad and Right oppositions. His extremism was apparent as he developed his specialism in agricultural policy, where his hostility to the kulaks and enthusiasm for collectivisation came to exceed that of even Stalin. The *komandirovki* he undertook were of key importance in forming his views.

The status that Molotov had achieved in the oligarchy ruling the USSR was recognised in December 1930 when he was appointed Sovnarkom chairman. In this position he showed that he was more than a bureaucrat and possessed at least some of the qualities of a statesman. His efforts to mediate in the disputes between the commissars; his attempts to keep the economy in balance and arbitrate the financial claims of warring departments; and the way in which he operated as chairman, endeavouring to ensure the smooth running of the institution; are among the clearest examples of this. His careful and painstaking attention to the detail of documents also indicates more than mere bureaucratism, as does his support for friends in Sovnarkom before the Terror. Here he was prepared to take an unpopular and perhaps unwise line. Molotov's ideological orthodoxy was also very apparent in his work as head of government in the first half of the decade. His visits to the Ukraine in 1932 demonstrated it again as did his continuing commitment to extreme policies in agriculture.

During the Terror, the process by which Stalin destroyed the ruling oligarchy and consolidated his dictatorship to become a despot or tyrant by 1938, a disagreement, in 1936, placed Molotov in considerable danger, but evidence indicates that this was not because he resisted the Terror. If Molotov was fierce in his attacks on his opponents before the Terror, in that process, he must be held personally responsible for sanctioning, if not initiating, mass murder. He showed that he was not willing to cross Stalin to protect friends, and in 1949 when his wife was arrested, even his own family. Although Molotov was committed to the Terror, it changed his relationship with Stalin. It was now based on fear, and there are striking examples of this in his correspondence with Stalin.

Molotov's appointment as Commissar for Foreign Affairs in 1939 is not surprising. Stalin's correspondence with Kaganovich whilst on leave, 1931–1936, demonstrates that foreign policy was one of Stalin's chief concerns,[1] and in the international crisis leading to the Second World War, it was logical that he should charge his chief lieutenant with responsibility for foreign policy. Molotov's immediate concern was Soviet security. On this excuse, in the time gained by the notorious Molotov–Ribbentrop pact, his bullying technique was used to expand Soviet territory into the Baltic States, and less successfully against Finland. Once Hitler had attacked, he was entrusted with more conventional negotiations for a wartime alliance and the opening of a Second Front. When it became clear that the USSR was going to be victorious in the war, Molotov was Stalin's instrument in guaranteeing Soviet post-war security and in expanding Soviet influence in what might be regarded as reversion to the patriotic and great power ambitions of Tsarist foreign policy. Of Molotov as an established foreign minister it has been written:

> With his pince-nez and pedantic fussiness which [later] caused Western diplomats to refer to him as 'Auntie Moll', he pursued his goal with the determined air of a maiden aunt who could not stand untidiness. ... [2]

He left a legacy of what has been described as 'grim professionalism'.[3]

Kennan observed that his imperturbability, stubbornness and lack of histrionics, the 'master chess player who never missed a move, who let nothing escape him,' often made him the ideal negotiator.[4] The evidence presented in this volume challenges the view of one authority that Molotov was 'one of the most inexorably stupid men to hold the foreign ministership of any major power' in the twentieth century. If he appeared 'ignorant, stupid, greedy and grasping, incurably suspicious and immovably obstinate',[5] these characteristics were sometimes useful as tactics in negotiation.

Asked in old age if he ever dreamt of Stalin, Molotov replied:

> Not often, but sometimes. The circumstances are very unusual – I'm in some sort of destroyed city, and I can't find my way out. Afterwards I meet with him. In a word, very strange dreams, very confused.[6]

These words must apply particularly to the last years of Stalin's life as Molotov struggled to serve the increasingly unpredictable dictator. He claimed publicly at the 'anti-party group' plenum in 1957 that there were occasions on which he had opposed Stalin,[7] and Khrushchev acknowledged this in his memoirs.[8] Molotov told Chuev, 'Bear in mind, I was not one to hang on Stalin's every word. I argued with him, told him the truth.'[9] In his memoirs, Zhukov wrote:

> Molotov was a strong-willed and opinionated person whom it was difficult to move when he had adopted a particular position. I observed in addition that he

exerted a serious influence on Stalin ... especially in foreign policy questions, in which Stalin, at that time, before the war considered him competent. It was another matter later, when all the calculations turned out to be incorrect ... more than once in my presence Stalin spoke angrily to Molotov about this. Even then Molotov by no means always kept silent.[10]

Gromyko too conceded that Molotov had considerable influence on Stalin on foreign policy where there were areas which Stalin delegated to him.[11] In contrast to many of Stalin's other lieutenants, who tried to predict the General Secretary's view, as Sovnarkom chairman, particularly up to the time of the Terror, Molotov appears to have been ready to reach his own conclusions on policy which he adapted if they clashed with Stalin's view. When he did resist Stalin, from the time of the Terror onwards, he must have been shrewd enough to know how far he could push his opposition. Documentary evidence overwhelmingly supports the conclusion that Molotov implicitly implemented the dictator's instructions on his missions abroad as foreign minister.

Molotov's behaviour under Khrushchev shows that his support for Stalin was more than an attempt to protect himself. If the death of the tyrant removed what had become a great restraining influence, Molotov demonstrated that he was an 'unrepentant Stalinist', and willing to stake his career on Stalinist policies. Sometimes perhaps, with Stalin's other lieutenants he may have been trying to protect himself by stopping the revelation of 'Stalin's crimes'; but in foreign policy, on the Virgin Lands and other domestic issues, this was clearly not the case. In the post-Stalin era the commitment to ideological orthodoxy, which had been apparent throughout Molotov's life, continued. He was less willing to adapt Marxism than most other soviet politicians and the rigidity that marked his whole career ultimately led to his downfall.

Notes

Notes to Pages 4–6

1 The Making of a Revolutionary, 1890–1917

1. *Rossiiskii Gosudarstvennyi Arkhiv Sotsial'no-Politicheskoi Istorii* (hereinafter *RGAS-PI*), 82/1/1, 7.
2. Larro, G. M., ed. *Goroda Rossii. Entsiklopediya*, Moscow: 1994, pp. 428–9.
3. *RGAS-PI*, 82/1/1/,7; Gambarova, Yu. S. *et al.*, eds, *Entsiklopedicheskii slovar' russkogo bibliograficheskogo instituta Granat* (hereinafter *Granat*), vol. 41, ch. II, Moscow: (n.d.), p. 58.
4. *RGAS-PI*, 82/1/1, 56; Chuev, F., *Molotov: poluderzhavnyi vlastelin* (hereinafter Chuev, *Molotov*) Moscow: 2000, p. 178. This revised and expanded edition of Chuev, F., *Sto sorok besed s Molotovym: iz dnevnika F. Chueva* (hereinafter Chuev, *Sto sorok*), Moscow: 1991, will be used throughout except where it does not contain information contained in Chuev, *Sto sorok*.
5. Eklof, B., *Russian Peasant Schools: Officialdom, Village Culture and Popular Pedagogy*, 1861–1914, Berkeley: 1986, pp. 215–20.
6. *RGAS-PI*, 82/1/1, 7.
7. *Ibid.*, 82/1/1, 7; Chuev, *Molotov*, p. 179.
8. *Bol'shaya Sovetskaya Entsiklopediya* (hereinafter *BSE*), 1st. edn, vol. 151, Moscow: 1945, p. 338.
9. See for instance, *Sobranie zakonov i rasporyazhenii raboche-krestyanskogo pravitel'stva SSSR* (hereinafter *SZ*), Part I, no. 7, 20 February 1931, pp. 80–84. This process changed quite suddenly and deliberately in February 1934. The last decree where Molotov was followed by the bracketed Skryabin was dated 17 February (*SZ*, 1934 Part I, 11–68), the first without 25 February (*Ibid.*, 12–70).
10. *Granat*, vol. 41, ch. II, p. 58.
11. Chuev, *Molotov*, pp. 181–3.
12. *Ibid.*, pp.179–80.
13. Larro, *Goroda Rossii*, p. 320.
14. Alston, P. L., *Education and the State in Tsarist Russia*, Stanford: 1969, pp. 86–7.
15. Chuev, *Molotov*, p. 185.
16. *RGAS-PI*, 82/1/8, 39.
17. *Granat*, vol. 41, ch. II, p. 58; Chuev, *Molotov*, pp. 187–8.
18. *RGAS-PI*, 82/1/130, 6.
19. Alston, *Education and the State*, pp. 95–6, 124–5, 160–2.
20. Chuev, *Molotov*, p. 185.
21. *RGAS-PI*, 82/1/8, 13.
22. See Service, R., *Lenin: a Biography*, London: 2000, p. 61.
23. *RGAS-PI*, 82/1/1, 79–80, 106–7, 8, 48. For these marks see Alston, *Education and the State*, p. 148.
24. Mosse, W. E., 'Makers of the Soviet Union', *The Slavic and East European Review*, vol. XLVI, no. 106, January 1968, p.148, states that of 231 Bolshevik leaders whose biographies appear in the *Granat* only about 7 were educated in a 'real school'.
25. Service, *Lenin*, pp. 67–9.
26. *Granat*, vol. 41, ch. II, p. 58. Tikhomirnov, G. A., *Vyacheslav Mikhailovich Molotov: kratkaya biografiya*, Moscow: 2nd edn, 1940, p. 8, makes more extensive claims for Molotov's revolutionary activities in this period not supported elsewhere, This work is a reprint, with minor additions of the entry in the 1st edn, of *BSE*, vol. 39, Moscow: 1938, columns 721–26. To avoid confusion with entries in other editions of *BSE*, I have used the *kratkaya biografiya* for the purposes of reference in these notes. *Cf.* Chuev, *Molotov*, p. 186.

27. *Ibid.*, p. 188. See below pp. 29, 145.
28. *RGAS-PI*, 82/1/18, 1; 130, 4.
29. Sokolov, V., 'Foreign Affairs Commissar Vyacheslav Molotov', *International Affairs*, no. 6, 1991, p. 84; Chuev, *Molotov*, p. 184.
30. *Ibid.*, p. 186.
31. For A. M. & V. M. Vasnetsov see *BSE*, 1st edn, vol. 9, Moscow: 1928, pp. 64–5.
32. *Granat*, vol. 41, part II, p. 59.
33. Chuev, *Molotov*, pp. 186–7; *RGAS-PI*, 82/1/6, 53.
34. *Ibid.*, 82/1/12, 212; 128, 21a.
35. *Ibid.*, 82/1/6, 54; Mal'tsev was to become a doctor and died during the defence of Moscow in 1941. Chuev, *Molotov*, p.188.
36. *Ibid.*, *RGAS-PI*, 82/1/147; Wolfe, B., *Three who Made a Revolution: a Biographical History*, Harmondsworth: 1966, p. 622. The Tikhomirnov family was to continue to be important in the history of Bolshevism and in Molotov's career. After 1917 Victor Tikhomirnov became a member of the *kollegiya* of NKVD, but died in the influenza epidemic of 1919. (See *BSE* 2nd edn, Moscow: 1954, vol. 42, p. 498.) The youngest brother, G. A. Tikhomirnov (1899–1955), after serving in the army and as a Chekist during the revolutionary period, became closely associated with Molotov on the Central Committee Secretariat in the early 1920s. He worked in the Secretariat of the Chairman of Sovnarkom 1937–1938 and was thus able to write the official *kratkaya biografiya* of Molotov. He later became director of the Marx–Engels Lenin Institute, *ibid.*; Bazhanov, B., *Vospominaniya vyshego sekretarya Stalina*, Paris: 1980, p. 23.
37. Chuev, *Molotov*, p. 188.
38. See Coates, W. P. & Z. K., 'A Biographical Sketch', in Molotov, V., *Soviet Peace Policy*, London: 1941, p. 86.
39. *RGAS-PI*, 82/1/4, 255.
40. Chuev, *Molotov*, pp. 186–7; *RGAS-PI*, 82/1/2, 3–4.
41. *Ibid.*, 82/1/6, 33–9, 54; Coates, 'Biographical Sketch', p. 86; Bazhanov, *Vospominaniya*, p. 22; Medvedev, R., *All Stalin's Men*, Oxford: 1983, p. 83.
42. Coates, 'Biographical Sketch,' p. 87. I have not been able to trace the original of this document.
43. *RGAS-PI*, 82/1/1, 47; 82/1/126, 14.
44. Melancon, M., *"Stormy Petrels"*, *the Socialist Revolutionaries in Russia's Labour Organisation, 1905–1914*, Carl Beck Papers in Russian and East European Studies, Pittsburgh: 1988, pp. 10–11, 21.
45. *Granat*, vol. 42, p. 60; Chuev, *Molotov*, pp. 192–3; *RGAS-PI*, 82/2/1495, 19.
46. *BSE*, 2nd edn, vol. 42, p. 498; Chuev, *Molotov*, pp. 188–9; *RGAS-PI*, 82/1/4, 2. Vyacheslav's brother Vladimir seems to have been involved in attempts to maintain the group after these arrests, see *Ibid.*, 82/1/18, 5.
47. *Ibid.*, 82/1/4, 116a–g.
48. *Ibid.*, 82/1/4, 260–6.
49. *Ibid.*, 82/1/2, 18–19; 82/1/4, 490; 82/1/6, 33–37, 53–4.
50. *Ibid.*, 82/1/ 130,4; 4, 41.
51. *Ibid.*, 82/1/4, 397.
52. *Ibid.* 82/1/7, 36–7.
53. Quoted Coates 'Biographical Sketch', p. 87.
54. *RGAS-PI*, 82/1/1, 71–2; 82/1/4, 527, Chuev, *Molotov*, pp. 188–9.
55. *RGAS-PI*, 82/1/13, 1–4.
56. Chuev, *Molotov*, p. 297.
57. *RGAS-PI*, 82/1/13, 10–13.
58. *Ibid.*, 14.
59. *Ibid.*, 82/1/4, 534.
60. *Ibid.*, 82/1/1, 49, 54, 83, 194; Tikhomirnov, *kratkaya biografiya*, p. 6; *Granat*, vol. 41, ch. II, p. 62; Chuev, *Molotov*, pp. 189, 297. Shortly after Molotov left Sol'vychegodsk Stalin arrived there, *ibid.*, p. 297.

61. *RGAS-PI*, 82/1/8, 60.
62. Milyukov, P. I., *Gosudarstvennoe khozyaistvo Rossii v pervoi chetverti xviii stoleta i reforma Petra Velikogo*, 1892.
63. *RGAS-PI*, 82/1/16, 3–6.
64. *Ibid.*, 1–2.
65. *Ibid.*, 82/1/128, 44.
66. Tikhomirnov, *kratkaya biografiya*, p. 6; *RGAS-PI*, 82/1/8, 32; 128,21.
67. Probably workers from the Mytishchenskii metal working plant who had been active in the 1905 rebellion. See Bonnell, V. E., *Roots of Rebellion: Workers Political Organisations in St. Petersburg and Moscow, 1900–1914*, Berkeley, CA: 1993, p.148.
68. *RGAS-PI*, 82/1/1, 172–210, 216–224; 8,71.
69. *Ibid.*, 82/1/126, 14.
70. *Ibid.*, 82/1/1, 134–7, 172; 8, 63.
71. *Ibid.*, 82/1/8, 71.
72. *Ibid.*, 212–20.
73. *Ibid.*, 82/1/128, 20–21; 1, 40.
74. *Ibid.*
75. *Ibid.*, 82/1/130, 1; Iroshnikov M. P. and Sheleaev, Yu. B. *Bez retushi, stranitsy sovetskoi istorii v fotografiyakh, dokumentakh vospominakh*, Leningrad: 1991, *T.* 1, p. 27.
76. *RGAS-PI*, 82/1/128, 9, 36.
77. *Ibid.*, 12.
78. *Ibid.*, 82/2/1495, 28.
79. Chuev, *Molotov*, p. 298.
80. Bailes, K.E., *Technology and Society under Lenin and Stalin: Origins of the Soviet Technical Intelligentsia, 1917–1941*, Princeton, NJ: 1978, pp. 26–7.
81. Chuev, *Molotov*, p. 180.
82. Bromage, B., *Molotov: the Story of an Era*, London: 1956, p. 69.
83. *Granat*, vol. 41, p. 61; Chuev, *Molotov*, pp. 188–9, 195. Hough, J. H. and Fainsod, M., *How the Soviet Union is Governed*, Cambridge, MA: 1979, p. 469 claim that Molotov was expelled from the Polytechnic in 1912. But in a deposition to the *Okhrana* in 1913 (*RGAS-PI* 82/1/10, 22), he stated that he was in the third year of his course, and in his memoirs he claimed that he studied economics there for part of each year until 1916. See Chuev, *Molotov*, p. 195.
84. *Ibid.*, p. 195. Bromage, *Molotov*, pp. 78–9 claims that Molotov was existing on a small allowance made available by his parents and that he rejected accommodation with a widowed aunt who lived in St. Petersburg, but I have found no supporting evidence.
85. See Mandel, D., *The Petrograd Workers and the Fall of the Old Regime: From the February Revolution to the July days, 1917*, London: 1984, pp. 50–54; Haimson, L. H., ' "The Problem of Political and Social Stability in Urban Russia on the Eve of War and Revolution" Revisited', *Slavic Review*, vol. 59, no. 4, 2000, p. 850.
86. *Ibid.*, p. 852. See also Hasegawa, T., *The February Revolution: Petrograd 1917*, Seattle: 1981, pp. 68–9.
87. Bromage, *Molotov*, p. 28.
88. Tikhomirnov, *kratkaya biografiya*, pp. 6–7; *BSE*, 2nd edn, vol. 28, p. 152; *RGAS-PI*, 82/2/1495, 76.
89. *Ibid.*, 82/1/131, 5.
90. See below p. 15.
91. *RGAS-PI*, 82/1/11, 205, 293–300.
92. *Ibid.*, 82/1/11, 31–2; 128, 21a.
93. *Ibid.*, 82/1/10, 86; 82/1/12, 212.
94. *Ibid.*, 82/1/11, 158, 162–3.
95. *Ibid.*, 82/1/12, 213.
96. Revolutionaries continued to use the old name rather than the more chauvinistic Petrograd.
97. Tikhomirnov, *kratkaya biografiya*, p. 8.

98. *RGAS-PI*, 82/1/12, 213; 128, 21a; 131, 5, but there is no correspondence to suggest that Lenin was directing Molotov's agitational work.
99. Elwood, R. C., 'Lenin and *Pravda*, 1912–1914', *Slavic Review*, vol. 31, no. 2, 1972, p. 356.
100. Tikhomirnov, *kratkaya biografiya*, p. 7; Yaroslavskii, E., *Istoriya VKP(b)*, ch. 2, Moscow: 1933, p. 376.
101. Bazhanov, *Vospominaniya*, p. 23; Elwood, 'Lenin and *Pravda*', p. 359; Wolfe, *Three who Made a Revolution*, p. 619. According to Elwood, besides the 3000 rubles Tikhomirnov donated, *Pravda* was financed initially by 3850 rubles from Russian workers, 4000 rubles from the Bolshevik Central Committee and 2000 rubles from Maxim Gorky. Wolfe's estimate of Tikhomirnov's donation at 100,000 rubles seems highly inaccurate. Elwood states that his legacy totalled 300,000 rubles. Molotov told Chuev that Tikhomirnov donated 3000 rubles to the Bolshevik Party, but this seems to be in the period when they were together in Kazan, Chuev *Molotov*, p. 188.
102. Lenin, V. I., *Polnoe sobranie sochinenii* (hereinafter *PSS*), 5th edn, Moscow: 1956–1965, vol. 17, pp. 417 *et seq.*, 510 *et seq.*
103. Istpart, *Iz epokhi 'Zvezdy' i 'Pravdy' 1911–1914 gg.*, *vypusk III*, Moscow: 1923, p. 21.
104. Bazhanov, *Vospominaniya*, p. 23; Elwood, 'Lenin and *Pravda*', p. 361; Wolfe, *Three who Made a Revolution*, p. 621; Tikhomirnov, *kratkaya Biografiya*, p. 7; *BSE*, 2nd edn, vol. 28, p. 152.
105. Contrary to Ispart, *Iz epokhi 'Zvezdy' i 'Pravdy' 1911–1914 gg.*, *vypusk I*, Moscow:1921, p. 41, Molotov was not arrested but went into hiding in October 1912. See above pp. 12–13.
106. *RGAS-PI*, 82/1/10, 22.
107. 'Novyi pod"em rabochego dvizheniya, 1910–1914', *Krasnyi Arkhiv*, no. 1, 1934, pp. 233–4.
108. *Iz epokhi 'Zvezdy' i 'Pravdy' 1911–1914 gg. vypusk III*, p.240. The Kadets were an important party in the Duma.
109. Wolfe, *Three who Made a Revolution*, p. 624; *cf.* Chuev, *Molotov*, p. 234; Lenin, *PSS*, vol. 48, pp. 76–7.
110. *Ibid.*, p. 78; part-quoted Trotsky, L., ed. and trans. Malmuth, C., *Stalin: An Appraisal of the Man and his Influence*, London: 1947, p. 141. The condemnation seems less personally directed against Molotov than Trotsky indicates. See also Loginov, V. T., *Leninskaya 'Pravda' (1912–1914gg.)*, Moscow: 1972, pp. 62–3.
111. Trotsky, *Stalin*, p. 141.
112. Chuev, *Molotov*, pp. 230, 298.
113. Lenin, V. I., *PSS*, 3rd. edn, vol. XVII, p. 696; Elwood, 'Lenin and *Pravda*', pp. 368–9, 371.
114. *Iz epokhi 'Zvezdy' i 'Pravdy' 1911–1914 gg.*, *vypusk*. III, p. 244.
115. Trotsky, *Stalin*, p. 147.
116. Elwood, 'Lenin and *Pravda*', p. 365.
117. Trotsky, *Stalin*, p. 141; *cf.* Petryakov, G.V., 'Deyatelnost' V.I. Lenin po rukovodstvu "*Pravdoi*" v 1912–1914 godakh', *Voprosy Istorii*, no. 11, 1956, pp. 3–16.
118. Trotsky, *Stalin*, p. 145; Ulam. A.B., *Stalin: the Man and his Era*, London: 1974, p. 118.
119. Tikhomirnov, *kratkaya biografiya*, p. 7; *Granat*, vol. 41, ch. II, p. 63; Badayev, A., *The Bolsheviks in the Tsarist Duma*, London: 1930, pp. 38–9; *RGAS-PI*, 82/1/9, 31–39, 82/1/10, 27.
120. Badayev, *The Bolsheviks in the Tsarist Duma*, pp. 4–5, 10, 178–9; Elwood, 'Lenin and *Pravda*', p. 357.
121. *RGAS-PI*, 82/1/10, 27.
122. Tikhomirnov, *krakaya biografiya*, p. 7; Bromage, *Molotov*, pp. 82–8.
123. Badayev, The *Bolsheviks in the Tsarist Duma*, pp. 10–11, 34.
124. *Russian Social Democracy and the Legal Labour Movement, 1906–1914*, London: 1983, pp. 133–58.
125. Elwood, 'Lenin and *Pravda*', p. 370.
126. Trotsky, *Stalin*, p. 147.
127. *Elwood, 'Lenin and Pravda'*, p. 371; Swain, *Russian Social Democracy*, p. 161.

128. *RGAS-PI*, 82/1/17, 1–2.
129. *Ibid.*, 82/2/1495, 76.
130. See the list at *Ibid.*, 82/1/89, 1–12. Unfortunately I have not been able to see copies of these early articles.
131. *Ibid.* See also Ist part, *Iz epokhi 'Zvezdy' i 'Pravdy' 1911–1914 gg., vypusk I*, p. 26 and Chuev, *Molotov*, p. 200.
132. *Granat*, vol. 41, ch. II, p. 63. This seems to be the source of the statement in Wolfe, *Three who Made a Revolution*, p. 624. I have not been able to trace these articles.
133. *Ibid.*; *RGAS-PI*, 82/1/89, 1–13. I. Vantrak, a 1935 biographer claimed that he wrote a single article in *Pravda*, just before the journal was finally closed in the late spring of 1914, signed 'A. Molotov', but I have been unable to find this, *ibid.*, 82/2/1495, 76. The first article I have been able to trace signed Molotov in *Pravda* is for 28 March 1917. It is signed 'A. Molotov'.
134. Terras, V., *Handbook of Russian Literature*, New Haven: 1985, pp. 47–50; Harkins, W. E., *Dictionary of Russian Literature*, New York: 1956, p. 506. See Pomyalovskii, N. G., *Meshchansko schast'e – Molotov – ocherki bursy*, Moscow: 1987.
135. Chuev, *Molotov*, pp. 208, 297.
136. Shlyapnikov, A., *Kanun semnadtsatogo* (hereinafter Shlyapnikov, *Kanun*), ch. 2, Moscow: 1922, p. 58; Shlyapnikov, A., *Semnadtsatyi god*, ch. 1, Moscow-Leningrad: 1923, p. 243.
137. *Pravda*, 25 April 1912.
138. *Ibid.*, 4 May 1912.
139. *Ibid.*, 26 May 1912.
140. *Ibid.*, 10, 15 and 16 June 1912.
141. See Haimson, L., 'The Problem of Social Stability in Urban Russia, 1905–1917', *Slavic Review*, vol .23, no. 4, 1964, pp. 619–22.
142. *Pravda*, 23 May; 5, 15, 19 and 28 June and 18 July.
143. *Ibid.*, 21 June 1912.
144. *Ibid.*, 5 and 24 July 1912.
145. *Ibid.*, 10 and 12 August 1912.
146. *Ibid.*, 9 October; 12 and 18 December 1912.
147. *Ibid.*, 20 December 1912.
148. *Ibid.*, 3 March 1913.
149. Wolfe, *Three Who Made a Revolution*, p. 629; Ulam, *Stalin*, p. 117; Badayev, *The Bolsheviks in the Tsarist Duma*, p. 171.
150. See the list at *RGAS-PI*, 82/1/89, 10–12.
151. *Pravda Truda*, 26, 27 September 1913.
152. *Ibid.*, 18,19 September, *Za Pravdu*. 25, 31 October, 6 November 1913.
153. *Ibid.*, 31 October 1913.
154. *Pravda Truda*, 29 September 1913. In 1913 he also made two contributions to periodicals, one to *Metallist* and one to *Prosveshchenie*.
155. See the list at *RGAS-PI*, 82/1/89, 13.
156. *Proletarskaya Pravda*, 21 January 1914.
157. *Put' Pravdy*, 28 January 1914.
158. *Ibid.*, 31 January 1914.
159. *Ibid.*, 5 March 1914.
160. *Ibid.*, 10 April 1914.
161. See above p. 13.
162. *Trudovaya Pravda*, 12 June 1914.
163. Lukovets, A. I. and Sybotskii, A. B., eds, *Lenin v 'Pravde': vospominaniya*, Moscow: 1970.
164. *Cf. Granat*, vol. 41, ch. 2, p. 64; Loginov, *Leninskaya 'Pravda'*, and Tikhomirnov, *kratkaya biografiya*; Drabkhina, F., 'Tsarskoe pravitel'stva i "Pravda" ', *Istoricheskii Zhurnal*, vol. 7, no3/4, March/April 1937, pp. 115–23. See also Molotov's article 'Iz proshlogo "Pravdy" ' and other articles in the tenth anniversary issue, *Pravda*, 6 May 1922.
165. Kochan, L., *Russia in Revolution*, London: 1970, pp. 176–9.

166. *RGAS-PI*, 82/1/12, 282.
167. *Granat*, vol. 41, ch. 2, p. 64. For the harassment of the St. Petersburg Bolsheviks see Shlyapnikov, *Kanun*, ch. I, p. 45 et seq.
168. *RGAS-PI*, 82/1/12, 124, 212, 282; 130, 5; Menitski, I., *Revolyutsionnoe dvizhenie voennykh godov, 1914–1917*, vol. 1, Moscow: 1925, pp. 226–7. I am indebted to Dr Ronald Kowalski for making sources available to me on Molotov's activities in Moscow in 1915.
169. Djilas, M., trans. Petrovich, M.B., *Conversations with Stalin*, Harmondsworth: 1963, pp. 56–7; Chuev, *Molotov*, p. 202; *RGAS-PI* 82/1/12, 125.
170. *Ibid.*, 82/1/12, 290.
171. *Ibid.*, 82/1/130, 9.
172. Menitski, *Revolyutsionnoe dvizhenie voennykh godov*, vol. 1, pp. 226–7; Ibraginov, Sh.N., 'O Lefortovskom raione (1915g. do nachala 1917g.)' in *Put' k Oktyabryu*, vol. 5, Moscow: 1926, pp. 144, 5,9; Latsis, M. I., *V poslednei ex Latve s tsarizma*, Moscow: 1935, p. 40; *Ocherki po istorii revolyutsionnogo dvizheniya i Bol'shevistskoi organizatsii v Baumanskom raione* (hereinafter *Baumanskom raione*) Moscow: 1926, pp. 59–61; *RGAS-PI* 82/1/12, 412–13.
173. *Ibid.*, 82/1/17, 1.
174. Institut istorii partii MGK i MK KPSS, *Lenin i Moskovskie Bol'sheviki*, Moscow: 1977, pp. 167–8.
175. *RGAS-PI*, 82/1/12, 128, 133–7.
176. For the Union of Municipalities see Katkov, G., *Russia 1917: The February Revolution*, London: 1969, pp. 57–9; Menitski *Revolyutsionnoe dvizhenie voennykh godov*, vol. 2, p. 265; *RGAS-PI*, 82/1/131, 5.
177. *Ibid.*, 82/1/12, 282; 131, 5–6.
178. Institut istorii partii MK and MGK KPSS, *Listovki Moskovskii organizatsii Bol'shevikov 1914–1925gg*, Moscow: 1954, pp. 13–14.
179. *Ibid.*, pp. 15–16. For the War Industry Committee see Katkov, *Russia 1917*, pp. 36–7.
180. Ibraginov, 'O Lefortovskom raione', pp. 144, 6; *RGAS-PI*, 82/1/12, 226–7, 282–4; 131, 5–6.
181. Ibraginov, 'O Lefortovskom raione', pp. 146, 148, 149–50.
182. *RGAS-PI*, 82/1/18, 10; 131, 6; *Baumanskom raione*, pp. 60–1; Ibraginov, 'O Lefortovskom raione', p. 146.
183. *RGAS-PI*, 82/1/10, 283–4, 327.
184. Tikhomirnov, *kratkaya biografiya*, p. 9.
185. *Baumanskom raione*, pp. 60, 64; Coates and Coates, 'A Biographical Sketch', p. 89.
186. *RGAS-PI*, 82/1/131, 5.
187. *Ibid.*, 82/1/18, 1–7. A translation which is considerably romanticised is quoted at Coates and Coates, *Biographical Sketch*, p. 90.
188. *RGAS-PI*, 82/1/18, 1–7. Latsis, later to become a senior CHEKA official, claimed specifically that he met Molotov during this period of exile, *Granat*, vol. 41, ch. II, p. 284.
189. Chuev, *Molotov*, p. 204; Bromage, *Molotov*, p. 105.
190. Ibraginov, 'O Lefortovskom raione', p. 65; Chuev, *Molotov*, pp. 205–6.
191. Service, *Lenin*, p. 224.
192. Tikhomirnov, *kratkaya biografiya*, p. 9; *BSE*, 1st edn, vol. 42, p. 451.
193. Carr, E.H., *The Bolshevik Revolution, 1917–1923*, vol. 1, Harmondsworth: 1966, p. 79. For the history of Bolshevism in St. Petersburg in 1915 see Shlyapnikov *Kanun*, ch. 1, pp. 97–136. Molotov is not mentioned. Chuev, *Molotov*, p. 209.
194. The importance of the last two, who do not figure in Shlyapnikov's memoirs, may be questioned. I have not been able to identify Comrade Emma.
195. *Kanun*, ch. 1, p. 292. *Granat*, vol. 41, p. 65 attributes the foundation of this group to Molotov, but this cannot be the case as he was in exile at the time it was founded.
196. Chuev, *Molotov*, pp. 206–8; *RGAS-PI*, 82/2/1495, 23.
197. Tikhomirnov, *kratkaya biografiya*, p. 10; Swain, *Russian Social Democracy*, p. 173.
198. Hasegawa, *The February Revolution*, pp. 87–8, 106; Milligan, S., 'The Petrograd Bolsheviks and Social Insurance, 1914–17', *Soviet Studies*, vol. XX, no. 3, 1968–1969, pp. 369–74.

199. Shlyapnikov, *Kanun*, ch. 1, p. 183, ch. 2, pp. 58–9. In his memoirs Molotov claimed that he was the editor of a literary journal in 1916 and did not become a full-time party official until six months before the October revolution. See Chuev, *Molotov*, p. 209.
200. *Cf.* White, J. D., 'The Sormovo-Nikolaev Zemlyachestvo in the February Revolution', *Soviet Studies*, vol. XXXI, no. 4, 1979, pp. 475–77; Chuev, *Molotov*, p. 209.
201. Shlyapnikov, *Kanun*, ch. 1, pp. 179, 183, 247, 250; Shlyapnikov, *Semnadtsatyi god*, vol. 1, p. 60.
202. Tikhomirnov, *kratkaya biografiya*, p. 9. For Shlyapnikov see *Granat*, vol. 41, ch. 3, pp. 244–51; Carr, The *Bolshevik Revolution*, vol. 1, p. 79. *Cf.* Shlyapnikov *Semnadtsatyi god*, vol. 1, p. 20.
203. Tikhomirnov, *kratkaya biografiya*, p. 9; *BSE*, 2nd edn, vol. 28, p. 152; Chuev, *Molotov*, p. 211.
204. Carr, *The Bolshevik Revolution*, vol. 1, p. 83; Shlyapnikov, *Kanun*, ch. 1, p. 248; Shlyapnikov, *Semnadtsatyi god*, vol. 1, p. 87; Chuev, *Molotov*, p. 211.
205. Trotsky, *Stalin*, p. 186.
206. Stasova, E. D., *Stranitsy zhizni o bor'by*, Moscow: 1957, pp. 88–91; Shlyapnikov, *Semnadtsatyi god*, vol. 1, p. 61, vol. 2, p. 170.
207. Shlyapnikov, *Kanun*, ch. 1, p. 183.

2 Forging the Bolshevik Regime

1. White, 'The Sormovo-Nikolaev Zemlyachestvo', pp. 475–6, 486, 495.
2. Longley, D., 'The Divisions of the Bolshevik Party in March 1917', *Soviet Studies*, vol. XXIV, no. 1, 1972, pp. 61–76.
3. Hasegawa, T., 'The Bolsheviks and the Formation of the Petrograd Soviet in the February Revolution' (hereinafter Hasegawa, 'The Bolsheviks'), *Soviet Studies*, vol. XXIX, no. 1, 1977, pp. 91, 96; Hasegawa, *The February Revolution*, p. 258.
4. Hasegawa, 'The Bolsheviks', p. 91; Shlyapnikov, *Semnadtsatyi god*, vol. 1, pp. 101–3.
5. Hasegawa, 'The Bolsheviks', pp. 92–3.
6. Shlyapnikov, *Semnadtsatyi god*, vol. 1, pp. 101–3, 158–9; White, 'The Sormovo-Nikolaev Zemlyachestvo', pp. 497–9, 504.
7. Shlyapnikov, *Semnadtsatyi god*, vol. 1, pp. 185–7; Carr, *The Bolshevik Revolution*, vol. 1, p. 85; Chuev, *Molotov*, pp. 212–13.
8. Longley, 'The Divisions of the Bolshevik Party in March 1917', p. 74.
9. Chuev, *Molotov*, pp. 211–12.
10. Tikhomirnov, *kratkaya biografiya*, p. 10; *BSE*, 2nd edn, vol. 28, p. 153; Tokarev, Yu. S., *Petrogradskii sovet rabochikh soldatskikh deputatov v marte-aprele 1917g.*, Leningrad: 1976, pp. 45–6; Shlyapnikov, *Semnadtsatyi god*, vol. 1, p. 149 *et seq*; Ferro, M., *The Russian Revolution of February 1917*, London: 1971, pp. 51, 184. *Cf.* Chuev, *Molotov*, p. 212.
11. Tokarev, *Petrogradskii sovet*, pp. 83–4. For a slightly different version of Molotov's words see Volobuev, P. V., *Petrogradskii sovet rabochhikh i soldatskikh deputatov v 1917 godu*, t. 1, *27 fevralya–31 marta 1917 godu*, Leningrad: 1971, pp. 36, 38.
12. *Proletarskaya Revolyutsiya*, no. 1 (13) 1923, pp. 109–10; Chuev, *Molotov*, p. 212.
13. Shlyapnikov, *Semnadtsatyi god*, vol. 1, pp. 228, 243.
14. Hasegawa, *The February Revolution*, p. 345; Tokarev, *Petrogradskii sovet*, pp. 46–8.
15. Sukhanov, N. N., trans. Carmichael, J., *The Russian Revolution 1917: a Personal Record*, London: 1955, pp. 107–8; Hasegawa, *The February Revolution*, p. 411. Molotov gives a romanticised view of this in his memoirs, Chuev, *Molotov*, p. 212.
16. Hasegawa, *The February Revolution*, p. 538.
17. Ferro, *The Russian Revolution of February 1917*, p. 184; Sukhanov, *The Russian Revolution*, p. 130.
18. *Ibid.*, p. 191.
19. Volobuev, *Petrogradskii Sovet*, p. 67; Tokarev, *Petrogradskii Sovet*, p. 97. Brackets in originals suggest missing words. A. Guchkov was the leader of the right-wing Octobrist party and A. Konavolov, an industrialist in the Duma.

20. Sukhanov, *The Russian Revolution*, p. 191.
21. *Ibid.*; Carr, *The Bolshevik Revolution*, vol. 1, p. 85; Kudelli, P. F., ed., *Pervyi legal'nyi Peterburgskii komitet bol'shevikov v 1917g.: sbornik materialov i protokolov zasedanii Peterburgskogo komiteta RSDRP(b) i ego ispolnitelnoi komissii za 1917g. i rechnoi V. I. Lenina*, Moscow-Leningrad: 1927, p. 17.
22. Longley, 'The Divisions of the Bolshevik Party in March 1917', p. 67.
23. Elwood, 'Lenin and *Pravda*, 1912–1914', p. 139; Shlyapnikov, *Semnadtsatyi god*, vol. 2, p. 180; 'Protokoly i rezolyutsii byuro TsK RSDRP(b) (mart 1917g.)' (hereinafter 'Protokoly'), *Voprosy Istorii KPSS*, 1962, no. 3, p. 136.
24. Shlyapnikov, *Semnadtsatyi god*, vol. 2, p. 180; Frank, P. and Kirkham, B. C., 'The Revival of *Pravda* in 1917', *Soviet Studies*, vol. XX, no. 3, 1968–1969, pp. 366–8.
25. Longley, 'The Divisions of the Bolshevik Party in March 1917', p. 68; Chuev, *Molotov*, pp. 213–14.
26. Carr, *The Bolshevik Revolution*, vol. 1, p. 84; 'Protokoly', pp. 140, 142.
27. Shlyapnikov, *Semnadtsatyi god*, vol. 2, pp. 179–80; Chuev, *Molotov*, p. 215.
28. 'Protokoly', p. 143; Ulam, A. B., *Stalin: the Man and his Era*, London: 1974, p. 135.
29. Longley, 'The Divisions of the Bolshevik Party in March 1917', pp. 70–1; 'Protokoly', pp. 142–4. *Cf.* Medvedev, R., *Let History Judge: the Origins and Consequences of Stalinism*, Oxford: 1989, pp. 41–2.
30. 'Protokoly', p. 146; Snegov, A. V., 'Neskolko stranitsii iz istorii partii', *Voprosy Istorii KPSS*, 1963, no. 2, p.19; Moskalev, M. A., *Byuro Tsentral'nogo Komiteta RSDRP v Rossii*, Moscow: 1964, pp. 288–9. For Stalin's activities changing the *Pravda* editorial board see Smith, E. E., *The Young Stalin: the Early Years of an Elusive Revolutionary*, London: 1967, pp. 329–30.
31. 'Protokoly', p. 146.
32. No. 8, 14 March.
33. No. 9, 15 March.
34. 'Protokoly', p. 148.
35. Volobuev, *Petrogradskii sovet*, pp. 471, 620.
36. Shlyapnikov, *Semnadtsatyi god*, vol. 2, pp. 185–6; 'Protokoly', p. 154.
37. Chuev, *Molotov*, pp. 216–7, 297.
38. Drabkina, F. I., 'Vserossiiskoe soveshchanie bol'shevikov v marte 1917 goda', *Voprosy Istorii*, no. 9, 1956, pp. 4–16.
39. 'The March 1917 Party Conference', in Trotsky, L., *The Stalin School of Falsification*, New York: 1971, pp. 274–6.
40. ' "Aprel'skie tezisy" Lenina i aprel'skaya konferentsiya bol'shevikov', *Bol'shevik* no. 9, 1937, p. 92.
41. Orakhelashvili, M. D., ed., *Sed'maya ('aprel'skaya') vserossiiskaya konferentsiya RSDRP (bol'shevkov) i Petrogradskaya obshchegorodskaya konferentsii RSDRP (bol'shevikov) aprel' 1917 goda, protokoly*, Moscow: 1958, pp.8, 22.
42. Slusser, R. M., *Stalin in October: the Man who Missed the Revolution*, Baltimore: 1987, pp. 115–16; Sobolev, P. I. *et al.*, eds, *Velikaya oktyabr'skaya sotsialisticheskaya revolyutsiya: khronika sobytii*, t. 2, *7 maya–25 iyunya 1917 god*, Moscow: 1957, pp. 7, 10; Siborov, A. L. ed., *Velikaya oktyabr'skaya sotsialisticheskaya revolyutsiya: documenti i materialy*, t. 2, Moscow: 1962, p. 5.
43. Slusser, *Stalin in October*, pp. 82, 101; Molotov, 'O Lenine', *Pravda*, 22 April 1957; Chuev, *Molotov*, p. 217.
44. Slusser, *Stalin in October*, pp. 114–15; *Pervyi legal'nyi Petersbugskskii komitet Bol'shevikov v 1917 goda*, Moscow-Leningrad: 1917, pp. 96–102.
45. *Leningradskaya Pravda*, 4 November 1927.
46. Siborov, *Velikaya oktyabr'skaya sotsialisticheskaya revolyutsiya*, p. 59.
47. Sazanov, I. S., 'Byuro pechato pri TsK RSDRP(b) v 1917 godu', *Istoricheskii Arkhiv*, (hereinafter *IA*) no. 5, 1955, p. 200.
48. Chuev, F., *Tak govoril Kaganovich: ispoved' stalinskogo apostola*. Moscow: 1992, p. 21.

49. Rabinowitch, A., *Prelude to Revolution: the Petrograd Bolsheviks and the July 1917 Uprising*, Bloomington: 1991, p. 158.
50. *Vtoraya i tret'ya Petrogradskie obshchegorodskie konferentsii bol'shevikov v iyule i oktyabre 1917 goda: protokoly*, Moscow-Leningrad: 1927, p. 85, quoted Rabinowitch, A., *The Bolsheviks Come to Power*, New York: 1976, pp. 59–60.
51. *Ibid.*, pp. 74–5.
52. *Ibid.*
53. Emal'yanov, N. A. 'Il'ich v Razlive', *Znamya*, no. 2 1957, p. 146.
54. *Shestoi s"ezd RSDRP (bol'shevikov) avgust 1917 goda: protokoly*, Moscow: 1958, pp. 136–7.
55. Tsukerman, S. I., 'Petrogradskii raionnyi komitet bol'shevikov v 1917 godu', *Krasnaya Letopis'*, no. 2 (53), 1933, pp. 101, 116.
56. *Shestoi s"ezd RSDRP (bol'shevikov) avgust 1917 goda*, pp. 136–7; Schapiro, L., *The Origin of the Communist Autocracy: Political Opposition in the Soviet State: First Phase 1917–1922*, London: 1977, p. 50.
57. *RGAS-PI*, 82/1/20, 4.
58. Kudelli, *Pervyi legal'nyi Peterburgskii komitet bol'shevikov v 1917g. p.* 303, quoted, Rabinowitch, *The Bolsheviks Come to Power*, p. 200.
59. See for instance Tsukerman, 'Petrogradskii raionnyi komitet bol'shevikov v 1917 godu', pp. 98, 101.
60. Chuev, *Molotov*, p. 220. For the Military Revolutionary Committee see Rigby, T. H., *Lenin's Government: Sovnarkom 1917–1922*, Cambridge: 1979, pp. 14–23.
61. *Istoriya vsesoyuznoi kommunisticheskoi partii (bol'shevikov): kratkii kurs*, Moscow: 1938, p. 197.
62. Bromage, *Molotov*, p. 121; Slusser, *Stalin in October*, p. 237; Bone, A., ed., *The Bolsheviks and the October Revolution: Minutes of the Central Committee of the Russian Social-Democratic Labour Party (Bolsheviks) August 1917–February 1918*, London: 1974, p. 123.
63. Molotov, V., 'Smolnyi i Zimnii', *Pravda*, 7 November 1924. See also Rabinowitch, *The Bolsheviks Come to Power*, pp. 289–90.
64. Chuev, *Molotov*, pp. 218–220.
65. Tsukerman, 'Petrogradskii raionnyi komitet bol'shevikov v 1917 godu', p. 116.
66. Tikhomirnov, *kratkaya biografiya*, pp. 10–11; McAuley, M., *Bread and Justice: State and Society in Petrograd, 1917–1922*, Oxford: 1991, pp. 140–1.
67. Keep, J. H., ed., *The Debate on Soviet Power: Minutes of the All-Russian Central Executive Committee, October 1917–January 1918*, Oxford: 1979, p. 68.
68. *Protokoly tsentral'nogo komiteta RSDRP(b) avgust 1917g.–fevral'ya 1918g.*, Moscow: 1958, p. 156.
69. *RGAS-PI*, 82/2/6.
70. McAuley, *Bread and Justice*, p. 159.
71. *Ibid.*, p. 141.
72. Sidorov, A. L. *et al.*, eds, *Velikaya oktiabr'skaya sotsialisicheskaya revolyutsiya*, t. 9, Moscow: 1963, p. 186, Protokol of the Executive Committee of the Petrograd Soviet 4 December 1917.
73. Rigby, *Lenin's Government*, pp. 15–16.
74. Bromage, *Molotov*, pp. 125–6, no source cited.
75. Rigby, *Lenin's Government*, p. 20.
76. McAuley, *Bread and Justice*, pp. 209–210.
77. *RGAS-PI*, 82/2/519, 2–4.
78. McAuley, *Bread and Justice*, pp. 142–7.
79. Tikhomirnov, *kratkaya biografiya*, p. 11; Ilyin-Zhevsky, A. F., *The Bolsheviks in Power: Reminiscences of the Year 1918*, New York: 1984, pp. 26–7; Chuev, *Molotov*, p. 222; McAuley, *Bread and Justice*, p. 147.
80. *RGAS-PI*, 82/2/519, 5–9.
81. McAuley, *Bread and Justice*, p. 88 quoting *M. I. Kalinin i piterskie rabochie*, Leningrad: 1947, p. 138.

82. McAuley, *Bread and Justice*, pp. 209–12.
83. *Trudy pervogo vserossiskogo s"ezda Sovetov Narodnogo Khozyaistva, 25 maya–4 iyunya 1918g.*, Moscow: 1918, pp. 232–8.
84. Carr, *The Bolshevik Revolution*, vol. 1, pp. 362–3.
85. McAuley, *Bread and Justice*, p. 201. For Lenin and piecework at this time see Carr, *The Bolshevik Revolution, 1917–1923*, vol. 2, Harmondsworth: 1966, pp. 115–17.
86. *RGAS-PI*, 82/2/1495, 24.
87. *Ibid.*, 82/2/519, 10–16.
88. *Kak rabochie stroyat sotsialisticheskoe khozyaistvo*, Moscow: 1918.
89. *Novyi Put'*, no. 3, 1 August 1918.
90. McAuley, M., 'Bread without the Bourgeoisie', in Koenker, D. P., Rosenberg, W. G., and Suny R. G., eds, *Party, State and Society in the Russian Civil War: Explorations in Social History*, Bloomington: 1989, pp. 158, 162.
91. McAuley, *Bread and Justice*, pp. 143–5.
92. *Ibid.*, p. 118.
93. *RGAS-PI*, 82/2/519, 25–29; 82/1/133, 10–11; 82/1/27, 1–10.
94. Varlamov, K. I. and Slamikhin, N. A., *Razoblachenie V. I. Leninym teorii i taktiki levykh kommunistov*, Moscow: 1964, pp. 353–4.
95. *Ibid.*, pp. 352–3.
96. McAuley, *Bread and Justice*, pp. 157, 230–1.
97. Quoted, *Ibid.*, pp. 212, 229–30.
98. *RGAS-PI*, 82/1/118, 4.
99. *Ibid.*, 82/1/30, 44.
100. McAuley, *Bread and Justice*, pp. 213–14.
101. *Vos'moi s"ezd RKP(b), Mart 1919 goda: Protokoly*, Moscow: 1959, pp. 186, 426, 466.
102. Bromage, *Molotov*, p. 134.
103. Tikhomirnov, *kratkaya biografiya*, p. 11; *RGAS-PI*, 82/2/8, 5.
104. *RGAS-PI*, 82/2/8, 13; Krupskaya, N., *Reminiscences of Lenin*, Moscow: 1959, pp. 524–5; *cf.* Lenin to Krupskaya, 15 July 1919 in Lenin, V. I., *PSS*, 5th edn, vol. 55, Moscow: 1965, p. 377; McNeal, R. H., *Bride of the Revolution*, London: 1973, p. 190; Kuznetsova, T. N. and Podvigina, E. P., eds, *O Nadezhde Krupskoi: vospominaya, ocherki, statii sovremenikov*, Moscow: 1988, p. 82.
105. *RGAS-PI*, 82/2/8, 5, 15, 17.
106. *Ibid.*, 82/2/1495, 24.
107. *Ibid.*, 82/2/8, 4, 6, 8, 18, 19; Obichin, G., *Nadezhda Konstantinova Krupskaya: biografiya*, Moscow: 1978, p. 192.
108. *RGAS-PI*, 82/2/8, 58; Kuntskaya, L. and Mashitakova, K., *Krupskaya*, Moscow: 1973, p. 249.
109. *Ibid.*, p. 250; *RGAS-PI*, 82/2/8, 23–31, 38.
110. *Ibid.*, 82/2/8, 30, 33, 36.
111. Kuntskaya, and Mashitakova, *Krupskaya*, pp. 253–5; Bromage, *Molotov*, p. 137.
112. *RGAS-PI*, 82/2/8, 37.
113. Lenin, *PSS*, vol. 55, p. 371; *RGAS-PI*, 82/2/8, 63.
114. Obichin, *Krupskaya: biografiya*, p. 195; McNeal, R. H., *Bride of the Revolution*, pp. 190–1; Kuntskaya, and Mashitakova, *Krupskaya*, p. 264.
115. *Ibid.*, pp. 253, 259–60.
116. *RGAS-PI*, 82/2/8, 38.
117. *Ibid.*, 82/2/9, 52.
118. *Ibid.*, 82/1/157, 38.
119. Chuev, *Molotov*, p. 184.
120. *RGAS-PI*, 82/1/157, 40, 41.
121. *Ibid.*, 82/2/8, 69.
122. Chuev, *Molotov*, pp. 481–2.
123. RGAS-PI, 82/2/8, 32–50, 66–68.
124. *Ibid.*, 82/2/8, 52.

125. *Ibid.*, 82/1/32, 4–10.
126. Service, R., *The Bolshevik Party in Revolution 1917–1923: a Study in Organisational Change*, London: 1979, pp. 106–110.
127. *RGAS-PI*, 82/2/8, 75–8.
128. Trotsky, L., *My Life: An Attempt at an Autobiography*, Harmondsworth: 1975, p. 413.
129. Rees, E. A., 'Red Terror and Party Rule in Nizhny Novgorod 1918–1919: Lazar Kaganovich's Big Secret', unpublished paper, CREES, Birmingham 1997, p. 5; Leggett, G., *The Cheka: Lenin's Political Police*, Oxford: 1981, pp. 103–4, 112, 148.
130. Rees, 'Red Terror and Party Rule in Nizhny Novgorod, pp. 21–5, 31–5.
131. Chuev, *Molotov*, p. 226.
132. *RGAS-PI*, 82/2/235, 11–25.
133. Chuev, *Molotov*, p. 235.
134. *RGAS-PI*, 82/2/1495, 77.
135. Chuev, *Molotov*, p. 230.
136. *Pravda*, 14 May 1920; *RGAS-PI*, 82/2/235, 26.
137. Mikoyan, A., *V nachale dvadtsatykh*, Moscow: 1975, pp. 25–6; Chuev, *Molotov*, pp. 716–17.
138. Quoted Mikoyan, *V nachale dvadtsatykh*, p. 26.
139. *XXII s"ezd kommunisticheskoi partii sovetskogo soyuza 17–31 oktyabrya 1961 god: stenograficheskii otchet*, Moscow: 1962 (hereinafter *XXII s"ezd: sten. ot*) t. 2, p. 352; *RGAS-PI*, 82/2/235, 10.
140. *Ibid.*, 82/1/134, 1–3.
141. *Ibid.*, 82/1/134, 5–15, 25–6, 32.
142. Mikoyan, A., *V nachale dvadtsatykh*, pp. 24–6; *cf.* Chuev, *Molotov*, pp. 227–8; Smirnov, V. V. and Khitrina, N. E., 'Ya ne veryu etomu' *IA*, no. 1, 2000, p. 17.
143. *Ibid.*
144. Chuev, *Tak govoril Kaganovich*, p. 25.
145. Deutscher, I., *Stalin: a Political Biography*, Harmondsworth: 1966, pp. 230–1.

3 Party Secretary

1. Chuev, *Molotov*, p. 229. In his memoirs in old age Molotov blamed the move to relocate him in Bashkiriya on the domination of the secretariat by the Trotskyists Krestinskii, Preobrazhenskii and L. Serebryakov.
2. *RGAS-PI*, 82/2/1495, 25; Yurchuk, V. I. *et al.* eds, *Kommunisticheskaya Partiya Ukrainu v rezolyutsiyakh i resheniyakh s"ezdov, konferentsii i plenumov TsK, t. 1, 1918–1941*, Kiev: 1976, p. 99.
3. Chuev, *Molotov*, p. 230.
4. Borys, J., *The Sovietisation of the Ukraine 1917–1923: the Communist Doctrine and Practice of Self–Determination*, Edmonton: 1980, pp. 88, 159, 295; Gill, G., *The Origins of the Stalinist Political System*, Cambridge: 1990, p. 48.
5. *RGAS-PI*, 82/1/34, 3.
6. *Shestoi S"ezd RSDRP: protokoly*, pp. 166–171. For this Congress see above p. 30.
7. *Kommunisticheskaya Partiya Ukrainu v rezolyutsiyakh*, Kiev: 1958, p. 147. N. I. Makhno was an anarchist leader of peasant terrorists during the Civil War.
8. *RGAS-PI*, 82/1/34, 7; 82/1/35, 1.
9. *Desyatyi s"ezd RKP(b) mart 1921 goda: stenograficheskii otchet*, Moscow: 1963 (hereinafter *X s"ezd: sten. ot.*), p. 732.
10. *Devyatyi s"ezd RKP(b) mart-aprel 1920 goda: protokoly*, Moscow: 1960, pp. 236–7.
11. *Ibid.*, p. 432.
12. *X s"ezd: sten. ot.*, p. 402.
13. For the trade union question see Schapiro, *Communist Autocracy*, p. 282 *et seq.*
14. *Istoriya vsesoyuznoi kommunisticheskoi partii (bol'shevikov): kratkii kurs*, p. 242.
15. Duranty, W., *Stalin & Co., the Politburo – the Men who Run Russia*, New York: 1949, pp. 92–3. Schapiro, *Comunist Autocracy*, p. 320, identifies those promoted at this time as

Stalin supporters, but there is no evidence of a growing association between Molotov and Stalin before 1921.

16. *X s"ezd: sten. ot.*, p. 402.
17. *RGAS-PI*, 17/2/62, 1.
18. Service, *The Bolshevik Party in Revolution*, p. 175.
19. Chuev, *Molotov*, pp. 230, 233, 717.
20. Tucker, R. C., *Stalin as Revolutionary 1879–1929: A Study in History and Personality*, London: 1974, p. 240, notes that it may have been at this time and not a year later that Lenin made his famous remark of Stalin 'This cook will concoct nothing but peppery dishes.' *Cf.* Schapiro, L., *The Communist Party of the Soviet Union*, London: 1970, p. 242.
21. Service, R., *Lenin: a Political Life*, vol. 3, *The Iron Ring*, Basingstoke: 1995, pp. 220–222. Service, *The Bolshevik Party in Revolution*, p. 176; Daniels, R. V. ' The Secretariat and the Local Organisation of the Russian Communist Party, 1921–1923', *The American Slavic and East European Review*, vol. XVI, 1957, no. 1, pp. 32–3.
22. Chuev, *Molotov*, p. 240.
23. Bazhanov, B., trans. Doyle D. W., *Bazhanov and the Damnation of Stalin*, Athens: 1980, p. 14.
24. See Sotheby's Catalogue, *Catalogue of Continental and Russian Books and Manuscripts, Science and Medicine*, April 1990, p. 255.
25. Chuev, *Molotov*, p. 231.
26. Zalesskii, K. D., *Imperiya Stalina: biograficheskii entsiklopedicheskii slovar'* Moscow: 2000, p.166. Claims in other authorities that she originated from the Ukraine seem to derive from the fact that she was based there from 1919. For her manners see Mikoyan, A., *Tak bylo*, Moscow: 1999, p. 299.
27. Medvedev, *All Stalin's Men*, p. 97; Vasilieva, L. trans. Porter, C., *Kremlin Wives*, London: 1994, p.127. Bromage, *Molotov*, pp. 138–9 appears to be in error in claiming that Molotov met her in the Ukraine. Molotov, in old age, seems to have confused Petrograd with Moscow as the place where they met, Chuev, *Molotov*, p. 231.
28. *Ibid.*, p. 284.
29. Gill, *The Origins of the Stalinist Political System*, pp. 65–72.
30. *Izvestiya TsK RKP(b)*, no 31, 21 July 1921, p. 7.
31. Chuev, *Molotov*, pp. 233–4. See below pp. 56–8.
32. Service, *Lenin*, vol. 3, p. 186.
33. *Ibid.*, pp. 206–10.
34. *Ibid.*, p. 210; *RGAS-PI*, 46/1/3, 5.
35. Service, *Lenin*, vol. 3, pp. 211, 221.
36. Venturi, F. *et al.*, eds, *Bol'shevistskoe rukovodstvo perepiska 1912–1927*, Moscow: 1997, pp. 235, 241; Lenin, *PSS*, vol. 44, pp. 121, 243, vol. 45, pp 17–21.
37. Pipes, R., ed., *The Unknown Lenin: From the Secret Archive*, New Haven: 1997, pp. 127, 130–1.
38. *RGAS-PI*, 17/3/192, 9; 5/2/315, 123–4; Lenin, *PSS*, vol. 53, p. 110.
39. *Ibid.*, pp. 36, 65–6, 94; vol. 54, pp. 105–6, 176, 181–2.
40. Meijer, J. M. ed., *The Trotsky Papers*, vol. 2, The Hague: 1971, pp. 446–7.
41. *Arkhiv Vneshnei Politiki Rossiiskoi Federatsii* (hereinafter *AVPRF*), 4/52/342/55312, 14.
42. Lenin, *PSS*, vol. 44, pp. 374–6, 380, 409; vol. 54, pp. 117–18, 133–7, 164, 170–1, 183, 194–5.
43. *Ibid.*, vol. 54, pp. 136–7.
44. *AVPRF*, 4/52/342a/55329, 13.
45. Chuev, *Molotov*, p. 8.
46. Lenin, *PSS*, vol. 52. p. 151 *et passim*, vol. 53, pp. 13–14.
47. *Leninskii sbornik*, vol. 35, Moscow: 1945, p. 233.
48. Service, *Lenin*, vol. 3, p. 323; Lenin, *PSS*, vol. 53, p. 17.
49. Pipes, *The Unknown Lenin*, p. 147; Lenin, *PSS*, vols. 44, 45, 54, *passim*.
50. *Ibid.*, vol. 54, pp. 32, 118.
51. *Ibid.*, pp. 65–6, 74.
52. *Ibid.*, pp. 92–4 *et passim*.
53. Service, *Lenin*, vol. 3, pp. 220–1; Lenin, *PSS*, vol. 53, p. 79.

54. *Ibid.*, vol. 52, pp. 147–8, 388.
55. Service, *The Bolshevik Party in Revolution*, pp. 176–7.
56. Pipes, *The Unknown Lenin*, pp. 152–4.
57. Leeds Russian Archive, Lomonosov Papers, 716/2/1/8, 386. I am most grateful to the Lomonosov family for allowing me to consult these papers, for the assistance of Mr. Richard Davies of the Leeds Russian archive, and to Dr. A Heywood for drawing my attention to this material.
58. Bazhanov, *Vospominaniya*, p. 26.
59. Bazhanov, *Bazhanov and the Damnation of Stalin*, p. 52; *cf.* Bazhanov, *Vospominaniya*, p. 74. The date of this incident is not clear and may be later than 1921–1922, but Trotsky's allusion to Molotov's nickname, 'stone bottom' apparently given to him by Radek, is clear.
60. *Izvestiya TsK*, 1921, nos. 31–34, 36 *passim*, 1922, nos. 1–3 *passim*.
61. Medvedev, *All Stalin's Men*, p. 85; Service, *Lenin*, vol. 3, p. 269.
62. *Odinatsiya s"ezd RKP(b): mart-aprel' 1922 goda: stenograficheskii otchet*, Moscow: 1961, pp. 45–59.
63. *Ibid.*, p. 46.
64. *Ibid.*, pp. 57–8.
65. *Ibid.*, pp. 98–151; Schapiro, *Communist Autocracy*, pp. 334–7; *cf.* Chuev, *Molotov*, pp. 180–1.
66. Schapiro, *Communist Autocracy*, pp. 337–8; *Protokoly s"ezdov i konferentsii vsesoyuznoi kommunisiticheskoi partii(b): odinatsyi s"ezd RKP(b) mart-aprel' 1922g.*, Moscow: 1936, pp. 52, 75–6.
67. *Pravda*, 4 April 1922.
68. Tucker, *Stalin as Revolutionary*, p. 220; Medvedev, *Let History Judge*, p. 17.
69. *Pravda*, 4 April 1922. The 'reception' times of the Secretariat were Monday to Saturday from 12 noon to 3 pm. Molotov was available with one of his colleagues on Mondays, Tuesdays, Wednesdays and Fridays.
70. *Izvestiya TsK*, 1922, no. 5, 84–6.
71. McNeal, R. H., ed., *Resolutions and Decisions of the Communist Party of the Soviet Union, 1917–1967*, vol. 2, Toronto: 1974, p. 178; Bazhnaov, *Bazhanov and the Damnation of Stalin*, pp. 12–13.
72. *RGAS-PI*, 17/112/722, 17, 32, 43, 49, 55b, 60.
73. Bazhanov, *Vospominaniya*, pp. 54–5.
74. It is interesting, for instance, that Molotov is often not included as a member of Stalin's first 'general staff.' See Hughes, J., 'Patrimonialism and the Stalinist System: the Case of S.I. Syrtsov', *Europe–Asia Studies*, vol. 48, no. 4, 1996, p. 554.
75. Trotsky, *My Life*, pp. 485, 496.
76. Lenin seems to have written only once to Molotov after Stalin's appointment as General Secretary, Lenin, *PSS*, vol. 54, p. 303.
77. *RGAS-PI*, 82/1/137, 1. Liquidation of women's sections seems to have occurred as a result of confusion when local party organisations implemented instructions to establish *Agitprop* departments. See Wood, E. A. *The Baba and the Comrade: Gender and Politics in Revolutionary Russia*, Bloomington: 1997, p. 133.
78. *RGAS-PI*, 82/2/125, 92–93.
79. *Ibid.*, 82/1/137, 6–7.
80. *Ibid.*, 82/1/137, 1–5.
81. *Ibid.*, 82/2/138, 1–43.
82. *(XII) Vserossiiskaya Konferentsiya RKP (bol'shevikov), Byulleten'*, no. 3, 8 August 1922, pp. 40–6, *Byulleten'* no. 4, 9 August 1922, pp. 1–5, 35–7; *Resolutions and Decisions of the CPSU*, vol. 2, p. 178; Bazhanov, *Vospominaniya*, p. 20.
83. Tucker, *Stalin as Revolutionary*, pp. 254–5.
84. *Ibid.*, p. 252; Pipes. R., *The Formation of the Soviet Union*, Cambridge, MA: 1964, pp. 265–74; Lewin, M., *Lenin's Last Struggle*, New York: 1968, pp. 43–63; Lenin, *PSS*, vol. 45, pp. 556–560.
85. Tucker, *Stalin as Revolutionary*, p. 252 *et seq.*

86. *RGAS-PI*, 17/2/148, 143–4; 17/2/151, 149.
87. Carr, E. H., *A History of Soviet Russia: The Interregnum 1923–1924*, Harmondsworth: 1969, p. 273.
88. Trotsky, *The Stalin School of Falsification*, p. 72.
89. Trotsky, L, *The Challenge of the Left Opposition (1923–1925)*, ed. Allen, N., New York: 1975, p. 62; Rees, E. A., *Rabkrin and the Soviet System of State Control, 1920–1930*, University of Birmingham PhD. thesis, 1982, pp. 83–137; Valentinov, N., ed. Bunyan, J. and Bytenko, U., *Novaya ekonomicheskaya politika i krizis partii posle smerti Lenina*, Stanford: 1971, pp. 204–7.
90. Rees, *Rabkrin and the Soviet System of State Control*, p.118 *et seq*; *Dvenadtsatyi s"ezd RKP(b), 17–25 aprelya 1923 goda: stenograficheskii otchet*, Moscow: 1968, p. 61.
91. Rees, *Rabkrin and the Soviet System of State Control*, p. 127.
92. Carr, *The Interregnum*, pp. 134–6.
93. *Ibid.*, pp. 350–1.
94. *Pravda*, 9 October 1923.
95. *Izvestiya*, 24 January 1924. The commission was chaired by Dzerzhinskii and the other members were N. I. Muralov, M. M. Lashevich, V. D. Bonch-Bruvich, Voroshilov, V. D. Zelensky and A. S. Enukidze.
96. It contained articles by Kamenev, Trotsky, Zinoviev and others.
97. Speakers included Kalinin, Krupskaya, Zinoviev, Stalin, Bukharin, Clara Zetkin and Kamenev.
98. Carr, *The Interregnum*, pp. 361, 363.
99. *RGAS-PI*, 17/2/128, 6–8.
100. See also his speech to the XIII Party Congress, *Trinadtsatyi s"ezd RKP(b), mai 1924, stenograficheskii otchet*, Moscow: 1963, pp. 487–510.
101. See for instance *RGAS-PI*, 17/2/129, 2, 11; 144, 25; 155,1, 15; 159, 1–3; 197, 82–4; 201, 2–6.
102. See Volkogonov, D., *Triumf i tragediya: politicheskii portret I.V. Stalina*, Moscow: 1989, kn.1, ch. 2, p. 152.
103. *Izvestiya TsK*, 1925, no. 38, 1–3. See also his report following his visit to Kursk, Tula and Tambov provinces, February 1925, below, p. 58.
104. Molotov, V.M., 'O proizvoditel'nosti truda', *Bol'shevik*, no. 11–12, 20 October 1924, pp. 3–9.
105. For example *Voprosy partinoi praktiki*, 1923; *Partiya i Leninski prizyv*, 1924; *Lenin i partiya za vremya revolyutsii*, 1924; *Ob urokakh trotskizma*, 1925 and speeches published in *Pravda*, 6 October 1926 and 4 February 1927.
106. *RGAS-PI*, 17/113/162, 4. Kosior was also available on Tuesday and E. G. Evdokimov on Wednesday.
107. Barmine, A., *One Who Survived*, New York: 1945, p. 128.
108. Bromage, *Molotov*, p. 161.
109. Bazhanov, *Bazhanov and the Damnation of Stalin*, pp. 25, 40.
110. *Ibid.*, p. 22.
111. *Izvestiya TsK*, March 1924, p. 50.
112. From 1924 to 1930 the number of Central Committee plenums was 1924 – 5, 1925 – 4, 1926 – 6, 1927 – 7, 1928 – 3, 1929 – 3, 1930 – 5. See *RGAS-PI*, 17/2/124, 460.
113. *Resolutions and Decisions of the Communist Party*, vol. 2, pp. 221–2, 245; *RGAS-PI*, 17/2/397, 1–9.
114. *Ibid.*, 17/113/175, 19–31.
115. *Ibid.*, 17/113/162, 3.
116. *Izvestiya TsK*, no. 17–18, 13 May 1927, pp. 1–5.
117. Kemp Welch, A., *Stalin and the Literary Intelligentsia, 1928–1939*, Basingstoke: 1991, p. 42.
118. *RGAS-PI*, 17/113/162, 4.
119. *Ibid.*, 17/113/158–346.
120. See for instance *ibid.*, 17/113/162.
121. *Ibid.*, 17/113/347–582.

122. *Cf. ibid.*, 17/113/811, 815, 824, 832, 848, 856.
123. For instance see *Ibid.*, 17/113/158, the Orgburo meeting which organised the group to go to Leningrad following the defeat of Zinoviev and Kamenev. See below p. 64.
124. See the votes recorded for the meeting of the Secretariat on 22 January 1926 at *ibid.*, 17/113/160.
125. *Resolutions and Decisions of the Communist Party*, vol. 2, pp. 221–2. This was not reported in the 1963 edition of the congress proceedings. See *XIII s"ezd RKP(b), mai 1924 goda: stenograficheskii otchet*.
126. Schapiro, *The Communist Party of the Soviet Union*, p. 647. For the circumstances of Molotov's promotion see below p. 64.
127. Compiled from *RGAS-PI*, 17/3/542–808.
128. For 1926 see *ibid.*, 17/3/547–8, 561, 582–4, 590, 597; for 1927 *ibid.*, 613, 617, 620, 621, 628, 640, 643, 646.
129. For 1926 see *ibid.*, 17/3/560, 571, 574, 582, 589; for 1927 *ibid.*, 621, 622, 638, 641, 651, 655, 656.
130. Samuelson, L., *Plans for Stalin's War Machine: Tukhachevskii and Military–Economic Planning, 1925–1941*, Basingstoke: 2000, p. 331.
131. For 1929 see *RGAS-PI*, 17/3/725, 729, 733–5, 738–9, 742, 745–6, 758, 763, 765; for 1930 see *ibid.*, 772, 776–784, 787, 797, 799, 805, 808.
132. *Ibid.*, 784, 793–4, 799, 805, 806.
133. *Ibid.*, 772, 775–6, 782, 783, 787, 791–4, 796, 799, 808.
134. *Ibid.*, 703, 705, 742, 787, 807.
135. *Ibid.*, 788, 792, 793, 797, 798, 806, 808.
136. Lih, L. T., Naumov, O. V. and Khlevniuk, O. V. eds, *Stalin's Letters to Molotov, 1925–1936*, New Haven: 1995, pp. 85–223.
137. Davies, R. W., 'Peaches from our Tree,' *London Review of Books*, 7 September 1995.
138. *Stalin's Letters to Molotov*, p. 89.
139. *Izvestiya TsK*, 1922, no. 1, pp. 68–9; Gill, G., *The Origins of the Stalinist Political System*, pp. 126–7.
140. Viola, L., *The Best Sons of the Fatherland: Workers in the Vanguard of Soviet Collectivisation*, New York: 1987, pp.18–22.
141. See for instance *RGAS-PI*, 17/2/125, 2. For a full account of the position of the Soviets and the campaign for their 're-vitalisation' see Carr, E. H., *A History of Soviet Russia: Socialism in One Country*, vol. 2, Harmondsworth: 1970, pp. 325–96.
142. *RGAS-PI*, 17/2/128, 53.
143. *BSE*, 2nd edn, vol. 28, p. 153.
144. *RGAS-PI*, 17/2/148/138–171; *Pravda*, 1 November 1924. A different version of this report, reflecting how party policy had evolved by 1927 was published in Molotov, V. M., *Politika partii v derevne*, Moscow: 1927, pp. 23–51.
145. *RGAS-PI*, 17/2/151/103–122.
146. For strengthening the rural party organisation and sending workers into the countryside at this time, see Viola, *The Best Sons of the Fatherland*, pp. 20–21.
147. Molotov, *Politika partii v derevne*, pp. 284–92.
148. Chuev, *Sto sorok*, p. 587.
149. Chuev, *Molotov*, p. 235.
150. Molotov, *Politika partii v derevne*, p. 222; *RGAS-PI*, 82/2/134, 113.
151. Viola, *The Best Sons of the Fatherland*, p. 23.
152. *RGAS-PI*, 82/2/134, 34.
153. There are reports from four different villages visited on 4, 5, 7 and 9 February. *Ibid.*, 56, 70, 82, 95.
154. *Ibid.*, 60–5.
155. *Ibid.*, 65–6.
156. *Ibid.*, 68–9. Of the remaining questions one related to international affairs, one to party organisational matters – about Trotsky; and two that he classified as 'other' concerned

the Communist party and showed the hostility of his audience towards it. The subject of a further question was not specified.

157. *RGAS-PI*, 82/2/134, 90–4.
158. *Ibid.*, 103–12.
159. *Ibid.*, 113–20.
160. *Ibid.*, 121–5.
161. *Ibid.*, 128–30.
162. *Ibid.*, 82/2/128, 2, 51, 69.
163. *Ibid.*, 15–16. For this speech see also Molotov, *Politika partii v derevne*, pp. 209–21.
164. *RGAS-PI*, 82/2/128, 30–1.
165. *Ibid.*, 36–8, 50.
166. *Ibid.*, 69–81.
167. Lewin, M., *Russian Peasants and Soviet Power: a Study of Collectivisation*, London: 1968, pp. 115–16.
168. Molotov, *Politika partii v derevne*, pp. 222–54.
169. *Izvestiya TsK*, 1925 no. 13–14, pp. 3–4.
170. Molotov, *Politika partii v derevne*, pp. 255–71.
171. Rees, E. A., 'Ukraine under Kaganovich, 1925–1928,' unpublished paper, CREES: University of Birmingham, 1997 quoting *Tsentral'nyi gosudarstvennyi Arkhiv Obshestvennykh Organizatsii Ukrainy, 1/6/60, 39*; Shapoval, Yu., *Lazar Kaganovich*, Kiev, 1994, p. 5; Kaganovich, L., *Pamyatnye zapiski rabochego kommunista-bol'shevika, profsoyuznogo, partiinogo i sovetsko-gosudarstvennogo rabotnika*, Moscow: 1996, p. 373.

4   The Struggle with the Oppositions 1925–1927

1. Valentinov, *Novaya ekonomicheskaya politika i krizis partii posle smerti Lenina*, p. 222 *et passim*; Bazhanov, *Vospominaniya*, pp. 117–18, 174, 185, 195.
2. 'Vnutrinapartiinye diskussii 20-kh godi', *Izvetiya TsK*, 1990, no, 7, pp. 175–92; Carr, *The Interregnum*, pp.113–15, 303–5.
3. Moscow-Leningrad: 1925, pp. 168–202.
4. *Pravda*, 9 December 1924.
5. *Za Leninizm*, p. 186.
6. *Stalin's Letters to Molotov*, pp. 18–24, 89–94, 241–9.
7. *Ibid.*, pp. 89–94.
8. *XIV s"ezd VKP(b) 18–31 dekabrya 1925 g.: stenograficheskii otchet*, Moscow: 1962, (hereinafter *XIV s"ezd: sten. ot.*), p. 84.
9. See above p. 55.
10. Molotov, *Politika partii v derevne*, pp. 295–303.
11. *Ibid.*, pp. 304–10.
12. *RGAS-PI*, 17/2/172,13–67. Cf. Molotov, *Politika partii v derevne*, pp. 52–81.
13. Carr, E. H., *A History of Soviet Russia: Socialism in One Country*, vol. 1, Harmondsworth: 1970, p. 274.
14. Molotov, *Politika partii v derevne*, pp. 92–3.
15. *Ibid.*, p. 94.
16. *Ibid.*, pp. 95–101.
17. Carr, *Socialism in One Country*, vol. 2, pp. 68–69.
18. *Cf*. Carr, *Socialism in One Country*, vol. 1, pp. 286–7.
19. *RGAS-PI*, 17/2/179, 41.
20. Carr, *Socialism in One Country*, vol. 1, p. 305.
21. Molotov, *Politika partii v derevne*, p. 84.
22. *Pravda*, 9 May 1925.
23. Carr, *Socialism in One country*, vol. 2, pp. 71, 84.
24. Deutscher, I., *The Prophet Unarmed: Trotsky 1921–1929*, London: 1959, pp. 242–5.

25. *Stalin's Letters to Molotov*, p. 95.
26. *RGAS-PI*, 17/2/197, 85., *cf.* Carr, *Socialism in One Country*, vol. 1, pp. 329–30. The first deviation implied 'neglect of the interests of the village poor and an underestimate of the kulak danger', the second 'neglect of the middle peasant and a breach of the "link" between proletariat and peasantry'.
27. *RGAS-PI*, 17/2/197, 55–8.
28. Lewin, M., *Russian Peasants and Soviet Power*, pp. 54–5.
29. Carr, *Socialism in One Country*, vol. 1, pp. 328–30.
30. *Ibid.*, pp. 322–5.
31. *Ibid.*, pp. 331–2; *Pravda*, 20, 24 October 1925.
32. *Pravda*, 13 December 1925.
33. Molotov, *Politika partii v derevne*, pp. 144–5.
34. *Ibid.*, pp. 151–2.
35. *XIV s"ezd: sten. ot*, pp. 446–7. *Cf.* Carr, *Socialism in One Country*, vol. 1, pp. 334–5.
36. *XIV s"ezd: sten. ot*, pp. 83–4, 468, 470–86.
37. *Ibid.*, pp. 156, 158, 163.
38. Chuev, *Molotov*, p. 250.
39. *RGAS-PI*, 17/2/209, 3–6.
40. Chuev, *Molotov*, pp. 370–2.
41. Carr, *Socialism in One Country*, vol. 2, pp. 169–70; Schapiro, *The Communist Party of the Soviet Union*, p. 310; *Istoriya vsesoyuznoi kommunisticheskoi partii (bol'shevikov): kratkii kurs*, p. 265.
42. Carr, *Socialism in One Country*, vol. 2, pp. 172–4.
43. *Izvestiya TsK*, no. 10–11, 1926, pp. 3–5.
44. *RGAS-PI*, 17/2/220, 34–7, 49–53, 63–4.
45. Molotov, *Politika partii v derevne*, pp. 316–20.
46. Reck, V. T., *Boris Pil'niak: a Soviet Writer in Conflict with the State*, Montreal: 1975, pp. 13–27. For Stalin and Molotov's visit to Frunze see *Pravda*, 1 November 1925.
47. Reck, *Boris Pil'niak*, pp. 20–34.
48. *RGAS-PI*, 17/3/560, 5–6; Reck, *Boris Pil'niak*, pp. 42–9.
49. *Stalin's Letters to Molotov*, p. 106.
50. *Ibid.*, pp. 106–7.
51. *Ibid.*, p. 112.
52. *RGAS-PI*, 17/2/246, 7.
53. *Ibid.*, 42–3, 45.
54. *Ibid.*, 50.
55. *Stalin's Letters to Molotov*, p. 116.
56. *RGAS-PI*, 17/2/246, 54.
57. *Stalin's Letters to Molotov*, pp. 117–18.
58. *Ibid.*, p. 121.
59. *Ibid.*, p. 127.
60. *Ibid.*, p. 120.
61. Chuev, *Molotov*, p. 250.
62. Khlevnyuk, O. V., *Stalin i Ordzhonikidze: konflikty v Politbyuro v 30-e gody*, Moscow: 1993, pp. 16–18.
63. *Ibid.*, pp. 122–5; Venturi, *et al.* eds, *Bol'shevistskoe rukovodstvo perepiska*, pp. 336–7.
64. *SZ*, 1926, II, 26-202.
65. *Izvestiya TsK*, 20 September 1926, pp. 1–2.
66. Carr, E. H., *A History of Soviet Russia: Foundations of a Planned Economy*, vol. 2, Harmondsworth: 1971, p. 111; *Izvestiya TsK*, 2 December 1926, pp. 1–2.
67. *XV konferentsiya VKP(b), stenograficheskii otchet*, Moscow: 1927, p. 669.
68. *Pravda*, 5 October 1926.
69. *Stalin's Letters to Molotov*, p.127.
70. *Izvestiya*, 5 October 1926; Carr, *Foundations of a Planned Economy*, vol. 2, p. 164.

71. *RGAS-PI*, 17/2/248, 2.
72. *Stalin's Letters to Molotov*, pp. 117, 122.
73. Carr, *Socialism in One Country*, vol. 1, pp. 377–8, 381–2.
74. *RGAS-PI*, 17/2/125, 28–39.
75. *Stalin's Letters to Molotov*, p. 132.
76. *Pravda*, 1, 30 January, 4 February 1927. *Cf.* Carr, *Foundations of a Planned Economy*, vol. 2, pp. 291–4.
77. *RGAS-PI*, 82/2/129, 46–7.
78. *Ibid.*, 17/2/276, 49–50.
79. *Ibid.*, 17/2/276(3), 12.
80. *Ibid.*, 12–15.
81. *Izvestiya TsK*, 30 April 1927, pp. 2–4.
82. *RGAS-PI*, 17/2/259, 3, 10; 283, 7–9; 317, 6, 18, 27.
83. This was a reference to the distance of the Germans from Paris in autumn 1914, drawing an analogy with the very dangerous situation then in existence. This had been used shortly before by Trotsky in his famous 'Clemenceau statement' and the reference would be familiar to Molotov's listeners, See Deutscher, *The Prophet Unarmed: Trotsky 1921–1929*, pp. 350–2.
84. *RGAS-PI*, 17/2/317, 35–8.
85. *Ibid.*, 47–8.
86. *Ibid.*, 58–9.
87. *Ibid.*, 67.
88. *Gosudarstvennyi Arkhiv Rossiiskoi Federatsii* (hereinafter *GARF*), 374/23/2470, 173–4, quoted Danilov, V., Vinogradov, V., Viola, L. *et al.*, *Tragediya sovetskoi derevni: kollektivizatsiya i raskulachivanii: dokumenty i materialy t. 1, mai 1927–noyabr' 1929*, Moscow: 1999 (hereinafter *TSD*), p. 95.
89. *RGAS-PI*, 17/2/318, 2.
90. *Ibid.*, 17/2/329, 63, 66.
91. *Ibid.*, 17/2/329, 13.
92. *Ibid.*, 24–9.
93. Carr, E. H. and Davies, R. W., *A History of Soviet Russia: Foundations of a Planned Economy*, vol. 1, Harmondsworth: 1974, pp. 37–38.
94. *Pravda*, 12 November 1927. For the opposition's complaints see *RGAS-PI*, 17/2/329, 34 *et seq.*
95. *Pravda*, 1, 5 November 1927; Carr, *Foundations of a Planned Economy*, vol. 2, pp. 43–4.
96. *Pravda*, 7 November 1927.
97. Brackman, R., *The Secret File on Joseph Stalin: a Hidden Life*, London: 2001, pp. 199–200.
98. *XV s"ezd VKP(b): Dekabr' 1927 goda: stenograficheskii otchet*, Moscow: 1962 (hereinafter *XV s"ezd: sten. ot.*), vol. 2, p. 1186; Carr, *Foundations of a Planned Economy*, vol. 2, p. 60.

5　Stalin's Lieutenant 1927–1929

1. *RGAS-PI*, 17/2/333, 1.
2. Carr and Davies, *Foundations of a Planned Economy*, vol. 1, p.40.
3. Chuev, *Molotov*, p. 454. This is not published in *XV s"ezd: sten. ot.* (1962).
4. *XV s"ezd: sten. ot., vol.* 2, p. 1183.
5. *Ibid.*, p. 1207.
6. *Ibid.*, p.1217. *Cf.* Carr, and Davies, *Foundations of a Planned Economy*, vol. 1, p. 132.
7. Lewin, M., *Russian Peasants and Soviet Power*, pp. 200, 205.
8. *Cf.* Cohen, S. F., *Bukharin and the Bolshevik Revolution: A Political Biography 1888–1938*, London: 1974, p. 266.
9. *XV s"ezd: sten. ot.*, vol. 2., pp. 1175–83, 1191.
10. *Ibid.*, pp. 1195–1203.
11. *Ibid.*, pp. 1210–11.

12. *Ibid.*, pp. 1219–23.
13. *Ibid.*, p. 1227.
14. *Ibid.*, p. 1229.
15. Antonov-Osvyenko, A., *The Time of Stalin: Portrait of a Tyranny*, trans. Saunders, G., New York: 1980, p. 41. This story does not appear in the more recent Russian edition of the book, Antonov-Osvyenko, A., *Portret Tirana*, Moscow: 1994, nor is Stalin's criticism apparent in *XV s"ezd: sten. ot.*
16. *XV s"ezd: sten. ot.* vol. 2, 1419–21. For Stalin's encouraging remarks see Volkogonov, *Triumf i tragediya*, kn. 1, ch. 2, pp. 14–15. *Cf.* Carr and Davies, *Foundations of a Planned Economy*, vol. 1, pp. 36, 38, 42, 214, 234.
17. *RGAS-PI*, 82/2/136, 1; 17/3/666, 1; 668, 7. Chuev, *Molotov*, p. 451. For the policy see Carr and Davies, *Foundations of a Planned Economy*, vol. 1, pp. 53–4. *Sotsialisticheskii Vestnik*, no. 14, 23 July 1928, appears to be in error in saying that Molotov accompanied Stalin.
18. 'Iz istorii kollektivizatsii', *Izvestiya TsK*, no. 5, 1991, pp. 195–6.
19. Carr and Davies, *Foundations of a Planned Economy*, vol. 1, pp. 56–7.
20. *RGAS-PI*, 82/2/136, 1.
21. Chuev, *Molotov*, pp. 451–2.
22. *RGAS-PI*, 82/2/136, 1–55.
23. *TSD*, p. 35. *Cf. GARF*, 5446/19/318, 17.
24. *TSD*, p. 292. *Cf.* Carr and Davies, *Foundations of a Planned Economy*, vol. 1, p. 59.
25. *RGAS-PI*, 82/2/136, 50–55. For the percentage of kulaks see Davies, R. W., *The Industrialisation of Soviet Russia, vol. 1, The Socialist Offensive: The Collectivisation of Soviet Agriculture, 1929–1930*, London: 1980, p. 26.
26. *TSD*, p. 35.
27. 'Iz istorii kollektivizatsii', *Izvestiya TsK*, no. 5, 1991, p. 201.
28. *RGAS-PI*, 82/2/134, 168, 170b.
29. *Ibid.*, 133b, 135.
30. *Ibid.*, 135–8.
31. *Ibid.*, 141b–6b.
32. *Ibid.*, 148–53b.
33. *Ibid.*, 159.
34. *Ibid.*, 161b–67.
35. *Ibid.*, 172.
36. *Ibid.*, 174–80, 189b
37. *Ibid.*, 17/85/410, 216.
38. *TSD*, p. 292.
39. *RGAS-PI*, 17/2/354, 18–19, 28.
40. Carr and Davies, *Foundations of a Planned Economy*, vol. 1, p. 62.
41. *RGAS-PI*, 17/3/683, 1–2.
42. *Ibid.*, 17/165/13, 1–102, 17/3/684, 18–20, printed *TSD*, pp. 237–262.
43. Tauger, M., 'Stalin, Soviet Agriculture and Collectivisation', Unpublished paper for XXIX conference of the Study Group on the Russian Revolution, January 2003, p. 29.
44. Carr and Davies, *Foundations of a Planned Economy*, vol. 1, pp. 168–70.
45. Ivnitskii, N. A. in Nesomov, A. N. *et al.*, *Problemy istochnikovediniya*, vol. IV, Moscow: 1955, pp. 62–66, 82–7.
46. *RGAS-PI*, 17/3/637, 15; 654, 20, 27; *XVI konferentsiya Vsesoyuznoi Kommunisticheskoi Partii(b): stenograficheskii otchet*, (hereinafter *XVI konf.: sten. ot.*) Moscow: 1962, p. 293.
47. *RGAS-PI*, 17/3/673, 6.
48. *Politika partii v derevne*, Moscow: 1926, 1927, 1928.
49. *RGAS-PI*, 17/163/736, 43–50, printed *TSD*, pp. 290–4. *Cf.* Carr and Davies, *Foundations of a Planned Economy*, vol. 1, pp. 78–9.
50. Stalin, I. V., *Sochineniya*, t. 11, Moscow: 1954, pp. 116–26; *RGAS-PI*, 17/163/736, 60–8, printed *TSD*, pp. 297–300.
51. Molotov, V. M., 'Partinaya liniya i khozyaistvennaya praktika', *Izvestiya.*, 5 August 1928.

52. *RGAS-PI*, 17/2/375b2, 16–17, 59–60.
53. *Ibid.*, 60–2.
54. *Ibid.*, 63–6.
55. *Ibid. Cf.* Carr and Davies, *Foundations of a Planned Economy*, vol. 1, pp. 79–82.
56. *RGAS-PI*, 17/2/375b2, 65.
57. *Ibid.*, 65–6.
58. *Ibid.*, 375b3, 19.
59. Molotov, V. M., '*K tekushchemu momentu*', *Izvestiya*, 5 August 1928. The title of the article was deliberately the same as the Astrov article, attacked at the July 1928 plenum. *Cf.* Carr and Davies, *Foundations of a Planned Economy*, vol. 1, pp. 89–90.
60. *Pravda*, 26 September 1928.
61. Carr and Davies, *Foundations of a Planned Economy*, vol. 1, p. 90.
62. *Ibid.*, pp. 90–6.
63. *RGAS-PI*, 17/2/397, 6–7.
64. *Pravda*, 4 December 1928.
65. *RGAS-PI*, 17/2/397, 26–7.
66. Carr and Davies, *Foundations of a Planned Economy*, vol. 1, pp. 621–2; Bourdiougov, G. A. 'The Transformation of the Policy of Extraordinary Measures into a Permanent System of Government', in Rosenfeldt, N. A. *et al.*, eds, *Mechanisms of Power in the Soviet Union*, Basingstoke: 2000, p. 126.
67. *Stalin's Letters to Molotov*, p. 89.
68. See Fitzpatrick, S., 'Stalin and the Making of a New Elite, 1928–1939', *Slavic Review*, vol. 38, no. 3, 1979, pp. 377–82.
69. *RGAS-PI*, 17/2/354, 18; Kislitsyn, S. A., *Shakhtinskoie delo: nachalo stalinskikh repressii protiv nauchno-tekhnicheskoi intelligentsii*, Rostov-on-Don: 1993, pp. 48–9, 52, 98.
70. *RGAS-PI*, 17/2/354, 20.
71. *Ibid.*, 20–1.
72. *Ibid.*, 23–5.
73. *Ibid.*, 43–4.
74. *Ibid.*, 17/2/355, 3.
75. *RGAS-PI*, 17/2/375, 22–36.
76. Bailes, K. E., *Technology and Society under Lenin and Stalin*, p. 135, quoting *Inzhernyi trud*, no. 6, 1929, p. 252.
77. *Pervaya Moskovskaya oblstnaya konferentsiya Vsesoyuznoi Kommunisticheskoi Partii (bol'shevikov): stenograficheskii otchet* [September 14–18 1929] Moscow: 1929, t. 1, pp. 161–4.
78. Carr, *Foundations of a Planned Economy*, vol. 2, pp. 64–6.
79. *Ibid.*, pp. 71, 76.
80. For this see below p. 87.
81. Kaganovich, *Tak govoril Kaganovich*, p. 75. Prince Shuisky, the leader of a boyar family, plotted to become Tsar.
82. Carr, *Foundations of a Planned Economy*, vol. 2, pp. 65–6; *Pravda*, 4, 5, 6 July 1928; *Izvestiya TsK*, 31 July 1928, p. 13.
83. Cohen, S. F., *Bukharin and the Bolshevik Revolution*, pp. 289–90, 448; Lewin, *Russian Peasants and Soviet Power*, pp. 304–5.
84. Khlevnyuk, O., *Politbyuro: mekhanizma politicheskoi vlasti v 30-e gody*, Moscow: 1996, p. 22.
85. Carr, *Foundations of a Planned Economy*, vol. 2, pp. 76–7.
86. *Ibid.*, p.77; *Pravda*, 26 September 1928.
87. *RGAS-PI*, 17/2/397, 7.
88. *Ibid.*, v2, 8–10. For Stalin's speech see *ibid.*, v1, 52.
89. *Ibid.*, v2, 21–25.
90. *Ibid.*, 27.
91. *Ibid.*, v3, 79.
92. Shimotomai, N., 'The Defeat of the Right Opposition in the Moscow Party Organisation, 1928', *Japanese Slavic and East European Studies*, vol. 4, 1983, p. 19.

93. *Ibid.*, pp. 19–26.
94. Colton, T. J., *Moscow: Governing the Socialist Metropolis*, Cambridge, MA: 1995, p. 198.
95. Quoted, Nebogin, O. B. and Samorodov, A. G., 'Diskussii v Moskovskoi partiinoi orga-nizatsii v 1928–1929 gg.', *Voprosy Istorii KPSS*, no. 6, 1990, pp. 69.
96. Merridale, C., *Moscow Politics and the Rise of Stalin: The Communist Party in the Capital 1925–1932*, Basingstoke: 1990, p. 59.
97. Shimotomai, 'The Defeat of the Right Opposition in the Moscow Party Organisation, 1928', pp. 28–9.
98. Carr, *Foundations of a Planned Economy*, vol. 2, p. 86; *Pravda*, 28 November 1928.
99. Avtorkhanov, A., *Stalin and the Communist Party*, London: 1959, p. 63.
100. Davies, *The Socialist Offensive*, p. 280. Bauman was attacked as a result of Stalin's 'Dizzy with Success' speech, Shimotomai, N., 'The Defeat of the Right Opposition in the Moscow Party Organisation 1928', p. 33.
101. *Ibid.*, pp. 15–34; Cohen, *Bukharin and the Bolshevik Revolution*, pp. 297–8; Merridale, *Moscow Politics and the Rise of Stalin*, pp. 58–9, 232, 347; Nebogin, and Samorodov, 'Diskussii v Moskovskoi partiinoi organizatsii v 1928–1929 gg.', pp. 64–74.
102. Zalesskii, *Imperiya Stalina*, p. 322.
103. Bessedovsky, G., *Revelations of a Soviet Diplomat*, Westport: 1977, pp. 177, 182–3. Cf. Duranty, *Stalin and Co.*, p. 98.
104. Nebogin, and Samorodov, 'Diskussii v Moskovskoi partiinoi organizatsii v 1928–1929 gg.', pp. 85–6; *Pravda*, 4 December 1928.
105. Avtorkhanov, *Stalin and the Communist Party*, pp. 96–7.
106. *Pravda*, 23, 26, 27 February, 1,2,7, March 1929; Carr and Davies, *Foundations of a Planned Economy*, vol. 1, pp. 265–6, 352.
107. *Pravda*, 30 March, 2 April 1929. For Kalinin wavering towards the right see Carr, *Foundations of a Planned Economy*, vol. 2, pp. 64–5 *et passim*.
108. *RGAS-PI*, 17/2/417, 40.
109. See Carr, *Foundations of a Planned Economy*, vol. 2, p. 96.
110. *RGAS-PI*, 17/2/417, 76.
111. *Bol'shevik*, no. 12, 30 June 1928, pp. 89–90.
112. *RGAS-PI*, 17/2/417, 78.
113. *Ibid.*, 78–9.
114. *Ibid.*, 108.
115. Carr, *Foundations of a Planned Economy*, vol. 2, pp. 97–8; Egorov, A. G. and Bogolyubov, K. M., eds, *Kommunisticheskaya partiya Sovetskogo Soyuza v rezolyutsiyakh i resheniyakh s"ezdov, konferentsii i plenumov TsK, t. 4, 1926–1929*, Moscow: 1984, p. 496; *XVI konf.: sten. ot.*, p. 584.
116. See below p. 90.
117. *Pravda*, 29 September 1929.
118. *Stalin's Letters to Molotov*, pp. 165–6, 68.
119. *Bol'shevik*, no. 2, January 31, 1930, p. 21.
120. *Stalin's Letters to Molotov*, pp. 160, 181.
121. Cohen, *Bukharin and the Bolshevik Revolution*, p. 334.
122. *RGAS-PI*, 17/2/441b, 57–9. This speech was published in slightly abbreviated form in *Bol'shevik*. No. 2, 31 January 1930, pp 7–26, under the title 'On two Fronts' (*Na dva fronta*).
123. *RGAS-PI*, 17/2/441b, 59–62.
124. Davies, *The Socialist Offensive*, p. 166; *RGAS-PI*, 17/2/422, 3,5–6.
125. Lazitch, B. and Drackovitch, M. M., *Biographical Dictionary of the Comintern*, Stanford: 1986, p. 321; *RGAS-PI*, 17/3/562,7; 583,4.
126. Carr, E. H., *A History of Soviet Russia: Foundations of a Planned Economy*, vol. 3, London: 1976, pp. 193–5, 227.
127. *Ibid.*, p. 227.
128. McDermott, K. and Agnew, J, *The Comintern: a History of International Communism from Lenin to Stalin*, Basingstoke: 1996, p. 78; Carr, *Foundations of a Planned Economy*, vol. 3,

pp. 193–5, 221, 227, 358, 447, 602–3; Lazitch and Drachkovitsh, *Biographical Dictionary*, p. 321.

129. Gomez, M., 'From Mexico to Moscow II', *Survey*, April 1965, pp. 119–21. On one occasion Gomez describes the VI Congress as 'the Molotov Congress', *Ibid.*, p. 122.
130. Carr, *Foundations of a Planned Economy*, vol. 3, p. 221.
131. *RGAS-PI*, 82/1/146, 1–60, especially l, 9–10, 13, 22–3, 28–30, 46–60; printed in shortened form in *Pravda*, 13 September 1928.
132. Carr, *Foundations of a Planned Economy*, vol. 3, pp. 451–2; Humbert-Droz, J., *De Lenine á Staline: Dix Ans au Service de l'Internationale Communiste, 1921–1931*, Neuchatel: 1971, pp. 341, 349–53, 356. Humbert-Droz, Swiss by birth was a member of the German party.
133. Carr, *Foundations of a Planned Economy*, vol. 3, pp. 608–11; *RGAS-PI*, 17/3/740, 6.
134. Carr, *Foundations of a Planned Economy*, vol. 3, p. 227; Humbert-Droz, *De Lènine á Staline*, pp. 374–5.
135. Carr, *Foundations of a Planned Economy*, vol. 2, p. 101; vol. 3, pp. 250, 556–7.
136. *Pravda*, 31 July and 4 August 1929; *cf.* Davies, *The Socialist Offensive*, p. 117.
137. *Pravda*, 31 July and 4 August 1929; *cf.* Carr, *Foundations of a Planned Economy*, vol. 3, pp. 462, 893–4.
138. *Pervaya Moskovskaya oblstnaya konferentsiya*, t. 1, pp. 150–1.
139. Carr, E. H., *The Twilight of Comintern*, London: 1982, pp. 10–11.
140. *Ibid.*, p. 18; *XVI s"ezd VKP(b) stenograficheskii otchet* (hereinafter *XVI s"ezd: sten. ot.*) Moscow: 1931, pp. 407–8.

6   Change and Consolidation 1929–1930

1. *Pravda*, 27 February 1929.
2. *RGAS-PI*, 17/2/398, 2.
3. *Pravda*, 20 July 1929. See above p. 85.
4. *Stalin's Letters to Molotov*, pp. 165–6, 168–9; *RGAS-PI*, 17/3/755, 3–4; 756, 14, printed *TSD*, pp. 691–3.
5. *Pervaya Moskovskaya oblastnaya konferentsiya*, t. 1, pp. 146–7.
6. *Stalin's Letters to Molotov*, p. 182.
7. Davies, *The Socialist Offensive*, pp. 385–6, quoting *Sel'skokhozyaistvennaya gazeta*, 6 October 1929.
8. Davies, *The Socialist Offensive*, p. 408.
9. Up to this point there had been no Commissariat of Agriculture of the USSR. See Watson, D., *Molotov and Soviet Government: Sovnarkom 1930–1941*, Basingstoke: 1996, pp. 15–16. Tucker, R. C., *Stalin in Power: the Revolution from Above, 1928–1941*, New York: 1990, p. 134 claims that Molotov made three speeches, but the third was a short introduction to the resolution proposing the Union Commissariat of Agriculture, *RGAS-PI*, 17/2/441b$_2$, 49–50.
10. See above p. 90 for his attack on the Right.
11. *RGAS-PI*, 17/2/441v$_2$, 28. For a published version see Molotov, V. M., 'O kolkhoznom dvizhenie', *Bol'shevik*, no. 22, 1929, pp. 10–23.
12. *RGAS-PI*, 17/2/441v$_2$ 49.
13. *Ibid.*, 29.
14. Davies, *The Socialist Offensive*, p. 316.
15. *Ibid.*, pp. 156, 9, 165, 322. *Cf.* Tucker, *Stalin in Power*, p. 134.
16. *RGAS-PI*, 17/2/441v$_2$, 29–31.
17. *Ibid.*, 31–2; *cf.* Davies, *The Socialist Offensive*, p. 265. For the use of industrial workers see Viola, *The Best Sons of the Fatherland*.
18. *RGAS-PI*, 17/2/441v$_2$, 49–50.
19. *Stalin's Letters to Molotov*, p. 183.

20. Chuev, *Tak govoril Kaganovich*, p. 36; Tucker, *Stalin as Revolutionary*, pp. 462–87.
21. *TSD*, t. 2, noyabr' 1929–dekabr' 1930, Moscow: 2000, p. 9, 76.
22. Stalin, *Sochineniya*, t. 12, Moscow: 1949, p. 173. See Davies, *The Socialist Offensive*, pp. 188, 194–7.
23. *Ibid.*, pp. 173–4, 216, 226, 228; *Pravda*, 21 January 1930.
24. *RGAS-PI*, 17/3/772, 3; Davies, *The Socialist Offensive*, pp. 232, 240; Ivnitskii, N. A., *Klassovaya bor'ba v derevne i likvidatsiya kulachestva kak klassa*, Moscow: 1972, p. 179.
25. *RGAS-PI*, 17/162/8, 64–9, see Viola, L., 'The Other Archipelago: Kulak Deportations to the North in 1930', *Slavic Review*, vol. 60, no. 4, 2001, p. 734.
26. *TSD2*, p. 11.
27. Quoted Viola, 'The Other Archipelago', p. 740.
28. *TSD2*, p. 131 quoting *RGAS-PI*, 558/11/38, 19; Davies, *The Socialist Offensive*, pp. 239–41.
29. *Ibid.*, p. 265.
30. *RGAS-PI*, 82/2/60, 154.
31. *Ibid.*, 82/2/103, 54–7.
32. *TSD2*, pp. 14–15.
33. *RGAS-PI*, 17/3/778, 5; 779, 9.
34. Davies, *The Socialist Offensive*, p. 252.
35. Chernopitskii, P. G., *Na velikom perelome: Sel'skie sovety Dona v period podgotovki i provideniya massovoi kollektivizatsii (1928–1931gg.)*, Rostov on Don: 1965, pp. 124–5.
36. *RGAS-PI*, 82/2/125, 42, 44.
37. Lewin, *Russian Peasants and Soviet Power*, p. 48.
38. *RGAS-PI*, 82/2/125, 62–3.
39. *Ibid.*, 52, 56–8.
40. Chernopitskii, *Na velikom perelome*, pp. 124–5.
41. *RGAS-PI*, 82/2/130, 132–6.
42. *Ibid.*, 137–143, 146–150.
43. *Ibid.*, 151–5, 165–74.
44. *Ibid.*, 17/3/787, 6, 792, 3, quoted *TSD2*, pp. 486, 581–2.
45. *Stalin's Letters to Molotov*, pp. 210–11.
46. *RGAS-PI*, 558/11/39, 74–5; 75, 39; quoted *TSD2*, p. 612.
47. For the procurement figures and their modification see Davies, *The Socialist Offensive*, pp. 340–58.
48. *RGAS-PI*, 82/2/61, 8.
49. *RGAS-PI*, 82/2/61, 1–30.
50. *RGAS-PI*, 82/2/61, 129–49. For the 'labour day' see Davies R.W., *The Industrialisation of Soviet Russia 2: The Soviet Collective Farm, 1929–1930*, London: 1980, pp. 140–2.
51. *Ekonomicheskaya Zhizn'*, 20 December 1930.
52. Vyshinskii, A., 'Glava sovetskogo pravitel'stva', *Sovetskoe Gosudarstvo i Pravo*, no. 2, 1940, pp. 4–5. Among Western historians Tucker, *Stalin in Power*, p. 134 also acknowledges this.
53. See for instance, Ivnitskii, N. A., 'Istoriya podgotovki postanovleniya TsK VKP(b) O tempakh kollektivizatsii sel'skogo khozyaistva ob 5 yanvarya 1930 g.', in *Istochnikovedenie istorii sovetskogo obshchestva*, Moscow: 1964, pp. 265–88.
54. Stalin, *Sochineniya*, t. 12, pp. 147–8, 192. *Cf.* Kemp-Welch, A., 'Stalinism and the Intellectual Order', in Rigby, T. H., Brown, A. and Reddaway, P., *Authority Power and Policy in the USSR: Essays Dedicated to Leonard Schapiro*, London: 1980, p. 122.
55. *Ibid.*; Molotov, V. M., 'O nashikh zadachakh,' *Bol'shevik*, no. 5, 1930, pp. 16–17.
56. *RGAS-PI*, 82/2/130, 82, 107.
57. *RGAS-PI*, 82/2/130, 110–25.
58. *Ibid.*, 126–31.
59. *Ibid.*, 174–7.
60. McDermott and Agnew, *The Comintern*, p. 96 argue that 'foreign "leftists" had taken the revolutionary posturings of Comintern too literally and in so doing had threatened the security of the isolated Soviet Union at a particularly sensitive time.'

61. *XVI s"ezd: sten. ot.*, pp. 719–55.
62. *Ibid.*, pp. 831–9.
63. *Ibid.*, pp. 719, 732, 737; Haslam, J., *Soviet Foreign Policy, 1930–1933: the Impact of the Depression*, London: 1983, p. 60; Carr, E. H., *The Twilight of Comintern*, p. 18.
64. *Cf.* Ulam, A.B., *Expansion and Coexistence: Soviet Foreign Policy 1917–73*, New York: 1974, pp. 191–2; McDermott and Agnew, *The Comintern*, pp. 99–101.
65. *Stalin's Letters to Molotov*, pp. 199–204.
66. *Ibid.* p. 204.
67. *Pravda*, 5 October 1930.
68. *Pravda*, 1, 2, 5, October 1930; Molotov, V., *V bor'be za sotsializm: rechi i stat"i*, Moscow: 1935, p. 50. *Cf.* Davies, R. W. *The Industrialisation of Soviet Russia, vol. 3, The Soviet Economy in Turmoil*, Basingstoke: 1989, p. 425.
69. Molotov, *V bor'be za sotsializm*, pp. 50–4.
70. *Pravda*, 5 October 1930.
71. *RGAS-PI*, 17/3/798, 3, 19.
72. *Stalin's Letters to Molotov*, p. 221.
73. *Ibid.*, pp. 216–8.
74. *Ibid.*, p. 219.
75. Chuev, *Tak govoril Kaganovich*, p. 60.
76. Vyshinskii, 'Glava sovetskogo pravitel'stva', p. 13.
77. Watson, *Molotov and Soviet Government*, p. 14.
78. *Ibid.*, p. 16; see above p. 90.
79. *Ibid.*, p. 26.
80. *Ibid.*, pp. 188–92.
81. *Ibid.*, pp. 27–33.
82. *Ibid*, pp. 33–4.
83. *Ibid.*, pp. 35–8.
84. *Stalin's Letters to Molotov*, pp. 206, 208.
85. Watson, *Molotov and Soviet Government*, p. 39.
86. Davies, *The Soviet Economy in Turmoil*, pp. 240–1.
87. *RGAS-PI*, 17/2/448, 1–4.
88. *Ibid.*, 17/2/460, 42–4.
89. *Ibid.*, 45.
90. *Ibid.*, 83–4. For Syrtsov and Lominadze see Davies, *The Soviet Economy in Turmoil*, pp. 411–15.
91. *RGAS-PI*, 17/2/460, 84–6.
92. *Ibid.*, 86–7. *Cf. Stalin's Letters to Molotov*, pp. 217–18.
93. Quoted Vorobechuk, G., and Zhurov, V., 'K voprosam ratsionalizatsii gosapparati,' *Organizatsiya upravleniya*, no. 5, 1932, p. 6.
94. *RGAS-PI*, 82/2/460, 87.

7   Head of Government

1. Khlevnyuk, O. V., Devis, R. U., (Davies, R. W.), Kosheleva, L. P., Ris, E. A. (Rees, E. A.) Rogovaya, L. A., eds, *Stalin i Kaganovich: perepiska. 1931–1936 gg*. Moscow: 2001, p. 5.
2. Khlevnyuk, O. V. *et al.*, *Stalinskoe politbyuro v 30-e gody: sbornik dokumentov*, Moscow: 1995, p. 99; Watson, *Molotov and Soviet Government*, p. 55.
3. Chuev, *Molotov*, p. 424.
4. Compiled from *RGAS-PI*, 17/3/808–1042 and Watson, *Molotov and Soviet Government*, pp. 55–7.
5. *Ibid.*, pp. 55–7.
6. Watson, D., 'STO (The Council of Labour and Defence) in the 1930s', *Europe–Asia Studies*, vol. 50, no. 7, 1998, pp. 1217–18.

7. Watson, *Molotov and Soviet Government*, pp. 46–7.
8. Watson, 'STO (The Council of Labour and Defence) in the 1930s', pp. 1215–16.
9. *Ibid.*, p. 1215.
10. For the STO Price Committee, established October 1931, see Barnett, V., 'The People's Commissariat of Supply and the People's Commissariat of Internal Trade', in Rees, E. A. ed., *Decision-Making in the Stalinist Command Economy, 1932–1937*, Basingstoke: 1997, pp. 180–1. For the Committee of Reserves see *SZ*, 1931, I, 64–421. For Molotov's report proposing the committee see *RGAS-PI*, 17/3/853, item 15, 854, item 16.
11. See for example *GARF*, 5446/3/10, 77.
12. Watson, *Molotov and Soviet Government*, pp. 19, 62–8. Krestinskii, as deputy commissar, attended 19 meetings and the commissariat was unrepresented at eight.
13. See for instance the visit of the Turkish prime minister and foreign minister in May 1932, Deev, G. *et al.* ed., *Dokumenty vneshnei politiki SSSR*, (hereinafter *DVP*), vol. XV, Moscow: 1969, pp. 283–6, 302–3.
14. Rees, E. A. and Watson, D. H., 'Politburo and Sovnarkom', in Rees, ed., *Decision-Making in the Stalinist Command Economy, 1932–1937*, p. 11.
15. Davies, R. W., Ilic, M. and Khlevnyuk, O., 'The Politburo and Economic Policy-making', in Rees, E. A., ed., *The Nature of Stalin's Dictatorship: the Politburo 1928–1953*, Basingstoke: 2003, p. 129.
16. Colton, *Moscow*, p. 259.
17. *RGAS-PI*, 17/3/827, item 53, 25 May and 17/3/833, item 18, 30 June. Cf. Davies, R. W., *The Industrialisation of Soviet Russia, vol 4, Crisis and Progress in the Soviet Economy, 1931–1933* (hereinafter *Crisis and Progress*) Basingstoke: 1996, p. 81.
18. Hoisington, S. S., ' "Even Higher": The Evolution of the Project for the Palace of Soviets', *Slavic Review*, vol. 62, no. 1, 2003, pp. 41–68.
19. Chuev, *Molotov*, pp. 322–3.
20. *Izvestiya*, 14, 15 May 1935.
21. Molotov, *V bor'be za sotsializm*, pp. 77–82.
22. *Stalin i Kaganovich: perepiska*, p. 31.
23. Molotov, *V bor'be za sotsializm*, pp. 83–4.
24. *Ibid.*, pp. 100–5.
25. *Ibid.*, pp. 109–14.
26. For this conference see Davies, *Crisis and Progress*, pp. 11–17.
27. Molotov, *V bor'be za sotsializm*, pp. 119–25.
28. Davies, *Crisis and Progress*, pp. 11–14, 61, 140; Davies, *The Soviet Economy in Turmoil*, p. 315.
29. See Davies, *Crisis and Progress*, p. 14.
30. *Stalin's Letters to Molotov*, p. 228.
31. Molotov, *V bor'be za sotsializm*, pp. 128–39.
32. See 'Vopros o prinuditel'nim trude v SSSR', *Byulleten' Ekonomicheskogo Kabineta S.N. Prokopovicha*, no. 88, May 1931, pp. 1–10.
33. Molotov, *V bor'be za sotsializm*, pp. 139–43.
34. Rees, E. A., 'The People's Commissariat of the Timber Industry', in Rees, ed., *Decision-Making in the Stalinist Command Economy*, p. 128.
35. Molotov, *V bor'be za sotsializm*, p. 145.
36. *Ibid.*, pp. 145–7.
37. *Ibid.*, pp. 170–85.
38. *SZ*, 1931, I, 16–157.
39. *GARF* 5442/82/7, 65–75.
40. *SZ*, 1931, I, 28–4.
41. For this conference see Davies, *Crisis and Progress*, p. 47 and Graham, L. A. *The Soviet Academy of Sciences and the Communist Party, 1927–1932*, Princeton: 1967, pp. 186–7.
42. Molotov, *V bor'be za sotsializm*, pp. 196, 200–1.
43. *RGAS-PI*, 17/2/473, 3.

44. *RGAS-PI*, 17/2/473, 461, 1, 22.
45. Chuev, *Molotov*, p. 483. See below p. 111.
46. For this conference see Davies, *Crisis and Progress*, pp. 67–70.
47. *RGAS-PI*, 85/28/7, 70, 140.
48. *Ibid.*, 70ii, 154–71.
49. *Ibid.*, 207–8. For Stalin's speech see Davies, *Crisis and Progress*, pp. 70–5.
50. *RGAS-PI*, 17/162/10, 122, quoted Davies, *Crisis and Progress*, p. 120.
51. *Ibid.*, p. 82.
52. The period of the vacation is suggested by the fact that he did not chair Sovnarkom from early August until mid-September, *GARF* 5446/1/61/633–634, 800. For his proximity to Stalin see *Stalin i Kaganovich: perepiska*, pp. 40, 41.
53. See for instance *ibid.*, pp. 46, 50, 65.
54. *Ibid.*, pp. 33–4, 40–2, 51.
55. *RGAS-PI*, 79/1/683, 2–4, printed Khlevnyuk, *Stalinskoe Politbyuro v 30-e gody*, p. 121.
56. *Stalin i Kaganovich: perepiska*, pp. 35, 79, 92–3.
57. *Ibid.*, pp. 80, 82, 83, 87–8, 92–3.
58. See Watson, *Molotov and Soviet Government*, pp. 84–5; *RGAS-PI*, 17/3/867, 11–12; Khlevnyuk, *Stalin i Ordzhonikidze*, pp. 132–3; Davies, *Crisis and Progress*, p. 204.
59. Mikoyan, *Tak bylo*, p. 324.
60. *RGAS-PI*, 558/11/779, 23, 29–31, 33; Khlevnyuk, *Politbyuro: mekhanizma politicheskoi vlasti v 1930-e gody*, pp. 84–5.
61. *Stalin i Kaganovich: perepiska*, p. 32.
62. *Ibid.*, pp. 118, 122–6.
63. Khlevnyuk, *Stalinskoe Politbyuro v 30-e gody*, pp. 140–1.
64. *Stalin i Kaganovich: perepiska*, pp. 111–12.
65. *Stalin's Letters to Molotov*, p. 228.
66. Davies, *Crisis and Progress*, pp. 168–9 quoting *GARF*, 8418/5/166, 47–50, 109–11, 115–20,
67. *RGAS-PI*, 17/3/863, item 3.
68. *GARF*, 5446/57/16, 152–7; see Davies, *Crisis and Progress*, p. 127.
69. *RGAS-PI*, 17/3/843, 2.
70. Molotov, *V bor'be za sotsializm*, p. 202–12.
71. *RGAS-PI*, 17/2/484, 53–5.
72. *Ibid.*, 17/3/866, 1.
73. Molotov, *V bor'be za sotsializm*, pp. 229–35.
74. Watt, D. C. ed., *British Documents on Foreign Affairs: Reports and Papers from the Foreign Office Confidential Print, Part II From the First to the Second World War, Series A, The Soviet Union 1917–1939*, vol. 16, *The Soviet Union 1930–1932*, Washington: 1992, p. 83.
75. *RGAS-PI*, 17/162/11, 39, 40, 49, 68, 98, 99, 101, 107, 111, 169. Stalin chaired this commission. Besides Molotov, Voroshilov, Kaganovich and Ordzhonikidze were members.
76. Molotov, *V bor'be za sotsializm*, pp. 262–3; *cf.* Stalin, *Sochineniya*, t. 12, p. 269.
77. *RGAS-PI*, 17/162/11, 10, 101; Davies, *Crisis and Progress*, p. 166.
78. Molotov, *V bor'be za sotsializm*, pp. 328–9.
79. *RGAS-PI*, 17/3a/101, 1; Davies, *Crisis and Progress*, pp. 138–9.
80. *XVII konferentsiya Vsesoyusnoi Kommunisticheskoi Partii (b): stenograficheskii otchet*, Moscow: 1932 (hereinafter *XVII konf.*) p. 8.
81. *Ibid.*, p. 143.
82. *Ibid.*, pp. 145, 147, quoted in Davies, *Crisis and Progress*, p. 134. For Molotov's views in 1955 on the question of the establishment of a socialist society see below p. 253.
83. *XVII konf.* pp. 154–5.
84. *Ibid.*, pp. 152, 154, 242, 265.
85. *Ibid.*, pp. 150–51.
86. *Ibid.*, p. 183.
87. *Ibid.*, p. 150.
88. Davies, *Crisis and Progress*, p. 137.

89. Molotov, *V bor'be za sotsializm*, p. 324.
90. See for instance Nove, A., *An Economic History of the USSR*, Harmondsworth: 1982, p. 207.
91. *RGAS-PI*, 17/3/883, 1.
92. *Byulleten' Oppozitsii*, July 1932, p. 3.
93. *Stalin i Kaganovich: perepiska*, p.129.
94. *Ibid.*, pp. 146, 151, 152, 262.
95. *Stalin's Letters to Molotov*, pp. 230–1, citing *RGAS-PI*, 17/3/890, 11. For this decree se *SZ*, 1932, I, 50–98. See also, Solomon, Jr, P. H., *Soviet Criminal Justice under Stalin*, Cambridge: 1996, p. 112.
96. For this law which imposed the death penalty for theft of state property see *ibid.* pp. 112–13; *Stalin i Kaganovich: perepiska*, pp. 235, 242. For the law itself see *SZ*, 1932, I, 62–260.
97. *Stalin i Kaganovich: perepiska*, pp. 240–1, 242, 245–6, 248, 273.
98. *Ibid.*, p. 270; *RGAS-PI*, 17/3/833, 2, 895, 2; *ibid.*, 82/2/1421, 258–60.
99. *Stalin i Kaganovich: perepiska*, pp. 230–1, 245.
100. *Ibid.*, pp. 238–9.
101. *Ibid.*, p. 281; *RGAS-PI*, 17/162/13, 63.
102. *Ibid.*, 17/2/488, 1a. For the main reports see *ibid.*, 17/2/500.
103. Davies, *Crisis and Progress*, pp. 244–55.
104. Molotov, *V bor'be za sotsializm*, pp. 345–60.
105. Khlevnyuk, *Stalin i Ordzhonikidze*, p.132; *GARF*, R-5446/27/4, 135–6.
106. *RGVA (Rossiiskii gosudarstvennyi voennyi arkhiv)* 33987/3/633, 20, quoted Davies, R. W. and Harrison, M., 'The Soviet Military–Economic Effort during the Second Five-Year Plan (1933–1937), unpublished paper, CREES, University of Birmingham, 1996, p. 18.
107. Davies, R. W. and Harrison, M., 'The Soviet Military–Economic Effort during the Second Five-Year Plan (1933–1937), *Europe–Asia Studies*, vol. 49, no. 3 1997, pp. 389–90.
108. Stalin, I. V., *Sochineniya*, t. 13, Moscow: 1955, pp. 414, 419.
109. Kemp Welch, A., *Stalin and the Literary Intelligentsia, 1928–1939*, pp. 127–32.
110. Chuev, *Molotov*, pp. 306–8; see also Vasilieva, *Kremlin Wives*, pp. 67–75; Alliluyeva, S., trans. Johnson, J., *Twenty Letters to a Friend*, Harmondsworth: 1968, pp. 97–100.
111. See above p. 112.
112. Vasil'ev, V., 'Tsena golodnogo khleba. Politika rukovodstva SSSR i USSR v 1932–1933gg.', in Vasil'ev, V. and Shapoval, Yu. eds, *Komandiry bol'shogo goloda: poezdki V. Molotova i L. Kaganovicha v Ukrainu i na Severnyi Kavkaz. 1932–1933gg*, Kiev: 2001, p. 83, citing *RGAS-PI*, 17/112/1, 110.
113. *Ibid.*, 82/2/137, 53.
114. *Ibid.* 30–2.
115. *Ibid.*, 4.
116. *Ibid.*, 104–5, 116, 118.
117. *Ibid.*, 23–44.
118. *Ibid.*, 70–80.
119. *Ibid.*, 111–12.
120. *Ibid.*, 69–72, 86–8.
121. Ivnitskii, N.A., 'Golod 1932–1933 godov: kto vinovat?', in Afanas'ev, Yu., N., ed., *Golod 1932–33*, Moscow: 1995, p. 45.
122. Davies, R.W. and Wheatcroft, S. G., *The Industrialisation of Soviet Russia 5, The Years of Hunger: Soviet Agriculture, 1931–1933*, Basingstoke: 2004, p. 100, quoting *RGAS-PI*, 558/11/43, 105.
123. See Bone J., in the discussion on H-Net on the Ukrainian famine in May 2002; Vasil'ev, 'Tsena golodnogo khleba', p. 87.
124. *GARF*, 5446/27/9, 98–9.
125. Vasil'ev, 'Tsena golodnogo khleba', p. 89 citing *RGAS-PI*, 17/162/12, 153.
126. *Stalin i Kaganovich: perepiska*, p. 133; *RGAS-PI*, 82/2/138, 124, 128.

127. *Stalin i Kaganovich: perepiska*, p. 133; *RGAS-PI*, 17/3/887, 9.
128. *Stalin's Letters to Molotov*, p. 230.
129. *Stalin i Kaganovich: perepiska*, pp. 196, 201; *RGAS-PI*, 17/3/890,8.
130. *Stalin i Kaganovich: perepiska*, pp. 205, 211.
131. *Ibid.*, p. 180, citing *RGAS-PI*, 17/3/890, 8; *ibid.*, pp. 210, 211.
132. *Ibid.*, p. 213, citing *RGAS-PI* 17/3/891, 10; *ibid.*, p. 218. The statement in Afanas'ev, *Golod 1932–33*, p. 8, saying that the figures were reduced by 1.1 million tons as a result of the conference seems to be in error, although they were reduced for the Ukraine and other areas on Stalin's proposal in August, *Stalin i Kaganovich: perepiska*, pp. 287, 289, 290, 297; Vasil'ev, 'Tsena golodnogo khleba', p. 101 citing *RGAS-PI*, 17/162/13, 76.
133. *Pravda*, 9 July 1932; Vasil'ev, 'Tsena golodnogo khleba', p. 96.
134. Molotov, *V bor'be za sotsializm*, p. 332.
135. *Ibid.*, p. 335.
136. *Ibid.*, pp. 336–8, 343.
137. *Stalin i Kaganovich: perepiska*, pp. 218–9.
138. Ivnitskii, 'Golod 1932–1933 godov: kto vinovat?', p. 59, citing *RGAS-PI*, 17/2/536, 9 although this reference appears to be erroneous; Vasi'lev, 'Tsena golodnogo khleba', p. 97.
139. Davies, *Crisis and Progress*, pp. 243–4.
140. Vasil'ev, 'Tsena golodnogo khleba', p. 104; *RGAS-PI*, 17/3/904, 10–11.
141. *Ibid.*, 82/2/141, 6.
142. *Ibid.*, 7.
143. *Ibid.*, 12–14.
144. *RGAS-PI*, 82/2/141, 18. For this law see above p. 114.
145. *RGAS-PI*, 17/3/906, 6.
146. Vasil'ev, 'Tsena golodnogo khleba', p. 106.
147. Ivnitskii, 'Golod 1932–1933 godov: kto vinovat?', p. 52.
148. *RGAS-PI*, 82/2/141, 42.
149. *Ibid.*, 24, 52.
150. Ivnitskii, 'Golod 1932–1933 godov: kto vinovat?', pp. 53–4.
151. i.e. the grain the peasant sold on the market in excess of that which he kept for food and as seed grain. There is a copy of the brochure entitled *Zadachi bol'shevikov ukrainoy v bor'be za khleb* at *RGAS-PI*, 82/2/141, 81–88.
152. *Ibid.*, 82/2/141, 75–6.
153. *Ibid.*, 77–80.
154. *Ibid.*, 74–5.
155. Ivnitskii, 'Golod 1932–1933 godov: kto vinovat?', p. 56.
156. *RGAS-PI*, 82/2/141, 102.
157. See above p. 108 and below pp. 253–4.
158. Ivnitskii, 'Golod 1932–1933 godov: kto vinovat?', pp. 57–8.
159. *Ibid.*, p. 59.
160. Conquest, R., *The Harvest of Sorrow*, London: 1986, p. 328.
161. Afanas'ev, *Golod 1932–33*, p. 11.
162. Chuev, *Molotov*, pp. 453–4.
163. *RGAS-PI*, 17/2/502, 4.
164. Molotov, *V bor'be za sotsializm*, pp. 363–86. Cf. Davies, *Crisis and Progress*, pp. 250, 322–3.
165. Ibid., pp. 326–7; *RGAS-PI*, 17/2/514ii, 55–7.
166. *Stalin's Letters to Molotov*, p. 232.
167. Davies, *Crisis and Progress*, pp. 381–3.
168. *RGAS-PI*, 17/3/92, 50–5, see Getty, J. Arch, ' "Excesses are not permitted": Mass Terror and Stalinist Governance in the Late 1930s', *The Russian Review*, vol. 61, 2002, p. 118.
169. *GARF*, 5446/82/26, 34–6.
170. *SZ*, 1933, I, 49–228.
171. *GARF*, 5446/82/26, 18–22.

172. *Pravda*, 23 August 1933.
173. *Stalin i Kaganovich: perepiska*, p. 315.
174. *RGAS-PI*, 17/163/989, 165.
175. *Stalin i Kaganovich: perepiska*, p. 315.
176. *Ibid.*, p. 318.
177. *RGAS-PI*, 17/3/929, 21; 930, 13; *Stalin i Kaganovich: perepiska*, pp. 303, 326.
178. *Stalin's Letters to Molotov*, pp. 233–4; Watson, *Molotov and Soviet Government*, p. 147; Davies, *Crisis and Progress*, pp. 350–1.
179. *Stalin i Kaganovich: perepiska*, p. 333.
180. *Stalin's Letters to Molotov*, p. 234.
181. *RGAS-PI*, 558/11/769, 126–9, quoted Fitzpatrick, S., 'Stalin, Molotov and the Practice of Politics', unpublished paper for the XXIX Conference of the Study Group on the Russian Revolution, Durham, 2003, p. 10.
182. Rees, E. A., *Stalinism and Soviet Rail Transport, 1928–41*, Basingstoke: 1995, pp. 75–6.
183. *Stalin's Letters to Molotov*, pp. 233–4.
184. Davies, R. W. and Khlevnyuk, O., 'Gosplan', in Rees, ed., *Decision-Making in the Stalinist Command Economy 1932–1937*, pp. 49–51; *XVII s"ezd vsesoyuznoi kommunisticheskoi partii (b): stenograficheskii otchet*, Moscow: 1934 (hereinafter *XVII s"ezd: sten. ot.*) pp. 351–80, 433–5, 522–4.
185. Davies, Ilic, and Khlevnyuk, 'The Politburo and Economic Policy-making', p. 117; *XVII s"ezd: sten. ot.*, pp. 351–380 and particularly pp. 532–4.
186. *RGAS-PI*, 79/1/798, 10–11, printed Khlevnyuk *et al.*, *Stalinskoe Politbyuro v 30-e gody*, p. 140.
187. Davies, *Crisis and Progress*, p. 341; quoting *SZ*, 1933, I, 33–195; *RGAS-PI*, 79/1/684, 18–20.
188. Davies, Ilic, and Khlevnyuk, 'The Politburo and Economic Policy-making', pp. 113–4; Davies, and Khlevnyuk, 'Gosplan', pp. 46–54; *Stalin's Letters to Molotov*, p. 234.
189. *Ibid.*, p. 235.
190. *Arkhiv Prezidenta Rossiskoi Federatsii* (hereinafter *APRF*) 45/1/769, 159–60, quoted Davies, R. W. and Khlevnyuk, O., 'Stakhanovism and the Soviet Economy', *Europe–Asia Studies*, vol. 54, no. 6, 2002, pp. 873–4.
191. *Stalin's Letters to Molotov*, p. 236, cited Davies, Ilic, and Khlevnyuk, 'The Politburo and Economic Policy-making', pp. 116–17.
192. *Ibid.*, p. 117 citing *APRF*, 45/1/769, 162–3.
193. Davies, and Khlevnyuk, 'Stakhanovism and the Soviet Economy', p. 887.
194. *RGAS-PI*, 17/2/536, 1–9; see Khlevnyuk, O., and Davies, R. W., 'The End of Rationing in the Soviet Union, 1934–1935', *Europe–Asia Studies*, vol. 51, no. 4, 1999, pp. 573–4. For Stalin's interruptions see *RGAS-PI*, 17/2/536,7.
195. Watson, *Molotov and Soviet Government*, p. 121.
196. *Stalin's Letters to Molotov*, pp. 238–9.
197. Pavlov, D, 'Eto eshche ne sotsialism: dve poslednie vstrechi s V.M. Molotovym,' *Literaturnaya Gazeta*, 18 April 1990.
198. Davies, Ilic, and Khlevnyuk, 'The Politburo and Economic Policy-making', p.109.
199. Bessedovsky, G., *Memoirs of a Soviet Diplomat*, New York: 1938, p. 247 *et seq.*
200. Public Record Office (hereinafter *PRO*), FO, 371/16338, 75.
201. Rees, E. A., 'Stalin as Leader 1924–1937: From Oligarch to Dictator', in Rees ed., *The Nature of Stalin's Dictatorship*, p. 42.
202. *RGAS-PI*, 17/3/ 867, 9, 11, 20, 24.
203. Davies, R. W., 'The Archives and the Soviet Economy', unpublished paper presented to the conference on 'Reappraising the Stalin Era', European University Institute, Florence, October 2002, pp. 7, 10.
204. I am indebted to Professor R.W. Davies for this information. See also Davies, R. W., Tauger, M. B. and Wheatcroft, S. G. 'Stalin, Grain Stocks and the Famine of 1932–1933', *Slavic Review*, no. 3, 1995, pp. 642–657.
205. Mikoyan, *Tak bylo*, pp. 519–20.
206. See above p. 115.

207. Khlevnyuk, *et al. Stalinskoe Politbyuro v 30-e gody*, pp. 90–93.
208. See above, p. 110.
209. Davies, R. W. *Soviet History in the Yeltsin Era*, Basingstoke: 1997, p. 153.
210. Chuev, F., *Tak govoril Kaganovich*, pp. 61, 129–130; *Stalin i Kaganovich: perepiska*, p. 21.
211. Chuev, F., *Tak govoril Kaganovich*, p. 61.
212. *Ibid.*, p. 130.
213. For this thesis see Getty, J. Arch, *Origins of the Great Purges: the Soviet Communist Party Reconsidered, 1933–1938*, Cambridge: 1985, pp. 129–30.
214. Watson, *Molotov and Soviet Government*, pp. 56–8, 70–3.
215. *GARF*, 5446/1/70b, 121, cited Davies, *Crisis and Progress*, p. 286.
216. *GARF*, 5446/82/53, 51–39. I am greatly indebted to Professor R. W. Davies for drawing my attention to this document and for his comments on Molotov's marking of the document.
217. *Ibid.*, 5446/82/53, 51–39. I am again indebted to Professor Davies for this information.
218. *Ibid.*, 5446/1/99, 261–3.
219. For Molotov's support for Rukhimovich see above p. 111. For Rukhimovich's support of investment on the railways see Rees, *Stalinism and Soviet Rail Transport*, pp. 32, 46–8, 55, 220. For Rukhimovich advising caution see Davies, *Crisis and Progress*, p. 42.
220. See below p. 140.

8   Molotov and the Terror 1934–1938

1. Chuev, *Molotov*, p. 489.
2. *Ibid.*, pp. 468–9.
3. *Ibid.*, p. 480.
4. See above p. 120.
5. Mandelstam, N.Y., *Hope Against Hope*, New York: 1970, p. 13.
6. Ibid., p. 160.
7. See for instance Conquest, R., *The Great Terror: a Reassessment*, London: 1990, p. 37.
8. Getty, J. Arch and Naumov, N., *The Road to Terror: Stalin and the Self-Destruction of the Bolsheviks, 1932–1939*, Hew Haven: 1999, pp. 141–2.
9. *XVII s" ezd: sten. ot.* pp. 124–9, 209–12, 236–9, 455–63, 492–7, 515–22.
10. *Ibid.*, pp 5–6, 331–80.
11. For the controversy over the plan see above p. 122.
12. Chuev, *Molotov*, p. 373. More than a hundred delegates allegedly did not vote for Molotov and Kaganovich, 125 or 126 refrained from voting for Stalin, i.e. their names were deleted from the ballot paper, 'V komissii Politbyuro TsK KPSS', *Izvestiya TsK*, no 7, 1989, p. 114.
13. Chuev, *Molotov*, p. 374. *Cf.* Davies, R. W., *Soviet History in the Gorbachev Revolution*, Basingstoke: 1989, p. 85.
14. Chuev, *Molotov*, pp. 375–6.
15. Brackman, R. *The Secret File on Joseph Stalin*, p. 233; Basseches, N. trans. Dicker, E. W., *Stalin*, London: 1952, p. 188. Other possibilities for this incident are in 1932, after the death of Stalin's wife; or in connection with repression in the countryside; or in connection with the Ryutin affair.
16. Knight, A., *Who Killed Kirov? The Kremlin's Greatest Mystery*, New York: 1999, pp.176–8.
17. Khlevnyuk, *Politbyuro: mekhanizma politicheskoi vlasti v 1930-e gody*, pp. 124–5.
18. See Benvenuti, F., 'The Reform of the NKVD, 1934', *Europe–Asia Studies*, vol. 49, no. 6, 1997, p. 1046, quoting *RGAS-PI*, 17/165/47, 154–64.
19. Knight, *Who Killed Kirov*, p. 182. Molotov signed no decrees between 3 and 27 September.
20. 'V komissii Politbyuro TsK KPSS', *Izvestiya TsK*, no. 9 1981, p. 47.
21. *Report of Court Proceedings in the Case of the Anti-Soviet Trotskyite Centre*, Moscow: 1937, p. 17; *Pravda*, 26 October 1961. In his Memoirs Molotov ascribed this to 1932, Chuev, *Molotov*, p. 452.

22. See above, pp. 123–4.
23. Chuev, *Molotov*, p. 423.
24. Korotkov, A. V. and Chernobaev, A. A., eds, 'Posetiteli kremlevskogo kabineta I.V. Stalina', (hereinafter 'Stalin's Office Diary') *IA*, no. 3, 1995, p. 144; Knight, *Who Killed Kirov*, p. 197. Conquest, R., *Stalin and the Kirov Murder*, London: 1989, p. 38, makes no mention of Kaganovich. In his memoirs, Molotov claimed that it was Medved, head of the Leningrad NKVD, who telephoned, Chuev, *Molotov*, p. 376.
25. *SZ*, 1934, I, 65–459. Conquest, *The Great Terror*, p. 41. 'Stalin's Office Diary', *IA*, no. 3, 1995, p. 144 makes clear that Conquest is incorrect in accepting Khrushchev's claim that 'the Politburo presented with a *fait accompli*, approved it "casually" ' on 2 December, although it is true that the matter does not appear in the Politburo *protokoly*.
26. Knight, *Who Killed Kirov*, p. 201. For the secret police members of the party see Conquest, *Stalin and the Kirov Murder*, p. 38.
27. 'Stalin's Office Diary', *IA*, no. 3, 1995, p. 146; Knight, *Who Killed Kirov*, p. 207.
28. Kirilina, A., *Rikoshet*, St. Petersburg: 1993, pp. 50–62.
29. Knight, *Who Killed Kirov*, pp. 213–4.
30. *Izvestiya*, 8 December 1934.
31. Knight, *Who Killed Kirov*, p. 215; Chuev, *Molotov*, p. 376.
32. *Izvestiya*, 27 December 1934.
33. Getty, ' "Excesses are not permitted" ', pp. 120–1.
34. Kurtsov, V. I. ed., *Stranitsy istorii KPSS. Fakty, problemy, uroki*, Moscow: 1989, vol. 2, pp. 647–50; 'Poshchadite zhe rodinu i nas', *Istochnik*, no. 1., 1995, pp. 138–45.
35. See Watson, *Molotov and Soviet Government*, p. 154. Evidence of foul play in Kuibyshev's death is not at all clear.
36. *Trotsky's Diary in Exile 1935*, trans. Zaradnaya E., Cambridge, MA: 1976, pp. 9–10, 54.
37. *SZ*, 1935, I, 19–155; Conquest, *The Great Terror*, p. 75.
38. Joint Sovnarkom-Central Committee secret decree no. 1232–191, printed Getty and Naumov, *The Road to Terror*, pp. 187–8.
39. Conquest, *The Great Terror*, pp. 77–8; *Pravda*, 26 May and 28 June 1935.
40. Getty and Naumov, *The Road to Terror*, pp. 161–6; *RGAS-PI* 17/2/544, 22.
41. Davies, R. W. and Khlevnyuk, O., 'Stakhanovism and the Soviet Economy', pp. 882–3.
42. *Za Industrializatsiya*, 18 October 1935; Benvenuti, F., 'Stakhanovism and Stalinism, 1934–8', unpublished paper, CREES, University of Birmingham, 1989, p. 25.
43. *RGAS-PI*, 17/2/548,2, 561, 83–4.
44. Thurston, R. W., *Life and Terror in Stalin's Russia*, New Haven: 1996, p.7, quoting *GARF*, 8131sch/27, 70, 103–6.
45. Getty and Naumov, *The Road to Terror*, p. 219.
46. *Ibid.*, pp. 239–43; Thurston, *Life and Terror in Stalin's Russia*, pp. 8–9.
47. *RGAS-PI*, 17/2/572, 32–3.
48. Krivitsky, W. G., *I Was Stalin's Agent*, London: 1939, p. 223.
49. *Byulleten' Oppozitsii*, 1937, no. 58–9, pp. 18–19.
50. Molotov, V. M., *Stat'i i rechi 1935–1936*, Moscow: 1937, pp. 231–2. Getty and Naumov, *The Road to Terror*, p. 252 suggest that Molotov's fall from grace was the result of criticising P. P. Postyshev and lack of enthusiasm for the Zinoviev–Kamenev trial, but produce no supporting evidence. Beloff, M., *The Foreign Policy of Soviet Russia*, vol. 2, London: 1949, pp. 153–4 seems to be in error in dating this interview to 14 March and claiming that there was no response until an article in *Izvestiya*, by Radek on 6 April. The article was published in *Pravda*, on 24 March and dated 19 March; there were reports on foreign press comments on the next day and Radek published an article in that paper on the interview on 27 March.
51. Molotov, *Stat'i i rechi*, p. 232.
52. See below p. 151.
53. Molotov, *Stat'i i rechi*, pp. 235–6.
54. Rittersporn, G. T., 'The State against Itself: Social Tension and Political Conflicts in the USSR, 1936–1938', *Telos*, no. 41, Fall 1979, p. 90; Siegelbaum, L. H., *Stakhanovism and the*

Politics of Productivity in the USSR, 1935–1941, Cambridge: 1988, pp. 127–35; Khlevnyuk, O., *Stalin i Ordzhonikidze*, pp. 63, 65–6; Rees, E. A., *The Purge on the Soviet Railways 1937*, unpublished paper, CREES, University of Birmingham: 1992, p. 2; Rees, E. A., *Stalinism and Soviet Rail Transport, 1928–1941*, pp. 138–9.

55. *Pravda*, 21, June 1936. Molotov may have accompanied Stalin twice to see the dying Gorky, see Spiridonova, L., 'Gorky and Stalin (According to New Materials from A.M. Gorky's Archive)', *The Russian Review*, vol. 54, no. 3, 1995, p. 423.
56. 'V komissii Politbyuro TsK KPSS', *Izvestiya TsK*, no. 8, 1989, pp. 100–15, printed Getty and Naumov, *The Road to Terror*, pp. 250–5.
57. *Report of Court Proceedings: the Case of the Trotskyite–Zinovievite Terrorist Centre*, Moscow: 1936, p. 10 *et passim.*
58. Orlov, A., *The Secret History of Stalin's Crimes*, London: 1954, pp. 162–3.
59. Mandelstam, *Hope Against Hope*, p. 316.
60. Chuev, *Molotov*, p. 486.
61. Montefiore, S. S., *Stalin: the Court of the Red Tsar*, London: 2003, p. 168.
62. *RGAS-PI*, 17/3/979, 3, quoted Getty and Naumov, *The Road to Terror*, p. 221.
63. 'Stalin's Office Diary', *IA*, no. 4, 1995, pp. 30–1.
64. He did not sign any of more than 250 Sovnarkom decrees issued between these dates. See *GARF*, 5446/1/104, *Pravda* reported his return from leave on 1 September.
65. *Stalin i Kaganovich: perepiska*, pp. 627–708. For the telegram to the chairman of Sovnarkom see pp. 640–1.
66. Orlov, *The Secret History of Stalin's Crimes*, pp. 163–4.
67. *Byulleten' Oppozitsii*, 1937, no. 58–9, p. 18.
68. Zalesskii, V.A., *Imperiya Stalina*, p. 324.
69. Conquest, *The Great Terror*, p. 91.
70. *RGAS-PI*, 17/162/20, 34.
71. 'V komissii Politbyuro TsK KPSS', *Izvestiya TsK*, 1989, no. 8, p. 92, no. 9, p. 42.
72. Lenin, *PSS*, vol. 44, pp. 396–400.
73. *RGAS-PI*, 558/11/767, 87–88, Molotov's letter to Stalin, quoted in Fitzpatrick, 'Stalin, Molotov and the Practice of Politics', p. 8.
74. *Stalin's Letters to Molotov*, p. 210.
75. *Ibid.*, pp. 211, 224. See also *RGAS-PI*, 558/11/769, 10, 22–3, 36–40; Fitzpatrick, 'Stalin, Molotov and the Practice of Politics', p. 10; *Stalin i Kaganovich: perepiska*, p. 337, see above p. 121.
76. Chuev, *Molotov*, pp. 474, 478, 479.
77. Getty and Naumov, *The Road to Terror*, p. 303; 'V komissii Politbyuro TsK KPSS', *Izvestiya TsK*, 1989, no. 5, p. 71. The Politburo representatives consisted of Kaganovich, Ezhov and Vyshinskii.
78. Conquest, *The Great Terror*, p. 136; 'V komissii Politbyuro TsK KPSS', *Izvestiya TsK*, 1989, no. 8, p. 92.
79. *Stalin i Kaganovich: perepiska*, pp. 682–3. The telegram was sent to 'Molotov, Kaganovich and other members of the Politburo'.
80. *SZ*, 1936, II, 28–277, 279, 280.
81. Chuev, *Molotov*, p. 467.
82. Shearer, D. R., 'Social Disorder, Mass Repression and the NKVD during the 1930s', *Cahiers du Monde Russe*, vol. 42, 2001, pp. 523–4, 527–8; Shearer, D. R., 'Crime and Social Disorder in Stalin's Russia', *ibid.*, vol. 39, 1996, pp. 119–48.
83. Chuev, *Molotov*, pp. 467, 492, 511.
84. *Pravda*, 20–26 November 1936.
85. *RGAS-PI*, 82/2/897, 8–10.
86. *Ibid.*, 17/2/575, 11–67.
87. *Ibid.*, 122. For Stalin's views on suicide at this time see Khlevnyuk, *Stalin i Ordzhonikidze*, p. 161.
88. *RGAS-PI*, 17/2/575, 125.
89. *Ibid.*, 127–30.

90. 'V komissii Politbyuro TsK KPSS', *Izvestiya TsK*, 1989, no. 5, p. 76.
91. Getty and Naumov, *The Road to Terror*, p. 328.
92. See for instance Fischer, L., *Men and Politics: an Autobiography*, New York: 1946, p. 98 who quotes Bukharin as saying in the late 1920s 'Molotov ... is a fool. He tries to teach me Marxism'.
93. Medevedev, R., 'The Murder of Bukharin', in Medvedev, Z. A. and Medvedev, R. A., *The Unknown Stalin*, London: 2003, p. 277.
94. 'V komissii Politbyuro TsK KPSS', *Izvestiya TsK*, 1989, no. 5, p. 76.
95. Marina, Yu., 'Vse, chto govorit Radek, – eto absolyutno zlostnaya kleveta ...', *Istochnik*, no. 1, 2001, pp. 64–71.
96. *Report of Court Proceedings in the Case of the Anti-Soviet Trotskyite Centre*, pp. 17, 70, 89, 218, 263, 328, 394.
97. Medvedev, R., *Let History Judge: the Origins and Consequences of Stalinism*, Manchester: 1976, p. 180.
98. See Khlevnyuk, *Stalin i Ordzhnoikidze*, pp. 111–18. The trial of Pyatakov, his deputy, seems to have seriously compromised Ordzhonikidze's position in resisting attacks on his commissariat. There seems little doubt that the death was suicide, following a quarrel with Stalin, but see Conquest, *The Great Terror*, pp. 168–72.
99. Medvedev, *Let History Judge*, p. 196; *Izvestiya*, 19 February 1937.
100. *Izvestiya*, 20, 21, 22 February 1937.
101. Chuev, *Molotov*, p. 250.
102. 'Materialy fevral'sko-martovskogo plenuma TsK VKP(b) 1937 goda', *Voprosy Istorii*, 1992, nos. 4–5, pp. 31–6; nos. 6–7, pp. 3–29. The record of the plenum published here is fuller than in the documents at *RGAS-PI*, 17/2/578–613.
103. *Voprosy Istorii*, nos. 8–9, 1992, pp. 18–29.
104. *Ibid.*, no. 2, 1993, pp. 6–9.
105. *Ibid.*, pp. 21, 33; *RGAS-PI*, 17/2/577, 4; Getty and Naumov, *The Road to* Terror, p. 411.
106. Khlevnyuk, O.V., *Stalin i Ordzhonikidze*, pp. 96–97.
107. *Ibid.* pp. 99, 112–13.
108. Khlevniuk, O., 'The Reasons for the "Great Terror": the Foreign Political Aspects', in Pons, S. and Romano, A., eds, *Russia in the Age of Wars*, Milan: 2000, p. 165.
109. *Voprosy Istorii*, no. 8, 1993, pp. 3–26.
110. Thurston, *Life and Terror in Stalin's Russia*, pp. 43–4.
111. *Voprosy Istorii* 1994, no. 8, pp. 17–29; 'Delo o tak nazyvaemoi "antisovetskoi–trotskistskoi voennoi organizatsii v krasnoi armii" ', *Izvestiya TsK*, 1989, no. 4, p. 45.
112. *Voprosy Istorii*, no. 12, 1994, pp. 20, 23; no. 2, 1995, pp. 8, 10, 12; no. 8, 1995, p. 17.
113. Starkov, B., 'Narkom Ezhov' in Getty, J. Arch and Manning, R. T., *Stalinist Terror: New Perspectives*, Cambridge: 1993, p. 27.
114. Alliluyeva, S., *Only One Year*, London: 1969, p. 388.
115. Getty and Naumov, *The Road to Terror*, p. 447.
116. Chuev, *Molotov*, pp. 484–7.
117. *Ibid.*, pp. 469, 489.
118. *Ibid.*, p. 469; Kovaleva, N.V. *et al.* 'Poslednyaya "antipartiinaya" gruppa: Stenograficheskii otchet iyun'skogo (1957g) plenuma TsK KPSS', (hereinafter 'Poslednyaya "antipartiinaya" gruppa ...') *IA*, no. 3, 1993, pp. 88–9.
119. Chuev, *Molotov*, pp. 490, 506.
120. *Stalin's Letters to Molotov*, p. 323; *Voenno-Istoricheskii Arkhiv*, 1997, no. 1. pp. 24–7; Khlevnyuk, *Politbyuro mekhanizma politicheskoi vlasti b 1930-e gody*, p. 37.
121. *RGAS-PI*, 17/163/1147, 133; *cf.* Pechenkin, A. A., '1937 god: Stalin i voennyi sovet', *Otechestvennaya Istoriya*, no. 1, 2003, p. 43.
122. *RGAS-PI*, 17/2/615, 68, printed Getty and Naumov, *The Road to Terror*, p. 448; *Oktyabr'* no. 12, 1988.
123. Main, S. J., 'The Arrest and Testimony of Marshal of the Soviet Union M. N. Tukhachevsky (May–June 1937)', *Journal of Slavic Military Studies*, vol. 10, no. 1, 1997, p. 153.

124. *Pravda*, 27 October 1961, Shelepin's speech to the XXII Congress.
125. *Izvestiya TsK*, 1989, no. 4, pp. 43–61; 'Stalin's Office Diary', *IA*, 1995, no. 4, pp. 54–6; Pechenkin, '1937 god: Stalin i voennyi sovet', p. 51.
126. Kumanev, G. A., 'V ogne tyazhelykh ispytanii (iyun 1941–noyabr' 1942g.)', *Istoriya SSSR*, no. 2, 1991, p. 6.
127. Reese, R. A., 'The Red Army and the Great Purges', in Getty and Manning, *Stalinist Terror: New Perspectives*, p. 213.
128. Chuev, *Molotov*, pp. 464, 486.
129. See for instance Khlevnyuk, O., 'The Objectives of the Great Terror, 1937–1938', in Cooper, J., Perrie, M. and Rees E. A. eds, *Soviet History 1917–1953: Essays in Honour of R.W. Davies*, Basingstoke: 1995, pp. 172–3.
130. *RGAS-PI*, 17/2/617, 175–210; 621, 50–52.
131. Starkov, B. A., 'Ar'ergardnye boi staroi partiino gvardii', in Afanas'ev, A. V. ed., *Oni ne molchali*, Moscow: 1991, p. 221; cf. *Moscow News*, no. 15, 1988, quoting Kaganovich's account of this incident.
132. For Andreev visiting Saratov and other areas see Getty and Naumov, *The Road to Terror*, p. 454. For Ezhov as a member of Molotov's delegation see Conquest, *The Great Terror*, p. 230.
133. Dedijer, V., *Tito Speaks*, London: 1954, p. 102; Vasil'ev, V., 'Politbyuro TsK KP(b) U v period otnositel'noi ekonomicheskoi stabilizatsiii i v usloviyakh "bol'shogo terrora" (1934 i 1937 gg.)', unpublished paper for EUI conference on 'Stalin's Politburo', Florence, 2000, p. 21.
134. *Izvestiya.*, 21 December 1937.
135. Getty, ' "Excesses are not Permitted" ', pp. 113–38.
136. *Ibid.*, p.130.
137. Zemskov, V.M., 'O nekotorykh problemakh "bol'shogo terrora" 1937–1938 godov', *Otechestvennaya Istoriya*, no. 1, 2000, p. 202.
138. Conquest, *The Great Terror*, p. 236, no source quoted.
139. Volkogonov, D.V., *Triumf i tragediya*, t. 1, ch. 2, pp. 300–1; cf. 'V komissii Politbyuro TsK KPSS', *Izvestiya TsK*, no. 4, 1989, p. 59.
140. Chuev, *Molotov*, pp. 480–1, 514.
141. *RGAS-PI*, 82/2/887, 66–9, 70, 133, 163.
142. Watson, *Molotov and Soviet Government*, p. 168.
143. *Ibid.*, p. 170.
144. *Foreign Relations of the United States: The Soviet Union 1933–1939* (hereinafter *FRUS*), Washington: 1952, p. 511.
145. *Pervaya sesssiya Verkhovnogo Soveta SSSR, 12–19 yanvarya 1938: stenograficheskii otchet*, Moscow: 1938, pp. 135–46; Watson, *Molotov and Soviet Government*, p. 170.
146. 'Massovye repressii opravdany byt' ne mogut', *Istochnik*, no. 1, 1995, pp. 124–5.
147. Uldricks, T. J., 'The Impact of the Great Purges on the People's Commissariat of Foreign Affairs', *Slavic Review*, vol. 36, 1977, pp. 188–92. A Soviet had replaced the *kollegiya* in each commissariat in 1934.
148. Watson, *Molotov and Soviet Government*, p. 55.
149. *Sobranie Postanovlenii i Rasporyazhenii Pravitel'stva SSSR*, (hereinafter *SP*), 1937, II, 38–333.
150. *Ibid.*, 1939, II, 8–55.
151. Martin, T., 'The Origins of Soviet Ethnic Cleansing', *Journal of Modern History*, vol. 70, no. 4, 1998, pp. 848–9.
152. 'Massovye repressii opravdany byt' ne mogut', p. 127.
153. Martin, 'The Origins of Soviet Ethnic Cleansing', p. 851. In the light of Stalin's belief in the increased threat of war and the dangers of a 'fifth column', this swing in the later stages of the 'mass operation' against national groups is not surprising. See Petrov, N. and Roginskii A., 'The "Polish Operation" of the NKVD, 1937–8', in McLoughlin, B., and McDermott, K. eds, *Stalin's Terror: High Politics and Mass Repression in the Soviet Union*, Basingstoke: 2003, pp. 163–5.

154. Chuev, *Molotov*, p. 483.
155. *RGAS-PI*, 17/2/639, 9–10, quoted Getty and Naumov, *The Road to Terror*, pp. 503–12. Postyshev had first come under attack in Stalin's speech to the February–March 1937 plenum. See Conquest, *The Great Terror*, pp. 176–7.
156. Adzhubei, A., 'Te desyat' let', *Znamya* no. 6, 1988, p. 96.
157. Chuev, *Molotov*, p. 487.
158. *Ibid.*, p. 489.
159. *Ibid.*, pp. 474, 478.
160. Molotov, V., 'O Vysshei Shkole', *Bol'shevik*, nos. 10–11, 1938, pp. 3–15.
161. *Moscow News* no. 15, 1988, quoting testimony of M. Mendeleyev.
162. Thurston, *Life and Terror in Stalin's Russia*, pp. 108–9 citing *GARF*, 8131sch/27/111, 13; Getty and Naumov, *The Road to Terror*, pp. 523–5.
163. Starkov, 'Narkom Ezhov', pp. 37–8, quoting archive source.
164. Chuev, *Molotov*, pp. 511–21; Mikoyan, *Tak bylo*, pp. 320–4.
165. Knight, A., *Beria: Stalin's First Lieutenant*, Princeton, NJ: 1994, p. 88.
166. Jansen, M., and Petrov, N., *Stalin's Loyal Executioner: People's Commissar Nikolai Ezhov, 1895–1940*, Stanford, CA: 2002, p. 146.
167. *Ibid.*, p. 164.
168. *Ibid.*, p. 177.
169. Chuev, *Molotov*, pp. 472–3.
170. *Ibid.*, p. 472; quoted Getty, ' "Excesses are not Permitted" ', p. 134.
171. *Moskovskie Novosti*, 21 June 1992, p.19; *RGAS-PI*, 17/3/1003, 85–7, printed Getty and Naumov, *The Road to Terror*, pp. 529–37.
172. *Izvestiya*, 10 November 1938.
173. Chuev, *Molotov*, pp. 480–1, 487.
174. Chuev, *Sto sorok*, pp. 428–9.
175. Chuev, *Molotov*, p. 465.
176. Aroseva, O. A., and Maksimova, V. A., *Bez grima*, Moscow: 1999, pp. 19–50.
177. *Ibid.*, p. 51.
178. *Ibid.*, pp. 27–9, 32.
179. *Ibid.*, p. 78.
180. *Ibid.*, pp. 73–5.
181. *Ibid.*, pp. 86–7.
182. *Ibid.*, pp. 30, 256.
183. *Ibid.*, pp. 256–7, 260.

9   1939 – Molotov Becomes Foreign Minister

1. Rees, E. A., 'Stalin as Leader, 1937–1953: From Dictator to Despot', in Rees, ed., *The Nature of Stalin's Dictatorship*, p. 207.
2. Rees, 'Stalin as Leader 1924–1937', p. 25.
3. Watson, *Molotov and Soviet Government*, pp. 55, 72.
4. *Ibid.*, p. 74. For the *opros* procedure see above p. xvi. There is no evidence of dissent from decisions taken in this way in the later 1930s.
5. Kuznetsov, N. G., 'Voenno-Morskoi Flot nakanune Velikoi Otechestvennoi voiny', *Voenno–istoricheskii Zhurnal*, no. 9, 1965, pp. 65–6.
6. *RGAS-PI*, 17/3/986, 53.
7. Rees, 'Stalin as Leader 1924–1937', p. 41; Rees, 'Stalin as Leader, 1937–1953', p. 204.
8. 'Stalin's Office Diary', *IA*, nos. 5–6, 1995, pp. 5–28; no. 6, 1994, pp. 27–44. For the importance of the meetings in Stalin's office see Rees, E. A., 'Stalin as Leader 1924–1937', p. 41.
9. Wheatcroft, S. G., 'From Team-Stalin to Degenerate Tyranny', in Rees, ed., *The Nature of Stalin's Dictatorship*, pp. 93–94, 99.
10. *Izvestiya*, 28 February, 1, 3 March 1939. Krupskaya, whose birthday had been celebrated a few days before, died on 27 February.

11. *XVIII s"ezd Vsesoyuznoi Kommunisticheskoi Partii (b) 10–21 marta 1939 g. stenograficheskii otchet* (hereinafter *XVIII s"ezd: sten. ot.*), Moscow: 1939, pp. 3–4.
12. 'Eto eshche ne sotsialism ...', *Literaturnaya Gazeta*, 18 April 1990.
13. *XVIII s"ezd: sten. Ot.*, pp. 282–315.
14. See above p. 46.
15. Belevich, Y. and Sokolov, V. 'Foreign Affairs Commissar Georgy Chicherin', *International Affairs*, no. 3, 1991, pp. 94–96.
16. Molotov, *V bor'be za sotsializm*, pp. 131–9.
17. *Ibid.*, p. 391, *et seq.*
18. Raymond, P. D., *Conflict and Consensus in Soviet Foreign Policy 1933–1935*, Pennsylvania State University D.Phil. thesis, 1979, pp. 190–242.
19. Such a dual strategy was not unique, see Gorodetsky, G., *Grand Delusion; Stalin and the German Invasion of Russia*, New Haven: 1999, p. 59.
20. Hilger, G. and Meyer, A. G., *The Incompatible Allies: A Memoir-History of German–Soviet Relations 1930–1941*, New York: 1983, p. 255; Haslam, J., *The Soviet Union and the Struggle for Collective Security in Europe, 1933–39* (hereinafter *The Struggle for Collective Security*), London: 1984, pp. 19–20.
21. Dolya, F. P., ed., *DVP*, t. 16, Moscow: 1970, pp. 445–8.
22. *Ibid.*, pp. 476–81; Carr, E. H., *The Twilight of Comintern*, p. 98, cites this document to illustrate the decline in Soviet–German relations, but Haslam, *The Struggle for Collective Security*, p. 22, stresses Molotov's pro-German attitude.
23. Sweet, P.R. *et al.*, eds, *Documents on German Foreign Policy 1918–1939* (hereinafter *DGFP*), Series C, vol. 1, 1933, London: 1957, p. 718.
24. *DGFP*, vol. 2, London: 1959, p. 40.
25. Molotov, *V bor'be za sotsializm*, pp. 452–3.
26. *FRUS: The Soviet Union 1933–1939*, p. 57.
27. *RGAS-PI*, 17/162/15, 155–6; *Istoriya Vtoroi Mirovoi Voiny, 1939–1945*, Moscow: 1983, vol. 1, p. 283; *DVP*, t. 16, pp. 876–7; Haslam, *The Struggle for Collective Security*, pp. 29–30.
28. Dunn, D., 'Maksim Litvinov: Commissar of Contradictions', *Journal of Contemporary History*, vol. 23, no. 2, April 1988, p. 222.
29. Haslam, *The Struggle for Collective Security*, pp. 30–1; Raymond, *Conflict and Consensus*, pp. 196–7.
30. Molotov, *V bor'be za sotsializm*, pp. 484–5.
31. Molotov, V. M., *Stat'i i rechi 1935–1936*, pp. 12, 20–21, *et passim*. This speech is described by Haslam, *The Struggle for Collective Security*, p. 46, as 'exceptionally effusive *vis à vis* Germany'. See also Phillips, H. D., *Between the Revolution and the West: a Political Biography of Maxim M. Litvinov*, Boulder, CO: 1992, pp. 147–9.
32. The Earl of Avon, *The Eden Memoirs, Vol. 1, Facing the Dictators*, London: 1962, pp. 152–6; Maiskii, I. M. *Vospominaniya sovetskogo diplomata 1925–1945*, Moscow: 1987, p. 317; Borisov, Yu., ed., *DVP*, t. 18, Moscow: 1973, pp. 246–51.
33. Haslam, *The Struggle for Collective Security*, pp. 89–95.
34. See Watt, D. C., 'The Initiation of the Negotiations Leading to the Nazi–Soviet Pact', in Abramsky, C. and Williams, B., *Essays in Honour of E.H. Carr*, London: 1974, p. 154.
35. Molotov, *Stat'i i rechi*, pp. 168–79.
36. *FRUS: The Soviet Union 1933–1939*, pp. 286, 514–15; Haslam, *The Struggle for Collective Security*, pp. 93–4.
37. *Ibid.*, p. 95, *Documents Diplomatiques Français*, 2e série (1936–1939) (hereinafter *DDF*), t. 1, Paris: 1963, p. 69.
38. Degras, J., *Soviet Documents on Foreign Policy*, vol. 3, 1933–1941, Oxford: 1953, p. 168.
39. Molotov, *Stat'i i rechi*, pp. 229–230.
40. See above p. 133.
41. Degras, *Soviet Documents on Foreign Policy*, vol. 3, pp. 170–82.
42. Molotov, *Stat'i i rechi*, pp. 260–4.
43. Lambert, M. *et al.*, eds, *DGFP*, series C, vol. 6, London: 1983, pp. 274–77; PRO, FO, 371/21056, 282.

44. *DGFP*, series C, vol. 6, pp. 358–63, 387, 454, 462, 464, 514–15.
45. *Pravda*, 21 April 1937. For Stalin's speech to the plenum see Stalin, I., *O nedostatkakh partiinoi raboty i merakh likvidatsii trotskistkikh i inykh dvurushnikov*, Moscow: 1937.
46. See for instance Deev, G. K. *et al.*, eds, *DVP*, t. 21, Moscow: 1977, pp. 250–1, 58–9, 72–3. *Cf.* Haslam, J., *The Soviet Union and the Threat from the East: Moscow Tokyo and the Prelude to the Pacific War* (hereinafter *The Threat from the East*), Basingstoke: 1992, p. 108.
47. See above p. 146.
48. Gromyko, A., trans. Shukman, H., *Memories, from Stalin to Gorbachev*, London: 1989, pp. 30, 33, 404.
49. Komplektov, V. G. *et al.*, eds, *DVP 1939*, t. 22, kn. 1, Moscow: 1992, pp. 1–324, *passim*.
50. *RGAS-PI*, 17/3/985, 19, 27, 40, 41; Roshchin, A., 'Soviet Pre-war Diplomacy: Reminiscences of a Diplomat', *International Affairs*, December 1987, p. 118.
51. Chuev, *Molotov*, p. 133.
52. Haslam, J., 'Litvinov, Stalin and the Road not Taken', in Gorodetsky, G., ed., *Soviet Foreign Policy, 1917–1991: a Retrospective*, London: 1994, p. 57.
53. *Pravda*, 9 November 1938. Recent research suggests that there was significant Soviet mobilisation in late September 1938, Ragsdale, H., 'Soviet Actions during the Czechoslovakian Crisis of 1938', *Bulletin of the Kennan Institute*, vol. XV, no. 18, 1998.
54. Roberts, G., 'The Fall of Litvinov: a Revisionist View', *Journal of Contemporary History*, 1992, p. 643; Volkogonov, D., *Triumf i tragediya*, t. II, ch. I, pp. 11–16.
55. *XVIII S"ezd: sten. ot*, p. 15. The strict translation of *zagrebat' zhar chuzhimi rukami* is 'to rake the fire with someone else's hands' or metaphorically to 'make a cat's-paw of'.
56. Beloff, M., *The Foreign Policy of Soviet Russia*, vol. 2, p. 219.
57. There were 29 interviews in 1937, 24 in 1938 and 15 in 1939 up to the time of Litvinov's dismissal. See 'Stalin's Office Diary', *IA*, no. 4, 1995, pp. 15–72; nos. 5–6, 1995, pp. 5–64.
58. *FRUS: The Soviet Union 1933–1939*, pp. 567–82, 594–601, The excuse for bypassing Litvinov was that the matter had originated in *Amtorg*, the real reason being that Stalin and Molotov regarded it as a priority to secure credits from the United States, particularly for the purchase of armaments.
59. Woodward, E. L. and Butler, R., eds, *Documents on British Foreign Policy* (hereinafter *DBFP*), 3rd. series, vol. IV, London: 1949, pp. 511–12, 523–4, 568–70, vol. V, 1952, p. 235.
60. *FRUS: The Soviet Union 1933–1939*, p. 737.
61. Gnedin, E., 'V Narkomindele 1922–1939: Interv'yu s E.A. Gnedinym', *Pamyat'*, New York/Paris, 1981–1982, no. 5, p. 391.
62. Roshchin, A., 'Soviet Pre-war Diplomacy: Reminiscences of a Diplomat', pp. 113–19.
63. Roberts, G., 'The Infamous Encounter? The Merekalov–Weizsäcker Meeting of 17 April 1939', *Historical Journal*, vol. 35, no. 4, 1992, pp. 921–4; Roberts, G. *The Unholy Alliance: Stalin's Pact with Hitler*, London: 1989, pp. 124–7; Roberts, G., *The Soviet Union and the Origins of the Second World War*, Basingstoke: 1995, pp. 69–71.
64. 'Stalin's Office Diary', *IA*, nos. 5–6, 1995, pp. 33–36; *DVP 1939*, t. 22 kn. 1, pp. 208, 209, 220, 230, 246, 269, 270, 275–8, 283, 297.
65. Resis, A., 'The Fall of Litvinov: Harbinger of the German–Soviet Non-aggression Pact', *Europe–Asia Studies*, vol. 52, no. 1, 2000, pp. 36–47.
66. Roberts, 'The Fall of Litvinov,' pp. 651–2; Resis, A., 'The Fall of Litvinov', p. 46.
67. Gromyko, A. A. *et al.*, eds, *SSSR v bor'be za mir nakanune vtoroi mirovoi voiny: (sentyabr' 1938g.–avgust 1939g.): dokumenty i materialy* (hereinafter *SSSR v bor'be za mir*), Moscow: 1971, p. 333; *DVP*, t. 22, kn. 1, pp. 278–9, 291–2.
68. Resis, A., The Fall of Litvinov, p. 47; 'Stalin's Office Diary', *IA*, nos. 5–6, 1995, p. 35.
69. Trubnikov, V. I., 'Sovetskaya diplomatiya nakanune Velikoi Otechestvennoi voiny: usiliya po protivodeistviyu fashistskoi agressii', in *60 let so dnya nachala velikoi otechestvennoi voiny: voenno–istoricheskaya konferentsiya, spetsial'ni vypusk, Voenno–istoricheskii Zhurnal*, Moscow: 2001, p. 15.
70. Sheinis, Z., *Maksim Maksimovich Litvinov: revolyutsioner, diplomat, chelovek*, Moscow: 1989, pp. 360–362, quoted Haslam, *The Threat from the East*, p. 129. This meeting dated by Maiskii as 27 April is more likely to have been the meeting on 21 April. See 'Stalin's

Office Diary', *IA*, nos. 5–6, 1995, pp. 33–6. The reason for Stalin's anger seems to have been an unauthorised meeting between Maiskii and the Finnish Foreign Minister Erkko in Helsinki. See Nekrich, A. M. trans., Freeze, G. L., *Pariahs, Partners, Predators: German–Soviet Relations, 1922–1941*, New York: 1997, p. 109.

71. *Pravda*, 2 May 1939.
72. Gnedin, E., *Katastrofa i vtoroe rozhdenie*, Amsterdam: 1977, pp. 105–10, 111; Sheinis, *Maksim Maksimovich Litvinov*, pp. 363–4.
73. *DBFP*, 3rd series, vol. 5, pp. 400, 410, 542.
74. Phillips, *Between the Revolution and the West*, p. 166, quoting an interview with Litvinov's daughter; 'Stalin's Office diary', *IA*, nos. 5–6, 1995, p. 36.
75. *RGAS-PI*, 17/3/1009, 18, 19.
76. Sokolov, V., 'People's Commissar Maxim Litvinov', *International Affairs*, May 1991, p. 103.
77. *AVPRF*, 59/1/313/2154, 45.
78. Sheinis, *Maksim Maksimovich Litvinov*, pp. 363–4.
79. Roshchin, A., 'People's Commissariat for Foreign Affairs before World War II', *International Affairs*, May 1988, pp. 112–13.
80. Gnedin, *Katastrofa i vtoroe rozhdenie*, pp. 114–15.
81. Shevchenko, A. N., *Breaking with Moscow*, New York: 1985, pp. 147–8.
82. Phillips, *Between the Revolution and the West*, p. 171, quoting memo of a conversation between Litvinov and Sumner Welles, 1943, *U.S. National Archives*.
83. See for instance Shevchenko, *Breaking with Moscow*, p. 81.
84. Chuev, *Molotov*, pp. 332–3.
85. Roshchin, 'Peoples Commissariat for Foreign Affairs before World War II', pp. 113–14.
86. Quoted Sokolov, 'People's Commissar Maxim Litvinov', p. 104.
87. Uldricks, T. J., 'The Impact of the Great Purges on the People's Commissariat of Foreign Affairs', p. 191.
88. *FRUS: The Soviet Union 1933–1939*, pp. 770–2.
89. Miner, S. M., 'His Master's Voice: Viacheslav Mihailovich Molotov as Stalin's Foreign Commissar', in Craig, G. A. and Lowenheim, F. Z., *The Diplomats, 1939–1979*, Princeton, NJ: 1994, p. 69.
90. Raymond, *Conflict and Consensus*, pp. 190–6.
91. McSherry, J.E., *Stalin, Hitler and Europe*, vol. 1, *The Origins of World War II 1933–1939*, Arlington: 1968, pp. 41–2, 144–5.
92. Roberts, 'The Fall of Litvinov', pp. 639–57.
93. Gnedin makes clear that from early 1939 NarkomIndel and the Central Committee apparatus were sent a list of members of the Politburo and government who could receive the 'daily collection of most interesting telegrams of foreign correspondents', 'V narkomindele 1922–1939', p. 381.
94. For the latest contribution to this debate see Resis, 'The Fall of Litvinov', pp. 33–56.
95. McSherry, *Stalin, Hitler and Europe*, vol. 1, p. 156; Banac, I., ed., *The Diary of Georgi Dimitrov 1933–1949*, New Haven: 2003, p. 116.
96. *SSSR v bor'be za mir*, pp. 383–7; Carley, M. J., 'End of the "Low, Dishonest Decade": Failure of the Anglo-Franco Soviet Alliance in 1939', *Europe–Asia Studies*, vol. 45, no. 2, 1993, p. 305.
97. *Ibid.*, pp. 314, 319.
98. *PRO, FO*, 371/23065,180; *DBFP*, vol. 5, pp. 469–71, 483–6; *AVPRF* 5/1a/25/8, 6–8.
99. *DBFP*, vol. 5, p. 571.
100. Roshchin, 'Soviet Pre-war Diplomacy', p. 120.
101. *AVPRF*, 6/16/27/1, 7–10. In August, when the pact with Germany had been negotiated, Molotov told the French ambassador that the Soviet government considered that the 1935 Soviet–French Pact of Mutual Assistance was made void by the Franco-German Non-Aggression Declaration of December 1938, Namier, L. B., *Diplomatic Prelude*, London: 1948, p. 289.
102. *DBFP*, vol. 5, p. 568; *PRO, FO*, 371/23071, 243–4; Aster, S., *1939: The Making of the Second World War*, London: 1973, p. 182; *AVPRF*, 69/23/66/1, 39–40.

103. *AVPRF*, 6/1a/26/18, 19–20, 121; *DBFP*, vol. 5, pp. 589–90, 558–9, 567–8.
104. *DBFP*, vol. 5, p. 737; *AVPRF*, 6/16/27/1, 7–10.
105. *DBFP*, vol. 5, p. 710; *PRO, FO*, 371/23067, 126–30.
106. *DBFP*, vol. 5, p. 680, 702, 712; Strang, W., *Home and Abroad*, London: 1956, p. 168. For the Soviet account of this interview, recorded by Potemkin, which confirms the words of Molotov, which struck Seeds and Strang most forcibly see *AVPRF*, 6/1/1/2, 41–7. References to the League of Nations had been introduced by Chamberlain to allow Britain to limit its commitments. See Watson, D., 'Molotov's Apprenticeship in Foreign Policy: The Triple Alliance Negotiations in 1939', *Europe–Asia Studies*, vol. 52, no. 4, 2000, p. 701.
107. Carley, 'End of the "Low, Dishonest Decade" ', p. 324.
108. *DBFP*, vol. 5, p. 722; *PRO, FO*, 371/23067, 49–50.
109. *AVPRF*, 6/1a/26/18, 146–7.
110. *AVPRF*, 59/1/301/2075, 186–7. Unfortunately, Maiskii did not see Halifax until 12 June, the day the Foreign Office representative left. Maisky, *Who Helped Hitler*, London: 1964, pp. 140–1; *AVPRF*, 59/1/300/2077, 59–61. Chamberlain not only discouraged Halifax, but also refused to allow Eden who had met Molotov in 1935, to go.
111. Roberts, G., 'The Alliance that Failed: Moscow and the Triple Alliance Negotiations, 1939', *European History Quarterly*, vol. 26, no. 3, 1996, p. 402.
112. Hansard, *Parliamentary Debates*, vol. 348, London: 1939, col. 2205, 21 June; vol. 349, London: 1939, col. 5, 26 June; vol. 350, London: 1939, col. 2036, 31 July.
113. *DBFP*, vol. 6, pp. 2–4; Sontag, R. J. and Beddie, J. S., *Nazi–Soviet Relations 1939–1941: Documents from the Archives of the German Foreign Office* (hereinafter *Nazi–Soviet Relations*), Westport: 1976, p. 60; Bondarenko, A. P., ed., *God krizisa 1938–1939: dokumenty i materialy* (hereinafter *God krizisa*), Moscow: 1990, t. 2, p. 270.
114. *Pravda*, 1 September 1939.
115. According to Aster, *1939, the Making of the Second World War*, p. 268, Molotov's desk '*appeared mistakenly* to be on a raised dais' [my italics].
116. Strang, *Home and Abroad*, p.175; *PRO, FO*, 371/23071,14.
117. 'Stalin's Office Diary', *IA*, 1995, no. 6, pp. 37–41.
118. For Molotov's achievements at school see above pp. 5–6.
119. Strang, *Home and Abroad*, p. 174; *DBFP*, vol. 6, pp. 138–9.
120. Strang, *Home and Abroad*, p. 165.
121. *DBFP*, vol. 6, pp. 85–7; *PRO, FO*, 371/23069, 36–7; *AVPRF*, 6/1a/25/10, 14–15.
122. *DBFP*, vol. 6, pp. 89, 119; Strang, *Home and Abroad*, pp. 176–7.
123. *DBFP*, vol. 6., pp. 173–4, 179–84, 193–4, 208–9; *PRO, FO*, 371/23069, 56–7, 63–5; *God krizisa*, t. 2, pp. 76–7.
124. *DDF*, 2e série, (1936–1939) Paris: 1963, t. xvii, pp. 125–7, 151–3; *DBFP*, vol. 6, pp. 229–33.
125. *Ibid.* vol. 6, pp. 266–70; *PRO, FO*, 371/23069, 94–5; 23070, 61–4. The frequently cited paradigm for 'indirect aggression' was the Austrian *Anschluss* of 1938, see Raymond, *Conflict and Consensus*, pp. 579, 635; Poltavskii, M. A., *Diplomatiya imperializma: malye strany Europy 1938–1939gg.*, Moscow: 1973, *passim*.
126. *DBFP*, vol. 6, p. 277; *PRO, FO*, 371/23069, 94–5; 23070, 53–5; Strang, *Home and Abroad*, p. 179.
127. *PRO, FO*, 371/23070, 165; *DDF*, t. xvii, pp. 262–3.
128. *DBFP*, vol. 6, p. 314; *PRO, FO*, 371/32070, 85.
129. Strang, *Home and Abroad*, p. 180.
130. *DBFP*, vol. 6, pp. 308–10; *PRO, FO*, 371/23070, 46–8, 156–7; *DDF*, t. xvii, pp. 278, 192–9.
131. 'Anglo-French–Soviet Talks in Moscow 1939', *International Affairs*, October 1969, p. 62; Haslam, *The Struggle for Collective Security*, p. 221; *SSSR v bor'be za mir*, pp. 459, 471.
132. *PRO, FO*, 371/23070, 164; *DBFP*, vol. 6, p. 313; *AVPRF*, 6/1a/26/16, 70.
133. *DDF*, t. xvii, pp. 268, 312–17; *DBFP*, vol. 6, p. 311–12.

134. *DBFP*, vol. 6, p. 379.
135. Aster, *1939, The Making of the Second World War*, p. 284.
136. 'Anglo-French-Soviet Talks in Moscow in 1939', pp. 115–6.
137. *DBFP*, vol. 6, pp. 375–7; PRO, FO, 371/23070, 215–19.
138. *SSSR v bor'be za mir*, p. 496.
139. *DBFP*, vol. 6, pp. 422–6; PRO, FO, 371/23071, 132–5.
140. *DDF*, t. xvii, p. 388; PRO, Cab 27/625, FP (36) 54th. Meeting, 26 June.
141. *DBFP*, vol. 6, pp. 456–60; PRO, FO, 371/23071, 69–74; *DDF*, t. xvii, pp. 469–7; Jakobson, M., *The Diplomacy of the Winter War*, Cambridge MA.: 1951, p. 89.
142. *DDF*, t. xvii, p. 539.
143. *DBFP*, vol. 6, pp. 509–10, 521–4; PRO, FO, 371/23071, 126–7, 173–9.
144. PRO, FO, 371/23072, 64–7; Aster, *1939 The Making of the Second World War*, p. 296.
145. PRO, FO, 371/23072, 7; 23073, 35; *DBFP*, vol. 7, p. 45.
146. Maisky, *Who Helped Hitler*, pp. 165–7; Aster, *1939, The Making of the Second World War*, p. 291.
147. Volkogonov, *Triumf i tragediya*, t. 2, ch. 1, p. 19.
148. PRO, FO, 371/23074, 47–54; *DBFP*, vol. 6, pp. 570–4; Strang, *Home and Abroad*, pp. 187–8; AVPRF, 6/1a/26/18, 218.
149. See below p. 168. See also *Nazi–Soviet Relations*, pp. 32–4; *God krizisa*, t. 2, pp. 136–40.
150. Strang, *Home and Abroad*, pp. 187–8; *DBFP*, vol. 6, pp. 575, 592, 682–3; AVPRF, 69/23/66/1, 53.
151. *DBFP*, vol. 7, p. 46; PRO, FO, 371/23073, 37.
152. AVPRF, 6/1/3/1, 2–6; *God krizisa*, t. 2, pp. 159–63.
153. AVPRF, 6/1/3/1, 21.
154. *DBFP*, vol. 7, p. 384; Carley, 'End of the "Low Dishonest Decade"', p. 330; See below p. 168.
155. McSherry, *Stalin, Hitler and Europe*, vol. 1, pp. 224–5, 7, quoting Bonnet, G., *La Défense de la Paix, 1936–1940*, Geneva: 1948, vol. 2, p. 286.
156. *DBFP*, vol. 7, p. 385.
157. PRO, FO, 371/23073, 80–1; *DBFP*, vol. 7, pp. 142–3, 385.
158. PRO, FO, 371/23103, 289.
159. *DBFP*, vol. 7, p. 225; PRO, FO, 371/23073, 199.
160. *DDF*, t. xvii, pp. 515–16.
161. Craig, G. A., 'Totalitarian Approaches to Diplomatic Negotiations', in Sorkisson, A. D., *Studies in Diplomatic History and Historiography in Honour of G.P. Gooch*, London: 1961, pp. 120–5.
162. Hayter, Sir W., *The Diplomacy of the Great Powers*, London: 1960, p. 22.
163. Craig, 'Totalitarian Approaches …', p. 122.
164. *Cf.* Hilger and Meyer, *The Incompatible Allies*, p. 290.

10　The Nazi–Soviet Pact and After 1939–1941

1. See below p. 180.
2. Watson, *Molotov and Soviet Government*, pp. 184–5.
3. PRO, FO, 371/24852, 28, 29.
4. *Nazi–Soviet Relations*, pp. 2–5.
5. *God krizisa*, t. 1, p. 459.
6. I have been unable to find any published dispatches of Litvinov that report the initial stages of the negotiations with Great Britain and France to the Soviet embassy.
7. Bezymenskii, L. A., 'Sovetsko–Germanskie dogovory 1939g.: novye dokumenty i starye problemy', *Novaya i Noveishaya Istoriya*, (hereinafter *NNI*) no. 4, 1998, p. 15.

8. *Nazi–Soviet Relations*, pp. 5–9; *God krizisa*, t. 1, pp. 482–4. For Molotov's understanding of foreign languages see above p. 5.
9. Haslam, J., 'Soviet–German Relations and the Origins of the Second World War: The Jury is Still Out', *Journal of Modern History*, vol. 69, 1997, p. 794.
10. *DGFP*, vol. 6, pp. 494–500.
11. Kershaw, I., *Hitler 1936–1945: Nemesis*, London: 2001, p. 192.
12. *Nazi–Soviet Relations*, pp. 15–17.
13. *Izvetsiya*, 1 June 1939.
14. Aster, *1939, The Making of the Second World War*, p. 262.
15. *Nazi–Soviet Relations*, pp. 17–28; Raymond, *Conflict and Consensus*, p. 589.
16. *Ibid.*, p. 590; *Nazi–Soviet Relations*, pp. 21–6; Bezymenskii, 'Sovetsko–Germanskie dogovory 1939g.', p. 17.
17. The non-aggression pact of Rapallo 1926, renewed in Berlin in 1933.
18. U.S. Department of State, *FRUS, Diplomatic Papers 1939*, vol. 1, Washington, DC: 1952, pp. 327–9.
19. *Nazi–Soviet Relations*, pp. 26–30; *God krizisa*, t. 2, pp. 65–7.
20. *Ibid.*, pp. 136–40; *Nazi–Soviet Relations*, pp. 32–6.
21. *God krizisa*, t. 2, p. 145; Bezymenskii, 'Sovetsko–Germanskie dogovory 1939g.', p. 18.
22. *God krizisa*, t. 2, pp. 157–8.
23. *Nazi–Soviet Relations*, pp. 39–41, 42–4, 46–8; *God krizisa*, t. 2, pp. 159–63; *FRUS Diplomatic Papers 1939*, vol. 1, p. 332.
24. *God krizisa*, t. 2, pp. 178–80.
25. *Ibid.*, p. 184; *Nazi–Soviet Relations*, pp. 48–9.
26. See Roberts, G., 'The Soviet Decision for a Pact with Nazi-Germany', *Europe–Asia Studies*, vol. 44, no. 1, 1992, p. 68.
27. *God krizisa*, t. 2, pp. 185–8, 208.
28. *Nazi–Soviet Relations*, p. 48.
29. *Ibid.*, pp. 52–6; *God krizisa*, t. 2, pp. 229–33; Roberts, 'The Soviet Decision for a Pact', p. 69.
30. *DGFP*, vol. 7, London: 1956, p. 87; *Nazi–Soviet Relations*, p. 57.
31. *Ibid.*, p. 58.
32. Bezymenskii, 'Sovetsko–Germanskie dogovory 1939g.', p. 19; 'Stalin's Office Diary', *IA*, No. 6, 1995, pp. 37–41.
33. *Nazi–Soviet Relations*, pp. 59–61; *God krizisa*, t. 2, pp. 269–73.
34. *DGFP*, vol. 7, pp. 132–3.
35. *Nazi–Soviet Relations*, pp. 61–3; *God krizisa*, t. 2, pp. 274–8; Bezymenskii, 'Sovetsko–Germanskie dogovory 1939g.', p. 19.
36. *DGFP*, vol. 7, p.158.
37. 'Stalin's Office Diary', *IA*, no. 6, 1995, p. 48.
38. *Nazi–Soviet Relations*, pp. 66–7; *God krizisa*, t. 2, p. 302. Bezymenskii, 'Sovetsko–Germanskie dogovory 1939g.', pp. 19–20.
39. *Nazi–Soviet Relations*, pp. 68–9; God krizisa, t. 2, p. 303.
40. ' "Avtobiograficheskii zametki" V. N. Pavlova – perevodchika I. V. Stalina', *NNI*, no. 4, 2000, p. 98.
41. Hilger and Meyer, *The Incompatible Allies*, p. 303.
42. 'Predistoriya 1939 goda', *Svobodnaya mysl'*, no. 7, 1999, p. 108.
43. *DGFP*, vol. 7, pp. 295–6.
44. *Nazi–Soviet Relations*, pp. 72–6.
45. Hilger and Meyer, *The Incompatible Allies*, p. 301.
46. Bezymenskii, 'Sovetsko–Germanskie dogovory 1939g.', pp. 3, 20–1.
47. Bezymenskii, L., 'The Secret Protocols of 1939 as a Problem of Soviet Historiography', in Gorodetsky, G., ed., *Soviet Foreign Policy 1917–1991: a Retrospective* London: 1994, p. 76.

48. Roberts, 'The Soviet Decision for a Pact', p. 71. See for instance 'Sobytiya 1939 Goda–Vzglyad s Poluvekovoi Distantsii', *Pravda*, 18 August 1989.
49. 'Vnov' o dogovore 1939 goda', *Vestnik ministerstva inostrannykh del SSSR*, 28 February 1991, pp. 56–63; Bezymenskii, L. A., 'Sekretnye protokoly 1939g. kak problema sovetskoi istoriografii', *Rossiya i sovremennyi mir*, no. 1(10) 1996, pp. 143–4.
50. Bezymenskii, 'Sovetsko–Germanskie dogovory 1939g.', p. 3. The Soviet originals were published for the first time in 1993, see 'Sovetsko–Germanskie dokumenty 1939–1941gg. iz arkhiva TsK KPSS,' *NNI*, no. 1 1993, pp. 83–95.
51. 'Stalin's Office Diary', *IA*, no. 6, 1995, p. 49.
52. Chuev, *Molotov*, pp. 25–6.
53. Raymond, *Conflict and Consensus*, p. 622; *DGFP*, vol. 7, pp. 350, 439–40; Roberts, 'The Soviet Decision for a Pact', p. 72.
54. *Pravda*, 1 September 1939.
55. 'Vnov' o dogovore 1939 goda', p. 56.
56. *DGFP*, vol. VII, pp. 296, 362–3, 379–80, 386–7, 408, 409, 419–20, 438–9, 446, 460, 466, 494, 509.
57. Sevestyanov, P., *Before the Nazi Invasion: Soviet Diplomacy in September 1939–June 1941*, Moscow: 1981, p. 75; Roberts, *The Unholy Alliance*, p. 157; Beloff. M., *The Foreign Policy of Soviet Russia*, vol. 2, 1936–41, London: 1949, pp. 280–2; McSherry, *Stalin, Hitler and Europe*, vol. 1, pp. 248–9, quoting *The Polish White Book*, London: 1940, pp. 187–8, 209–10.
58. *Nazi–Soviet Relations*, pp. 86–7.
59. Roberts, *The Unholy Alliance*, pp. 158–9.
60. *Nazi–Soviet Relations*, pp. 90–91; Roberts, *The Unholy Alliance*, p. 159.
61. *Nazi–Soviet Relations*, pp. 89–96.
62. Degras, *Soviet Documents on Foreign Policy*, vol. 3, pp. 374–6.
63. Nevezhin, V. A., 'The Making of Propaganda Concerning USSR Foreign Policy 1939–1941', in Rosenfeldt, N. E., Jensen, B. and Kulavig, E., *Mechanisms of Power in the Soviet Union*, Basingstoke: 2000, p. 154.
64. *Izvestiya*, 18 September 1939; Degras, *Soviet Documents on Foreign Policy*, vol. 3, p. 374.
65. Beloff, *The Foreign Policy of Soviet Russia*, vol. 2, p. 283.
66. *Izvestiya*, 18 September 1939.
67. Weinberg, G. L., *Germany and the Soviet Union, 1939–1941*, Leiden: 1954, p. 56.
68. Vinton, L., 'The Katyn Documents: Politics and History', Radio Free Europe/Radio Liberty *Research Report*, vol. 2, no. 4, 1993 p. 23.
69. Chuev, *Molotov*, p. 103.
70. *DGFP*, vol. VIII, London: 1954, pp. 104–5, 109–10, 122–3.
71. *Nazi–Soviet Relations*, p. 101; Nekrich, *Pariahs, Partners, Predators*, p. 131.
72. *Nazi–Soviet Relations*, p. 103, 105–7; Fleischhauer, I., 'The Molotov–Ribbentrop Pact: the German Version', *International Affairs*, August 1991, pp. 119, 120, 122.
73. *Nazi–Soviet Relations*, p. 108.
74. *Soviet Peace Policy*, pp. 33–4.
75. *DGFP*, vol. VIII, pp. 306, 310.
76. Smulkstys, J., 'The Incorporation of the Baltic States in the Soviet Union', *Lituanus*, vol. 14, no. 2, 1968, pp. 25–6.
77. Miner, 'His Master's Voice', p. 76.
78. Gubergrits, A., ed., *Ot pakta Molotova–Ribbentropa do dogovora o basakh*, Talinin: 1990, p. 44.
79. *DGFP*, vol. VI, p. 1076, 806. See Tarulis, A. N., *Soviet Policy towards the Baltic States 1918–1940*, Notre Dame: 1959, pp. 119–20, 148.
80. Testimony of Estonian Foreign Minister, K. Selter, in 'Documents: Negotiating in the Kremlin: the Estonian Experience of 1939', *Lituanus*, vol. 14, no. 2, 1968, p. 55; Tarulis, *Soviet Policy towards the Baltic States*, pp. 148–9. For these negotiations see also Mel'tyukhov, M. I., 'Narashchivanie sovetskogo voennogo prisutstviya v pribaltike v 1939–1941 godakh', *Otechestvennaya istoriya*, no. 4, 1999, p. 48.

81. Tarulis, *Soviet Policy Towards the Baltic States*, p. 150; 'Negotiating in the Kremlin: the Estonian Experience of 1939', p. 67.
82. Dallin, D. J., *Soviet Russia's Foreign Policy, 1939–1942*, New Haven: 1942, p. 83; Tarulis, *Soviet Policy Towards the Baltic States*, p. 151.
83. *Ibid.*, p. 152.
84. *Izvestiya*, 18 September 1939. McSherry, J.E., *Stalin, Hitler and Europe, vol. 2, The Imbalance of Power 1939–1941*, Arlington: 1970, p. 11; 'Negotiating in the Kremlin: the Estonian Experience of 1939', pp. 57–60, 78; *Ot pakta Molotova – Ribbentropa do dogovora o basakh*, pp. 134–43, 167–73, 173–180, 180–9.
85. Dallin, *Soviet Russia's Foreign Policy*, p. 86.
86. Tarulis, *Soviet Policy Towards the Baltic States*, p. 155. See also Mel'tyukhov, 'Narashchivanie sovetskogo voennogo prisutstviya v pribaltike v 1939–1941 godakh', p. 51.
87. Beloff, *The Foreign Policy of Soviet Russia*, vol. 2, p. 280; Tarulis, *Soviet Policy Towards the Baltic States*, p. 154.
88. *Ibid.*, p. 155.
89. Smulkstys, 'The Incorporation of the Baltic States in the Soviet Union', p. 27.
90. Roberts, *The Unholy Alliance*, p. 163; Beloff, *The Foreign Policy of Soviet Russia*, vol. 2, p. 186.
91. *Nazi–Soviet Relations*, p. 112.
92. *Ibid.*, p. 114.
93. *Ibid.*, p. 118; Tarulis, *Soviet Policy Towards the Baltic States*, pp. 138–42.
94. *Ibid.*, p. 157.
95. Kaslas, B. J., 'The Lithuanian Strip in Soviet–German Secret Diplomacy, 1939–1941', *Journal of Baltic Studies*, vol. 4, no. 3, 1973, p. 215.
96. *Soviet Peace Policy*, p. 36.
97. Mel'tyukhov, 'Narashchivanie sovetskogo voennogo prisutstviya v pribaltike v 1939–1941 godakh', pp. 53–4.
98. Tarulis, *Soviet Policy Towards the Baltic States*, pp. 162–3, 165; *FRUS: the Soviet Union 1933–1939*, p. 966.
99. McSherry, *Stalin, Hitler and Europe, vol. 2*, pp. 90–97; Mel'tyukhov, 'Narashchivanie sovetskogo voennogo prisutstviya v pribaltike v 1939–1941 godakh', pp. 56–68; 'The Baltic Countries Join the Soviet Union (Documents on the USSR's Relations with the Baltic Countries in 1939 and 1940),' *International Affairs*, no. 4, April 1990, pp. 97–124.
100. *Nazi–Soviet Relations*, p. 124.
101. Sevestyanov, *Before the Nazi Invasion*, p. 197.
102. Roberts, *The Unholy Alliance*, p. 168–9.
103. See documents published in Morozova, I. and Takhnenko, G., ' "The Winter War": Documents on Soviet–Finnish Relations 1939–40', *International Affairs*, no. 9, 1989, pp. 53–4 and McSherry, *Stalin. Hitler and Europe, vol. 2*, p. 17; Van Dyke, C., *The Soviet Invasion of Finland 1939–1940*, London: 1997, pp. 4, 6; Tanner, V., *The Winter War: Finland against Russia, 1939–1940*, Stanford: 1950, pp. 74–6.
104. Degras, *Soviet Documents on Foreign Policy*, vol. 3, pp. 337–9; Tanner, *The Winter War*, p. 77.
105. Jakobson, M. *The Diplomacy of the Winter War*, pp. 105–6.
106. *Ibid.*, p.120.
107. Dallin, *Soviet Russia's Foreign Policy*, p. 119.
108. *Ibid.*, pp. 115–21; *Nazi–Soviet Relations*, p. 110; *DGFP*, vol. VIII, pp. 124–5.
109. *Soviet Peace Policy*, pp. 38–42.
110. *DGFP*, vol. VIII, p. 427. McSherry, *Stalin, Hitler and Europe, vol. 2*, p. 32; Upton, A. F., *Finland 1939–1940*, London: 1974, p. 39.
111. Tanner, *The Winter War*, pp. 66–7; Upton, *Finland 1939–1940*, p. 40. For an overview of these negotiations see Van Dyke, *The Soviet Invasion of Finland 1939–1940*, pp. 14–20; Jakobson, *The Diplomacy of the Winter War*, p. 135.
112. McSherry, *Stalin, Hitler and Europe, vol. 2*, pp. 34–5.
113. Kollontai, A., ' "Seven Shots" in the Winter of 1939', *International Affairs*, January 1990, pp. 185–6.

114. Jakobson, *The Diplomacy of the Winter War*, pp. 147–54; McSherry, *Stalin, Hitler and Europe, vol. 2*, pp. 37–9; Dallin, *Soviet Russia's Foreign Policy*, pp. 130–3.
115. Degras, *Soviet Documents on Foreign Policy*, vol. 3, pp. 404–5.
116. Dallin, *Soviet Russia's Foreign Policy*, pp. 131–2.
117. Hull, C., *The Memoirs of Cordell Hull*, New York: 1948, p. 706.
118. Talbot, S., ed., *Khrushchev Remembers*, London: 1971, p. 151.
119. Jakobson, *The Diplomacy of the Winter War*, p. 164.
120. Degras, *Soviet Documents on Foreign Policy*, vol. 3, p. 410.
121. McSherry, *Stalin, Hitler and Europe, vol. 2*, pp. 41–4; Dallin, *Soviet Russia's Foreign Policy*, pp. 133–4, 143, 149–151; Van Dyke, *The Soviet Invasion of Finland 1939–1940*, pp. 71–72.
122. Mamedov, G. *et al.*, eds, *DVP*, t. XXIII, kn. 2, ch. 1, Moscow: 1998, pp. 441–2.
123. *DGFP*, vol. VIII, p. 644.
124. Dallin, *Soviet Russia's Foreign Policy*, pp. 182–3.
125. Jakobson, *The Diplomacy of the Winter War*, p. 216.
126. Sokolov, V. V., 'K 200-letiyu MID ROSSII', *Diplomaticheskii Vestnik*, no. 7, 2002, p. 147.
127. Dallin, *Soviet Russia's Foreign Policy*, pp. 181, 184.
128. Quoted, Tanner, *The Winter War: Finland against Russia, 1939–1940*, p. 125.
129. Jakobson, *The Diplomacy of the Winter War*, p. 218.
130. *Ibid.*, pp. 237–8.
131. *Ibid.*, p. 250.
132. McSherry, *Stalin, Hitler and Europe, vol. 2*, pp. 48–9, 62–5; Van Dyke, *The Soviet Invasion of Finland 1939–1940*, pp. 125–6; Upton, *Finland 1939–1940*, pp. 138–48.
133. Quoted *Ibid.*, p. 140.
134. Molotov, *Soviet Peace Policy*, p. 57.
135. Van Dyke, *The Soviet Invasion of Finland 1939–1940*, p. 214.
136. Molotov, *Soviet Peace Policy*, pp. 55, 60.
137. Upton, *Finland 1939–1940*, pp. 150–157.
138. Dallin, *Soviet Russia's Foreign Policy*, p. 196 quoting *Blue-White Book of Finland*.
139. McSherry, *Stalin, Hitler and Europe, vol. 2*, p. 196.
140. Van Dyke, *The Soviet Invasion of Finland 1939–1940*, p. 190.
141. Mar'ina, V. V., 'Dnevnik G. Dimitrova', *Voprosy Istorii*, no. 7, 2000, p. 41. The text of Molotov's speech is not available but the tenor was presumably the same as that to the Supreme Soviet, two days later.
142. Sheinis, *Maksim Maksimovich Litvinov*, pp. 367–8; Haslam, J., 'Soviet Foreign Policy 1939–1941: Isolation and Expansion', *Soviet Union/Union Soviétique*, vol. 18, 1991, pp. 116–17.
143. *Izvestiya*, 2 August 1940.
144. Dallin, *Soviet Russia's Foreign Policy*, pp. 286–96.
145. McSherry, *Stalin, Hitler and Europe, vol. 2*, pp. 186–7.
146. *Ibid.*, pp. 84–7; Sipols, V. Ya., 'Torgovo-ekonomicheskie otnosheniya mezhdu SSSR i Germaniei v 1939–1941gg. v svete novykh arkhivnykh dokumnetov', *NNI*, no. 2, 1997, p. 31; Nekrich, *Pariahs, Partners, Predators*, pp. 149, 155–6.
147. Dallin, *Soviet Russia's Foreign Policy*, pp. 200–201.
148. *Nazi–Soviet Relations*, pp. 134–7.
149. *Ibid.*, pp. 138–9; Nekrich, *Pariahs, Partners, Predators*, pp. 176–7, 183–5.
150. *Ibid.*, pp. 177–81; Haslam, 'Soviet Foreign Policy 1939–41: Isolation and Expansion', pp. 112–16; *Nazi–Soviet Relations*, pp. 157–64.
151. McSherry, *Stalin, Hitler and Europe vol. 2*, pp. 112–24; Dallin, *Soviet Russia's Foreign Policy*, pp. 233–6; Degras, *Soviet Documents on Foreign Policy*, vol. 3, pp. 458–61.
152. Dallin, *Soviet Russia's Foreign Policy*, pp. 241–53; *Nazi–Soviet Relations*, p. 154.
153. See above p. 175.
154. Kaslas, 'The Lithuanian Strip in Soviet–German Secret Diplomacy, 1939–1941', pp. 213, 218–20; Weinberg, *Germany and the Soviet Union*, p. 130; *Nazi–Soviet Relations*, pp. 166, 174, 176, 178–88, 189–94.

155. *Ibid.*, pp. 206–7; Weinberg, *Germany and the Soviet Union*, pp. 128–36.
156. *Ibid.*, p. 136; *Nazi–Soviet Relations*, pp. 195–9, 201–3.
157. *Ibid.*, pp. 207–13.
158. *Ibid.*, pp. 214–15. Schulenburg explained the delay because of the necessity of translating the letter: 'translations made by the Soviets are bad and full of inaccuracies'.
159. Weinberg, *Germany and the Soviet Union*, p. 141.
160. *Ibid.*, p. 140; Kershaw, *Hitler 1936–1945: Nemesis*, pp. 332–4.
161. Bezymenskii, L. A., 'Direktivy I. V. Stalina V. M. Molotovu pered poezdkoi v Berlin v noyabre 1940g.', *NNI*, no. 4, 1995, pp.76–9. *Cf.* Roberts, G., 'Stalin, the Pact with Germany and the Origins of Postwar Soviet Diplomatic Historiography', *Journal of Cold War Studies*, vol. 4, no. 2, 2002, p. 99.
162. Dallin, *Soviet Russia's Foreign Policy*, p. 270, 273. For the British reaction see Watson, D., 'Molotov, the Making of the Grand Alliance and the Second Front 1939–1942', *Europe–Asia Studies*, vol. 54, no. 1, 2002, pp. 53–4.
163. Waddington, G. T., 'Ribbentrop and the Soviet Union, 1937–1941', in Erickson, J. and Dilks, D., *Barbarossa: the Axis and the Allies*, Edinburgh: 1994, pp. 21–2.
164. Dallin, *Soviet Russia's Foreign Policy*, p. 271 estimates the size of the group as 32; *Izvestiya*, 13 November 1940, Bezymenskii, L. A., 'Vizit V. M. Molotova v Berlin v noyabre 1940g. v svete novykh dokumentov', *NNI*, no. 6, 1995, p. 131; Kershaw, *Hitler 1936–1945: Nemesis*, p. 334 states that the *Internationale* was not played, to avoid the possibility of the Berliners, familiar with the words, joining in.
165. Volkov, V. K. 'Sovetsko–germanskie otnosheniya vo vtoroi polovine 1940 goda', *Voprosy istorii*, no. 2, 1997, pp. 8–9, quoting *APRF*, 56/1/1161, 147–55; Bezymenskii, 'Direktivy I.V.Stalina V.M. Molotovu pered poezdkoi v Berlin v noyabre 1940g.', pp. 76–9.
166. See Bezymenskii, L., *Gitler i Stalin pered skhvatkoi*, Moscow: 2000, pp. 346–50; Gorlov, S. A., ed., 'Perepiska V.M. Molotova s I.V. Stalinym noyabr' 1940 goda', *Voenno–istoricheskii Zhurnal*, no. 9, 1992, pp. 18–21. Stalin's Office Diary contains no record of Molotov meeting him there in the days immediately prior to the visit.
167. Pechatnov, V. O., trans. Zubok, V. M. ' "The Allies are Pressing on You to Break Your Will …" Foreign Policy Correspondence between Stalin and Molotov and Other Politburo Members, September 1945-December 1946', *Cold War International History Project, Working Paper no. 26*, Washington, DC: 1999, p. 1. See also Zubok, V., and Pleshakov, C., *Inside the Kremlin's Cold War: from Stalin to Khrushchev*, Cambridge MA: 1996, pp. 86–7.
168. Schmidt, P., *Statist auf diplomatischer Bühne 1923–1945*, Bonn: 1954, pp. 515–16.
169. *Nazi–Soviet Relations*, pp. 217–25; The Soviet record of the discussions from *APRF* are printed in Sevost'yanov, G. N., 'Poezdka V. M. Molotova v Berlin v noyabre 1940 g.', *NNI*, no. 5, 1993, pp. 69–99. They make no reference to Molotov's question about the USSR turning south, *ibid.*, pp. 69–73.
170. 'Perepiska V. M. Molotova s I. V. Stalinym noyabr' 1940 goda', p. 18.
171. *Nazi–Soviet Relations*, pp. 226–32.
172. Schmidt, *Statist auf diplomatischer Bühne*, pp. 520–1.
173. *Nazi–Soviet Relations*, pp. 232–4; 'Poezdka V.M.Molotova v Berlin v noyabre 1940 g.', pp. 74–8. The Soviet record of these discussions is far less detailed than the German.
174. Berezhkov, V., *History in the Making (Memoirs of World War II Diplomacy)*, Moscow: 1998, pp. 26–7.
175. Hilger and Meyer, *The Incompatible Allies*, pp. 291, 322.
176. 'Perepiska V. M. Molotova s I. V. Stalinym noyabr' 1940 goda', pp. 19–20.
177. *Nazi–Soviet Relations*, pp. 234–47; 'Perepiska V. M. Molotova s I. V. Stalinym noyabr' 1940 goda,' p. 20; 'Poezdka V. M. Molotova v Berlin v noyabre 1940 g.,' pp. 80–88.
178. 'Perepiska V. M. Molotova s I. V. Stalinym Noyabr' 1940 goda,' p. 20.
179. See below p. 199. See also Berezhkov, V. M., *S diplomaticheskoi missiei v Berlin 1940–1941*, Moscow: 1966, p. 47.
180. *Nazi–Soviet Relations*, pp. 247–54; 'Poezdka V. M. Molotova v Berlin v noyabre 1940 g.', pp. 88–94.

322   Notes to Pages 186–190

181. Bezymenskii, L., 'On the Eve: Vyacheslav Molotov's Talks in Berlin in November 1940',
     International Affairs, no. 9, 1991, p. 85.
182. Chuev, *Molotov*, p. 40.
183. Sipols, 'Torgovo-ekonomicheskie otnosheniya mezhdu SSSR i Germaniei v 1939–1941gg.
     v svete novykh arkhivnykh dokumentov', p. 37.
184. Sevestyanov, *Before the Nazi Invasion*, p. 274.
185. *Pravda*, 15 November 1940.
186. Gorlov, S. A., 'Peregovory V. M. Molotova v Berlin v noyabre 1940 goda',
     Voenno–istoricheskii Zhurnal, no. 6–7, 1992, p. 46.
187. 'Perepiska V. M. Molotova s I. V. Stalinym noyabr' 1940 goda', pp. 20–1.
188. Sipols, V. Ya., *Tainy diplomaticheskie kanun Velikoi Otechestvennoi Voiny*, Moscow: 1997,
     p. 275.
189. McSherry, *Stalin, Hitler and Europe, vol. 2*, pp. 174–5.

11   The Great Patriotic War

1. Gorodetsky, *Grand Delusion*, pp. 102–4; *Nazi–Soviet Relations*, pp. 270–1, 274, 277–9.
2. Gorodetsky, *Grand Delusion*, pp. 144–150; McSherry, *Stalin, Hitler and Europe, vol. 2*,
   pp. 209–11.
3. 'Kanun voiny: preduprezhdeniya diplomatov', *Vestnik MID*, no. 8 (66), 30 April 1990,
   pp. 76–7.
4. Kuznetsov, N., 'Voennoi-Morskoi Flot nakanune Velikoi Otechestvennoi voiny', p. 73.
5. Assarsen, V., 'The Moscow Diplomatic Corps in 1941', *International Affairs*, July 1991, p. 127.
6. Gorodetsky, *Grand Delusion*, pp. 190–8; Chuev, *Molotov*, p. 39.
7. *DVP*, t. 23, kn. 2, ch. 2, Moscow: 1998, pp. 631–3.
8. Nevezhin, V. A., 'Stalin's 5 May Addresses: the Experience of Interpretation', *Journal of
   Slavic Military Studies*, vol. 11, no. 1, 1998, p. 132.
9. *Ibid.*, p. 137, quoting Lyashchenko, N.G., 'S ognem i krov'yu popolam ...',
   Voenno-istoricheskii Zhurnal, no. 2, 1995, p. 23.
10. *RGAS-PI*, 17/3/1039, 10.
11. *Izvestiya*, 7 May 1941.
12. *Nazi–Soviet Relations*, p. 335.
13. Gorodetsky, *Grand Delusion*, p. 211; Nekrich, *Pariahs, Partners, Predators*, p. 223.
14. *Nazi–Soviet Relations*, pp. 345–6; McSherry, *Stalin, Hitler and Europe, vol. 2*, p. 233.
15. *The Times*, 20 June 1941; Dallin, *Soviet Russia's Foreign Policy, 1939–1942*, p. 375.
16. Hilger and Meyer, *The Incompatible Allies*, pp. 335–6; *Nazi–Soviet Relations, 1939–1941*,
    pp. 355–6; *DVP*, t. XXIII, kn. 2, ch. 2, pp. 751–2.
17. Gor'kov, Yu., *Gosudarstvennyi komitet oborony postanovlyaet (1941–1945): tsifry, dokumenty*,
    Moscow: 2002, p. 17; Zhukov, G.K., *Vospominaniya i razmyshleniya*, t. 2 , Moscow: 1990,
    pp. 8–10.
18. *DVP*, t. XXIII, kn. 2, ch. 2, pp. 753–4; Hilger and Meyer, *The Incompatible Allies*, p. 336;
    Chuev, *Molotov*, p.58.
19. Shakhurin, A. I. 'Aviatsionnaya promyshlennost' nakanune i v gody Velikoi
    Otechestvennoi voiny', in Pospelov, P. N., ed., *Sovetskii tyl v Velikoi Otechestvennoi voine*,
    t. 2, Moscow: 1974, p. 77.
20. Erickson, J., *The Road to Stalingrad: Stalin's War with Germany*, vol. 1, London: 1985,
    pp. 162–77, Gor'kov, *Gosudarstvennyi komitet oborony postanovlyaet*, p. 17; Zhukov,
    Vospominaniya, t. 2, p. 10.
21. 'Iz vospominanii o voennykh godakh', *Politicheskoe Obrazovanie*, no. 9, 1988, p. 74.
22. Chuev, *Molotov*, p. 59; Banac, ed., *The Diary of Georgi Dimitrov*, pp. 166–7.
23. Molotov's halting delivery was commented on by a number of listeners. See for
    instance, Werth, A., *Russia at War 1941–1945*, London: 1964, p. 162; Erickson, *The Road
    to Stalingrad*, p. 177.
24. *DVP*, t. XXIII, kn. 2, ch. 2, pp. 764–5.

25. Assarsen, V., 'The Moscow Diplomatic Corps in 1941', p. 126.
26. Erickson, *The Road to Stalingrad*, p. 177.
27. Overy, R., *Russia's War*, London: 1997, p. 74; Radzinsky, E., *Stalin*, London: 1996, p. 447.
28. Erickson, *The Road to Stalingrad*, p. 191; Watson, *Molotov and Soviet Government*, pp. 104–8.
29. Gor'kov, *Gosudarstvennyi komitet oborony postanovlyaet*, pp. 494–5, 501–2 citing *RGAS-PI*, 644/2/3, 23–6; Erickson, *The Road to Stalingrad*, p. 191; Zhukov, *Vospominaniya*, t. 2, pp. 12, 70, 72.
30. 'Stalin's Office Diary', *IA*, no. 2, 1996, p. 54.
31. *PRO, FO*, 371/29466 N3231/3/38.
32. Chuev, *Molotov*, p. 59; Mikoyan, *Tak bylo*, p. 391. See Main, S.J., 'Stalin in June 1941: A Comment on Cynthia Roberts', *Europe–Asia Studies*, vol. 48, no. 5, 1996, pp. 837–9; 'Stalin's Office Diary', *IA*, no. 2, 1996, p. 54.
33. Mikoyan, *Tak bylo*, pp. 389–90; Chuev, *Molotov*, pp. 58–60; Radzinsky, *Stalin*, pp. 451–2, quoting Chadaev's manuscript diary. This incident is dated as 29 June by Mikoyan and 27 June by Chadaev, but from 'Stalin's Office Diary', *IA*, no. 2, 1996, p. 54, can be dated as 28 June.
34. Radzinsky, *Stalin*, pp. 451–4.
35. Beria, S., *Beria, My Father: Inside Stalin's Kremlin*, London: 1999, pp. 70, 324.
36. Mikoyan, *Tak bylo*, p. 391.
37. *Ibid.*; Mikoyan, S., 'Barbarossa and the Soviet Leadership', in Erickson and Dilks, eds, *Barbarossa: the Axis and the Allies*, p. 128; Radzinsky, *Stalin*, p. 455.
38. Gor'kov, *Gosudarstvennyi komitet oborony postanovlyaet*, p. 39.
39. *RGAS-PI*, 17/3/1041, no. 130; *Vedomosti Verkhovnogo Soveta SSSR* (hereinafter *VVS*), no. 31, 6 July 1941.
40. Medvedev, *All Stalin's Men*, p. 92; Zalesskii, *Imperiya Stalina*, p. 325.
41. *Voenno-istoricheskii Zhurnal*, no. 9, 1988, pp. 26–8.
42. *Izvestiya TsK*, no. 9, 1990, p. 209.
43. *RGAS-PI*, 558/11/492, 29–33.
44. Chuev, *Molotov*, p. 63; Erickson, *The Road to Stalingrad*, pp. 262–3; *Izvestiya TsK*, no. 9, 1990, p. 209.
45. *Ibid.*, pp. 211–12.
46. Courtois, S., Werth, N. *et al.*, *The Black Book of Communism: Crimes Terror and Repression*, Cambridge, MA: 1999, p. 218.
47. *Izvestiya TsK*, no. 10, 1990, p. 217.
48. Medvedev, *All Stalin's Men*, p. 92; Erickson, *The Road to Stalingrad*, pp. 306–8; Zhukov, K., 'Vospominaniya komanduyushchego frontom', in *Bitva za Moskvu*, Moscow: 1966, pp. 55–77.
49. See Watson, D., 'Molotov, the Making of the Grand Alliance and the Second Front, 1939–1942', *Europe–Asia Studies*, vol. 54, no. 1, 2002, p. 56.
50. Sherwood, R.E., *The White House Papers of Harry Hopkins*, vol. 1, London: 1949, pp. 332–34.
51. *Izvestiya TsK*, no. 12, 1990, p. 217.
52. *PRO, FO*, 181/962/3; 371/29558, 123, quoted Gorodetsky, G., *Sir Stafford Cripps Mission to Moscow, 1940–1942*, Cambridge: 1984, p. 251.
53. *Neizvestnaya Rossiya XX vek*, t. III, Moscow: 1993, p. 177; Barber, J., 'The Moscow Crisis of October 1941', in Cooper, Perrie and Rees, eds, *Soviet History, 1917–1953*, p. 206.
54. *Neizvestnaya Rossiya XX vek*, t. III, p. 178; *Izvestiya TsK.*, no. 4, 1991, p. 218; Barber, J., 'The Moscow Crisis of October 1941', p. 212. See 'Stalin's Office Diary', *IA*, no. 2, 1996, p. 68, for Molotov's presence in Moscow on this date.
55. Gor'kov, *Gosudarstvennyi komitet oborony postanovlyaet*, pp. 90–5, quoting Stadnyuk, I., *Ispoved' kommunista*, Moscow: 1993, p. 346.
56. Barber, J. and Harrison, M., *The Soviet Home Front, 1941–1945*, London: 1991, pp. 54–5; Volkogonov, *Triumf i tragediya*, kn. 2, ch. 1, pp. 172–3.
57. Kot, S., *Conversations with the Kremlin and Dispatches from Russia*, London: 1963, p. 71.

58. Eden Papers, Birmingham University Library (hereinafter Eden Papers) AP33/9/1, vol. 24, ff. 455–9; I am grateful to Lady Avon for allowing me to use and cite these papers. Miner, S. M., *Between Churchill and Stalin, the Soviet Union and the Origins of the Grand Alliance*, Chapel Hill: 1988, p. 171.
59. Citrine, W., *In Russia Now*, London: 1942, p. 91.
60. Kot, *Conversations with the Kremlin*, pp. 76, 79.
61. This was the third visit to the front 'to spur on Zhukov,' Molotov referred to in his memoirs, Chuev, *Molotov*, p. 63.
62. Kot, *Conversations with the Kremlin*, pp. xviii, 106–16.
63. Gor'kov, *Gosudarstvennyi komitet oborony postanovlyaet*, pp. 45–6.
64. See the numerous references in Banac, ed., *The Diary of Georgi Dimitrov*, pp. 197–380.
65. See below pp. 200–4.
66. 'Stalin's Office Diary', *IA*, no. 2, 1996, pp. 3–72; no. 7, 1996, pp. 4–85; no. 8, 1996, pp. 66–110.
67. 'Materialy plenuma TsK VKP(b) (1944g.)', *IA*, no. 1, 1992, pp. 61–5. This was to give the USSR a number of votes when UNO was formed.
68. Mikoyan, *Tak bylo*, p. 464; Khrulev, A., 'Stanovlenie strategicheskogo tyla v Velikoi Otechestvennoi voine', *Voenno-istoricheskii Zhurnal*, no. 6, 1961, pp. 68–9.
69. Mikoyan, *Tak bylo*, p. 463.
70. Zhukov, G. K., *Vospominaniya i razmyshleniya*, t. 3, Moscow: 1990, p. 214; t. 2, p. 112.
71. 'Beseda professora G. A. Kumaneva s M. G. Pervukhinym', *NNI*, No. 5, 2003, p. 136.
72. Nepomniashchii, K., *Polki idyut na zapad*, Moscow: 1964, pp. 238–41.
73. Zhukov, *Vospominaniya*, t. 3, pp. 170–3.
74. Gor'kov, *Gosudarstvennyi komitet oborony postanovlyaet*, p. 48.
75. Tsikulin, V. A., *Istoriya gosudarstvennykh uchrezhdenii SSSR, 1936–1965gg.*, Moscow: 1968, p. 69; Gor'kov, *Gosudarstvennyi komitet oborony postanovlyaet*, pp. 33–4, 69.
76. *Ibid.*, p. 101.
77. *RGAS-PI*, 644/2/36, 32–5; Zhukov, *Vospominaniya*, t. 2 , p. 73.
78. Gor'kov, *Gosudarstvennyi komitet oborony postanovlyaet*, pp. 55, 70.
79. 'Beseda professora G. A. Kumaneva s M. G. Pervukhinym', p. 128.
80. Gor'kov, *Gosudarstvennyi komitet oborony postanovlyaet*, pp. 72–3, 122.
81. *RGAS-PI*, 664/2/184, 159.
82. Mikoyan, *Tak bylo*, p. 425.
83. *Pravda*, 1 October 1943.
84. Holloway, D., *Stalin and the Bomb: the Soviet Union and Atomic Energy 1939–1946*, New Haven: 1994, pp. 74, 84, 87–8.
85. Chuev, *Molotov*, p. 108.
86. Zhukov, *Vospominaniya*, t. 3, p. 334.
87. Holloway, *Stalin and the Bomb*, pp. 115, 129.
88. *RGAS-PI*, 644/2/116, 56–57; Gor'kov, *Gosudarstvennyi komitet oborony postanovlyaet* pp. 31, 36, 80, 101; Petrov, Yu. P., 'KPSS – organizator i rukovoditel' pobedy sovetskogo naroda v Velikoi Otechestvennoi voine', *Voprosy Istorii*, no. 5, 1970, p. 13.
89. *RGAS-PI*, 644/3/1–6.
90. Gor'kov, *Gosudarstvennyi komitet oborony postanovlyaet*, pp. 101, 110.
91. Khlevnyuk, *Politbyuro: mekhanizma politicheskoi vlasti v 1930-e gody*, pp. 251–3. The other members were Voznesenskii, Mikoyan, Bulganin, Beriya, Kaganovich and Andreev.
92. Mikoyan, *Tak bylo*, p. 389.
93. A small number of the Protokols are available among Molotov's papers, *RGAS-PI*, 82/2/392, but I am indebted to Dr. Oleg Khlevnyuk for providing me with a computerised listing of a full set from documents at *GARF* yet to be catalogued.
94. *Pravda*, 17 August 1942; Chuev, *Molotov*, p. 62.
95. See above.
96. See uncatalogued protokols at *GARF*.

97. Gor'kov, *Gosudarstvennyi komitet oborony postanovlyaet*, pp. 102–3, citing archive version of Mikoyan's memoirs.
98. Redlich, S., *War, Holocaust and Stalinism: A Documented History of the Jewish Anti-Fascist Committee in the USSR*, Luxembourg: 1995, pp. 47–8.
99. Rubenstein, J. and Naumov, V. P., eds, *Stalin's Secret Pogrom: the Postwar Inquisition of the Jewish Anti-Fascist Committee*, New Haven: 2001, pp. 7, 10, 14.
100. *Khrushchev Remembers*, p. 240; Redlich, S., *Propaganda and Nationalism in Wartime Russia: The Jewish Antifascist Committee in the USSR, 1941–1948*, Boulder: 1982, p. 55.
101. Rubenstein and Naumov, *Stalin's Secret Pogrom*, p. 20.
102. *Khrushchev Remembers*, p. 240.
103. *Literaturnaya Gazeta*, 7 July 1993. For the letter see Kostyrchenko, G., *Out of the Red Shadows: Anti-Semitism in Stalin's Russia*, New York: 1995, pp. 45–9.
104. Rubenstein and Naumov, *Stalin's Secret Progrom*, p. 24 quoting *RGAS-PI*, 17/125/246, 184–4b.

12   The Diplomat at War

1. Watson, 'Molotov, the Making of the Grand Alliance ...', pp. 52–4.
2. *Ibid.*, p. 56.
3. *Ibid.*, pp. 54–5. The term, 'Second Front', 'of Russian origin, had come to signify in Moscow parlance an Anglo-American invasion of France across the English channel; it carried the insulting connotation that the Soviet Union alone was really fighting,' Mastny, V., *Russia's Road to the Cold War: Diplomacy. Warfare and the Politics of Communism, 1941–1945*, New York: 1970, p. 46.
4. Harvey, J., ed., *The War Diaries of Oliver Harvey*, London: 1978, pp. 78–80.
5. Rzheshevsky, O. A., ed., *War and Diplomacy: the Making of the Grand Alliance: Documents from Stalin's Archives* (hereinafter *War and Diplomacy*), Amsterdam: 1996, pp. 35–40; *PRO, FO,* 371/32874, 56–58A.
6. *Eden Papers*, AP 20/3/3; *The Earl of Avon, The Eden Memoirs: the Reckoning*, London: 1965, p. 295.
7. Watson, 'Molotov, the Making of the Grand Alliance. ...', p. 58.
8. *The Eden Memoirs: the Reckoning*, pp. 302–3; Churchill, W. S., *The Second World War*, vol. 2, *Their Finest Hour*, London: 1952, p. 463. See above p. 185.
9. *AVPRF*, 6/3/8/82, 89–96.
10. Arbatov, G. A. *et al.*, eds, *Sovetsko-amerikanskie otnosheniya vo vremya Velikoi Otechestvennoi voiny, 1941–1945*, t. 1, 1941–1943, Moscow: 1984 (hereinafter *Sovetsko-amerikanskie otnosheniya*), pp. 150–1.
11. Kynin, G.P. *et al.*, eds, *Sovetsko-angliiskie otnosheniya vo vremya Velikoi Otechestvennoi voiny, 1941–1945*, t. 1, 1941–1943, Moscow: 1983 (hereinafter *Sovetsko-angliiskie otnosheniya*) pp. 217–8; *PRO, FO,* 371/32879, 112.
12. *Sovetsko-amerikanskie otnosheniya*, pp. 159–60; *FRUS 1942*, vol. III, *Europe*, Washington: 1961, p. 543.
13. Eden Papers, AP/33/9/1, vol. 25, 88; *PRO, FO,* 371/32879, 89.
14. *Sovetsko-amerikanskie otnosheniya*, p. 164.
15. Stoler, M. A., *The Politics of the Second Front: American Military Planning and Diplomacy in Coalition Warfare, 1941–1943*, Westport: 1977, p. 43.
16. Chuev, *Molotov*, pp. 83, 87; *PRO, FO,* 371/32882, 158; 32908, 53.
17. *Eden Papers*, AP33/9/1/, vol. 25, 142,164, 172–3; *FRUS, 1942*, vol. III, p. 553.
18. Dilks, D., ed., *The Diaries of Alexander Cadogan 1938–1941*, London: 1971, pp. 451–3.
19. *War Diaries of Oliver Harvey*, p. 119.
20. *Cadogan Diaries*, p. 453.
21. Churchill, W. S., *The Second World War*: vol. 4, *The Hinge of Fate*, London: 1952, pp. 278–9.
22. Chuev, *Molotov*, p. 84.

23. *AVPRF*, 6/4/5/47, 4–5; *War and Diplomacy*, p. 67; *PRO, FO*, 371/32882, 36. There is a difference between the English and Soviet reports here; the British implying that Molotov said that the 'Second Front' was the *more* important question.
24. *War and Diplomacy*, pp. 66–81.
25. *Cadogan Diaries*, p. 454.
26. *War and Diplomacy*, pp. 89–96. Stalin had mentioned the figure of 40 divisions to Churchill as early as September 1941. See Ministry of Foreign Affairs of the USSR, *Stalin's Correspondence with Churchill, Attlee, Roosevelt and Truman 1941–1945*, London: 1955, pp. 20–2.
27. *AVPRF*, 6/4/5/47, 49–57; *War and Diplomacy*, pp. 96–101; *Cf*. Miner, *Between Churchill and Stalin*, p. 247. I have rechecked both the Foreign Office documents and the Eden Papers for a copy of the record of this meeting.
28. *War and Diplomacy*, pp. 102–4; *Sovetsko-angliiskie otnosheniya*, pp. 230–1.
29. *AVPRF* 6/4/5/47, 8–69; *PRO, FO*, 371/32882, 46–48; *War and Diplomacy*, pp. 106–14.
30. *Ibid.*, p. 119.
31. *Ibid.*, pp. 122–3.
32. Miner, *Between Churchill and Stalin*, pp. 258–9.
33. *War and Diplomacy*, pp. 138–9.
34. Molotov told Winant that the new draft treaty was interesting and that the Soviet government would discuss it, *AVPRF*, 6/4/5/48, 4.
35. *Ibid.*, 6/4/5/47, 89–94; *War and Diplomacy*, pp. 122–3, 139–43; *PRO, FO*, 371/32882, 53–4; *Sovetsko-angliiskie otnosheniya*, pp. 232–5.
36. *AVPRF*, 6/4/5/47, 1.
37. Eden Papers, AP/33/9/1, vol. 25, 248.
38. Chuev, *Molotov*, pp. 85–6, 131–2; *War and Diplomacy*, pp. 163, 176, 224, 254.
39. *Ibid.*, p. 173.
40. *Ibid.*, pp.176–9, 225. *Sovetsko-amerikanskie otnosheniya*, pp. 178–80. *FRUS, 1942*, vol. III, pp. 568–71, 572–4. It seems clear that Roosevelt was committing British troops for there was little possibility of an American landing in 1942.
41. Sherwood, R. E., ed., *The White House Papers of Harry L. Hopkins: An Intimate History by Robert E. Sherwood*, vol. 2, January–July 1942, London: 1949, p. 564.
42. *War and Diplomacy*, pp.183–9; *Sovetsko-amerikanskie otnosheniya*, pp. 181–7; *FRUS 1942*, vol. III, pp. 575–8; Sherwood, *The White House Papers of Harry L. Hopkins*, vol. 2, pp. 566–9.
43. *War and Diplomacy*, pp. 193, 228.
44. Sherwood, *The White House Papers of Harry L. Hopkins*, vol. 2, p. 569; *FRUS 1942*, vol. III, p. 577.
45. *War and Diplomacy*, pp. 198–9; *Sovetsko-amerikanskie otnosheniya*, pp. 187–192; *FRUS 1942*, vol. III, p. 582.
46. Sherwood, *The White House Papers of Harry L. Hopkins*, vol. 2, p 579. *Cf*. Harriman, W. A. and Abel, E. *Special Envoy to Churchill and Stalin, 1941–1946*, New York: 1975, p. 137; *FRUS 1942*, vol. III, pp. 582–3.
47. *War and Diplomacy*, p. 205.
48. *Ibid.*, pp. 207–9.
49. Typically, Stalin used the familiar second person singular when writing to Molotov, to show that he was writing personally, but then signed the telegram *Instantsiya* – the highest authority – the term usually used to refer to the Central Committee or Politburo
50. *War and Diplomacy*, pp. 210–11.
51. Eden Papers, AP33/9/1, vol. 25, 250–1.
52. *War and Diplomacy*, pp. 212–13, 219–20. Harriman later commented on the statement on the Second Front:

    That single sentence was to be to be interpreted, misinterpreted and over-interpreted for many years to come. In accepting of Molotov's version, Roosevelt provided employment for a whole generation of Cold War publicists and historians who solemnly argued its meaning in dozens of books and hundreds of articles.

    Harriman and Abel, *Special Envoy*, p. 138.

53. *Ibid.*, pp. 215–17.
54. Gromyko, *Memories*, p. 401.
55. *War and Diplomacy*, p. 220.
56. *Ibid.*, pp. 222–30.
57. *Ibid.*, p. 254.
58. Kimball, W. F., ed., *Churchill and Roosevelt: the Complete Correspondence*, vol. 1, *Alliance Emerging, October 1933–November 1942*, Princeton, NJ: 1984, p. 508.
59. *War and Diplomacy*, pp. 264–7.
60. *Ibid.*, pp. 267–74; AVPRF, 6/4/5/47, 110–120; Eden Papers, AP33/9/1, vol. 25, 257–60; *Sovetsko-angliiskie otnosheniya*, pp. 244–7. The result of these plans was the Dieppe raid of August 1942.
61. PRO, FO, 371/32882, 216.
62. *War and Diplomacy*, pp. 283–4; *Sovetsko-angliiskie otnosheniya*, pp. 246–7.
63. AVPRF, 6/4/5/49, 5–73. The deleted passage is in l. 73.
64. *War and Diplomacy*, pp. 306–7.
65. Chuev, *Molotov*, pp. 83–4.
66. Churchill, W. S, *The Second World War:* vol. 1, *The Gathering Storm*, London: 1950, p. 301.
67. For a detailed discussion of the conference see Watson, D., 'Molotov et la Conférence de Moscou Octobre 1943', *Communisme*, no. 74/75, 2003, pp. 71–99.
68. Churchill, *The Second World War*, vol. 4, pp. 389–407.
69. *Ibid.*, p. 396.
70. Birse, A. H., *Memoirs of an Interpreter*, London: 1967, p. 137; Werth, *Russia at War*, p. 674.
71. Overy, R., *Russia's War*, pp. 184, 209–10.
72. Mastny, V., 'Soviet War Aims at the Moscow and Teheran Conferences of 1943', *Journal of Modern History*, vol. 47, 1975, p. 493.
73. FRUS: Diplomatic Papers 1943, vol. 3, *British Commonwealth, Eastern Europe and the Far East*, Washington: 1963, pp. 536, 544–5.
74. Marion, C. J., *Ministers in Moscow*, Indiana University PhD. thesis, 1970, pp. 20–2; Zubok and Pleshakov, *Inside the Kremlin's Cold War*, p. 28. FRUS, 1943, vol. 3, pp. 564–5, 567–8.
75. AVPRF, 6/5/17/159, 75 published Kynin, G.P. and Laufer, I., eds, *SSSR i Germanskii vopros, 22 iyunya 1941g.–8 maya 1945g.* t. 1, Moscow: 1996, p. 225.
76. Eden Papers, AP20/10, 198.
77. FRUS: 1943, vol. 1, *General*, Washington, DC: 1963, pp. 497–8.
78. Eden Papers, AP20/10, 250.
79. Gromyko, A. A. *et al.*, eds, *Sovetskii Soyuz na mezhdunarodnykh konferentsiyakh perioda Velikoi Otechestvennoi voiny 1941–1945gg.*, T. 1, *Moskovskaya konferentsiya ministrov inostrannykh del SSSR, SShA i Velikobritaniii (19–30 oktyabrya 1943g.): sbornik dokumentov*, (hereinafter, *Moskovskaya konferentsiya*), Moscow: 1978, pp. 41–2.
80. *Ibid.*, p. 42; Sainsbury, K., *The Turning Point: Roosevelt, Stalin, Churchill and Chiang-Kai-Shek, 1943, The Moscow, Cairo and Teheran Conferences*, New York: 1985, pp. 11, 329.
81. *Moskovskaya konferentsiya*, p. 43; FRUS, 1943, vol. 1, pp. 515–6.
82. *Ibid.*, pp. 518–31; Sainsbury, *The Turning Point*, pp. 8–11; *Moskovskaya konferentsiya*, pp. 43–53.
83. FRUS, 1943, vol. 1, pp. 518–20.
84. *Ibid.*, p. 531; *Moskovskaya konferentsiya*, pp. 52–3.
85. 'Stalin's Office Diary', *IA*, no. 3, 1996, pp. 82–4.
86. ' "Zanyat'sya Podgotovkoi Budushchego Mira" ', *Istochnik*, no. 4, 1995, pp. 114–17, quoting APRF, 3/63/237, 1–8.
87. *Ibid.*, pp. 118–24 quoting APRF 3/63/242, 1–8.
88. Many of these documents are published in Kynin and Laufer, *SSSR i Germanskii vopros*, pp. 236–329. I am indebted to Dr Geoffrey Roberts for drawing my attention to them.
89. AVPRF, 6/5/39/5, 36–50; Kynin and Laufer, *SSSR i Germanskii vopros*, pp. 277–86.
90. *Ibid.*, pp. 252–65, 286–312, 320–27.
91. *Ibid.*, pp. 326–7.

92. *Moskovskaya konferentsiya*, pp. 53–6; *FRUS 1943*, vol. 1, pp. 534–5.
93. *Ibid.*, pp. 535–6; Sainsbury, *The Turning Point*, pp. 31–2.
94. See Watson, 'Molotov's Apprenticeship in Foreign Policy', p. 699; Watson, 'Molotov, the Making of the Grand Alliance ...', p. 64.
95. *Izvestiya*, 1 October 1943.
96. *PRO, FO*, 371/36951, 213.
97. *FRUS 1943*, vol. 1, p. 568; *Eden Memoirs: the Reckoning*, p. 410. Oliver Harvey recorded in his diary: 'A guard of honour ... did a little march up and down, terrific smartness and precision including goose-step,' *War Diaries of Oliver Harvey*, p. 309.
98. Marion, *Ministers in Moscow*, p. 69.
99. *Moskovskaya konferentsiya*, p. 65; *FRUS 1943*, vol. 1, p. 547.
100. *Pravda*, 9 October 1943; *PRO, FO*, 371/36951, 77.
101. Bohlen, C. E., *Witness to History, 1929–1969*, London: 1963, p. 130. Photographs of Molotov show that after 1943 the belt and dagger were discarded. Many thanks to David King for help on this point. When ranks for diplomatic workers were reintroduced on 14 June 1943, Molotov was designated 'ambassador extraordinary and plenipotentiary', *VVS*, 17 June 1943; *PRO, FO*, 371/36950, 11–12.
102. *FRUS 1943*, vol. 1, pp. 577–8; *Moskovskaya konferentsiya*, pp. 91–92; *PRO, FO*, 371/37031, 231.
103. See Watson, 'Molotov's Apprenticeship in Foreign Policy', p. 714.
104. *Moskovskaya konferentsiya*, pp. 95–6; *PRO, FO*, 371/37030, 11.
105. *War Diaries of Oliver Harvey*, p. 310; *FRUS 1943*, vol. 1, pp. 589–90.
106. *Eden Memoirs: the Reckoning*, p. 411.
107. *FRUS 1943*, vol. 1, pp. 577–8; *Moskovskaya konferentsiya*, pp. 113–14.
108. *PRO, FO*, 371/37030, 34; *FRUS 1943*, vol. 1, p. 590.
109. *Ibid.*, pp. 123–8; *PRO, FO*, 371/37031, 241–3. *FRUS 1943*, vol. 1, pp. 596–8.
110. *Ibid.*, pp. 604–8; *PRO, FO*, 371/37031, 244–7; *Moskovskaya konferentsiya*, pp. 131–41.
111. *Ibid.*, pp. 148–52; *FRUS 1943*, vol. 1, pp. 613–16.
112. *Moskovskaya konferentsiya*, pp. 153–64; *FRUS, 1943*, vol. 1, pp. 617–21; *PRO, FO*, 371/37031, 249–53; Hull, *Memoirs*, p. 1285.
113. 'Stalin's Office Diary', *IA*, no. 3, 1996, p. 83.
114. Hull *Memoirs*, p. 1285.
115. Berezhkov, *History in the Making*, p. 221.
116. The term is a reference to a law passed during the English Civil War.
117. Harriman and Abel, *Special Envoy*, p. 245.
118. This was a mutual aid treaty for the post-war period and aimed at dealing with new aggression from Germany.
119. *PRO, FO*, 371/ 37031, 254–7; *FRUS 1943*, vol. 1, pp. 624–7; *Moskovskaya konferentsiya*, pp. 164–72. *Cf.* Sainsbury, *The Turning Point*, pp. 74–5, 80–1.
120. Mastny, V., 'The Beneš–Stalin–Molotov Conversations in December 1943: New Documents', *Jahrbücher für Geschichte Osteuropas*, 20, 1972, p. 387.
121. Mosely, P. E., *The Kremlin and World Politics: Studies in Soviet Policy and Action*, New York: 1960, p. 19. For Eden's capitulation see Mastny, 'Soviet War Aims,' pp. 486–8; Mastny, *Russia's Road to the Cold War*, pp. 116–17.
122. Molotov's views were fully in accord with the proposals propounded by the Litvinov commission, see Roberts, G., 'Ideology, Calculation and Improvisation: Spheres of Influence and Soviet Foreign Policy 1939–1945', *Review of International Studies*, vol. 25, 1999, p. 666.
123. See Narinsky, M. M. and Filitov, A. M., *Sovetskaya vneshnaya politika v period vtoroi mirovoi voiny*, Moscow: 1999, pp. 103–5.
124. *Moskovskaya konferentsiya*, pp. 176–85; *PRO, FO*, 371/ 37031, 259–62; *FRUS 1943*, vol. 1, pp. 629–33.
125. Marion, *Ministers in Moscow*, pp. 221–2.
126. *FRUS 1943*, vol. 1, pp. 633–4; *Moskovskaya konferentsiya*, pp. 185–9; *PRO, FO*, 371/ 37031, 263–4.

127. Marion, *Ministers in Moscow*, p. 205.
128. *FRUS, 1943*, vol. 1, pp. 637–9, 762–3; *PRO, FO*, 371/ 37031, 265–6; *Moskovskaya konferentsiya*, pp. 189–195. It should perhaps be noted that the same states would be involved irrespective of the purpose of the *cordon sanitaire*.
129. *Moskovskaya konferentsiya*, pp. 196–203; *PRO, FO*, 371/ 37031, 266–7; *FRUS, 1943*, vol. 1, pp. 639–42.
130. *Ibid.*, pp. 738–9; Sainsbury, *The Turning Point*, pp. 94–5.
131. *FRUS, 1943*, vol. 1, pp. 651–2; *PRO, FO*, 371/ 37031, 269–70; *Moskovskaya konferentsiya*, pp. 206–9.
132. *Moskovskaya konferentsiya, pp.* 212–20.
133. *Ibid.*, pp. 225–30; *FRUS, 1943*, vol. 1, pp. 656–9.
134. *Ibid.*, pp. 665–6; *Moskovskaya konferentsiya*, pp. 246–51; *PRO, FO*, 371/ 37031, 278–9. *Cf.* Sainsbury, *The Turning Point*, pp. 101–3.
135. Berezhkov, *History in the Making*, p. 209.
136. *Moskovskaya konferentsiya*, pp. 252–4; *FRUS 1943*, vol. 1, pp. 667–8; *PRO, FO*, 371/ 37031, 279–81.
137. Hull, *Memoirs*, pp. 1306–7; *FRUS, 1943*, vol. 1, pp. 670–71.
138. Eden, *Memoirs: the Reckoning*, p. 415.
139. *Moskovskaya konferentsiya*, pp. 259–70; *FRUS, 1943*, vol. 1, pp. 679–83; *PRO, FO*, 371/ 37031, 282–5. *Cf.* Mastny, 'Soviet War Aims,' p. 491.
140. *PRO, FO*, 371/37031, 12.
141. *Ibid.*, 97.
142. *Ibid.*, 192.
143. Mastny, *Russia's Road to the Cold War*, p. 121.
144. *Eden Memoirs: the Reckoning*, p. 565.
145. See *Pravda* and *Izvestiya*, 2 November 1943.
146. Mastny, 'Soviet War Aims' p. 493.
147. *FRUS, 1943*, vol. 1, p. 589.
148. Bohlen, *Witness to History*, p. 130.
149. Hull, *Memoirs*, pp. 1308–9; *Eden Memoirs: the Reckoning*, p. 410.
150. Harriman and Abel, *Special Envoy*, p. 243.
151. *Eden Memoirs: the Reckoning*, pp. 302–3; Churchill, *The Second World War*, vol. 2, p. 463.
152. Harriman and Abel, *Special Envoy*, p. 247.
153. See above p. 133.
154. Haslam, 'Litvinov, Stalin and the Road not Taken', p. 57; Haslam, *The Soviet Union and the Threat from the East*, p. 44.
155. Gromyko, A.A. *et al.*, eds, *Sovetskii Soyuz na mezhdunarodnykh konferentsiyakh perioda Velikoi Otechestvennoi voiny 1941–1945 gg., T. II Tegeranskaya konferentsiya rukovoditelei trekh soyuznykh derzhav – SSSR, SShA i Velikobritanii (25 noyabrya–1 dekabrya 1943g.): sbornik dokumentov*, Moscow: 1978 (hereinafter *Tegeranskaya konferentsiya*), p. 66.
156. *Ibid.*, pp. 69–70.
157. *Ibid.*, p. 73.
158. *Ibid.*, p. 74.
159. Sainsbury, *The Turning Point*, p. 135. Stalin was uneasy about the Japanese reaction to Soviet involvement in discussions with its enemy.
160. *Ibid.*, pp. 219–20; *Tegeranskaya konferentsiya*, pp. 85–6; Eden Papers AP20/3/5.
161. Sainsbury, *The Turning Point*, pp. 219–20.
162. *Tegeranskaya konferentsiya*, pp. 92–102, 121–34, 140–3, 150–67.
163. Churchill, W.S., *The Second World War*, vol. 5, *Closing the Ring*, London: 1952, p. 294.
164. Kennedy-Pipe, C., *Stalin's Cold War: Soviet Strategies in Europe, 1943 to 1956*, Manchester: 1995, p. 42.
165. *Ibid.*, pp. 42–3; Sainsbury, *The Turning Point*, pp. 262–5; *Tegeranskaya konferentsiya*, pp. 144–9.

166. *Tegeranskaya konferentsiya*, pp. 144–9.
167. Sainsbury, *The Turning Point*, pp. 270–1; *Tegeranskaya konferentsiya*, p. 157.
168. *Ibid.*, p. 159.
169. *Ibid.*, p. 167; Sainsbury, *The Turning Point*, p. 276.
170. Mastny, 'The Beneš–Stalin–Molotov Conversations in December 1943', pp. 397, 399.
171. *Ibid.*, p. 397.
172. *Izvestiya*, 2 February 1944; Mastny, *Russia's Road to the Cold War*, p. 143.
173. Pons, S., 'In the Aftermath of the Age of Wars: the Impact of World War II on Soviet Security Policy', in Pons, S., and Romano, A., eds, *Russia in the Age of Wars*, Milan: 1998, pp. 283–91.
174. *Ibid.*, p. 299 quoting *AVPRF*, 7/10/6/64, 4.
175. Churchill, W. S., *The Second World War*: vol. 6, *Triumph and Tragedy*, London: 1954, pp. 194–5.
176. Rzheshevskii, O. A., 'Operatsiya "Tolstoi". Vizit U. Cherchilya v Moskvu v oktyabre 1944g.', *NNI*, no. 5, 2003, pp. 111, 116.
177. 'Angliya dolzhna imet' pravo reshayushchego golosa v Gretsii', *Istochnik*, no. 2, 2003, p. 50.
178. ' "Zanyat'sya Podgotovkoi Budushchego Mira" ', pp. 148–52.
179. *PRO, PREM* 3/434/2; 'Operatsiya "Tolstoi" ', pp. 116–20.
180. Eden Papers 20/3/9, Notebook of Journey to Moscow.
181. 'Operatsiya "Tolstoi" ', pp. 116–20, the Soviet record of these discussions.
182. Eden Papers 20/3/9, Notebook of Journey to Moscow. Mastny, *Russia's Road to the Cold War*, p. 208 claims that they reached no agreement.
183. *PRO, PREM* 3/434/2.
184. For the latest contribution to this debate see Roberts, G., 'Beware Greek Gifts: The Stalin–Churchill "Percentages" Agreement of October 1944', Paper presented at the Foreign Office Seminar "Churchill–Stalin", London: 2002.
185. Kennedy-Pipe, *Stalin's Cold War*, p. 46.
186. Mastny, *Russia's Road to the Cold War*, p. 210. For a detailed account of these negotiations see Resis, A., 'The Churchill–Stalin Secret "Percentages" Agreement on the Balkans, Moscow, 1944', *American Historical Review*, vol. 83, no. 2, 1978, pp. 368–87.
187. *FRUS, Diplomatic Papers, 1945*, vol. 5, *Europe*, Washington: 1967, pp. 942–4.
188. Bohlen, *Witness to History*, p.186; *FRUS, 1945*, vol 5, pp. 1008–9.
189. *Ibid.*, pp. 91–2, 103; Mastny, *Russia's Road to the Cold War*, p. 232.
190. Kennedy-Pipe, *Stalin's Cold War*, pp. 48–9.
191. Gromyko, A. A. *et al.*, eds, *Sovetskii Soyuz na mezhdunarodnykh konferentsiyakh perioda Velikoi Otechestvennoi voiny 1941–1945 gg., T. IV Krymskaya konferentsiya rukovoditelei trekh soyuznykh derzhav – SSSR, SShA i Velikobritanii (4–11 fevralya 1945g), sbornik dokumentov* Moscow: 1979 (hereinafter *Krymskaya konferentsiya*), pp. 46–273; *FRUS Diplomatic Paper, The Conferences at Malta and Yalta 1945*, Washington: 1955, pp. 539–934.
192. *Ibid.*, p. 716; *FRUS, 1945*, vol 5, pp. 123–4; Mastny, *Russia's Road to the Cold War*, pp. 246–8.
193. *Ibid.*, pp. 250–1; *Krymskaya konferentsiya*, pp. 182, 187; *FRUS, The Conferences at Malta and Yalta 1945*, p. 848.
194. Mastny, *Russia's Road to the Cold War*, p. 251.
195. *FRUS, The Conferences at Malta and Yalta 1945*, pp. 608–10, 656–7, 700–1.
196. *Ibid.*, p. 736. This interjection is not included in the Soviet record of the meeting, *Krymskaya konferentsiya*, p. 134.
197. Ministry of Foreign Affairs of the USSR, *Correspondence between the Chairman of the Council of Ministers of the USSR and the Presidents of the U.S.A. and the Prime Ministers of Great Britain during the Great Patriotic War of 1941–1945*, vol. 2, Moscow: 1957, pp. 197, 199.
198. Mastny, *Russia's Road to the Cold War*, pp. 257–8; *FRUS, 1945*, vol. 5, pp. 134, 142–4, 180–2, 196–8; *FRUS 1945*, vol. 3, *European Advisory Commission, Austria and Germany*, Washington, DC: 1968, pp. 731–12.

199. *FRUS, 1945*, vol. 5, pp. 825–6.
200. *Ibid.*, pp. 825–7, 839. In his memoirs Molotov wrongly claimed that he was on a train in the United States when Roosevelt's death was announced. Chuev, *Molotov*, p. 95.
201. Sherwin, M. J., *A World Destroyed: the Atomic Bomb and the Grand Alliance*, New York 1997, pp. 171–3.
202. *FRUS, 1945*, vol. 5, pp. 235–6, 256–8. The first conversation took place on the day of Molotov's arrival.
203. *Ibid.*, pp. 237–52, 259–62.
204. Truman, H. S., *Year of Decisions, 1945*, London: 1955, p. 85.
205. See for instance, Yergin, D., *Shattered Peace: the Origins of the Cold War and National Security State*, London: 1978, p. 83.
206. See Roberts, G., 'Sexing up the Cold War: New Evidence on the Molotov–Truman Talks of April 1945', *Cold War History*, vol. 4, no. 3, 2004, pp. 105–125, which prints the Soviet record of the conversations; Bohlen, *Witness to History*, p. 213.
207. Truman, *Year of Decisions*, pp. 202–3.
208. Duranty, *Stalin & Co.*, p. 114.
209. *Ibid.*, pp. 114–15; *Documents of the United Nations Conference on International Organization San Francisco 1945*, vol. 1, London: 1945, p. 281.
210. Zubok and Pleshakov, *Inside the Kremlin's cold War*, p. 34.
211. Butler, R. and Pelly, M. E., eds, *Documents on British Policy Overseas*, series 1, vol. 1, *The Conference at Potsdam, July–August 1945* (hereinafter *DBPO1*), London: 1984, p. 455.
212. *FRUS*, 1945, vol. 5, p. 272–6.
213. Davies, N., 'The Soviet Occupation of Poland, 1944–45', in Bennett, G., ed., *The End of the War in Europe*, London: 1995, p. 197.
214. *FRUS*, 1945, vol. 5, pp. 281–4.
215. Bromage, *Molotov*, p. 210.
216. Yakovlev, A.S. *Tsel' zhizni*, Moscow: 1966, pp. 373–7.
217. Duranty, *Stalin & Co.*, p. 93.
218. *FRUS, Diplomatic Papers: The Conference of Berlin (The Potsdam Conference), 1945*, vol. 1, Washington: 1960, p. 24.
219. *Ibid.*, pp. 28, 31, 85.
220. *Ibid.* p.58; *FRUS, 1945*, vol. 5, pp 309–13.
221. *Ibid.*, p.61.
222. *Ibid.*, pp. 164–73.
223. *Ibid.*, p. 233.
224. Mastny, *Russia's Road to the Cold War*, p. 293; Gromyko, A.A. *et al.*, eds, *Sovetskii Soyuz na mezhdunarodnykh konferentsiyakh perioda Velikoi Otechestvennoi voiny 1941–1945 gg., T.6, Berlinskaya konferentsiya rukovoditelei trekh soyuznykh derzhav – SSSR, SShA i Velikobritanii (17 iyulya–2 avgusta 1945 g.) sbornik dokumentov*, Moscow: 1980, p. 38.
225. *Ibid.*, p. 41–2.
226. *Ibid.*, p. 44.
227. *Ibid.*, pp. 35, 69, 92, 271–2.
228. Mastny, *Russia's Road to the Cold War*, p. 296.
229. *DBPO1*, p. 357.
230. In addition, the Western powers as a priority wanted to settle the nature of the 'liberation' in the territories the Red Army now occupied and the meaning of 'free elections', although they were less concerned about reparations. Dilks, D., 'The Conference at Potsdam, 1945', in Bennett, ed., *The End of the War in Europe*, p. 78.
231. Mastny, *Russia's Road to the Cold War*, pp. 294–300; Kennedy-Pipe, *Stalin's Cold War*, p. 82; Zubok and Pleshakov, *Inside the Kremlin's Cold War*, p. 32. For Molotov pressing hard on reparations see *DBPO1*, pp. 445, 577–80, 931–5, 1019–36.
232. See above p. 196. Zhukov, *Vospominanya*, t. 3, p. 334.
233. Harriman and Abel, *Special Envoy to Churchill and Stalin*, p. 491.
234. *DBPO1*, p. 957; Chuev, *Molotov*, p. 115.

235. Sir Frank Roberts, quoted Dilks, 'The Conference at Potsdam, 1945', p. 97.
236. During the election campaign Churchill had tried to provoke fears of 'a Labour Party Gestapo'. See Thomson, D., *England in the Twentieth Century: 1914–1963*, Harmondsworth: 1965, pp. 218–9.
237. *DBPO1*, pp. 1063–4.
238. Mastny, *Russia's Road to the Cold War*, pp. 301, 303; Dilks, 'The Conference at Potsdam, 1945', p. 95.
239. *DBPO1*, p. 1064.
240. *Ibid.*, p. 1150.
241. Banac, ed., *The Diary of Georgi Dimitrov 1933–1949*, p. 377.

13   Stalin's Last Years 1945–1953

1. Roschin, N., 'The UN in the Cold War Years', *International Affairs*, January 1990, p. 216; Ward, P. D., *The Threat of Peace: James F. Byrnes and the Council of Foreign Ministers, 1945–1946*, Kent, Ohio: 1979, pp. 145–6, 155.
2. See above p. 219.
3. Bullen, R., Pelly, M. E. *et al.*, eds, *Documents on British Policy Overseas,* series 1, vol II, London: 1985 (hereinafter *DBPO2*), p. 77.
4. Pechatnov, ' "The Allies are Pressing on You ..." ', p.3, quoting *AVPRF*, 0431/1/1/1, 14–15.
5. *DBPO2*, pp. 106–7.
6. *Ibid.*, p. 103.
7. *Ibid.*, p. 153.
8. *Ibid.*, p. 253.
9. *Ibid.*, pp. 162–3.
10. *Cf. Ibid.*, p. 349.
11. *Ibid.*, pp. 163–6, 174–8.
12. *FRUS, Diplomatic Papers 1945*, vol. 2, *General: Political and Economic Matters*, Washington: 1967, pp. 163–6, 200.
13. Pechatnov, ' "The Allies are Pressing on You ..." ', p. 2.
14. *DBPO2*, p. 256.
15. Pechatnov, ' "The Allies are Pressing on You ..." ', p. 2.
16. *FRUS, 1945*, vol. 2, p. 243.
17. *DBPO2*, p. 274.
18. *Ibid.*, pp. 284–6.
19. Quoted, Pechatnov, ' "The Allies are Pressing on You ..." ', p. 4.
20. *Ibid.*, p. 5; *FRUS, 1945*, vol. 2, p. 268.
21. Pechatnov, ' "The Allies are Pressing on You ..." ', p. 4.
22. *FRUS, 1945*, vol. 2, pp. 313–15; *DBPO2*, pp. 292–4.
23. *Ibid.*, pp. 298–300.
24. *Ibid.*, pp. 388–90, 397–9, 405–7, 422–6, 449–57.
25. *Ibid.*, 390.
26. *Ibid.*, p. 429.
27. *Ibid.*, pp. 450–1.
28. *Ibid.*, pp. 354–8; ' "The Allies are Pressing on You ..." ', pp. 5–6.
29. *Ibid.*, p. 6; *DBPO2*, p. 372.
30. *Ibid.*, p. 391.
31. Pechatnov, ' "The Allies are Pressing on You ..." ', pp. 6–7.
32. *Ibid.*, p. 7; *DBPO2.*, p. 439; Ward, *The Threat of Peace*, p. 41; Bohlen, *Witness to History*, p. 246.
33. Pechatnov, ' "The Allies are Pressing on You ..." ', p. 7.
34. *Ibid.*, pp. 7–8.

35. *DBPO2*, p. 474.
36. Ward, *The Threat of Peace*, p. 47.
37. *Ibid.*, pp. 52–3.
38. Pechatnov, ' "The Allies are Pressing on You ..." ', p. 14.
39. Ward, *The Threat of Peace*, p. 71.
40. Pechatnov, ' "The Allies are Pressing on You ..." ', p.14.
41. Ward, *The Threat of Peace*, p. 72.
42. Pechatnov, ' "The Allies are Pressing on You ..." ', p.14.
43. *Ibid.*, p. 14; Ward, *The Threat of Peace*, p. 71; Bohlen, *Witness to History*, p. 249; *cf.* below p. 237.
44. Ward, *The Threat of Peace*, pp. 79–83.
45. *Pravda*, 8 February 1946.
46. Ward, *The Threat of Peace*, p. 83.
47. *Ibid.*, pp. 93–8; Pechatnov, ' "The Allies are Pressing on You ..." ', pp. 16–17.
48. *Ibid.*, p. 16.
49. *Ibid.*, p. 18.
50. Ward, *The Threat of Peace*, p. 110.
51. Pechatnov, ' "The Allies are Pressing on You ..." ', pp. 18–19.
52. Ward, *The Threat of Peace*, p. 125.
53. *Ibid.*, pp. 115–16.
54. *Ibid.*, pp. 122–3.
55. *Ibid.*, pp. 129–32.
56. *Ibid.*, p. 135.
57. *Ibid.*, pp. 145–7, 150.
58. Pechatnov, ' "The Allies are Pressing on You ..." ', p. 20.
59. Novikov, N. V., *Vospominaniya diplomata: Zapiski 1938–1947*, Moscow: 1989, pp. 351–4.
60. Parrish, S., 'A Diplomat Reports', *Cold War International History Project, Bulletin*, no. 1, 1992, p. 21.
61. Jensen, K. N., ed., *Origins of the Cold War: the Novikov, Kennan and Roberts 'Long Telegrams' of 1946, Revised Edition with Three New Commentaries*, Washington DC: 1993, pp. 3–16.
62. Pechatnov, ' "The Allies are Pressing on You ..." ', p. 22.
63. Ward, *The Threat of Peace*, pp. 155–9.
64. *Ibid.*, pp. 159–60.
65. *Ibid.*, p. 161.
66. *Ibid.*, pp. 161–4; Pechatnov, ' "The Allies are Pressing on You ..." ', p. 21.
67. *Ibid.*, p. 21; Ward, *The Threat of Peace*, pp. 164–7.
68. Pechatnov, ' "The Allies are Pressing on You ..." ', pp. 22–3.
69. Ward, *The Threat of Peace*, p. 176.
70. Parrish, S. D. and Narinsky, M. N., 'New Evidence on the Soviet Rejection of the Marshall Plan, 1947: Two Reports', *Cold War International History Project, Working Paper no. 9*, Washington: DC: 1994, p. 1.
71. *Ibid.*, pp. 7–9, 13.
72. *Ibid.*, p. 14.
73. Zubok and Pleshakov, *Inside the Kremlin's Cold War*, p. 104.
74. Parrish and Narinsky, 'New Evidence on the Soviet Rejection of the Marshall Plan pp. 16–19.
75. *Ibid.*, pp. 21–4.
76. *Ibid.*, p. 25.
77. *Ibid.*, p. 45.
78. *Ibid.*, p. 26 quoting *AVPRF*, 59/18/22/151, 87.
79. *Ibid.*, p. 29.
80. *Ibid.*, pp. 28–31.
81. *Ibid.*, pp. 32–40.
82. Mastny, V., *The Cold War and Soviet Insecurity: the Stalin Years*, New York: 1996, p. 26.

83. Zubok and Pleshakov, *Inside the Kremlin's Cold War*, p. 107.
84. Deighton, A., *Britain, the Division of Germany and the Origins of the Cold War*, Oxford: 1993, pp. 209–10.
85. Smyser, W. R. *From Yalta to Berlin: the Cold War Struggle over Germany*, New York: 1999, pp. 58–9. The term 'Mr. *Nyet*' is more often applied to Gromyko, but for its use in describing Molotov see the obituaries in *The Daily Telegraph* and *The Independent*, 12 November 1986.
86. Smyser, *From Yalta to Berlin*, pp. 59–60; Clay, L.D. *Decision in Germany*, Westport, CT: 1970, p. 348.
87. Smyser, *From Yalta to Berlin*, pp. 74, 76; Narinskii, M.N., 'The Soviet Union and the Berlin Crisis, 1948–9', in Gori, F. and Pons, S., eds, *The Soviet Union and Europe in the Cold War*, 1943–53, Basingstoke: 1996, pp. 62–4, 69–71.
88. Djilas, M., *Conversations with Stalin*, pp. 133–43; Dedijer, V., *Tito Speaks: His Self Portrait and Struggle with Stalin*, London: 1954, pp. 278–83, 294–5, 306–13, 324–33, 339–43, 354–65.
89. *Pravda*, 22 July 1951. *Cf.* Dallin, D. J., *Soviet Foreign Policy after Stalin*, London: 1962, p. 122.
90. For the most recent attempt to argue that the Politburo tried to marginalize Stalin see Zhukov, Yu. N., *Tainy Kremliya: Stalin, Molotov, Beriya, Malenkov*, Moscow: 2000. For the defeat of a 'moderate' faction see Hahn, W.G. *Postwar Soviet Politics: the Fall of Zhdanov and the Defeat of Moderation 1946–1953*, Ithaca: 1982.
91. See Gorlizki, Y. and Khlevniuk, O., *Cold Peace: Stalin and the Soviet Ruling Circle, 1945–1953*, Oxford: 2004, pp. 5–11, 17.
92. *Ibid.*, p. 19.
93. *RGAS-PI*, 17/3/1053, 50.
94. *RGAS-PI*, 17/3/1053, 43, 430–2; Khlevnyuk, O.V., Gorlitskii, I., *et al.* eds, *Politbyuro TsK VKP(b) i Sovet Ministrov SSSR 1945–1953* (hereinafter *Politbyuro TsK i Sovet Ministrov*), Moscow: 2002, pp. 438–64.
95. *GARF*, R7523/35/13a, 115–8, printed *Politbyuro TsK i Sovet Ministrov*, p. 27.
96. *GARF*, R5446/1/275/121–4, printed *Politbyuro TsK i Sovet Ministrov*, pp. 30–32.
97. *RGAS-PI*, 17/3/1063, 32–7, printed *Politbyuro TsK i Sovet Ministrov*, pp. 39–43.
98. *GARF*, R5446/1/275, 35, printed *Politbyuro TsK i Sovet Ministrov*, p. 30.
99. Gorlizki and Khlevniuk, *Cold Peace*, p. 57.
100. *Politbyuro TsK i Sovet Ministrov*, pp. 464–88.
101. *Ibid.*, pp. 39–43, 488–511.
102. *RGAS-PI*, 17/3/1070, 2, printed *Politbyuro TsK i Sovet Ministrov*, p. 57.
103. *Ibid.*, pp. 517–30.
104. *Ibid.*, pp. 530–34.
105. *Ibid.*, pp. 534–9.
106. *RGAS-PI*, 17/3/1080, 81, printed *Politbyuro TsK i Sovet Ministrov*, p. 83.
107. *Ibid.*, pp. 539–63.
108. *Ibid.*, pp. 421–31.
109. Gorlizki and Khlevniuk, *Cold Peace*, pp. 46–7.
110. Wheatcroft, 'From Team-Stalin to Degenerate Tyranny', pp. 93–5.
111. Compiled from 'Stalin's Office Diary', *IA*, no. 4, 1996, pp. 92–131, no. 5–6, 1996, pp. 4–61; no. 1, 1997, pp. 5–38.
112. Chuev, *Molotov*, pp. 329, 116.
113. Gorlizki and Khlevniuk, *Cold Peace*, pp. 8, 17; *Pravda*, 10 October 1945; *Politbyuro TsK i Sovet Ministrov*, p. 398.
114. Gorlizki and Khlevniuk, *Cold Peace*, pp. 19, 21.
115. *Izvestiya.*, 7 November 1945.
116. Pechatnov, ' "The Allies are Pressing on You …" ' p. 11.
117. *Ibid.*, p. 12.
118. *RGAS-PI*, 558/11/99, 86, 92–3, printed *Politbyuro TsK i Sovet Ministrov*, pp. 195–7.
119. *RGAS-PI*, 558/11/99, 95, printed *Politbyuro TsK i Sovet Ministrov*, pp. 197–8.
120. *RGAS-PI*, 558/11/99, 103–5, printed *Politbyuro TsK i Sovet Ministrov*, pp. 198–9.

121. *RGAS-PI*, 558/11/99, 120, printed *Politbyuro TsK i Sovet Ministrov*, p. 200.
122. *RGAS-PI*, 558/11/99, 121, printed *Politbyuro TsK i Sovet Ministrov*, p. 201.
123. *RGAS-PI*, 558/11/99, 127, printed *Politbyuro TsK i Sovet Ministrov*, pp. 201–2.
124. *RGAS-PI*, 558/11/99, 167, printed Chubaryan, A.O. and Pechatnov, V.O., ' "Molotov the Liberal": Stalin's 1945 Criticism of his Deputy', *Cold War History*, vol. 1, no. 1, August 2000, p. 139.
125. Danilov, A. A., 'Stalinskoe Politbyuro v poslevoennye gody', in Erofeev, N.D. *et al.* eds, *Politichestkie partii Rossii: stranitsy istorii*, Moscow: 2000, pp. 199, 201.
126. McCagg, W. O., Jr, *Stalin Embattled 1943–1948*, Detroit: 1978, pp. 255, 390; Mileikovskii, A. G., ed., *Mezhdunarodnye otnosheniya posle vtoroi mirovoi voiny, T. 1, 1945–1949gg.*, Moscow: 1962, pp. 254–5.
127. Pechatnov, 'The Allies are Pressing on you ...', pp. 23–4.
128. Krementsov, N., 'The "KR Affair": Soviet Science on the Threshold of the Cold War', *History and Philosophy of the Life Sciences*, vol. 17, 1995, pp. 423, 432, 436; Kneen, P., 'Physics, Genetics and Zhdanovschina', *Europe–Asia Studies*, vol. 50, no. 7, 1998, p. 1197. I am indebted to Dr P. Kneen for drawing my attention to this episode.
129. Zubok and Pleshakov, *Inside the Kremlin's Cold War*, p. 87; Sudoplatov, P. and Sudoplatov, A. *et al.*, *Special Tasks: the Memoirs of an Unwanted Witness – a Soviet Spymaster*, London: 1994, pp. 235–7.
130. Zubok, V.M., 'Soviet Intelligence and the Cold War: the "Small" Committee of Information, 1952–53', *Cold War International History Project, Working Paper, no. 4*, Washington DC: 1992, p. 5.
131. Zhirnov, E., 'Nashi dos"e pri likvidatsii komiteta byli unichtozheny', *Kommersant' vlast*, 15 August 2000, pp. 52–3.
132. Beria, *Beria, My Father*, p.190.
133. Khlevnyuk, O., 'Zadavlennye oligarkhi. Stalin i ego okruzhenie v poslevoennye gody', Unpublished Paper for Conference 'Rethinking the Stalin Era', University of Toronto, 1999, p. 12, quoting *RGAS-PI*, 17/163/1509, 247. See above p. 234.
134. Gorlizki and Khlevniuk, *Cold Peace*, p. 75.
135. Quoted, Brent, J. and Naumov, V.P., *Stalin's Last Crime: the Doctors' Plot*, London: 2003, pp. 69–70.
136. Torchinov, V.A. and Leontyuk, A.M., *Vokrug Stalina – istorio-biograficheskii spravochnik*, Saint Petersburg: 2000, p. 220.
137. Zalesski, *Imperiya Stalina*, p. 166.
138. Ivkin, V.I., *Gosudarstvennaya vlast' SSSR: vysshe organy vlasti i upravleniya i ikh rukovoditeli 1923–1991*, Moscow: 1999, pp. 307–8.
139. Redlich, *War, Holocaust and Stalinism*, pp. 133, 322–5, 341–4, 358, 458–64.
140. Chuev, *Molotov*, p. 551; Vasilieva, *Kremlin Wives*, p. 132.
141. Rubenstein and Naumov, *Stalin's Secret Progrom*, p. 46; Redlich, *War, Holocaust and Stalinism*, p. 149.
142. Medvedev, Zh.A., 'Stalin i "delo vrachei". Novye materialy', *Voprosy Istorii*, no. 1, 2003, pp. 101–2.
143. Chuev, *Molotov*, p. 549.
144. Gorlizki and Khlevniuk, *Cold Peace*, p. 76.
145. *Ibid.*, quoting *RGAS-PI*, 17/163/1518, 164.
146. Medvedev, *All Stalin's Men*, p. 99, quoting, Mikunis, S., *Vremya i my*, no. 48, 1971, p. 162.
147. *RGAS-PI*, 17/3/1074, 58 printed *Politbyuro TsK i Sovet Ministrov*, p. 68.
148. Gorlizki and Khlevniuk, *Cold Peace*, p. 77.
149. Haslam, J., 'Russian Archival Revelations and Our Understanding of the Cold War', *Diplomatic History*, vol. 21, no. 2, 1997, p. 223.
150. Mlechlin, L., 'Vyacheslav Molotov: On dazhe ne mog spasti svoyu zhenu', *Novoe Vremya*, nos. 43–44, 1998, pp. 40, 42.
151. *RGAS-PI*, 17/3/1075, 54, printed *Politbyuro TsK i Sovet Ministrov*, p. 75; Gorlizki and Khlevniuk, *Cold Peace*, p. 77.

152. Gorlizki and Khlevniuk, *Cold Peace*, p. 77; *RGAS-PI*, 17/3/1075, 38, printed *Politbyuro TsK i Sovet Ministrov*, p. 74.
153. *RGAS-PI*, 17/3/1075, 29 printed *Politbyuro TsK i Sovet Ministrov*, p. 73.
154. Gorlizki and Khlevniuk, *Cold Peace*, pp. 77–8.
155. *Ibid.*, p. 78.
156. *Ibid.*, p. 70.
157. *Ibid.*, p. 78.
158. *RGAS-PI*, 17/163/1526, 166, printed *Politbyuro TsK i Sovet Ministrov*, p. 76.
159. *Pravda*, 17 December 1949; Goncharov, S.N., Lewis, J.W. and Litai, X, *Uncertain Partners: Stalin, Mao and the Korean War*, Stanford: 1993, pp. 85, 93–5, 103.
160. *RGAS-PI*, 17/3/1080, 3, 1088, 2, printed *Politbyuro TsK i Sovet Ministrov*, pp. 81–2, 86.
161. *GARF*, R5446/1/411, 247 printed *Politbyuro TsK i Sovet Ministrov*, pp. 82–3.
162. Bonvesch, B., ed, ' "Skostit' polovinu summy reparatsii ... my mozhem" ', *Istochnik*, no. 3, 2003, pp. 100–28.
163. Gorlizki and Khlevniuk, *Cold Peace*, pp. 78–9, 107. See for instance *RGAS-PI*, 17/163/1616, 132–5, printed *Politbyuro TsK i Sovet Ministrov*, pp. 117–9; Khlevnyuk, 'Zadavlennye oligarkhi', p. 16.
164. Troyanovskii, O., *Cherez gody i rastoyaniya: istorii odnoi sem'i*, Moscow: 1997, p. 166.
165. *RGAS-PI*, 17/3/1080, 81, printed *Politbyuro TsK i Sovet Ministrov*, p. 83.
166. Gorlizki and Khlevniuk, *Cold Peace*, pp. 105–6, 144.
167. Gorlizki, Y., 'Stalin's Cabinet: the Politburo and Decision Making in the Post-war Years', *Europe–Asia Studies*, vol. 53, no. 2, 2001, pp. 296–7.
168. *RGAS-PI*, 81/3/52, 9–14; *GARF*, R5446/86/10265, 371–90, 38, printed *Politbyuro TsK i Sovet Ministrov*, pp. 167–81.
169. Chuev, *Molotov*, pp. 432–3.
170. *Pravda*, 21 December 1949.
171. *Pravda*, 9 March 1950.
172. See Kozlov, V. A. and Mironenko, S. V., eds, *Arkhiv noveishei istorii Rossii, t. 2, 'Osobaya papka' V. M. Molotova*, Moscow: 1994, pp. 61–85, 117–39, 161–77.
173. Gorlizki and Khlevniuk, *Cold Peace*, p. 146.
174. *Pravda*, 6 October 1952.
175. Chuev, *Molotov*, p. 541.
176. Gorlizki and Khlevniuk, *Cold Peace*, pp. 145–8; *Pravda*, 15 October 1952.
177. Conquest, R., *Power and Policy in the U.S.S.R: the Study of Soviet Dynastics*, London: 1962, p. 395.
178. *Khrushchev Remembers*, pp. 279–80; *Rossiiskii Gosudarstvennyi Arkhiv Noveishei Istorii*, (hereinafter *RGANI*), 2/1/21, 1, printed *Politbyuro TsK i Sovet Ministrov*, p. 89.
179. Khrushchev's Secret Speech in *Khrushchev Remembers*, pp. 615–16.
180. Mawdsley, E. and White, S., *The Soviet Elite from Lenin to Gorbachev: the Central Committee and its Members, 1917–1991*, Oxford: 2000, pp. 103–4.
181. Gorlizki and Khlevniuk, *Cold Peace*, p. 149.
182. Rubenstein and Naumov, *Stalin's Secret Pogrom*, p. 260.
183. *Dos'e glasnosti spetsvypusk*, 13 December 2001.
184. See Gorlizki and Khlevniuk, *Cold Peace*, p. 151.
185. Simonov, K., *Glazami cheloveka moego pokoleniya*, Moscow: 1988, pp. 242–3.
186. Mikoyan, *Tak bylo*, pp. 557–8.
187. Gorlizki and Khlevniuk, *Cold Peace*, pp. 150.
188. Sudoplatov, *Special Tasks*, p. 327; *cf.* above p. 170.
189. Gorlizki, 'Stalin's Cabinet', p. 302.
190. *Politbyuro TsK i Sovet Ministrov*, pp. 432–3.
191. *RGAS-PI*, 83/1/7, 71–3, printed *Politbyuro TsK i Sovet Ministrov*, pp. 89–91.
192. *Ibid.*, p. 98.
193. *Khrushchev Remembers*, pp. 281, 309–10.
194. Danilov, 'Stalinskoe Politbyuro v poslevoennye gody', p. 217.
195. Chuev, *Molotov*, p. 395.

196. *Ibid.*, p. 339.
197. *Khrushchev Remembers*, pp. 280, 615.
198. Gorlizki and Khlevniuk, *Cold Peace*, p. 154.
199. Vasilieva, *Kremlin Wives*, p. 144.
200. Brent and Naumov, *Stalin's Last Crime*, pp.178, 181, 285; *cf. Politbyuro TsK i Sovet Ministrov*, p. 434.
201. Goudover, A.P. van, *The Limits of Destalinisation in the Soviet Union: Political Rehabilitation in the Soviet Union since Stalin*, London: 1986, p. 62; Berezhkov, V., *Kak ya stal perevodchikom Stalina*, Moscow: 1993, p. 360.
202. Gorlizki and Khlevniuk, *Cold Peace*, p. 159.
203. *Pravda*, 6, 10 March 1953.
204. Beria, *Beria, My Father*, pp. 249–50.
205. Chuev, *Molotov*, p. 549; Medvedev, *All Stalin's Men*, pp. 102–3.
206. Beria, *Beria, My Father*, p. 273.

14   Unrepentant Stalinist 1953–1957

1. *Politbyuro TsK i Sovet Ministrov*, pp. 436–8.
2. *Ibid.*, p. 103.
3. Simonov, *Glazami cheloveka moego pokoleniya*, p. 260.
4. *Politbyuro TsK i Sovet Ministrov*, p. 103.
5. *Izvestiya TsK*, no. 1, 1991, p. 161; Zubok and Pleshakov, *Inside the Kremlin's Cold War*, p. 156.
6. Dallin, *Soviet Foreign Policy after Stalin*, p. 121.
7. Taubman, W., *Khrushchev: the Man and his Era*, London: 2003, pp. 245–8; Knight, *Beria: Stalin's First Lieutenant*, pp. 184, 186–91.
8. *Izvestiya*, 10 March 1953.
9. *Pravda*, 16 March 1953.
10. Zubok and Pleshakov, *Inside the Kremlin's Cold War*, p. 155; Mastny, *The Cold War and Soviet Insecurity*, pp. 172–3.
11. See Brooks, J., *When The Cold War Did Not End: The Soviet Peace Offensive of 1953 and the American Response*, Kennan Institute Occasional Papers, no. 278, Washington DC: 2000, pp. 7–9.
12. Knight, *Beria: Stalin's First Lieutenant*, p. 186; Beria, *Beria, My Father*, pp. 263–4.
13. Zubok and Pleshakov, *Inside the Kremlin's Cold War*, p. 157.
14. Beria, *Beria, My Father*, p. 264.
15. Dallin, *Soviet Foreign Policy after Stalin*, p. 122.
16. Knight, *Beria: Stalin's First Lieutenant*, pp. 191–3; Chuev, *Molotov*, pp. 403–4; Taubman, *Khrushchev*, pp. 247–8; Zubok and Pleshakov, *Inside the Kremlin's Cold War*, pp. 160–1.
17. *Khrushchev Remembers*, p. 333.
18. Taubman, *Khrushchev*, p. 254.
19. *Khrushchev Remembers*, p. 337.
20. *Izvestiya TsK*, no. 1, 1991, p. 145.
21. *Ibid.*, pp. 156–60.
22. *Ibid.*, pp. 161–71.
23. 'Lavrentii Beriya: "Cherez 2–3 goda ya krepko ispravlyus' ... " ', *Istochnik*, no. 4, 1994, pp. 6–7; Taubman, *Khrushchev*, p. 256.
24. *Ibid.*, pp. 259–60.
25. *Ibid.*, p. 266.
26. Schecter, J. L. and Luchkov, V. V., eds, *Khrushchev Remembers: the Glasnost Tapes*, Boston: 1990, pp. 86–7.
27. *Ibid.*, p. 77.
28. *Ibid.*, pp. 75–6, 87.

29. Varsori, A., 'Britain and the Death of Stalin', in Gori, and Pons, *The Soviet Union and Europe in the Cold War, 1943–53*, pp. 342–3.
30. Bar-Noi, U., 'The Soviet Union and Churchill's Appeals for High-Level Talks, 1953–54: New Evidence from the Russian Archives', *Diplomacy and Statecraft*, vol. 9, no. 3, 1998, pp. 112–14.
31. *Ibid.*, pp. 114–15.
32. *Ibid.*, pp. 120–1, 124.
33. *Pravda*, 14 November 1953; Dallin, *Soviet Foreign Policy after Stalin*, p. 139.
34. *Ibid.*, pp. 132, 140.
35. *Ibid.*, p. 142.
36. *Ibid.*, pp. 142–3; Mastny, *The Cold War and Soviet Insecurity*, pp. 176–7.
37. Dallin, *Soviet Foreign Policy after Stalin*, pp. 143–5.
38. *Ibid.*, pp. 145–6; Zubok and Pleshakov, *Inside the Kremlin's Cold War*, pp. 169–70.
39. Dallin, *Soviet Foreign Policy after Stalin*, p. 146.
40. Roberts, F., *Dealing with Dictators: the Destruction and Revival of Europe, 1930–1970*, London: 1991, p. 168.
41. Dallin, *Soviet Foreign Policy after Stalin*, pp. 147–50; Bell, C., *Royal Institute of International Affairs, Survey of International Affairs 1954*, London: 1957, pp. 271–8.
42. *Ibid.*, pp. 42–73; Dallin, *Soviet Foreign Policy after Stalin*, pp. 151–5.
43. Ulam, *Expansion and Coexistence*, p. 354.
44. *FRUS 1952–1954*, vol. 16, *The Geneva Conference*, Washington: 1981, pp. 899, 904, 642.
45. Bar-Noi, U., 'The Soviet Union and Churchill's Appeals for High-Level Talks, 1953–54', pp. 125–6.
46. *Ibid.*, p. 126–7, citing AVPRF, 6/13/129/12, no 547. See *Exchange of Letters between Sir Winston Churchill and Mr. Molotov ... 1954 ... CMD. 9418*, London: 1955 and *Further Correspondence between Her Majesty's Government and the Soviet Government regarding Collective Security*, CMD 9281, London: 1954.
47. Bar-Noi, U., 'The Soviet Union and Churchill's Appeals for High-Level Talks, 1953–54', p. 128.
48. Zubok and Pleshakov, *Inside the Kremlin's Cold War*, pp. 166–8.
49. Taubman, *Khrushchev*, pp. 264–5.
50. *RGANI*, 3/8/388, 23–5, printed Fursenko, A. A., ed., *Prezidium TsK KPSS 1954–1964, t. 1, Chernovye protokol'nye zapisi zasedanii, Stenogrammy* (hereinafter Fursenko, *Prezidium TsK*), Moscow: 2003, pp. 35–6.
51. 'Poslednyaya "antipartiinaya" gruppa ... ', *IA*, no. 2, 1994, p. 9.
52. Taubman, *Khrushchev*, pp. 265–6. Cf. 'Plenum Transcripts Excerpts, 1955–1957', *Cold War International History Project Bulletin*, no. 10, March 1998, pp. 35–7, quoting *RGANI*, 2/1/127, and Zubok and Pleshakov, *Inside the Kremlin's Cold War*, p. 168.
53. *Pravda*, 9 February 1955.
54. Taubman, *Khrushchev*, p. 266, quoting *RGANI*, 2/1/176, 290–1.
55. *Ibid.*, pp. 261–3.
56. Talbot, S., ed., *Khrushchev Remembers, vol. 2, The Last Testament* (hereinafter *Khrushchev Remembers 2*), Harmondsworth: 1974, p. 159.
57. Chuev, *Molotov*, pp. 416–7.
58. Taubman, *Khrushchev*, p. 267 quoting *RGANI*, 2/1/176, 290–91, 294.
59. *Khrushchev Remembers 2*, pp. 163–4.
60. Taubman, *Khrushchev*, p. 376.
61. *Khrushchev Remembers 2*, pp. 136–7.
62. Taubman, *Khrushchev*, p. 267.
63. *Ibid.*
64. Supplement to *Études Soviétiques*, no. 84, 1955, p. 6, quoted Pethybridge, R., *A Key to Soviet Politics: the Crisis of the 'Anti-Party' Group*, London: 1962, pp. 62–3.
65. *Pravda*, 9 February 1955.
66. Schecter and Luchkov, eds, *Khrushchev Remembers: the Glasnost Tapes*, pp. 74–8.

67. *Pravda*, 12 March 1955.
68. Dallin, *Soviet Foreign Policy after Stalin*, pp. 255–9. Zubok and Pleshakov, *Inside the Kremlin's Cold War*, p. 171.
69. Taubman, *Khrushchev*, p. 268; Fursenko, *Prezidium TsK*, p. 889.
70. *Khrushchev Remembers* 379. Cf. Taubman, *Khrushchev*, p. 268.
71. *RGANI*, 2/8/388, 35–9, printed Fursenko, *Prezidium TsK*, p. 42.
72. *RGANI*, 3/8/388, 40–2, printed Fursenko, *Prezidium TsK*, pp. 44–6.
73. Taubman, *Khrushchev*, p. 268.
74. *RGANI*, 3/8/388, 53–7, printed Fursenko, *Prezidium TsK*, pp. 51–4.
75. 'Sovetsko–yugoslavskie otnosheniya: Iz dokumentov iyul'skogo plenuma TsK KPSS 1955g', *IA*, no. 5, 1999, pp. 1–12.
76. *Ibid.*, p. 22.
77. Taubman, *Khrushchev*, pp. 268–9, quoting *RGANI*, 2/1/172; 2/1/161, 229; Fursenko, *Prezidium TsK*, p. 889.
78. Taubman, *Khrushchev*, p. 269, quoting *RGANI*, 2/1/176, 295.
79. *Khrushchev Remembers*, p. 394.
80. Dallin, *Soviet Foreign Policy after Stalin*, pp. 277–83.
81. *Ibid.*, pp. 284–5.
82. *RGANI*, 3/8/388, 61–5, printed Fursenko, *Prezidium TsK*, pp. 58–60.
83. Dallin, *Soviet Foreign Policy after Stalin*, p. 285.
84. *Pravda*, 9 February 1955.
85. Chuev, *Molotov*, pp. 417–19. In one place Molotov speaks of Rumyantsev as the second author of the letter, in another P. A. Satyukov.
86. *Kommunist*, no. 14, 1955, pp. 127–8.
87. *Ibid.*, p. 4.
88. See above pp. 108.
89. *RGANI*, 3/8/389, 43–51, printed Fursenko, *Prezidium TsK*, pp 88–93.
90. *Pravda*, 15 February 1956.
91. *Ibid.*, 20 February 1956.
92. Taubman, *Khrushchev*, p. 278. Cf. *RGANI*, 3/8/389, 30–5, printed Fursenko, *Prezidium TsK*, p. 79.
93. Taubman, *Khrushchev*, pp. 278–9.
94. *RGANI*, 3/8/389, 52–4, printed Fursenko, *Prezidium TsK*, pp. 95–7.
95. *RGANI*, 3/8/389, 56–62, printed Fursenko, *Prezidium TsK*, pp. 101–3. Cf. Taubman, *Khrushchev*, pp. 279–80.
96. *RGANI*, 3/8/389, 66, printed Fursenko, *Prezidium TsK*, p. 106.
97. Taubman, *Khrushchev*, p. 281.
98. *Ibid.*, p. 273.
99. Khrushchev's Secret Speech in *Khrushchev Remembers*, pp. 575, 615. For Stalin's telegram see above p. 136 and for Molotov as a potential victim in 1952 see above p. 243.
100. Chuev, *Molotov*, pp. 419–21.
101. Knight, *Stalin and the Kirov Murder*, p. 263; Chuev, *Molotov*, p. 423; Taubman, *Khrushchev*, p. 288.
102. *Ibid.*, p. 287; Mićunović, V, trans. Floyd, D., *Moscow Diary*, London: 1980, pp. 23, 34, 38.
103. *Ibid.*, pp. 43–5.
104. *RGANI*, 3/12/1004, 48–9, printed Fursenko, *Prezidium TsK*, pp. 135–6.
105. *RGANI*, 3/12/1004, 50, printed Fursenko, *Prezidium TsK*, pp. 136–7.
106. *RGANI*, 3/12/1004, 50–1, printed Fursenko, *Prezidium TsK*, pp. 137–8.
107. *VVS*, 1955, 12–251.
108. Mićunović, *Moscow Diary*, pp. 62–3, 66–7.
109. *Ibid.*, pp. 81–4.
110. *RGANI*, 3/12/1004, 52–67, 1005, 1–3, printed Fursenko, *Prezidium TsK*, pp. 139–50.
111. *Ibid.*, pp. 953–61.
112. *RGANI*, 3/12/1005, 32–48, 1006, 1–5, printed Fursenko, *Prezidium TsK*, pp. 167–77.

113. See Gluchowski, L. W., 'Poland 1956: Khrushchev, Gomulka and the "Polish October" ', *Cold War International History Project Bulletin*, no. 5, 1995, pp. 1, 38–45.
114. Taubman, *Khrushchev*, p. 293.
115. *Ibid.*, p. 294.
116. *RGANI*, 3/12/1006, 4–5, printed Fursenko, *Prezidium TsK*, pp. 176–7.
117. Taubman, *Khrushchev*, p. 295.
118. *RGANI*, 3/12/1005, 53, 54–61, 62–3, printed Fursenko, *Prezidium TsK*, pp. 179–87.
119. See Kramer, M., 'New Evidence on Soviet Decision-Making and the 1956 Polish and Hungarian Crises', *Cold War International History Project Bulletin*, no. 8–9, Winter 1996/1997, pp. 367–8.
120. *RGANI*, 3/12/1006, 6–14, printed Fursenko, *Prezidium TsK*, pp. 187–91. *Cf.* Kramer, 'New Evidence on Soviet Decision-Making', p. 368.
121. *RGANI*, 3/12/1006, 15–18, printed Fursenko, *Prezidium TsK*, pp. 191–3.
122. Taubman, *Khrushchev*, p. 298; Kramer, 'New Evidence on Soviet Decision-Making', pp. 373–4.
123. *Ibid.*, pp. 375–6; *RGANI*, 3/12/1006, 31–3, printed Fursenko, *Prezidium TsK*, pp. 201–2.
124. *Ibid.*, 3/12/1006, 41–6, printed Fursenko, *Prezidium TsK*, pp. 204–7.
125. Kramer, 'New Evidence on Soviet Decision-Making', p. 376.
126. *VVS*, 1955, 23–508.
127. Fursenko, *Prezidium TsK*, p. 997.
128. Zalesskii, *Imperiya Stalina*, p. 326.
129. Taubman, *Khrushchev*, p. 301.
130. *Ibid.*, pp. 300–3.
131. *RGANI*, 3/12/1006, 54, 57, printed Fursenko, *Prezidium TsK*, pp. 212–13 215–16.
132. Conquest, *Power and Policy*, p. 293.
133. *RGANI*, 3/12/1006, 63–5, printed Fursenko, *Prezidium TsK*, pp. 221–3.
134. *RGANI*, 3/12/1007, 22–6, printed Fursenko, *Prezidium TsK*, pp. 236–9.
135. *Ibid*, pp. 999–1000. *Cf.* Chuev, *Molotov*, p. 347.
136. *RGANI*, 3/12/1007, 32–5, printed Fursenko, *Prezidium TsK*, pp. 239–42.
137. *Ibid.*, p. 1000.
138. *RGANI*, 3/12/1007, 32–5, printed Fursenko, *Prezidium TsK*, pp. 242–6.
139. Taubman, *Khrushchev*, pp. 304–5.
140. *RGANI*, 3/12/1007, 43–4, 47–8, printed Fursenko, *Prezidium TsK*, pp. 249–53.
141. *RGANI*, 3/12/1007, 45–6, printed Fursenko, *Prezidium TsK*, pp. 251–2.
142. *RGANI*, 3/12/1007, 52–3, printed Fursenko, *Prezidium TsK*, p. 255.
143. *RGANI*, 3/12/1007, 54–6, printed Fursenko, *Prezidium TsK*, p. 257; *Pravda*, 3 March 1957. *Cf. Conquest, Power and Policy*, pp. 296, 306.
144. *RGANI*, 3/12/1007, 54–6, printed Fursenko, *Prezidium TsK*, p. 257.
145. *Ibid.*, p. 1008.
146. Taubman, *Khrushchev*, pp. 305–6.
147. Quoted *Ibid.*, p. 306.
148. *Plenum TsK KPSS, 15–19 dekabriya 1958 goda, sten ot.* Moscow: 1958, pp. 421–3.
149. Taubman, *Khrushchev*, p. 310.
150. *Ibid.*, pp. 310–11; Barsukov, N., *XX s"ezd KPPSS i ego istoricheskie real'nost*, Moscow: 1991, p. 47.
151. 'Poslednyaya "antipartiinaya" gruppa', *IA*, no. 2, 1994, p. 9.
152. Taubman, *Khrushchev*, pp. 311–14.
153. *RGANI*, 3/12/1007, 57, printed Fursenko, *Prezidium TsK*, p. 258. *Cf.* Taubman, *Khrushchev*, p. 315.
154. *Pravda*, 15 July 1957.
155. *RGANI* 3/12/1007, 58, printed Fursenko, *Prezidium TsK*, pp. 258–9.
156. Taubman, *Khrushchev*, p. 316.
157. *Ibid.*, p. 317.

158. Kaganovich, *Pamyatnye zapiski*, pp. 518–21.
159. Taubman, *Khrushchev*, p. 318.
160. Barsukov, N., 'Proval "antipartiinoi gruppy" ', *Kommunist*, no. 8, 1990, p. 101.
161. 'Poslednyaya "antipartiinaya" gruppa', *IA*, no. 4, 1993, p. 57.
162. Schapiro, *The Communist Party of the Soviet Union*, p. 569.
163. Tompson, W. J., *Khrushchev: a Political Life*, Basingstoke: 1997, p.180; Taubman, *Khrushchev*, pp. 318–20.
164. 'Poslednyaya "antipartiinaya" gruppa', *IA*, no. 3, 1993, p. 5.
165. *Ibid.*, p. 6.
166. *Ibid.*, pp. 7–12.
167. *Ibid.*, pp. 17–18. See above p. 140.
168. *Ibid.*, pp. 24–45.
169. *Ibid.*, p. 46.
170. *Ibid.*, pp. 49, 50.
171. *Ibid.*, pp. 54–69.
172. *Ibid.*, pp. 70–1.
173. *Ibid.*, pp. 72–84.
174. *Ibid.*, pp. 85–7.
175. *Ibid.*, *IA*, no. 4 1993, pp. 4–9.
176. *Ibid.*, pp. 11–13.
177. *Ibid.*, pp. 13–76; *Ibid.*, *IA*, no. 5, 1993, pp. 4–75; *IA*, no. 6, 1993, pp. 4–72; *IA*, no. 1, 1994, pp. 4–75.
178. *Ibid.*, p. 17.
179. *Ibid.*, *IA*, no. 6, 1993, p. 58.
180. *Ibid.*, *IA*, no. 5, 1993, pp. 25–32.
181. See for instance *Ibid.*, *IA*, no. 6, p. 57.
182. *Ibid.*, *IA*, no. 4, 1993, pp. 26, 62; *IA*, no. 5, 1993, pp.15, 16, 24, 27, 28; *IA*, no. 6, 1993, p. 58.
183. *Ibid.*, *IA*, no. 1, 1994, pp. 36–42.
184. *Ibid.*, pp. 42–5.
185. *Ibid.*, pp. 45–65.
186. *Ibid.*, p. 52; Chuev, *Molotov*, p. 424.
187. 'Poslednyaya "antipartiinaya" gruppa', *IA*, no. 2, 1994, pp. 4–8.
188. *Ibid.*, pp. 9–11.
189. *Ibid.*, p. 13.
190. *Ibid.*, pp. 17–18, 20, 22.
191. *Ibid.*, pp. 24–9.
192. *Ibid.*, pp. 32–3.
193. *Ibid.*, pp. 36, 39.
194. *Ibid.*, pp. 46–7.
195. *Ibid.*, pp. 60, 61.
196. *Ibid.*, pp. 60–1.
197. *Ibid.*, pp. 61–2.
198. *Ibid.*, pp. 62–3.
199. *Pravda*, 4 July 1957.
200. 'Poslednyaya "antipartiinaya" gruppa', *IA*, no. 2, 1994, pp. 64–5.
201. Tompson, *Khrushchev: a Political Life*, pp. 182–3.
202. *Pravda*, 4 July 1957. *Cf.* 'Poslednyaya "antipartiinaya" gruppa', *IA*, no. 2, 1994, p. 69.
203. *Ibid.*, pp. 72–83.
204. *VVS*, 1957, 15–385–7.
205. *RGANI*, 3/12/1007, 63, printed Fursenko, *Prezidium TsK*, p. 262; *VVS*, 1957, 18–475.
206. Pethybridge, *A Key to Soviet Politics*, p. 135; Mićunović, *Moscow Diary*, p. 245.

15   The Outcast

1. Chuev, *Molotov*, p. 677.
2. Mićunović, *Moscow Diary*, p. 295.
3. *Ibid.*, pp. 350–75 *passim*.
4. *Ibid.*, pp. 351–5.
5. Medvedev, *All Stalin's Men*, pp. 106–7.
6. Mićunović, *Moscow Diary*, p. 355.
7. *Ibid.*, p. 352.
8. Chuev, *Molotov*, p. 164.
9. Medvedev, *All Stalin's Men*, p. 107.
10. *RGANI, 3/12/1009, 48*, printed Fursenko, *Prsezidium TSK*, p. 334.
11. Pethybridge, *A Key to Soviet Politics*, pp. 166–74; Sokolov, V., 'Foreign Affairs Commissar Vyacheslav Molotov', *International Affairs*, no. 6 1991, p. 95.
12. *VVS*, 1960, 39–362.
13. Sokolov, V., 'Foreign Affairs Commissar Vyacheslav Molotov', p. 95.
14. Medvedev, *All Stalin's Men*, p. 107; *KR2*, p. 558.
15. Zubok and Pleshakov, *Inside the Kremlin's Cold War*, p. 60.
16. *Ibid.*, quoting *RGANI*, KPK/13/76/1, 122–3.
17. See above p. 260.
18. Chuev, *Molotov*, p. 544.
19. *XXII s"ezd: sten. ot.*, t. 2, pp. 352–4.
20. Chuev, *Molotov*, p. 584.
21. *XXII s"ezd sten. ot.*, t. 1, pp. 15–92, 148–257.
22. *Ibid.*, p. 107.
23. Taubman, *Khrushchev*, pp. 514–5.
24. *XXII s"ezd, sten. ot.*, t. 2, p. 216.
25. *Ibid.*, p. 404.
26. *Ibid.*, pp. 579–93.
27. *Ibid.*, p. 585.
28. *Ibid.*, p. 586.
29. *The Guardian*, 31 January 1962.
30. Chuev, *Molotov*, p. 428.
31. Medvedev, *All Stalin's Men*, p. 108.
32. Sokolov, V., 'K 200 letiyu MID ROSSII: Molotov Vyascheslav Mikhailovich ... ', p. 150.
33. Chuev, *Molotov*, p. 677.
34. *Ibid.*, pp. 678–9; Vasilieva, *Kremlin Wives*, p. 148.
35. Mlechin, V., 'Vyacheslav Molotov: On dazhe ne mog spasti svoyu zheny', p. 43.
36. Alliluyeva, S., trans. Chavchavadze, P., *Only One Year*, London: 1969, p. 384.
37. Aroseva, *Bez grima*, pp. 257–64; see above p. 145.
38. Medvedev, *All Stalin's Men*, p. 109.
39. Chuev, *Molotov*, p. 678.
40. Chuev, *Tak govoril Kaganovich*, p. 59.
41. Kumanev, G.A., *Ryadom so Stalinym: otkrovennye svidetel'stva*, Moscow: 1999, p.13.
42. Medvedev, *All Stalin's Men*, pp. 109–11.
43. Chuev, *Sto sorok*, p. 3.
44. Kosolapov, R., 'Govoril li tak Molotov', *Marksist*, no. 2, 1994, pp. 111–17.
45. Chuev, *Molotov*, p. 693.
46. *Ibid.*, pp. 699–701.
47. 'More documents from the Russian Archives, VII, Excerpts from the Politburo Minutes, 1983–6', *Cold War International History Project Bulletin*, no. 4, 1994, p.81.
48. *Daily Telegraph*, 3 July 1986.
49. *Cf. Izvestiya.*, 11 November 1986 with *The Guardian*, or *The Daily Telegraph* or *The Times*, 12 November 1986.

50. Chuev, *Molotov*, p. 12.
51. *The Guardian*, 13 November 1986.

Conclusion

1. Davies, Ilic and Khlevnyuk, 'The Politburo and Economic Policy-Making', p. 129.
2. Roetter, C., *The Diplomatic Art: an Informal History of World Diplomacy*, Philadelphia: 1963, p. 108.
3. US Congress Committee on Foreign Affairs, *Soviet Diplomacy and Negotiating Behaviour: Emerging New Context for US Diplomacy*, Washington: 1979, p. xlviii.
4. Kennan, G., *Russia and the West under Lenin and Stalin*, Toronto: 1960, p. 335.
5. Watt, D. C., *How War Came: the Immediate Origins of the Second World War*, London: 1989, p. 113.
6. Chuev, *Molotov*, p. 340.
7. See above p. 264.
8. *Khrushchev Remembers: the Glasnost Tapes*, p. 77.
9. Chuev, *Molotov*, p. 362.
10. Simonov, K., 'Zametki k biografiii G.K. Zhukhova', *Voenno-istoricheskii Zhurnal*, no. 9, 1987, p. 49.
11. Gromyko, *Memories*, p. 404.

Bibliography

Archives

Russian archives

Rossiiskii Gosudarstvennyi Arkhiv Sotsial'no-Politicheskoi Istorii (referred to as *RGAS-PI*)
Fond 5	Lenin's Secretariat
Fond 17	Central Committee Papers
Fond 79	Kuibyshev Papers
Fond 82	Molotov Papers
Fond 85	Ordzhonikidze Papers
Fond 558	Stalin Papers
Fond 644	State Defence Committee (GKO) Papers

Arkhiv Vneshnei Politiki Rossiiskoi Federatsii (referred to as *AVPRF*)
Fond 6	Molotov's Secretariat
Fond 69	English Affairs
Fond 129	US Affairs

Gosudarstvennyi Arkhiv Rossiiskoi Federatsii (referred to as *GARF*)
Fond 5446	Sovnarkom Papers
Unclassified	Sovnarkom Bureau Papers

Russian archival sources are referred to by the name of the archive followed by fond/opis'/delo, list

Other archives

Birmingham University Library	Eden Papers	
Leeds Russian Archive	Lomonosov Papers	
Public Record Office	FO371	Foreign Office Papers
	Cab	Cabinet Papers

Printed documents and collections of documents

In Russian

Arbatov, G. A. *et al.*, eds, *Sovetsko–amerikanskie otnosheniya vo vremya Velikoi Otechestvennoi voiny, 1941–1945*, t. 1, 1941–1943, Moscow: 1984.

Bezymenskii, L. A., 'Direktivy I. V. Stalina V. M. Molotovu pered poesdkoi v Berlin v Noyabre 1940g.', *Novaya i noveishaya istoriya*, no. 4 1995, pp. 76–79.

Bondarenko, A. P., ed., *God krizisa 1938–1939: dokumenty i materialy* (referred to as *God krizisa*), t. 2, Moscow: 1990.

Danilov, V., Vinogradov, V., Viola, L. *et al.*, eds, *Tragediya sovetskoi derevni: kollektivizatsiya i raskulachivanii: dokumenty i materialy*
—— t. 1, *mai 1927–noyabr' 1929*, Moscow: 1999.
—— t. 2, *noyabr' 1929–dekabr' 1930*, Moscow: 2000.

Desyatyi s"ezd RKP(b) mart 1921 goda: stenograficheskii otchet, Moscow: 1963.

Devyatyi s"ezd RKP(b) mart–aprel 1920 goda: protokoly, Moscow: 1960.

Dokumenty vneshnei politiki SSSR (referred to as DVP), t. 15, Moscow: 1969, t. 16, Moscow: 1970, t. 18, Moscow: 1973, t. 21, Moscow: 1977, t. 22, kn. 1, Moscow: 1992, t. 23, kn. 2, ch. 1 Moscow: 1998.

Dvenadtsatyi s"ezd RKP(b), 17–25 aprelya 1923 goda: stenograficheskii otchet, Moscow: 1968.

Fursenko, A. A. ed., *Prezidium TsK KPSS 1954–1964, t. 1, Chernovye protokol'nye zapisi zasedanii, Stenogrammy* (referred to as Fursenko, *Prezidium TsK*) Moscow: 2003.

Gorlov, S. A. ed., 'Perepiska V. M. Molotova s I. V. Stalinym noyabr' 1940 goda', *Voenno–istoricheskii Zhurnal*, no. 9, 1992, pp. 18–23.

Gromyko, A. A. *et al.*, eds, *Sovetskii Soyuz na mezhdunarodnykh konferentsiyakh perioda Velikoi Otechestvennoi voiny 1941–1945 gg.*,

—— *t. I, Moskovskaya konferentsiya ministrov inostrannykh del SSSR, SShA i Velikobritaniii (19–30 oktyabyra 1943g.): sbornik dokumentov*, (referred to as *Moskovskaya konferentsiya*) Moscow: 1978.

—— *t. II, Tegeranskaya konferentsiya rukovoditelei trekh soyuznykh derzhav – SSSR, SShA i Velikobritanii (25 noyabrya–1 dekabrya 1943g.): sbornik dokumentov* (referred to as *Tegeranskaya konferentsiya*) Moscow: 1978.

—— *t. IV, Krymskaya konferentsiya rukovoditelei trekh soyuznykh derzhav–SSSR, SShA i Velikobritanii (4–11 fevralya 1945g), sbornik dokumentov*, Moscow: 1979.

—— *t. VI, Berlinskaya konferentsiya rukovoditelei trekh soyuznykh derzhav–SSSR, SShA i Velikobritanii (17 iyulya–2 avgusta 1945 g.) sbornik dokumentov*, Moscow: 1980.

Gromyko. A. A. *et al.*, eds, *SSSR v bor'be za mir nakanune vtoroi mirovoi voiny: (sentyabr' 1938g.–avgust 1939g.): dokumenty i materialy* (referred to as *SSSR v bor'be za mir*), Moscow: 1971.

Khlevnyuk, O. V., Devis, R. U. (Davies, R.W.), Kosheleva, L. P., Ris, E. A. (Rees, E. A.) Rogovaya, L. A., eds, *Stalin i Kaganovich: perepiska. 1931–1936 gg.* Moscow: 2001.

Khlevnyuk, O. V., Gorlitskii, I. *et al.*, eds, *Politbyuro TsK VKP(b) i Sovet Ministrov SSSR 1945–1953* (referred to as *Politbyuro TsK i Sovet Ministrov*), Moscow: 2002.

Korotkov, A. V. and Chernobaev, A. A. eds, 'Posetiteli kremlevskogo kabineta I.- V. Stalina' (referred to as 'Stalin's Office Diary'), *Istoricheskii Arkhiv*, no. 6, 1994, pp. 4–43; no. 2, 1995, 128–199; no. 3, 1995, pp. 119–77; no. 4, 1995, pp. 15–73; nos. 5–6, 1995, pp. 4–64; no. 2, 1996, pp. 3–72; no. 3, 1996, pp. 4–86; no. 4, 1996, pp. 66–121; nos. 5–6, 1996, pp. 3–61; no. 1, 1997, pp. 3–39.

Kovaleva, N. V. *et al.*, 'Poslednyaya "antipartiinaya" gruppa: Stenograficheskii otchet iyun'skogo (1957g) plenuma TsK KPSS' (referred to as 'Poslednyaya "antipartiinaya" gruppa ...', *Istoricheskii Arkhiv*, no. 3, 1993, pp. 4–95; no. 4, 1993, pp. 4–82; no. 5, 1993, pp. 4–78; no. 6, 1993, pp. 4–78; no. 2, 1994, pp. 4–88.

Kudelli, P. F., ed., *Pervyi legal'nyi Peterburgskii komitet bol'shevikov v 1917g.: sbornik materialov i protokolov zasedanii Peterburgskogo komiteta RSDRP(b) i ego ispolnitelnoi komissii za 1917g i rechnoi V. I. Lenina*, Moscow-Leningrad: 1927.

Kynin, G. P. and Laufer, I., eds, *SSSR i Germanskii Vopros, 22 iyunya 1941g.–8 maya 1945g, t. 1*, Moscow: 1996.

Kynin, G. P. *et al.*, eds, *Sovetsko-angliiskie otnosheniya vo vremya Velikoi Otechestvennoi voiny, 1941–1945, t. 1, 1941–1943*, Moscow: 1983.

Mar'ina, V.V., 'Dnevnik G. Dimitrova', *Voprosy Istorii*, no. 7, 2000, pp. 32–55.

'Materialy fevral'sko-martovskogo plenuma TsK VKP(b) 1937 goda', *Voprosy Istorii*, no. 2/3, 1992, pp. 3–45; no.4/5, 1992, pp. 3–36; no. 6/7, 1992, pp. 3–29; no. 8/9, 1992, pp. 3–29; no. 10, 1992, pp. 3–36; no. 11/12, 1992, pp. 3–19; no. 2, 1993, pp. 3–33; no. 5, 1993, pp. 3–21; no. 6, 1993, pp. 3–30; no. 7, 1993, pp. 3–24; no. 8, 1993, pp. 3–26; no. 9, 1993, pp. 3–32; no. 1, 1994, pp. 12–28; no. 2, 1994, pp. 3–29; no. 6, 1994, pp. 3–23; no. 8, 1994, pp. 3–29; no. 10, 1994, pp. 3–27; no. 12, 1994, pp. 3–29; no. 2, 1995, pp. 3–26; no. 3, 1995, pp. 3–15; no. 4, 1995, pp. 3–18; no. 5/6, 1995, pp. 3–24; no. 7, 1995, pp. 3–25; no. 8, 1995, pp. 3–25; no. 10, 1995, pp. 3–28; no. 11/12, 1995, pp. 13–23.

'Materialy plenuma TsK VKP(b) (1944g.)', *Istoricheskii Arkhiv*, no. 1, 1992, pp. 61–5.

Odinatsiya s"ezd RKP(b): mart–aprel' 1922 goda: stenograficheskii otchet, Moscow: 1961.

Pervaya Moskovskaya oblastnaya konferentsiya Vsesoyuznoi Kommunisticheskoi Partii (bol'she-vikov): stenograficheskii otchet [September 14–18, 1929], t. 1, Moscow: 1929.

Pervaya sesssiya Verkhovnogo Soveta SSSR, 12–19 yanvarya 1938: stenograficheskii otchet, Moscow: 1938.

'Protokoly i rezolyutsii byuro TsK RSDRP(b) (mart 1917g.)', *Voprosy Istorii KPSS*, 1962, no. 3, pp. 134–57.

Protokoly s"ezdov i konferentsii vsesoyuznoi kommunisiticheskoi partii(b): odinatsyi s"ezd RKP(b) mart–aprel' 1922g., Moscow: 1936.

Protokoly tsentral'nogo komiteta RSDRP(b) avgust 1917g.–fevral'ya 1918g., Moscow: 1958.

Sevost'yanov, G.N., 'Poezdka V. M. Molotova v Berlin v noyabre 1940 g.', *Novaya i Noveishaya Istoriya*, no. 5, 1993, pp. 64–99.

Shestoi s"ezd RSDRP (bol'shevikov) avgust 1917 goda: protokoly, Moscow: 1958.

Siborov, A. L. ed. *Velikaya oktyabr'skaya sotsialisticheskaya revolyutsiya: documenti i materialy*, t. 2, Moscow: 1962.

'Sovetsko–germanskie dokumenty 1939–1941gg. iz arkhiva TsK KPSS', *Novaya i Noveishaya Istoriya*, no. 1, 1993, pp. 83–95.

'Sovetsko–yugoslavskie otnosheniya: Iz dokumentov iyul'skogo plenuma TsK KPSS 1955g.', *Istoricheskii Arkhiv*, no. 5, 1999, pp. 1–50.

Trinadtsatyi s"ezd RKP(b), mai 1924, stenograficheskii otchet, Moscow: 1963.

Venturi F. *et al.*, eds, *Bol'shevistskoe rukovodstvo perepiska 1912–1927*, Moscow: 1997.

Vos'moi s"ezd RKP(b), Mart 1919 goda: Protokoly, Moscow: 1959.

Vtoraya i tret'ya Petrogradskie obshchegorodskie konferentsii bol'shevikov v iyule i oktyabre 1917 goda: protokoly, Moscow-Leningrad: 1927.

(XII) Vserossiiskaya Konferentsiya RKP (bol'shevikov), Byulleten' no. 3, 8 August 1922; *Byulleten'* no. 4, 9 August 1922.

XIV s"ezd VKP(b) 18–31 dekabrya 1925 g.: stenograficheskii otchet, Moscow: 1962.

XV konferentsiya VKP(b), stenograficheskii otchet, Moscow: 1927.

XV s"ezd VKP(b): Dekabr' 1927 goda: stenograficheskii otchet, Moscow: 1962.

XVI konferentsiya Vsesoyuznoi Kommunisticheskoi Partii(b): stenograficheskii otchet, Moscow: 1962.

XVI s"ezd Vsesoyuznoi Kommunisticheskoi Partii(b) stenograficheskii otchet, Moscow: 1931.

XVII konferentsiya Vsesoyuznoi Kommunisticheskoi Partii(b): stenograficheskii otchet, Moscow: 1932.

XVII s"ezd Vsesoyuznoi Kommunisticheskoi Partii(b): stenograficheskii otchet, Moscow: 1934.

XVIII s"ezd Vsesoyuznoi Kommunisticheskoi Partii(b) 10–21 marta 1939 g. stenograficheskii otchet, Moscow: 1939.

XXII s"ezd Kommunisticheskoi Partii Sovetskogo Soyuza 17–31 oktyabrya 1961 god: stenograficheskii otchet, Moscow: 1962.

In English and other languages

Banac, I., ed., *The Diary of Georgi Dimitrov 1933–1949*, New Haven, CT: 2003.

Butler, R. and Pelly, M. E., eds, *Documents on British Policy Overseas*, Series 1, vol. 1, London: 1984; vol. 2, London: 1985.

Degras, J., *Soviet Documents on Foreign Policy*, vol. 3, 1933–1941, Oxford: 1953.

Documents Diplomatiques Français, 2e série (1936–1939) referred to as *DDF*, t. 1, Paris: 1963.

'Documents: Negotiating in the Kremlin: the Estonian Experience of 1939', *Lituanus*, vol. 14, no. 2, 1968, pp. 52–84.

Documents of the United Nations Conference on International Organization San Francisco 1945, vol. 1, London: 1945.

Exchange of Letters between Sir Winston Churchill and Mr. Molotov ... 1954, CMD 9418, London: 1955.

Further Correspondence between Her Majesty's Government and the Soviet Government regarding Collective Security, CMD 9281, London: 1954.

Gluchowski, L. W., 'Poland 1956: Khrushchev, Gomulka and the "Polish October" ', *Cold War International History Project Bulletin*, no. 5, 1995, pp. 1, 38–45.

'More documents from the Russian Archives, VII Excerpts from the Politburo Minutes, 1983–6', *Cold War International History Project Bulletin*, no. 4, 1994, pp. 76–85.

Morozova, I. and Takhnenko, G., ' "The Winter War": Documents on Soviet–Finnish relations 1939–40', *International Affairs*, no. 9, 1989, pp. 49–71.

'Plenum Transcripts Excerpts, 1955–1957', *Cold War International History Project Bulletin*, no. 10, March 1998, pp. 27–60.

Rzheshevsky, O. A., ed., *War and Diplomacy: the Making of the Grand Alliance: Documents from Stalin's Archives*, Amsterdam: 1996.

Sontag R. J. and Beddie J.S., eds, *Nazi–Soviet Relations 1939–1941: Documents from the Archives of the German Foreign Office*, Westport: 1976.

Sweet, P.R. *et al.*, eds, *Documents on German Foreign Policy 1918–1939* (referred to as *DGFP*) Series C, vols. 1, 6, 7, 8, London: 1953–1958.

'The Baltic Countries Join the Soviet Union (Documents on the USSR's Relations with the Baltic Countries in 1939 and 1940)', *International Affairs*, no. 4, April 1990, pp. 97–124.

US Department of State, *Foreign Relations of the United States: Diplomatic Papers* (referred to as *FRUS*).

—— *The Soviet Union 1933–1939*, Washington, DC: 1952.

—— *1939*, vol.1, Washington, DC: 1952.

—— *1942*, vol. 3, *Europe*, Washington, DC: 1961.

—— *1943*, vol. 1, *General*, Washington, DC: 1963.

—— *1943*, vol. 3, *British Commonwealth, Eastern Europe and the Far East*, Washington, DC: 1963.

—— *1945, The Conference of Berlin (The Potsdam Conference), 1945*, vol. 1, Washington, DC: 1960.

—— *1945*, vol. 2, *General: Political and Economic Matters*, Washington, DC: 1967.

—— *1945, The Conferences at Malta and Yalta 1945*, Washington, DC: 1955.

—— *1945*, vol. 3, *European Advisory Commission, Austria and Germany*, Washington, DC: 1968.

—— *1945*, vol. 5, *Europe*, Washington, DC: 1967.

—— *1952–1954*, vol. 16, *The Geneva Conference*, Washington, DC: 1981.

Watt, D. C., ed., *British Documents on Foreign Affairs: Reports and Papers from the Foreign Office Confidential Print, Part II From the First to the Second World War, Series A, The Soviet Union 1917–1939*, vol. 16, *The Soviet Union 1930–1932*. Washington, DC: 1992.

Woodward, E. L. and Butler, R., eds, *Documents on British Foreign Policy*, (referred to as *DBFP*), 3rd. series, vols. 4–7, London: 1949–1956.

Newspapers and journals

Bol'shevik.
Byulleten' Oppozitsii.
Ekonomicheskaya Zhizn'.
Izvestiya TsK KPSS.
Izvestiya TsK RKP(b).
Izvestiya.
Kommunist.
Leningradskaya Pravda.
Literaturnaya Gazeta.
Moscow News.
Moskovskie Novosti.
Organizatsiya Upravleniya.
Pravda Truda.

Pravda.
Proletarskaya Pravda.
Proletarskaya Revolyutsiya.
Put' Pravdy.
Sotsialisticheskii Vestnik.
Trudovaya Pravda.
Vedomosti Verkhovnogo Soveta SSSR.
Za Industrializatsiyu.
Za Pravdu.

Books and articles in Russian

Adzhubei, A., 'Te desyat' let', *Znamiya,* no. 6, 1988, pp. 81–123.
'Angliya dolzhna imet' pravo reshayushchego golosa v Gretsii', *Istochnik,* no. 2, 2003, pp. 45–56.
' "Aprel'skie tezisy" Lenina i aprel'skaya konferentsiya bol'shevikov', *Bol'shevik* no. 9, 1937, pp. 86–101.
Aroseva, O.A. and Maksimova, V.A., *Bez grima,* Moscow: 1999.
' "Avtobiograficheskii zametki" V.N.Pavlova – perevodchika I.V.ytalina', *Novaya i Noveishaya Istoriya,* no. 4, 2000, pp. 92–104.
Barsukov, N., 'Proval "antipartiinoi gruppy" ', *Kommunist,* no. 8, 1990, pp. 98–108.
Bazhanov, B., *Vospominaniya vyshego sekretarya Stalina,* Paris: 1980.
Berezhkov, V. M., *S diplomaticheskoi missiei v Berlin 1940–1941,* Moscow: 1966.
'Beseda professora G. A. Kumaneva s M. G. Pervukhinym', *Novaya i Noveishaya Istoriya,* no. 5, 2003, pp. 123–9.
Bezymenskii, L. A., 'Vizit V. M. Molotova v Berlin v noyabre 1940g. v svete novykh dokumentov', *Novaya i Noveishaya Istoriya,* no. 6, 1995, pp. 121–43.
Bezymenskii, L. A., *Gitler i Stalin pered skhvatkoi,* Moscow: 2000.
Bezymenskii, L. A., 'Sekretnye protokoly 1939g. kak problema sovetskoi istoriografii', *Rossiya i Sovremennyi Mir,* no. 1(10), 1996, pp. 129–50.
Bezymenskii, L. A., 'Sovetsko–Germanskie dogovory 1939g.: novye dokumenty i starye problemy', *Novaya i Noveishaya Istoriya,* no. 4, 1998, pp. 3–26.
Bol'shaya Sovetskaya Entsiklopediya, (referred to as *BSE*), 1st. edn, vol. 151, Moscow: 1945; vol. 9, Moscow: 1928; 2nd. edn, Moscow: 1949–1958.
Bonvesch, B., ed., ' "Skostit' polovinu summy reparatsii ... my mozhet" ', *Istochnik,* no. 3, 2003, pp. 100–28.
Chernopitskii, P. G., *Na velikom perelome: Sel'skie Sovety Dona v period podgotovki i provideniya massovoi kollektivizatsii (1928–1931gg.),* Rostov-on-Don: 1965.
Chuev, F., *Molotov: poluderzhavnyi vlastelin,* Moscow: 2000.
Chuev, F., *Sto sorok besed s Molotovym: iz dnevnika F. Chueva,* Moscow: 1991.
Chuev, F., *Tak govoril Kaganovich: ispoved' stalinskogo apostola,* Moscow: 1992.
Danilov, A. A., 'Stalinskoe Politbyuro v poslevoennye gody', in Erofeev, N. D. *et al.,* eds, *Politichestkie partii Rossii: stranitsy istorii,* Moscow: 2000, pp. 193–201.
'Delo o tak nazyvaemoi "antisovetskoi–trotskistskoi voennoi organizatsii v krasnoi armii" ', *Izvestiya TsK,* 1989, no. 4, pp. 42–80.
Drabkhina, F., 'Tsarskoe pravitel'stva i "Pravda" ', *Istorcheskii Zhurnal,* vol. 7, no. 3/4, March/April 1937, pp. 115–23.
Drabkina, F. I., 'Vserossiiskoe soveshchanie bol'shevikov v marte 1917 goda', *Voprosy Istorii,* no. 9, 1956, pp. 4–16.
Egorov, A. G. and Bogolyubov, K. M., eds, *Kommunisticheskaya Partiya Sovetskogo Soyuza v rezolyutsiyakh i resheniyakh s"ezdov, konferentsii i plenumov TsK,* t. 4, 1926–1929, Moscow: 1984.
Emal'yanov, N. A., 'Il'ich v Razlive', *Znamya,* no. 2, 1957, pp. 143–7.

Gambarova, Yu. S. *et al.*, eds, *Entsiklopedicheskii slovar' russkogo bibliograficheskogo instituta Granat*, Moscow: n.d.

Gnedin, E., 'V Narkomindele 1922–1939: Interv'yu s E. A. Gnedinym', *Pamyat'*, New York/Paris, 1981–1982, no. 5, pp. 357–93.

Gnedin, E., *Katastrofa i vtoroe rozhdenie*, Amsterdam: 1977.

Gor'kov, Yu., *Gosudarstvennyi Komitet Oborony postanovlyaet (1941–1945): tsifry dokumenty*, Moscow: 2002.

Gorlov, S.A., 'Peregovory V. M. Molotova v Berlin v noyabre 1940 goda', *Voenno–istoricheskii Zhurnal*, no. 6–7, 1992, pp. 45–8.

Gubergrits A., ed., *Ot pakta Molotova-Ribbentropa do dogovora o basakh*, Talinin: 1990.

Ibraginov, Sh. N., 'O Lefortovskom raione (1915g. do nachala 1917g.)' in *Put' k Oktyabryu*, vol. 5, Moscow: 1926.

Institut istorii partii MK and MGK KPSS, *Listovki Moskovskii organizatsii Bol'shevikov 1914–1925gg*, Moscow: 1954.

Istoriya Vsesoyuznoi Kommunisticheskoi Partii (bol'shevikov): kratkii kurs, Moscow: 1938.

Istpart, *Iz epokhi 'Zvezdy' i 'Pravdy' 1911–1914 gg.*, *vypusk I*, Moscow: 1921; *vypusk III*, Moscow: 1923.

Ivnitskii, N. A., 'Istoriya podgotovki postanovleniya TsK VKP(b) o tempakh kollektivizatsii sel'skogo khozyaistva ob 5 yanvarya 1930 g.', in *Istochnikovedenie istorii sovetskogo obshchestva*, Moscow: 1964, pp. 265–88.

Ivnitskii, N. A., 'Golod 1932–1933 godov: kto vinovat?', in Afanas'ev, Yu. N., ed., *Golod 1932–33*, Moscow: 1995, pp. 43–65.

Ivnitskii, N.A., *Klassovaya bor'ba v derevne i likvidatsiya kulachestva kak klassa*, Moscow: 1972.

'Iz istorii kollektivizatsii', *Izvestiya TsK*, no. 5, 1991, pp. 193–203.

Kaganovich, L. *Pamyatnye zapiski rabochego kommunista-bol'shevika, profsoyuznogo, partiinoi sovetsko-gosudarstvennogo rabotnika*, Moscow: 1996.

'Kanun voiny: preduprezhdeniya diplomatov', *Vestnik MID*, no. 8 (66), 30 April 1990, pp. 71–80.

Khlevnyuk, O. V. *et al.*, *Stalinskoe politbyuro v 30-e gody: sbornik dokumentov*, Moscow: 1995.

Khlevnyuk, O., *Politbyuro: mekhanizma politicheskoi vlasti v 30-e gody*, Moscow: 1996.

Khlevnyuk, O. V., *Stalin i Ordzhonikidze: konflikty v Politbyuro v 30-e gody*, Moscow: 1993.

Kislitsyn, S.A., *Shakhtinskoie delo: nachalo stalinskikh repressii protiv nauchno-tekhnicheskoi intelligentsii*, Rostov-on-Don: 1993.

Kommunisticheskaya Partiya Ukrainu v rezolyutsiyakh, Kiev: 1958.

Kosolapov, R., 'Govoril li tak Molotov', *Marksist*, no. 2, 1994, pp. 111–17.

Kozlov, V. A. and Mironenko, S. V., eds, *Arkhiv noveishei istorii Rosiii, t. 2, 'Osobaya papka' V.M. Molotova*, Moscow: 1994.

Kumanev, G. A., *Ryadom so Stalinym: otkrovennye svidetel'stva*, Moscow: 1999.

Kuntskaya, L. and Mashitakova, K., *Krupskaya*, Moscow: 1973.

Kurtsov, V. I., ed., *Stranitsy istorii KPSS. Fakty, problemy, uroki*, vol. 2, Moscow: 1989.

Kuznetsov N. G., 'Voenno-Morskoi Flot nakanune Velikoi Otechestvennoi voiny', *Voenno–istoricheskii Zhurnal*, no. 9, 1965, pp. 59–76.

'Lavrentii Beriya: "Cherez 2–3 goda ya krepko ispravlyus" ..." ', *Istochnik*, no. 4, 1994, pp. 3–14.

Lenin, V.I., *Polnoe sobranie sochinenii*, (referred as Lenin, *PSS*), 5th. edn, Moscow: 1956–1965.

Loginov, V.T, *Leninskaya "Pravda" (1912–1914gg.)*, Moscow: 1972.

Lukovets, A. I. and Sybotskii, A. B., eds, *Lenin v 'Pravde': vospominaniya*, Moscow: 1970.

Lyashchenko, N. G., 'S ognem i krov'yu po polam ... ', *Voenno–istoricheskii Zhurnal*, 1995, pp. 22–8.

Maiskii, I. M. *Vospominaniya sovetskogo diplomata 1925–1945*, Moscow: 1987.

Marina, Yu., 'Vse, chto govorit Radek-eto absolyutno elostnaya kleveta ...', *Istochnik*, no. 1, 2001, pp. 63–77.

'Massovye repressii opravdany byt' ne mogut', *Istochnik*, no. 1, 1995, pp. 117–32.

Mel'tyukhov, M. I., 'Narashchivanie sovetskogo voennogo prisutstviya v pribaltike v 1939–1941 godakh', Otechestvennaya Istoriya, no. 4, 1999, pp. 46–70.
Menitski, I., Revolyutsionnoe dvizhenie voennykh godov, 1914–1917, vol. 1, Moscow: 1925.
Mikoyan, A., Tak bylo, Moscow: 1999.
Mikoyan, A., V nachale dvadtsatykh, Moscow: 1975.
Mlechlin, L., 'Vyacheslav Molotov: On dazhe ne mog spasti svoyu zhenu', Novoe Vremya, nos. 43–44, 1998, pp. 40–43.
Molotov, V. M., 'O proizvoditel'nosti truda', Bol'shevik, no. 11–12, 1924, pp. 3–9.
Molotov, V. M., 'O Vysshei Shkole', Bol'shevik, nos. 10–11, 1938, pp. 3–15.
Molotov, V. M., 'Ob urokakh trotskizma', in Za Leninizm, sbornik statei, Moscow: 1925, pp. 168–200.
Molotov, V. M., Kak rabochie stroyat sotsialisticheskoe khozyaistvo, Moscow: 1918.
Molotov, V. M., V bor'be za sotsializm: rechi i stat'i, Moscow: 1935.
Molotov, V. M., 'O kolkhoznom dvizhenie', Bol'shevik, no. 22, 1929, pp. 10–23.
Molotov, V. M., 'O nashikh zadachakh', Bol'shevik, no. 5, 1930, pp. 9–25.
Molotov, V. M., Politika partii v derevne, Moscow: 1927.
Molotov, V. M., Stat'i i rechi 1935–1936, Moscow: 1937.
Moskalev, M. A., Byuro Tsentral'nogo Komiteta RSDRP v Rossii, Moscow: 1964.
Nebogin, O. B. and Samorodov, A. G., 'Diskussii v Moskovskoi partiinoi organizatsii v 1928–1929 gg.', Voprosy Istorii KPSS, 1990, no. 6, pp. 64–74.
Nepomniashchii, K., Polki idyut na zapad, Moscow: 1964.
Novikov, N.V., Vospominaniya diplomata: Zapiski 1938–1947, Moscow: 1989.
'Novyi pod''em rabochego dvizheniya, 1910–1914', Krasnyi Arkhiv, no. 1, 1934.
Ocherki po istorii revolyutsionnogo dvizheniya i bol'shevistskoi organizatsii v Baumanskom raione, Moscow: 1926.
Pavlov, D., 'Eto eshche ne sotsialism: dve poslednie vstrechi s V.M. Molotovym', Literaturnaya Gazeta, 18 April 1990.
Pechenkin, A. A., '1937 god: Stalin i voennyi sovet', Otechestvennaya Istoriya, no. 1, 2003, pp. 35–53.
Pomyalovskii, N. G., Meshchansko schast'e – Molotov – ocherki bursy, Moscow: 1987.
'Poshchadite zhe rodinu i nas', Istochnik, no. 1, 1995, pp. 138–45.
'Predystoriya 1939 goda', Svobodnaya Mysl', no. 7, 1999, pp. 108–12.
Rzheshevskii, O. A., 'Operatsiya "Tolstoi", Vizit U. Cherchilya v Moskvu v oktyabre 1944g.', Novaya i Noveishaya Istoriya, no. 5, 2003, pp. 104–21.
Sazanov, I. S., 'Byuro pechato pri TsK RSDRP(b) v1917 godu', Istoricheskii Arkhiv, no. 5, 1955, pp. 199–201.
Sheinis, Z., Maksim Maksimovich Litvinov: revolyutsioner, diplomat, chelovek, Moscow: 1989.
Shlyapnikov, A., Kanun semnadtsatogo, ch. 2, Moscow: 1922.
Shlyapnikov, A., Semnadtsatyi god, ch. 1, Moscow-Leningrad: 1923.
Simonov, K., Glazami cheloveka moego pokoleniya, Moscow: 1988.
Sipols, V. Ya., 'Torgovo-ekonomicheskie otnosheniya mezhdu SSSR i Germaniei v 1939–1941gg. v svete novykh arkhivnykh dokumnetov', Novaya i Noveishaya Istoriya, no. 2, 1997, pp. 29–41.
Sipols, V. Ya., Tainy diplomaticheskie kanun Velikoi Otechestvennoi Voiny, Moscow: 1997.
Smirnov, V. V. and Khitrina, N. E., 'Ya ne veryu etomu', Istoricheskii Arkhiv, no. 1, 2000, pp. 9–20.
Sobolev, P. I. et al., eds, Velikaya Oktyabr'skaya Sotsialisticheskaya Revolyutsiya: khronika sobytii, t. 2, 7 maya–25 iyunya 1917 god, Moscow: 1957.
Sobranie Postanovlenii i Rasporyazhenii Pravitel'stva SSSR (referred to as SP).
Sobranie Zakonov i Rasporyazhenii Raboche-krest'yanskogo Pravitel'stva SSSR (referred to as SZ).
Sokolov, V.V., 'K 200-letiyu MID ROSSII', Diplomaticheskii Vestnik, no. 7, 2002, pp. 145–50.
Stalin, I. V. Sochineniya, (13 vols.) Moscow: 1946–1949.
Starkov, B. A., 'Ar'ergardnye boi staroi partiino gvardii', in Afanas'ev, A.V., ed., Oni ne molchali, Moscow: 1991, pp. 215–25.

Tikhomirnov, G.A., *Vyacheslav Mikhailovich Molotov: kratkaya biografiya*, 2nd edn, Moscow: 1940.
Tokarev, Yu. S., *Petrogradskii sovet rabochikh soldatskikh deputatov v marte-aprele 1917g.*, Leningrad: 1976.
Troyanovskii, O., *Cherez gody i rastoyaniya: istorii odnoi sem'i*, Moscow: 1997.
Trubnikov, V. I., 'Sovetskaya diplomatiya nakanune Velikoi Otechestvennoi voiny: usiliya po protivodeistviyu fashistskoi agressii', in *60 let so dnya nachala Velikoi Otechestvennoi voiny: voenno-istoricheskaya konferentsiya, spetsial'ni vypusk, Voenno–Istoricheskii Zhurnal*, Moscow: 2001, pp. 12–19.
Trudy pervogo vserossiskogo s"ezda Sovetov Narodnogo Khozyaistva, 25 maya – 4 iyunya 1918g., Moscow: 1918.
Tsukerman, S. I., 'Petrogradskii raionnyi komitet bol'shevikov v 1917 godu', *Krasnaya Letopis'*, no. 2 (53), 1933, pp. 88–122.
Valentinov, N., ed, Bunyan, J. and Bytenko, U., *Novaya ekonomicheskaya politika i krizis partii posle smerti Lenina*, Stanford, CA: 1971.
Varlamov, K. I. and Slamikhin, N. A., *Razoblachenie V. I. Leninym teorii i taktiki levykh kommunistov*, Moscow: 1964.
Vasil'ev, V., 'Tsena golodnogo khleba. Politika rukovodstva SSSR i USSR v 1932–1933gg.', in Vasil'ev, V. and Shapoval, Yu., eds, *Komandiry bol'shogo goloda: poezdki V. Molotova i L. Kaganovicha v Ukrainu i na Severnyi Kavkaz, 1932–1933gg*, Kiev: 2001, pp. 81–164.
'V komissii Politbyuro TsK KPSS', *Izvestiya TsK KPSS*, no. 4, 1989, pp. 42–80; no. 5, 1989; pp. 67–92; no. 8, 1999, pp.78–115; no. 9, 1989, pp. 30–50.
'Vnov' o dogovore 1939 goda', *Vestnik Ministerstva Inostrannykh del SSSR*, 28 February 1991, pp. 56–63.
'Vnutrinapartiinye diskussii 20-kh godi', *Izvetiya TsK*, 1990, no. 7, pp. 175–92.
Volkogonov, D., *Triumf i tragediya: politicheskii portret I. V. Stalina*, Moscow: 1989.
Volkov, V. K., 'Sovetsko-germanskie otnosheniya vo vtoroi polovine 1940 goda', *Voprosy Istorii*, no. 2, 1997, pp. 3–17.
Volobuev, P. V., *Petrogradskii sovet rabochhikh i soldatskikh deputatov v 1917 godu*, t.1, *27 fevralya–31 marta 1917 godu*, Leningrad: 1971.
Vyshinskii, A., 'Glava sovetskogo pravitel'stva', *Sovetskoe Gosudarstvo i Pravo*, no. 2., 1940, pp. 3–22.
Yaroslavskii, E., *Istoriya VKP(b)*, ch. 2. Moscow: 1933.
Yurchuk, V.I. *et al.*, eds, *Kommunisticheskaya Partiya Ukrainu v rezolyutsiyakh i resheniyakh s"ezdov, konferentsii i plenumov TsK*, t. 1, 1918–1941, Kiev: 1976.
Zalesskii, K.D., *Imperiya Stalina: biograficheskii entsiklopedicheskii slovar'*, Moscow: 2000.
' "Zanyat'sya Podgotovkoi Budushchego Mira" ', *Istochnik*, no. 4, 1995, pp. 114–58.
Zemskov, V. M., 'O nekotorykh problemakh "bol'shogo terrora" 1937–1938 godov', *Otechestvennaya Istoriya*, no. 1, 2000, pp. 200–5.
Zhukov, G. K., *Vospominaniya i razmyshleniya*, t. 2, 3, Moscow: 1990.

Unpublished material in Russian

Khlevnyuk, O., 'Zadavlennye oligarkhi. Stalin i ego okruzhenie v poslevoennye gody', unpublished paper for conference 'Rethinking the Stalin Era', University of Toronto, 1999.
Vasil'ev, V., 'Politbyuro TsK KP(b) U v period otnositel'noi ekonomicheskoi stabilizatsiii i v usloviyakh "bol'shogo terrora" (1934 i 1937 gg.)', unpublished paper for European University Institute conference on 'Stalin's Politburo', Florence, 2000.

Books and articles in English and other languages

Alliluyeva, S., trans. Chavchavadze, P., *Only One Year*, London: 1969.
Alliluyeva, S., trans. Johnson, J., *Twenty Letters to a Friend*, Harmondsworth: 1968.
'Anglo-French-Soviet Talks in Moscow 1939', *International Affairs*, October 1969, pp. 61–8.

Antonov-Osvyenko, A., *The Time of Stalin: Portrait of a Tyranny*, trans. Saunders, G., New York: 1980.
Assarsen, V., 'The Moscow Diplomatic Corps in 1941', *International Affairs*, July 1991, pp. 123–31.
Aster, S., *1939: The Making of the Second World War*, London: 1973.
Avtorkhanov, A., *Stalin and the Communist Party*, London: 1959.
Badayev, A., *The Bolsheviks in the Tsarist Duma*, London: 1930.
Bailes, K. E., *Technology and Society under Lenin and Stalin: Origins of the Soviet Technical Intelligentsia, 1917–1941*, Princeton, NJ: 1978.
Barmine, A., *One Who Survived*, New York: 1945.
Barnett, V., 'The People's Commissariat of Supply and the People's Commissariat of Internal Trade', in Rees, E. A., ed., *Decision-Making in the Stalinist Command Economy, 1932–1937*, Basingstoke: 1997, pp. 176–202.
Bar-Noi, U., 'The Soviet Union and Churchill's Appeals for High-Level Talks, 1953–54: New Evidence from the Russian Archives', *Diplomacy and Statecraft*, vol. 9, no. 3, 1998, pp. 110–33.
Basseches, N. trans. Dicker, E.W., *Stalin*, London: 1952.
Bazhanov, B., trans. Doyle D. W., *Bazhanov and the Damnation of Stalin*, Athens, OH: 1980.
Belevich, Y. and Sokolov, V., 'Foreign Affairs Commissar Georgy Chicherin', *International Affairs*, no. 3, 1991, pp. 90–9.
Bell, C., *Royal Institute of International Affairs, Survey of International Affairs 1954*, London: 1957.
Beloff, M., *The Foreign Policy of Soviet Russia*, vol. 2, London: 1949.
Benvenuti, F., 'The Reform of the NKVD, 1934', *Europe–Asia Studies*, vol. 49, no. 6, 1997, pp. 1037–56.
Berezhkov, V., *History in the Making (Memoirs of World War II Diplomacy)*, Moscow: 1998.
Beria, S., *Beria, My Father: Inside Stalin's Kremlin*, London: 1999.
Bessedovsky, G., *Memoirs of a Soviet Diplomat*, New York: 1938.
Bezymenskii, L., 'On the Eve: Vyacheslav Molotov's Talks in Berlin in November 1940', *International Affairs*, no. 9, 1991, pp. 84–122.
Bezymenskii, L., 'The Secret Protocols of 1939 as a Problem of Soviet Historiography', in Gorodetsky, G., ed., *Soviet Foreign Policy 1917–1991: a Retrospective*, London: 1994, pp. 75–85.
Birse, A.H., *Memoirs of an Interpreter*, London: 1967.
Bohlen, C.E., *Witness to History, 1929–1969*, London: 1963.
Brackman, R., *The Secret File on Joseph Stalin: a Hidden Life*, London: 2001.
Brent, J. and Naumov, V. P., *Stalin's Last Crime: the Doctors' Plot*, London: 2003.
Bromage, B., *Molotov: the Story of an Era*, London: 1956.
Brooks, J., *When The Cold War Did Not End: The Soviet Peace Offensive of 1953 and the American Response*, Kennan Institute Occasional Papers, no. 278, Washington, DC: 2000.
Carley, M. J., 'End of the "Low, Dishonest Decade": Failure of the Anglo-Franco Soviet Alliance in 1939', *Europe–Asia Studies*, vol. 45, no. 2, 1993, pp. 303–42.
Carr, E. H., *A History of Soviet Russia*:
—— *The Interregnum 1923–1924*, Harmondsworth: 1969.
—— *Socialism in One Country*, vols.1 and 2, Harmondsworth: 1970.
—— with Davies, R.W., *Foundations of a Planned Economy*, vol. 1, Harmondsworth: 1974.
—— *Foundations of a Planned Economy*, vol. 2, Harmondsworth: 1971, vol. 3, Harmondsworth: 1976.
Carr, E.H., *The Bolshevik Revolution, 1917–1923*, vols. 1, 2, Harmondsworth: 1966.
Carr, E. H., *The Twilight of Comintern*, London: 1982.
Chubaryan, A. O. and Pechatnov, V. O., ' "Molotov the Liberal": Stalin's 1945 Criticism of his Deputy', *Cold War History*, vol. 1, no. 1, August 2000, pp. 129–40.
Churchill, W.S., *The Second World War*:
—— vol. 1, *The Gathering Storm*, London: 1950.

—— vol. 4, *The Hinge of Fate*, London: 1952.

—— vol. 5, *Closing the Ring*, London: 1952.

—— vol. 6, *Triumph and Tragedy*, London: 1954.

Coates, W. P. & Z. K., 'A Biographical Sketch', in Molotov, V., *Soviet Peace Policy*, London: 1941.

Cohen, S.F., *Bukharin and the Bolshevik Revolution: A Political Biography 1888–1938*, London: 1974.

Colton, T. J., *Moscow: Governing the Socialist Metropolis*, Cambridge, MA: 1995.

Conquest, R., *Power and Policy in the U.S.S.R: the Study of Soviet Dynastics*, London: 1962.

Conquest, R., *Stalin and the Kirov Murder*, London: 1989.

Conquest, R., *The Great Terror: a Reassessment*, London: 1990.

Craig, G.A., 'Totalitarian Approaches to Diplomatic Negotiations', in Sorkisson, A. D., *Studies in Diplomatic History and Historiography in Honour of G.P. Gooch*, London: 1961, pp. 115–31.

Dallin, D. J., *Soviet Foreign Policy after Stalin*, London: 1962.

Dallin, D. J., *Soviet Russia's Foreign Policy, 1939–1942*, New Haven: 1942.

Daniels, R.V., 'The Secretariat and the Local Organisation of the Russian Communist Party, 1921–1923', *The American Slavic and East European Review*, vol. XVI, no. 1, 1957, pp. 32–49.

Davies, N., 'The Soviet Occupation of Poland, 1944–45', in Bennett, G., ed., *The End of the War in Europe*, London: 1995, pp. 183–230.

Davies R.W., *The Industrialisation of Soviet Russia*:

—— vol. 1, *The Socialist Offensive: The Collectivisation of Soviet Agriculture, 1929–1930*, London: 1980.

—— vol. 2, *The Soviet Collective Farm, 1929–1930*, London: 1980.

—— vol. 3, *The Soviet Economy in Turmoil, 1929–1930*, Basingstoke: 1989.

—— vol. 4, *Crisis and Progress in the Soviet Economy, 1931–1933*, Basingstoke: 1996.

—— vol. 5, *The Years of Hunger: Soviet Agriculture, 1931–1933*, Basingstoke: 2004.

Davies, R. W., 'Peaches from our Tree', *London Review of Books*, 7 September 1995.

Davies, R. W., *Soviet History in the Gorbachev Revolution*, Basingstoke: 1989.

Davies, R. W., *Soviet History in the Yeltsin Era*, Basingstoke: 1997.

Davies, R. W. and Harrison, M., 'The Soviet Military–Economic effort during the Second Five-Year Plan (1933–1937), *Europe–Asia Studies*, vol. 49, no. 3, 1997, pp. 369–406.

Davies, R. W. and Khlevnyuk, O., 'Gosplan', in Rees, E. A., ed., *Decision–Making in the Stalinist Command Economy 1932–1937*, Basingstoke: 1997, pp. 32–66.

Davies, R. W. and Khlevnyuk, O., 'Stakhanovism and the Soviet Economy', *Europe–Asia Studies*, vol. 54, no. 6, 2002, pp. 867–904.

Davies, R. W., Ilic, M. and Khlevnyuk, O., 'The Politburo and Economic Policy-making', in Rees, E. A., ed., *The Nature of Stalin's Dictatorship: the Politburo 1928–1953*, Basingstoke: 2003, pp. 108–33.

Dedijer, V., *Tito Speaks: His Self Portrait and Struggle with Stalin*, London: 1954.

Deutscher, I., *The Prophet Unarmed: Trotsky 1921–1929*, London: 1959.

Dilks, D., 'The Conference at Potsdam, 1945', in Bennett, G., ed., *The End of the War in Europe*, London: 1995, pp. 77–100.

Dilks, D., ed., *The Diaries of Alexander Cadogan 1938–1941*, London: 1971.

Djilas, M., trans. Petrovich, M. B., *Conversations with Stalin*, Harmondsworth: 1963.

Dunn, D., 'Maksim Litvinov: Commissar of Contradictions', *Journal of Contemporary History*, vol. 23, no. 2, April 1988, pp. 221–4.

Duranty, W., *Stalin & Co., the Politburo – the Men who Run Russia*, New York: 1949.

Elwood, R. C., 'Lenin and *Pravda*, 1912–1914', *Slavic Review*, vol. 31, no. 2, 1972, pp. 349–80.

Erickson, J., *The Road to Stalingrad: Stalin's War with Germany*, vol. 1, London: 1985.

Ferro, M., *The Russian Revolution of February 1917*, London: 1971.

Fischer, L., *Men and Politics: an Autobiography*, New York: 1946.

Fleischhauer, I., 'The Molotov–Ribbentrop Pact: the German Version', *International Affairs*, August 1991, pp. 114–29.

Frank, P. and Kirkham, B. C., 'The Revival of *Pravda* in 1917', *Soviet Studies*, vol. XX, no. 3, 1968–69, pp. 366–8.

Getty, J. Arch, ' "Excesses are not permitted": Mass Terror and Stalinist Governance in the Late 1930s', *The Russian Review*, vol. 61, 2002, pp. 113–38.

Getty, J. Arch, *Origins of the Great Purges: the Soviet Communist Party Reconsidered, 1933–1938*, Cambridge: 1985.

Getty, J. Arch and Naumov, N., *The Road to Terror: Stalin and the Self-Destruction of the Bolsheviks, 1932–1939*, New Haven, CT: 1999.

Gill, G., *The Origins of the Stalinist Political System*, Cambridge: 1990.

Gomez, M., 'From Mexico to Moscow II', *Survey*, April 1965, pp. 116–25.

Goncharov, S. N., Lewis, J. W. and Litai X, *Uncertain Partners: Stalin, Mao and the Korean War*, Stanford, CA: 1993.

Gorlizki, Y. and Khlevniuk, O., *Cold Peace: Stalin and the Soviet Ruling Circle, 1945–1953*, Oxford: 2004.

Gorlizki, Y., 'Stalin's Cabinet: the Politburo and Decision Making in the Post-war Years', *Europe–Asia Studies*, vol. 53, no. 2, 2001, pp. 291–312.

Gorodetsky, G., *Grand Delusion; Stalin and the German Invasion of Russia*, New Haven: 1999.

Gorodetsky, G., *Sir Stafford Cripps' Mission to Moscow, 1940–1942*, Cambridge: 1984.

Gromyko, A., trans. Shukman, H., *Memories, from Stalin to Gorbachev*, London: 1989.

Harriman, W. A. and Abel, E., *Special Envoy to Churchill and Stalin, 1941–1946*, New York: 1975.

Harvey, J., ed., *The War Diaries of Oliver Harvey*, London: 1978.

Hasegawa, T., 'The Bolsheviks and the Formation of the Petrograd Soviet in the February Revolution', *Soviet Studies*, vol. XXIX, no. 1, 1977, pp. 86–107.

Hasegawa, T., *The February Revolution: Petrograd 1917*, Seattle: 1981.

Haslam, J., 'Litvinov, Stalin and the Road not Taken', in Gorodetsky, G., ed., *Soviet Foreign Policy, 1917–1991: a Retrospective*, London: 1994, pp. 55–64.

Haslam, J., 'Russian Archival Revelations and Our Understanding of the Cold War', *Diplomatic History*, vol. 21, no. 2, 1997, pp. 217–28.

Haslam, J., 'Soviet Foreign Policy 1939–1941: Isolation and Expansion', *Soviet Union/Union Soviétique*, vol. 18, 1991, pp. 103–21.

Haslam, J., 'Soviet–German Relations and the Origins of the Second World War: The Jury is Still Out', *Journal of Modern History*, vol. 69, 1997, pp. 785–97.

Haslam, J., *Soviet Foreign Policy, 1930–1933: the Impact of the Depression*, London: 1983.

Haslam, J., *The Soviet Union and the Struggle for Collective Security in Europe, 1933–39*, London: 1984.

Haslam, J., *The Soviet Union and the Threat from the East: Moscow, Tokyo and the Prelude to the Pacific War*, Basingstoke: 1992.

Hayter, Sir W., *The Diplomacy of the Great Powers*, London: 1960.

Hilger, G. and Meyer, A. G., *The Incompatible Allies: A Memoir-History of German–Soviet Relations 1930–1941*, New York: 1983.

Hoisington, S.S., ' "Even Higher": The Evolution of the Project for the Palace of Soviets', *Slavic Review*, vol. 62, no. 1, 2003, pp. 41–68.

Holloway, D., *Stalin and the Bomb: the Soviet Union and Atomic Energy 1939–1946*, New Haven, CT: 1994.

Hough, J. H. and Fainsod, M., *How the Soviet Union is Governed*, Cambridge, MA: 1979.

Hughes, J., 'Patrimonialism and the Stalinist System: the Case of S.I. Syrtsov', *Europe–Asia Studies*, vol. 48, no. 4, 1996, pp. 551–68.

Hull. C., *The Memoirs of Cordell Hull*, New York: 1948.

Humbert-Droz, J., *De Lenine á Staline: Dix Ans au Service de l'Internationale Communiste, 1921–1931*, Neuchatel: 1971.

Ilyin-Zhevsky, A.F., *The Bolsheviks in Power: Reminiscences of the Year 1918*, New York: 1984.

Jakobson, M., *The Diplomacy of the Winter War*, Cambridge, MA: 1951.

Jansen, M., and Petrov, N., *Stalin's Loyal Executioner: People's Commissar Nikolai Ezhov, 1895–1940*, Stanford: 2002.

Jensen, K. N., ed., *Origins of the Cold War: the Novikov, Kennan and Roberts 'Long Telegrams' of 1946, Revised Edition with Three New Commentaries*, Washington, DC: 1993.

Kaslas, B. J., 'The Lithuanian Strip in Soviet–German Secret Diplomacy, 1939–1941', *Journal of Baltic Studies*, vol. 4, no. 3, 1973, pp. 204–19.

Kemp Welch, A., *Stalin and the Literary Intelligentsia, 1928–1939*, Basingstoke: 1991.

Kemp-Welch, A., 'Stalinism and the Intellectual Order', in Rigby, T. H., Brown, A. and Reddaway, P., eds, *Authority Power and Policy in the USSR: Essays Dedicated to Leonard Schapiro*, London: 1980, pp. 118–34.

Kennedy-Pipe, C., *Stalin's Cold War: Soviet Strategies in Europe, 1943 to 1956*, Manchester: 1995.

Khlevniuk, O., 'The Reasons for the "Great Terror": the Foreign Political Aspects', in Pons, S. and Romano, A., eds, *Russia in the Age of Wars*, Milan: 2000, pp. 159–70.

Khlevnyuk, O., 'The Objectives of the Great Terror, 1937–1938', in Cooper, J., Perrie, M. and Rees, E. A., eds, *Soviet History 1917–1953: Essays in Honour of R.W. Davies*, Basingstoke: 1995, pp. 158–76.

Khlevnyuk, O. and Davies, R.W., 'The End of Rationing in the Soviet Union, 1934–1935', *Europe–Asia Studies*, vol. 51, no. 4, 1999, pp. 557–610.

Kneen, P., 'Physics, Genetics and Zhdanovschina', *Europe–Asia Studies*, vol. 50, no. 7, 1998, pp. 1183–202.

Knight, A., *Beria: Stalin's First Lieutenant*, Princeton, NJ: 1994.

Knight, A., *Who Killed Kirov? The Kremlin's Greatest Mystery*, New York: 1999.

Kostyrchenko, G., *Out of the Red Shadows: Anti-Semitism in Stalin's Russia*, New York: 1995.

Kot, S., *Conversations with the Kremlin and Dispatches from Russia*, London: 1963.

Kramer, M., 'New Evidence on Soviet Decision-Making and the 1956 Polish and Hungarian Crises', *Cold War International History Project Bulletin*, no. 8–9, Winter 1996/1997, pp. 358–84.

Krementsov, N., 'The "KR Affair": Soviet Science on the Threshold of the Cold War', *History and Philosophy of the Life Sciences*, vol. 17, 1995, pp. 419–46.

Krivitsky, W. G., *I Was Stalin's Agent*, London: 1939.

Lazitch, B. and Drackovitch, M. M., *Biographical Dictionary of the Comintern*, Stanford: 1986.

Lewin, M., *Lenin's Last Struggle*, New York: 1968.

Lewin, M., *Russian Peasants and Soviet Power: a Study of Collectivisation*, London: 1968.

Lih, L. T., Naumov, O. V. and Khlevniuk, O. V., eds, *Stalin's Letters to Molotov, 1925–1936*, New Haven, CT: 1995.

Longley, D., 'The Divisions of the Bolshevik Party in March 1917', *Soviet Studies*, vol. XXIV, no. 1, 1972, pp. 61–76.

Main, S. J., 'The Arrest and Testimony of Marshal of the Soviet Union M. N. Tukhachevsky (May–June1937)', *Journal of Slavic Military Studies*, vol. 10, no. 1, 1997, pp. 151–95.

Mandel, D., *The Petrograd Workers and the Fall of the Old Regime: From the February Revolution to the July days, 1917*, London: 1984.

Mandelstam, N. Y., *Hope Against Hope*, New York: 1970.

Martin, T., 'The Origins of Soviet Ethnic Cleansing', *Journal of Modern History*, vol. 70, no. 4, 1998, pp. 813–60.

Mastny, V., *Russia's Road to the Cold War: Diplomacy, Warfare and the Politics of Communism, 1941–1945*, New York: 1970.

Mastny, V., 'Soviet War Aims at the Moscow and Teheran Conferences of 1943', *Journal of Modern History*, vol. 47, 1975, pp. 481–504.

Mastny, V., 'The Beneš–Stalin–Molotov Conversations in December 1943: New Documents,' *Jahrbücher für Geschichte Osteuropas*, 20, 1972, pp. 369–402.

Mastny, V., *The Cold War and Soviet Insecurity: the Stalin Years*, New York: 1996.

Mawdsley, E. and White, S., *The Soviet Elite from Lenin to Gorbachev: the Central Committee and its Members, 1917–1991*, Oxford: 2000.

McAuley, M., *Bread and Justice: State and Society in Petrograd, 1917–1922*, Oxford: 1991.

McAuley, M., 'Bread without the Bourgeoisie', in Koenker, D. P., Rosenberg, W. G. and Suny, R .G., eds, *Party, State and Society in the Russian Civil War: Explorations in Social History*, Bloomington: 1989, pp. 158–72.

McCagg, W. O., Jr, *Stalin Embattled 1943–1948*, Detroit: 1978.

McDermott, K. and Agnew, J., *The Comintern: a History of International Communism from Lenin to Stalin*, Basingstoke: 1996.

McNeal, R. H., ed., *Resolutions and Decisions of the Communist Party of the Soviet Union, 1917–1967*, vol. 2, Toronto: 1974.

McSherry, J. E., *Stalin, Hitler and Europe*,
—— vol. 1, *The Origins of World War II 1933–1939*, Arlington: 1968.
—— vol. 2, *The Imbalance of Power*, Arlington: 1970.

Medvedev, R., *All Stalin's Men*, Oxford: 1983.

Medvedev, R., *Let History Judge: the Origins and Consequences of Stalinism*, 1st edn, Manchester: 1976, 2nd. edn, Oxford: 1989.

Medvedev, Z. A. and Medvedev, R. A., *The Unknown Stalin*, London: 2003.

Meijer, J. M., ed., *The Trotsky Papers*, vol. 2, The Hague: 1971.

Merridale, C., *Moscow Politics and the Rise of Stalin: The Communist Party in the Capital 1925–1932*, Basingstoke: 1990.

Mićunović, V, trans. Floyd, D., *Moscow Diary*, London: 1980.

Mikoyan, S., 'Barbarossa and the Soviet Leadership', in Erickson J. and Dilks, D., eds, *Barbarossa: the Axis and the Allies*, Edinburgh 1994, pp. 123–32.

Milligan, S., 'The Petrograd Bolsheviks and Social Insurance, 1914–17', *Soviet Studies*, vol. XX, no. 3, 1968–69, pp. 369–74.

Miner, S.M., *Between Churchill and Stalin, the Soviet Union and the Origins of the Grand Alliance*, Chapel Hill: 1988.

Miner, S.M., 'His Master's Voice: Viacheslav Mihailovich Molotov as Stalin's Foreign Commissar', in Craig, G. A. and Lowenheim, F. Z., eds, *The Diplomats, 1939–1979*, Princeton, NJ: 1994, pp. 65–99.

Molotov, V., *Soviet Peace Policy*, London: 1941.

Montefiore, S. S., *Stalin: the Court of the Red Tsar*, London: 2003.

Mosse, W. E., 'Makers of the Soviet Union', *The Slavic and East European Review*, vol. XLVI, no. 106, January 1968, pp. 141–54.

Narinskii, M. N., 'The Soviet Union and the Berlin Crisis, 1948–9', in Gori, F. and Pons, S., *The Soviet Union and Europe in the Cold War, 1943–53*, Basingstoke: 1966, pp. 56–75.

Nekrich, A.M., trans. Freeze, G.L., *Pariahs, Partners, Predators: German–Soviet Relations, 1922–1941*, New York: 1997.

Nevezhin, V. A., 'Stalin's 5 May Addresses: the Experience of Interpretation', *Journal of Slavic Military Studies*, vol. 11, no. 1, 1998, pp. 116–46.

Orlov, A., *The Secret History of Stalin's Crimes*, London: 1954.

Parrish, S. D., and Narinsky, M. N., 'New Evidence on the Soviet Rejection of the Marshall Plan, 1947: Two Reports', *Cold War International History Project, Working Paper no. 9*, Washington, DC: 1994.

Parrish, S., 'A Diplomat Reports', *Cold War International History Project, Bulletin no. 1*, 1992, pp. 16, 21–2.

Pechatnov, V.O., trans. Zubok, V.M. ' "The Allies are Pressing on You to Break Your Will ..." Foreign Policy Correspondence between Stalin and Molotov and Other Politburo Members, September 1945–December 1946', *Cold War International History Project, Working Paper no. 26*, Washington, DC: 1999.

Pethybridge, R., *A Key to Soviet Politics: the Crisis of the 'Anti-Party' Group*, London: 1962.

Phillips, H. D., *Between the Revolution and the West: a Political Biography of Maxim M. Litvinov*, Boulder: 1992.

Pipes, R., ed., *The Unknown Lenin: From the Secret Archive*, New Haven, CT: 1997.

Pons, S., 'In the Aftermath of the Age of Wars: the Impact of World War II on Soviet Security Policy', in Pons, S. and Romano, A., eds, *Russia in the Age of Wars*, Milan: 1998, pp. 277–307.

Rabinowitch, A., *Prelude to Revolution: the Petrograd Bolsheviks and the July 1917 Uprising*, Bloomington: 1991.

Rabinowitch, A., *The Bolsheviks Come to Power*, New York: 1976.

Radzinsky, E., *Stalin*, London: 1996.

Redlich, S., *Propaganda and Nationalism in Wartime Russia: The Jewish Antifascist Committee in the USSR, 1941–1948*, Boulder: 1982.

Redlich, S., *War, Holocaust and Stalinism: A Documented History of the Jewish Anti-Fascist Committee in the USSR*, Luxembourg: 1995.

Rees, E. A., 'The People's Commissariat of the Timber Industry', in Rees, ed., *Decision-Making in the Stalinist Command Economy*, Basingstoke: 1997, pp. 124–49.

Rees, E. A., 'Stalin as Leader 1924–1937; From Oligarch to Dictator', in Rees, ed., *The Nature of Stalin's Dictatorship: the Politburo 1928–1953*, Basingstoke: 2003, pp. 19–58.

Rees, E. A., 'Stalin as Leader, 1937–1953: From Dictator to Despot', in Rees, ed., *'The Nature of Stalin's Dictatorship: the Politburo 1928–1953*, Basingstoke: 2004, pp. 200–39.

Rees, E. A., *Stalinism and Soviet Rail Transport, 1928–41*, Basingstoke: 1995.

Rees, E. A. and Watson, D. H., 'Politburo and Sovnarkom', in Rees, ed., *Decision-Making in the Stalinist Command Economy, 1932–1937*, Basingstoke: 1997, pp. 9–31.

Report of Court Proceedings in the Case of the Anti-Soviet Trotskyite Centre, Moscow: 1937.

Report of Court Proceedings: the Case of the Trotskyite–Zinovievite Terrorist Centre, Moscow: 1936.

Resis, A., 'The Churchill-Stalin Secret "Percentages" Agreement on the Balkans, Moscow, 1944', *American Historical Review*, vol. 83, no. 2, 1978, pp. 368–87.

Resis, A., 'The Fall of Litvinov: Harbinger of the German–Soviet Non-aggression Pact', *Europe–Asia* Studies, vol. 52, no. 1, 2000, pp. 33–56.

Roberts, F., *Dealing with Dictators: the Destruction and Revival of Europe, 1930–1970*, London: 1991.

Roberts, G., 'Ideology, Calculation and Improvisation: Spheres of Influence and Soviet Foreign Policy 1939–1945', *Review of International Studies*, vol. 25, 1999, pp. 655–73.

Roberts, G., 'Sexing up the Cold War: New Evidence on the Molotov–Truman Talks of April 1945' *Cold War History* vol. 4, no. 3, 2004, pp. 105–125.

Roberts, G., 'Stalin, the Pact with Germany and the Origins of Postwar Soviet Diplomatic Historiography', *Journal of Cold War Studies*, vol. 4, no. 2, 2002, pp. 93–103.

Roberts, G., 'The Alliance that Failed: Moscow and the Triple Alliance Negotiations, 1939', *European History Quarterly*, vol. 26, no. 3, 1996, pp. 383–414.

Roberts, G., 'The Fall of Litvinov: a Revisionist View', *Journal of Contemporary History*, 1992, pp. 639–57.

Roberts, G., 'The Infamous Encounter? The Merekalov–Weizsäcker Meeting of 17 April 1939', *Historical Journal*, vol. 35, no. 4, 1992, pp. 921–26.

Roberts, G., 'The Soviet Decision for a Pact with Nazi-Germany', *Europe–Asia Studies*, vol. 44, no. 1, 1992, pp. 57–78.

Roberts, G., *The Soviet Union and the Origins of the Second World War*, Basingstoke: 1995.

Roberts, G., *The Unholy Alliance: Stalin's Pact with Hitler*, London: 1989.

Roshchin A., 'People's Commissariat for Foreign Affairs before World War II', *International Affairs*, May 1988, pp. 108–14.

Roshchin, A., 'Soviet Pre-war Diplomacy: Reminiscences of a Diplomat', *International Affairs*, December 1987, pp. 113–20.

Roschin, A., 'The UN in the Cold War Years', *International Affairs*, January 1990, pp. 216–21.

Rubenstein, J. and Naumov, V.P., eds, *Stalin's Secret Pogrom: the Postwar Inquisition of the Jewish Anti-Fascist Committee*, New Haven, CT: 2001.

Sainsbury, K., *The Turning Point: Roosevelt, Stalin, Churchill and Chiang-Kai-Shek, 1943, The Moscow, Cairo and Teheran Conferences*, New York: 1985.

Samuelson, L., *Plans for Stalin's War Machine: Tukhachevskii and Military–Economic Planning, 1925–1941*, Basingstoke: 2000.

Schapiro L., *The Communist Party of the Soviet Union*, London: 1970.

Schapiro L., *The Origin of the Communist Autocracy: Political Opposition in the Soviet State: First Phase 1917–1922*, London: 1977.

Schecter, J. L. and Luchkov, V. V., eds, *Khrushchev Remembers: the Glasnost Tapes*, Boston: 1990.

Schmidt, P., *Statist auf diplomatischer Bühne 1923–1945*, Bonn: 1954.

Service, R., *Lenin: a Biography*, London: 2000.

Service, R., *Lenin: a Political Life*, vol. 3, *The Iron Ring*, Basingstoke: 1995.

Service, R., *The Bolshevik Party in Revolution 1917–1923: a Study in Organisational Change*, London: 1979.

" 'Seven Shots" in the Winter of 1939', *International Affairs*, January 1990, pp. 180–201.

Sevestyanov, P., *Before the Nazi Invasion: Soviet Diplomacy in September 1939–June 1941*, Moscow: 1981.

Shearer, D. R., 'Crime and Social Disorder in Stalin's Russia', *Cahiers du Monde Russe*, vol. 39, 1996, pp. 119–48.

Shearer, D. R., 'Social disorder, Mass Repression and the NKVD during the 1930s', *Cahiers du Monde Russe*, vol. 42, 2001, pp. 505–34.

Sherwood, R. E., ed., *The White House Papers of Harry L. Hopkins: An Intimate History by Robert E. Sherwood*, vols. 1 and 2, London: 1949.

Shevchenko, A. N, *Breaking with Moscow*, New York: 1985.

Shimotomai, N., 'The Defeat of the Right Opposition in the Moscow Party Organisation, 1928', *Japanese Slavic and East European Studies*, vol. 4, 1983, pp. 15–34.

Slusser, R. M., *Stalin in October: the Man who Missed the Revolution*, Baltimore: 1987.

Smulkstys, J., 'The Incorporation of the Baltic States in the Soviet Union', *Lituanus*, vol. 14, no. 2, 1968.

Smyser, W. R., *From Yalta to Berlin: the Cold War Struggle over Germany*, New York: 1999.

Sokolov, V., 'Foreign Affairs Commissar Vyacheslav Molotov', *International Affairs*, June, 1991, pp. 83–96.

Sokolov, V., 'People's Commissar Maxim Litvinov', *International Affairs*, May 1991, pp. 93–107.

Solomon, Jr, P. H., *Soviet Criminal Justice under Stalin*, Cambridge: 1996.

Sotheby's, *Catalogue of Continental and Russian Books and Manuscripts, Science and Medicine*, April 1990.

Spiridonova, L., 'Gorky and Stalin (According to New Materials from A. M. Gorky's Archive)', *The Russian Review*, vol. 54, no. 3, 1995, pp. 413–23.

Starkov, B., 'Narkom Ezhov', in Getty, J. Arch and Manning R.T., *Stalinist Terror: New Perspectives*, Cambridge: 1993, pp. 21–39.

Strang, W., *Home and Abroad*, London: 1956.

Sukhanov, N. N., trans. Carmichael, J., *The Russian Revolution 1917: a Personal Record*, London: 1955.

Swain, G., *Russian Social Democracy and the Legal Labour Movement, 1906–1914*, London: 1983.

Talbot, S., ed., *Khrushchev Remembers*, London: 1971.

Talbot, S., ed., *Khrushchev Remembers, vol. 2, The Last Testament*, Harmondsworth: 1974.

Tanner, V., *The Winter War: Finland against Russia, 1939–1940*, Stanford, CA: 1950.

Tarulis, A. N., *Soviet Policy towards the Baltic States 1918–1940*, Notre Dame: 1959.

Taubman, W., *Khrushchev: the Man and his Era*, London: 2003.

The Earl of Avon, *The Eden Memoirs*,

—— vol. 1, *Facing the Dictators*, London: 1962.

—— vol. 2, *The Reckoning*, London: 1965.

Thurston, R. W., *Life and Terror in Stalin's Russia*, New Haven, CT: 1996.

Tompson, W. J., *Khrushchev: a Political Life*, Basingstoke: 1997.

Trotsky, L., *My Life: An Attempt at an Autobiography*, Harmondsworth: 1975.

Trotsky, L., ed. and trans. Malmuth, C., *Stalin: An Appraisal of the Man and his Influence*, London: 1947.

Trotsky, L., *The Stalin School of Falsification*, New York: 1971.

Trotsky's Diary in Exile 1935, trans. Zaradnaya E., Cambridge, MA: 1976.

Truman, H. S., *Year of Decisions, 1945*, London: 1955.

Tucker, R. C., *Stalin as Revolutionary 1879–1929: A Study in History and Personality*, London: 1974.

Tucker, R. C., *Stalin in Power: the Revolution from Above, 1928–1941*, New York: 1990.
Ulam A. B., *Expansion and Coexistence: Soviet Foreign Policy 1917–73*, New York: 1974.
Ulam A. B., *Stalin: the Man and his Era*, London: 1974.
Uldricks, T. J., 'The Impact of the Great Purges on the People's Commissariat of Foreign Affairs', *Slavic Review*, vol. 36, 1977, pp. 187–204.
Upton, A. F., *Finland 1939–1940*, London: 1974.
Van Dyke, C., *The Soviet Invasion of Finland 1939–1940*, London: 1997.
Vasilieva, L., trans. Porter, C., *Kremlin Wives*, London: 1994.
Vinton, L., 'The Katyn Documents: Politics and History', Radio Free Europe/Radio Liberty *Research Report*, vol. 2, no. 4, 1993, pp. 19–31.
Viola, L., 'The Other Archipelago: Kulak Deportations to the North in 1930', *Slavic Review*, vol. 60, no. 4, 2001, pp. 734–55.
Viola, L., *The Best Sons of the Fatherland: Workers in the Vanguard of Soviet Collectivisation*, New York: 1987.
Waddington, G. T., 'Ribbentrop and the Soviet Union, 1937–1941', in Erickson, J. and Dilks, D., eds, *Barbarossa: the Axis and the Allies*, Edinburgh: 1994, pp. 7–33.
Ward, P. D., *The Threat of Peace: James F. Byrnes and the Council of Foreign Ministers, 1945–1946*, Kent, Ohio: 1979.
Watson, D., 'Molotov et la Conférence de Moscou Octobre 1943', *Communisme*, no. 74/75, 2003, pp. 71–99.
Watson, D., 'Molotov, the Making of the Grand Alliance and the Second Front 1939–1942', *Europe–Asia Studies*, vol. 54, no.1, 2002, pp. 51–85.
Watson, D., 'Molotov's Apprenticeship in Foreign Policy: The Triple Alliance Negotiations in 1939', *Europe–Asia Studies*, 52, 4, 2000, pp. 695–722.
Watson, D., 'STO (The Council of Labour and Defence) in the 1930s', *Europe–Asia Studies*, vol. 50, no. 7, 1998, pp. 1203–27.
Watson, D., *Molotov and Soviet Government: Sovnarkom 1930–1941*, Basingstoke: 1996.
Watt, D. C., 'The Initiation of the Negotiations Leading to the Nazi–Soviet Pact', in Abramsky, C., and Williams, B., *Essays in Honour of E. H. Carr*, London: 1974, pp. 152–70.
Weinberg, G. L., *Germany and the Soviet Union, 1939–1941*, Leiden: 1954.
Werth, A., *Russia at War 1941–1945*, London: 1964.
Wheatcroft, S. G., 'From Team-Stalin to Degenerate Tyranny', in Rees, E. A., ed., *The Nature of Stalin's Dictatorship; the Politburo 1928–1953*, Basingstoke: 2004, pp. 79–107.
White, J. D., 'The Sormovo–Nikolaev Zemlyachestvo in the February Revolution', *Soviet Studies*, vol. XXXI, no. 4, 1979, pp. 475–504.
Wolfe, B., *Three who Made a Revolution: a Biographical History*, Harmondsworth: 1966.
Zubok, V. and Pleshakov, C., *Inside the Kremlin's Cold War: from Stalin to Khrushchev*, Cambridge, MA: 1996.
Zubok, V. M., 'Soviet Intelligence and the Cold War: the "Small" Committee of Information, 1952–53', *Cold War International History Project, Working Paper, no. 4*, Washington DC: 1992.

Theses and other unpublished material in English

Benvenuti, F., 'Stakhanovism and Stalinism, 1934–8', unpublished paper, CREES (Centre for Russian and East European Studies), University of Birmingham, 1989.
Davies, R. W., 'The Archives and the Soviet Economy', unpublished paper presented to the conference on 'Reappraising the Stalin Era', European University Institute, Florence, October 2002.
Davies, R.W. and Harrison, M., 'The Soviet Military–Economic Effort during the Second Five-Year Plan (1933–1937), unpublished paper, CREES, University of Birmingham, 1996.
Fitzpatrick, S., 'Stalin, Molotov and the Practice of Politics', unpublished paper for the XXIX Conference of the Study Group on the Russian Revolution, Durham, 2003.
Marion, C. J., *Ministers in Moscow*, Indiana University PhD. thesis, 1970.
Raymond, P. D., *Conflict and Consensus in Soviet foreign Policy 1933–1935*, Pennsylvania State University DPhil. thesis, 1979.

Rees, E. A., *Rabkrin and the Soviet System of State Control, 1920–1930*, University of Birmingham Ph D. thesis, 1982.

Rees, E. A., 'Red Terror and Party Rule in Nizhny Novgorod 1918–1919: Lazar Kaganovich's Big Secret', unpublished paper, CREES, University of Birmingham, 1997.

Rees, E.A., 'Ukraine under Kaganovich, 1925–1928', unpublished paper, CREES: University of Birmingham, 1997.

Roberts, G., 'Beware Greek Gifts: The Stalin–Churchill "Percentages" Agreement of October 1944', Paper presented at the Foreign Office Seminar "Churchill–Stalin" ', London: 2002.

Tauger, M., 'Stalin, Soviet Agriculture and Collectivisation', unpublished paper for XXIX Conference of the Study Group on the Russian Revolution, January 2003.

Name Index

Subject Index